Language
Network

Grammar • Writing • Communication

McDougal Littell
A HOUGHTON MIFFLIN COMPANY

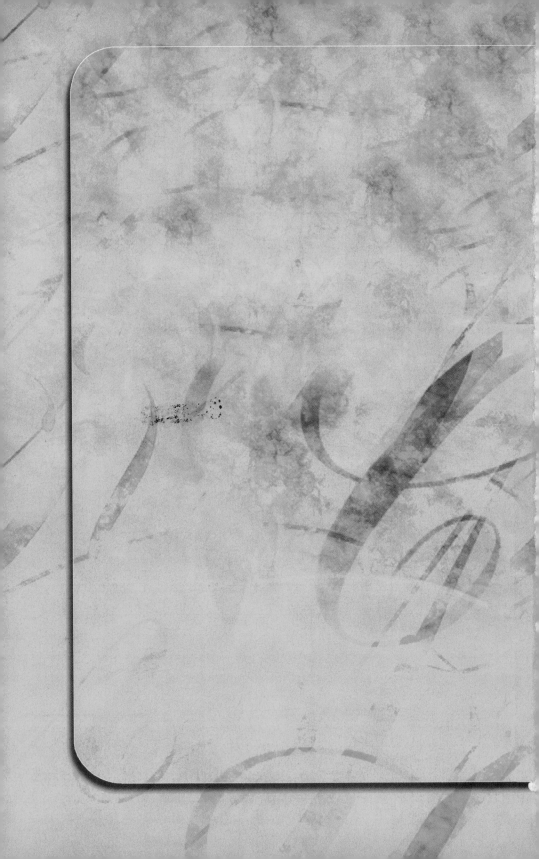

Language
Network

- Grammar, Usage, and Mechanics
- Essential Writing Skills
- Writing Workshops
- Communicating in the Information Age

McDougal Littell
A HOUGHTON MIFFLIN COMPANY

ISBN-13: 978-0-395-96741-6   ISBN-10: 0-395-96741-4

2004 Impression.

40058042

Acknowledgments begin on page 693.

12 13 14 15 16 17 18 – DCI – 09 08 07 06

Teacher Panels

The teacher panels helped guide the conceptual development of *Language Network*. They participated actively in shaping and reviewing prototype materials for the pupil edition, determining ancillary and technology components, and guiding the development of the scope and sequence for the program.

Cynda Andrews, Western Hills High School, Fort Worth School District, Fort Worth, Tex.
Gay Berardi, Evanston Township High School, Evanston School District, Evanston, Ill.
Nadine Carter-McDaniel, Townview Academic Center, Dallas School District, Dallas, Tex.
Sandra Dean, English Department Chairperson, Kerr High School, Alief School District, Houston, Tex.
Delia Diaz, English Department Chairperson, Rio Grande City High School, Rio Grande City School District, Rio Grande City, Tex.
Cynthia Galindo, Bel Air High School, Yselta School District, El Paso, Tex.
Ellen Geisler, English/Language Arts Department Chairperson, Mentor Senior High School, Mentor School District, Mentor, Ohio
Dr. Paulette Goll, English Department Chairperson, Lincoln West High School, Cleveland City School District, Cleveland, Ohio
Myron Greenfield, Davis High School, Houston School District, Houston, Tex.
Lorraine Hammack, Executive Teacher of the English Department, Beachwood High School, Beachwood City School District, Beachwood, Ohio
James Horan, Hinsdale Central High School, Hinsdale Township High School, Hinsdale, Ill.
Marguerite Joyce, English Department Chairperson, Woodridge High School, Woodridge Local School District, Peninsula, Ohio
Christi Lackey, North Side High School, Fort Worth School District, Fort Worth, Tex.
Jane McGough, Wichita Falls High School, Wichita Falls School District, Wichita Falls, Tex.
Dee Phillips, Hudson High School, Hudson Local School District, Hudson, Ohio
Dr. Bob Pierce, English Department Chairperson, Conroe High School, Conroe School District, Conroe, Tex.
Cyndi Rankin, John Jay High School, Northside School District, San Antonio, Tex.
Mary Ross, English Department Chairperson, Tascosa High School, Amarillo School District, Amarillo, Tex.
Robert Roth, Evanston Township High School, Evanston, Ill.
Carol Steiner, English Department Chairperson, Buchtel High School, Akron City School District, Akron, Ohio
Nancy Strauch, English Department Chairperson, Nordonia High School, Nordonia Hills City School District, MacEdonia, Ohio
Sheila Treat, Permian High School, Ector County School District, Odessa, Tex.
Ruth Vukovich, Hubbard High School, Hubbard Exempted Village School District, Hubbard, Ohio

Content Specialists

Dr. Mary Newton Bruder, former Professor of Linguistics at University of Pittsburgh; (creator of the Grammar Hotline Web site)
Rebekah Caplan, High School and Middle Grades English/Language Arts Specialist, New Standards Project, Washington, D.C.
Dr. Sharon Sicinski Skeans, Assistant Professor, University of Houston-Clear Lake, Houston, Tex.
Richard Vinson, Retired Teacher, Provine High School, Jackson, Miss.

Technology Consultants

Dr. David Considine, Media Studies Coordinator, Appalachian State University, Boone, NC (author of *Visual Messages: Integrating Imagery into Instruction*)
Heidi Whitus, Teacher, Communication Arts High School, San Antonio, Tex.
Anne Clark, Riverside-Brookfield High School, Riverside, Ill.
Pat Jurgens, Riverside-Brookfield High School, Riverside, Ill.
Ralph Amelio, Former teacher, Willowbrook High School, Villa Park, Ill.
Cindy Lucia, Horace Greeley High School, New York, N.Y.
Aaron Barnhart, Television writer for the *Kansas City Star* and columnist for *Electronic Media*, Kansas City, Mo.

ESL Consultants

Dr. Andrea B. Bermúdez, Professor of Studies in Language and Culture; Director, Research Center for Language and Culture; Chair, Foundations and Professional Studies, University of Houston-Clear Lake, Clear Lake, Tex.
Inara Bundza, ESL Director, Kelvyn Park High School, Chicago, Ill.
Danette Erickson Meyer, Consultant, Illinois Resource Center, Des Plaines, Ill.
John Hilliard, Consultant, Illinois Resource Center, Des Plaines, Ill.
John Kibler, Consultant, Illinois Resource Center, Des Plaines, Ill.
Barbara Kuhns, Camino Real Middle School, Las Cruces, N.M.

Teacher Reviewers

Nadine Carter-McDaniel, Townview Magnet Center, Dallas ISD, Dallas, Tex.
Frances Capuana, Director of ESL, Curtis High School, Staten Island, N.Y.
Lucila A. Garza, ESL Consultant, Austin, Tex.
Dan Haggerty, Drama Department Chair, Lewis and Clark High School, Vancouver, Wash.
Betty Lou Ludwick, Wakefield Senior High School, Arlington, Va.
Linda Maxwell, MacArthur High School, Houston, Tex.
Linda Powell, Banning High School, Wilmington, Calif. (Los Angeles Unified School District)
Cindy Rogers, MacArthur High School, Houston, Tex.
Lynnette Russell, Lewis and Clark High School, Vancouver, Wash.
Joan Smathers, Language Arts Supervisor, Brevard School-Secondary Program, Viera, Fla.
Sharon Straub, English Department Chair, Joel Ferris High School, Spokane, Wash.
Mary Sylvester, Minneapolis North High School, Minneapolis, Minn.
Shirley Williams, English Department Chair, Longview High School, Longview, Tex.

Student Reviewers

Saba Abraham, Chelsea High School
Julie Allred, Southwest High School
Nabiha Azam, East Kentwood High School
Dana Baccino, Downington High School
Christianne Balsamo, Nottingham High School

Luke Bohline, Lakeville High School
Nathan Buechel, Providence Senior High School
Melissa Cummings, Highline High School
Megan Dawson, Southview Senior High School
Michelle DeBruce, Jurupa High School
Brian Deeds, Arvada West High School
Ranika Fizer, Jones High School
Ashleigh Goldberg, Parkdale High School
Jacqueline Grullon, Christopher Columbus High School
Dimmy Herard, Hialeah High School
Sean Horan, Round Rock High School
Bob Howard, Jr., Robert E. Lee High School
Rebecca Iden, Willowbrook High School
Agha's Igbinovia, Florin High School
Megan Jones, Dobson High School
Ed Kampelman, Parkway West High School
David Knapp, Delmar High School
Eva Lima, Westmoor High School
Ashley Miers, Ouachita High School
Raul Morffi, Shawnee Mission West High School
Sakenia Mosley, Sandalwood High School
Sergio Perez, Sunset High School
Jackie Peters, Westerville South High School
Kevin Robischaud, Waltham High School
Orlando Sanchez, West Mesa High School
Selene Sanchez, San Diego High School
Sharon Schaefer, East Aurora High School
Mica Semrick, Hoover High School
Julio Sequeira, Belmont High School
Camille Singleton, Cerritos High School
Solomon Stevenson, Ozen High School
Tim Villegas, Dos Pueblos High School
Shane Wagner, Waukesha West High School
Swenikqua Walker, San Bernardino High School
Douglas Weakly, Ray High School
Lauren Zoric, Norwin High School

Student Writers

Yursa Ahmad, Glenbard East High School
Jake Berlin, Francis Parker School
Paige Blake, New Trier High School
Stephanie Butler, Glenbard East High School
Dave Donaldson, Thomas High School
Sarah Hospelhorn, New Trier High School
Jacqueline Jimerson, Homewood High School
Mary Ellen Shuttleworth, Yorktown High School
Jennifer Stiers, R.O.W.V.A. High School

Contents Overview

Grammar, Usage, and Mechanics

Essential Writing Skills

Writing Workshops

Communicating in the Information Age

Student Resources

Grammar, Usage, and Mechanics

3 Using Clauses

4 Using Verbs 104

5 Subject-Verb Agreement 130

Other Punctuation at a Glance

   Uses for Other Punctuation *An Important Brief*

   Commas, Dashes, or Parentheses? *A Simple Verdict*

   The Bottom Line *Checklist for Other Punctuation*

Quick-Fix Editing Machine

Essential Writing Skills

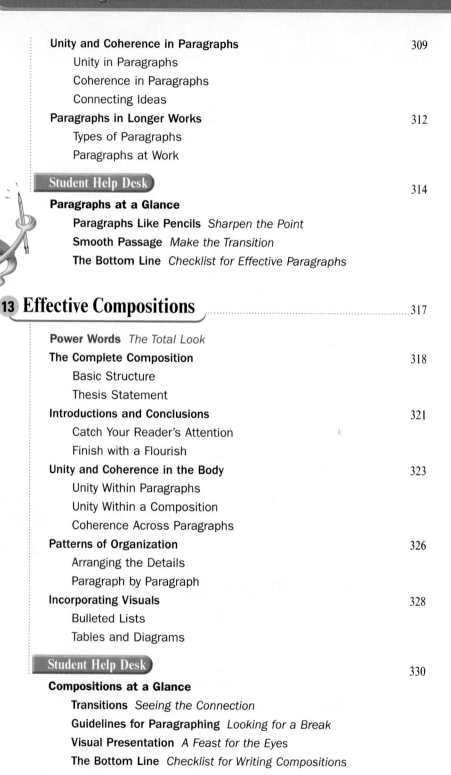

Writing Workshops

Literary Analysis

19 Literary Interpretation

Informative Exposition

20 Comparison-and-Contrast Essay

Narrative/Literary Writing

23 Short Story 434

Research Report

24 Research Report 444

Communicating in the Information Age

Viewing and Representing

28 Persuasion and the Media

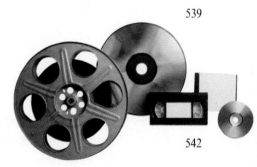

Special Features

Real World Grammar

Grammar in Literature

Power Words: Vocabulary for Precise Writing

Quick-Fix Editing Machine

Student Resources

Grammar, Usage, and Mechanics

Quick-Fix Editing Machine

You Hold the Keys

You know that feeling of having your keys
just within reach. There's a similar security in
understanding language. Once you've learned
about sentence parts and the intricate ways
in which they work, you'll have a valuable set
of keys at hand. These are keys that will
enable you to unlock meanings.

Parts of Speech

Do you remember the parts of speech? Just as sky jumpers need to carry their chutes for a safe landing, you'll need to know those eight building blocks of language before moving on. Try taking the self-check at the right to find out if you are ready to leap ahead. If you find that you forgot a thing or two (like adjectives and conjunctions?), then pull the ripcord and read this review chapter.

Hey! Prepare first, and you can

An **interjection** is a word or phrase used to express emotion. (p. 23)

A **verb** expresses an action, a condition, or a state of being. (p. 13)

A **conjunction** connects words, phrases, or clauses in a sentence. (p. 21)

A **pronoun** replaces a noun or another pronoun. (p. 9)

Write the part of speech of each numbered word.

It's true! People **rarely**[(1)] talk **about**[(2)] **adjectives**.[(3)] If **you**[(4)] **confuse**[(5)] prepositions **and**[(6)] interjections, the **world**[(7)] **will**[(8)] **not**[(9)] come to an **abrupt**[(10)] **halt**.[(11)] However, you need to learn the **parts**[(12)] of speech so you **can**[(13)] talk **about**[(14)] **your**[(15)] language and writing. **Moreover**,[(16)] if you make many **grammatical**[(17)] mistakes **in**[(18)] your writing, you can **kiss**[(19)] a good job—and possibly a **secure**[(20)] future—goodbye.

Self-Check Answers (upside down)

20. adjective	15. pronoun	10. adjective	5. verb
19. verb	14. preposition	9. adverb	4. pronoun
18. preposition	13. verb	8. verb	3. noun
17. adjective	12. noun	7. noun	2. preposition
16. adverb	11. noun	6. conjunction	1. adverb

leap ahead with real confidence.

An **adverb** describes or tells more about a verb, an adjective, or another adverb. (p. 17)

A **preposition** shows the relationship between a noun or pronoun and another word in the sentence. (p. 19)

An **adjective** describes or tells more about a noun or a pronoun. (p. 16)

A **noun** names a person, place, thing, or idea. (p. 6)

Nouns

❶ Review the Basics

A **noun** is a word that names a person, place, thing, or idea.

PERSONS	**brother, scientist, Rita, Governor Lee**
PLACES	**porch, stadium, Chicago, Africa**
THINGS	**television, cactus, hurricane, Holland Tunnel**
IDEAS	**truth, democracy, ability, safety**

Common and Proper Nouns

A **common noun** is a general name for a person, place, thing, or idea. A **proper noun** is the name of a particular person, place, thing, or idea. Capitalize proper nouns.

Common and Proper Nouns	
Common nouns (general)	**Proper nouns (particular)**
man	Albert Einstein, Michael Jordan, Jackson Pollock
holiday	Earth Day, Labor Day, Presidents' Day
language	Spanish, English, Mandarin, Hebrew
city	Miami, London, Dallas, Beijing

Unsure which nouns to capitalize? See pp. 202–214.

Singular and Plural Nouns

Singular nouns name one person, place, thing, or idea. **Plural nouns** name more than one. To make most nouns plural, add –s or –es to the singular form.

SINGULAR NOUNS	**award**	**horse**	**knife**	**coach**	**woman**
PLURAL NOUNS	**awards**	**horses**	**knives**	**coaches**	**women**

Collective Nouns

A **collective noun** names a group—people or things that are regarded as a unit.

COLLECTIVE NOUNS **tribe, litter, flock, committee, batch**

Abstract and Concrete Nouns

A **concrete noun** names something perceptible to the senses—something that can be seen, heard, smelled, touched, or tasted. An **abstract noun** names something that cannot be perceived through the senses, such as an idea, quality, emotion, or state. An abstract noun names something that you can think about but cannot see or touch.

CONCRETE NOUNS   **coin, hand, fire, computer**
ABSTRACT NOUNS   **jealousy, freedom, laziness**

Compound Nouns

A **compound noun** consists of two or more words used together as a single noun. A compound noun may be written as one word, as two words, or as a hyphenated word.

Compound Nouns		
As one word	**As two words**	**Hyphenated**
bookcase	ice cream	great-grandmother
candlelight	New York	one-third
sunshine	attorney general	father-in-law

Possessive Nouns

A **possessive noun** shows ownership or belonging. Add an apostrophe and s to a singular noun to make it possessive.

Ricky Martin's first CD, a dog's bark

Add only an apostrophe to a plural noun ending in s to make it possessive.

horses' manes, book-lovers' delight

© 2000 by Sidney Harris

"I miss the good old days when all we had to worry about was nouns and verbs."

❷ Nouns in Action

You can use concrete nouns to add power to descriptive writing. Notice how Ambrose Bierce precisely names the things that his character sees, feels, and hears.

LITERARY MODEL

He was now in full **possession** of his physical **senses**. ... He looked at the **forest** on the **bank** of the **stream**, saw the individual **trees**, the **leaves** and the **veining** of each **leaf**—saw the very **insects** upon them: the **locusts**, the brilliant-bodied **flies**, the gray **spiders** stretching their **webs** from **twig** to **twig**. He noted the prismatic **colors** in all the **dewdrops** upon a million **blades** of grass. The **humming** of the **gnats** that danced above the **eddies** of the **stream**, the **beating** of the **dragon-flies'** **wings**, the **strokes** of the **water-spiders' legs**, like **oars** which had lifted their **boat**—all these made audible **music**. A **fish** slid along beneath his **eyes** and he heard the **rush** of its **body** parting the **water**.

—Ambrose Bierce, "An Occurrence at Owl Creek Bridge"

REVIEW: Nouns

The nouns in the following exercise are taken from the Literary Model. Use the following categories to identify each noun: *concrete noun, proper noun, abstract noun, possessive noun,* or *compound noun.* You will use two or more categories to identify some nouns.

1. Owl Creek Bridge
2. colors
3. gnats
4. dewdrops
5. Ambrose Bierce
6. water-spiders'
7. oars
8. senses
9. dragon-flies'
10. rush

For more practice, see the EXERCISE BANK, p. 590.

Pronouns

❶ Review the Basics

A **pronoun** is a word used in place of a noun or another pronoun. The word that a pronoun stands for is called its **antecedent.** It may be found in the same sentence or in an earlier sentence.

Jasmine is celebrating her birthday. She is 17.
     ANTECEDENT   PRONOUNS

Personal Pronouns

Personal pronouns refer to the first person (I), second person (you), and third person (he, she, it).

SPEAKER   SPOKEN TO   SPOKEN ABOUT
I think you should be nicer to him.

A personal pronoun has three cases that indicate how it is used in a sentence: **nominative, objective,** and **possessive.** The nominative case is used for subjects and predicate nominatives. The objective case is used for objects of verbs and prepositions. The possessive case is used to show ownership or belonging.

NOMINATIVE   OBJECTIVE   POSSESSIVE
She let me borrow her helmet.

Personal Pronouns			
	Nominative	**Objective**	**Possessive**
First person *(speaker)*	I; we	me; us	my, mine; our, ours
Second person *(spoken to)*	you	you	your, yours
Third person *(spoken about)*	he, she, it; they	him, her, it; them	his, her, hers, its; their, theirs

Gender Personal pronouns in the third-person singular also have gender. These pronouns are *masculine, feminine,* or *neuter,* depending on whether they refer to a male, a female, or a thing.

WATCH OUT

A pronoun has to match the person, number, and gender of its antecedent.

PARTS OF SPEECH

Parts of Speech   **9**

Possessive Pronouns

A **possessive pronoun** shows ownership or belonging. The following possessive pronouns are used to replace possessive nouns: *mine, yours, hers, his, its, ours, theirs.*

That bike is mine.   **The bike carrier is ours.**

The following possessive pronouns are used as adjectives to modify nouns: *my, your, his, her, its, our, their.* The possessive pronoun *his* can be used both ways.

That is my map.   **That is his compass.**

Reflexive and Intensive Pronouns

Both reflexive and intensive pronouns are formed by adding *–self* or *–selves* to a personal pronoun. Although these two types of pronouns look identical, they are used in different ways. A **reflexive pronoun** reflects an action back on a preceding noun or pronoun.

Kim helped herself to seconds of every buffet item.

An **intensive pronoun** adds emphasis to a noun or pronoun in the same sentence.

No one asked the doctor herself if she needed help.

Reflexive and Intensive Pronouns	
First person	myself; ourselves
Second person	yourself; yourselves
Third person	himself, herself, itself; themselves

Is it a reflexive or an intensive pronoun? If it can be removed without changing the meaning of the sentence, then it's an *intensive pronoun.*

Sara ~~herself~~ went to the game.

Interrogative Pronouns

An **interrogative pronoun** is used to ask a question.

who   whom   which   what   whose

Whose wallet is this?
What can we do while it rains?

Demonstrative Pronouns

A **demonstrative pronoun** points out specific persons, places, things, or ideas. *This* and *these* point out persons or things that are near in space or time. *That* and *those* point out persons or things that are more distant in space or time. Demonstrative pronouns may come before or after their antecedents.

Did you get her new CD? I'm dying to hear that.
ANTECEDENT

Read the instructions, even those in small print.
ANTECEDENT

 Demonstrative pronouns are commonly used as adjectives. In these cases, they come immediately before the noun they modify.

Relative Pronouns

A **relative pronoun** introduces a subordinate clause.

who   whom   which   whose   that

SUBORDINATE CLAUSE

Schliemann was the archaeologist who discovered Troy.

For more on subordinate clauses, see pp. 78–80.

Indefinite Pronouns

An **indefinite pronoun** does not refer to a specific person or thing.

Someone left the phone off the hook.
The snowstorm closed most of the schools.

Common Indefinite Pronouns	
Singular	another, anybody, anyone, anything, each, either, everybody, everyone, everything, much, neither, nobody, no one, nothing, one, somebody, someone, something
Plural	both, few, many, several
Singular or Plural	all, any, more, most, none, some

For more on using pronouns correctly, see pp. 152–179.

❷ Pronouns in Action

Several pronouns below refer to people or things mentioned earlier in the passage, thereby making the writing both tight and unified. You can use pronouns in dialogue to identify frequent changes of speakers, persons addressed, and ideas.

> **LITERARY MODEL**
>
> "**What** do **I** care about Louise? **I** just thought **she** was a friend of **yours**, **that**'s all. **That**'s why **I** never even noticed **her**."
>
> "Well, **you** certainly took an awful lot of notice of **her** today," **she** said. On **our** wedding day! **You** said **yourself** when **you** were standing there in the church **you** just kept thinking of **her**...."
>
> "Listen honey," **he** said, "**I** never should have said **that**. How does **anybody** know **what** kind of crazy things come into **their** heads when **they**'re standing there waiting to get married?"
>
> —Dorothy Parker, "Here We Are"

REVIEW: Pronouns

Refer to Dorothy Parker's passage above to complete these exercises.

1. Find an example of each of these kinds of pronouns in the passage: *personal, intensive, possessive, relative, demonstrative, indefinite, and interrogative.*
2. Identify the nominative pronoun and the objective pronoun in this sentence: "That's why I never even noticed her."
3. Write the antecedent of *she* and *her* that appears in the first paragraph.
4. What kind of pronoun is *yourself* in the second paragraph?
5. To what does *that* refer in the last paragraph?

For more practice, see the EXERCISE BANK, p. 590.

Verbs

REVIEW 3

❶ Review the Basics

A **verb** is a word used to express action, condition, or a state of being. The two main categories of verbs are action verbs and linking verbs.

Action Verbs

An **action verb** expresses an action. That action may be physical or mental.

PHYSICAL ACTION   **wince create gallop steal chew**
MENTAL ACTION   **visualize believe recall desire know**

Transitive and Intransitive Verbs

Action verbs may be transitive or intransitive. A **transitive verb** transfers the action from the subject toward a **direct object.**

ACTS ON

A group of volunteers painted a mural on the wall.

An **intransitive verb** does not transfer action so it does not have an object.

I waited patiently.

Linking Verbs

A **linking verb** connects the subject with a word or words that identify or describe the subject. It can connect the subject with a noun, the predicate nominative.

LINKS TO

Judge Bianca is also a professor of law.

A linking verb can also connect the subject to a pronoun or an adjective in the predicate.

LINKS TO

Michelle felt ill after the barbecue.

LINKS TO

The decision remains his, and his alone.

Most linking verbs are forms of *be*.

Common Linking Verbs	
Forms of *be*	am, is, are, was, were, being, be, can be, may be, might be, will be, could be, would be, must be, has been, have been, had been, shall have been, could have been, would have been, will have been
Other common linking verbs	appear, become, feel, grow, look, remain, seem, smell, sound, stay, taste, turn

Forms of *be* are always linking verbs when used as the main verb.

Form of be: **We were so hungry.**

Some verbs can also be used as linking verbs.

The veggie burgers tasted scrumptious.

Some verbs can function as both action and linking verbs.

ACTS ON

Used as action verb: **We grew pumpkins in the fall.**
Used as linking verb: **The laborer grew hungry.**

LINKS

Is it a linking verb or an action verb? It's a linking verb if it can be replaced by a form of the verb *be* and still make sense. Example: It *sounds* loud. It *is* loud.

Auxiliary Verbs

Auxiliary verbs, also called **helping verbs,** help the main verb express action or make a statement. Auxiliary verbs help indicate voice, mood, or tense. A **verb phrase** is made up of a main verb and one or more auxiliary verbs.

Common Auxiliary Verbs					
am	are	has	does	can	might
is	be	had	did	could	shall
was	being	have	will	may	should
were	been	do	would	must	

AUXILIARY VERBS   MAIN VERB
The officers had been planning the raid for months.

Many contractions are formed by combining an auxiliary verb with a pronoun or the word *not* (*I'll, don't*). In such cases, remember to break apart the contraction in order to identify which part is the verb (I'll = I will, don't = do not).

❷ Verbs in Action

Well-chosen verbs can make your writing more vigorous and interesting. Notice how both action and linking verbs in the following passage vividly capture sounds and movements in nature.

PROFESSIONAL MODEL

Bighorn sheep **clung** to the canyon walls above the river, and bison **trailed** across the floodplain. Fresh grizzly tracks **punctured** the mud at a melting snowbank's edge. But the creature that **held** my attention here in Yellowstone National Park **was** the one that **seemed** to be talking to itself. Hunched among the pine branches, it **gabbled, growled,** and **mewled** without pause. At times the voice **resembled** liquid gurgling through a pipe. Then it **became** a drum and, soon after, a rattle. I **felt** as if I'**d happened** upon a shaman in the midst of his prayers. . . .

I **don't mean** to make this sound too mysterious. The birds **were** only common ravens.

—Douglas H. Chadwick, "Ravens"

REVIEW: Verbs

Refer to the passage above to complete these exercises.

1. Write the sentence from the last paragraph that contains a linking verb. Underline the two words that are connected by the linking verb.

2. Write two verb phrases from the passage. Underline the auxiliary verbs in each phrase. If the phrase contains a contraction, write the full verb contained within the contraction.

3. Find examples of two transitive verbs in the first paragraph. Write the transitive verbs and the direct objects that receive their actions. Example: unfold their wings

4. Write three action verbs from the passage that describe sounds. Then write three action verbs of your own that describe other sounds in nature.

For more practice, see the **EXERCISE BANK, p. 591.**

Adjectives and Adverbs

❶ Review the Basics

Adjectives and **adverbs** are modifiers—they describe other words in a sentence. An *adjective* modifies a noun or a pronoun.

MODIFIES NOUN **Hawaii has titanic waves.**

MODIFIES PRONOUN **They can be intimidating.**

An *adverb* modifies a verb, an adjective, or another adverb.

MODIFIES ADVERB **The waves crash very dangerously.**

MODIFIES VERB **Yet surfers ride them gracefully.**

MODIFIES ADJECTIVE **It's quite beautiful.**

Adjectives

An adjective qualifies or specifies the meaning of the noun it modifies. It answers one of these questions:

WHAT KIND? **silver ornaments, huge serving, lively writing**

WHICH ONE? **this fossil, another book, those computers**

HOW MANY? **three rings, some exhibitors, few volunteers**

HOW MUCH? **enough help, abundant harvest, little chance**

Nouns, pronouns, and even articles can function as adjectives, modifying the nouns they precede.

Nouns as Adjectives
   mouse pad   business letter   tuna fish salad

Possessive Pronouns as Adjectives
   his portfolio   our Web site   their supervisor

Demonstrative Pronouns as Adjectives
   that application   this uniform   those menus

Articles
   an undertaking   a game   the one I want

Proper adjectives are formed from proper nouns. They are always capitalized, as are proper nouns.

Proper Adjectives	
Proper Nouns	**Proper Adjectives**
America	American
French	French
Jefferson	Jeffersonian

Predicate adjectives follow linking verbs and modify the subject of a sentence. Unlike most adjectives, predicate adjectives are separated from the words they modify.

MODIFIES

My cat is unpredictable.

MODIFIES

The parakeet looks nervous.

For guidelines on capitalizing proper adjectives, see p. 202.

For guidelines on capitalizing proper adjectives, see p. 202.

Adverbs

Most adverbs end in *-ly*. They answer these questions about the words they modify: How? Where? When? To what extent?

Adverbs	
How?	opened **slowly**, praised **profusely**, hummed **softly**
Where?	waddled **away**, sank **lower**, rode **east**
When?	shipped **yesterday**, arrived **early**, slept **late**
To what extent?	**so** early, **very** sorry, **really** pleased

The word *not* is an adverb that tells to what extent. Though it often comes between the parts of the verb, it is not part of the verb. Example: could not go; verb = could go

❷ Adjectives and Adverbs in Action

Notice the central role that adjectives and adverbs play in this description. Not every adjective and adverb is highlighted.

It was a **rainy July** morning, and Bernd Blossey's beetles were **sluggish**. Or maybe they were **shy**.... Blossey wasn't worried. When they were **ready,** the **tiny brown** beetles he and his assistants had set **free** would start devouring the **purple** loosestrife strangling the refuge's wetlands.

... [L]oosestrife grows in North America like, well, a weed. When the **tall, hardy** plants with **bright purple, conelike** flowers **first** arrived from Europe in the **19th** century, they found **no** enemies, **just fertile** soil. In marshes, **especially,** loosestrife took over like kudzu. **Now,** a century **later, this** unchecked growth threatens **local** wildlife, which depends on **other** plants for nesting materials and food. In **another** time, hard-pressed naturalists might have reached for pesticides or poisons, but **today those** are **environmentally incorrect**—and **often plain dangerous.** Instead, scientists looked for a "**biological** control" for the **loosestrife** problem. In **other** words, they sought to turn Mother Nature against one of **her** own.

—"Pest vs. Pest," *Newsweek*, Aug. 4, 1997

REVIEW: Adjectives and Adverbs

For each underlined word, identify: (a) whether the word is an adjective or adverb; (b) the word it modifies; (c) the part of speech of the word it modifies.

"When the <u>tall</u>, <u>hardy</u> plants with <u>bright</u> <u>purple</u>, <u>conelike</u>
     (1)   (2)   (3)   (4)   (5)
flowers <u>first</u> arrived from Europe in the 19th century, they
      (6)
found <u>no</u> enemies, <u>just</u> <u>fertile</u> soil. In marshes, <u>especially</u>,
   (7)   (8)   (9)   (10)
loosestrife took over like kudzu."

For a SELF-CHECK and more practice, see the EXERCISE BANK, p. 592.

REVIEW

Prepositions

❶ Review the Basics

A **preposition** is a word used to show the relationship between a noun or pronoun and some other word in the sentence.

Each preposition below relates *yelled* to *child*, but notice how the meaning of the sentence changes.

He yelled to the child.

He yelled at the child.

He yelled about the child.

He yelled near the child.

The Far Side by Gary Larson

"Goldberg, you idiot! Don't play tricks on those things—they can't distinguish between "laughing with" and "laughing at"!

Common Prepositions				
about	before	during	off	toward
above	behind	except	on	under
across	below	for	out	underneath
after	beneath	from	outside	until
against	beside	in	over	unto
along	between	inside	past	up
among	beyond	into	since	upon
around	but	like	through	with
as	by	near	throughout	within
at	down	of	to	without

Prepositional Phrase

A preposition always introduces a phrase called a **prepositional phrase.** A prepositional phrase ends in a noun or pronoun called the **object of the preposition.** If the object has modifiers, they are also part of the prepositional phrase.

PREPOSITION   MODIFIERS   OBJECT OF PREPOSITION

Drag the cursor to the very last item.

PREPOSITIONAL PHRASE

Compound Prepositions and Objects

A **compound preposition** is a preposition that consists of more than one word.

Compound Prepositions	
according to	on account of
in addition to	in place of
prior to	in spite of
by means of	aside from

Compound objects are two or more objects of a single preposition.

Reza bought T-shirts for Eva, Rob, and Choi.

COMPOUND OBJECTS

❷ Prepositions in Action

You can use a short, simple preposition to clarify complex relationships. In the excerpt below, Flannery O'Connor uses several prepositions to clarify location, time, gesture, and action.

LITERARY MODEL

The old woman and her daughter were sitting **on** their porch when Mr. Shiftlet came **up** their road **for** the first time. The old woman slid **to** the edge **of** her chair and leaned forward, shading her eyes **from** the piercing sunset **with** her hand. The daughter could not see far **in** front **of** her and continued to play **with** her fingers. Although the old woman lived **in** this desolate spot **with** only her daughter and she had never seen Mr. Shiftlet before, she could tell, even **from** a distance, that he was a tramp and no one to be afraid of.

—Flannery O'Connor, "The Life You Save May Be Your Own"

REVIEW: Prepositions

For each boldfaced preposition in the first two sentences above, write the entire prepositional phrase. Label the preposition with *P*, the object of preposition with *OP*, and any modifiers with *M*.

For more practice, see the EXERCISE BANK, p. 592.

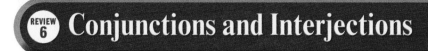

Conjunctions and Interjections

❶ Review the Basics

A **conjunction** is a word used to join words or groups of words.

Coordinating Conjunctions

A **coordinating conjunction** connects words or word groups that have equal importance in a sentence.

and	**but**	**or**	**for**	**so**	**yet**	**nor**

The Three Stooges are Larry, Moe, and Curly.

We thought about going to a movie, but we rented one instead.

A **conjunctive adverb** is an adverb used to clarify the relationship between clauses of equal weight in a sentence.

We figured Noah wasn't home; still, we rang his doorbell.

A conjunctive adverb can also be used parenthetically within a sentence.

Michelangelo, moreover, is known as both a sculptor and a painter.

Conjunctive Adverbs			
accordingly	finally	indeed	otherwise
also	furthermore	meanwhile	still
besides	hence	moreover	then
consequently	however	nevertheless	therefore

Correlative Conjunctions

Correlative conjunctions are pairs of conjunctions that connect words or groups of words. Always used in pairs, they *correlate* with one another.

Neither motorboats nor jet skis are allowed.
Both my cousin and my brother know how to sail.

Correlative Conjunctions	
both . . . and	not only . . . but also
neither . . . nor	whether . . . or
either . . . or	

PARTS OF SPEECH

Subordinating Conjunctions

Subordinating conjunctions introduce subordinate clauses—clauses that cannot stand alone as complete sentences. A subordinating conjunction joins a subordinate clause to an independent clause—a clause that can stand alone as a complete sentence.

SUBORDINATE CLAUSE   INDEPENDENT CLAUSE

After Paco tried snowboarding, he was hooked on the sport.

Common Subordinating Conjunctions

after	because	since	when
although	before	so that	whenever
as if	even if	than	where
as long as	even though	though	wherever
as much as	in order that	unless	while
as soon as	provided that	until	

❷ Conjunctions in Action

You can use conjunctions to provide flow and logic by connecting and differentiating the various relationships among the words.

LITERARY MODEL

They found him under a big cottonwood tree. His Levi jacket **and** pants were faded light-blue **so that** he had been easy to find. The big cottonwood tree stood apart from a small grove of winterbare cottonwoods **which** grew in the wide, sandy arroyo. He had been dead for a day **or** more, **and** the sheep had wandered **and** scattered up **and** down the arroyo. . . . He [Leon] squinted up at the sun **and** unzipped his jacket—it sure was hot for this time of year. **But** high **and** northwest the blue mountains were still deep in snow.

—Leslie Marmon Silko, "The Man to Send Rain Clouds"

The phrases and clauses below are taken from the Literary Model. Write the conjunction in each phrase or clause and identify whether it is a coordinating or a subordinating conjunction.

1. his Levi jacket and pants
2. so that he had been easy to find
3. cottonwoods which grew in the wide, sandy arroyo
4. dead for a day or more
5. sheep had wandered and scattered

For more practice, see the EXERCISE BANK, p. 593.

Interjections

An **interjection** is a word or short phrase used to express emotion. It has no grammatical connection to other words in a sentence. Interjections are usually set off from the rest of a sentence by a comma or by an exclamation mark.

Wow! We won!
My, I've heard everything now.

Many English words are used for more than one part of speech. If you're sometimes confused, remember that you are in good company! To determine the part of speech of a word, you need to check how it's used within a sentence.

Here's How Which Part of Speech Is It?

Noun or adverb?

Yesterday was drizzly.	➡ **Noun.** Serves as subject.
Did you hike **yesterday?**	➡ **Adverb.** Modifies verb. Tells when.

Preposition or adverb?

Do you color **outside** the lines?	➡ **Preposition.** Has an object, *lines.*
Let's go **outside.**	➡ **Adverb.** Modifies verb. Tells where.

Adjective or pronoun?

She wears **several** rings.	➡ **Adjective.** Modifies noun *rings.*
Several are gold.	➡ **Pronoun.** Serves as subject.

Conjunction or preposition?

Learn Spanish **before** you travel.	➡ **Conjunction.** Connects clauses.
Can you meet me **before** class?	➡ **Preposition.** Has an object, *class.*

Chapter 1

Parts of the Sentence

0   1   2   3   4

INCHES

Theme: Oddities of Nature

You Won't Believe This!

Good grief, what do you think this is? It's actually a life-sized goliath beetle that weighs about as much as a medium-sized apple. Even though it's a giant among insects, it's made up of the same parts as any other bug. Sentences are like bugs in that way. They all have the same basic parts, no matter how long or short and complex or simple they are.

Write Away: Phenomenal Phenomenon

There are many oddities in nature in addition to enormous bugs: amazing storms, unusual land forms, and strange animal behavior. Write a paragraph about the strangest natural phenomenon you've ever experienced. Save your paragraph in your  **Working Portfolio.**

CD-ROM **Grammar Coach**

Choose the letter of the term that correctly identifies each numbered part of the passage.

Some of our planet's oddest creatures <u>live in the ocean</u>. For example,
(1)

anglerfish attract <u>prey</u> with fleshy, quivery "fishing poles" protruding from
(2)

their heads. Sponges are another <u>example</u> of ocean oddities. Many people
(3)

call them <u>plants,</u> but sponges are actually animals that eat very small
(4)

plants and animals. Other ocean-dwelling animals, like lantern fish, have

special <u>organs</u> that give off light. <u>Imagine if humans had such organs.</u>
(5)   (6)

Then there are <u>the nudibranchs, or sea slugs</u>. They may sound <u>ugly</u>, but
(7)   (8)

sea slugs are some of the most beautifully colored and varied organisms

in the oceans. Scientists <u>appreciate</u> their variety and <u>have given</u> them
(9)

names that match their appearance. For example, a bumpy orange

covering gave the <u>orange-peel nudibranch</u> its mouthful of a label.
(10)

---

1. A. complete predicate
   B. simple predicate
   C. compound verb
   D. direct object

2. A. indirect object
   B. predicate nominative
   C. direct object
   D. objective complement

3. A. predicate adjective
   B. simple predicate
   C. direct object
   D. predicate nominative

4. A. predicate nominative
   B. objective complement
   C. predicate adjective
   D. indirect object

5. A. objective complement
   B. direct object
   C. indirect object
   D. predicate nominative

6. A. inverted sentence
   B. declarative sentence
   C. imperative sentence
   D. interrogative sentence

7. A. objective complement
   B. direct object
   C. compound subject
   D. complete subject

8. A. predicate adjective
   B. direct object
   C. indirect object
   D. objective complement

9. A. predicate nominative
   B. compound verb
   C. complete predicate
   D. simple predicate

10. A. simple subject
    B. direct object
    C. indirect object
    D. predicate adjective

Subjects and Predicates

❶ Here's the Idea

▶ **A sentence is a group of words that expresses a complete thought. Every sentence can be divided into two parts—the subject and the predicate.**

The Atacama Desert in Chile	is one of the driest places on earth.
SUBJECT	PREDICATE

Some areas of the Atacama	get rain only a few times a century.
SUBJECT	PREDICATE

Simple Subjects and Simple Predicates

The most basic elements of a sentence are the simple subject and the simple predicate, or verb. Neither one includes modifiers but each may be made up of more than one word.

▶ **The simple subject tells who or what performs the action in a sentence.**

The slender Arctic **tern** migrates remarkable distances.

It may travel over 22,000 miles in the course of its yearly trek.

▶ **The simple predicate tells what the subject did or what happened to the subject.**

Many terns **have flown** from the Arctic Circle to the Antarctic Circle and back again.

They generally **follow** the same migratory route.

> **Here's How** Finding Simple Subjects and Simple Predicates
>
> • To find the **simple subject**, ask "Who or what is or does the action?"
> • To find the **simple predicate**, ask "What does the subject do?" or "What happens to it?"
>
> **One three-month-old tern from Nova Scotia migrated as far as southern South Africa.**
> What did the action? **tern**   What did the subject do? **migrated**

Complete Subjects and Complete Predicates

▶ **The complete subject includes the simple subject and all the words that modify it.**

> **More tornadoes** occur in the United States than anywhere else.
> ↖ SIMPLE SUBJECT

▶ **The complete predicate includes all the words that tell what the subject did or what happened to the subject.**

> **Some tornadoes** produce winds of over 250 miles per hour.
> ↖ SIMPLE PREDICATE

▶ **A sentence fragment is a group of words that is only part of a sentence. It may lack a subject, a predicate, or both.**

Sentence or Fragment?		
Fragment	**Problem**	**Sentence**
A much lower average daily temperature than most deserts.	The fragment needs a subject and a predicate.	**The Atacama has** a much lower average daily temperature than most deserts.
Daytime temperatures in the 60s typical even in summer.	The fragment needs a predicate.	Daytime temperatures in the 60s **are** typical even in summer.

❷ Why It Matters in Writing

Both subject and predicate are needed to make the meaning of a sentence clear.

STUDENT MODEL

DRAFT

Have you ever seen a fish walking? One example, the climbing perch. Walks by using its tail and the edges of its gill covers as legs. A rocking motion.

REVISION

Have you ever seen a fish walking? One example **is** the climbing perch. **It** walks by using its tail and the edges of its gill covers as legs. **The "walk" is** actually a rocking motion.

> Add predicate.

> Add subject.

> Add subject and predicate.

❸ Practice and Apply

A. CONCEPT CHECK: Subjects and Predicates

Copy each sentence below. Draw a vertical line between the complete subject and the complete predicate. Then underline the simple subject once and the simple predicate twice.

Example: Some animals move in unexpected ways.
Answer: Some <u>animals</u> | <u>move</u> in unexpected ways.

Look, Ma—I'm Flying!

1. No one thinks twice about flying birds, insects, or bats.
2. Flying lizards are an entirely different matter.
3. The Asian flying dragon has folds of skin stretched over its ribs.
4. The animal can unfold this skin to form "wings."
5. It soars from tree to tree on these outstretched "wings."
6. Some squirrel species also have folds of skin between their front and back legs.
7. Observers of flying squirrels have measured glides of 200 feet.
8. Certain fish fling themselves out of the sea with their powerful tails.
9. They glide above the water surface on large, winglike fins.
10. North America has both flying squirrels and flying fish.

➡ For a SELF-CHECK and more practice, see the EXERCISE BANK, p. 594.

B. REVISING: Correcting Sentence Fragments

Revise the paragraph below, changing sentence fragments to complete sentences.

STUDENT MODEL

Hold Your Breath!

Before 1995, the green iguana unknown on the Caribbean island of Anguilla. In September 1995, two hurricanes the Caribbean region. One month later, about 15 green iguanas ashore at Anguilla. Had apparently traveled 200 miles from an island in Guadeloupe. The lizards were probably perched in their trees on the island when the hurricanes uprooted the trees. Flung into the sea. Where they formed a natural "raft." Ocean currents must have carried them to their new home.

Compound Sentence Parts

❶ Here's the Idea

Every sentence must have a subject and a verb. Either or both of these basic parts may be compound.

Compound Sentence Parts		
	Definition	**Examples**
Compound subject	Two or more subjects that share a verb	The **aurora borealis** and the **aurora australis** are two of nature's great light shows.
Compound verb	Two or more verbs or verb phrases that share the same subject	The lights **glimmer** and **ripple** across the night sky.
Compound predicate	A compound verb and all the words that go with each verb	A magnetic storm in the upper atmosphere **causes the lights** and **creates their eerie, shifting patterns**.

Join compound subjects and verbs with a conjunction that makes the relationship between the parts clear.

- Use *or* or *either . . . or* to show a choice.
- Use *neither . . . nor* to show a negative choice.
- Use *and* to show a combination.

"*Your mother and I are feeling overwhelmed, so you'll have to bring yourselves up.*"

© New Yorker Collection 1999 David Sipress

❷ Why It Matters in Writing

Using compound sentence parts allows writers to combine several ideas into one sentence.

PROFESSIONAL MODEL

In 1966, the 44,000-ton *Michelangelo,* an Italian steamship carrying 775 passengers, encountered a single massive wave in an otherwise unremarkable sea. Her bow fell into a trough and the wave stove in her bow, flooded her wheelhouse, and killed a crewman and two passengers.

—Sebastian Junger, *The Perfect Storm*

> The compound verb combines four actions in one sentence.

❸ Practice and Apply

A. CONCEPT CHECK: Compound Sentence Parts

Write the compound subjects and compound verbs in the following sentences.

Blame It on El Niño

1. The 1997–1998 El Niño ranked as the strongest in history and took the blame for every odd weather event.
2. At various times El Niño either terrified or annoyed people.
3. Television comedians and other jokesters blamed El Niño for every problem in people's lives.
4. The warming effect of El Niño caused droughts and wildfires in some places and brought floods and mud slides to others.
5. Exceptionally violent tornadoes and hurricanes struck the United States and Latin America.
6. Hurricane Georges and Hurricane Mitch were especially devastating.
7. The hurricanes killed thousands of people and destroyed property worth billions of dollars.
8. Oceanographers and other scientists found El Niño fascinating.
9. Neither government officials nor ordinary people regretted El Niño's end though.
10. A related phenomenon, La Niña, followed El Niño and cooled the Pacific Ocean waters.

➡ **For a SELF-CHECK and more practice, see the EXERCISE BANK, p. 594.**

Write five sentences describing this picture of an ice storm caused by El Niño. Choose a subject, a predicate, or both from the list below for each sentence.

people and animals

warm mittens and waterproof boots

glazed tree branches and sagging telephone lines

cars or snowplows

parents or children

neither streets nor sidewalks

neither businesses nor schools

snow and ice

glistened like a crystal necklace and crackled like popping corn

cleared the paths and shoveled the streets

trudged through the snow or cross-country skied

enjoyed the break from the routine or complained about the inconvenience

either skidded or got stuck

blew and drifted

SENTENCE PARTS

Subjects in Sentences

❶ **Here's the Idea**

▶ There are four types of sentences, each with a specific function.

Types of Sentences		
	Function	**Example**
Declarative	To state a fact, wish, intent, or feeling	**Severe thunderstorms** can cause some unusual droppings from the sky.
Interrogative	To ask a question	Have **you** heard about fish-falls in northern Australia?
Imperative	To give a command, request, or direction	**(You)** Read some firsthand reports from people with dead fish on their roofs.
Exclamatory	To express strong feeling	How unnerving **the thump of fish bodies** must be!

As the chart shows, in most sentences the subject comes before the verb. Common exceptions to this S-V order include inverted sentences and sentences beginning with *here* or *there.*

Remember, the subject of imperative sentences is *you,* even though it is not written or spoken.

Inverted Sentences

▶ **Inverted sentences are sentences in which the subject follows the verb or comes in the middle of a verb phrase.**

Inverted word order is used

• in most interrogative sentences

> **Have any botanists in your area** encountered **an insect-eating cobra lily?**

• to change the emphasis in declarative or exclamatory sentences

> **Within its long, slippery leaves** lies **a death trap for careless bugs.**

Sentences That Begin with *Here* or *There*

▶ The words *here* and *there* almost never function as subjects of sentences. In sentences that begin with these words, the subject usually follows all or part of the verb.

There are several other carnivorous plants besides the cobra lily.

Here are some examples: Venus flytraps, sundews, and bladderworts.

To find the simple subject in a sentence beginning with *here* or *there,* first find the verb. Then ask who or what performs that action or has that state of being.

There are carnivorous plants growing throughout the world. Who or what are growing? **plants**

SENTENCE PARTS

❷ Why It Matters in Writing

A long series of declarative sentences can be boring to read. Using different types of sentences allows writers to vary the pace, tone, and mood of their message.

PROFESSIONAL MODEL

Have you ever heard of a flower whose seeds are carried and spread by elephants? Well, meet the rafflesia. Found in the rain forests of Sumatra, this unusual blossom is the world's largest flower, measuring three feet in diameter!

—Elizabeth Tambor

INTERROGATIVE SENTENCE

IMPERATIVE SENTENCE

EXCLAMATORY SENTENCE

❸ Practice and Apply

A. CONCEPT CHECK: Subjects in Sentences

For each sentence below, identify the type (D, Int, Imp, or Ex) and write the subject and the verb.

Really Big, Really Old Trees

1. Redwoods rank among the world's largest living things.
2. One tree in Redwood National Park stands about 368 feet tall!
3. Spectacular redwoods also soar high above the forest floor of Muir Woods National Monument.
4. To many people, there is nothing more awesome.
5. Think about the redwood's relative, the giant sequoia.
6. Do giant sequoias grow as tall as redwoods?
7. Giant sequoias have shorter but wider trunks than redwoods.
8. Both redwoods and giant sequoias can live to a ripe old age.
9. Do you want to see the world's most massive tree?
10. Visit Sequoia National Park on your next vacation.
11. Here the General Sherman Tree has stood for more than 2,200 years!
12. There are few things in nature harmful to a giant sequoia or a redwood.
13. Giant sequoias are protected by the U.S. government and live largely undisturbed by humans.
14. Listen, though, to the unmistakable sounds of chain saws in some redwood forests.
15. Should people harvest redwoods for their lumber?

➜ For a SELF-CHECK and more practice, see the EXERCISE BANK, p. 595.

Choose five sentences from Exercise A. Rewrite each sentence by inverting the word order for emphasis.

B. REVISING: Using a Variety of Sentences

In your 🗀 **Working Portfolio,** find the paragraph you wrote for the **Write Away** on page 24. Revise it to include several different types of sentences. Use at least one inverted sentence or sentence beginning with *here* or *there*.

Complements

❶ Here's the Idea

A subject and a verb alone often can't convey the whole meaning in a sentence. Many sentences require complements, words or word groups that follow the verb and complete its meaning. There are four types of complements: direct objects, objective complements, indirect objects, and subject complements.

Direct and Indirect Objects

▶ **A direct object is a noun or pronoun that tells who or what receives the action of a verb.**

> Nothing can escape a black hole.
>   DIRECT OBJECT

Sentences with direct objects may also have **indirect objects,** nouns or pronouns that tell to or for whom or what the action of the verb is done.

> The Hubble telescope showed scientists an enormous black hole.
>   INDIRECT OBJECT   DIRECT OBJECT

> It offered them only a roundabout view, however.
>   INDIRECT OBJECT   DIRECT OBJECT

Indirect objects never follow prepositions. A phrase that begins with *to* or *for* is a prepositional phrase, not an indirect object.

> Pairs of orbiting stars gave the first clue to researchers.
>   PREPOSITIONAL PHRASE

> Pairs of orbiting stars gave researchers the first clue.
>   INDIRECT OBJECT

Objective Complements

▶ **An objective complement is a noun or adjective that follows the direct object and identifies or describes it.** Only certain verbs, and their synonyms, can be followed by objective complements.

Verbs That Signal Objective Complements				
appoint	choose	elect	keep	name
call	consider	find	make	think

Over 1,500 species of fish call **the Great Barrier Reef** home.

  DIRECT OBJECT ➶   OBJECTIVE ➘
                     COMPLEMENT—NOUN

Its colorful coral formations make **the reef** unique. ◀

  DIRECT OBJECT ➶   OBJECTIVE COMPLEMENT
                     —ADJECTIVE

Subject Complements

▶ **A subject complement follows a linking verb and identifies or describes the subject.** Linking verbs include *be* and sense verbs such as *feel, seem, consider, smell, sound,* and *taste.*

A subject complement may be either a predicate nominative or a predicate adjective.

A **predicate nominative** is a noun used as a subject complement.

SAME AS

The Amazon is **a very wide river—over six miles in places.**

  ⬆ PREDICATE NOMINATIVE

A **predicate adjective** is an adjective used as a subject complement.

MODIFIES

In places, neither bank is **visible from the middle of the river.**

  ⬆ PREDICATE ADJECTIVE

❷ Why It Matters in Writing

Complements convey important information about the subject and verb in a sentence. Notice how incomplete this passage about tsunamis (waves generated by earthquakes) would be without the details in the complements.

> **PROFESSIONAL MODEL**
>
> A huge tsunami struck Hawaii in 1946. It was that state's worst-ever natural disaster. The massive wave killed 159 people and did some 25 million dollars' worth of damage. A tsunami caused by an earthquake off Chile in 1960 was the most destructive in recent history.
>
> —Michael Magada

DIRECT OBJECT

PREDICATE NOMINATIVE

PREDICATE ADJECTIVE

❸ Practice and Apply

A. CONCEPT CHECK: Complements

Identify each italicized complement as a direct object (DO), an indirect object (IO), an objective complement (OC), a predicate nominative (PN), or a predicate adjective (PA).

Not Your Ordinary Rocks

1. The American West offers *residents* and *tourists* an *abundance* of beautiful rock formations weirdly eroded.
2. For example, Bryce Canyon in Utah is *popular* among sightseers and photographers.
3. Visitors find its multicolored *formations* unspeakably *gorgeous.*
4. Geologists call the oddly shaped rock *columns* "hoodoos."
5. In visitors' imaginations, some formations become *cathedrals* or *castles.*
6. The federal government made *Bryce Canyon* a *national park* in 1928.
7. The huge sandstone arches, windows, and towers of Utah's Arches National Park also show *humans* the *power* of erosion.
8. Faced with such grandeur, park visitors feel *small* and *humble.*
9. Monument Valley in Utah and Arizona has been the *site* of many Hollywood Westerns.
10. Moviemakers apparently consider Monument Valley's towering sandstone *formations symbolic* of the Old West.

➡ For a SELF-CHECK and more practice, see the EXERCISE BANK, p. 595.

B. REVISING: Using Complements to Improve Writing

Revise the following student model, replacing vague or weak complements with more precise ones from the list that follows it.

STUDENT MODEL

Ocean water is salty and lake water is fresh—right? Well, Utah's Great Salt Lake is something else. The lake lies many miles from any ocean, but its water is several times saltier than ocean water! The resulting buoyancy can give people something unexpected. No matter how hard they try, they cannot stay under. The salty water keeps them up.

- effortlessly afloat
- even the strongest swimmers and divers
- the surprise of their lives
- submerged for long
- an exception to that natural "rule"

Sentence Diagramming

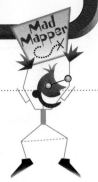

Mad Mapper

① Here's the Idea

Diagramming is a way of visually representing the structure of a sentence. It can help you understand how a sentence works by showing relationships among the parts.

Watch me for diagramming tips!

Simple Subjects and Verbs

The simple subject and the verb are written on one line and are separated by a vertical line that crosses the main line.

Comets orbit.

| Comets | orbit |

Remember: A simple subject and a verb can consist of more than one word.

Comet Hale-Bopp has orbited.

| Comet Hale-Bopp | has orbited |

Compound Subjects and Compound Verbs

For a compound subject or verb, split the main line. Write the conjunction on a dotted line connecting the split lines.

Comets and asteroids orbit.

Compound Subject

Comets
and
asteroids

orbit

Some asteroids collide and break apart.

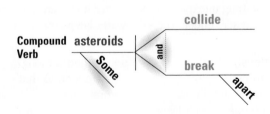

Compound Verb

asteroids
Some
and
collide
break
apart

Put adverbs and adjectives on slanted lines below the words they modify.

CHAPTER 1

SENTENCE PARTS

A. CONCEPT CHECK: Subjects and Verbs

Diagram these sentences, using what you have learned.

1. Amateur astronomers stargaze.
2. Some comets travel quickly and glow brightly.
3. Asteroids and comets differ dramatically.

Direct and Indirect Objects

A direct object follows the verb on the same line. It is separated by a vertical line that does not cross the main line.

Comets sometimes have ghostly white tails.

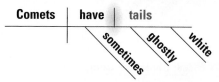

To show a compound predicate with direct objects, split the line and show both parts of the predicate on parallel lines.

Scientists observe comets and record information.

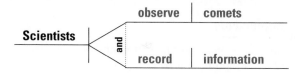

Write an indirect object below the verb on a horizontal line connected to the verb with a slanted line.

Comet Hale-Bopp gave all observers a spectacular show.

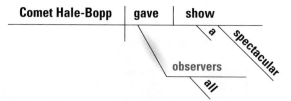

B. CONCEPT CHECK: Direct and Indirect Objects

Diagram these sentences, using what you have learned.

1. Alan Hale and Thomas Bopp discovered a new, faraway comet.
2. Reporters told the world the fantastic story.
3. The huge, bright comet met every expectation.

Objective Complements

An objective complement is written on the main line after the direct object and separated from it by a slanted line.

Astronomers often call comets dirty snowballs.

Some ancient people considered comets evil.

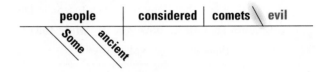

C. CONCEPT CHECK: Objective Complements

Diagram these sentences, using what you have learned.

1. Modern people find comets interesting.
2. Astronomers consider a comet strike possible.
3. This possibility makes comet location a priority.

Subject Complements

A subject complement is written on the main line after the verb and separated from it by a slanted line.

A falling star is actually a luminous dust particle.

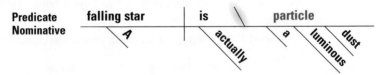

The name is deceptive.

The slanted line between a verb and a complement does not cross the main line because the complement is part of the predicate.

D. CONCEPT CHECK: Subject Complements

Diagram these sentences, using what you have learned.

1. The correct name is "meteor."
2. The sudden bright streak looks awesome.
3. Meteor showers are simply multiple meteors.

E. MIXED REVIEW: Diagramming

Diagram the following sentences. Pay special attention to the sentence parts you have learned about.

1. A cloud may surround a comet's icy nucleus.
2. This dusty, gaseous cloud is the coma.
3. Gas and dust may also give the comet a tail.
4. Asteroids are often quite large.
5. Astronomers consider asteroids minor planets.
6. Asteroids have struck the earth and have caused major damage.
7. Astronomers give their fellow citizens a warning.
8. An asteroid or a comet could hit the earth again.
9. The results might be disastrous.
10. That prospect makes many people nervous.

SENTENCE PARTS

Don't panic when you come up against a complicated sentence. Just reach into your memory bank and pull out these two diagramming patterns. Then find the subject and the predicate of your sentence and insert them in the diagram. Finally, identify and place modifiers and complements.

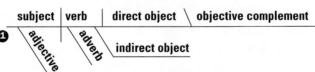

Real World Grammar

Field Report

Imagine that you volunteered to present a report on a natural oddity to your science club. You observed your subject carefully and took lots of notes. Now you have to turn those notes into an engaging, informative presentation. You're going to need all the skills you learned about sentence parts to turn your notes into clear, complete sentences.

Look at this student's draft of a report about a partial solar eclipse, along with comments from a friend he asked to read it.

FIELD REPORT

Shouldn't look during an eclipse—not even with sunglasses—or your eyes might be permanently damaged. To observe the sun indirectly, I found two pieces of stiff white cardboard—one for a "projector" and the other for a "screen." I took a safety pin. Then I punched a pinhole in the center of the projector cardboard.

The next day I went outside. With my back to the sun, I held the projector in my left hand. At the same time, I held the screen in my right hand. Keeping my eyes on the screen, I raised my left hand and moved it around until the sunlight came through the pinhole. I was told that an image of the eclipse would form on the screen. I was

shocked that it actually did. It looked like a cookie with a bite taken out of it. The bite got bigger. The cookie got smaller. There were noticeable changes every minute.

Who shouldn't look? And not look at what?

A little choppy. Can you combine the sentences or something?

Where did you go? At what time?

All these sentences are pretty much alike. How about some variety?

This must have been exciting, but it sounds pretty boring. Can you give more details?

Using Grammar in Writing

Compound parts	Use compound parts to combine sentences and present information more concisely. Just make sure those compound parts are parallel, or in the same grammatical structure or form.
Sentence variety	Use different kinds of sentences for the various parts of your field report—straightforward declarative sentences for the methods and materials section and more varied descriptive sentences for the observations and results.

REVISED FIELD REPORT

You shouldn't look at the sun during an eclipse —not even with sunglasses—or your eyes might be permanently damaged. To observe the sun indirectly, I found two pieces of stiff white cardboard—one for a "projector" and the other for a "screen." I punched a pinhole in the center of the projector cardboard with a safety pin.

This is much better. It feels as if I'd seen the eclipse myself.

The next day I went into my backyard about half an hour before the eclipse was supposed to peak. With my back to the sun, I held the projector in my left hand and the screen in my right hand. Keeping my eyes on the screen, I moved the projector until the sunlight came through the pinhole. There it was—an image of the eclipse! There were noticeable changes in the image with each passing minute. At first it looked like a cookie with a bite taken out of it. The bite grew bigger and bigger and the cookie smaller and smaller as the shadow gobbled up the sun.

PRACTICE AND APPLY: Revising

Below is another passage from the student's report on the solar eclipse. Revise it, using the writing tips at the top of the page.

ROUGH DRAFT

In addition to watching my "screen," paid attention to what was happening around me. You might expect that day became, but that's not what happened. The sky stayed blue, though it a dark, grayish blue. Shadows seemed sharper than usual. At the peak of the eclipse, the birds stopped. I realized I had goose bumps. The dimness was eerie. The silence was eerie too.

SENTENCE PARTS

Mixed Review

A. Subjects, Predicates, and Kinds of Sentences Read the passage below. Then write the answers to the questions that follow.

(1) Australia's weird and rare creatures include the platypus and the echidna, egg-laying mammals. (2) The platypus's furry body and wide, flat tail might remind you of a beaver. (3) However, its broad, hairless snout resembles the bill of a duck! (4) The spine-covered echidna uses its slender sensitive snout and long sticky tongue to sniff out and to lick up ants and termites. (5) Here is something really strange. (6) After an echidna egg hatches, the young echidna lives in its mother's pouch for several weeks before emerging.

(7) Tasmanian devils, another Australian oddity, scavenge for dead animals and hunt live animals. (8) With great ease do they tear the flesh and crunch the bones of their victims. (9) Why is this animal called a "devil"? (10) Just look at its fierce face and listen to its shrill scream.

1. What are the simple subject and the complete subject in sentence 1?
2. Is the subject in sentence 2 simple or compound?
3. What kind of sentence is sentence 3?
4. What are the simple and complete predicates in sentence 4?
5. What is the subject in sentence 5?
6. What kind of sentence is sentence 6?
7. What is the complete predicate in sentence 7?
8. What is the subject in sentence 8?
9. What kind of sentence is sentence 9, and what is its simple subject?
10. What are the simple subject and the compound verb in sentence 10?

B. Complements In the paragraph below, identify each underlined word as a direct object (DO), an indirect object (IO), an objective complement (OC), a predicate nominative (PN), or a predicate adjective (PA).

PROFESSIONAL MODEL

The idea of "living fossils" may seem **(1)** <u>silly</u> at first. Scientists call **(2)** <u>organisms</u> living **(3)** <u>fossils</u> if they have existed for millions of years without dying out or changing their form. The coelacanth is probably the most famous living **(4)** <u>fossil</u>. In 1938, some South African fishermen brought the **(5)** <u>curator</u> of a local museum an unusual **(6)** <u>fish</u>. The curator, Marjorie Courtenay-Latimer, was **(7)** <u>curious</u> about by the creature. It had hard, bony scales and muscular, almost limblike fins. Soon one of Courtenay-Latimer's colleagues gave **(8)** <u>her</u> the stunning news. The fish was a **(9)** <u>coelacanth</u>. Until that moment, experts had considered the coelacanth **(10)** <u>extinct</u> for at least 65 million years.

—Jennifer Knauf

Choose the letter of the term that correctly identifies each numbered part
of the passage.

Volcanic eruptions are not <u>true natural oddities</u>. At any moment, nearly
(1)
two dozen eruptions <u>shake</u> the earth's surface or <u>explode</u> unseen on the
(2)
ocean floor. However, the "birth" of a new volcano is extremely <u>rare</u>. In the
(3)
Western Hemisphere, such a birth last occurred in 1943.

<u>On February 20 of that year, a Mexican farmer named Dionisio Pulido</u>
(4)
<u>discovered a long crack in the ground that had not been there the day</u>

<u>before.</u> Soon, gray <u>smoke</u> and hot <u>stones</u> were coming out of the crack.
(5)
<u>Here was a chance for geologists to witness a once-in-a-lifetime event.</u>
(6)
The new volcano reached a height of about 500 feet within a week.

Named Parícutin after a nearby village, the volcano brought the local

<u>people</u> much <u>suffering</u>. <u>Ash and lava buried and destroyed</u> their fields,
(7)   (8)   (9)
homes, and other buildings. In 1952, Paricutin suddenly became <u>silent</u>.
(10)

1. A. indirect object
   B. objective complement
   C. predicate nominative
   D. simple subject

2. A. simple subject
   B. compound verb
   C. direct object
   D. objective complement

3. A. indirect object
   B. direct object
   C. objective complement
   D. predicate adjective

4. A. declarative sentence
   B. imperative sentence
   C. inverted sentence
   D. sentence fragment

5. A. direct object
   B. predicate nominative
   C. compound subject
   D. subject complement

6. A. sentence fragment
   B. imperative sentence
   C. inverted sentence
   D. interrogative sentence

7. A. predicate nominative
   B. indirect object
   C. direct object
   D. objective complement

8. A. objective complement
   B. indirect object
   C. predicate nominative
   D. direct object

9. A. complete subject and complete
      predicate
   B. simple subject and predicate
   C. sentence fragment
   D. compound subject and verb

10. A. predicate adjective
    B. predicate nominative
    C. objective complement
    D. indirect object

SENTENCE PARTS

Student Help Desk

Sentence Parts at a Glance

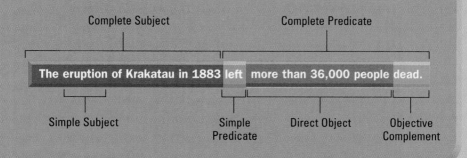

Complete Subject   Complete Predicate

The eruption of Krakatau in 1883 | left | more than 36,000 people | dead.

Simple Subject   Simple Predicate   Direct Object   Objective Complement

Inversion Version

Use various types of sentence inversion to vary the effect of your writing.

Basic Sentence

Dark smoke was pouring out of the crater of the volcano.

Method	Inversion	Effect
Change into a question.	Was dark smoke pouring out of the crater?	Asks a question
Begin with a prepositional phrase.	Out of the crater of the volcano was pouring dark smoke.	Changes the emphasis of the sentence
Begin with *here* or *there*.	There was dark smoke pouring out of the crater of the volcano.	Softens the impact of the sentence

Sentence Styling Salon

Do	Why?	How?
Use compound sentence parts.	Combining related parts makes your writing flow more smoothly.	The veil of volcanic dust dimmed the light of the sun. ~~It also~~ *and* created dramatic sunsets in North America and Europe.
Use mostly sentences beginning with words that carry information, rather than with *here* and *there*.	*Here* and *there* delay readers' getting to the point.	~~There was a drop in~~ *T*he world's temperature *dropped* ≡ for several years afterwards.
Use a variety of sentence types.	Varied sentences give your writing a lively rhythm that pulls readers along.	*What an* The explosion ~~was very loud~~ *that must have been!* It *The blast* was heard 3,000 miles away. ~~It~~ even set off huge ocean waves that traveled all the way around the globe.

The Bottom Line

Checklist for Parts of the Sentence

Have I . . .

____ made sure each sentence has a subject and predicate?

____ used appropriate complements to complete the meaning of a sentence?

____ used compound sentence parts to connect related ideas?

____ included a variety of sentence structures?

____ inverted sentence order when necessary or appropriate?

Using Phrases

That's one small step, one giant leap.

Theme: History Makers
How Shall I Phrase It?

Does the sentence above seem familiar yet somehow incomplete? Notice the difference as you read the famous quotation in full.

"That's one small step for man, one giant leap for mankind."
—Neil Armstrong, July 20, 1969

This historic message just doesn't have the same distinguished ring without its well-placed phrases. A **phrase** is a group of words, without a subject or predicate, that functions as a single part of speech. By using phrases effectively, you can make your writing more precise, more descriptive, and more memorable.

Write Away: Recording Your Own History
Where, when, and under what circumstances did you reach a turning point in your personal "history"? Write a paragraph describing a person, place, or event that changed your life. Save your paragraph in your **Working Portfolio**.

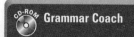
Grammar Coach

Choose the letter of the description that correctly identifies each underlined group of words.

What weighed approximately 185 pounds, was about the size <u>of a</u> ₍₁₎ <u>basketball</u>, and traveled <u>around the earth</u> at 18,000 miles per hour? The ₍₂₎ answer is *Sputnik I, <u>the world's first artificial satellite</u>*. (The satellite ₍₃₎ *Sputnik II*, the world's second piece of hardware to orbit the earth, was ₍₄₎ much larger and heavier.) <u>Launched on October 4, 1957, by the Soviet</u> ₍₅₎ <u>Union</u>, *Sputnik I* stunned Americans. In fact, the <u>completely unexpected</u> ₍₆₎ event that took place on that October day kicked off a new era. As a direct result of <u>the successful launching of *Sputnik I*</u>, <u>winning the technological</u> ₍₇₎ ₍₈₎ <u>competition with the Soviet Union</u> became one of the U.S. government's highest priorities. The space age had begun.

1. A. gerund phrase
   B. prepositional phrase
   C. participial phrase
   D. infinitive phrase

2. A. infinitive phrase acting as a subject
   B. infinitive phrase acting as an adjective
   C. prepositional phrase acting as an adverb
   D. prepositional phrase acting as an adjective

3. A. absolute phrase
   B. nonessential appositive phrase
   C. essential appositive phrase
   D. past participial phrase

4. A. absolute phrase
   B. nonessential appositive phrase
   C. essential appositive phrase
   D. past participial phrase

5. A. participial phrase
   B. infinitive phrase
   C. prepositional phrase
   D. appositive phrase

6. A. gerund phrase acting as a noun
   B. prepositional phrase acting as an adverb
   C. participial phrase acting as an adjective
   D. infinitive phrase acting as a noun

7. A. gerund phrase
   B. participial phrase
   C. infinitive phrase
   D. appositive phrase

8. A. gerund phrase acting as the subject
   B. infinitive phrase acting as the subject
   C. gerund phrase acting as the object of a preposition
   D. infinitive phrase acting as the object of a preposition

Prepositional Phrases

❶ Here's the Idea

▶ **A prepositional phrase consists of a preposition, its object, and any modifiers of the object.**

PREPOSITION ◢ ◢ MODIFIER ◢ OBJECT

Basketball was first played with real baskets.

A sentence can include more than one prepositional phrase.

James Naismith invented the game of basketball for a class at a YMCA in Springfield, Massachusetts.

The preposition in a prepositional phrase can have more than one object.

It was in Crawfordsville, Indiana, and nearby towns that basketball truly caught on.

For lessons on parts of a sentence, see pp. 24–37. For a list of common prepositions, see p. 19.

Adjective and Adverb Phrases

A prepositional phrase can function as either an adjective or an adverb. When a prepositional phrase modifies a noun or a pronoun, it acts as an adjective and is called an **adjective phrase**. An adjective phrase tells *what kind* or *which one*.

The original rules of the game were written in 1892.

MODIFIES A NOUN

When a prepositional phrase modifies a verb, an adjective, or an adverb, it acts as an adverb and is called an **adverb phrase**. An adverb phrase tells *where, when, how, why,* or *to what extent*.

Early hoops were constructed of peach baskets .

MODIFIES A VERB

Sometimes a prepositional phrase modifies the object of another phrase.

The baskets were mounted on the tops of tall poles.

MODIFIES PHRASE

Placement of Prepositional Phrases

▶ **In general, prepositional phrases should be placed before or immediately after the words they modify.** A misplaced prepositional phrase can make a sentence awkward, unclear, or even unintentionally humorous.

AWKWARD

Wild applause broke out for the team from the stands.

REVISED

From the stands, wild applause broke out for the team.

AWKWARD

Our coach paid tribute to the gym teacher who invented the game of basketball at last night's awards dinner.

REVISED

At last night's awards dinner, our coach paid tribute to the gym teacher who invented the game of basketball.

❷ Why It Matters in Writing

By using prepositional phrases as adjectives and adverbs, you can clarify time or location and add other essential details to your descriptions. Notice how this sports columnist uses prepositional phrases to give a precise and memorable account of what made Michael Jordan stand out as a rookie college player.

PROFESSIONAL MODEL

During the first few Tar Heel practices, coach Dean Smith realized something from one-on-one drills. Despite the presence of such stars as James Worthy and Sam Perkins, no one could keep up with this skinny freshman, "Mike" Jordan. He was respectful of the various egos among teammates, but afforded no mercy on the court.

—Bob Condor, *Chicago Tribune*

❸ Practice and Apply

A. CONCEPT CHECK: Prepositional Phrases

Write each prepositional phrase in the sentences below, along with the word or phrase it modifies. Then indicate whether the prepositional phrase is an adjective phrase or an adverb phrase.

Example: Michael Jordan's jersey, number 23, was officially retired at Chicago's United Center.

Answer: at Chicago's United Center; was retired—adverb phrase

Michael Jordan's Farewell

1. The historic news conference occurred on January 13, 1999.
2. Michael Jordan of the Chicago Bulls announced that he was retiring from basketball.
3. After the announcement, the reporters asked Jordan about his reasons, his emotions, and his plans.
4. Jordan explained that basketball no longer presented him with a strong mental challenge.
5. Although Jordan's love for the game of basketball remained unchanged, he chose to pursue new goals.

➡ For a **SELF-CHECK** and more practice, see the **EXERCISE BANK**, p. 595.

B. WRITING: Using Prepositional Phrases

The following information tells about notable events in the history of women's basketball. Use the facts given in each item below to write a complete sentence about the event cited. Include at least two prepositional phrases in each sentence, and underline each prepositional phrase that you use.

The Women's Game: Historical Highlights

1. When: 1895; Who: college instructor Clara Gregory Baer; What: publishes first set of rules—women's basketball
2. When: April 4, 1896; Where: San Francisco; What: first women's intercollegiate basketball game; Who: Stanford University team and University of California at Berkeley team
3. When: 1918; What: basket with open bottom becomes official, replacing closed basket with pull chain
4. When: July 1976; What: women's basketball makes its debut as an Olympic sport; Where: Montreal summer games
5. When: June 21, 1997; Who: the eight founding teams of the Women's National Basketball Association; What: officially begin their first season of pro basketball

LESSON 2 Appositives and Appositive Phrases

❶ Here's the Idea

▶ **An appositive is a noun or pronoun that identifies or renames another noun or pronoun.** An **appositive phrase** consists of an appositive plus its modifiers.

> **Passengers in a hot-air balloon ride in the gondola, a small basket beneath the balloon.**
> APPOSITIVE PHRASE

Essential and Nonessential Appositives

Appositives and appositive phrases can be essential or nonessential.

▶ **An essential or restrictive appositive is needed to make the meaning of the sentence complete.**

If you mentally cross out the appositive in the following sentence, the meaning of the sentence is incomplete.

> ESSENTIAL APPOSITIVE
> **The British tycoon Richard Branson has made several attempts to circle the world nonstop in a balloon.**

▶ **A nonessential or nonrestrictive appositive adds extra information to a sentence. It is not needed to make the meaning of the sentence clear.**

> NONESSENTIAL APPOSITIVE PHRASE
> **Steve Fossett, an American financier, is another dedicated competitor in around-the-world ballooning.**

Take another look at the sentences above. Notice that no commas are used with an essential appositive. A nonessential appositive, on the other hand, is set off with commas.

❷ Why It Matters in Writing

You can use appositive phrases to clarify terms in science reports, history papers, music reviews, and other pieces of nonfiction writing. Appositives help to identify or explain people, places, or things, as illustrated in the following account of the last flight of aviation pioneer Amelia Earhart.

PHRASES

PROFESSIONAL MODEL

In 1937 a round-the-world flight (another first) was planned, to test long-range performance of crew and aircraft. After an unsuccessful attempt, on June 1st Amelia Earhart and navigator Fred Noonan left Miami, Florida, flying east on an equatorial route that took them across the Atlantic Ocean, Africa, and the Indian Ocean. At Lae, New Guinea, on July 2, they took off to fly 2570 miles to Howland Island, **a spot in the Pacific scarcely longer than its runway.** They never reached it. Hours after they were due, the Coast Guard cutter *Itaska,* near Howland, received their last voice messages: "... gas is running low ... " and "We are on a line of position. ..." Sea and air searches found nothing.

—Vincent Wilson, Jr., "Amelia Earhart"

❸ Practice and Apply

CONCEPT CHECK: Appositives and Appositive Phrases

Write the appositives and appositive phrases in these sentences, and indicate whether they are essential or nonessential.

Around the World in 20 Days

1. On March 20, 1999, Swiss psychiatrist Bertrand Piccard and British balloon instructor Brian Jones made history.
2. As they flew over Mauritania, a country in northwestern Africa, the two completed the world's first nonstop balloon flight around the world.
3. The journey had begun 19 days earlier, on March 1, Piccard's birthday.
4. Piccard, who had just turned 41, and Jones, who was 51, had taken off from Château-d'Oex, a small town in the Swiss Alps.
5. Piccard comes from a family of adventurers. His father, Jacques Piccard, traveled to the greatest ocean depth ever reached using a bathyscaph, a deep-sea research vessel.

➡ **For a SELF-CHECK and more practice, see the EXERCISE BANK, p. 596.**

Prepositional and Appositive Phrases Read the following passage and then write the answers to the questions.

(1) Margaret Bourke-White, one of the most famous American photojournalists, documented many of the developments and events that shaped the second quarter of the 20th century. **(2)** Bourke-White first became interested in photography during her college years. **(3)** She began her professional career as an architectural photographer, but soon she developed an intense interest in modern industry and technology. **(4)** Her dynamic pictures of skyscrapers and steel mills won praise and attention. **(5)** They also landed her a job with *Fortune*, a newly founded business magazine.

(6) During the 1930s, Bourke-White journeyed to the Soviet Union, photographing Soviet farms and factories. **(7)** She also traveled widely within the United States, photographing farm families who lived in the Dust Bowl, a huge area of the Southwest and northern Great Plains that was devastated by the effects of erosion and drought. **(8)** It was also during this decade that Bourke-White pioneered the photo essay, a group of pictures that tell a story.

(9) *Life*, which became a leading American magazine in the 1940s, hired Bourke-White as a staff photographer. **(10)** Bourke-White's 285 assignments for *Life*, covering a wide range of events, took her around the world.

1. What is the appositive phrase in sentence 1?
2. What are the two prepositional phrases in sentence 2?
3. There are two prepositional phrases in sentence 3. What words do they modify?
4. Does the prepositional phrase in sentence 4 act as an adjective or an adverb?
5. Is the appositive in sentence 5 essential or nonessential?
6. What are the prepositional phrases in sentence 6?
7. What is the appositive phrase in sentence 7?
8. Is the appositive phrase in sentence 8 essential or nonessential?
9. There are two prepositional phrases in sentence 9. Which one is an adjective phrase? Which one is an adverb phrase?
10. Identify the prepositional phrases in sentence 10.

Verbals: Participial Phrases

A **verbal** is a verb form that acts as a noun, an adjective, or an adverb. There are three types of verbals: participles, gerunds, and infinitives. Each of these verbals can be used to form phrases. A **verbal phrase** consists of a verbal plus its modifiers and complements.

❶ Here's the Idea

▶ **A participle is a verb form that functions as an adjective.**

There are two kinds of participles: present participles and past participles. The present participle always ends in *-ing*. Most past participles end in *-d* or *-ed*. Others are irregularly formed.

PRESENT PARTICIPLE

The **falling** prices were good news for would-be buyers.

PAST PARTICIPLE

The **improved** designs made the automobiles cheaper and more reliable.

PAST PARTICIPLE

Known as "motoring," car travel soon became a popular pastime.

Auxiliary verbs can be added to past participles, as in *having improved*, *being improved*, and *having been improved*. Even though the auxiliary verb may end in *-ing,* the participle is still past.

Participial Phrases as Adjectives

▶ **A participial phrase consists of a participle plus its modifiers and complements.**

PARTICIPLE   PARTICIPIAL PHRASE   MODIFIES

Launching the first moving assembly line, Henry Ford revolutionized the automobile industry.

Because a participle is formed from a verb, it may have an object. If it does, the object is part of the participial phrase, as are any modifiers of the object.

PARTICIPIAL PHRASE   OBJECT

Driving their own automobiles, middle-class Americans enjoyed a sense of freedom and prosperity.

Don't confuse a participle with the main verb in a verb phrase. Note the difference in these examples.

> VERB: The trip to Venus was **cancelled**.

> VERBAL: Another passenger filled the **cancelled** appointment.

Absolute Phrases

▶ **An absolute phrase consists of a participle and the noun or pronoun it modifies.** An absolute phrase has no grammatical connection to the rest of the sentence. It does not function as a part of speech, and it does not belong to either the complete subject or the complete predicate. Usually, an absolute phrase relates to the rest of the sentence by providing additional details about circumstances or time.

ABSOLUTE PHRASE

Its popularity waning, **the Model T was retired from production in 1927.**

ABSOLUTE PHRASE

Our deadline fast approaching, **we realized that we would have to test our solar-powered lawn mower or else go back to our first idea.**

❷ Why It Matters in Writing

You can use participial phrases to show a close connection between the ideas in your sentences. These phrases also provide an economical way of adding interesting details. You will find them particularly helpful when writing brief pieces, such as the one-page essays often required on college and job applications.

STUDENT MODEL

Building on an intense interest in filmmaking, I bought my first video camera at the age of 14. The props and materials used in my first film were homemade or inexpensive. My ambition to learn documentary production still not satisfied, I decided to apply for your Young Filmmakers program.

PRESENT PARTICIPIAL PHRASE

PAST PARTICIPIAL PHRASE

ABSOLUTE PHRASE

❸ Practice and Apply

A. CONCEPT CHECK: Participial Phrases

Write the participial phrase in each sentence.

Henry Ford Builds an Affordable Car

1. Envisioning better automobile production, Henry Ford revolutionized the early automotive industry.
2. Borrowing an idea from the meat-packing industry, he introduced a conveyor belt to the assembly line.
3. By 1914, he had thoroughly perfected the new assembly system, allowing the production of Model Ts at the incredible rate of one every 93 minutes.
4. Priced beyond most people's means, automobiles had been owned almost exclusively by the wealthy.
5. Costing a great deal less because of the increased efficiency at Ford's plants, the Model T was a car that the average American could own.

➡ For a SELF-CHECK and more practice, see the EXERCISE BANK, p. 597.

B. WRITING: Using Participial Phrases

Combine each pair of sentences into a single sentence by using a participial phrase. Add or change words where necessary.

Example: The popularity of cars increased from year to year. Cars led to changes in the American lifestyle and landscape.
Answer: Increasing in popularity from year to year, cars led to changes in the American lifestyle and landscape.

1. Roads and highways proliferated. They were punctuated by roadside gas stations, motels, and diners.
2. A network of interstate highways gave the automobile industry a boost during the 1940s. The network was funded by the federal government.
3. Henry Ford established the first brand-name auto dealerships. Ford was always looking for ways to increase sales.
4. The architectural style of homes changed and began to include a garage or carport and a driveway. This resulted in smaller lawns.
5. Automobiles gave formerly isolated rural families new mobility. Automobiles allowed them to travel not only to cities but also to distant vacation spots.

Verbals: Gerund Phrases

LESSON 4

❶ Here's the Idea

▶ **A gerund is a verb form that ends in _–ing_ and functions as a noun.** Like any noun, a gerund can be used as a subject, an object of a preposition, a direct object, an indirect object, or a predicate nominative.

SUBJECT

Skiing **is a winter sport.**

OBJECT OF PREPOSITION

Thank you for listening.

▶ **A gerund phrase consists of a gerund plus its modifiers and complements.** Because a gerund is formed from a verb, it may have an object. If it does, the object and any modifiers of the object are part of the gerund phrase.

GERUND PHRASE

Tim Berners-Lee is known for inventing the World Wide Web.

GERUND ⬆   ⬆ OBJECT

Both gerunds and present participles end in _–ing_, but they function as different parts of speech. Remember, present participles function as adjectives, while gerunds function as nouns.

PRESENT PARTICIPLE

What does a blinking **cursor mean?**

GERUND

Blinking **can be a sign of eye strain.**

Which four _–ing_ words in the cartoon are gerunds? Which three are not?

Calvin & Hobbes by Bill Watterson

❷ Why It Matters in Writing

Gerunds can help you make your writing more concise and specific. Notice how gerunds are used effectively in the passage on the next page.

It turns out you can "enquire" [British spelling] about nearly anything online these days.... Click once to go to a site in Nairobi and enquire about booking shuttle reservations there. Click again, and zip off to Singapore, to a company that specializes in "pet moving." Enquire about buying industrial-age nuts and bolts from "the Bolt Boys" in South Africa, or teddy bears in upstate New York.

GERUNDS

GERUND PHRASES

—Joshua Quittner, "Tim Berners-Lee," *Time*

❸ Practice and Apply

CONCEPT CHECK: Gerund Phrases

Write each gerund phrase contained in the sentences below. Then underline the gerund within each phrase.

The Original Web Master

1. Today, visiting Web sites is practically as common as going to the movies.
2. Clicking your mouse can take you almost anywhere.
3. When you think about the history of inventing, Tim Berners-Lee probably doesn't come to mind.
4. The next time you try e-mailing someone or researching a topic on a computer, think about the efforts of this unsung hero.
5. Tim Berners-Lee's specialty was creating software.
6. While he worked at a physics lab in Switzerland, he devised an efficient system for organizing his copious notes.
7. Linking words within various documents and then following the trail of links gave him easy access to his files.
8. Discovering how to link documents was a huge milestone in developing the World Wide Web.
9. Linking the documents of other users to his was next.
10. By making it possible for any computer user anywhere in the world to access the system, Berners-Lee created the World Wide Web.

➜ For a SELF-CHECK and more practice, see the EXERCISE BANK, p. 597.

❶ Here's the Idea

▶ **An infinitive is a verb form that usually begins with the word**
to **and functions as a noun, an adjective, or an adverb.**

INFINITIVE

Eileen Collins had a goal to pursue.

▶ **An infinitive phrase consists of an infinitive plus its modifiers**
and complements. Like other verbals, an infinitive phrase may
have an object.

In 1995, Collins became the first female pilot
to command a space mission.
INFINITIVE PHRASE

An infinitive or an infinitive phrase can function as a noun, an
adjective, or an adverb.

Functions of Infinitive Phrases	
Acting as a **noun** (predicate nominative)	Her lifelong dream was **to fly in space**.
Acting as an **adjective** (modifies noun, *woman*)	The first American woman **to fly in space** was Dr. Sally Ride.
Acting as an **adverb** (modifies verb, *endured*)	She endured rigorous training **to fly in space**.

PHRASES

Split Infinitives

A modifier placed between the word *to* and the verb of an infinitive
is said to "split" the infinitive. Usually, a split infinitive sounds
awkward and should be avoided.

AWKWARD

Astronauts need to rigorously train
for space missions.

BETTER

Astronauts need to train rigorously
for space missions.

Formerly, the use of split infinitives was always avoided. Now they
may be used when needed, for maintaining clarity or smooth reading.

My goal is to really understand this chapter.

❷ Why It Matters in Writing

Infinitives or infinitive phrases can help you clarify details in your writing.

Jerrie Cobb

PROFESSIONAL MODEL

Thirty-eight years after becoming NASA's first female astronaut candidate, [Jerrie] Cobb has emerged from the [Amazon] jungle to crusade for the space shot she was promised. John Glenn's return to orbit ... at age 77 has given Cobb—and her supporters—hope. "I would give my life to fly in space. I really would," says Cobb.

—Marcia Dunn, Associated Press

INFINITIVE PHRASES

PREPOSITIONAL PHRASE

❸ Practice and Apply

CONCEPT CHECK: Infinitive Phrases

Write each infinitive phrase, indicating whether it acts as a noun, an adjective, or an adverb.

Space Adventurer

1. Since Jerrie Cobb was a record-setting pilot who had logged more than 10,000 hours in aircraft, NASA decided to tap her as a potential astronaut.
2. To become an astronaut, Cobb had to pass torturous tests and to show that she had the ability to endure sensory deprivation for more than ten hours.
3. Jerrie Cobb and 12 other exceptional women pilots were accepted and trained by NASA but ultimately were denied the chance to participate in the space program.
4. Cobb left for the Amazon jungle to serve as a missionary pilot, and she was still there when NASA chose John Glenn to fly again in 1998.
5. Although Cobb was not able to fly in space, she was nominated for a Nobel Peace Prize for her missionary work.

➡ **For a SELF-CHECK and more practice, see the EXERCISE BANK, p. 598.**

CHAPTER 2

A. Verbals: Participial, Gerund, and Infinitive Phrases Read the following passage and then write the answers to the questions.

PROFESSIONAL MODEL

> **(1)** For four years, I sought . . . to collect images [taken during the Apollo moon missions] that offered the viewer a sense of direct experience, of actually being there. **(2)** I also wanted to emphasize a sense of intimacy: the fragile humanness of the Apollo endeavor drove me to try and find every decent in-flight portrait the astronauts made of each other. **(3)** The mythic aspects of Apollo—the small vulnerable human venturing out into the heart of the unknown—were one of the things that drew me to the archive in the first place. . . . **(4)** To view such photographs, even from the safety of Earth, is to feel both ecstatic and imperiled.
>
> —Michael Light, *Full Moon*

1. What is the infinitive in sentence 1?
2. What is the participial phrase in sentence 1?
3. What is the gerund phrase in sentence 1?
4. What is the first infinitive phrase in sentence 2?
5. What is the participial phrase in sentence 3?
6. Is the participial phrase in sentence 3 past or present?
7. In sentence 3, are the words *drew me to the archive* part of an infinitive phrase?
8. What is the first infinitive phrase in sentence 4?
9. Does the first infinitive phrase in sentence 4 function as a noun, an adjective, or an adverb?
10. In sentence 4, is the word *imperiled* a past participle or a gerund?

B. Verbals Identify each underlined group of words as a participial phrase, a gerund phrase, or an infinitive phrase.

(1) Trained as a zoologist, Rachel Carson worked for the U.S. Fish and Wildlife Service from 1936 to 1952. She was also a **(2)** remarkably gifted writer. **(3)** Working full-time at her job, Carson managed **(4)** to write two books about the natural world, **(5)** eventually publishing *Under the Sea-Wind* and *The Sea Around Us*. **(6)** Nationally acclaimed, *The Sea Around Us* came out in 1951. In this masterpiece, Carson succeeded in **(7)** describing the biological richness of the sea. After **(8)** completing one more book, she decided **(9)** to turn her attention to the dangers of chemical pesticides. The result of her efforts was *Silent Spring,* a book generally credited with **(10)** starting the environmental movement.

Avoiding Problems with Phrases

LESSON 6

❶ Here's the Idea

Misplaced Modifiers

A **misplaced modifier** is a word or phrase that is placed so far away from the word it modifies that the meaning of the sentence is unclear or incorrect.

MISPLACED PARTICIPIAL PHRASE:

The school district is issuing new desks to students made of molded plastic.

> Are students made of plastic?

REVISION:

The school district is issuing new desks made of molded plastic to students.

> Phrase near word it modifies

Dangling Modifiers

A **dangling modifier** is a word or phrase that does not clearly modify any noun or pronoun in a sentence. To correct a sentence containing a dangling modifier, you will need to supply the word being modified. You will also need to add or rearrange other words to make the sentence clear and complete.

DANGLING PARTICIPIAL PHRASE:

Looking around, objects made of plastic fill our homes, our offices, and our schools.

> Are the plastic objects looking?

REVISION:

Looking around, we realized that objects made of plastic fill our homes, our offices, and our schools.

> Added words make meaning clear.

❷ Why It Matters in Writing

Misplaced modifiers often result in unintended, absurd meanings. What would you think if you saw the following headlines in your local newspaper?

Gold Coin Found by 11th-Grader from 18th Century

REVISION:

Gold Coin from 18th Century Found by 11th-Grader

New Life Forms Found by Scientists from Mars

REVISION:

New Life Forms from Mars Found by Scientists

❸ Practice and Apply

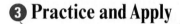

CONCEPT CHECK: Avoiding Problems with Phrases

Rewrite these sentences, eliminating problems caused by misplaced or dangling phrases. If a sentence has no error, write *Correct*.

Pioneer in Plastics

1. Now hailed as a substance that changed the world, Leo Baekeland invented the first all-synthetic plastic.
2. Born in Belgium, the United States became his home in 1889.
3. Having invented a new kind of photographic paper, a million-dollar fortune came to Baekeland relatively early in his career.
4. The chemist continued to perform experiments involving new substances instead of abandoning science.
5. For his next scientific challenge, Baekeland attempted to formulate a synthetic substitute for shellac.
6. Made from the secretions of the lac insect, manufacturers of early electrical equipment commonly used shellac as an insulator.
7. In 1909, after several years of experimentation, Baekeland successfully developed the first all-synthetic plastic.
8. Calling the newly patented substance Bakelite, uses ranged from electrical parts to buttons and billiard balls.
9. Innovative product designers found the material perfect for their needs, easily molded and shaped.
10. Thought of as important artifacts of modern technology and design, kitchenware, jewelry, and small appliances made from Bakelite have become collectors' items.

➡ **For a SELF-CHECK and more practice, see the EXERCISE BANK, p. 598.**

Sentence Diagramming

Here's the Idea

Diagramming is a powerful visual tool for understanding how the parts of a sentence fit together.

For a review of the basic steps in diagramming, see pp. 38–41.

Watch me for diagramming tips!

Prepositional Phrases

• Write the preposition on a slanted line below the word the prepositional phrase modifies.

• Write the object of the preposition on a horizontal line attached to the slanted line and parallel to the main line.

• Write words that modify the object of the preposition on slanted lines below the object.

Adjective Phrase

People use electrical appliances of many kinds.

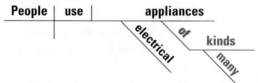

Adverb Phrase

Electricity flows to every household.

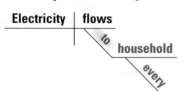

The preposition goes on a slanted line.

A. CONCEPT CHECK: Prepositional Phrases

Diagram these sentences, using what you have learned.

1. Large appliances plug into wall outlets.
2. Tiny batteries provide power for watches.

Appositive Phrases

• Write an appositive in parentheses after the word it identifies or renames.

• Place words that modify the appositive on slanted lines below it.

CHAPTER 2

The appositive goes inside parentheses.

Thales, an ancient Greek philosopher, may have conducted the first electrical experiments.

| Thales (philosopher) | may have conducted | experiments |

an, ancient, Greek / the, first, electrical

B. CONCEPT CHECK: Appositive Phrases

Diagram these sentences, using what you have learned.

1. Thales rubbed amber, a stonelike substance, with fur.

2. The English word *electricity* comes from the Greek word for amber.

Participial Phrases

- The participle curves along a bent line below the word it modifies.

- Diagram an object or a subject complement on the horizontal part of the bent line in the usual way.

- Place any modifiers on slanted lines below the words they modify.

Carefully observing the results, Thales repeated his experiment.

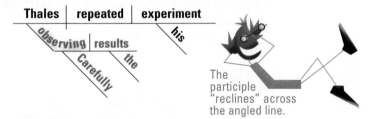

| Thales | repeated | experiment |

observing | results
Carefully, the
his

The participle "reclines" across the angled line.

C. CONCEPT CHECK: Participial Phrases

Diagram these sentences, using what you have learned.

1. Rubbing the amber, Thales created a charge.

2. Now electrically charged, the amber attracted light objects.

Gerund Phrases

- The gerund curves over a line that looks like a step.
- With a vertical forked line, connect the step to the part of the diagram that corresponds to the role of the gerund phrase in the sentence.
- Diagram complements and modifiers in the usual way.

Gerund Phrase as Subject

Studying electricity became Benjamin Franklin's goal in the mid-1700s.

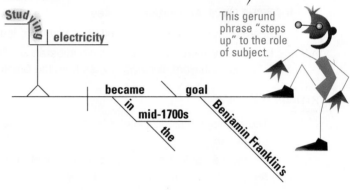

This gerund phrase "steps up" to the role of subject.

D. CONCEPT CHECK: Gerund Phrases

Diagram these sentences, using what you have learned.

1. Discovering the true nature of lightning was his objective.
2. Franklin proved his hypothesis by receiving a shock.

Infinitive Phrases

- Write the infinitive on a bent line, with the word *to* on the slanted part and the verb on the horizontal part.
- When the infinitive or infinitive phrase functions as a noun, use a forked vertical line to connect the infinitive to the part of the diagram that corresponds to its role in the sentence.
- When the phrase functions as a modifier, place the bent line below the word it modifies.
- Add any complements or modifiers, using the procedures you've learned.

Infinitive Phrase as Subject

To attract lightning is extremely dangerous.

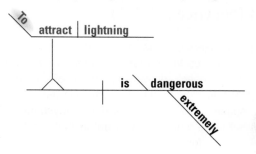

The infinitive has a fork but no step.

Infinitive Phrase as Direct Object

Franklin wanted to explore the secrets of electricity.

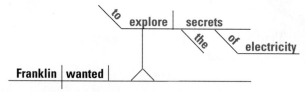

E. CONCEPT CHECK: Infinitive Phrases

Diagram these sentences, using what you have learned.

1. To study lightning became Franklin's obsession.
2. Franklin tried to invent a practical lightning rod next.

F. MIXED REVIEW: Diagramming

Diagram the following sentences. Look for all the types of phrases you have learned about.

1. Static electricity occurs in nature.
2. Thales's aim was to describe this phenomenon.
3. Generating friction causes a static charge.
4. An electrically charged object will attract neutral objects.
5. Franklin, a brilliant scientist, also studied the physical world.
6. Scientists had long wondered about lightning.
7. Constantly conducting experiments, Franklin became an authority on the subject.
8. Electricity was not harnessed until the 19th century.
9. Developing electrical machines was a great breakthrough.
10. Thales and Franklin laid the groundwork for this achievement.

Grammar in Literature

Achieving Eloquence with Phrases

Forceful speakers use rhetorical devices such as parallel and repeated phrases to express their ideas with eloquence. The following speech, delivered by President Abraham Lincoln in 1863, is enhanced by the effective use of phrases. Lincoln spoke these famous words in Gettysburg, Pennsylvania, the site of a bitter Civil War battle that resulted in staggering losses for both sides.

The Gettysburg Address
Abraham Lincoln

Four score and seven years ago, our fathers brought forth on this continent a new nation, conceived in liberty, and dedicated to the proposition that all men are created equal. Now we are engaged in a great civil war, testing whether that nation, or any nation so conceived and so dedicated, can long endure. We are met on a great battlefield of that war. We have come to dedicate a portion of that field as a final resting place for those who here gave their lives that that nation might live. It is altogether fitting and proper that we should do this. But, in a larger sense, we cannot dedicate—we cannot consecrate—we cannot hallow—this ground. The brave men, living and dead, who struggled here have consecrated it far above our poor power to add or detract. The world will little note nor long remember what we say here, but it can never forget what they did here. It is for us, the living, rather, to be dedicated here to the unfinished work which they who fought here have thus far so nobly advanced. It is rather for us to be here dedicated to the great task remaining before us—that from these honored dead we take increased devotion to that cause for which they gave the last full measure of devotion; that we here highly resolve that these dead shall not have died in vain; that this nation, under God, shall have a new birth of freedom; and that government of the people, by the people, for the people, shall not perish from the earth.

Paired participial phrases clarify Lincoln's vision of the "new nation."

The infinitive phrase explains why the people present have come together for the dedication.

A gerund functions as an appositive to emphasize the contrast between the living and the dead.

Parallel infinitive phrases emphasize the need and the reasons for the dedication.

Three parallel prepositional phrases convey core principles of democracy.

Ways You Can Use Phrases in Writing	
Prepositional phrases	Use a series of prepositional phrases for effective parallel repetition.
Appositive phrases	Use appositive phrases to add emphasis to important terms, names, and ideas.
Participial phrases	Use participial phrases to clarify relationships between key ideas and to emphasize important concepts.
Gerund phrases	Use gerund phrases at the beginning of sentences to add variety.
Infinitive phrases	Use infinitive phrases in pairs or in a series to achieve a smooth, parallel flow of ideas.

PRACTICE AND APPLY: Writing

Think about a place you've visited or an event you've attended—such as a reenactment of the Battle of Gettysburg—that gave you a fresh perspective on people or events from history. Write a paragraph about your experience and the insights it provided. Try to incorporate in your paragraph the types of phrases listed in the chart above.

When you are finished, exchange papers with a classmate. Identify the prepositional, appositive, and verbal phrases in each other's paragraphs, and discuss how the phrases affect the writing. Also identify and correct any misplaced or dangling modifiers.

PHRASES

Reenactment of the Battle of Gettysburg; Gettysburg, Pennsylvania

Mixed Review

A. Kinds of Phrases Read this passage from "Armistice," a short story by Bernard Malamud, that is set in New York during the early days of World War II. Then write the answers to the questions.

> **LITERARY MODEL**
>
> (1) Thirty years later Morris, a widower who owned a small grocery and delicatessen store in a Scandinavian neighborhood in Brooklyn, could recall the scene of the pogrom with the twisting fright that he had felt at fifteen. (2) He often experienced the same fear since the Nazis had come to power.
>
> (3) The reports of their persecution of the Jews that he heard over the radio filled him with dread, but he never stopped listening to them. (4) His fourteen-year-old son, Leonard, a thin, studious boy, saw how overwrought his father became and tried to shut off the radio, but the grocer would not allow him to. (5) He listened, and at night did not sleep, because in listening he shared the woes inflicted upon his race.
>
> —Bernard Malamud, "Armistice"

1. What is the appositive phrase in sentence 1? Is it essential or nonessential?
2. Is "to power" in sentence 2 a prepositional phrase or an infinitive phrase? What word or words does the phrase modify?
3. What is the gerund phrase in sentence 3? Does it act as the object of a preposition or as a direct object?
4. What is the infinitive phrase in sentence 4?
5. What is the participial phrase in sentence 5? What does it modify?

B. Avoiding Problems with Phrases Identify each underlined group of words as a misplaced modifier or a dangling modifier. Then rewrite the faulty sentences correctly.

One of the most extraordinary but least-publicized military operations on the Pacific front during World War II was carried out by a specially trained group of American marines recruited from the Navajo nation. **(1)** <u>Based on the highly complex Navajo language</u>, the Navajo marines devised a code in order to transmit radio messages about troop movements, enemy attacks, and rescue operations. **(2)** <u>Never having encountered anything similar before</u>, the encoded messages were completely baffling. Japanese intelligence officers were unable to crack the code. **(3)** <u>Transmitted in more conventional forms of encryption</u>, American forces, on the other hand, were usually able to decode enemy messages. These valiant members of the Marine Corps **(4)** <u>known as the Navajo code talkers</u> helped win a number of key battles, including the Battle of Iwo Jima.

Choose the letter of the correct answer for each numbered item below the passage.

   In a 1961 speech, President John F. Kennedy declared, "I believe that
   (1)
this nation should commit itself to achieving the goal before this decade is

out, of landing a man on the moon and returning him safely to earth." On
          (2)
July 20, 1969, with a little over five months remaining in the decade, half
                                                  (3)
of that goal was reached. Millions watched and listened as the American

astronaut Neil Armstrong transmitted one of the most memorable
          (4)
announcements of the century: "The *Eagle* has landed."

   Eagle was the name of the lunar module that had been ferried into
                      (5)
space by the *Columbia,* the command module of the *Apollo 11* spacecraft.
                              (6)
Piloted by Armstrong and Edwin "Buzz" Aldrin, the *Eagle* touched down
          (7)
on the lunar surface at 4:17 P.M. Eastern Daylight Time. A few hours later,

after climbing down a ladder, Armstrong himself "touched down,"

becoming the first human being ever to set foot on the moon.
                                      (8)

---

1. The underlined section is
   A. a gerund phrase
   B. an infinitive phrase
   C. a prepositional phrase
   D. a participial phrase

2. The underlined section is
   A. a prepositional phrase
   B. an absolute phrase
   C. a gerund phrase
   D. an infinitive phrase

3. The underlined section is
   A. a gerund phrase
   B. an appositive phrase
   C. a past participial phrase
   D. a present participial phrase

4. The essential appositive *Neil Armstrong*
   A. does not belong in the sentence
   B. completes the meaning of the sentence
   C. acts as the subject
   D. acts as a direct object

5. The prepositional phrase modifies
   A. a noun
   B. a verb
   C. an adjective
   D. an adverb

6. The underlined section is
   A. an essential appositive
   B. a nonessential appositive
   C. a misplaced modifier
   D. a dangling modifier

7. All participial phrases, including this one, modify
   A. adjectives
   B. nouns and pronouns
   C. verbs
   D. other participial phrases

8. The underlined section is
   A. a prepositional phrase
   B. an appositive phrase
   C. a participial phrase
   D. an infinitive phrase

PHRASES

Student Help Desk

Phrases at a Glance

Kind of Phrase	Function	Example
Prepositional phrase	Adverb	What will happen on "All My Phrases"?
	Adjective	That's the question on everyone's mind.
Appositive phrase	Noun	Ally, the debating captain, has laryngitis.
Participial phrase	Adjective	Thinking quickly, she asks Joe for help.
Gerund phrase	Noun	Debating today was not in his plans.
Infinitive phrase	Noun	Will he agree to save the day?
	Adverb	He's happy to help.
	Adjective	It's Joe's turn to be a hero.

Fixing Phrase Problems   A Turn for the Better

Split Infinitives	The debaters had to **quickly** think.	AWKWARD
	The debaters had to think **quickly**.	SMOOTH
Misplaced Modifier	**Turning plump and red,** the gardener watched his tomatoes.	CONFUSING
	The gardener watched his tomatoes **turning plump and red.**	CLEAR
Dangling Modifier	**Standing at the mountain summit,** the view was spectacular.	DANGLING
	Standing at the mountain summit, the hikers admired the spectacular view.	CLEAR

Punctuating Appositives — A Matter of Essentials

Nonessential Appositive: not needed to make the sentence clear	Use commas.	Marc García, **the newspaper editor,** assigns a reporter to the story.
Essential Appositive: needed to make the sentence complete	Don't use commas.	Ace reporter **Susan Wright** rushes to the scene.

Phrases in Writing — The Phrase Craze

Infinitive Phrase	Since my hope was to be on the debating team, I took Advanced Speech.
Participial Phrase	Hoping to be on the debating team, I took Advanced Speech.
Gerund Phrase	In hopes of making the debating team, I took Advanced Speech.
Prepositional Phrase	My hope for a place on the debating team led me to take Advanced Speech.

PHRASES

The Bottom Line

Checklist for Phrases

Have I . . .

_____ used prepositional phrases to clarify time, location, and other conditions?

_____ used appositive phrases to identify or explain nouns?

_____ used participial phrases to describe nouns and pronouns?

_____ used gerund phrases to specify actions and activities?

_____ used infinitive phrases as nouns, adjectives, and adverbs?

Using Clauses

Take This Quiz to Discover More About the Real You!

1. <u>When you are going to be alone for a whole day,</u> your plan would probably be to
   a. repaint your room and refinish the furniture in it.
   b. see three movies in a row.
   c. call a couple of old friends you haven't seen in a while.

2. <u>If you could choose a perfect vacation spot,</u> it would be
   a. along the French Riviera.
   b. on a dude ranch in Wyoming.
   c. in an Earth colony on Mars.

3. <u>After you heard a juicy bit of gossip about someone,</u> you most likely would

Theme: Personality

The Real You

You've probably seen quizzes like the one illustrated above in magazines or books. While such quizzes can be fun, the complex traits that make up your personality probably can't be explained by a simple multiple-choice answer.

No matter who you are, describing your personality can present an interesting challenge. One way to write about a subject as complex as yourself is to use sentences made up of different types of clauses like those underlined above. Using clauses, groups of words that contain a subject and a verb, can help you express a variety of ideas in your writing.

Write Away: I am the kind of person who . . .
Write a paragraph describing your personality. Use specific examples to support the points you make about yourself. Save your paragraph in your 📁 **Working Portfolio**.

CD-ROM Grammar Coach

Diagnostic Test: What Do You Know?

Choose the letter of the term that describes each underlined passage.

> You've probably heard people say <u>that someone has "no personality."</u>
> (1)
> They may say this about a person <u>because he or she seems dull.</u> In this
> (2)
> case, people are using the word *personality* to refer to only those traits
> <u>that are generally considered desirable,</u> such as a sense of humor.
> (3)
> <u>However, many psychologists and other experts define personality</u>
> (4)
> <u>differently.</u> Most view personality as an overall temperament or
> combination of traits, <u>which may or may not be desirable.</u> <u>These traits are</u>
> (5)
> <u>fairly stable; the person reacts nearly the same in most situations.</u> One
> (6)
> reason experts study personality is to learn more about <u>how people</u>
> (7)
> <u>change and interact.</u> <u>Not to limit them with labels.</u> Terms like "the
> (8)
> confident type" or "the shy type" may describe personality <u>better, however,</u>
> (9)
> <u>even this categorization describes</u> only the trait or two <u>that make the</u>
> (10)
> <u>biggest impression,</u> not the whole person.

1. A. adjective clause
   B. independent clause
   C. noun clause
   D. adverb clause

2. A. adjective clause
   B. independent clause
   C. noun clause
   D. adverb clause

3. A. adjective clause
   B. independent clause
   C. noun clause
   D. adverb clause

4. A. simple sentence
   B. compound sentence
   C. complex sentence
   D. compound-complex sentence

5. A. essential adjective clause
   B. nonessential adjective clause
   C. adverb clause
   D. noun clause

6. A. simple sentence
   B. compound sentence
   C. complex sentence
   D. compound-complex sentence

7. A. noun clause as direct object
   B. noun clause as subject
   C. noun clause as object of
      preposition
   D. noun clause as appositive

8. A. independent clause
   B. sentence fragment
   C. run-on sentence
   D. complex sentence

9. A. independent clause
   B. sentence fragment
   C. run-on sentence
   D. simple sentence

10. A. essential adjective clause
    B. nonessential adjective clause
    C. adverb clause
    D. noun clause

CLAUSES

Kinds of Clauses

1 Here's the Idea

▶ **A clause is a group of words that contains a subject and a verb.**

There are two types of clauses: independent clauses and subordinate clauses.

Independent Clauses

▶ **An independent, or main, clause expresses a complete thought and can stand alone as a sentence.**

Many people love to read about their personalities.
　　　　　↑　　↑
　　 SUBJECT　VERB

Subordinate Clauses

▶ **A subordinate, or dependent, clause does not express a complete thought and cannot stand alone as a sentence.**

If current studies are correct
　　　　↑　　　↑
　 SUBJECT　VERB

To form a complete sentence, combine a subordinate clause with an independent clause.

If current studies are correct, many people love to read about their personalities.

Words That Introduce Clauses

▶ **Subordinating conjunctions and coordinating conjunctions are two kinds of words that link or introduce clauses.**

Use a coordinating conjunction to join two independent clauses.

Some researchers define 3 or 4 personality types,
yet others identify as many as 16!
　↑
COORDINATING CONJUNCTION

Use a subordinating conjunction to introduce a subordinate clause.

Defining personality types is still an inexact science,
although research began over 80 years ago.
　　↑
SUBORDINATING CONJUNCTION

Conjunctions Used with Clauses	
Coordinating Conjunctions	**Subordinating Conjunctions**
and, but, for, nor, or, yet	after, although, as, as if, as though, because, before, even though, if, in order that, provided, since, so that, than, unless, until, when, where, whereas, wherever, while

For more information on conjunctions, see pp. 21–23.

Varying your use of independent clauses and subordinate clauses to start sentences can help to make your writing more interesting.

❷ Why It Matters in Writing

When doing many kinds of writing, including personal essays like the one below, you can use subordinate clauses to express complex ideas or cause-and-effect relationships.

STUDENT MODEL

Whenever I have free time, the first thing I do is call my friends. I'm a social person, and spending time with people helps me relax. Although I may have just seen my best friend two hours earlier on the bus, we can talk for hours about the things that happened at school that day. If my parents didn't object, I would probably talk on the phone for hours.

SUBORDINATE CLAUSE

INDEPENDENT CLAUSE

CLAUSES

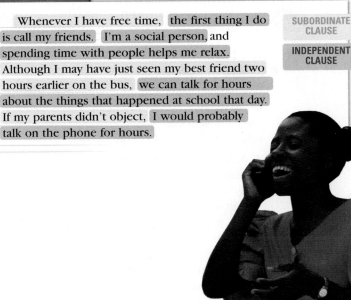

❸ Practice and Apply

A. CONCEPT CHECK: Kinds of Clauses

Identify the italicized clause in each sentence below as either independent or subordinate.

The Urge to Classify

1. *The Greek physician Hippocrates grouped traits into four personality types,* but he based the types on faulty ideas about the proportions of various fluids in the body.
2. By the early 20th century, *many observers of human behavior had come to believe in the basic sameness of all people.*
3. Carl Jung challenged that belief *when he published a book called* Psychological Types *in the 1920s.*
4. According to Jung, extroverts naturally focus on the people and events in the outside world, *while introverts naturally focus on their own thoughts and feelings.*
5. American psychologist David Keirsey and others consider all personality types equally valuable, *since each type has its own strengths and weaknesses.*

➡ **For a SELF-CHECK and more practice, see the EXERCISE BANK, p. 599.**

For sentences 1, 4, and 5, identify the conjunction and write whether it is subordinating or coordinating.

B. REVISING: Using Subordinate Clauses

Use the conjunction in the parentheses that follow each sentence below to combine the two independent clauses into a complex sentence with one independent and one subordinate clause. You may change other words as needed.

1. An extrovert enjoys interacting with others. An extrovert gets energy from others. (because)
2. By contrast, an introvert loses energy. An introvert interacts with others. (when)
3. Few people are either total introverts or total extroverts. They may tend toward one or the other. (although)
4. An extrovert may be talkative. An introvert may be quiet. (while)
5. Some extroverts think out loud. Introverts may prefer to think their ideas through before speaking. (whereas)

Adjective and Adverb Clauses

LESSON 2

❶ Here's the Idea

Subordinate clauses can function as adjectives, adverbs, or nouns. Adjective clauses and adverb clauses, like adjectives and adverbs, modify other words in a sentence.

Adjective Clauses

▶ **An adjective clause is a subordinate clause used as an adjective to modify a noun or a pronoun.**

An adjective clause sometimes is called a **relative clause** because it relates to and modifies a specific word within a sentence. Like an adjective, an adjective clause answers the questions *What kind of . . . ?* or *Which . . . ?*

MODIFIES NOUN

Some psychologists rely on tests that determine specific personality types.

MODIFIES PRONOUN

Someone who takes such a test may not always agree with the results, however.

Words Used to Introduce Adjective Clauses	
Relative Pronouns	**Relative Adverbs**
that, which, who, whom, whose	after, before, since, when, where, why

Essential and Nonessential Adjective Clauses

An **essential adjective clause** contains information that is critical to the identity of a modified word or to the meaning of a sentence as a whole.

MODIFIES NOUN

Kiki took the personality test that has ten questions.

(Which test did she take? She took the one with ten questions.)

A **nonessential adjective clause** adds information that is nice to have, but it is not absolutely necessary.

MODIFIES NOUN

Kiki took the personality test, which has ten questions.

(Which test did she take? She took the only one there was. By the way, it had ten questions.)

CLAUSES

Using Clauses **81**

As the examples on the preceding page show, you can use the same adjective clause as either an essential or a nonessential clause. Therefore, when you write a sentence with an adjective clause, you must decide whether it contains information that is essential to your sentence. Your use of punctuation (commas or no commas around the clause) can help readers interpret your writing correctly.

For more on using commas, see p. 226.

Adverb Clauses

▶ **An adverb clause is a subordinate clause that modifies a verb, an adjective, or another adverb.**

Like adverbs, adverb clauses answer several specific questions, such as *Where? When? Why? How?* and *To what extent?*

MODIFIES VERB

Al panics **whenever he takes a test.**

However, this time, the answers came

MODIFIES ADVERB

to him more easily **than he had expected.**

MODIFIES ADJECTIVE

Al felt better **after he took the test.**

Words Used to Introduce Adverb Clauses	
Subordinating Conjunctions	**Show**
after, as, as long as, as soon as, before, since, until, when, whenever, while	time
because	cause
as, than	comparison
although, as long as, even if, even though, if, provided that, though, unless, until, whereas	condition
in order that, so that	purpose
as, as if, as though	manner
where, wherever	place

Sometimes some of the words in an adverb clause are implied rather than stated. Because these omitted words are often verbs, the clauses may seem to be phrases at first glance. Such clauses are called **elliptical**, which means "marked by the omission of one or more words."

When (you are) taking a personality test, **try to answer all items honestly.**

No one can describe your traits and behaviors **as accurately as you (can) yourself.**

❷ Why It Matters in Writing

Adjective clauses can help you add details to describe *who* or *what* you're writing about, and adverb clauses can help to describe *where, when, why, how,* or *to what extent.* Feature articles, travel writing, and news articles often need the types of specific details that these clauses can quickly convey.

PROFESSIONAL MODEL

Anna and Susan have been close friends for over twenty-five years—**since they met at college.** But nine times out of ten, it will be Extraverted Anna **who calls Introverted Susan** to catch up on the news.... [S]ince her own life is so self-contained, it seldom occurs to [Susan] to seek the company of others....

—Paul D. Tieger and Barbara Barron-Tieger, *The Art of SpeedReading People*

Adverb clause tells *where* they became friends.

Essential adjective clause adds information about *who,* or *what kind of* person, Anna is.

Adverb clause answers *why* Susan seldom calls Anna.

❸ Practice and Apply

A. CONCEPT CHECK: Adjective and Adverb Clauses

For each sentence below, write the adjective or adverb clause and identify whether it is an adjective or an adverb clause.

Testing, Testing

1. You can find dozens of self-scoring personality tests if you look in magazines and on the Internet.
2. Such tests can be fun and even enlightening, as long as you don't take them too seriously.
3. These personality tests have simple scoring keys, which anyone can use.
4. Magazine and Internet tests are usually unscientific, whereas standardized tests approach personality traits scientifically.
5. One such personality test is the Myers-Briggs Type Indicator, or MBTI, which Katharine C. Briggs and Isabel Briggs Myers developed.
6. Your school counselor might give you this or another personality test that can help you make educational or career choices.
7. These personality tests are given so that characteristics of personality can be determined and categorized.
8. The answers are analyzed for characteristics that help to reveal your preferences.
9. Whenever you take a personality test, you are providing a self-report.
10. After all, you know yourself better than anyone else does.

➜ **For a SELF-CHECK and more practice, see the EXERCISE BANK, p. 600.**

Identify each adjective clause as essential or nonessential.

B. WRITING: Using Adjective and Adverb Clauses

Create a personality quiz for people your age. The test items must include complete sentences for people to identify as true or false about themselves. Write ten quiz statements and make sure each one includes at least one adjective clause or one adverb clause.

Example: I prefer a room that is tidy rather than messy.
True or false?

Noun Clauses

❶ Here's the Idea

▶ **A noun clause is a subordinate clause used as a noun.**

You can use a noun clause as a subject, a direct object, an indirect object, a predicate nominative, or an object of a preposition.

SUBJECT
Whatever you want to do is fine with me.

DIRECT OBJECT
Some people say **that heredity determines personality.**

INDIRECT OBJECT
They give **whatever we have as our genetic makeup** the credit or blame for many personality traits.

PREDICATE NOMINATIVE
Another influence can be **whom you select as friends.**

OBJECT OF A PREPOSITION
You may be influenced by **what you learn from your family.**

You can often tighten your writing by eliminating *that* from a noun clause.

Some people say ~~that~~ heredity determines personality.

You can also use a noun clause as the direct object of a verbal or as an appositive.

DIRECT OBJECT OF A GERUND
Learning **how birth order can influence personality** can be interesting.

DIRECT OBJECT OF AN INFINITIVE
To understand **how the human personality develops,** you can read books on the subject.

APPOSITIVE
How does attitude, **whatever your outlook is,** relate to personality?

For a review of complements, see pp. 35–36.

Words Used to Introduce Noun Clauses	
Pronouns	what, whatever, which, whichever, who, whoever, whom, whomever, whose
Subordinating conjunctions	how, that, when, where, whether, why

To decide whether to use *whoever* or *whomever*, look only at the clause itself. Try mentally substituting the words *he* and *him* in the clause. If *he* fits, use *who* or *whoever*. If *him* works, use *whom* or *whomever*.

Sari befriends whoever is nice to her.

~~He~~
~~Him~~ is nice to her.

❷ Why It Matters in Writing

Noun clauses can be useful for condensing ideas. Notice the way that using noun clauses improves each draft below.

STUDENT MODEL

DRAFT
These things I realized. I was an oldest child. My parents had high expectations for me. I loved drawing more than anything. Unfortunately, my parents decided against art as a career. They felt it was not realistic.

REVISION
I realize that I was an oldest child and my parents had high expectations for me. I loved drawing more than anything, but unfortunately my parents had decided that it would not be a realistic career.

NOUN CLAUSE

NOUN CLAUSE

DRAFT
I am strong-willed. I am a perfectionist. These traits may have something to do with my birth order.

REVISION
That I am a strong-willed perfectionist may have something to do with my birth order.

NOUN CLAUSE

❸ Practice and Apply

Write the noun clause or clauses in each of the following sentences.

Does Birth Order Matter?

1. Why even very young children differ in terms of irritability, calmness, shyness, and other traits is an intriguing question for biologists, psychologists, and others.

2. Heredity must play some role in determining a child's personality, but experts disagree about what that role is.

3. Some experts assert that specific inherited genes influence and perhaps even control many personality traits, such as a tendency to seek out new experiences ("novelty seeking") and a tendency to worry a great deal.

4. One theory about genes' influence on personality is that certain genes affect the actions of the brain's natural mood-affecting chemicals, such as dopamine and serotonin.

5. That each human cell contains about 50,000 to 100,000 genes poses a huge challenge for genetic researchers.

6. Some scientists are trying to determine which plays a more important role in shaping personality—heredity or life experiences.

7. This leads to the question of whether a child's birth order affects his or her personality.

8. Numerous popular books and magazine articles describe how first-born children tend to be bossy, how middle children tend to be diplomatic, how youngest children tend to be fun-loving, and so on.

9. In the late 1990s, scholar Frank Sulloway offered a mass of evidence in an effort to prove that later-born children are more likely than first-born children to have rebellious personalities.

10. According to Sulloway, whoever is born first into a family identifies strongly with established authority, while later-born children are family underdogs who tend to question authority.

➡ **For a SELF-CHECK and more practice, see the EXERCISE BANK, p. 600.**

Identify the function of each noun clause in sentences 1–5.

CHALLENGE

CLAUSES

Sentence Structure

LESSON 4

❶ Here's the Idea

A sentence is classified according to its structure, that is, the number and kinds of clauses it contains.

▶ **There are four kinds of basic sentence structures: simple, compound, complex, and compound-complex.**

Simple Sentences

A **simple sentence** consists of one independent clause and no subordinate clauses.

Different personality types may share similar interests.

A simple sentence can contain a compound subject, a compound verb, or both.

Extroverts and introverts may love books and fear dogs.
 ▲ COMPOUND ▶   ▲ COMPOUND ▶
   SUBJECT   VERB

Compound Sentences

A **compound sentence** contains two or more independent clauses joined together. The clauses in many compound sentences are joined with a coordinating conjunction.

| Some people like change, | but | others like stability. |
| INDEPENDENT CLAUSE | | INDEPENDENT CLAUSE |

Compound sentences can also be joined with just a semicolon or with a semicolon and a conjunctive adverb such as *however, nevertheless, finally,* or *then.*

| Some people like change; | others like stability. |

| Some people like change; | however, | others like stability. |

For more about coordinating conjunctions and conjunctive adverbs, see p. 21.

CHAPTER 3

Complex Sentences

A complex sentence contains one independent clause and one or more subordinate clauses.

Although only-children differ,	they often share many traits.
SUBORDINATE CLAUSE	INDEPENDENT CLAUSE

A sentence that contains a noun clause as part of the independent clause is still considered complex. In the following sentence, a subordinate noun clause functions as the subject of a complex sentence.

Whoever lives in this house must love the color red.

SUBORDINATE NOUN CLAUSE

Compound-Complex Sentences

A compound-complex sentence has two or more independent clauses and one or more subordinate clauses.

INDEPENDENT CLAUSE   SUBORDINATE CLAUSE

Researchers have studied couples who have contrasting personalities, and the results have been interesting.

INDEPENDENT CLAUSE

For more on sentence structures, see p. 24.

➋ Why It Matters in Writing

Varying sentence structures can help to maintain readers' interest.

LITERARY MODEL

I keep seeing your face, which is also the face of your father and my brother. Like him, you are tough, dark, vulnerable, moody—with a very definite tendency to sound truculent because you want no one to think you are soft. You may be like your grandfather in this, I don't know, but certainly both you and your father resemble him very much physically.

COMPLEX SENTENCES

COMPOUND SENTENCE

—James Baldwin, "My Dungeon Shook: Letter to My Nephew"

CLAUSES

❸ Practice and Apply

A. CONCEPT CHECK: Sentence Structure

Identify each sentence below as simple, compound, complex, or compound-complex.

Dealing with Differences

1. Everyone has ideas about the influence of personality on relationships.

2. "Birds of a feather flock together" is an old maxim; it implies that people prefer to be with others who are similar to themselves.

3. On the other hand, another old saying asserts that "opposites attract."

4. Both maxims are generalizations, and both probably have some truth in them.

5. Psychologist David Keirsey thinks that people whose personality types are similar in some ways and different in others tend to get along well.

6. According to Keirsey, the biggest problems in relationships occur when two people are initially attracted by the differences between their personalities but later try to change one another.

7. Of course, parents and teachers have an obligation to help foster and encourage appropriate behavior.

8. Yet, everyone is responsible for his or her own behavior, and everyone should make allowances for personality differences.

9. An important step in accepting differences is avoiding name-calling.

10. Negative labeling that makes people feel defensive can interfere with effective interaction, and it goes against another old maxim, "Live and let live."

➡ For a SELF-CHECK and more practice, see the EXERCISE BANK, p. 601.

B. WRITING AND REVISING: Varying Sentence Structure

Write a paragraph describing the relationship you imagine these people share; then exchange papers with a partner. Comment on each other's use of sentence structure. Can you find all four sentence structures? What would improve the paragraph? Revise your work, taking your partner's comments into consideration.

Fragments and Run-Ons

❶ Here's the Idea

Sentence fragments and run-on sentences are common writing errors. Understanding clauses and sentence structure can help you avoid these problems.

Sentence Fragments

▶ **A sentence fragment is only part of a sentence.**
A complete sentence has a subject and a verb and expresses a complete thought.

Phrase Fragments A phrase has neither subject nor verb. Correct a phrase fragment by combining it with a related sentence or by adding a subject and verb.

FRAGMENT:
At the beginning of a job search.

REVISED:
Many experts recommend having your personality analyzed at the beginning of a job search.

Clause Fragments A subordinate clause contains a subject and a verb, but it does not express a complete thought. Correct a clause fragment by connecting the subordinate clause to an independent clause, or rewrite the fragment to express a complete thought.

FRAGMENT:
If you are the outgoing sort.

REVISED:
You might want to become a teacher or a lawyer if you are the outgoing sort.

REVISED:
You are the outgoing sort.

Other Kinds of Fragments Forgetting to include the subject, a verb, or part of a linking verb in a sentence also results in a fragment.

FRAGMENT:
Librarians inaccurately stereotyped as quiet.

REVISED:
Librarians are inaccurately stereotyped as quiet.

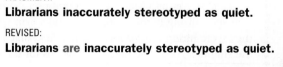

CLAUSES

Run-On Sentences

▶ **A run-on sentence consists of two or more sentences written as if they were one sentence.** Often, run-on sentences are two independent clauses joined by a comma, an error known as the **comma splice.** One way to fix a run-on sentence is to break it into two separate sentences. Another way is to combine the clauses by using any one of the following:

- a comma and a coordinating conjunction
- a semicolon
- a semicolon and a conjunctive adverb

RUN-ON:
Many people resent this practice, one "wrong" answer could disqualify them.

REVISED (with a coordinating conjunction):
Many people resent this practice, for one "wrong" answer could disqualify them.

RUN-ON:
Some firms give personality tests at job interviews they want to see if people will fit in.

REVISED (with a semicolon):
Some firms give personality tests at job interviews ; they want to see if people will fit in.

❷ Why It Matters in Writing

Although you sometimes will find fragments in advertising copy, using fragments and run-ons in your writing might confuse your readers.

STUDENT MODEL

DRAFT

I decided I wanted to go into computer mapmaking. After carefully analyzing my personal strengths. I found a firm specializing in this field, they were hiring interns for the summer. They gave me a personality test. Which I thought I aced.

REVISION

After carefully analyzing my personal strengths, I decided I wanted to go into computer mapmaking. I found a firm specializing in this field that was hiring interns for the summer. They gave me a personality test, which I thought I aced.

❸ Practice and Apply

A. CONCEPT CHECK: Fragments and Run-Ons

Identify each item in the paragraph below as a phrase fragment (PF), a clause fragment (CF), or a run-on sentence (RO). If an item is correct, write *Correct*.

Putting Personality to Work

(1) If certain personality types are best suited to certain careers. (2) How can a person determine his or her personality type and then put that information to use?

(3) Knowing your personality type can guide your career planning in a general way, it cannot tell you exactly what career to choose. (4) When you are choosing a career. (5) Learning who you are, however, can help you decide how to spend your working life. (6) You can consult books on personality types and careers, you also can take a personality test, such as the Myers-Briggs Type Indicator. (7) In discussing test results with a test interpreter or a career guidance counselor.

(8) Also, remember that your career choice must take your talents into account, if you can't play the piano well, the career of concert pianist may suit your personality but not your ability. (9) Because according to experts there are many different suitable careers and jobs within career fields. (10) For every personality type.

➡ For more practice, see the EXERCISE BANK, p. 602.

B. REVISING: Eliminating Fragments and Run-Ons

Rewrite one of the paragraphs in the student model above to eliminate all fragments and run-on sentences. Remember that there can be more than one acceptable way to eliminate a fragment or a run-on.

Sentence Diagramming

❶ Here's the Idea

Diagramming compound, complex, and compound-complex sentences can help you understand how they work. For a review on diagramming simple sentences, see pages 38–41.

Watch me for diagramming tips!

Compound Sentences

- Diagram the independent clauses on parallel horizontal lines.
- Connect the verbs in the two clauses by a dotted line with a step.

Most female chimpanzees are quite lenient mothers, but they differ somewhat in their nurturing styles.

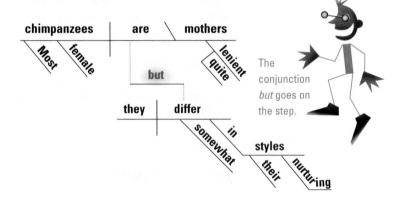

The conjunction *but* goes on the step.

A. CONCEPT CHECK: **Simple and Compound Sentences**

Use what you learned to diagram these sentences.

1. All human beings share similar DNA, yet people's personalities might be quite different.
2. Jane Goodall has observed depression in chimpanzees.
3. Chimps and humans share most of their DNA, and the variations in the personalities of chimps are similar to those in humans.

CHAPTER 3

Complex Sentences

Adjective and Adverb Clauses
- Diagram the subordinate clause on its own horizontal line below the main line, as if it were a sentence.
- Use a dotted line to connect the word introducing the clause to the word it modifies.

Adjective Clause Introduced by a Relative Pronoun
A monkey who acts aggressively may show high levels of the brain chemical serotonin.

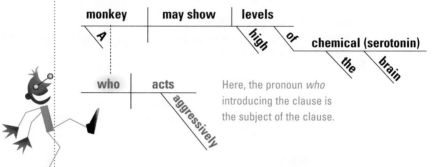

Here, the pronoun *who* introducing the clause is the subject of the clause.

Adjective Clause Introduced by a Relative Adverb
The place where J. Dee Higley studied monkeys' personalities was Morgan Island.

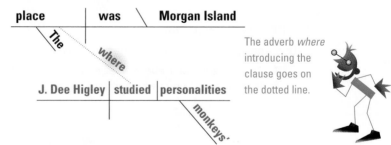

The adverb *where* introducing the clause goes on the dotted line.

Adverb Clause
When scientists study shyness, they may focus on monkeys.

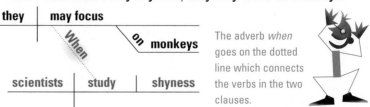

The adverb *when* goes on the dotted line which connects the verbs in the two clauses.

CLAUSES

B. CONCEPT CHECK: Adjective and Adverb Clauses

Use what you have learned to diagram these sentences.

1. Monkeys who act shy may have low serotonin levels.

2. When humans act shy, the same cause may sometimes apply.

Noun Clauses

- Diagram the subordinate clause on a separate line that is attached to the main line with a forked line.
- Place the forked line in the diagram according to the role of the noun clause in the sentence.
- Diagram the word introducing the noun clause according to its function in the clause.

Noun Clause Used as a Subject

What we know about animal personalities changes with each new study.

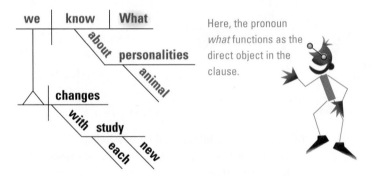

Here, the pronoun *what* functions as the direct object in the clause.

C. CONCEPT CHECK: Noun Clauses

Use what you learned to diagram these sentences.

1. Scientists wonder about what causes timid behavior in cats.

2. Another question is why humans are sometimes timid.

Compound-Complex Sentences

Diagram the independent clauses first; then attach each subordinate clause to the word it modifies.

People who have several cats may love each pet equally, but often the owners can identify differences in the cats' personalities.

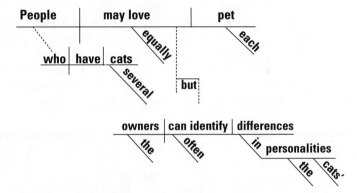

D. CONCEPT CHECK: Compound-Complex Sentences

Use what you learned to diagram these sentences.

1. One cat may greet all visitors with loud purrs, but another cat in the same household may hide whenever a stranger enters the room.
2. One cat's outgoing personality would seem obvious to some people, and they might marvel at how two cats can have different personalities.

E. MIXED REVIEW: Diagramming

Diagram the following sentences. Look for all types of clauses.

1. Dogs have been pets longer than any other animals have.
2. The long human association with dogs may be the reason that we know about the personalities of dogs.
3. Surveys reveal many dog adoptions fail because the owner's personality and the pet's personality are incompatible.
4. How people can determine the best dog breeds for their personalities is the focus of a book by Stanley Coren, a professor of psychology.
5. The book may appeal to whoever has an interest in dogs' personalities.

Grammar in Literature

Varying Sentence Structure

Writers craft their sentences carefully by using a variety of structures to add interest and rhythm to their writing. Adverb and adjective clauses, for example, provide descriptive details to engage a reader's imagination. They can also establish mood, tone, and setting. A variety of types of sentences can change the rhythm of writing or call attention to certain ideas.

In the following excerpt, Garrison Keillor uses clauses and varied sentence structures to create a colorful, humorous description of his personality when he was younger.

gary keillor
Garrison Keillor

When I was sixteen years old, I stood six feet two inches tall and weighed a hundred and forty pounds. I was intense and had the metabolism of a wolverine. I ate two or three lunches a day and three full dinners at night, **as my family sat around the kitchen table and observed,** and I cleaned off their plates too **when they had poor appetites or were finicky.** There was no food I disliked except muskmelon, which smelled rotten and loathsome. **Everything else I ate.** (It was Minnesota so we didn't have seafood, except fish sticks, of course.) **I was a remarkable person. I was a junior in high school, Class of 1960.** I was smart, so smart that poor grades didn't bother me in the slightest; I considered them no reflection on my intelligence. **I read four books a week, and I sometimes walked home from school, all twelve miles, so I could relive favorite chapters out loud, stride along the shoulder of the highway past the potato farms, and say brilliant and outrageous things, and sing in a big throbbing voice great songs like "Til There Was You" and "Love Me Tender."**

Adverb clause establishes time.

Adverb clauses add a more complete description.

Simple sentences stand in sharp contrast to other more complex sentences.

Lengthy sentence reflects his physical and emotional intensity.

You can use your knowledge of sentence structure to create a particular rhythm and to improve your writing when you revise.

Using Clauses to Vary Sentence Structure in Writing	
Using a single independent clause	Can slow down the momentum of a passage; in a series, can create a choppy rhythm that demands attention
Combining independent clauses	Connects ideas by pointing out the relationship between them; can balance the rhythm of short and long sentences
Adding subordinate clauses	Adds complexity by elaborating on main ideas; can build momentum and create a fluid rhythm

PRACTICE AND APPLY: Revising Sentence Structure

Use the directions below to revise the following paragraph. In some cases, you will have to make changes in the wording.

(1) I had a lot of friends, both male and female, in eighth grade. **(2)** I was talkative, both inside and outside class. **(3)** Then my family moved to another town. **(4)** I didn't know anyone. **(5)** Everyone in my new high school had known each other since kindergarten. **(6)** It seemed that way. **(7)** I felt shy, uncomfortable, and out of it all through high school. **(8)** College was a completely different story. **(9)** No one knew me there. **(10)** It freed me to become my more outgoing self once again.

1. Combine sentences 1 and 2 to form a compound-complex sentence.
2. Combine sentences 3 and 4 to form a complex sentence.
3. Combine sentences 5 and 6 to form a compound sentence.
4. Combine sentences 7 and 8 to form a compound sentence.
5. Combine sentences 9 and 10 to form a complex sentence with one adjective clause. Begin your sentence with *Somehow, the fact.*

After you have revised the paragraph, read the original and your revised version of the paragraph aloud with a partner. Discuss the differences you notice.

Working Portfolio: Choose a piece of your own writing and revise it to include all four kinds of sentence structures—simple, compound, complex, and compound-complex. Include at least one adjective clause, adverb clause, and noun clause.

Mixed Review

A. Kinds of Conjunctions, Clauses, and Sentence Structures Read the passage. Then write the answers to the questions below it.

Possible Health Tip: Avoid Hostility

(1) In the 1950s, two heart specialists, whose names were Meyer Friedman and Ray Rosenman, began studying the behavior patterns of heart-disease patients. **(2)** The doctors' research led them to coin the term *Type A personality,* which they described as aggressive, competitive, tense, and impatient. **(3)** The doctors then used the term *Type B* for people who have relaxed, patient, and easygoing personalities.

(4) As a result of this research, many doctors and patients now believe a Type A person is more likely to have a heart attack than a Type B person. **(5)** While recent studies clarify that many Type A traits such as aggressiveness and competitiveness do not play a role in heart attacks, one trait—chronic hostility—apparently does. **(6)** One possible explanation for this is that feelings of hostility make the heart beat faster and raise blood pressure. **(7)** Still under investigation is whether people with hostile attitudes also tend to follow poor health practices.

1. What is the adjective clause in sentence 1?
2. Is the adjective clause essential or nonessential in sentence 1?
3. What is the sentence structure of sentence 2?
4. What is the essential adjective clause in sentence 3?
5. What is the sentence structure in sentence 3?
6. What is the subordinating conjunction in sentence 4?
7. What is the sentence structure of sentence 5?
8. What is the type of clause that is introduced by *that* in sentence 5?
9. What is the noun clause in sentence 6? What is its function?
10. What is the noun clause in sentence 7? What is its function?

B. Identifying Sentence Structures, Fragments, and Run-Ons Identify each numbered group of words as either a simple, a compound, a complex, or a compound-complex sentence, a phrase fragment, a clause fragment, or a run-on.

> ## Hoping for Good Health
>
> **(1)** Can an optimistic, hopeful personality help you stay healthy? **(2)** Depending on whom you ask. **(3)** Research into the possible relationship between personality and disease has yielded some results, but they are contradictory. **(4)** No studies have shown that optimistic, hopeful people are less likely to develop cancer than other people, but some studies do suggest that cancer patients who are optimistic and hopeful have a better chance of recovery. **(5)** If that is true, perhaps personality has a direct effect on the body's ability to recover.

Write the letter of the term that describes each underlined passage.

Has this ever happened to you? You decide to take a personality quiz, <u>which you found on the Internet</u>. <u>You add up your score, and you eagerly</u>
(1)
<u>read the paragraph that supposedly describes your personality type</u>.
(2)
However, <u>when you finish reading</u>, you feel horrible. The reason is not
(3)
<u>because you don't recognize yourself</u>, but because you do! <u>When a scenario</u>
(4)   (5)
<u>like this occurs</u>, keep these points <u>in mind, first, the quiz results</u> may not
(6)
be completely accurate. <u>Taking a personality test while in a rotten mood</u>.
(7)
It can skew the results. Second, personality quizzes vary in quality. Even
highly respected tests <u>that professionals use</u> may have flaws. <u>Finally, even</u>
(8)
<u>if your quiz results are accurate, you could turn the situation into a</u>
(9)
<u>learning experience</u>. You might try to change <u>whatever attitudes and</u>
(10)
<u>behaviors you'd like to improve</u>, or you could choose to accept yourself as
you are.

1. A. noun clause
   B. adjective clause
   C. adverb clause
   D. independent clause

2. A. simple sentence
   B. compound sentence
   C. complex sentence
   D. compound-complex sentence

3. A. noun clause
   B. adjective clause
   C. adverb clause
   D. independent clause

4. A. noun clause as subject
   B. noun clause as direct object
   C. noun clause as predicate
      nominative
   D. adverb clause

5. A. noun clause
   B. adjective clause
   C. adverb clause
   D. independent clause

6. A. independent clause
   B. sentence fragment
   C. run-on sentence
   D. simple sentence

7. A. independent clause
   B. sentence fragment
   C. run-on sentence
   D. simple sentence

8. A. essential adjective clause
   B. nonessential adjective clause
   C. adverb clause
   D. noun clause

9. A. simple sentence
   B. compound sentence
   C. complex sentence
   D. compound-complex sentence

10. A. noun clause as subject
    B. noun clause as direct object of
       an infinitive
    C. noun clause as indirect object
    D. essential adjective clause

Student Help Desk

Clauses at a Glance

A clause contains a subject and a verb.

An independent clause expresses a complete thought.

A subordinate clause does not express a complete thought.

Though everyone has basic traits	ADVERB SUBORDINATE CLAUSE
that make up their personalities,	ADJECTIVE SUBORDINATE CLAUSE
we also have some ability to change	INDEPENDENT CLAUSE
who we are.	NOUN SUBORDINATE CLAUSE

Which is *Which?*   *That's* a Good Question!

Use *that* . . .	Example
to introduce essential adjective clauses	Some shy people develop tricks that help them talk to strangers.
to introduce noun clauses	These people have learned that questions often break the ice.

Use *which* . . .	Example
to introduce adjective clauses	They may ask a question about work, which most people like to talk about.
to introduce noun clauses	Which parts of a job are most annoying can be a great conversation starter.

Sentence Structures: For Variety's Sake

Structure	Example
Simple	Leah has many interests, from basketball to books.
Compound	She enjoys learning new things, but she has difficulty focusing on any one interest for very long.
Complex	Although Leah would love to be a musician, being a Web designer also sounds great to her.
Compound-Complex	Leah has many different friends, who range from bookish to athletic to artistic types, and she seldom finds herself bored.

Who or Whom?

Use *who* ...	Example
as the subject	We all have friends **who** break into every conversation.
as a predicate nominative	They couldn't care less about **who** the next speaker should be.

Use *whom* ...	Example
as a direct object	One "interrupter" **whom** I've known for years finally cured himself.
as the object of a preposition	He bites his tongue until everyone with **whom** he's speaking has stopped talking.

The Bottom Line

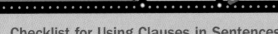

Checklist for Using Clauses in Sentences

Have I . . .

____ varied my sentence structure with independent and subordinate clauses?

____ put my most important ideas in independent clauses?

____ introduced clauses with appropriate conjunctions or pronouns?

____ punctuated clauses correctly?

____ avoided fragments and run-on sentences?

Using Verbs

PUT A S.T.A.R.
ON YOUR
CALENDAR!

Attend the
Students Take Action Rally
to rise funds for flood
victims in our community.
Does bring canned goods
and usable clothing.
Will have been held
Wednesday
at 3 P.M. in the gym.

YOU MAKES THE
DIFFERENCE!

Theme: Fighting for a Cause

Where Do You Stand?

Does this poster inspire you to help flood victims? Or does it make you feel stranded at sea? Instead of spurring you to action, the verbs, in particular, may leave you wondering what to do where and when.

Verbs are the movers and shakers of the grammar world. And to become movers and shakers in the real world, writers and speakers must choose powerful verbs and use them correctly. This chapter will show you how.

Write Away: This I Believe

Write a paragraph about a cause you think is worth fighting for. Tell why the cause is important to you and what action you would take. Save your paragraph in your 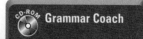 **Writing Portfolio.**

Grammar Coach

Choose the letter that indicates the best way to rewrite each underlined section.

Mohandas Gandhi grow up in India, where he learned the moral
(1)
value of nonviolence from his mother, a devout Hindu. As a young man,

Gandhi was sended to London to study law. He began his career in
(2)
South Africa, where he is fighting racial prejudice. When he returned to
(3)
India, he rised his voice to demand independence from British rule.
(4)
Civil disobedience was practiced by him in the form of hunger strikes
(5)
and nonviolent protest marches. He was arrested and imprisoned
(6)
several times for these activities. Britain finally have granted India's
(7)
independence in 1947, however. Gandhi spends his last years working to
(8)
end religious strife between Hindus and Muslims. Had he not been
(9)
assassinated by a Hindu fanatic, he succeeded in this cause as well.
(10)

1. A. Mohandas Gandhi was growing up
   B. Mohandas Gandhi grew up
   C. Mohandas Gandhi had grown up
   D. Correct as is

2. A. Gandhi was send to London
   B. Gandhi was being sent to London
   C. Gandhi was sent to London
   D. Correct as is

3. A. where he fought racial prejudice
   B. where he has fought racial prejudice
   C. where he has been fighting racial prejudice
   D. Correct as is

4. A. he had risen his voice
   B. he did rise his voice
   C. he raised his voice
   D. Correct as is

5. A. Civil disobedience being practiced by him
   B. He practiced civil disobedience
   C. He practices civil disobedience
   D. Correct as is

6. A. They arrested and imprisoned him
   B. He would have been arrested and imprisoned
   C. They arrest and imprisoned him
   D. Correct as is

7. A. Britain finally granted
   B. Britain finally had granted
   C. Britain finally grants
   D. Correct as is

8. A. Gandhi has spent his last years
   B. Gandhi spent his last years
   C. Gandhi was spending his last years
   D. Correct as is

9. A. Didn't someone assassinate him
   B. Haven't someone assassinated him
   C. Have he not been assassinated
   D. Correct as is

10. A. he may have been succeeding
    B. he may be succeeding
    C. he may have succeeded
    D. Correct as is

Principal Parts of Verbs

LESSON 1

❶ Here's the Idea

Calvin and Hobbes by Bill Watterson

A **verb** is a word that shows action, condition, or state of being.

- An **action verb,** such as *believe* and *protest,* shows either mental or physical activity.

- A **linking verb,** such as *feel* and *be,* describes a state of being and connects the subject with a word in the predicate.

▶ **Every verb has four principal parts: present, present participle, past, and past participle.** Use these to form the various verb tenses and to create other verb forms.

Principal Parts of Verbs			
Present	Present Participle	Past	Past Participle
protest	(is) protesting	protested	(has) protested
organize	(is) organizing	organized	(has) organized
speak	(is) speaking	spoke	(has) spoken
write	(is) writing	wrote	(has) written

Verbs can be regular or irregular. Most verbs are regular and form their principal parts similarly. Irregular verbs follow several patterns.

Regular Verbs

▶ **Create the past and past participle of regular verbs by adding *-d* or *-ed* to the present.**

Regular Verbs			
Present	Present Participle	Past	Past Participle
protest	(is) protesting	protested	(has) protested
organize	(is) organizing	organized	(has) organized

CHAPTER 4

Irregular Verbs

▶ The past and past participle of irregular verbs are formed in several ways. Most can be grouped into one of five spelling patterns.

Common Irregular Verbs

Spelling Pattern	Present	Present Participle	Past	Past Participle
Group 1 Present, past, and past participle are the same.	**let** put split spread	(is) letting (is) putting (is) splitting (is) spreading	**let** put split spread	(has) **let** (has) put (has) split (has) spread
Group 2 Past and past participle are the same.	**bring** get lead teach	(is) bringing (is) getting (is) leading (is) teaching	**brought** got led taught	(has) **brought** (has) got or gotten (has) led (has) taught
Group 3 Form past participle by adding -*n* or -*en* to past.	**beat** bite choose speak	(is) beating (is) biting (is) choosing (is) speaking	**beat** bit chose spoke	(has) **beaten** (has) bitten (has) chosen (has) spoken
Group 4 Change *i* in the present form to *a* for the past and to *u* for the past participle.	**begin** ring sink spring	(is) beginning (is) ringing (is) sinking (is) springing	**began** rang sank or sunk sprang or sprung	(has) **begun** (has) rung (has) sunk (has) sprung
Group 5 Change vowel of present to form past. Add -*n* or -*en* to form most past participles.	**do** fall see write	(is) doing (is) falling (is) seeing (is) writing	**did** fell saw wrote	(has) **done** (has) fallen (has) seen (has) written

For more about irregular verbs, see p. 129.

The principal parts of some regular and irregular verbs require spelling changes.

For more about spelling changes in regular verbs, see pp. 640–642.

❷ Why It Matters in Writing

The improper use or spelling of the principal parts of verbs—especially irregular verbs—accounts for many errors in writing. Be particularly watchful for these words when you proofread.

STUDENT MODEL

As a young girl, Bethany Wait ~~become~~ *became* interested in amateur,

or ham, radio. She quickly learned Morse Code and ~~sended~~ *sent*

codes from her private radio station at school. In the summer

of 1985, Hurricane Elena hit Florida. Having ~~got~~ *gotten* to her school,

Bethany spread urgent radio messages about the emergency.

~~Ignoreing~~ *Ignoring* her own sore eyes and aching back,

she got help for desperate hurricane victims.

❸ Practice and Apply

A. CONCEPT CHECK: Principal Parts of Verbs

Complete each sentence by writing the principal part of the verb indicated in parentheses.

Spokesperson for the Environment
1. Before she became an environmental activist, Rachel Carson (*work*—past) as a marine biologist for the U.S. Fish and Wildlife Service.
2. In her first three books, Carson dealt with the oceans, (*emphasize*—present participle) their importance as an ecosystem.
3. One of these books, *The Sea Around Us,* (*win*—past) the National Book Award for nonfiction in 1952.
4. Her message that all life is interdependent has (*inspire*—past participle) generations of nature lovers and ecologists.
5. A later book, *Silent Spring,* was published in 1962, (*earn*—present participle) Carson even greater recognition.
6. In this book Carson (*document*—past) the destructive effects of pesticides on the environment.

7. *Silent Spring* (*lead*—past) to a federal investigation and to stricter regulation of pesticide use.
8. In our ecologically aware society, Rachel Carson is (*consider*—past participle) a pioneer of environmental activism.
9. By (*combine*—present participle) scientific knowledge with beautiful descriptive writing, Carson's books reach a large audience.
10. Her writings (*be*—present) required reading for people concerned with the environment.

➡ **For a SELF-CHECK and more practice, see the EXERCISE BANK, p. 602.**

B. PROOFREADING: Using Principal Parts of Irregular Verbs

Write the correct principal part of each underlined verb.

Activism at Work

The chemical pesticide known as DDT was <u>putted</u> to use during World War II to kill body lice and fleas. Later, it was so effective that farmers <u>seen</u> a pest-free future. We now know, however, that chemical pesticides may be <u>done</u> more harm than good to humans and the environment. Problems <u>begun</u> in the 1950s. Resistant species of insects evolved, because the insecticide was killing natural predators and helpful parasites along with harmful insects. The pest population <u>spreaded</u> out of control. Scientists <u>teached</u> that pesticide residues in food were harmful to humans and wildlife. In early 1960, Rachel Carson <u>write</u> *Silent Spring,* which <u>brung</u> attention to these problems. Largely due to Carson's work, many people now <u>chose</u> a more ecologically sound approach to pest control instead of <u>let</u> chemicals do the job alone.

Rachel Carson

Verb Tenses

LESSON 2

❶ Here's the Idea

▶ **Verb tenses indicate when an action or a state of being occurs—in the past, present, or future.**

There are three **simple tenses** (past, present, and future) and three **perfect tenses** (past perfect, present perfect, and future perfect). These tenses are formed from the principal parts of verbs and make up the verb's **conjugation.** They give writers many ways to describe past, present, and future events.

Forming and Using Simple Tenses

Conjugation of Simple Tenses		
	Singular	**Plural**
Present Use the present part.	I talk you talk he, she, it talks	we talk you talk they talk
Past Add *-ed* to the present part for regular verbs.	I talked you talked he, she, it talked	we talked you talked they talked
Future Add *will* or *shall* to the present part.	I will (shall) talk you will (shall) talk he, she, it will (shall) talk	we will (shall) talk you will (shall) talk they will (shall) talk

Using the Present Tense Use the present tense to describe an action or a state of being . . .

• happening as it is being reported

   This biography of Mother Teresa inspires me.

• that is regularly occurring or habitual

   Mother Teresa's followers do important and exhausting work.

• that will take place in the future—when the verb is modified by an adverb or adverbial phrase indicating future time

   The presentation on Mother Teresa's life begins in an hour.

Writers often use the **historical** or **literary present tense** to tell about a past action or state of being as though it were happening now. This tense is often used to discuss literature.

> *A Simple Path,* a biography of Mother Teresa, describes her tireless work with the needy people of India.

Using the Past Tense Use the past tense to describe an action or a state of being that began and ended in the past.

> During the 1920s, a young girl of Albanian descent, Agnes Gonxha Bojaxhiu, joined a religious order in Ireland and took the name Sister Teresa.

Using the Future Tense Use the future tense to describe an action or a state of being that will take place some time after the present moment.

> Generations of social activists will honor Mother Teresa as one of the greatest Nobel Peace Prize recipients.

Forming and Using Perfect Tenses

Conjugation of Perfect Tenses		
	Singular	**Plural**
Present Perfect Add *has* or *have* to the past participle.	I have talked you have talked he, she, it has talked	we have talked you have talked they have talked
Past Perfect Add *had* to the past participle.	I had talked you had talked he, she, it had talked	we had talked you had talked they had talked
Future Perfect Add *will have* or *shall have* to the past participle.	I will (shall) have talked you will (shall) have talked he, she, it will (shall) have talked	we will (shall) have talked you will (shall) have talked they will (shall) have talked

Using the Present Perfect Tense Use the present perfect tense to express an action or a state of being . . .

- completed at an indefinite time in the past

  Historians have noted Mohandas Gandhi's tremendous impact on social activists such as Dr. Martin Luther King, Jr.

- that started in the past and continues into the present.

  Gandhi's philosophy of nonviolence has left a lasting impression on the world.

Using the Past Perfect Tense Use the past perfect tense to express a past action or state of being that occurred before another in the past.

Gandhi had embraced the principles of nonviolent protest long before he organized a demonstration against an unfair tax.

Using the Future Perfect Tense Use the future perfect tense to express a future action or state of being that will take place before another in the future.

By the year 2010, Gandhi's reforms will have been in practice for more than 60 years.

❷ Why It Matters in Writing

The correct use of verb tenses clarifies the sequence of events and can help readers understand causes and effects.

PROFESSIONAL MODEL

One Sunday, [Dr. Martin Luther] King [, Jr.] attended a lecture in Philadelphia by Dr. Mordecai W. Johnson, the president of Howard University. . . . "I had heard of Gandhi," King recalled, but he had never given him much thought. Yet as Johnson described the man and his movement, King became intrigued. What he heard, he said, "was so profound and fascinating that I left the meeting and bought a half dozen books on Gandhi's life and works."

—Robert Jakoubek, *Martin Luther King, Jr., Civil Rights Leader*

Past perfect tense shows events that happened before other past events.

Simple past tense shows what happened in the more recent past.

❸ Practice and Apply

A. CONCEPT CHECK: Verb Tenses

For each sentence, correct the error in the underlined verb and identify the correct tense.

The Fight for Civil Rights

1. In 1619, the first enslaved Africans <u>arrive</u> in the Virginia colony.
2. The long struggle of African Americans to obtain their civil rights <u>will have begun</u>.
3. During the American Civil War, President Lincoln <u>issue</u> the Emancipation Proclamation to end slavery.
4. After the war, Congress <u>has adopted</u> constitutional amendments to prohibit slavery.
5. In 1875, the first Civil Rights Act <u>make</u> segregation illegal in public places.
6. By 1896, however, the Supreme Court <u>will have judged</u> "separate but equal" facilities for blacks and whites legal.
7. This ruling stood until 1954, when the Supreme Court <u>had overruled</u> it.
8. In protest to the slow pace of desegregation, Dr. Martin Luther King, Jr., <u>leads</u> his followers in passive resistance.
9. He <u>will influence</u> Rosa Parks, a black woman, arrested for refusing to give up her bus seat to a white person.
10. The struggle for universal civil and human rights <u>has continued</u> today, all over the world.

➡ **For a SELF-CHECK and more practice, see the EXERCISE BANK, p. 603.**

B. REVISING: Correcting Verb Tenses

Revise the underlined verbs in the following paragraph to correct errors and show the proper sequence of events.

Ongoing Struggle

Despite Dr. King's successes, in the early 1960s, violence <u>erupts</u> all over the South. In 1963, an assailant <u>shooted</u> Medgar Evers, a black activist, in the back as he <u>had been walking</u> home. In 1965, some 600 blacks <u>join</u> a protest march from Selma to Montgomery, Alabama. After police <u>attack</u> them, 70 of the marchers were injured. In response, President Johnson <u>had called</u> in the National Guard to protect Dr. King and his followers on a third march. That time, 25,000 enthusiastic supporters <u>will have arrived</u> in Montgomery.

LESSON 3 Progressive and Emphatic Forms

❶ Here's the Idea

The progressive and emphatic forms of verbs give writers additional options in describing actions or states of being.

Using Progressive Forms

▶ **The progressive form of a verb describes an ongoing action or state of being.**

Nelson Mandela is working for better understanding among people.

Each of the six tenses has a progressive form. To create these forms, combine the appropriate simple or perfect tense of *be* with the present participle of the main verb.

Progressive Tenses		
Use this Tense	**Use to Describe an Action or State of Being . . .**	**Example**
Present	in progress	In Africa, followers of Nelson Mandela **are striving** for justice.
Past	ongoing in the past	Even as a prisoner, Mandela **was teaching.**
Future	ongoing in the future	Many high school students **will be emulating** Mandela's commitment to justice in their future work.
Present perfect	that started in the past and continues in the present	Nelson Mandela **has been acting** as a goodwill ambassador since his release from prison in 1990.
Past perfect	interrupted by another past action	Mandela **had been touring** the United States when former New York governor Mario Cuomo described him as "a symbol of hope for the world."
Future perfect	that will take place by a specified future time	Like Gandhi, by the year 2010, Mandela **will have been effecting** social change for more than 60 years.

CHAPTER 4

Using Emphatic Forms

▶ **The emphatic form of a verb (*do* + verb) is used to make a verb more forceful.**

Use this form to add emphasis to your writing.

> **There's no question that Mandela does influence human rights policy.**

There are two emphatic forms—present tense and past tense. To create them, add the appropriate tense of the auxiliary verb *do* to the present form of the verb.

> **Activists around the world do emulate the democratic ideals of Nelson Mandela.**

PRESENT EMPHATIC

> **To underscore his commitment to human rights, Mandela did join the African National Congress in 1944.**

PAST EMPHATIC

USING VERBS

❷ Why It Matters in Writing

When revising your writing, use progressive verb forms to show the ongoing nature of events and emphatic forms to emphasize the action or state of being.

STUDENT MODEL

By the time Nelson Mandela reached his 60th birthday, he **had been serving** time in jail for 14 years. Human rights activists **had begun using** his birthday to call attention to his long, unjust imprisonment. Mail carriers **were delivering** bundles of cards and letters from all over the world to Mandela's wife, Winnie.

Although prison **did rob** Mandela of his youth, it also provided an opportunity for him to display his humanity and courage.

Past perfect progressive shows events that happened during ongoing past actions.

Past progressive shows ongoing action in the past.

Past emphatic stresses impact of prison on Mandela.

❸ Practice and Apply

A. CONCEPT CHECK: **Progressive and Emphatic Verb Forms**

Identify each progressive and emphatic verb form in the following sentences. Write the verb, its tense, and its form.

Fighting for the Homeless

1. Author and social activist Studs Terkel has been fighting for the rights of poor people and workers for most of his adult life.
2. Terkel had been working as a Chicago TV actor in the 1950s when he became interested in social issues.
3. Among the causes Terkel did fight for in early years were racial justice, the labor movement, and the struggle to end the war in Vietnam.
4. In the past decade he has been turning his attention to the plight of the homeless.
5. The number of homeless people is increasing so fast that there are not enough shelters for them.
6. In Chicago, however, many homeless people do find places to sleep beside the heating grates under the streets.
7. Up to 80 people a night have been sleeping there on old mattresses, boxes, carpeting, and blankets.
8. The property owners in the area were threatening the homeless with a lockout.
9. However, Terkel did organize a meeting between property owners and advocates for the homeless in January 1999.
10. His activism will be affecting public policy for years to come.

➡ **For a SELF-CHECK and more practice, see the EXERCISE BANK, p. 603.**

B. WRITING PRACTICE: **Eyewitness Report**

Imagine you had attended this rally for the homeless with Studs Terkel in Chicago. In a short paragraph, describe the rally, using the following progressive and emphatic verbs.

are attending
were sleeping
did threaten
is saying
did win

Active and Passive Voice

LESSON 4

❶ Here's the Idea

▶ **The voice of an action verb indicates whether the subject performs or receives the action.**

A verb is in the **active voice** when the subject performs the action.

A verb is in the **passive voice** when the action is received by the subject.

SUBJECT   VERB

Mary Harris "Mother" Jones supported child labor laws.

> **Active Voice** The subject performs the action.

SUBJECT   VERB

Child labor laws were supported by Mary Harris "Mother" Jones.

> **Passive Voice** The subject receives the action.

Form the passive voice by using a form of the verb *be* and the past participle of the main verb. Use it to 1) emphasize the receiver of the action or 2) show that the doer of the action is unimportant or unknown.

Millions of women and children have been helped by Mother Jones's activism.   FORM OF BE ⬈   ⬉ PAST PARTICIPLE

     ⬋ FORM OF BE

Jones was known as "the mother of the laboring class."
       ⬉ PAST PARTICIPLE

Only transitive verbs—ones that can take direct objects—can be used in the passive voice.

❷ Why It Matters in Writing

Voice is your choice! Choose active or passive based on whether you want to emphasize the doer or the receiver of the action.

> **PROFESSIONAL MODEL**
>
> This is not the first time that girls **have been burned** alive in the city. Every year thousands of us **are maimed**.... I **know** from my experience it is up to the working people to save themselves.
>
> —Rose Schneiderman, Women's Trade Union League

> **Passive voice** emphasizes women workers as victims.

> **Active voice** emphasizes the writer's knowledge.

USING VERBS

❸ Practice and Apply

A. CONCEPT CHECK: Active and Passive Voice

Write the main verb in each sentence and identify it as either in the active or passive voice.

Workers Unite!

1. Around the turn of the 20th century, industrial workers in American cities were grossly underpaid.

2. Labor leaders recognized unions as a source of power for workers.

3. The first successful labor union, the American Federation of Labor (AFL), was founded in 1886 by Samuel Gompers.

4. Gompers had simple goals for workers: higher wages, shorter hours, safety, and the right to organize.

5. Under his leadership, the AFL grew from 140,000 members in 1886 to nearly one million in 1900.

6. Unfortunately, however, unskilled workers, African Americans, and women were excluded from the union.

7. Disagreements between business managers such as Andrew Carnegie and Henry Clay Frick and their workers sometimes resulted in violent battles.

8. Eugene Debs, an organizer of railroad workers, saw business owners as workers' enemies.

9. As a result, Debs formed the American Railway Union in 1893.

10. Debs, however, was defeated in his battle with the Pullman Palace Car Company in Chicago in 1894.

➡ For a SELF-CHECK and more practice, see the EXERCISE BANK, p. 604.

B. REVISING: Using Active and Passive Voice Effectively

Revise the following paragraph, changing verbs from passive to active voice where appropriate.

Pullman Against the Railroad Union

Pullman was a company town in which all aspects of its workers' lives were controlled by management. After the Panic of 1893, wages were cut by Pullman, and many workers were laid off. But prices in the town stores and rents in company housing remained the same. Many workers joined Eugene Debs's American Railroad Union and went on strike. In a fight with federal troops, scores of workers were killed. Debs was arrested. Despite this devastating defeat, the groundwork in the fight for a better life for working people was laid by Debs.

❶ Here's the Idea

▶ **The mood of a verb indicates the status of the action or state of being it describes.**

There are three moods: **indicative, imperative,** and **subjunctive.**

Indicative Mood

A verb in the indicative mood expresses a fact or asks a question. Verbs in most sentences are in the indicative mood.

Twelve-year-old Andrew Holleman fought to save a wooded wetland near his Massachusetts home.

Didn't he show courage in standing up to a large real estate developer?

Imperative Mood

A verb in the imperative mood gives a command or makes a request.

Imagine a sixth grader or seventh grader circulating petitions and raising money for lawyers' fees.

Subjunctive Mood

A verb in the subjunctive mood expresses a 1) wish or condition that is contrary to fact or 2) a command or request after the word *that.*

If only I were able to stand up more strongly for my beliefs, I could help build a better world.

Teachers should demand that more young people be able to act on their principles.

The subjunctive form of *be* is always *be* or *were,* even with singular subjects.

If only she were more confident in herself, she'd really go far.

His mother asked that he be more like his father.

USING VERBS

❷ Why It Matters in Writing

The subjunctive mood enables writers to discuss situations that don't exist while alerting readers to that fact.

Everyone has unique talents and beliefs, and if each of us **were** to discover our special strengths and work to develop them, we'd be happier, get along better with others, and make a difference in the world.

> **Subjunctive mood** indicates a wish for the way people could live

❸ Practice and Apply

A. CONCEPT CHECK: Mood of Verbs

Identify the mood of the underlined verb in each sentence.

Lock Out Land Mines!

1. Armies <u>have been using</u> land mines to terrorize.
2. Land mines <u>are</u> hidden bombs that explode when someone steps on them.
3. Much farmland also <u>has been contaminated</u> by land mines and has been abandoned.
4. <u>Think</u> of all the suffering these devices are inflicting on innocent people.
5. The International Campaign to Ban Landmines (ICBL) has demanded that the use of land mines <u>be prohibited.</u>

➜ For a SELF-CHECK and more practice, see the EXERCISE BANK, p. 604.

B. REVISING: Using the Imperative and Subjunctive Moods

Revise four of the following sentences to put the verbs in the imperative or subjunctive mood.

Even if land mines are banned in the future, what should be done about the estimated 100 million mines that already exist? Should the international community demand that the mines are removed? A land mine costs as little as $3, but removing one can cost up to $1,000. If this figure was multiplied by the number of mines, the cost could be in the billions. How does this price compare with the value of a single human life that would be saved?

Problems with Verbs

❶ Here's the Idea

As useful as verbs are, they can also spell trouble. Common problems include misuse of tenses and confusion of similar verbs.

Misuse of Tenses

▶ **Use the same tense to express two or more actions that occur at the same time.**

> **STUDENT MODEL**
>
> The Romanian-born writer and social activist Elie Wiesel **survived** one of the blackest times of human history. His parents and sister **were killed** in the Nazi concentration camps, and he **was forced** to work as a slave laborer. These experiences **changed** his life and **provided** the material for his many books.

All actions occurred at a similar time in the past, so all verbs should be in the past tense.

▶ **To show a sequence of past events, use the past perfect or past progressive tense to describe the older event and the simple past to describe the more recent one.**

> **STUDENT MODEL**
>
> After he **had suffered** the terrors of the Holocaust, Wiesel **wrote** about his experiences in his first book, *Night*. Once he **had put** that nightmare into words, he **began** addressing the larger issues of what the Holocaust **said** about human nature in several other books.

Wiesel first experienced the Holocaust and then wrote about it.

He first dealt with the Holocaust in *Night* and then wrote other books about it.

Commonly Confused Verbs

Watch out for pairs of verbs that are spelled similarly and may sound alike.

Commonly Confused Verbs			
	Meaning	**Conjugation**	**Example**
leave	to go away from	leave, (is) leaving, left, (have) left	The protesters have left the mayor's office.
let	to allow	let, (is) letting, let, (have) let	The law enforcers let them protest peacefully.
lie	to rest in a flat position	lie, (is) lying, lay, (have) lain	The protesters are lying in the street.
lay	to place	lay, (is) laying, laid, (have) laid	Lay the posters down and take your place in line.
rise	to go upward	rise, (is) rising, rose, (have) risen	The voice of the rally organizer rises above the crowd.
raise	to lift	raise, (is) raising, raised, (have) raised	The committee is raising money for the crash victims.
sit	to occupy a seat	sit, (is) sitting, sat, (have) sat	Sit down so the meeting can begin.
set	to put or place	set, (is) setting, set, (have) set	The speaker set forth the group's policies and programs.

❷ Why It Matters in Writing

Using confusing verbs and verb forms incorrectly can confuse your readers even more. To be bright, you have to do it right!

STUDENT MODEL

I had just ~~set~~ *sat* down to do my homework, when my friend called me. "~~Leave~~ *Let* it ~~lay~~ *lie* where it is," he said breathlessly, "and come over to the football field on the double. The Save-the-Park folks are ~~rising~~ *raising* a huge model of a garbage dump as a protest." So, what could I do? I ~~let~~ *left* my homework behind.

Using Verb Tenses and Forms for Effect

Tense	Use a variety of tenses to show the sequence of events over time.
Voice	Use the active voice to emphasize the doer of an action; use the passive voice to emphasize the action, not the doer.
Mood	Use the imperative mood to engage readers or listeners directly or the subjunctive mood to discuss situations that do not exist.

PRACTICE AND APPLY: Varying Verb Tenses and Forms

Read the paragraph below, which was written by a South African who lived under its now-abolished system of racial apartheid. Work with a partner to address the items that follow.

(1) To relieve my tormented conscience, I <u>convinced</u> myself that it was futile, it was suicidal, to fight bullets and truncheons with stones, armoured vehicles and tear gas with shouts of *"Amandla! Awethu!"* and fists clenched in black power salutes. (2) I <u>led</u> myself to believe that there were other ways of fighting the awesome apartheid machinery besides fleeing the country and joining the ANC [African National Congress] as a freedom fighter. (3) As I grappled with my conscience, in me <u>became born</u> a fanatical determination that if I ever <u>left</u> South Africa alive, I would devote every minute of my time, every ounce of my strength, to fighting for the liberation of my countrymen. (4) What my weapons would be I didn't know.

—Mark Mathabane, *Kaffir Boy*

1. What is the tense of the underlined verbs in sentences 1 and 2?
2. What voice are the verbs in the phrases *convinced myself* and *led myself to believe* in sentences 1 and 2?
3. Why do you think Mathabane used the passive voice *became born* in sentence 3?
4. How would you rewrite the verb *left* in that same sentence in the subjunctive mood using the verbs *were* and *leave*?
5. Write a short statement about the effect of the passage on you.

Working Portfolio Return to the writing you did on page 104 about a cause you think is worth fighting for. Revise it by varying verb tenses and forms to create a greater impact on your readers.

Mixed Review

A. Verb Tenses and Emphatic Forms Correct all errors of verb usage in the following sentences.

1. The scientific study of genetics, or the transmission of characteristics from parents to children, was began by Gregor Mendel, an Austrian monk.
2. He was doing a series of experiments on garden peas in the 1850s and 1860s.
3. Throughout the late 19th and early 20th centuries, scientists search for the chemical secrets of life.
4. In 1944, scientists has identified the substance responsible as deoxyribonucleic acid (DNA).
5. Its chemical makeup and operation in the genes was still being a mystery, however.
6. In the 1950s, scientists does know the importance of DNA in the production of proteins in cells.
7. Then by the end of 1953, a breakthrough occur.
8. In 1953, James Watson and Francis Crick proposed that DNA is having a coil of two strands in a double helix.
9. The strands peel apart, they said, and each create its matching half.
10. With this knowledge, other geneticists are being able to map and clone genetic material.
11. It is now possible that manipulation of genes will have been used to cure hereditary diseases.
12. Some scientists even do envisioned the use of normal genes as a cure for diseases.
13. Many people are feeling, however, that this power to change human beings' genetic makeup is dangerous.
14. Others had argued that the search for scientific knowledge must continue.
15. Gregor Mendel certainly open up a big can of worms.

B. Voice, Mood, and Problems with Verbs Edit and proofread the following paragraph, correcting all errors in verb usage and awkward use of voice.

Before modern medicine, it was believed that disease was caused by evil spirits or other imaginary substances. In the 19th century, it was discovered that infectious diseases were caused by microorganisms. Major contributions were made by Louis Pasteur, Robert Koch, and their followers, eventually identifying the causes of such fatal diseases as malaria, tuberculosis, cholera, and plague. If only someone can develop a way to prevent those diseases. A major victory was achieved by Pasteur in 1885 with his discovery of an effective vaccine against rabies. After Pasteur's success, other victories quickly had followed. Joseph Lister applied Pasteur's germ theory to create antiseptic conditions, which has led to safer, more infection-free surgery.

Choose the letter that indicates the best way to rewrite each underlined section.

Social worker Jane Addams choosed to be a leader of reform
(1)
movements throughout most of her life. Hull House, which she founded in
(2)
Chicago in 1899, is providing care for the urban poor and homeless.
(3)
Modeled after settlement houses Addams seen in England, Hull House
(4)
become a center for social activism in the United States and a model for
(5)
the rest of the world. Addams also lead the fight for women's suffrage,
(6)
and, later, a controversial stand as a pacifist was taken by her during
(7)
World War I. She has been elected president of the Women's International
(8)
League for Peace and Freedom, and in 1931, was being awarded the Nobel
(9)
Prize for peace. She also does write several books on social questions,
(10)
including her autobiography, *Twenty Years at Hull-House*.

1. A. Social worker Jane Addams
     has chosen
   B. Social worker Jane Addams
     was choosing
   C. Social worker Jane Addams
     chose
   D. Correct as is

2. A. which she has founded
   B. which she had found
   C. which she did find
   D. Correct as is

3. A. provided
   B. will be providing
   C. had provided
   D. Correct as is

4. A. Addams was seeing
   B. Addams have seen
   C. Addams had seen
   D. Correct as is

5. A. became
   B. had become
   C. is becoming
   D. Correct as is

6. A. Addams also leads
   B. Addams also was leading
   C. Addams also led
   D. Correct as is

7. A. a controversial stand as a
     pacifist is taken by her
   B. she had taken a controversial
     stand as a pacifist
   C. she took a controversial stand
     as a pacifist
   D. Correct as is

8. A. She have been elected
   B. She was elected
   C. She is elected
   D. Correct as is

9. A. has been awarded
   B. had been awarded
   C. was awarded
   D. Correct as is

10. A. She also wrote
    B. She also had written
    C. She also has been writing
    D. Correct as is

USING VERBS

Student Help Desk

Using Verbs at a Glance

Verbs are the **movers** and **shakers** of the grammar world.

Principal Parts: **Tense** **Form** **Voice** **Mood**

Using Verb Tenses

It's About Time

Writing About the Past

Past
I **studied** verbs every day last week.

Present perfect
I **have studied** many subjects, but never one like verbs.

Past progressive
I **was studying** verbs when the roof caved in.

Past perfect
I **had studied** everything else before I tackled verbs.

Past perfect progressive
I **had been studying** verbs when the roof caved in.

Writing About the Present

Present
I **study** best in the morning.

Present progressive
I **am studying** verbs in my sleep.

Present perfect
It seems as if I **have studied** verbs forever.

Present perfect progressive
I **have been studying** verbs as long as I remember.

Writing About the Future

Future
I **will study** verbs, I promise.

Present progressive + adverb
I **am studying** verbs tomorrow.

Future progressive
I **will be studying** verbs tomorrow.

Future perfect
I **will have studied** verbs for six hours when I finally give up.

Future perfect progressive
By my birthday, I **will have been studying** verbs for two-thirds of my life.

Irregular Verbs

All Shook Up

Group 1—Present, past, and past participle are the same.

bid	cut	let	shut
burst	hit	put	split
cost	hurt	set	spread

Group 2—Past and past participle are the same.

bring	get	sit
catch	lead	sting
fight	lend	swing
flee	lose	teach
fling	say	

Group 3—Form past participle by adding -n or -en to past.

bear	break	speak	tear
beat	choose	steal	wear
bite	freeze	swear	

Group 4—Change the vowel *i* in present to *a* for past and to *u* for past participle.

begin	shrink	swim
drink	sing	spring
ring	sink	

Group 5—Change vowel of present to form past. Form most past participles by adding -n or -en to present.

blow	eat	know	shake
come	fall	ride	slay
do	give	rise	take
draw	go	run	throw
drive	grow	see	write

The Bottom Line

Checklist for Using Verbs

Have I . . .

____ used the correct verb form?

____ used the right helping verb?

____ used the correct spelling for the principal parts of regular and irregular verbs?

____ used a variety of moods?

____ used the correct tense?

____ used the appropriate tenses to show a sequence of actions?

____ used the passive voice only when the doer of an action is not known or is not important?

____ chosen the correct form of confusing verbs?

Subject-Verb Agreement

Be an individual.
Everybody else are.

Theme: Outstanding Individuals

What's Your Fame?

What makes this bumper sticker humorous? Do you think a similar error in an essay or a newspaper article would cause laughter—or raised eyebrows? As much as you may want to stand out from the crowd, you probably don't want the reason to be your bad grammar.

In this chapter, you'll learn how to make your subjects and verbs agree. By doing so, you will make your writing clear, correct, and a true reflection of who you—a singular individual—are.

Write Away: Unique Contributions
Write a paragraph about a unique contribution you can make to the world. Save your paragraph in your 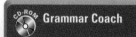 **Working Portfolio.**

Grammar Coach

Choose the letter of the best revision for each underlined section.

Many athletes has been famous in their day, but few have ever been as
(1)   (2)
admired as Muhammad Ali. Most regards him as one of history's greatest
(3)
boxers. His boxing career and personal life has been controversial since
(4)
the 1960 Olympics were the scene of his winning a gold medal, however.
(5)
Neither public criticism nor the removal of his title were enough to convince
(6)
him to serve in the military. Nevertheless, no amount of controversy have
(7)
lessened his popularity. An army of fans was watching emotionally as their
(8)
ailing hero lit the Olympic flame in 1996. How does people account for his
(9)
popularity? There are no simple answers to that question, but clearly
(10)
Muhammad Ali is the Greatest.

1. A. Many athletes have been
   B. Many an athlete have been
   C. Many athlete has been
   D. Correct as is

2. A. few was ever
   B. few has ever been
   C. few were not ever
   D. Correct as is

3. A. Most is regarding
   B. Most regard
   C. Most does regard
   D. Correct as is

4. A. His boxing career and personal
      life were being
   B. His boxing career and personal
      life was
   C. His boxing career and personal
      life have been
   D. Correct as is

5. A. the 1960 Olympics is
   B. the 1960 Olympics was
   C. the 1960 Olympics are
   D. Correct as is

6. A. Neither public criticism nor the
      removal of his title were not
   B. Neither public criticism nor the
      removal of his title have been
   C. Neither public criticism nor the
      removal of his title was
   D. Correct as is

7. A. no amount of controversy has
      lessened
   B. no amount of controversy lessen
   C. no amount of controversy are
      lessening
   D. Correct as is

8. A. An army of fans has watched
   B. An army of fans watches
   C. An army of fans were watching
   D. Correct as is

9. A. How has people accounted
   B. How do people account
   C. How is people accounting
   D. Correct as is

10. A. There is no simple answers
    B. There is not no simple answers
    C. There was no simple answers
    D. Correct as is

Agreement in Person and Number

❶ Here's the Idea

▶ **A verb must agree with its subject in person and number.**

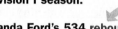
AGREE

Cindy Brown is famous for scoring 974 | THIRD–PERSON SINGULAR
points in the 1986–1987 NCAA women's
Division I season.
AGREE

Wanda Ford's 534 rebounds were the | THIRD–PERSON PLURAL
most ever collected in a single season.

Agreement in Person and Number

▶ **Singular subjects take singular verbs; plural subjects take plural verbs.**

The form of a verb also depends on the person of its subject.

Forms of Verbs		
	Singular	**Plural**
First person	I excel	we excel
Second person	you excel	you excel
Third person	he/she/it/Cindy excel**s**	they/Cindy and Wanda excel

In the present tense of all verbs except *be*, the third-person singular form is the only form that differs from the base form. Add -s to create that form.

Even this rule has exceptions. You can remember them by thinking OY! To create the third-person singular form of
• a verb ending in **o,** add -es (do → does)
• a verb ending in **y,** change the *y* to *i* and add -es (try → tries)

For more information about spelling rules, see p. 640.

The forms of *be* are a special case.

Forms of *Be*				
	Present		**Past**	
	Singular	**Plural**	**Singular**	**Plural**
First person	I am	we are	I was	we were
Second person	you are	you are	you were	you were
Third person	he/she/it is	they are	he/she/it was	they were

Don't get confused! **Nouns** that end in s are usually plural. **Verbs** that end in s are usually singular.

For more information about singular and plural forms of nouns, see p. 6.

Words That Separate Subjects and Verbs

When the subject and verb in a sentence are separated by other words, mentally screen out those words and make the verb agree with the subject.

The individual scoring title for 1967–1968, ~~as well as those for 1968–1969 and 1969–1970,~~ was won by Pete Maravich.

❷ Why It Matters in Writing

Words that separate the subject and the verb are the most common cause of errors in agreement, so watch for them carefully.

> **STUDENT MODEL**
>
> **DRAFT**
> Kevin Granger, along with Marcus Brown and Bubba Wells, stand out for scoring over 26 points per game in the 1995–1996 NCAA season.
>
> **REVISION**
> Kevin Granger, ~~along with Marcus Brown and Bubba Wells,~~ stands out for scoring over 26 points per game in the 1995–1996 NCAA season.

❸ Practice and Apply

A. CONCEPT CHECK: Agreement in Person and Number

Choose the correct verb form in parentheses to complete each of the following sentences.

All-Around Star

1. If you follow politics, you (is, are) familiar with Bill Bradley.
2. Others, especially sports fans, (remembers, remember) his sports career.
3. At Princeton University, Bradley's energy (was, were) actually focused more on studying than on playing basketball.
4. His mother, as well as casual acquaintances, (was, were) not surprised when he received a prestigious Rhodes scholarship to study at Oxford University.
5. Ivy League athletes such as Bradley rarely (achieves, achieve) national recognition in their sports, despite their academic honors.
6. His athletic accomplishments (includes, include) being a three-time All-American and being captain of the gold-medal-winning 1964 U.S. Olympic basketball team.
7. Athletes, even great ones, often (disappears, disappear) from the spotlight once they retire.
8. You already (knows, know) that Bill Bradley is an exception.
9. His three terms in the U.S. Senate (leaves, leave) a legacy of important tax and social reform laws.
10. Bradley's accomplishments, in addition to these, (includes, include) three published books on sports, politics, and life.

➜ **For a SELF-CHECK and more practice, see the EXERCISE BANK, p. 605.**

B. WRITING: Using Subjects and Verbs

Write a one-paragraph memo to your school administration, recommending that a sports figure you admire be asked to speak at your graduation ceremony. Include the following information, making sure that your subjects and verbs agree.

• the person's sports accomplishments
• other important achievements of the person
• qualities that make him or her a good role model for students

Indefinite Pronouns as Subjects

❶ Here's the Idea

▶ When used as subjects, some indefinite pronouns are always singular and some are always plural. Others can be either singular or plural, depending on how they're used.

Indefinite Pronouns

Always Singular

each	everyone	nobody	anything
either	everybody	nothing	someone
neither	everything	anyone	somebody
one	no one	anybody	something
another	much		

One of the Nobel Prize winners for chemistry, Richard Kuhn, was told by his government to refuse the award.

Always Plural

several	few	both	many

Many of the Nobelists in medicine since 1970 have been from the United States.

Singular or Plural

some	all	most	none
any	more		

REFERS TO

Most of the Nobel Prizes for literature have been awarded to men.

> *Most* refers to a number of individuals, so the verb, *have been awarded*, is plural.

REFERS TO

Most of the money for the Nobel Prizes comes from interest on a fund established by the will of Alfred Nobel, a Swedish chemist and engineer.

> *Most* refers to an amount, so the verb, *comes*, is singular.

S-V AGREEMENT

Don't be confused by nonessential phrases that come between indefinite-pronoun subjects and verbs. Subjects are never found in these phrases. Remember to mentally screen out these words and then make the verbs agree with the subjects.

Nobody, ~~not even Nobel laureates in literature,~~ is perfect.

Most of us, ~~even textbook editors,~~ make usage errors once in a while.

➋ Why It Matters in Writing

Indefinite pronouns appear as subjects in all types of communications—from press releases to sales reports. Using verb forms that agree with them can make people take your message—and you—seriously.

> **PROFESSIONAL MODEL**
>
> Few of the nation's college seniors, or even professional educators, are able to match the achievements of the University of Chicago Rhodes scholarship winner Mira Lutgendorf. She is fluent in Hindi and Italian, has written two novels, and teaches creative writing and literature to elementary school students.

➌ Practice and Apply

A. CONCEPT CHECK: Indefinite Pronouns as Subjects

Identify the sentences with subjects and verbs that don't agree. In each case, write the correct verb.

Beyond Remarkable
1. All of the world's best-known scientists has been remarkable people.
2. But one of them, Stephen Hawking, stands out.
3. Some thinks that his being born exactly 300 years after Galileo's death is significant.
4. Many of these people also mentions his position as Cambridge's Lucasian Professor of Mathematics—a chair which was once held by Isaac Newton.
5. No one else in modern history, except perhaps Albert Einstein, have had as brilliant a scientific mind.

6. Many of his writings has been about the strange phenomenon of black holes.
7. One of his most important discoveries were that black holes emit radiation.
8. Most of us nonscientists knows him for his popular book *A Brief History of Time.*
9. One of the episodes of *Star Trek: The Next Generation* have even featured an appearance by Hawking.
10. Something make his achievements even more remarkable, however.
11. Few of us is stricken with the disabling disease amyotrophic lateral sclerosis (ALS), but unfortunately Hawking is one who was.
12. Some of the symptoms of the disease is loss of muscular control and difficulty in speaking.
13. Hawking uses a wheelchair, and all of his thoughts are communicated with the aid of a computer.
14. However, none of the symptoms prevents him from traveling through the vast reaches of the universe in his imagination.
15. Everything about Hawking are a source of inspiration.

➡ **For a SELF-CHECK and more practice, see the EXERCISE BANK, p. 606.**

B. PROOFREADING: Correcting Agreement Errors

The following paragraph contains five errors in subject-verb agreement. Identify the errors and rewrite the sentences correctly.

Top Young Scientist
   In the early 1940s some of the world's top scientists was brought to Los Alamos, New Mexico, to work on developing a nuclear weapon. One of these physicists were 24-year-old Richard Feynman. Anyone who worked with him on that project vividly recall his vital contributions. For example, one of the systems he devised for the storage of radioactive materials are credited with saving the lives of many personnel. All of the project directors' opinions of his talents were so high that he was made a group leader in the theoretical division. Many of Feynman's accomplishments at Los Alamos ranks among the century's most important scientific achievements.

Compound Subjects

❶ Here's the Idea

A compound subject contains two or more simple subjects.
Compound subjects can take either singular or plural verbs.

Parts Joined by *And*

▶ **A compound subject whose parts are joined by *and* usually requires a plural verb.**

Michael Jackson and the Eagles have sold **over 22 million copies of single albums.**

A subject containing *and* takes a singular verb, however, if it

• names a single thing

Rhythm and blues is a music style developed in the South.

• consists of singular parts modified by *each, every,* or *many a*

Almost every teenager and young adult has been influenced **by the music of Elvis Presley.**

Parts Joined by *Or* or *Nor*

▶ **When the parts of a compound subject are joined by *or* or *nor*, the verb should agree with the part closest to it.**

AGREE

Wolfgang Amadeus Mozart or Johann Sebastian Bach is often **named as the greatest composer of classical music.**

AGREE

Neither Mozart nor the five Bachs have left **as much music as Georg Philipp Telemann, however.**

❷ Why It Matters in Writing

When revising your writing, you may combine sentences by creating compound subjects. The verbs in these combined sentences must agree with their subjects.

DRAFT

The American engineer Harry Olson was responsible for developing the first electronic sound synthesizer. The American engineer Herbert Belar worked with him to develop it.

REVISION

The American engineers **Harry Olson and Herbert Belar were** responsible for developing the first electronic sound synthesizer.

> The compound subject requires a plural verb.

❸ Practice and Apply

A. CONCEPT CHECK: Compound Subjects

Correct the sentences that have errors in subject-verb agreement.

A Gem of a Singer

1. *Singer* and *songwriter* is words that cannot completely convey the appeal of Jewel Kilcher.
2. Neither difficult sacrifices nor lack of recognition were enough to discourage her.
3. Carrot sticks and peanut butter was what Jewel survived on while she was performing in a San Diego coffeehouse.
4. "Rock 'n' roll" do not best describe Jewel's style, which was influenced by Tracy Chapman and Ella Fitzgerald.
5. *Pieces of You* and *Spirit* has sold in the millions.

➜ For a SELF-CHECK and more practice, see the EXERCISE BANK, p. 606.

B. REVISING: Using Compound Subjects to Combine Sentences

Rewrite the following paragraph, using compound subjects to combine sentences.

Sisters in Song

Jewel has won praise for her distinctive singing style. Lauryn Hill has too. Lauryn didn't imagine her first solo album would top many critics' lists. The other members of her group, the Fugees, didn't imagine that either. Hip-hop rhythms are one distinctive element of *The Miseducation of Lauryn Hill*. Another is the album's soulful sounds. In 1999 *Time* featured Lauryn on its cover. So did *Rolling Stone*.

LESSON 4 · Other Confusing Subjects

❶ Here's the Idea

Sometimes the number of a subject can be hard to determine. To decide whether the subject takes a singular or a plural verb, ask yourself, Does it refer to a number of individuals or to a single unit?

Collective Nouns

▶ **Collective nouns, which name groups of people or things, can take either singular or plural verbs, depending on how they are used.**

Examples of collective nouns include *committee, family, team, crowd,* and *herd.*

At one time, the family of Samuel S. Must of Fryburg, Pennsylvania, consisted of 824 direct descendants.	*Family* refers to a unit, so it takes a singular verb.

The family have gone their separate ways.	*Family* refers to individuals, so it takes a plural verb.

For more information about collective nouns, see p. 6.

Phrases and Clauses

▶ **Phrases or clauses used as subjects always take singular verbs.**

Infinitive Phrase

To have grown fingernails totaling 241 inches on his left hand is Shridhar Chillal's claim to fame.

Gerund Phrase

Finding herself in *The Guinness Book of World Records* was a life-changing experience for Sandy Allen, the tallest woman in the world at 7 feet 7¼ inches.

Noun Clause

What is hard to believe is that Michel Lotito of France has eaten 18 bicycles, 15 supermarket carts, 7 television sets, 6 chandeliers, a small airplane, and a computer since 1959.

Singular Nouns That End in *S*

▶ **Some nouns that end in *s* look plural but are actually singular. When used as subjects, these nouns take singular verbs.**

Examples include *news, mumps,* and *economics.*

> **The news reports that a 42-year-old Canadian woman swallowed 2,533 objects—including 947 bent pins.**

 Some words that end in *s* and describe a thing with two equal parts—such as *scissors, pants, trousers, binoculars,* and *tweezers*—take plural verbs.

> **Tweezers are the instrument the doctor used to remove all those objects from the woman's stomach.**

Numerical Amounts and Titles

▶ **Numerical amounts and titles often look like plurals. However, they usually refer to single units and take singular verbs.**

> **Seventeen years and ten months was the age at which Balamurali K. Ambati earned his M.D. degree.**

> **The Guinness Book of Records includes a special feature about Dr. Ambati.**

 A fractional number can take either a singular or a plural verb, depending on its meaning in the sentence.

> REFERS TO
>
> **Nine-tenths of the *Guinness Book of Records* is about people.**

Refers to an amount, so the verb is singular

> REFERS TO
>
> **Nine-tenths of my friends have read it.**

Refers to a number of individuals, so the verb is plural

Relative Pronouns as Subjects

▶ **When the relative pronoun *who, which,* or *that* is the subject of an adjective clause, its number is determined by its antecedent.**

> REFERS TO
>
> **Delia Gray is a British ballerina who is famous for doing 166 spins on one leg without stopping.**

Has a singular antecedent, so it takes a singular verb

It was Wayne Sleep's 158 leaps REFERS TO **in two minutes that** have landed **him in** *The Guinness Book of Records.*

> Has a plural antecedent, so it takes a plural verb

For more information on relative pronouns and adjective clauses, see pp. 11, 81–82.

❷ Why It Matters in Writing

By using verbs that agree with these special subjects, you can convey information without confusing your reader.

STUDENT MODEL

A team of people from all over the world discusses who should appear in *The Guinness Book of Records.*

> *Team* refers to a number of individuals and requires a plural verb.

❸ Practice and Apply

CONCEPT CHECK: Other Confusing Subjects

Write the verb form that should replace each incorrect form in the following sentences.

Woman at the Wheel

1. Driving the powerful race cars called dragsters are Shirley Muldowney's passion.
2. Her crew frequently has been the target of nasty remarks.
3. At least three-fourths of the problems Muldowney has faced stems from her being a woman in a field dominated by men.
4. What is truly remarkable are Muldowney's records.
5. Her 18 top-speed titles is an extraordinary achievement.
6. Racing in eight nationals in 1996 were a chance for Muldowney to set speed records.
7. Muldowney became the first woman racer who were elected to the Motorsports Hall of Fame.
8. News of her award from Congress were not surprising.
9. The making of a movie about Muldowney's life, *Heart Like a Wheel,* have given her national renown.
10. To encourage women are one of her major goals.

➔ **For a SELF-CHECK and more practice, see the EXERCISE BANK, p. 607.**

1 Here's the Idea

The form of some sentences can make identifying their subjects difficult.

Inverted Sentences and Questions

▶ **In inverted sentences and in many questions, subjects follow verbs. When writing such a sentence, identify the subject and make the verb agree.**

> **Here's How** Dealing with Verbs That Precede Subjects
>
> Put the subject and verb in normal order.
>
> | Inverted Order | Normal Order |
> |---|---|
> | Was the longest tennis match in a Grand Slam tournament one lasting 5 hours 26 minutes? | match was AGREE |
> | Don't Stefan Edberg and Michael Chang hold that record? | Stefan Edberg and Michael Chang don't hold AGREE |
> | Into the record book have gone Edberg and Chang because of that 1992 U.S. semifinal. | Edberg and Chang have gone AGREE |

Imperatives and *Here* and *There* Sentences

▶ **The subject of an imperative sentence is almost always *you*.**

(You) Think about the training and dedication that earned 17-year-old Bob Mathias the Olympic decathlon title in 1948.

▶ **In sentences beginning with *here* or *there*, the subjects usually follow the verbs.**

There have been no older female Olympic track-and-field medalists than the 37-year-old javelin thrower Dana Zátopková of Czechoslovakia.

Here is a feat of track history—Jesse Owens set five world records and tied a sixth in 45 minutes in 1935.

S-V AGREEMENT

Sentences with Predicate Nominatives

▶ **In a sentence containing a predicate nominative, the verb must agree with the subject, not the predicate nominative.**

Mentally screen out the predicate nominative and make the verb agree with the subject.

Team activities **are** ~~an enjoyable and productive pastime.~~

> Plural subject requires a plural verb.

One enjoyable and productive pastime **is** ~~team activities.~~

> Singular subject requires a singular verb.

For more information about predicate nominatives, see p. 36.

For more information about predicate nominatives, see p. 36.

❷ Why It Matters in Writing

As you revise your writing, you can use these special sentence structures to add variety and interest. Make sure you don't create problems in subject-verb agreement in the process.

STUDENT MODEL

DRAFT

The marathon was named for a famous run by a Greek soldier who supposedly dashed about 25 miles from Marathon to Athens with news of a military victory. A Greek runner, Spyridon Louis, won the first Olympic marathon in Athens in 1896. Only one runner from Greece has won any Olympic track event since that time. In 1992, Paraskevi Patoulidou won the women's 100-meter hurdles.

REVISION

The marathon was named for a famous run by a Greek soldier who supposedly dashed about 25 miles from Marathon to Athens with news of a military victory. A Greek runner, Spyridon Louis, won the first Olympic marathon in Athens in 1896. **Do you know** that only one runner from Greece has won any Olympic track event since that time? **Think** about how proud Paraskevi Patoulidou must have been when she won the women's 100-meter hurdles in 1992.

❸ Practice and Apply

A. CONCEPT CHECK: Special Agreement Problems

Correct the sentences with errors in subject-verb agreement.

Very Special Athletes

1. There is few athletic training and competition programs as respected as Special Olympics.
2. You can't find a program with a more worthy purpose.
3. Here is some questions that people often ask about the program.
4. Isn't Special Olympics events held only every four years?
5. There is Special Olympics events held every year in the United States at the local, area, and state levels.
6. Were the idea for Special Olympics conceived in ancient Greece?
7. Actually, the creator of the program were President John F. Kennedy's sister, Eunice Kennedy Shriver.
8. Her goal were to reward the efforts of the mentally disabled.
9. How do she account for the idea of giving these athletes the opportunity to succeed?
10. Her inspiration, say Shriver, was her mentally disabled sister, Rosemary.
11. Doesn't many athletes participate in Special Olympics events?
12. There has been more than 1 million Special Olympians from over 150 countries.
13. Included in the competition is 26 sports, such as figure skating, basketball, and long-distance running.
14. Here are a chance for athletes to build self-respect and pride.
15. Here are the Special Olympics oath: "Let me win. But if I cannot win, let me be brave in the attempt."

➜ For a SELF-CHECK and more practice, see the EXERCISE BANK, p. 607.

B. REVISING

In your **Working Portfolio** 🗂 find the paragraph you wrote for the **Write Away** on page 130. Revise it so that it includes some inverted sentences and sentences beginning with *here* and *there*. Pay particular attention to subject-verb agreement.

Real World Grammar

Survey Results

Conducting a survey is a good way to collect and compare information from a large number of individuals. In summarizing the data you collect, you'll need to use numerical amounts, indefinite pronouns, and other words that can cause problems in subject-verb agreement. One student decided to survey her classmates to find out who their heroes were. Before publishing the results, she asked a friend to read and comment on them.

SURVEY RESULTS

Who's Your Heroes?

Here, at last, are the results of my survey. Surprising to me are the areas in which you all agree. For instance, three-fifths of the responders admires some political figure. Also, there is fewer athletes on the final list than I thought there would be: sports provides only one of your top ten heroes.

Stars from the movies contributes several names to the list; but some, to be fair, are active in other fields, such as politics. Neither literature nor art seem significant in your choice of names: only two writers are among anybody's top five heroes.

And one of you should know that using the names of cartoon characters were not acceptable!

This title sounds funny to me. Is the grammar ok?

Sounds like only one of them was active in politics.

This is confusing: did the person just use unacceptable names for the characters, or what?

Using Grammar in Writing

Indefinite pronouns	Remember that some indefinite pronouns are always singular, some are always plural, and some can be either singular or plural, depending on how they're used.
Compound subjects	Compound subjects can be tricky. Their number can depend on the numbers of their parts, as well as on the conjunction that joins the parts.
Numerical amounts	Numerical amounts usually take singular verbs. Watch out for fractions, though. They are singular when they refer to amounts but plural when they refer to numbers of items.

REVISED SURVEY RESULTS

Who Are Your Heroes?

Here, at last, are the results of my survey. Surprising to me are the areas in which you all agree. For instance, three-fifths of the responders admire some political figure. Also, there are fewer athletes on the final list than I thought there would be: sports provide only one of your top ten heroes.

Stars from the movies contribute several names to the list; but some, to be fair, are active in other fields, such as politics. Neither literature nor art seems significant in your choice of names: only two writers are among anybody's top five heroes.

And one of you should know that using the names of cartoon characters was not acceptable!

This information is much clearer. You learned a lot from doing the survey, didn't you?

PRACTICE AND APPLY: Revising

This is the last paragraph of the student's account of the survey results. Rewrite it, correcting all errors.

> Doing this survey have raised important questions for me about my friends and myself. Many of us doesn't seem to look up to anybody at all. In fact, nearly one-third of the students I gave the survey to was unwilling to fill it out. What do that say about students today? One of our most important requirements are good role models. Both you and I has to figure out what kind of people we want to be. Neither books nor just thinking about it help as much as walking in a hero's footsteps. Everyone need to look up to somebody. Start now!

Mixed Review

A. Subject-Verb Agreement Correct all errors of subject-verb agreement in the following sentences.

1. The Japanese-born violinist Midori, though not yet 30, have been performing for almost 20 years.
2. No one attending her debut with the New York Philharmonic at the age of 11 were able to believe her skill.
3. Playing the violin has been the focus of her life from a very early age.
4. Incredibly swift have been the spread of her fame.
5. Was other musicians able to make such a mark so early in life?
6. There has been many child prodigies in music.
7. Few, however, has been able to sustain a career as Midori has done.
8. Concerts and recitals seems to leave her little time for other activities.
9. Nevertheless, neither practice nor a busy professional calendar has kept her from fulfilling other commitments.
10. To expose children to classical music are one of her important goals.
11. Her foundation, Midori & Friends, concentrate on bringing music to schools all over New York City.
12. Her group travel all over the city, delighting students with the beauty of the classical tradition.
13. Works by composers of many nationalities and from several centuries makes her concerts interesting.
14. The arts boasts of few individuals who have contributed more in so short a time.
15. Here, indeed, are an amazing artist and individual.

B. Subject-Verb Agreement Edit and proofread the following paragraph, correcting all errors in subject-verb agreement.

STUDENT MODEL

There has been several amazing child prodigies in music but none more astonishing than Wolfgang Amadeus Mozart. Mozart were playing tunes on the piano at the age of three! From the time he was six, he and his sister Anna, also a prodigy, was taken on concert tours by their father. Neither royalty nor nobility were able to resist the charm and talent of the two young artists. All of the gifts and money they received was kept by their father. Do the life of such a prodigy, praised but exploited, sound like fun? His arguments with his stern and demanding father were a constant source of tension. However, few finds any hint of gloom or depression in most of his music. Though Mozart died before his 36th birthday, his legacy of great compositions are a timeless gift to the world.

Choose the letter of the best revision for each underlined section.

Do wrapping islands, trees, and buildings seem like art to you? Bulgarian-
(1)
born Christo Javacheff and his wife, Jeanne-Claude, believe that it is. Many

of the admirers of their work agrees. In Riehen, Switzerland, there stand a
(2)   (3)
grove of 178 trees that Christo wrapped in miles of polyester fabric and rope.

Photographs of the project shows the fabric stretched into fascinating
(4)
sculptures by the tree branches. Wrapping huge objects are not Christo's
(5)
only form of expression, however. In California were built his *Running Fence*,
(6)
some 18 feet high and 24½ miles long. The press were skeptical at first.
(7)
Neither criticism nor technical difficulty have discouraged Christo from
(8)
expressing his unique ideas, though.

1. A. Do wrapping islands, trees,
   and buildings seems
   B. Does wrapping islands, trees,
   and buildings seems
   C. Does wrapping islands, trees,
   and buildings seem
   D. Correct as is

2. A. Many admirer of their
   work agree.
   B. Many admirers of their
   work agrees.
   C. Many of the admirers of their
   work agree.
   D. Correct as is

3. A. there stands a grove of
   178 trees
   B. there a grove of 178 trees stand
   C. a grove of 178 trees stand there
   D. Correct as is

4. A. Photographs of the project
   does show
   B. Photographs of the project show
   C. Photographs of the project
   has shown
   D. Correct as is

5. A. Wrapping huge objects were not
   B. Wrapping huge objects is not
   C. Wrapping huge objects have
   not been
   D. Correct as is

6. A. have been built his
   Running Fence
   B. his *Running Fence* were built
   C. was built his *Running Fence*
   D. Correct as is

7. A. The press was
   B. The press are
   C. The press have been
   D. Correct as is

8. A. Neither criticism nor
   technical difficulty have
   been discouraging
   B. Neither criticism nor technical
   difficulty has discouraged
   C. Neither criticism nor technical
   difficulty discourage
   D. Correct as is

S-V AGREEMENT

Student Help Desk

Subject-Verb Agreement at a Glance

Verbs must agree with their subjects in person and number.

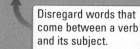

Every clause and sentence, even imperatives, needs subject-verb agreement.

> Pay special attention to a subject that has an unusual form or position in a sentence.

> Disregard words that come between a verb and its subject.

Agreement Problems  Subjects

Type of Subject	Number of Verb	Example
Indefinite pronoun	Singular or plural	**None** of the people **agree.** **None** of the argument **makes** sense.
Compound, with parts joined by *and*	Plural	**You and your conscience decide.**
Compound, with parts joined by *or* **or** *nor*	Number of closest part of subject	**Neither her brother nor her parents understand. Neither her parents nor her brother understands.**
Collective noun	Singular or plural	**Her team supports** her. **Her team take** sides.
Phrase or clause	Singular	**Getting along is** hard.
Singular noun ending in s	Singular	**Measles is** preferable.
Numerical amount	Singular	**A thousand miles away is** too close.
Title	Singular	***Men Are from Mars, Women Are from Venus* has** it right.

Agreement Problems Sentence Snags

Type of Sentence	Problem	Example
Inverted	Subject follows verb.	On and on **go** the **excuses**.
Question	Subject follows verb or helping verb.	**Can anyone settle** this argument?
Imperative	Subject (*you*) may not be expressed.	**(You)** Just **live** with it.
Sentence beginning with *here* or *there*	Subject follows verb.	There **is** a constructive **way** to criticize.
Sentence containing predicate nominative	Predicate nominative does not affect number of verb.	**Human beings are** an interesting species.

The Bottom Line

Checklist for Subject-Verb Agreement

Have I . . .

____ mentally screened out words between subjects and verbs?

____ determined the number of each indefinite-pronoun subject?

____ used correct verb forms with compound subjects?

____ paid attention to special agreement problems?

____ put inverted sentences and questions in normal order to check agreement?

____ used correct verb forms in imperative sentences?

____ located the true subjects in sentences beginning with *here* or *there*?

____ ignored predicate nominatives in checking agreement?

Using Pronouns

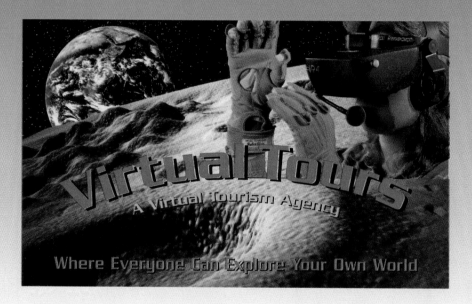

Theme: Explorers and Discoveries

Going Nowhere Fast

Where do you think VirtualTours could take you? Does it sound as if the sky—and beyond—is the limit? Or does it sound as if virtual visitors would be beating a path to *your* door? The problem with this slogan is the pronouns. They make the advertisement hard to understand.

You already know that a pronoun is a word used in place of a noun. Pronouns prevent you from saying something ridiculous like "Pat read Pat's book while Pat's dog barked at Pat." Of course, you have to know how to use pronouns. Using pronouns correctly may not open up new worlds for you, but it will make your writing clearer.

Write Away: Virtual Pronouns
Rewrite the advertisement slogan above, correcting the pronoun error. Then place the slogan in your 🗀 **Working Portfolio.**

Grammar Coach

Choose the letter that identifies the correct form of the underlined pronoun.

In 1804, Meriwether Lewis and William Clark began <u>his</u> expedition to
(1)
the land west of the Mississippi. Both were familiar with the frontier
through <u>his or her</u> service in the army. Lewis and Clark hired Toussaint
(2)
Charbonneau as interpreter and guide. With him came his Indian wife,
Sacajawea, <u>whom</u> was the sister of a Shoshone chief. The married couple,
(3)
Charbonneau and <u>her</u>, accompanied the group even though Sacajawea
(4)
had recently given birth to a baby boy. She carried <u>them</u> on her back and
(5)
was an invaluable Indian interpreter.

The group encountered many hardships on <u>their</u> journey. At one point,
(6)
ten of the men struck off on <u>his</u> own; the party skirmished with a group of
(7)
Native Americans. Later, Lewis <u>himself</u> was accidentally shot by one of his
(8)
men. After Lewis recovered, Clark and <u>himself</u> continued to St. Louis and
(9)
their journey's end. No American explorers had been as successful as <u>them</u>.
(10)

1. A. his or her
   B. their
   C. its
   D. Correct as is

2. A. their
   B. his
   C. whose
   D. Correct as is

3. A. who
   B. whose
   C. whoever
   D. Correct as is

4. A. hers
   B. he
   C. she
   D. Correct as is

5. A. it
   B. her
   C. him
   D. Correct as is

6. A. his
   B. its
   C. his or her
   D. Correct as is

7. A. their
   B. its
   C. your
   D. Correct as is

8. A. he
   B. him
   C. hisself
   D. Correct as is

9. A. them
   B. whoever
   C. he
   D. Correct as is

10. A. themselves
    B. they
    C. he
    D. Correct as is

Nominative and Objective Cases

❶ Here's the Idea

▶ **Personal pronouns take on different forms, depending on how they are used in sentences. These forms are called cases.**

There are three pronoun cases: nominative, objective, and possessive. This chart shows the personal pronouns (singular and plural) used in each case.

Personal Pronouns			
	Nominative	**Objective**	**Possessive**
Singular			
First person	I	me	my, mine
Second person	you	you	your, yours
Third person	he, she, it	him, her, it	his, her, hers, its
Plural			
First person	we	us	our, ours
Second person	you	you	your, yours
Third person	they	them	their, theirs

Nominative Case

▶ **The nominative case of a personal pronoun is used when the pronoun functions as a subject or a predicate nominative.**

I went on the trip.
　SUBJECT

They came along, too.
　SUBJECT

The nominative case is also used when the pronoun is part of a compound subject.

Carlos and he planned the trip.
　COMPOUND SUBJECT

When a pronoun functions as a predicate nominative, it is called a **predicate pronoun.** It immediately follows a linking verb and identifies the subject of the sentence.

SUBJECT　PREDICATE PRONOUN
It was she who led the expedition.
　LINKING VERB

In informal speech or writing, it can be acceptable to use the wrong case for a predicate pronoun: **It's me.** However, be sure to use the nominative case for predicate pronouns in formal writing: **It's I.**

Objective Case

▶ **The objective case of a personal pronoun is used when the pronoun functions as a direct object, an indirect object, or the object of a preposition.**

The group found me after a day-long search.
               DIRECT OBJECT OF A VERB

The mysterious stranger gave us the treasure map.
                           INDIRECT OBJECT OF A VERB

Midori climbed the mountain with them.
OBJECT OF A PREPOSITION

The objective case is also used when a pronoun is part of a compound object.

Suddenly the earth opened up between Josh and me.
COMPOUND OBJECT OF A PREPOSITION

To make sure you're using the correct pronoun case in a compound construction, look at each part separately.

Here's How Choosing the Correct Pronoun Case

Ben and (I, me) explored the outback.

Erin went with Ben and (I, me).

1. Try each pronoun choice alone in the sentence.

I explored the outback. Me explored the outback.
(nominative case correct)

Erin went with I. Erin went with me.
(objective case correct)

2. Choose the correct case for the sentence.

Ben and I explored the outback.

Erin went with Ben and me.

---

❷ Why It Matters in Writing

When you write a narrative or essay, you will be expected to use the correct pronoun case.

Anthropologists Louis and Mary Leakey searched for the remains of early humans in East Africa. The Leakeys' discovery in 1959 of a 1.8-million-year-old skull was a great breakthrough for Louis and ~~she~~. *her* Although Mary is not always given credit for the discovery, it was actually ~~her~~ *she* who found the fossil.

❸ Practice and Apply

CONCEPT CHECK: Nominative and Objective Cases

Choose the correct pronoun from those shown in parentheses.

On Top of the World

1. In the late 1800s, American explorer Annie Smith Peck set out to prove that (she, her) could climb some of the world's highest mountains.
2. The explorer wanted to climb higher than any woman before (she, her).

Annie Smith Peck

3. Peck's ambitions may seem normal to (we, us), but people in the Victorian age were shocked by this woman's behavior.
4. In particular, the climbing gear worn by Peck scandalized (they, them).
5. By 1900, Peck had decided that the first woman to climb Peru's highest mountain, Mount Huascarán, would be (she, her).
6. Accompanied by male porters, Peck attempted to climb the mountain, but howling winds and treacherous conditions thwarted the men and (she, her).
7. On five occasions the porters and (she, her) were forced to return to camp.
8. Actually, it was (they, them) who wanted to turn back.
9. Recalling the experience, Peck wrote that she "longed for a man with the pluck and determination to stand by (I, me) to the finish."
10. After Peck finally conquered the mountain in 1908, the press showered (she, her) with praise.

➡ **For a SELF-CHECK and more practice, see the EXERCISE BANK, p. 608.**

Possessive Case

❶ Here's the Idea

▶ **Personal pronouns that show ownership or relationships are in the possessive case.**

Possessive pronouns can be used in two ways:

1. The possessive pronouns *mine, ours, yours, his, hers, its,* and *theirs* can be used in place of a noun. The pronoun can function as a subject or an object.

I need to see a map of the whole region.

Can I see yours? Mine is missing.
DIRECT OBJECT ➤   ↖SUBJECT

2. The possessive pronouns *my, our, your, his, her, its,* and *their* can be used to modify a noun or a gerund. The pronoun precedes the noun or gerund it modifies.

Our searching the area led to their recovery.
GERUND   NOUN

Remember that a gerund acts as a noun. That's why the possessive pronoun can modify it.

Do use a possessive pronoun with a gerund.

No one objected to his climbing the mountain alone.
POSSESSIVE ➤   ↖GERUND

Do not use a possessive pronoun with a participle.

We saw him climbing the mountain alone.
OBJECTIVE ➤   ↖PARTICIPLE

Don't confuse the possessive pronouns *their, its,* and *your* with the contractions *they're* ("they are"), *it's* ("it is"), and *you're* ("you are"). Use context to figure out the correct word.

❷ Why It Matters in Writing

If you want to emphasize the *-ing* word, or action, use a possessive pronoun plus the gerund.

My running must have frightened the animals away.

If you want to emphasize the person or thing performing the action, use an objective pronoun plus the participle.

They watched me running away.

PRONOUNS

STUDENT MODEL

From the submarine's porthole, the group watched **him swimming** to the sunken ship. Suddenly, a shark emerged; the group saw **it stalking** the diver. Terrified, they shouted and pounded on the window, but **their screaming** fell on deaf ears.

Objective pronoun plus participle *swimming* emphasizes that the group watched *him.*

Objective pronoun plus participle *stalking* emphasizes that the group saw *it.*

Possessive pronoun plus gerund *screaming* emphasizes the action of screaming.

❸ Practice and Apply

CONCEPT CHECK: Possessive Case

For each sentence, choose the correct pronoun from those shown in parentheses. If either pronoun could be correct, choose one and explain what you want to emphasize.

To the North Pole

1. In 1891, American explorer Robert Peary undertook his first expedition to the North Pole; (him, his) teaming with Matthew Henson, an African American, probably created some controversy.
2. Peary first saw (him, his) working in a store.
3. For several years, (them, their) trekking across the treacherous ice ended in defeat.
4. Reading about the difficulties they faced ended (me, my) daydreaming about exploring unknown lands.
5. However, even (him, his) losing his toes to frostbite didn't stop Peary from fulfilling his goal.
6. Henson's skills contributed enormously to (their, them) finally reaching the North Pole in 1909.
7. Eighteen years after their first attempt, a photograph shows (them, their) waving the American flag on the North Pole.
8. Henson's account of the journey, *A Negro Explorer at the North Pole,* aids (us, our) understanding of the achievement.
9. (Him, His) being an African American often prevented Henson from receiving the recognition he deserved.
10. In 1944, Henson's family watched (him, his) being awarded a congressional medal.

➡ **For a SELF-CHECK and more practice, see the EXERCISE BANK, p. 608.**

Who and Whom

❶ Here's the Idea

▶ **The case of the pronoun *who* is determined by the pronoun's function in a sentence.**

Here are the nominative, objective, and possessive forms of *who* and *whoever*.

Forms of *Who* and *Whoever*	
Nominative	who, whoever
Objective	whom, whomever
Possessive	whose, whosever

Who and *whom* can be used to ask questions and to introduce subordinate clauses.

Who and *Whom* in Questions

In a question, the nominative pronoun *who* is used as a subject or as a predicate pronoun.

Who discovered radium?   **The scientist was who?**
SUBJECT   PREDICATE PRONOUN

In a question, the objective pronoun *whom* is used as a direct object, an indirect object, or the object of a preposition.

Whom did Marie Curie marry?   **With whom did she work?**
DIRECT OBJECT   OBJECT OF PREPOSITION

Here's How Choosing *Who* or *Whom* in a Question

To (who, whom) were the findings given?

1. Rewrite the question as a statement.

   The findings were given to (who, whom).

2. Figure out whether the pronoun is used as a subject, an object, a predicate pronoun, or the object of a preposition.

   The findings were given to whom.
   (*Whom* is the object of the preposition *to*.)

3. Use the correct form in the original question.

   To whom were the findings given?

Who and *Whom* in Subordinate Clauses

When deciding whether to use *who* or *whom* in a subordinate clause, consider only how the pronoun functions within the clause. Use *who* when the pronoun is the subject of the clause.

He's the climber who planted the flag.
SUBJECT ▸ SUBORDINATE CLAUSE

Use *whom* when the pronoun is an object in the subordinate clause.

The climber whom we all know planted the flag.
DIRECT OBJECT ▸ SUBORDINATE CLAUSE

Here's How Choosing *Who* or *Whom* in a Clause ————

Eileen Collins is an astronaut (who, whom) I admire.

1. Identify the subordinate clause in the sentence.

(who, whom) I admire

2. Determine how the pronoun is used in the clause. Is it a subject or an object? You may have to rearrange the clause to figure this out.

I admire (who, whom)

The pronoun is a direct object, so the correct form is *whom*.

I admire whom

3. Use the correct pronoun in the sentence.

Eileen Collins is an astronaut whom I admire.

Don't assume that you should use *whomever* after a preposition. Choose *whoever* or *whomever* based on the pronoun's function in the subordinate clause.

Share your discovery with (whoever, whomever) is interested.

Share your discovery with whoever is interested.
SUBJECT ▸ SUBORDINATE CLAUSE

❷ Why It Matters in Writing

You will be expected to use *who* and *whom* correctly in formal writing situations, including essays, letters, and reports.

STUDENT MODEL

David Livingstone, ~~whom~~ *who* was a Scottish medical doctor,

became a renowned explorer of Africa. In the mid-1800s, he

went to southern Africa to work with the people, ~~who~~ *whom* he

hoped to convert to Christianity.

❸ Practice and Apply

CONCEPT CHECK: *Who* and *Whom*

Choose the correct pronoun from those shown in parentheses.

Life's Ups and Downs

1. Writer Vince Rause, (who, whom) is afraid of roller coasters, decided to ride them and write about his experiences.
2. Rause told (whoever, whomever) would listen that he had shunned roller coasters since he was nine years old.
3. The writer undertook the challenge for his baby daughter, (who, whom), he fears, will someday want to ride roller coasters with her father.
4. (Whoever, Whomever) has ridden a roller coaster recently can recall its speed, twists, and upside-down thrills.
5. Rause, (who, whom, whose) fear of coasters had only increased, asked some friends to accompany him.
6. It was one of those friends (who, whom) told Rause to hold his arms over his head during his first ride.
7. Rause, for (who, whom) the ride's start was sheer torture, could only scream in terror.
8. During the ride, however, he found that he loved the sensation of weightlessly hurtling through the air—as those (who, whom) he bored with his new coaster stories will confirm.
9. (Who, Whom) would have thought that Rause would discover that he actually enjoys riding roller coasters?
10. (Whoever, Whomever) thinks that people can't overcome their fears should talk to Vince Rause.

➡ **For a SELF-CHECK and more practice, see the EXERCISE BANK, p. 609.**

Pronoun-Antecedent Agreement

LESSON 4

❶ Here's the Idea

▶ **A pronoun must agree with its antecedent in number, gender, and person.** An **antecedent** is the noun or pronoun to which a pronoun refers.

Agreement in Number

If the antecedent of a pronoun is singular, use a singular pronoun. If the antecedent is plural, use a plural pronoun.

REFERS TO

Neil Armstrong knew early in life that he wanted a career in aviation.

REFERS TO

Astronauts undergo strenuous training before they can blast off into space.

In Compound Subjects A plural pronoun is used to refer to nouns or pronouns joined by *and.*

REFERS TO

Armstrong and Aldrin have taken their place in history.

A pronoun that refers to nouns or pronouns joined by *or* or *nor* should agree with the noun or pronoun nearest to it.

REFERS TO

Neither the astronauts nor NASA neglected its duties.

SINGULAR PRONOUN

REFERS TO

Neither NASA nor the astronauts neglected their duties.

PLURAL PRONOUN

With Collective Nouns A collective noun, such as *crew, team, audience,* or *family,* may be referred to by either a singular or a plural pronoun. The collective noun's number is determined by its meaning in the sentence.

A pronoun that refers to a collective noun should be singular if the collective noun names a group acting as a unit.

REFERS TO

The crew is completing its countdown to the launch.
(The crew is acting as a single unit.)

A pronoun that refers to a collective noun should be plural if the collective noun names the members or parts of a group acting individually.

REFERS TO

The crew will carry out their assignments.
(The crew members are acting individually.)

Agreement in Gender and Person

The gender of a pronoun must be the same as the gender of its antecedent. When the antecedent could be either feminine or masculine, use the phrase "he or she" or "his or her."

During the flight, an astronaut conducts his or her experiments.

You can often avoid the awkward "he or she" construction by making both the pronoun and its antecedent plural. Notice that you may also need to change the verb to a plural form.

During the flight, astronauts conduct their experiments.

The person of the pronoun must agree with the person of its antecedent.
                                                                their
All astronauts should take ~~your~~ responsibilities seriously.
                                                    ∧

❷ Why It Matters in Writing

If your pronouns don't agree with their antecedents, your readers won't be able to understand your ideas or follow your argument. In the revised paragraph below, notice that pronoun changes also required changes in the verb forms.

STUDENT MODEL

When Christopher Columbus landed on Cuba, he insisted it

was part of China. Neither Columbus nor his men ever really
                    they were
knew where ~~he was~~. The crew sensed they were lost during
            ∧

the voyage, but landing on the island Columbus first called
                    their
Juana ended ~~its~~ threats of mutiny.
            ∧

❸ Practice and Apply

A. CONCEPT CHECK: Pronoun-Antecedent Agreement

For each sentence, choose the correct pronoun from those shown in parentheses.

Women in Space

1. Sally Ride became the first American woman in space when (she, they) flew on a *Challenger* space-shuttle flight in 1983.
2. Her team took six days to complete (its, their) mission.
3. When I met Mae Jemison, the first African-American woman in space, she encouraged (me, us) to improve my grades.
4. Jemison and the other American crew members undertook (her, their) mission on the space shuttle *Endeavour* with a team of Japanese astronauts.
5. Neither Shannon Lucid nor the Russian crew members aboard the space station *Mir* could know that (her, their) mission would be such a success.

➡ **For a SELF-CHECK and more practice, see the EXERCISE BANK, p. 610.**

B. REVISING: Correcting Pronoun-Antecedent Agreement

Rewrite the following paragraph, correcting pronoun-antecedent errors and making any other necessary changes.

STUDENT MODEL

Real Estate on the Moon

What do scientists look for when he wants to find a good spot for a human colony on the moon? The same thing we look for on earth when you want to buy a house: location, location, location. In particular, when a scientist studies locations on the moon, he looks for a place that provides good sunlight and some water. You may not think that the moon has any water. However, in 1998, NASA and its top scientists announced that it had discovered evidence of ice around the moon's two poles. The group announced their findings, claiming that the water could support a colony for about a hundred years. Now researchers have found three locations near the moon's south pole that he and she think might be good sites for a lunar colony. In the not too distant future, then, either you or the children of tomorrow might build your home on the moon.

Indefinite Pronouns as Antecedents

❶ Here's the Idea

▶ **An indefinite pronoun may be the antecedent of a personal pronoun.**

The number of an indefinite pronoun is not always clear. The following chart shows the number of some common indefinite pronouns.

Indefinite Pronouns				
Always singular	another	each	everything	one
	anybody	either	neither	somebody
	anyone	everybody	nobody	someone
	anything	everyone	no one	
Always plural	both	few	many	several
Singular or plural	all	most	none	some
	any			

Singular Indefinite Pronouns

Use a singular personal pronoun to refer to a singular indefinite pronoun.

 REFERS TO

Each of the discoveries has its own special value.
🔺 SINGULAR INDEFINITE PRONOUN   🔺 SINGULAR PERSONAL PRONOUN

The phrase "his or her" is considered a singular personal pronoun.

No one wants his or her discoveries discounted.

When one or more nouns come between a personal pronoun and its indefinite-pronoun antecedent, make sure that the personal pronoun agrees with the indefinite pronoun and not with a noun.

INCORRECT: **One of the explorers broke their leg.**
(The personal pronoun should agree with the indefinite pronoun, not the noun.)

CORRECT: **One of the explorers broke his leg.**
(The personal pronoun agrees with the indefinite pronoun.)

HOT TIP

You may have trouble remembering that *everyone* and *everybody* are singular, because they seem to be plural in meaning. To help you recall that the pronouns are singular, remember that the endings *body* and *one* are always singular.

PRONOUNS

Plural Indefinite Pronouns

Use a plural personal pronoun to refer to a plural indefinite pronoun.

REFERS TO

Both of the scientists presented their findings at the meeting.
PLURAL INDEFINITE PRONOUN   PLURAL PERSONAL PRONOUN

Several of the researchers pledged their support.

Singular or Plural Indefinite Pronouns

Some indefinite pronouns can be singular or plural. Use the meaning of the sentence to determine whether a personal pronoun that refers to such an indefinite pronoun should be singular or plural.

If the indefinite pronoun refers to a part of a whole, use a singular personal pronoun.

None of the gold found on the ship has lost its glitter.

If the indefinite pronoun refers to the members of a group, use a plural personal pronoun.

None of the guests left their seats during the lecture.

❷ Why It Matters in Writing

Indefinite pronouns are frequently used in business writing. If your personal pronouns don't agree with their indefinite-pronoun antecedents, your readers may be confused by your writing. Notice the confusion caused by the pronouns in this report draft.

I spoke before State University's most eminent

scientists and discussed our proposal to track alien

his or her
signals. Each confided to me ~~their~~ fascination with the
           ∧

possibility of extraterrestrial life. Dr. Kevin Yamamoto was

particularly interested in our search. Unfortunately, none

their
of the people I spoke to wanted to invest ~~his~~ money in
           ∧

our "great Martian chase."

❸ Practice and Apply

A. CONCEPT CHECK: Indefinite Pronouns as Antecedents

For each sentence, choose the correct pronoun from those shown in parentheses.

A Fossil Hunter Named Sue

1. Most paleontologists have heard of (his or her, their) unorthodox colleague Sue Hendrickson.
2. Just about everyone who has tried to earn (his or her, their) living in the field knows that Hendrickson discovered the remains of a *Tyrannosaurus rex,* which was later named Sue.
3. One of the team members explained Hendrickson's motivation when (he, they) said that she simply loves to learn.
4. Both of these scientists had (his or her, their) picture taken as (he or she, they) posed together in front of the dinosaur's head.
5. However, none of the others on Hendrickson's team were with her when she discovered the *T. rex* because (he, they) weren't as persistent.
6. Hendrickson doesn't have a college degree, but few can boast that (he or she, they) can match her achievements.
7. Many people feel overwhelmed when (he or she, they) are in Hendrickson's presence.
8. Some of the paleontologists discredit Hendrickson's achievements; (he or she, they) say that she collects fossils for money, not for science.
9. However, Sue, bought at auction by a museum, became yet another of Hendrickson's discoveries to find (its, their) way into such an institution.
10. Several of the insects in an exhibition of amber had something in common with Sue: (it, they) too had been collected by Hendrickson.

➡ **For a SELF-CHECK and more practice, see the EXERCISE BANK, p. 610.**

B. WRITING: Using Indefinite Pronouns

Reread the advertisement slogan you corrected for the **Write Away** and placed in your 📁 **Working Portfolio.** Then write a paragraph of advertisement copy in which you urge readers to explore new worlds at VirtualTours. Be sure to use at least two indefinite pronouns that are antecedents of personal pronouns.

Other Pronoun Problems

LESSON 6

❶ Here's the Idea

▶ Pronouns may be used with an appositive, in an appositive, or in a comparison. Pronouns can also be used reflexively or intensively.

Pronouns and Appositives

The pronouns *we* and *us* are often followed by an **appositive,** a noun that identifies the pronoun.

We explorers meet on Mondays.
APPOSITIVE

The task was assigned to us students.
APPOSITIVE

Here's How *We* and *Us* with Appositives

(We, Us) divers refused to explore the ship.

1. Rewrite the sentence without the appositive.

   (We, Us) refused to explore the ship.

2. Determine whether the pronoun is a subject or an object. In this sentence, the pronoun is a subject.

3. Write the sentence, using the correct case.

   We divers refused to explore the ship.

Sometimes a pronoun is used in an appositive. The pronoun helps to identify a preceding noun. Notice that pronouns used in appositives take the nominative case as a subject and the objective case if they function as an object.

SUBJECT   NOMINATIVE PRONOUN
The guides, Emilio and I, met for lunch.
                APPOSITIVE

Here's How Using Pronouns in Appositives

The museum paid the explorers, Ron and (she, her), for the find.

1. Rewrite the sentence, using the appositive by itself.

   The museum paid Ron and (she, her) for the find.

2. Determine whether the pronoun is a subject or an object. In this sentence, the pronoun is a direct object.

3. Write the sentence, using the correct case.

   The museum paid the explorers, Ron and her, for the find.

Pronouns in Comparisons

A comparison can be made by using *than* or *as* to begin a clause.

Linda is a more successful explorer than he is.

No one was as adventurous as he was.

When you omit one or more words from the final clause in a comparison, the clause is said to be **elliptical.**

No one was as adventurous as he.

If you have trouble determining the correct pronoun to use in an elliptical clause, fill in the unstated words.

None of the guides were as experienced as (he, him). [was]

None of the guides were as experienced as he.

Notice that the case of the pronoun you use in a comparison can affect the meaning of the sentence.

I depend more on Raul than he.
(This means "I depend more on Raul than he does.")

I depend more on Raul than him.
(This means "I depend more on Raul than on him.")

PRONOUNS

Reflexive and Intensive Pronouns

You can use a pronoun ending in *-self* or *-selves* reflexively or intensively.

Reuben did not consider himself an explorer.   REFLEXIVE
(*Himself* reflects back to the subject.)

Rita herself chose to take part in the expedition.   INTENSIVE
(*Herself* adds emphasis to *Rita.*)

Don't use reflexive or intensive pronouns alone. Pronouns ending in *-self* or *-selves* must have an antecedent in the same sentence.

Jesse and myself found the tracks together.
(incorrect, since there is no antecedent for *myself*)

Hisself and *theirselves* are never correct. Do not use them.

❷ Why It Matters in Writing

Writers sometimes use pronouns with appositives incorrectly when writing in the first person. When you write a personal narrative or some other piece of first-person writing, make sure you use the correct pronoun with or in an appositive.

> **STUDENT MODEL**
>
> As we waved and shouted, the helicopter lowered the rope
>
> ladder for ~~we~~ survivors. *us* The last ones to board the chopper
>
> were the leaders, Aaron and ~~me.~~ *I*

❸ Practice and Apply

CONCEPT CHECK: Other Pronoun Problems

Choose the correct pronoun from those shown in parentheses.

Leo Africanus Explores Timbuktu

1. Our history teacher assigned (we, us) students to read about al-Hassan Ibn Mohammad al-Wassan al-Zayyati, who became known as Leo Africanus.
2. Leo was born in the kingdom of Granada in 1485 and lived there until 1492, when the Muslims, thousands of others and (he, him), were expelled.
3. His family, his parents and (he, him), settled in Morocco.
4. Several years later, two capable people, his uncle and (he, him), traveled to Timbuktu on a diplomatic mission.
5. Strangers, visiting merchants and (they, them), were greatly impressed with the wealth and learning of the city.
6. The Muslim women veiled their faces and could not talk to them, Leo's uncle and (he, him).
7. (We, Us) students were surprised to learn that salt was an expensive commodity in Timbuktu.
8. Pirates eventually captured the pair, his uncle and (he, him), and presented Leo as a slave to Pope Leo X.
9. The pope freed Leo and commissioned him to write a detailed survey of Africa, which (we, us) students were astonished to learn he composed in Italian.
10. The teacher asked us, Juanita and (I, me), to present a report on Leo Africanus and his impressions of Timbuktu.

➡ **For a SELF-CHECK and more practice, see the EXERCISE BANK, p. 611.**

Pronoun-Reference Problems

❶ Here's the Idea

If a pronoun's antecedent is missing or unclear, or if there is more than one antecedent, readers will be confused.

General Reference

Problems can occur when the pronoun *it, this, that, which,* or *such* is used to refer to a general idea rather than a specific noun. You can often fix the problem by rewording the sentence to eliminate the pronoun.

Fixing General-Reference Problems	
Awkward	**Revised**
High winds and driving snow assailed the mountaintop. **This** trapped the climbers in their tents.	When high winds and driving snow assailed the mountaintop, the climbers became trapped in their tents.
The mummified bodies were excavated from the ice on an Andean peak, **which** was a great find.	The mummified bodies excavated from the ice on an Andean peak were a great find.

Indefinite Reference

An indefinite reference occurs when the pronoun *it, you,* or *they* does not refer to a specific person or thing. You can fix this problem by rewording the sentence to eliminate the pronoun.

Fixing Indefinite-Reference Problems	
Awkward	**Revised**
It stated in the newspaper article that the expedition was a success.	The newspaper article stated that the expedition was a success.
In some schools, **you** can take part in an archaeological dig.	In some schools, students can take part in an archaeological dig.

In formal writing, don't use the pronoun *you* to refer to people in general. The pronoun should only be used to address the reader directly.

PRONOUNS

Ambiguous Reference

The word *ambiguous* means "having two or more possible meanings." An ambiguous reference occurs when a pronoun has two or more possible antecedents. You can fix an ambiguous-reference problem by rewording the sentence to clarify what the pronoun refers to.

Fixing Ambiguous-Reference Problems

Awkward	Revised
When Joe called Kwok, he was preparing to set sail.	When Kwok was preparing to set sail, he received a call from Joe.
After the men removed the sail from the mast, they began to repair it.	The men began to repair the sail after they removed it from the mast.
When the shovel struck the buried pottery jar, it broke in half.	The buried pottery jar broke in half when it was struck by the shovel.

❷ Why It Matters in Writing

Ambiguous references can result in confusing and unintentionally humorous writing. What would you think if you read the first sentence below?

When the diver encountered the shark, he bit him.

INCORRECT

The diver was bitten by the shark he encountered.

REVISED

❸ Practice and Apply

A. CONCEPT CHECK: Pronoun-Reference Problems

Correct the pronoun-reference problems in these sentences.

The Fruits of Mendel's Garden

1. Gregor Mendel, an Austrian monk, crossbred pea plants. This led to his discovery of the basic laws of heredity in 1866.
2. In my book, it says that Mendel gave up his research when he became an abbot.
3. They ignored his published findings until 1900.
4. Mendel's theory—that you can predict traits handed down from parent plants to offspring—transformed agriculture.
5. Modern farmers cross inbred seeds until they produce offspring that outperform either parent.
6. Corn is bred this way. It has been called the greatest success story of modern genetics.
7. The development of a high-yielding dwarf wheat saved millions of lives, which was wonderful.
8. When agriculturists used Mendel's laws to produce tangelos and broccoflower, they became very popular.
9. Scientists also crossed a firefly gene with tobacco. It resulted in glow-in-the-dark tobacco.
10. In this biology book, you learn that Mendel is considered the father of genetics.

➡ **For a SELF-CHECK and more practice, see the EXERCISE BANK, p. 611.**

Identify the pronoun problem in each sentence above.

B. REVISING: Correcting Ambiguous-Reference Problems

Revise the following, correcting any ambiguous-reference problems.

Rosalind Franklin: Unsung Hero of DNA's Discovery

In 1951, Rosalind Franklin joined a team of scientists at King's College in London to study living cells. When the leader of the team introduced Franklin to Maurice Wilkins, the laboratory's second-in-command, he assumed she would be his assistant. From the start, then, the relationship between Wilkins and Franklin was strained.

The two scientists began studying DNA fibers, entering the race to discover their structure. Then Wilkins and James Watson arranged a meeting, during which he shared Franklin's data—without her consent. Shortly thereafter, Watson and Francis Crick discovered the structure of DNA.

Grammar in Literature

Achieving Clarity with Pronouns

When careful writers describe their own experiences, they don't let pronoun errors confuse their readers. In the following excerpt from *La Relación* by Spanish explorer Álvar Núñez Cabeza de Vaca, the writer's use of pronouns helps readers follow the chain of events. The report, written for the King of Spain, details Cabeza de Vaca's expedition in 1527 to Florida. This passage describes Cabeza de Vaca's ordeal after a wave capsizes his barge off the coast of Galveston Island, near present-day Texas.

from
Álvar Núñez Cabeza de Vaca
La Relación

We lost only those the barge took down; but the **survivors** escaped as naked as **they** were born, with the loss of everything we had. That was not much, but valuable to us in that bitter November cold, our bodies so emaciated we could easily count every bone and looked the very picture of death. **I** can say for **myself** that from the month of May I had eaten nothing but corn, and that sometimes raw. **I** never could bring **myself** to eat any of the horse-meat at the time our beasts were slaughtered; and fish I did not taste ten times. On top of everything else, a cruel north wind commenced to complete **our killing.**

The Lord willed that we should find embers while searching the remnants of our former fire. We found more wood and soon had big fires raging. Before them, with flowing tears, we prayed for mercy and pardon, **each** filled with pity, not only for **himself** but for all **his** wretched fellows.

> Agreement between *they* and its antecedent helps readers understand the men's condition.

> In both sentences, the reflexive pronoun *myself* refers to the preceding pronoun *I* and helps clarify the writer's own attitude.

> The possessive pronoun *our* places the focus on the act of *killing*.

> The pronouns *himself* and *his* refer to the indefinite pronoun *each* and help clarify the sentence's complex construction.

If your pronouns don't refer clearly to their antecedents, your readers will have trouble understanding your writing. Here is a review of tips for avoiding common pronoun-reference problems that can make your writing hard to follow.

Avoiding Common Pronoun-Reference Problems	
General reference	Make sure the pronouns *it, this, that, which,* and *such* refer to a specific noun rather than a general idea.
Indefinite reference	Avoid using *it, they,* and *you* if the pronouns don't refer to a particular person or thing.
Ambiguous reference	When a pronoun follows two or more antecedents, be sure the pronoun clearly refers to only one of them.

PRACTICE AND APPLY: Revising

Revise the following passage, eliminating any pronoun-reference problems.

In 1996, American astronaut Shannon Lucid and two Russian cosmonauts traveled to the space station *Mir* for what would become a six-month stay. It was difficult training for the mission. For one thing, Lucid had to become fluent in Russian, which was hard enough. She also had to learn the systems and operations on *Mir* and *Soyuz* because that was the spacecraft that would be attached to *Mir* throughout Lucid's stay in space.

Once the mission began, the crew members quickly developed a routine, beginning with meals. Particularly popular were the Russian soup and mayonnaise; the cosmonauts added it to nearly everything they ate. Also, when you live in space, you have to exercise every day to keep your muscles from atrophying. During much of the day, the crew members maintained *Mir*'s systems and conducted experiments. That was the most important daily activity. Yet even with their busy schedules, the astronauts found time to talk. They discussed their homelands and their childhood fears and discovered that they were groundless.

Mixed Review

A. Using Pronouns For each sentence, choose the correct pronoun from those shown in parentheses.

Accidental Discoveries

1. Legend credits the discovery of quinine to a South American Indian (who, whom) drank from a jungle pool tainted with the bark of the nearby cinchona, or quina, trees.
2. According to the legend, the man was suffering from malaria; (his, him) drinking from the pool cured him.
3. Edward Jenner's discovery of a cure for smallpox was the result of (his, their) medical treatment of farmers and milkmaids.
4. It was (he, him) who discovered that an exposure to cowpox provided an immunity to smallpox.
5. In 1844, during a demonstration of "laughing gas," or nitrous oxide, a volunteer became violent, fell, and cut (him, himself) deeply but was unaware of his injury.
6. Dentist Horace Wells, who was sitting in the audience, realized that the gas could be used when pulling a patient's teeth to prevent causing (him or her, them) pain.
7. In 1974, when Chinese peasants discovered life-sized terra-cotta figures made around 221 B.C., no one was more surprised than (they, them).
8. The 1947 discovery of the Dead Sea Scrolls by a Bedouin boy searching for his goat has always been a favorite of (we, us) history students.
9. As George de Mestral pulled cockleburs off of his jacket, he got an idea for a popular fastener that almost everyone has used at least once in (his or her, their) life.
10. Most of these people don't realize that the name of (his, their) favorite fastener is derived from the words *velour* and *crochet.*

B. Pronoun Agreement and Reference Problems Rewrite the following paragraph, correcting any errors in pronoun usage.

The Discovery of Self-Stick Notes

Anyone who has covered their computer or refrigerator with self-stick notes knows the value of these handy bits of paper. However, few know how his favorite adhesive scratch pad came to be. Actually, it was the result of an accident. When Spencer Silver and Art Fry were working at the 3M company, he discovered an adhesive but discarded it because it was not very strong. Fry remembered his colleague's discovery one Sunday after they had marked songs in his choir book with scraps of paper. As frequently happened, the scraps fell out while Fry was singing, which was annoying. When Fry returned to work on Monday, he himself began using Silver's adhesive to develop a temporary bookmark. After he worked the bugs out of the bookmarks, he showed them to 3M executives. They say the rest is history. Although Fry pursued the discovery, credit should go to both scientists, Silver and he.

Choose the letter that identifies the best way to correct the underlined pronoun.

From about 1503 to 1480 B.C., Egypt was ruled by Queen Hatshepsut, whom encouraged commerce. In 1493 B.C., they sent a fleet of ships to the
(1)   (2)
land of Punt, near present-day Somalia. Queen Hatshepsut ordered that

it was to be primarily a trading expedition. Centuries before, Punt had
(3)
furnished Egypt, their rulers and people, with frankincense and myrrh.
                (4)
Queen Hatshepsut decided that he would renew that trade.
                              (5)
    When the ships returned home loaded with valuable items, the queen

had them immortalized on the walls of her beautiful temple. In addition
    (6)
to murals depicting myrrh and frankincense, the artists painted
                                                (7)
themselves pictures of the fish and plants collected on the trip. The

expedition shows you that the ancient Egyptians had amassed knowledge
              (8)
that allowed them to undertake seafaring adventures. Them traveling to
              (9)   (10)
Punt also helped pave the way for later expeditions to the south of Africa.

---

1. A. whomever
   B. which
   C. who
   D. Correct as is

2. A. she
   B. he
   C. herself
   D. Correct as is

3. A. that
   B. Punt
   C. the journey
   D. Correct as is

4. A. its
   B. our
   C. them
   D. Correct as is

5. A. they
   B. she
   C. he or she
   D. Correct as is

6. A. they
   B. it
   C. the items
   D. Correct as is

7. A. artists painted
   B. artists painted theirselves
   C. they
   D. Correct as is

8. A. reveals
   B. shows them
   C. reveals to you
   D. Correct as is

9. A. him
   B. they
   C. him or her
   D. Correct as is

10. A. Her
    B. Their
    C. Themselves
    D. Correct as is

Student Help Desk

Using Pronouns at a Glance

Nominative Case

I	we
you	you
he	they
she	
it	

Use this case when
- the pronoun is a **subject**
- the pronoun is a **predicate nominative**

Objective Case

me	us
you	you
him	them
her	
it	

Use this case when
- the pronoun is the **direct object of a verb**
- the pronoun is the **indirect object of a verb**
- the pronoun is the **object of a preposition**

Possessive Case

my/mine	our/ours
your/yours	your/yours
his	their/theirs
her/hers	
its	

Use this case for
- pronouns that show ownership or relationship

Agreement Problems

Digging Up Solutions

Problem: A pronoun is part of an elliptical clause.

Example: No one found more interesting specimens than (he, him). [did]

Solution: • Add the words that are missing from the elliptical clause. (For this sentence, you would add "did.")
- Choose the correct pronoun case for the sentence.

Problem: A pronoun is used with an appositive.

Example: They wouldn't let (we, us) students go on the expedition.

Solution: • Rewrite the sentence without the appositive. (For this sentence, you would drop "students.")
- Choose the correct pronoun case for the sentence.

Problem: A pronoun is used in an appositive.

Example: The leaders, Rhonda and (I, me), will meet to discuss the trip.

Solution: • Drop the words identified by the appositive. (For this sentence, you would drop "The leaders.")
- Choose the correct pronoun case for the sentence.

Reference Problems

General-Reference Problem: The pronoun *it, this, that, which,* or *such* refers to a general idea rather than a specific noun.

Example: He had to give up his search, which was a shame.

Solution: Reword the sentence to eliminate the pronoun.

Revision: That he had to give up his search was a shame.

Indefinite-Reference Problem: The pronoun *it, you,* or *they* does not refer to a specific person or thing.

Example: During the launch, you heard the astronauts' conversation.

Solution: Reword the sentence to eliminate the pronoun.

Revision: During the launch, the astronauts' conversation could be heard.

Ambiguous-Reference Problem: A pronoun has two or more possible antecedents.

Example: When Ron found Al, he breathed a sigh of relief.

Solution: Reword the sentence to clarify what the pronoun refers to.

Revision: Al breathed a sigh of relief when Ron found him.

The Bottom Line

Checklist for Using Pronouns

Have I . . .

_____ used the nominative case for pronouns functioning as subjects or predicate nominatives?

_____ used the objective case for pronouns functioning as objects?

_____ made all pronouns agree with their antecedents in number, gender, and person?

_____ used the possessive case for pronouns that show ownership or relationship?

_____ used *who* and *whom* correctly?

_____ used the correct case for pronouns in compound structures, comparisons, and appositives?

_____ eliminated any pronoun-reference problems?

Using Modifiers

Sports & Fitness

Attitude & Fitness:
The Hidden Connection

Exercises You Can't
Hardly Believe!

Achieving Your
Personal Best

Your Complete
Guide to Total Fitness

How Good Are You at Determining Your Wellness?

Theme: Health/Wellness

Feeling Fit

Any time you describe how you feel, you use modifiers. Whether you're fit and trim or fitness-challenged, modifiers can help get your writing in shape. Consider the modifiers in the headlines above. Which one needs to be shaped up?

Write Away: A Work-Out for the Brain
Correct the headline that contains a modifier error. Then choose any one of the five headlines above and write a paragraph that might follow as part of an article inside the magazine. Save the paragraph in your 📁 **Working Portfolio.**

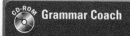

Grammar Coach

Write the letter that indicates the best way to revise each underlined section.

Since health is one of your most precious possessions, always try hard to keep yourself <u>fittest</u>. You might feel defeated if your eating habits are
(1)
not the <u>most good</u> they could be for a day, but there are a lot of things
(2)
<u>more bad</u> than that! One day of not having the most nutritious meals in
(3)
the world won't matter much in the long run. What you eat is no more important than <u>any aspect</u> of your total fitness program. What does
(4)
matter is to plan a program that works for you: don't worry that your routine is less strenuous than <u>your friend</u>. A well-rounded program
(5)
involves aerobics, stretching, and strength-building. <u>These type of</u>
(6)
<u>exercises</u> should all be included. <u>Exercising on a regular basis, both</u>
(7)
<u>strength and stamina will increase.</u> But remember not to overdo it. For instance, it isn't good to exercise if you have a cold and <u>feel bad</u>.
(8)

1. A. best fit
   B. most fittest
   C. fit
   D. Correct as is

2. A. best
   B. good
   C. better
   D. Correct as is

3. A. worse
   B. more badly
   C. worst
   D. Correct as is

4. A. an aspect
   B. any other aspect
   C. one aspect
   D. Correct as is

5. A. your friend is
   B. your friend was
   C. your friend's is
   D. Correct as is

6. A. These kind of exercises
   B. Those type of exercise
   C. These types of exercises
   D. Correct as is

7. A. Exercising on a regular basis, strength and stamina increase.
   B. Strength will be increased exercising on a regular basis and stamina.
   C. Exercising on a regular basis, you will increase both strength and stamina.
   D. Correct as is

8. A. feel badly
   B. feel worse
   C. feel worst
   D. Correct as is

MODIFIERS

LESSON 1 Using Adjectives and Adverbs

❶ Here's the Idea

Modifiers are words that describe or restrict the meanings of other words. Adjectives and adverbs are common modifiers.

Using Adjectives

▶ **An adjective modifies a noun or a pronoun.**

Adjectives answer the following questions.

Which one? He injured his **left** leg.
What kind? She is allergic to **long-haired** cats.
How many? He has **16** stitches.
How much? She needs **some** sleep.

Other words can often be used as adjectives.

Words Used as Adjectives	
Articles	**an** illness, **a** hospital, **the** rest
Nouns	**laser** surgery, **asthma** attack, **health** club
Participles	**throbbing** pain, **bleeding** wound, **healing** art
Possessive nouns and pronouns	**Kayla's** physical, **his** eyes, **her** recovery
Demonstrative pronouns	**this** cut, **that** cure, **these** patients, **those** doctors
Indefinite pronouns	**all** dust, **few** symptoms, **many** athletes
Numbers	**one** day, **20** minutes

Predicate adjectives follow linking verbs and modify the subject of a clause.

MODIFIES
She seems fine.

MODIFIES
He looks good.

Using Adverbs

▶ **An adverb modifies a verb, an adjective, or another adverb.**

You can use adverbs to answer the following questions.

When? He injured his leg **yesterday.**
Where? She ran **farther** than he did.
How? The doctor **patiently** listened to her symptoms.
To what extent? The sore healed **completely.**

For a review of adjectives and adverbs, see pp. 16–18.

❷ Why It Matters in Writing

Notice the variety of adverbs and adjectives in the excerpt that follows. How do they add to the richness of the writing?

Everyone in the community called her "Miss Mag." She was a giant of a woman, with paper-sack brown skin that was smooth as a summer peach. For Big Mama, visiting the sick was just as natural as wearing her apron every day. She often gave more respect to people when they were sick or dead than when they were alive and well.

—Ethel Morgan Smith, "A Conspiracy of Grace"

PREDICATE ADJECTIVE

ADJECTIVES

ADVERBS

❸ Practice and Apply

CONCEPT CHECK: Using Adjectives and Adverbs

Identify the words that function as adjectives or adverbs in the following sentences. Do not identify articles.

Number One Children's Illness
1. Asthma is now the leading chronic illness among children.
2. Asthma affects almost 5 million children.
3. According to a prominent medical association, asthma has increased nearly 79 percent since 1982.
4. This sharp rise may be from an increase in some allergens.
5. Asthma tightens airways and can quickly restrict a person's breathing ability.
6. Repeated infections or exposure to allergens can chronically inflame a child's bronchial tubes.
7. During an asthma attack, the bronchial tubes constrict and the simple intake of air becomes very difficult.
8. Dust mites or animal dander may trigger asthma attacks.
9. In the past, the detection of asthma rarely took place in its early stages; today doctors can identify asthma much earlier.
10. Researchers undoubtedly will continue their search for new asthma medications that have minimal side effects.

➡ For a SELF-CHECK and more practice, see the EXERCISE BANK, p. 612.

MODIFIERS

Making Comparisons

LESSON 2

❶ Here's the Idea

You can use modifiers to compare two or more things in your writing. The following chart shows you the two ways that modifiers form comparisons: in the comparative degree and in the superlative degree.

Degrees of Comparisons	
The **positive** (base) form of the adverb or adjective makes no comparison.	Atlas Fitness Center is a **good** facility.
The **comparative** form compares two persons, places, or things.	Shamrock Fitness Center is a **better** facility than Atlas.
The **superlative** form compares three or more persons, places, or things.	Health Bridge Fitness Center is the **best** facility in the area.

Regular Comparisons

Most modifiers change in predictable (regular) ways to show comparisons.

Regular Comparisons			
Rule	**Positive Form**	**Comparative**	**Superlative**
For one-syllable words, add -er or -est.	fit strong	fitter stronger	fittest strongest
For many two-syllable words, add -er or -est.	healthy happy	healthier happier	healthiest happiest
For most words of more than two syllables and adverbs ending in *ly*, use *more* or *most*.	flexible quickly	more flexible more quickly	most flexible most quickly

HOT TIP

Some two-syllable modifiers sound awkward when you add -er or -est. If so, use *more* or *most*. For example:

> **more tired** (*not* tireder), **most tired** (*not* tiredest)

CHAPTER 7

To show a negative comparison, use the words *less* and *least,* or *fewer* and *fewest,* the opposites of *more* and *most,* with most modifiers.

This gym is less crowded than Top Fitness is.

This gym is the least crowded of any that I've used.

Don't confuse *less* and *fewer. Less* means a smaller quantity of something. *Fewer* means a smaller (countable) number of individual things.

I drank less water tonight at the gym because I did fewer sit-ups than last night.

Irregular Comparisons

Some modifiers have irregular comparative and superlative forms.

Common Irregular Modifiers		
Positive Form	Comparative	Superlative
good/well	better	best
bad/ill	worse	worst
many/much	more	most

Some modifiers are absolutes, words that cannot be compared. Examples include unique, complete, and total.

unique (*not* more unique, most unique)

❷ Why It Matters in Writing

Most writing about athletic activities, especially competitive sports, requires comparisons. Notice the superlative forms this sportswriter uses to question how newspapers rank high school football teams.

PROFESSIONAL MODEL

Should the rankings be based on who plays the **toughest** competition? Who gains the **most** yards and scores the **most** points? Or who permits the **fewest** points? . . . Or who wins by the **widest** margins?

—Taylor Bell, *Chicago Sun-Times*

❸ Practice and Apply

A. CONCEPT CHECK: Making Comparisons

For each sentence write the correct comparative or superlative form.

Fitting Fitness into Your Day

1. Do you think your exercise regimen is (less strenuous, least strenuous) than you would like it to be?
2. If you really want to be (fitter, more fit) than you are, you don't need an expensive health club membership or a time-consuming workout schedule.
3. Recent research on fitness has come up with (gooder, better) news than ever: as little as 30 minutes of moderate exercise on most days is all you need.
4. Even (helpfuller, more helpful) than this is that the 30 minutes do not have to be all at one time.
5. The (easier, easiest) way of all to "fit in" fitness is by using time whenever it is available throughout the day.
6. For instance, you are (less likely, least likely) to arrive as early as your friends if you walk rather than ride home from school, but you will be increasing your fitness level.
7. During the day, it is a (good, better) idea to vary your exercise activities than to do the same exercises all the time.
8. Of the two aerobic activities of bicycling and running, running is the (vigorouser, more vigorous).
9. Doing stretching exercises while you watch TV may make you the (more flexible, most flexible) member of your family.
10. Using weights or just doing calisthenics will make you (stronger, strongest) than you once were.

➜ For a SELF-CHECK and more practice, see the EXERCISE BANK, p. 612.

B. WRITING: Using Comparisons Correctly

Study the information listed in the chart below. Write a paragraph using modifiers in their correct comparative forms to describe which swimming events you imagine to be the most and least difficult. Include details from the chart or your own experience.

| Swimming Records | | | |
Swimmer	Event	Distance	Time
Aleksandr Popov	Freestyle	100 meters	48.21
Jeff Rouse	Backstroke	100 meters	53.86
Pablo Morales	Butterfly	100 meters	52.84

Problems with Comparisons

① Here's the Idea

The explanations that follow will help you to avoid three of the most troublesome constructions dealing with comparisons—double comparisons, illogical comparisons, and incomplete comparisons.

Frank and Ernest by Bob Thaves

© 1992 Thaves/Reprinted with permission.

Double Comparisons

▶ **Do not use both -er and more at the same time to form a comparative or both -est and most at the same time to form a superlative.**

NONSTANDARD **Playing high school sports can be more harder on students' bodies than other activities are.**

STANDARD **Playing high school sports can be harder on students' bodies than other activities are.**

NONSTANDARD **Spinal injuries may be the most hardest of all athletic injuries to recover from.**

STANDARD **Spinal injuries may be the hardest of all athletic injuries to recover from.**

Illogical and Incomplete Comparisons

▶ **Use the word other or else to compare an individual with the rest of its group.** In the following sentence, the writer's wording is confusing. Does the writer mean that basketball is not a sport?

NONSTANDARD **Basketball can result in more injuries than any sport.**

Because basketball is a type of sport, the writer should have written the sentence this way:

STANDARD **Basketball can result in more injuries than any other sport.**

▶ **Complete whatever comparison you are making.** When you are making a compound comparison, use *than* or *as* after the first modifier to avoid an incomplete comparison.

NONSTANDARD **Young people recover more quickly from injuries.**

STANDARD **Young people recover more quickly from injuries than older people do.**

▶ **Fully state both parts of a comparison if there is any chance of readers misunderstanding your sentence.** In the following sentence, the writer compares the care needed to heal a sports injury with an illness itself, not with the *care* needed to heal an illness.

NONSTANDARD **The care required to heal a sports injury may be as extensive as an illness.**

In this sentence, the writer is clearly comparing the care needed to heal a sports injury with the care needed to heal an illness.

STANDARD **The care required to heal a sports injury may be as extensive as that for an illness.**

❷ Why It Matters in Writing

Writers sometimes try too hard to emphasize a point and end up making double or illogical comparisons.

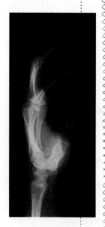

STUDENT MODEL

Injuries in school sports occur much **more** oftener than most people know. Sprinters in track may get shin splints, a condition in which shin muscles separate, and other even **more serious** injuries. Football players can suffer serious knee or back injuries, and even **worser** concussions. When basketball players fall or crash into each other, they can break bones, get deep lacerations or contusions, and injure their heads. Volleyball players injure their knees **more frequently** than other parts of their bodies. From tennis elbow to swimmer's ear, injuries from competitive sports take a toll on athletes' bodies. People who deal with sports injuries are busier than ever they have ever been before.

> Here the writer correctly uses *more* to modify *serious*.

➌ Practice and Apply

A. CONCEPT CHECK: Problems with Comparisons

Rewrite the following sentences to make the comparisons clear and correct. For the three sentences that have no comparison problems, write *Correct*.

Robot Surgeons

1. Can a robot be a more skillfuller surgeon than a real doctor?
2. Certain specialized surgeries require a higher degree of accuracy than doctors alone can achieve.
3. The accuracy rate of a robotic arm is higher than a human doctor.
4. A robot, guided by a doctor, may be 20 times as accurate if not more than a surgeon working without such help.
5. Many doctors also believe the robotic arm to be more safer and less invasive.
6. The robotic arm is also generally faster than any surgical tool.
7. For performing tedious operating room tasks, robots are as good if not better than humans.
8. Some surgeons already know that robots make good assistants in the operating room.
9. Dr. Y. S. Kwoh of Long Beach prefers a robot as an assistant more than some surgeons.
10. The robotic arm provides a much more easier way to perform certain procedures.
11. Dr. Kwoh is as skilled as any doctor in using the robotic arm.
12. Kwoh is more on the cutting edge of medicine than many doctors are.
13. A surgeon working with a robot can be as competent as any team in the operating room.
14. Your chances of a successful operation with a robot are as good with a human surgeon, if not better.
15. In the future, robots will only become more usefuller than they are now.

➡ For a SELF-CHECK and more practice, see the EXERCISE BANK, p. 613.

B. REVISING: Using Comparisons Correctly

In your 🗎 **Working Portfolio,** find your **Write Away** paragraph from page 180. Make your writing clearer by finding and revising any modifier and comparison errors.

LESSON 4 — **Other Modifier Problems**

❶ Here's the Idea

Misplaced and dangling modifiers, double negatives, and the misuse of demonstrative pronouns and predicate adjectives are common modifier errors.

This/That, These/Those, and *Them*

This, that, these, and *those* are demonstrative pronouns used as adjectives. Three rules cover all situations.

1. These words must agree in number with the words they modify. Be especially careful when modifying *kind, kinds, sort,* and *sorts.*

> **This headache is not just in my mind.** (SINGULAR)

> **These kinds of migraine symptoms are awful.** (PLURAL)

2. Never use *here* or *there* with one of these words. The adjective already points out which one; it doesn't need any help.

> **This ~~here~~ migraine hurts even my teeth.**

3. Never use the pronoun *them* as an adjective in place of *these* or *those.*

> USAGE ERROR   **Stress often contributes to them attacks.**

> CORRECT USAGE   **Stress often contributes to those attacks.**

Good/Well and *Bad/Badly*

Note the correct usage of the following pairs of modifiers.

> **_Good_ = Adjective, Predicate Adjective**
>
> MODIFIES
> **A good workout may leave you sore.**
>
> MODIFIES
> **Seth feels good today.** (*good,* that is, happy)
>
> **_Well_ = Adverb, Predicate Adjective**
>
> MODIFIES
> **That warmup routine works well.**
>
> MODIFIES   ADVERB
> **Moe looks well today.** (*well,* that is, healthy)
>   ADJECTIVE

CHAPTER 7

Bad = Adjective, Predicate Adjective

Tina has a bad ankle. (*bad,* that is, injured ankle)

MODIFIES

Tina felt bad after her race. (*bad,* that is, sick or unhappy)

Badly = Adverb

She ran badly. (*badly,* that is, poorly)

Misplaced and Dangling Modifiers

▶ **A misplaced modifier is a word or phrase that is placed so far away from the word it modifies that the meaning of the sentence is unclear or incorrect.**

MISLEADING

> The doctor explained how to help migraine sufferers at a recent convention.

CLEARER

> At a recent convention, the doctor explained how to help migraine sufferers.

▶ **A dangling modifier is a word or phrase that does not clearly modify any noun or pronoun in a sentence.**

MISLEADING

> Learning how to relax, my migraines improved.

CLEARER

> As I learned how to relax, my migraines improved.

MISLEADING

> Often misunderstood, myths about migraines abound.

CLEARER

> Myths about migraines abound.
>
> OR
>
> Migraines are often misunderstood.

For more about misplaced and dangling modifiers, see pp. 64–65.

MODIFIERS

Double Negatives

▶ **A double negative is the use of two or more negative words to express a single negation.**

Remember that the words *hardly, barely,* and *scarcely* function as negatives, so they should not be used with other negative words.

AWKWARD

Headache-free people can't hardly imagine what a migraine is like.

REVISED

Headache-free people can't imagine what a migraine is like.

Headache-free people can hardly imagine what a migraine is like.

> Use of the words *can't* and *hardly* in the same sentence creates a double negative.

> Eliminating either of the negative words creates a correct sentence.

 Although people often use *can't help but* and *haven't but* in speech, these constructions should not be used in formal writing because they create double negatives.

❷ Why It Matters in Writing

Instructors and employers consider the use of double negatives to be one of the most obvious signs that a writer has weak language skills. Be sure not to send this message in your own writing.

STUDENT MODEL

DRAFT

I **can't say nothing** about headaches, but my sister certainly can. From the age of eight years, migraine attacks have made her life miserable. I **can't help but feel** sorry for her. She **can't hardly ever** eat chocolate any more.

REVISION

I **can't say anything** about headaches, but my sister certainly can. From the age of eight years, she has suffered from migraine attacks that have made her life miserable. I **can't help feeling** sorry for her. She **can hardly ever** eat chocolate any more.

❸ Practice and Apply

Correct the sentences that have modifier errors. If a sentence has no errors, write *Correct.*

What's in Your Head Can Affect Your Body

1. Vivach had a pain in his chest that often made him feel badly.
2. This here pain was sometimes dull and throbbing and sometimes sharp.
3. Playing soccer, the pain didn't bother him, though.
4. However, he didn't do good in several of his classes.
5. The doctor can't not help but think that the pain has an emotional cause.
6. Why might a person's body develop these sort of physical symptoms based on emotions?
7. In Vivach's case, the pain began just when his grandfather developed asthma and no longer felt well.
8. Something wasn't not quite right in Vivach's life, and his brain may have been reacting to it.
9. Diagnosed with psychosomatic symptoms such as Vivach's, doctors still need to treat patients.
10. These kinds of symptoms are often related to stress.

➜ **For a SELF-CHECK and more practice, see the EXERCISE BANK, p. 614.**

Proofread and revise the modifier errors in the following paragraph.

A Physician Can Help

Do you have some of them persistent aches and pains that really make you feel badly? Don't delay; get a family physician. Don't never just think you can figure out what is wrong with you and then go see a specialist. These type of decisions need to be made by a doctor who knows you good. A competent family physician will rarely treat you bad. After examining you carefully, he or she will make a diagnosis. Or, if your physician doesn't find no explanation for your illness, then you might be referred to a specialist.

MODIFIERS

Grammar in Literature

Describing Health and Emotions with Modifiers

Physicians of the past have not always been aware of just how strong an effect emotions can have on a patient's physical state. Today, we know that some physical disorders, such as tension headaches, chest pain, upset stomachs, and ulcers, may be related to stress. In the following literature excerpt, the narrator relies on modifiers to describe her emotional and physical state, which her physician husband does not seem to understand.

THE YELLOW WALLPAPER

CHARLOTTE PERKINS GILMAN

John is a physician, and *perhaps*—(I would not say it to a living soul, of course, but this is dead paper and a great relief to my *mind*)—*perhaps* that is one reason I do not get well faster.

You see he does not believe I am sick!

And what can one do?

If a physician of high standing, and one's own husband, assures friends and relatives that there is really nothing the matter with one but temporary nervous depression— a slight hysterical tendency—what is one to do?

My brother is also a physician, and also of high standing, and he says the same thing.

So I take phosphates or phosphites—whichever it is, and tonics, and journeys, and air, and exercise, and am absolutely forbidden to "work" until I am well again.

Personally, I disagree with their ideas.

Personally, I believe that congenial work, with excitement and change, would do me good.

But what is one to do? I did write for a while in spite of them; but it *does* exhaust me a good deal—having to be so sly about it, or else meet with heavy opposition.

I sometimes fancy that in my condition if I had less opposition and more society and stimulus—but John says the very worst thing I can do is to think about my condition, and I confess it always makes me feel bad.

Repetition of adverb *not* helps set tone.

Opposite adjectives express narrator's confusion: *living/dead; well/sick; good/bad.*

Adverb/adjective combinations show husband's attempt to downplay his wife's condition.

Adverb *personally* creates emphasis.

Comparative and superlative degrees of adjectives show narrator's dissatisfaction with her situation.

Effects of Modifiers in "The Yellow Wallpaper"

Effects	Examples
Carefully chosen adjectives and adverbs can show a character's attitude toward people, things, and events.	*dead* paper, *congenial* work, *heavy* opposition
Comparatives and superlatives can be used to show contrast between situations.	*less* opposition, *more* society and stimulus
Contrasting modifiers can show the character's conflicting thoughts or denials.	*temporary* nervous condition, *slightly* hysterical tendencies

PRACTICE AND APPLY: Using Modifiers

Rewrite the following letter, choosing from any of the modifiers listed below to show tone, emphasis, and attitude in each numbered space. Share your letter with a partner to see how the modifiers you each chose affect the tone of the letter.

much	good	little	unfairly
dear	well	less	right
very	great	certainly	really
best	worst	perhaps	sincere
better	deeply	too	more

My (1) _____ friend,
    I hope that this letter finds you feeling better. Try not to be (2) _____ impatient about your illness; these types of ailments take time to heal. I believe John cares (3) _____ about you and thinks he is making the (4) _____ decision about your treatment. He (5) _____ loves you, as you must know, barring nothing. He is (6) _____ correct in thinking that you should not overexert yourself. Staying in the country sounds like the (7) _____ idea.
    I (8) _____ do miss you and can't wait for you to come back and resume your normal activities. I'm trying to be patient but expect to see you (9) _____ soon. Meanwhile, my hope is that you'll feel (10) _____ better as each day passes.

Love,
Elizabeth

A. Adjectives and Adverbs Read the following passage. Then answer the questions below it.

Protecting Your Skin

(1) If you're ever out in the sun, skin damage from invisible rays is a health concern you should take seriously. **(2)** In the past, sunshine seemed harmless to many people. **(3)** However, these days people are more knowledgeable than they once were about the dangers of ultraviolet-A (UVA) and ultraviolet-B (UVB) rays. **(4)** They recognize that no UV ray is really safe. **(5)** The American Academy of Dermatology has consistently advised caution for sun lovers. **(6)** It recommends using broad-spectrum sunscreens to protect your skin from sunburn. **(7)** Sunburn pain comes more quickly than you might suppose: by night you might be suffering from exposure early that same afternoon. **(8)** Soothing lotions and aloe can help relieve sore, hot skin. **(9)** Remember, though, that a little caution today can prevent skin problems in the future. **(10)** This is true whether you're vacationing at a Mexican resort or sitting in your own backyard.

1. What are the two nouns used as adjectives in sentence 1?
2. What is the predicate adjective in sentence 2?
3. Which adjective is used in the comparative form in sentence 3?
4. What question does the adverb *really* in sentence 4 answer?
5. What does the adverb in sentence 5 modify?
6. What pronoun is used as an adjective in sentence 6?
7. Which adverb is in the comparative form in sentence 7?
8. What is the participle in sentence 8?
9. Which adverb in sentence 9 answers the question *when*?
10. What is the proper adjective in sentence 10?

B. Fixing Modifier Problems Proofread and revise the following paragraph, correcting any modifier errors.

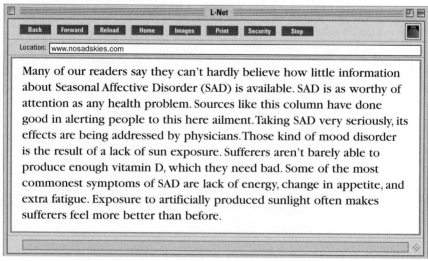

L-Net

Back Forward Reload Home Images Print Security Stop

Location: www.nosadskies.com

Many of our readers say they can't hardly believe how little information about Seasonal Affective Disorder (SAD) is available. SAD is as worthy of attention as any health problem. Sources like this column have done good in alerting people to this here ailment. Taking SAD very seriously, its effects are being addressed by physicians. Those kind of mood disorder is the result of a lack of sun exposure. Sufferers aren't barely able to produce enough vitamin D, which they need bad. Some of the most commonest symptoms of SAD are lack of energy, change in appetite, and extra fatigue. Exposure to artificially produced sunlight often makes sufferers feel more better than before.

Write the letter that indicates the best way to revise each underlined section.

It seems that teens, especially teenage boys, <u>can't hardly</u> get enough to
(1)
eat sometimes. However, they may not be eating the foods that are <u>most</u>
(2)
<u>best</u> of all for their health. In one Gallup poll, 87 percent of teens listed
their favorite foods as hamburgers, cheeseburgers, pizza, and luncheon
meats. <u>These type</u> of foods are generally very high in fat and sodium. Not
(3)
surprisingly, American teens have more access to fast food <u>than any teens</u>
(4)
in the world. Teens who don't eat a variety of foods from the Food Guide
Pyramid often <u>feel badly</u> after meals. Yet other teens may <u>have never even</u>
(5)   (6)
heard of this guide. According to some experts, using the pyramid and
avoiding fast foods can help Americans eat <u>more healthful</u> than they do
(7)
now. It also helps them consume <u>less</u> fat calories. So you would do <u>well</u> to
(8)   (9)
follow the experts' advice. It may be <u>indispensably</u> to maintaining your
(10)
health over time.

1. A. cannot hardly
   B. can hardly
   C. can't barely
   D. Correct as is

2. A. more better
   B. best
   C. bestest
   D. Correct as is

3. A. These types
   B. Those type
   C. This types
   D. Correct as is

4. A. than any other teens
   B. than the teens
   C. than teens
   D. Correct as is

5. A. feels badder
   B. feels badly
   C. feel bad
   D. Correct as is

6. A. have not never even
   B. haven't never even
   C. haven't not ever even
   D. Correct as is

7. A. more healthfully
   B. more healthfuller
   C. most healthful
   D. Correct as is

8. A. less
   B. much lesser
   C. fewer
   D. Correct as is

9. A. good
   B. gooder
   C. more well
   D. Correct as is

10. A. indispensabler
    B. very indispensably
    C. indispensable
    D. Correct as is

MODIFIERS

Student Help Desk

Modifiers at a Glance

Unfortunately, the slight **itching on** my big **toe spread** overnight **into** an incredibly bad **case of athlete's foot.**

Adjectives describe *which one, what kind, how many,* or *how much.*

Adverbs describe *how, where, when,* or *to what extent.*

Commonly Confused Modifiers — From Bad to Good

Modifier	Example	Use
bad	It's a **bad** idea to exercise before bed.	*bad* as an adjective
	I felt **bad.**	*bad* as a predicate adjective
badly	The workout went **badly.**	*badly* as an adverb
good	Running is a **good** choice for aerobic exercise.	*good* as an adjective
	I always feel **good** after I run.	*good* as a predicate adjective
well	Karl seems **well.**	*well* as a predicate adjective
	Karl is sprinting **well** now.	*well* as an adverb

Double Negatives to Avoid — Knots of Not

Example	Revision
That recent injury **can't help but** hurt her performance on the track.	That recent injury **can't help** hurting her performance on the track.
I haven't but a few more sit-ups to go.	**I have but** a few more sit-ups to go. OR **I have only** a few more sit-ups to go.

HÄGAR the Horrible by Dik Browne

Degrees of Comparison More or Less

Modifier	Example	Use to . . .
-er	My left foot is **itchier** than my right foot.	compare two things
-est	My toes are the **itchiest** spot on my body right now.	compare three or more things
more	My toes are **more sensitive** today than they were yesterday.	compare two things
most	My big toe is the **most sensitive** of all my toes.	compare three or more things
less	I hope my feet are **less sensitive** tomorrow.	negatively compare the smaller (quantity) of two things
fewer	I seem to have **fewer** bouts of athlete's foot now that I wear sandals during the summer.	negatively compare the smaller (number) of two individual things
least	Oddly, my little toe itches the **least** of all my toes.	negatively compare three or more things

The Bottom Line

Checklist for Using Modifiers

Have I . . .

____ used modifiers to provide the necessary detail in my writing?

____ placed each modifier as closely as possible to the word it modifies?

____ chosen the correct adjective and adverb forms?

____ avoided using *here* or *there* with demonstrative pronouns?

____ used no more than one negative word such as *not* in a single negative?

____ avoided double or illogical comparisons?

____ formed complete comparisons by including words such as *than* or *as*?

MODIFIERS

Capitalization

Last night, the unthinkable occurred—
and before a huge crowd of agonized onlookers.
The hurricanes destroyed the tigers. It pains
me to even write the words. How could this
have happened?

Last night, the unthinkable occurred—
and before a huge crowd of agonized onlookers.
The Hurricanes destroyed the Tigers. It pains
me to even write the words. How could this
have happened?

Theme: Sports

Capitalizing on the News

In which part of the newspaper do you think you'd find the first statement? On the front page? In the weather section? Now read the second statement. Where do you think this statement belongs? Without capitals, the first sentence is confusing—and somewhat alarming. The capitals in the second sentence clear up the confusion. Or at least they give you a sporting chance.

Used correctly, capitalization can help prevent your readers from misunderstanding what you have to say. It's all a matter of learning the rules.

Write Away: Creative Capitalization

Write a paragraph that develops one of the highlighted statements above. Think about how the capitalization—or lack thereof—affects the meaning of the statements. Place the paragraph in your ▭ **Working Portfolio.**

Grammar Coach

Choose the letter that indicates the best way to correct each underlined section.

Badminton is alive and well in Indonesia, according to <u>R. A. J. Gosal,</u>
(1)
<u>General Secretary</u> of the <u>Indonesian Badminton Association (iba).</u> In the
(2)
17th century, <u>Dutch colonists brought the european game to Asia.</u> The
(3)
sport's popularity surged before <u>World war II</u> and continues to attract new
(4)
fans today. <u>"Badminton," as one man said, "Is my life."</u> The government in
(5)
<u>Jakarta, the capital of Indonesia,</u> has tried to focus this enthusiasm on
(6)
international competitions. <u>athletes put in long hours in centers</u>
(7)
<u>throughout the country.</u> Working hours are also intense for the employees

of the <u>Gadjah Mada company,</u> maker of shuttlecocks. Villagers in the town
(8)
of Solo dream of <u>Olympic Gold medals.</u> In fact, the town square is a
(9)
badminton court where people play from <u>6:30 a.m. to midnight.</u>
(10)

1. A. R. A. J. gosal
   B. general secretary
   C. General secretary
   D. Correct as is

2. A. indonesian badminton
      association
   B. Indonesian badminton
      association
   C. (IBA)
   D. Correct as is

3. A. dutch
   B. European
   C. asia
   D. Correct as is

4. A. World War II
   B. world war II
   C. world War II
   D. Correct as is

5. A. "badminton
   B. As
   C. "is
   D. Correct as is

6. A. jakarta
   B. Capital
   C. indonesia
   D. Correct as is

7. A. Athletes
   B. Centers
   C. Country
   D. Correct as is

8. A. gadjah mada company
   B. Gadjah mada company
   C. Gadjah Mada Company
   D. Correct as is

9. A. olympic
   B. gold
   C. Medals
   D. Correct as is

10. A. A.m.
    B. A.M.
    C. Midnight
    D. Correct as is

Names

❶ Here's the Idea

Proper Nouns and Adjectives

A **common noun,** which is not capitalized, names a general class or type of person, place, or thing. A **proper noun,** which is capitalized, names a specific person, place, or thing. A **proper adjective** is formed from a proper noun and is also capitalized. Compare these three types of items in the following chart.

Nouns and Adjectives		
Common Nouns	**Proper Nouns**	**Proper Adjectives**
country	Germany	German pastry
religion	Buddhism	Buddhist monk
director	Spielberg	Spielberg film
river	Nile	Nile crocodile
team	Yankees	Yankees hat

When proper nouns and adjectives occur in compound words, capitalize only those parts that would be capitalized alone. Prefixes such as *pre-, anti-,* and *sub-* are not capitalized when joined with proper nouns and adjectives.

　　pre-Civil War　　anti-American journal　　sub-Saharan nation

Names of Individuals

▶ **Capitalize the names and initials of persons.**

　　Madeleine Albright　　Samuel L. Jackson　　F. Scott Fitzgerald

Many names contain parts such as *de, Mac, O',* and *van.* Capitalization of these parts varies. Always verify the capitalization of a name with the person, or check the name in a reliable reference source. Here are some examples.

Daphne du Maurier	W. E. B. Du Bois
Douglas MacArthur	Terry McMillan
Robert De Niro	Elizabeth Borton de Treviño
Vincent van Gogh	Ludwig Mies Van Der Rohe

Abbreviations The abbreviations *Jr.* and *Sr.,* which fall after a person's name, are part of the name and should always be capitalized. The abbreviations are always preceded by a comma. Within a sentence, they are also followed by a comma if they don't come at the end of the sentence.

In 1995, Cal Ripken, Jr., broke Lou Gehrig's record by playing in his 2,131st consecutive game.

Cal Ripken, Jr.

Titles of Individuals

▶ **Capitalize titles and the abbreviations of titles used with personal names.**

Reverend Jesse Jackson   Senator Dianne Feinstein

Dr. Antonia Novello   Benjamin Spock, M.D.

Prof. Wong   William Cosby, Ed.D.

Capitalize titles when they are used in direct address, that is, when the speaker uses the title to address the person. In general, don't capitalize a title when it follows a person's name or when it is used alone.

What effect will the latest polls have on your policies, Mayor?

Richard J. Daley was the mayor of Chicago for more than 20 years.

However, capitalize the following titles when they are used alone to refer to the current holders of the positions.

the President (of the United States)   the Queen (of England)

the Vice-President (of the United States)   the Pope

Don't capitalize the prefix *ex-,* the suffix *-elect,* or the words *former* or *late* when used with a title.

Governor-elect Jones   the late Congressman Bono

In formal writing, use the word *former* rather than the suffix *ex-:* former President Bush, rather than ex-President Bush.

Family Relationships

▶ **Capitalize family names used before a proper noun or used in place of the name. Don't capitalize family names preceded by articles or possessive words.**

When Grandma drove to her kickboxing class, she saw Uncle Edward.

After my father moved here, he called his cousin.

❷ Practice and Apply

CONCEPT CHECK: Names

Identify and rewrite the words that contain capitalization errors in the following sentences.

From Couch to Basketball Court

1. My parents recall that in the 1960s, president lyndon b. johnson promoted physical fitness for america's youths.

2. Yet, according to my mom and dad, young people in the united states are less fit today than ever before.

3. Since my couch-potato habits over the past winter have left me looking more like jabba the Hut than luke skywalker, my parents started me on their own fitness campaign.

4. From a recent article that he read, dad learned that james o. hill, ph.d., has been exploring teen fitness.

5. An experimental program conducted by dr. hill at a high school in denver, colorado, has had great success in increasing the students' overall health.

6. Despite my argument that we live in portland, oregon, not denver, my parents insisted that I stop watching sports on television and start playing them.

7. Since mom knew that basketball is my favorite sport, she pointed out that it was invented in 1891 by james naismith as a physical-education program.

8. With the help of uncle dave, who once tried out for the trailblazers basketball team, we set up a hoop in our backyard and started playing regularly.

9. Now my uncle looks as good as he ever has in his post-trailblazer days.

10. I think dr. hill would be pleased to know that I am another teen in the united states who has left the couch behind.

➜ For a SELF-CHECK and more practice, see the EXERCISE BANK, p. 615.

❶ Here's the Idea

Capitalize the names of nationalities, languages, places, and religions. Also capitalize certain geographical names, regions, and historical and calendar items.

People and Cultures

▶ **Capitalize the names of ethnic groups, races, languages, and nationalities, as well as adjectives formed from these names.**

> **LITERARY MODEL**
>
> I could smell the chicken soup immediately, and I had only taken two or three steps when Manya, our Russian housekeeper, came running out of the kitchen.... She planted a wet kiss on my forehead, then held me at arm's length and began to babble in Ukrainian.
>
> —Chaim Potok, *The Chosen*

NAMES A NATIONALITY

NAMES A LANGUAGE

Religious Terms

▶ **Capitalize all names referring to religions and their followers, sacred days, sacred writings, and specific deities.**

Religious Terms		
Religions and followers	Judaism	Jew
	Islam	Muslim
Sacred days	Easter	Ramadan
	Passover	Sabbath
Sacred writings	Bible	Torah
	Koran	Gospel
Specific deities	God	Vishnu
	Allah	Holy Trinity

The words *god* and *goddess* are not capitalized when they refer to the deities of ancient mythology.

The Olympic athletes honored Nike, the Greek goddess of victory.

CAPITALIZATION

Geographical Names

▶ **Capitalize the names of specific places and regions.**

Geographical Names and Regions		
Cities, states	San Francisco Hong Kong	North Dakota Texas
Regions	West East Coast	New England Pacific Northwest
Countries	Pakistan Somalia	Brazil Canada
Parts of the world	North America Asia	Southern Hemisphere Middle East
Land features	Rocky Mountains Sahara	Channel Islands Balkan Peninsula
Bodies of water	Caribbean Sea Indian Ocean	Lake Michigan Bay of Bengal
Streets, highways	1600 Pennsylvania Avenue Sunset Boulevard	Highway 101 Indiana Tollroad

Capitalize words that refer to sections of the country but not to directions of the compass.

The South has produced many great writers.

These days, fewer city birds head south for the winter.

Historical and Calendar Items

▶ **Capitalize the names of historical events, historical periods, and calendar items, including days, months, and holidays.**

Historical and Calendar Items		
Historical events	Revolutionary War Boxer Rebellion	World War II Reign of Terror
Historical periods	Renaissance Jurassic Period	Victorian Era Middle Ages
Calendar items	Friday November	Groundhog Day Father's Day

Don't capitalize the name of seasons: spring, summer, winter, autumn.

❷ Practice and Apply

A. CONCEPT CHECK: Other Names and Places

Identify and rewrite the words that contain capitalization errors in the following sentences.

World of Sports

1. After world war II, india gained its independence from england, but british influence is reflected in india's love of cricket.
2. *Chariots of Fire* tells the story of two british runners: Eric Liddell, a devout christian who refused to run on sundays, and Harold Abrahams, a jew who battled anti-semitism.
3. Bullfighting is a popular spectacle in spain, mexico, and portugal; but a form of the sport was practiced on the island of crete as long as 6,000 years ago.
4. Many of the top runners in kenya—which arguably produces the best distance runners in the world—come from a small area around the rift valley.
5. Jai alai, which means "merry festival" in the basque language, developed over three centuries ago in the basque area of spain's pyrenees mountain range.

→ **For a SELF-CHECK and more practice, see the EXERCISE BANK, p. 615.**

B. PROOFREADING: Capitalizing Names and Places

Rewrite the following paragraph from a travel brochure, correcting any capitalization errors.

Traditional Sports

Sports fans may be interested in witnessing an unusual ball game, which takes place on the island of kyushu in japan. Every january, men play the game before a shinto shrine in the city of fukuoka. The name of the game in english is "the ball struggle of Hakozaki Shrine." It is played shortly after new year's day; the winning team will have good luck throughout the year. To people from the west, the game may seem senseless. Two teams of japanese players, dressed in loincloths, push and shove in an effort to grab the wooden ball and place it before the shrine. If the team representing the Sea wins, a big catch of fish should be in store; if the team representing the Land wins, a good harvest is expected.

A. Capitalizing Names and Places For each sentence, write the words that should be capitalized.

The Grand Slam

1. The four major tournaments in tennis—known as "the grand slam"— are held in australia, france, england, and the united states.
2. The british tournament, called Wimbledon, is held in a suburb of london.
3. Some of Wimbledon's past male champions include arthur ashe, jr., bjorn borg, john mcenroe, jr., and pete sampras.
4. The Australian Open, held in melbourne, is played in january.
5. Players at the Australian Open don't freeze, however, because in the southern hemisphere, january is a summer month.
6. The French Open is played in paris in late may–early june.
7. The central stadium at the French Open is named after french aviator roland garros, a world war I hero who was shot down in october 1918.
8. The U.S. Open—sometimes called the toughest tournament in tennis—is played in september just outside of new york city.
9. Fans of the U.S. Open include david dinkins, the former mayor of new york city, and bill cosby, ed.d.
10. Many of the major tournaments coincide with holidays: the French Open with memorial day, Wimbledon with the fourth of july, and the U.S. Open with labor day.

B. Proofreading for Capitalization Identify and rewrite the words that contain capitalization errors in the following paragraphs.

History of Tennis

Many historians believe that the first recognizable form of tennis—or Real Tennis, as it is called in great britain—was played in the 11th century in french and italian monasteries. There, christian monks played the game by hitting the ball with their hands. The monks apparently enjoyed the game so much that the pope eventually banned it. The game became a pastime of the french and english nobility and, by the 16th century, was virtually indistinguishable from the game that's played today.

Tennis gained great popularity in england in the tudor and stuart periods. In fact, king henry VIII became such an avid player that many of his gambling debts were due to wagers lost on the tennis court. The game was even less kind to king james I, who tried to hide from his assassins in a drain but found his path blocked by tennis balls.

Organizations and Other Subjects

LESSON 3

① Here's the Idea

Capitalize the names of organizations and institutions, certain astronomical terms, vehicles, and landmarks. Some school terms and the names of awards, special events, and brand names should also be capitalized.

Organizations and Institutions

▶ **Capitalize all important words in the names of organizations, including teams and businesses. Capitalize all important words in the names of institutions, including schools, hospitals, and government and political bodies.**

Organizations and Institutions	
Organizations	National Organization for Women Houston Astros
Businesses	General Motors Corporation Columbia Records
Institutions	Tulane University Mayo Clinic
Government bodies	Supreme Court House of Representatives
Political parties	Democratic Party Libertarian Party

Don't capitalize words such as *democratic, republican,* and *communist* when they refer to principles or forms of government. Capitalize them when they refer to specific political parties.

China's communist government discourages dissenting views.

The Republican Party will hold its convention here next year.

Astronomical Terms

▶ **Capitalize the names of stars, planets, galaxies, constellations, and other heavenly bodies.**

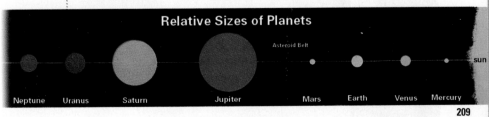

Relative Sizes of Planets

Asteroid Belt

sun

Neptune   Uranus   Saturn   Jupiter   Mars   Earth   Venus   Mercury

CAPITALIZATION

209

Do not capitalize *sun* and *moon*. Capitalize *earth* only when it is used in context with other capitalized astronomical terms. Never capitalize *earth* when it is preceded by the article *the*.

> Students compared their weights on Earth, Mars, and Venus.

> After returning to earth, the astronaut stared wistfully at the moon.

Vehicles and Landmarks

▶ **Capitalize the names of specific ships, trains, airplanes, and spacecraft. Also capitalize the names of monuments, memorials, and other landmarks.**

Titanic	*Challenger*
Orient Express	Navajo National Monument
Spirit of St. Louis	Vietnam Veteran Memorial

Notice that the names of ships, trains, airplanes, and spacecraft are italicized.

School Subjects and Terms

▶ **Capitalize the names of school subjects when they refer to specific courses. Do not capitalize the general names of school subjects—except language courses. Capitalize the words *freshman*, *sophomore*, *junior*, and *senior* only when they are part of a proper noun.**

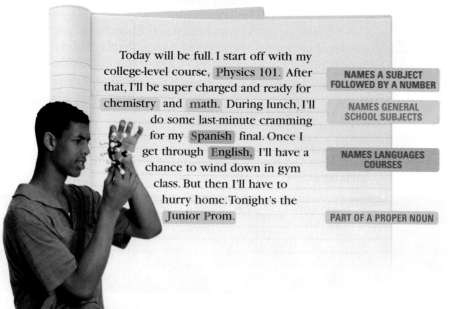

Today will be full. I start off with my college-level course, Physics 101. After that, I'll be super charged and ready for chemistry and math. During lunch, I'll do some last-minute cramming for my Spanish final. Once I get through English, I'll have a chance to wind down in gym class. But then I'll have to hurry home. Tonight's the Junior Prom.

NAMES A SUBJECT FOLLOWED BY A NUMBER

NAMES GENERAL SCHOOL SUBJECTS

NAMES LANGUAGES COURSES

PART OF A PROPER NOUN

Awards, Special Events, and Brand Names

▶ **Capitalize the names of awards, special events, and brand names.**

Awards, Special Events, and Brand Names	
Awards	Purple Heart, Oscar, National Book Award
Special events	Boston Marathon, Olympics (but Olympic games), Indiana State Fair
Brand names	Cat's Meow, Tendertouch, InfoComp

❷ Practice and Apply

A. CONCEPT CHECK: Organizations & Other Subjects

Identify and rewrite the words that contain capitalization errors in the following sentences.

Diana Golden: Going for the Gold

1. At the age of 12, Diana Golden was admitted to a Hospital, where her cancerous leg was removed.
2. Even though she had hated Gym Class, she loved to ski and soon learned to perform the sport on one leg.
3. When Diana was a Junior at lincoln-sudbury high school, the skiing coach talked her into working out with the ski team.
4. By her Senior year, Diana was competing in the world games for the disabled in Geilo, Norway.
5. Soon she had won the downhill event at the world games for the disabled.
6. When she was a Sophomore at dartmouth, the pressure of being considered a role model became overwhelming.
7. Diana didn't think a Monument should be erected to her and quit skiing for a few years.
8. When Diana returned to the sport, she asked the rossignol ski company to sponsor her.
9. Diana went on to win ten gold medals at the world games for the disabled.
10. She dominated the world disabled ski championships from 1986 to 1990.

➔ For a SELF-CHECK and more practice, see the EXERCISE BANK, p. 616.

B. EDITING: Using Capitalization Correctly

Look in your 📁 **Working Portfolio** at the paragraph you wrote for page 200. Use what you've learned to correct any capitalization errors.

First Words and Titles

❶ Here's the Idea

Capitalize the first word in a sentence and the important words in titles.

First Words

▶ **Capitalize the first words of sentences and direct quotations that are complete sentences.** The first word of this sentence is capitalized.

Tickets to the championship game are very expensive.

Capitalize the first word of a direct quotation if it is a complete sentence. Do not capitalize a direct quotation if it is a fragment of a sentence.

"We bought tickets," Al said, "in the nose-bleed section."

The announcer said that it was "a great day at the ballpark."

▶ **Capitalize the first word of each item in an outline and the letters that introduce major subsections.** Notice the use of capitalization in the following outline.

> I. Overview of basketball
> A. Rules of the game
> B. Legendary players
>   1. Past heroes
>   2. Present champions

▶ **Capitalize the first word in each line of traditional poetry.**

> **LITERARY MODEL**
>
> What could I do but yell *vivas*
>
> To baseball, milkshakes, and those sociologists
>
> Who would clock me
>
> As I jog into the next century
>
> On the power of a great, silly grin.
>
> —Gary Soto, "Mexicans Begin Jogging"

When quoting fewer than four lines of poetry, use slash marks to separate the lines, and imitate the capitalization of the original poem.

"Success is counted sweetest / By those who ne'er succeed."

The first lines of some poems are not capitalized—particularly in modern poetry. A prime example is E. E. Cummings, whose poetry is usually presented in lowercase.

Pronoun *I*

▶ **Always capitalize the pronoun *I*.**

I grabbed the ball and ran with it as if I'd been intercepting passes all my life.

Titles

▶ **Capitalize the first, last, and all other important words in titles, including verbs. Do not capitalize conjunctions, articles, or prepositions with fewer than five letters.**

Book Title	*Coming of Age in Mississippi*
Short Story Title	"In the American Society"
Movie Title	*Life Is Beautiful*
Song Title	"Rock Around the Clock"

❷ Practice and Apply

CONCEPT CHECK: First Words and Titles

Identify and rewrite the words that contain capitalization errors in the following sentences.

A Long Day at the Ballpark

1. Bud and Jim, the hosts of the popular talk-radio show *super fans and fanatics,* prepared to call the game.
2. the batter connected on the first pitch. "that ball," said Jim, rising for a better look, "is going, going, gone."
3. at the end of the first inning, the game was close at 6-5. "Folks, this is not," said Bud, "What i'd call a pitchers' duel."
4. At the seventh-inning stretch, Bud led the crowd in an off-key rendition of "take me out to the ballgame."
5. people began streaming out of the stadium when the game tied in the ninth. one woman shook her head saying, "you know, i can't take extra innings of this."

➡ **For a SELF-CHECK and more practice, see the EXERCISE BANK, p. 616.**

CAPITALIZATION

Abstract

LESSON 5 **Abbreviations**

❶ Here's the Idea

Capitalize abbreviations of place names, abbreviations related to time, and abbreviations of organizations and government agencies.

Place Names

▶ **Capitalize the abbreviations of cities, states, countries, and other places.**

NJ	U.S.	Washington, **D.C.**
NYC	U.K.	Eur.

Use a state abbreviation only in an address or reference, not in formal writing.

Time

▶ **Capitalize the abbreviations B.C., A.D., A.M., and P.M.**

The ancient Greek Olympics lasted from at least 776 **B.C.** to **A.D.** 393.

I practice my serve from 10:00 **A.M.** until 3:00 **P.M.**

Organizations and Agencies

▶ **Capitalize the abbreviations of organizations and agencies by using the initial letters of the complete name. Notice that these abbreviations do not usually take periods.**

FBI (Federal Bureau of Investigation)

UNICEF (United Nations International Children's Emergency Fund)

UN (United Nations)

Non Sequitur by Wiley

② Practice and Apply

Identify and rewrite any abbreviation errors in the following sentences.

Mere Mortals

1. In a.d. 400 in Constantinople, spectators cheered their gladiators to an often bloody victory.
2. In a.d. 200, Tertullian wrote that the champions of the chariot races did not deserve the devotion of the spectators.
3. According to writer Sean Paige, hero worship of today's nba and nfl players is as undeserved as the worship of gladiators in Roman times.
4. Paige has written that sports figures are now covered 24 hours a day by espn, abc, nbc, and the other television networks.
5. Paige's concerns echo those of sport writers across the u.s. who say they have seen a decline in good sportsmanship over the past few years.
6. Around the clock, a.m. or p.m., sports fans can tune in to a wide assortment of unsportsmanlike behavior, often displayed by superstar players.
7. Now many critics are concerned about the rise in popularity of the wwf and wcw, two professional wrestling leagues that have attracted fans once devoted to other sports.
8. Using promotional tactics that are reminiscent of circus sideshows, these leagues have even lured nba players into the ring.
9. An abc news show examined the fact that young viewers nationwide are imitating their favorite wrestlers in violent backyard games.
10. Viewers from l.a. to Washington, d.c., need to accept that the heroes they imitate are mere mortals.

➡ **For a SELF-CHECK and more practice, see the EXERCISE BANK, p. 617.**

CAPITALIZATION

Real World Grammar

Sports Article

When you write a sports article, you know your readers expect to find out the results of a game or learn about a favorite player. This means that you need to get quotes and the names of teams, players, and places right. Errors in capitalization can confuse your readers and detract from your writing. Luckily, the reporter who wrote the following article had an eagle-eyed editor proofread her work. Which of these errors have you seen in sports articles?

Capitalize the important words in titles.

Capitalize the names of teams.

Capitalize place names but not directions.

Capitalize special events.

Soccer sensations sock it to seals

The much anticipated soccer match last night between the Ramblers and the seals didn't disappoint. The Ramblers took control early and drove the ball down Owen field. The Seal defense seemed sluggish as, again and again, they allowed the team from the North side of town to dictate play.

Then, with the Ramblers up 2–0 at the beginning of the second period, the Seals came to life. Guard Rosa Chen stole the ball and passed it to teammate Chantal D'antonio. In a move worthy of the world cup, Chantal deftly lofted the ball over the Rambler goalie to cut the lead in half.

An indirect free kick awarded to the Seals resulted in a 2–2 tie with two minutes left in the period. That's when Rambler Senior Erin Andrews stepped up and dribbled the ball all the way down the field. Over the cheers of the crowd, coach Washington directed play. "Run the ball," he yelled to Erin. "find the opening." Erin found the opening over the goalie's head. Her last-minute drive gave the Ramblers a 3–2 edge and the game.

Capitalize school terms properly.

Capitalize personal titles.

Check the Capitalization of the player's names.

Capitalize quotations correctly.

The

Today a new writer i joining The Condor. name is John Stein He is a Senior at E High School. In h time he enjoys wri soccer, and baseb are very happy th will be joining the

Using Grammar in Writing

Personal names and titles	Verify the spelling of players' and coaches' names and capitalize any titles used with the names.
Names of teams	Be sure to capitalize properly the names of teams and leagues.
Place names	Properly capitalize the names of places, including playing fields, but don't capitalize directions of the compass.
School terms	Remember that the words *freshman, sophomore, junior,* and *senior* are capitalized only when they are part of a proper noun.
Names of special events	If you refer to a special sporting event, such as the Olympics or World Cup, be sure to capitalize its name.
Quotations	Be sure to quote your sources accurately and pay particular attention to the capitalization of divided quotations.

PRACTICE AND APPLY: Writing

The following are notes taken during a post-game interview with Ramblers star forward Erin Andrews. As you can see, the reporter wrote the notes using only lowercase letters. Use the notes to write a one-paragraph article on Erin. Be sure to use capitalization correctly.

> born in grand rapids, michigan
>
> became interested in soccer after watching the olympics
>
> graduates in the fall; plans to go to nyu
>
> "i'd like to major in french," she says, "with possibly a minor in p.e."
>
> immediate future: preparing for play-off game next friday at 4 p.m.

Mixed Review

A. Using Capitalization Correctly For each sentence, identify and rewrite the words and abbreviations that contain capitalization errors.

Olympics: Past, Present, and Future

1. In a.d. 393, emperor theodosius banned the greek olympics because gambling and cheating had ruined the games.
2. In 1896, a parisian nobleman named baron pierre de coubertin founded the modern olympic movement.
3. he wanted to unite the countries of the Earth in a global spirit of sportsmanship, but the games have frequently been affected by international events.
4. adolf hitler wanted to use the 1936 olympics in berlin to prove aryan superiority.
5. In the 1972 munich olympic games, arab terrorists took israeli athletes as hostages and killed two other athletes from israel.
6. After the ussr invaded afghanistan, president carter called a u.s. boycott of the games in moscow in 1980.
7. Likewise, moscow boycotted the 1984 olympic games in l.a.
8. In 1996, the olympic games in atlanta were marred by the presence of a terrorist armed with a pipe bomb.
9. Scandals involving salt lake city's bid for the 2002 olympics rocked the ioc, the international olympic committee.
10. Nonetheless, the heroics and artistry of athletes such as american gymnast kerri strug and ukrainian figure skater oksana baiul consistently restore people's faith in the olympics.

B. Identifying Errors in Capitalization Proofread the following letter, rewriting any words or abbreviations that contain capitalization errors.

Letter from a Figure Skating Fan
(1) ms. josephine whey
(2) Sporting book nook
(3) 555 Bo Peep lane
(4) Clear Lake, mi 48332

Dear Ms. Whey,
(5) For many years my Sister and I have read everything about figure skating. (6) Now there is one book i am anxious to find, but i don't know its title. (7) My sister said, "write to ms. whey. she'll find it." (8) I can tell you that the book was written by a reporter for the *washington post*. (9) The author follows the lives of figure skaters from october 1994 to february 1995 and includes interviews with olympic judges. (10) Anyway, i'm desperate; so if you know the book, please call me any evening after 7:30 p.m., and let me know its title.

Choose the letter that indicates the best way to rewrite each underlined section.

Many people know the great <u>basketball player reggie miller</u>, but few
(1)

know the physical obstacles he had to overcome. <u>because</u> he was born with
(2)

deformed hips and ankles that turned inward, Reggie had to wear metal

braces when he was a boy. The doctors told him that he would never walk

without a limp. <u>However, his Mother</u> never stopped believing in her son.
(3)

"The doctors," she said to Reggie, "<u>Are wrong. You'll</u> walk again." The
(4)

braces came off when Reggie entered <u>Elementary School</u>. After his legs
(5)

gained strength, he began running and playing basketball with <u>his sister</u>
(6)

<u>Cheryl</u>. Her more experienced game challenged him to improve his own

shots—and it paid off. Years later, he was drafted by the <u>nba</u>. In 1996, as a
(7)

member of the <u>american dream team</u>, he won a gold medal at the <u>olympic</u>
(8)   (9)

<u>games in atlanta</u>. He is certainly destined for entry in the <u>basketball hall</u>
(10)

<u>of fame</u>.

---

1. A. Basketball player Reggie Miller
   B. Basketball Player Reggie Miller
   C. basketball player Reggie Miller
   D. Correct as is

2. A. Because
   B. "Because
   C. "because
   D. Correct as is

3. A. however, his Mother
   B. However, his mother
   C. however, his mother
   D. Correct as is

4. A. "are wrong. you'll
   B. "are wrong. You'll
   C. "Are wrong. you'll
   D. Correct as is

5. A. Elementary school
   B. elementary School
   C. elementary school
   D. Correct as is

6. A. his Sister Cheryl
   B. his sister cheryl
   C. his Sister cheryl
   D. Correct as is

7. A. NBA
   B. Nba
   C. NbA
   D. Correct as is

8. A. American Dream Team
   B. American dream team
   C. American Dream team
   D. Correct as is

9. A. Olympic Games in Atlanta
   B. olympic games in Atlanta
   C. Olympic games in Atlanta
   D. Correct as is

10. A. Basketball Hall of Fame
    B. basketball Hall of Fame
    C. basketball Hall of fame
    D. Correct as is

Student Help Desk

Capitalization at a Glance

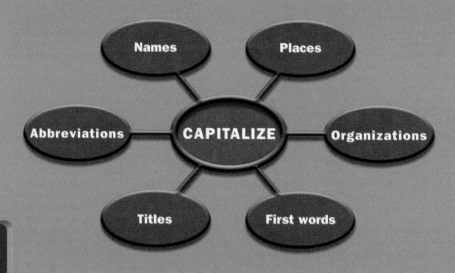

Capitals and Lowercase Letters

Major and Minor League Players

Caps	No Caps
Governor Fong	the governor
Aunt Mildred	her aunt
Venus, Andromeda, Orion	moon, sun, the earth
Southwest, East Coast	south, east
Shiva	goddess
December, Mother's Day	winter, spring
Democratic Party	democratic principles
Chemistry 101	chemistry class

Word Acronyms

laser	(**l**)ight (**a**)mplification by (**s**)timulated (**e**)mission of (**r**)adiation
PIN	(**P**)ersonal (**I**)dentification (**N**)umber
radar	(**ra**)dio (**d**)etecting (**a**)nd (**r**)anging
RAM	(**R**)andom (**A**)ccess (**M**)emory
ROM	(**R**)ead-(**O**)nly (**M**)emory
scuba	(**s**)elf-(**c**)ontained (**u**)nderwater (**b**)reathing (**a**)pparatus
sonar	(**so**)und (**na**)vigation and (**r**)anging
SWAT team	(**S**)pecial (**W**)eapons (**A**)nd (**T**)actics

Capitals Online Play by the Rules

Case-Sensitive Addresses	Capital and lowercase letters are important in e-mail addresses. You won't be able to make a connection if you use them incorrectly. Record them accurately and save them.
Case-Sensitive Systems	The names of many systems and search engines have specialized capitalization. For example: the World Wide Web, *WebCrawler*, *AltaVista*.
Shouting	DON'T SEND A MESSAGE IN ALL CAPITALS. Doing so is referred to as "shouting" and will offend your readers.

End Marks and Commas

NOT A
THROUGH
STREET

NO
OUTLET

Theme: Driving Experiences

Please, Give Me a Sign!

Most of the time, you probably pay little attention to street signs. However, if you've ever been lost, as either a driver or a passenger, you know how frustrating a poorly marked street sign and unclear directions can be. In your writing, end marks and commas provide similar visual guidance. Without these clues, most readers would have trouble following your ideas from point A to point B. This chapter will show you how to use end marks and commas correctly in your writing to keep your readers headed in the right direction.

Write Away: Get Me Out of Here

Think about a time that you were lost. Write a paragraph about the experience, and then place your writing in your
📁 **Working Portfolio.**

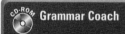
CD-ROM **Grammar Coach**

Diagnostic Test: What Do You Know?

Write the letter of the best revision for each underlined section.

> If you're looking for a scenic road trip, consider taking a drive on
> <u>Route 66 which</u> runs through many towns from <u>Chicago, Illinois, to Los
> (1)   (2)
> Angeles, California</u>. With its legendary <u>road signs, gas stations and burger
> (3)
> shacks, Route 66</u> offers a taste of the U.S.A. <u>in all its vintage glory.</u> Born of
> (4)
> the Transportation <u>Act of 1921, the road, stretches</u> over 2,400 miles and
> (5)
> across eight states. Route 66 was conceived by <u>Cyrus Stevens Avery a
> (6)
> highway commissioner</u> from Oklahoma. Completed in 1926, the road
> symbolized freedom to many travelers. Some early motorists called Route
> 66 the <u>Mother Road, others America's</u> Main Street. Today, drivers still
> (7)
> celebrate the road with Web sites, rallies, and clubs. Some drivers plan
> trips along the road's surviving stretches. The longest is in <u>Arizona,
> (8)
> obviously</u> Route 66 may not be the fastest U.S. highway, but to some
> people who love this historic road, the drive is the whole point of the trip!

1. A. Route 66, which
   B. Route 66 (which
   C. Route 66. Which
   D. Correct as is

2. A. Chicago Illinois to Los Angeles
   B. Chicago, Illinois to Los Angeles,
   C. Chicago Illinois, to Los Angeles
   D. Correct as is

3. A. road signs, gas stations and
      burger shacks. Route 66
   B. road signs, gas stations, and
      burger shacks, Route 66
   C. road signs, gas stations and
      burger shacks Route 66
   D. Correct as is

4. A. in all its vintage glory!
   B. in all it's vintage glory.
   C. in all, its vintage glory.
   D. Correct as is

5. A. Act of 1921 the road stretches
   B. Act of 1921, the road stretches
   C. Act of 1921, the road stretches,
   D. Correct as is

6. A. Cyrus Stevens Avery, a
      highway commissioner
   B. Cyrus Stevens Avery a
      highway commissioner,
   C. Cyrus Stevens Avery, a
      highway commissioner,
   D. Correct as is

7. A. Mother Road; others, America's
   B. Mother Road. Others America's
   C. Mother Road, others, America's
   D. Correct as is

8. A. Arizona. Obviously!
   B. Arizona obviously,
   C. Arizona. Obviously,
   D. Correct as is

Periods and Other End Marks

❶ Here's the Idea

End marks include periods, question marks, and exclamation points. This chart shows you how to use them correctly.

End Marks

Using End Marks		
End Mark	**Use after . . .**	**Example**
Period	• a declarative sentence	The key to good driving is concentration.
	• an imperative sentence	Follow that car.
	• an indirect question	He asked if I was too tired to drive.
Exclamation point	• an exclamatory sentence	What phenomenal skill she has!
	• a strong interjection	Oh, no!
	• words that express a sound	Crash!
Question mark	• an interrogative sentence	Did you check the oil?
	• a declarative sentence that asks a question	You ran out of gas?

For more about using end marks with direct quotations and parentheses, see p. 252 and p. 256.

Other Uses of Periods

Periods are also used with abbreviations and in outlines.

Putting Periods in the Proper Places		
Usage	**Rule**	**Example**
Abbreviations	Use a period with abbreviations or initials.	Mr. Emil T. Schmidt, Sr., Sat., 2 A.M., A.D., 1 hr., 32 ft., Main St., Ala., Speedy Tires Ltd.
Outlines	Use a period after each number or letter in an outline or list.	A. Longest traffic jam B. Oldest driver C. Biggest car

CHAPTER 9

Do not include periods with these abbreviations: metric measurements (cm ml kg g l), acronyms (NATO UNICEF NASA NASCAR), abbreviations that are pronounced letter by letter (CIA NBA IRS), state names in postal addresses (TX CA FL), points on a compass (N E S W).

❷ Practice and Apply

CONCEPT CHECK: Periods and Other End Marks

Add periods, question marks, and exclamation points as needed in the following sentences.

Driving for Fun and Profit

1. If someone said that you could earn money with your driving skills, what would your response be
2. As a part-time driver, you could probably earn more than minimum wage, without working from 9 AM to 5 PM every Saturday and Sunday
3. Most driving jobs can be divided into two categories:
   1 chauffeuring passengers
   2 delivering goods.
4. Should absolutely every teen apply for a driving job
5. Oh, no; absolutely not
6. Someone who speeds down the street like a NASCAR racer need not apply, for a paid driver must have an outstanding record
7. You might wonder what types of people would pay for driving services
8. Your neighbors might be interested in hiring you to run errands—especially when they see what a safe driver you are
9. What kinds of businesses do you think might hire you
10. Think about all of the local businesses, from Joe Jr's Pizza Shop to Margie's Main St Flowers Ltd, that deliver goods every day

➡ **For a SELF-CHECK and more practice, see the EXERCISE BANK, p. 618.**

COMMAS

Commas in Sentence Parts

1 Here's the Idea

When you speak, you rely on certain cues, such as pauses and body language, to help express your ideas. When you write, your use of such punctuation as commas supplies similar cues. The following rules for comma usage will help you communicate your ideas more clearly.

Commas with Introductory Elements

▶ **Use a comma after mild interjections or introductory words such as *oh, yes, no,* and *well.***

Yes, I admit that I love to watch the Daytona 500.

▶ **Use a comma after an introductory prepositional phrase that contains additional prepositional phrases.**

In the middle of the race, the lead car blew out a tire.

▶ **Use a comma after an introductory adverb or adverbial clause.**

Unfortunately, that car is out of the race.

After the pace car exits the track, drivers may reach speeds of over 200 mph.

▶ **Use a comma after an infinitive or participial phrase that serves as an introductory element.**

INFINITIVE PHRASE

To cover their expenses, racing teams solicit sponsors.

PARTICIPIAL PHRASE

Smiling politely, the driver accepted a $200,000 check.

For more on phrases, see p. 48, and for more on clauses, see p. 76.

Commas with Interrupters

▶ **Use commas to set off nouns of direct address.** A noun of direct address is the word naming the person or persons spoken to.

Marisa, have you ever worked as part of a pit crew?

Mother Goose & Grimm by Mike Peters

▶ **Use commas to set off parenthetical expressions, such as** ***however, therefore, for example, I suppose, moreover,*** **and** ***by the way.*** A parenthetical expression interrupts the flow of thought in a sentence.

PARENTHETICAL

By the way, your favorite driver will participate in the next heat.

NOT PARENTHETICAL

You can tell by the way Janet Guthrie drives that she has a great deal of experience.

Use a comma to separate a question tagged onto the end of a sentence.

That's a fairly common way of speaking, isn't it?

Commas with Nonessential Clauses and Phrases

▶ **Use commas to set off nonessential clauses and nonessential participial phrases.**

NONESSENTIAL CLAUSE

The pit crew manager, who also serves as the chief engineer, advised the driver of the car's condition.

NONESSENTIAL PARTICIPIAL PHRASE

The team, working hard for its driver's success, has won several races this year.

NONESSENTIAL CLAUSE

The woman, **who won last year,** will compete today.
(By the way, that woman won last year.)

ESSENTIAL CLAUSE

The woman **who won last year** will compete today.
(Last year's winner is competing again.)

▶ **Use commas to set off nonessential appositives and appositive phrases.**

Eddie Cheever's racing team, **Team Cheever,** has won the Indy 500.

Professional auto racing, **often a very dangerous sport,** requires extensive training and well-maintained equipment.

For more on phrases, see p. 48, and for more on clauses, see p. 76.

Commas with Compound Sentences

▶ **Use a comma before the conjunction that joins the two independent clauses of a compound sentence.**

Ted had the best opening lap, but he lost the race.

 Make sure you're punctuating a compound sentence, not a simple sentence with a compound predicate.

Ted had the best opening lap but lost the race.

For more about compound sentences, see p. 88.

Commas with Series or Lists

▶ **In a series of three or more items, use a comma after each item except the last one.**

Racetracks can have **dirt, asphalt, or concrete** surfaces.

▶ **Use a comma between two or more adjectives of equal rank that modify the same noun.**

A **skilled, athletic** pit crew should be able to get a driver back on the racetrack in less than 20 seconds.

Do not use a comma if one adjective in a series modifies another.

The driver in the **olive green** car is winning.

 To tell if two or more adjectives modifying the same noun require any commas, place the word *and* between the adjectives. If the sentence still makes sense, replace *and* with a comma.

❷ Practice and Apply

A. CONCEPT CHECK: Commas in Sentence Parts

Nineteen commas are missing from the sentences below.
Write the word before and the word after each missing
comma, adding the comma between them.

Avoid That Lemon!
1. Your first car may not be a brand-new model
   but you don't have to settle for a lemon either.
2. Affordable reliable used cars do exist.
3. To help you get the most for your money here is some time-
   tested advice.
4. Always bring along a responsible adult when you check out
   any car new or old you'd like to purchase.
5. Also if possible have a used car checked out by an
   experienced dependable mechanic.
6. When you take a test drive pay attention to how well the car
   accelerates the brakes function and the gears shift.
7. Be certain that all equipment (including the lights windshield
   wipers gauges and engine) is in good condition.
8. Also find out whether the car comes with a warranty.
9. In addition by consulting the *Kelley Blue Book* listing you can
   determine whether the price is fair.
10. Finally no matter how desperately you want a car always
    shop around before making a purchase.

➔ For a SELF-CHECK and more practice, see the EXERCISE BANK, p. 618.

B. EDITING: Revising Sentences with Commas

In your 🗀 **Working Portfolio,** find the writing you created for the
Write Away on page 222. Proofread your writing for correct comma
usage, and revise it as necessary.

C. WRITING: Using Commas in Sentences

Combine the words in the columns below to create four descriptive
phrases; then write a paragraph about a driving adventure,
including at least two of the phrases you created. Be sure to
correctly punctuate your writing with commas and end marks.

twisting	mountain passes
icy	snow-covered roads
clear	open highway
brand-new	shiny vehicle

LESSON 3 Using Commas for Clarity

❶ Here's the Idea

The following rules can help you use commas to clarify your ideas for readers.

Adding Commas for Clarity

▶ **Use a comma to separate words that might be misread.**

Unclear: Outside the trees seemed to race past the car windows.

Clear: Outside, the trees seemed to race past the car windows.

▶ **Use a comma to replace an omitted word or words.**

Some car or RV travelers prefer to drive all day; others prefer to drive all night.

Some car or RV travelers prefer to drive all day; others, all night.

▶ **When making a contrast, use a comma with antithetical phrases that use words such as *not* and *unlike*.**

Driving to another state, unlike flying, allows you to pack all the clothing you want for a trip.

Read your writing aloud to find awkward sentences that might need commas or additional reworking.

Eliminating Comma Splices

A **comma splice** occurs when you use a comma to separate two main clauses. To correct this error, you can replace the comma with a period or a semicolon, or you could add a coordinating conjunction, such as *and, or, so,* or *but* after the comma.

Comma splice: Travelers who car camp don't actually sleep in their cars, they camp out in sleeping bags or tents.

Possible fixes: Travelers who car camp don't actually sleep in their cars. **They** camp out in sleeping bags or tents.

Travelers who car camp don't actually sleep in their cars; **they** camp out in sleeping bags or tents.

Travelers who car camp don't actually sleep in their cars, **but** they camp out in sleeping bags or tents.

CHAPTER 9

❷ Practice and Apply

A. CONCEPT CHECK: Using Commas for Clarity

Add commas, as needed, to clarify sentences. Revise sentences
that contain comma splices.

Road Rallying

1. Road rallies unlike the Grand Prix or Indy 500 may be open
to standard automobiles and amateur drivers.

2. With courses on the open road rallies began in the 1890s.

3. Some road rallies test endurance and speed, other rallies
penalize drivers for speeding.

4. Today, some road rallies take place on paved roadways;
others on rugged back roads.

5. Dating back to 1910, the famous Monte Carlo rally begins in
a different city each year, it ends in the beautiful city that
gave the rally its name.

6. Because the Monte Carlo and other rallies are run on real
highways and streets not oval tracks drivers must use
special caution.

7. Odometers record mileage; stopwatches time.

8. Aware of average speeds officials penalize drivers who arrive
at rally checkpoints before or after the specified times.

9. In a rally drivers face the challenging demands of a strict
timetable and unfamiliar roadways.

10. Yet, rallying continues to be a popular American event, the
contests are held all over the United States.

➡ **For a SELF-CHECK and more practice, see the EXERCISE BANK, p. 619.**

B. REVISING: Correcting Comma Usage

Correct any comma errors to create correctly punctuated
sentences for each of the following bumper sticker statements.

Example: The kids drive me crazy, I drive them everywhere.
Correction: The kids drive me crazy. I drive them everywhere.

1. Go on, I'll see you at the next light.

2. Do not wash, this vehicle is undergoing a scientific, dirt test.

3. Except from a vending machine change is inevitable.

4. I used to be indecisive, now I'm not so sure.

5. Don't laugh, it's paid for.

Create your own correctly punctuated bumper sticker or slogan.

Other Comma Rules

❶ Here's the Idea

Other Uses for Commas

Use a comma . . .	Example
to set off a personal title or a business abbreviation	Even Janina Popek, Ph.D., failed her first driver's test.
in the salutation of a personal letter and the closing of any letter	Dear Tyla, Is your car still for sale? Your friend, Lan
between the day of the month and the year (and after the year in a complete date within a sentence)	The next driver's ed class starts June 16, 2001, at Wayne High School. The class runs until August 2001.
to separate the street, city, and state in addresses and names of places	I sold my car to Wylie Autos, 121 Clark St., Austin, Texas, last year.
in numbers of more than three digits to denote thousands	In 1999, I drove over 20,000 miles.
to set off a direct quotation from the rest of the sentence	"Turn left at the light," he said.

For more about using commas with quotation marks, see p. 252.

For more about using commas with quotation marks, see p. 252.

Notice how commas are used in the personal letter below.

STUDENT MODEL

Dear Kyle, — SALUTATION

This is just a quick note to remind you, my favorite cousin, that I will finally turn 16 on May 3, 2001, and — DATE
officially become a legal driver! To celebrate, my family is throwing a party on Saturday, June 10, at
Westside Park, 181 W. Elm St., Milwaukee. I'd love for — ADDRESS
you to join us!

Janina will be driving from Normal, Illinois, on — CITY AND STATE
Friday and can pick you up when she passes through Chicago. I'll call you soon to see whether you can come to the party and if you need a ride.

Sincerely, — CLOSING

Marta

❷ Practice and Apply

A. CONCEPT CHECK: Other Comma Rules

Read the following sentences. Identify and correct all errors in comma usage.

> **Bound for the Autobahn**
>
> **1.** Last month the principal of Beatty High School received a letter from an old friend in Germany that read as follows: "Dear Lee Would you like to launch a student-exchange program with a European sister school?"
>
> **2.** On May 7 2003 six members of the junior class will leave for a German study-abroad experience.
>
> **3.** Dr. Cleary the principal will stay at his friend's home in Frankfurt Germany for six weeks, and the students will stay with host families.
>
> **4.** The group wants to drive on the Autobahn to tour Germany; they've scheduled driving trips to Siena Italy and Strasbourg France as well.
>
> **5.** To convince Dr. Cleary to drive rather than take the train to France, the students reported "The Autobahn is one of the best-maintained roads in the world."

➡ **For a SELF-CHECK and more practice, see the EXERCISE BANK, p. 620.**

For a SELF-CHECK and more practice, see the EXERCISE BANK, p. 620.

B. PROOFREADING: Correcting Comma Usage

Read the following e-mail and make corrections in comma usage.

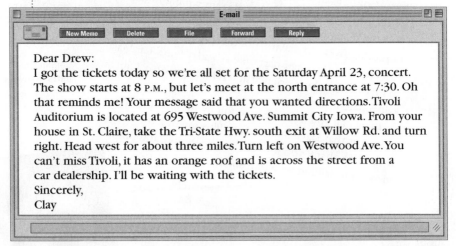

Dear Drew:
I got the tickets today so we're all set for the Saturday April 23, concert. The show starts at 8 P.M., but let's meet at the north entrance at 7:30. Oh that reminds me! Your message said that you wanted directions. Tivoli Auditorium is located at 695 Westwood Ave. Summit City Iowa. From your house in St. Claire, take the Tri-State Hwy. south exit at Willow Rd. and turn right. Head west for about three miles. Turn left on Westwood Ave. You can't miss Tivoli, it has an orange roof and is across the street from a car dealership. I'll be waiting with the tickets.
Sincerely,
Clay

Real World Grammar

Application Letter

An application or cover letter briefly describes to a potential employer why you might be a good candidate for a particular job. Punctuation errors in an application letter may convince a potential employer you're careless with your work. Notice how using end marks and commas correctly helps Jake Bell create a positive impression in the letter below.

1943 Lisa Lane
Tempe, AZ 88523
April 18, 2001

> Commas separate **name from title**, **city from state**, and **date from year**.

Ms. Angela Carson, Dealership Manager
Dave Mann's Auto Plus
Tempe, AZ 88523

Dear Ms. Carson:

Recently, Bob Carroll, a member of your sales staff, recommended that I contact you about possible job openings at your dealership. I met Mr. Carroll when he spoke to my class at Allemande High School, where I told him about my interest in working in the auto industry after I graduate next year.

Although I know you have not been advertising for help, I am confident that I could bring valuable skills to your dealership. I am a hard worker and am willing to do anything possible to get a start at your dealership, from washing cars to posting flyers to making photocopies for the sales staff. Last summer, I worked part-time at Sudzy Sue's Car Wash, so I have related experience and references. Also, I am an avid amateur mechanic.

I will call you next week to follow up on any part-time openings that Dave Mann's Auto Plus might have. In the meantime, thank you for your consideration, and I look forward to talking with you soon.

> In business letters, a **colon**, not a comma, follows the salutation.

> Uses commas with **appositive phrases.**

> Commas follow **introductory clauses** and make **complex sentences** easier to read.

> Commas clarify parts of **compound sentences.**

Sincerely,
Jake Bell
Jake Bell

Using Commas in Business Letters

Commas for format	Use commas in the date and address lines to indicate parts of the date, your and the recipient's addresses, and the recipient's professional title. Use a comma after the closing.
Commas for clarity	Use commas to clarify sentences that might be misread and to indicate parts of compound sentences.

PRACTICE AND APPLY: Revising

Use Jake Bell's application letter to help you improve the letter below. As you revise, be sure to correct any errors in comma, end mark, and period usage.

1555 N Harlem Ave
Oak Park I.L. 60153
April 30 2002

Ms Marlee Mills; Managing Editor
Popular Autos
213 Scoville St
River Forest IL 60614

Dear Ms. Mills;
    Enclosed is my resume, which I hope you will consider for the "Young Drivers" car reviewer position advertised last week. I am a high school student and I have a strong interest in cars the subject that your Web site covers.
    Currently, I write for the school newspaper at Walt Whitman High School where I am a junior, my father works at a car dealership, so I know a great deal about cars. I could send you a writing sample, if you'd like. Also, because I love to read about cars I've been following your Web site every week since I received my driver's license on January 15.
    Thank you very much. I hope to hear from you soon?

Sincerely,
Celia James
Celia James

A. Using End Marks and Commas Correctly For each sentence, make corrections in end mark, period, and comma usage as needed.

Is Bigger Necessarily Better?

1. On your way to school one day, ask yourself how many types of vehicles breeze down Main St U.S.A., on the average?
2. You may discover a large number of sports cars minivans, station wagons, motorcycles and trucks.
3. In addition you'll probably also see a large number of SUVs sport utility vehicles on the road.
4. With their hefty size, driving power and multiple uses, these vehicles enjoy great popularity among motorists.
5. Some people drive these large versatile vehicles for status; others for practical reasons.
6. Yet their size and different driving capabilities sometimes make SUVs difficult for new inexperienced SUV drivers to handle.
7. An S.U.V. unlike many cars does not get good gas mileage, but it can haul almost anything.
8. Students from Portland, Oregon to New York NewYork have been able to move their prized possessions from home to the dorms in the family's SUV.
9. However, watch out, if you're driving a smaller vehicle a collision with an SUV can be especially disastrous.
10. Do you think more or fewer people should drive SUVs

B. Editing Errors in End Marks and Commas Edit the following note, correcting any end mark or comma errors.

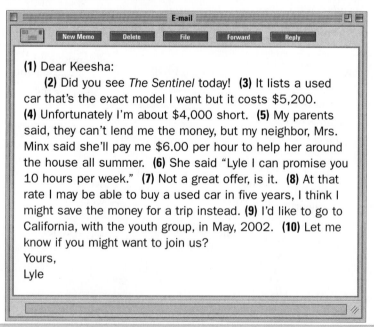

(1) Dear Keesha:

(2) Did you see *The Sentinel* today! **(3)** It lists a used car that's the exact model I want but it costs $5,200. **(4)** Unfortunately I'm about $4,000 short. **(5)** My parents said, they can't lend me the money, but my neighbor, Mrs. Minx said she'll pay me $6.00 per hour to help her around the house all summer. **(6)** She said "Lyle I can promise you 10 hours per week." **(7)** Not a great offer, is it. **(8)** At that rate I may be able to buy a used car in five years, I think I might save the money for a trip instead. **(9)** I'd like to go to California, with the youth group, in May, 2002. **(10)** Let me know if you might want to join us?

Yours,

Lyle

Write the letter of the best revision for each underlined section.

> Some motorcycling fans might ask what ever happened to Sammy
> Miller, the great British motorcycle racer of <u>the 1950s and 1960s</u>. "I'm right
> (1)
> here in <u>New Milton England" he</u> might say if he heard them. "Why not
> (2)
> stop by for a visit?" <u>Surprisingly it's true.</u> His fans can actually visit him
> (3)
> from <u>10:00 A.M. to 4:30 P.M., daily</u>. On the southern <u>coast of the UK Miller</u>
> (4) (5)
> runs a motorcycle shop and the Sammy Miller Motorcycle Museum. <u>The
> museum located in</u> a restored barn, displays roughly 150 bikes, many of
> (6)
> which he <u>once raced, all are in</u> working condition. Visitors might note that
> (7)
> <u>Miller unlike some museum owners</u> doesn't just collect bikes; he restores
> (8)
> them. How many people can say they were successful <u>motorcycle racers
> mechanics and museum owners</u> all in a <u>40-year span</u>!
> (9) (10)

1. A. the 1950s and 1960s?
   B. the 1950s, and 1960s.
   C. the 1950s, and 1960s?
   D. Correct as is

2. A. New Milton, England," he
   B. New Milton, England", he
   C. New Milton England," he
   D. Correct as is

3. A. Surprisingly it's true!
   B. Surprisingly! It's true!
   C. Surprisingly, it's true!
   D. Correct as is

4. A. 10:00 AM to 4:30 PM daily.
   B. 10:00 AM to 4:30 PM, daily.
   C. 10:00 A.M. to 4:30 P.M. daily.
   D. Correct as is

5. A. coast, of the UK, Miller
   B. coast of the U.K., Miller
   C. coast of the U.K. Miller,
   D. Correct as is

6. A. The museum, located in
   B. The museum, located in,
   C. The museum located, in
   D. Correct as is

7. A. once raced all are in
   B. once raced? All are in
   C. once raced. All are in
   D. Correct as is

8. A. Miller, unlike some museum
      owners
   B. Miller, unlike some museum
      owners,
   C. Miller; unlike some museum
      owners,
   D. Correct as is

9. A. motorcycle racers, mechanics,
      and museum owners
   B. motorcycle, racers, mechanics,
      and museum owners
   C. motorcycle racers mechanics,
      and museum owners
   D. Correct as is

10. A. 40-year span?
    B. 40-year span.
    C. 40-year span!"
    D. Correct as is

Student Help Desk

End Marks and Commas at a Glance

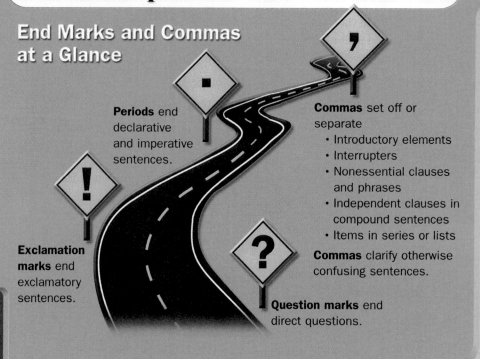

Periods end declarative and imperative sentences.

Exclamation marks end exclamatory sentences.

Commas set off or separate
- Introductory elements
- Interrupters
- Nonessential clauses and phrases
- Independent clauses in compound sentences
- Items in series or lists

Commas clarify otherwise confusing sentences.

Question marks end direct questions.

When a Comma Isn't Necessary

Clear Roads Ahead

Do not use a comma . . .	Example Sentence
with most statements that you have paraphrased	Imagine that your parents ask you to drive their new car to school.
after the name of a state (without a city) in a sentence	One city in Texas has a law against parking boats in front yards.
after a partial date within a sentence	Kato's driver's license expires in July 2006 on his birthday.
in a simple sentence with a compound predicate	I failed my first driving test but aced my second one.
with two unequal adjectives	My dad keeps an old snow shovel in the car trunk.
with an essential clause or phrase	I trust only those friends who have perfect driving records to drive my car.

When to Use a Comma Curves Ahead

Use a comma . . .	Example Sentence
to set off a direct quotation in a sentence	Imagine hearing your parents say, "Why don't you drive our new car to school today?"
after a city and state in a sentence	Bryan, Texas, has a law against parking boats in front yards.
after a complete date in a sentence	Kato's driver's license expires July 13, 2006, on his birthday.
to clarify an awkward sentence	Driving into my driveway, he nearly knocked over that tree.
to show a compound sentence	I failed my first driving test, but I aced my second one.
before *and* in a series	Remember to bring extra blankets, boots, and gloves on long-distance winter driving trips.
with two or more equal adjectives	Young, talkative passengers can be dangerous distractions to new drivers.
with a parenthetical or an antithetical expression	Cars, unlike passengers, can be moved before medical technicians arrive at an accident scene.
with a nonessential clause or phrase	Jules, who happens to be the mayor's son, has a perfect driving record.

The Bottom Line

Checklist for End Marks and Commas

Have I . . .

____ used the correct end mark?

____ made sure I haven't used exclamation points too often?

____ placed a comma after an introductory element?

____ set off nonessential clauses, phrases, and appositives with commas?

____ used a comma before the conjunction that joins the clauses of a compound sentence?

____ used commas to separate items in a series or list?

____ added commas when they are needed for clarity?

____ checked for and corrected comma splices?

____ used periods and commas correctly with dates, addresses, salutations, etc.?

Other Punctuation

DIRECT EXAMINATION BY MR. RUSSO

Q Mr. Klein, what did you do on the morning of May 21?

A First, I went to the coffee shop you know, the one on Second and second, I went to the Cooks place to recover the armchair, say about 800 however, thats when I saw the doctor lying on the kitchen floor. The news 5 weather was just starting.

Theme: The Quest for Justice

In Defense of Punctuation

If you were handed this transcript to review as a member of a jury, what would you think? Might you issue this verdict: guilty of missing punctuation? Notice how the course of events becomes clearer when punctuation—such as brackets, colons, and hyphens—is added to the account:

> **First, I went to the coffee shop (you know, the one on Second); and second, I went to the Cooks' place to re-cover the armchair—say, about 8:00; however, that's when I saw the doctor lying on the kitchen floor. The *News 5* weather was just starting.**

Write Away: A Reliable Witness

Think of a disagreement or incident that you have witnessed. It might be a fender-bender in a parking lot or an argument in the cafeteria. Write a paragraph about the incident, including as many details as you can remember. Save the paragraph in your
📁 **Working Portfolio.**

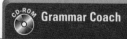
Grammar Coach

For each numbered item, choose the letter of the response that corrects the error.

In the late 1500s, one French village's residents didnt think it was
(1)
strange to try animals in court. Swarms of vine weevils were destroying the

grape crops in St. Julien, a well known village in the wine-making region.
(2)
The people sought recourse against these ever-present, devillike creatures.
(3)
Desperate, the villagers hired lawyers; two of them, in fact, to bring the
(4)
insects to justice. The lawyers met with their clients, as a result, the lawyers
(5)
wrote a statement. The lawyers asked for three things appointment of a
(6)
lawyer for the weevils, inspection of the fields, and anathematization of the

insects. According to the _American Heritage Dictionary,_ the Greek word
(7)
anathema, in this case, means, "an ecclesiastical ban, curse, or excommuni-
(8)
cation." (Among the legal precedents was a case in which the court excom-

municated moles in Italy (A.D. 824).) The trial lasted some eight months, but
(9)
no one knows how it ended, the last page of the archives was destroyed.
(10)

1. A. 1500's
   B. villages
   C. didn't
   D. Correct as is

2. A. well-known
   B. wine making region
   C. wine-making-region
   D. Correct as is

3. A. re-course
   B. ever present
   C. devil-like
   D. Correct as is

4. A. lawyers; two of them, in fact;
   B. lawyers—two of them, in fact—
   C. lawyers . . . two of them, in fact
   D. Correct as is

5. A. clients;
   B. clients:
   C. clients.
   D. Correct as is

6. A. for three things;
   B. for three things—
   C. for three things:
   D. Correct as is

7. A. "American Heritage Dictionary,"
   B. American Heritage Dictionary,
   C. American Heritage "Dictionary,"
   D. Correct as is

8. A. _anathema_
   B. "anathema"
   C. _an ecclesiastical ban, curse,_
      or excommunication.
   D. Correct as is

9. A. Italy—A.D. 824—.)
   B. Italy [A.D. 824].)
   C. Italy: A.D. 824.)
   D. Correct as is

10. A. ended: the last page
    B. ended, (the last page
    C. ended, [the last page
    D. Correct as is

Apostrophes

❶ Here's the Idea

Writers use apostrophes (') to show possession, to make contractions, and to form certain plurals.

Possessives

▶ **Use an apostrophe to form the possessive of nouns and indefinite pronouns.**

Using Apostrophes to Form Possessives		
Type of Word or Case	**To Form the Possessive**	**Examples**
Singular noun	Add apostrophe and *s* ('s).	nation's secrets Judge Ness's verdict
Plural noun ending in *s*	Add apostrophe only (').	reporters' questions the Joneses' defense
Plural noun not ending in *s*	Add apostrophe and *s* ('s).	the children's fate the people's outcries
Compound noun	Add apostrophe and *s* to last word of compound ('s).	sister-in-law's gift sisters-in-law's gifts
Individual possession	Change each noun to its possessive form.	the attorney's and the experts' fees
Joint possession	Change only last noun to its possessive form.	Jack and Claudia's alibi
Indefinite pronoun	Add apostrophe and *s* ('s).	someone's umbrella anybody's guess
Compound indefinite pronoun	Add apostrophe and *s* to the last word ('s).	someone else's parka no one else's watch
Noun expressing time or amount	Add apostrophe and *s* to a singular noun ('s); add apostrophe to a plural noun (').	one day's proceedings ten hours' deliberation

Exception: You often add just an apostrophe when using the singular possessive form of classical and biblical names ending in s.

Odysseus' wanderings   Jesus' disciples

Hercules' labors   Moses' leadership

Never add an apostrophe to a possessive pronoun *(yours, hers, his, its, ours, theirs, whose)*. In particular, remember that *it's* is a contraction meaning "it is."

It's time for the jury to state its verdict.
   ↑ CONTRACTION   ↑ POSSESSIVE PRONOUN

Contractions and Other Omissions

▶ **Use apostrophes in contractions to show the omission of letters.**

they're = they are   couldn't = could not   she's = she is

▶ **Use apostrophes to show where sounds have been omitted in poetry or in dialect.**

> **LITERARY MODEL**
>
> "I don't know too much 'bout Ohio," Unc Isom said, coming out in the road. "Where it at or where it s'pose to be, I ain't for sure."
>
> —Ernest J. Gaines, *The Autobiography of Miss Jane Pittman*

▶ **Use an apostrophe to indicate missing digits in a year number.**

the class of '08   back in '98

Special Plurals

▶ **Use an apostrophe and an s ('s) to form the plural of an individual letter or numeral, a word referred to as a word, or an abbreviation containing a period.**

In the handwriting sample, the b's looked like 6's.

▶ **Any punctuation that follows a word ending with an apostrophe should be placed after the apostrophe. Notice that this treatment departs from the usual rule, which dictates that a period or comma be placed within other punctuation.**

We thought the drawings were the architects', but they were the district attorneys'.

 Do not use an apostrophe to form the plural of dates, such as decades and centuries.

CORRECT: 1900s   INCORRECT: 1900's

❷ Practice and Apply

A. CONCEPT CHECK: Apostrophes

Identify and correct errors in the use of apostrophes.

Example: In cases of espionage, federal judge's rulings
arent always consistent.
Answer: judges'; aren't

Julius and Ethel
Rosenberg

Did the Punishment Fit the Crime?
1. During the Cold War of the 1950's, distrust of the Soviet Unions' power fueled fears for our nation's security.
2. The FBIs' investigations led to several peoples' arrests.
3. A physicists' arrest for passing atomic secrets to the Soviet Union eventually led to the arrest of others, including David Greenglass and his wife.
4. David Greenglass testified to his sisters and brother-in-laws roles as go-betweens.
5. As a result of Greenglass' testimony, his sister Ethel and her husband, Julius Rosenberg, were arrested in the summer of 1950.
6. The jurys' verdict of guilty placed sentencing in Justice Irving Kaufmans' hands.
7. Greenglass was sentenced to 15 years imprisonment.
8. Everyones shock at the Rosenberg's sentence of death made headlines.
9. The Supreme Courts refusal to hear their appeal didnt stop Justice William O. Douglas from issuing a stay of execution.
10. In a special session, six justice's votes upheld the sentence, and Julius and Ethel's executions took place on June 19, 1953.

➜ For a SELF-CHECK and more practice, see the EXERCISE BANK, p. 620.

B. PROOFREADING: Using Apostrophes

Correct all errors in the use of apostrophes.

Twelve Fair Jurors
(1) Before the mid-1960's, many states did not draft women to serve in their court's juries. (2) However, in 1975, the Supreme Courts ruling on this issue emphasized every defendants right to an impartial jury. (3) The court ruled that all jury's had to be selected from a true cross section of the defendant's community. (4) Womens rights were protected by the 75 ruling. (5) Not until 1986 were minority groups representation on juries protected by law.

Hyphens, Dashes, and Ellipses

LESSON 2

❶ Here's the Idea

A **hyphen** (-) connects words, word elements, or the parts of a compound word. A **dash** (—) sets off an abrupt change of thought or an explanation. An **ellipsis** (. . .) shows that a word, phrase, line, or paragraph has been omitted.

Hyphens

▶ **Use a hyphen to divide a word at the end of a line.**

In casual speech, confidence artists are often called **scam-mers** and grifters.

Rules for Hyphenating at the End of a Line		
Hyphenating Rule	**Incorrect**	**Correct**
Divide a word only between syllables.	gua-ranteed	guar-anteed
Make sure that at least two letters of the hyphenated word fall on each line.	nondair-y	non-dairy
Divide an already-hyphenated word at the hyphen.	self-satis-fied	self-satisfied
Do not divide a one-syllable word.	kni-ves	knives

▶ **Use a hyphen in compound numbers from twenty-one to ninety-nine and with fractions.**

sixty-two years   **three-fourths** of a cup

▶ **Use a hyphen in certain compound nouns.**

self-restraint   brother-in-law   vice-president

▶ **Hyphenate a compound adjective when it comes before the noun it modifies.**

He was a **well-informed** candidate.

In general, do not hyphenate a compound adjective when it follows the noun it modifies.

During the debate, the candidate seemed **well informed.**

PUNCTUATION

▶ **Use a hyphen with the prefixes *ex-*, *self-*, *quasi-*, and *all-* and with the suffix *-elect*.**

ex-officer   self-made   all-around   president-elect

▶ **Use a hyphen to avoid confusion or to avoid repeating a vowel or consonant.** When in doubt, check a dictionary.

re-create (as opposed to *recreate*)   anti-itch   shell-like

STUDENT MODEL

A **self-confident** trickster duped the Junior Class. **Mayor-elect** Kim is heading an **all-out** effort to catch the con artist who talked the juniors into an **unsound** investment. With **childlike** gullibility, the class officers handed three thousand dollars to the trickster, who had promised a **tenfold** increase in only two months. Unfortunately, the company that manufactures **anti-intruder** devices never existed.

Hyphen needed to set off prefix or suffix

No hyphen needed

Hyphen needed to avoid repeating a vowel

Dashes

▶ **Use a dash to signal an abrupt change or an idea that breaks into the thought of a sentence.**

Victims of scams often do not report the crime— embarrassment hurts more than financial loss.

▶ **Use dashes to set off explanatory, supplementary, or parenthetical material in sentences.** Note that parentheses and commas may be used for the same purpose.

Certain traits in the victim—**greed, neediness, gullibility**—make the con artist's job easier.

PROFESSIONAL MODEL

Since we aren't always at home, the Fourth [Amendment] applies not only to houses but to such places as business offices, cars, hotel rooms, and—**far-fetched though it sounds**—even to telephone booths. . . .

In most cases, the law requires that searches and seizures be made only with a warrant—**a legal document that permits such action.**

—Bernice Kohn, *The Spirit and the Letter*

Dashes set off break in thought.

Dashes set off explanatory phrase.

CHAPTER 10

Some computers or word-processing programs have the dash—also known as the em dash—as a character. If you can't find this character, type two hyphens (--).

For guidelines on using commas, dashes, and parentheses to set off explanatory material, see p. 263.

Ellipses

▶ **Use an ellipsis (also called ellipsis points) to show that one or more words have been omitted within a quoted sentence.**
An ellipsis consists of three periods preceded and followed by spaces (. . . , not ...).

"The judge raised her gavel and . . . demanded order."

▶ **Use a period and three ellipsis points to show the following types of omissions within quoted material:**

1. omission of the last part of a sentence
2. omission of the first part of the following sentence
3. omission of an entire sentence or more
4. omission of an entire paragraph or more

LITERARY MODEL

When the magician's engagement closed there was but one person . . . who did not believe in mesmerism and I was the one. All the others were converted but I was to remain an implacable and unpersuadable disbeliever in mesmerism and hypnotism. . . .

—Mark Twain, *The Autobiography of Mark Twain*

Ellipsis: words omitted from middle of sentence

Period and ellipsis: words omitted from last part of sentence

▶ **In fiction or informal writing, three ellipsis points may also be used to indicate that an idea or a character's voice trails off.**
Notice such a use of ellipsis points in the following cartoon.

Dilbert

A. CONCEPT CHECK: Hyphens, Dashes, and Ellipses

Copy the sentences, correcting errors in the use of hyphens, dashes, and ellipses. Circle your corrections.

If It Seems Too Good to Be True, It Probably Is

1. Approximately eighty four years ago, Louis Enricht, an inventor, claimed to have created a substitute for gasoline.
2. An oil crisis at the time long before concern about toxic emissions, inspired his remarkable claim.
3. Cleverly deemphasizing obvious problems, Enricht convinced people that he had invented a car that could run on water.
4. Initially, he duped many people reporters, the automaker Henry Ford, and other businessmen by giving foolproof demonstrations and inviting close inspections.
5. About five sixths of the tank was filled with water, and the remainder was filled with Enricht's "secret formula."
6. His invention led to lucrative offers one for a million dollars.
7. O. Henry's words fit the scam: "It was. . . . simple as all truly great swindles are."
8. One eager investor was keen to advertise the penny a gallon fuel and paid Enricht $100,000 for the formula.
9. Later, this truly inventive scammer announced another plan to distill fuel from peat.
10. Investors rushed to give him money, and the district attorney rushed to prosecute this quasi inventor.

➡ For a SELF-CHECK and more practice, see the EXERCISE BANK, p. 621.

B. PROOFREADING: Using Hyphens, Dashes, and Ellipses

Identify and correct all errors in the use of hyphens, dashes, and ellipses. If a sentence contains no errors, write Correct.

Reporter's Notes: Con Artist Nabbed

(1) With moves worthy of an all star football player, Detective Sonia Lopez tackled Willie Smith as he attempted to escape a well engineered sting operation. **(2)** Smith is wanted in four states Ohio, Kentucky, Florida, and Texas for bilking patriotic but gullible citizens of their savings. **(3)** One victim said, "I felt so stupid . . . I should have known the Washington Monument wasn't for sale." **(4)** Undercover officer Laura Hernández, forty two, posed as a wealthy widow looking for a nest egg. **(5)** Ex-uding selfconfidence, Smith had presented quasiauthentic shares in the Washington Monument.

Semicolons and Colons

❶ Here's the Idea

A **semicolon** (;) separates elements in a sentence. It indicates a more definite break than a comma. A **colon** (:) is used after a word introducing a quotation, an explanation, an example, or a series.

Semicolons

▶ **Use a semicolon to join the independent clauses of a compound sentence in which no coordinating conjunction is used.** Coordinating conjunctions are *and, but, for, nor, or, so,* and *yet*.

independent clause	**;**	independent clause

The Magna Carta protected citizens from royal abuses of power **;** the Bill of Rights protects citizens from federal abuse of power.

▶ **Use a semicolon between independent clauses that are joined by a conjunctive adverb or transitional phrase.**

CONJUNCTIVE ADVERB

The Constitution prohibits "unreasonable searches" **; however,** the courts need to decide what's "unreasonable."

TRANSITIONAL PHRASE

Free speech is a complex issue **; for example,** should conversations in Internet chat rooms be considered private or public?

Common Conjunctive Adverbs and Transitional Phrases	
Conjunctive adverbs	finally, consequently, nevertheless, also, moreover, therefore, otherwise, however
Transitional phrases	as a result, for example, in fact, in other words, that is, for instance

Use a comma, not a semicolon, to separate a phrase or subordinate clause from an independent clause.

SUBORDINATE CLAUSE

Although the Constitution has been amended many times **,** the Bill of Rights has never been amended.

INDEPENDENT CLAUSE

> **Use a semicolon between independent clauses joined by a conjunction if either clause contains commas.**

In 1896, the Supreme Court, in a seven-to-one vote, ruled that racial segregation was constitutional; but, on May 17, 1954, by a unanimous vote, the Supreme Court overturned that ruling.

> **Use a semicolon to separate items in a series if one or more of the items contain commas.**

These liberties are guaranteed in the Bill of Rights: freedom of speech, press, and religion, by the First Amendment; right to privacy, by the Fourth Amendment; and due process of law, by the Fifth Amendment.

Colons

> **Use a colon after an independent clause to introduce a list of items.**

Among the notable Supreme Court justices are the following: **Warren Burger, William O. Douglas, Thurgood Marshall, and Sandra Day O'Connor.**

> **Use a colon between two independent clauses when the second explains or elaborates the first.**

Thurgood Marshall received valuable experience by working as legal counsel for the NAACP: he argued 32 civil-rights cases before the Supreme Court.

Do not use a colon directly after a verb.

Marshall believed the government should provide: education, legal services, and access to the courts.

Here are some further rules for using colons.

- **Use a colon to introduce a long or formal quotation.**

  The Eighth Amendment has the following wording: "Excessive bail shall not be required, nor excessive fines imposed, nor cruel and unusual punishments inflicted."

- **Use a colon after the salutation of a business letter.**

  Dear Ms. Yamaguchi:

- **Use a colon between numerals indicating hours and minutes.**

  At 12:01 P.M., the court adjourned for lunch.

- **Use a colon to separate numerals in references to certain religious works, such as the Bible, the Qur'an (Koran), and the Talmud.**

  Solomon's famous ruling is found in 1 Kings 3:16–28.

❷ Practice and Apply

Identify and correct all errors in semicolons and colons. Write the word immediately preceding the semicolon or colon that needs to be added or deleted.

Example: The Bill of Rights does not gather dust, in fact, it continues to be tested: to this day.

Answer: dust; tested⤴

Vigilance of Rights

1. In his first inaugural address, Abraham Lincoln stated the following "While the people retain their virtue and vigilance, no administration . . . can very seriously injure the government in the short space of four years."
2. Lincoln's words refer to the length of a president's term, Supreme Court justices are appointed for life.
3. The Bill of Rights protects rights that are precious to citizens in a democracy, freedom of speech, free exercise of religion, freedom of the press, and due process of law.
4. The Constitution may declare our rights however, only through vigilance can those rights be preserved.
5. At one time, law enforcement officials could enter a person's home without a warrant and search through: drawers, closets, boxes, cabinets, and files.
6. Now, officers cannot simply enter and search a person's house or wiretap a suspect's phone they must get a warrant first.
7. The Supreme Court has defended a citizen's right to privacy, for example, it overturned the conviction of Charles Katz in 1967.
8. Katz, a gambler: who often made phone calls from a public booth, had his calls tapped by the FBI.
9. The court ruled that the FBI had "seized" Katz's conversation, in effect, the FBI had taken a piece of Katz's property.
10. The right to privacy is a complicated issue, for instance, should passengers' belongings be searched preflight?

➡ For a SELF-CHECK and more practice, see the EXERCISE BANK, p. 622.

PUNCTUATION

Quotation Marks and Italics

LESSON 4

① Here's the Idea

Quotation marks (" ") set off direct quotations, titles, and words used in special ways. **Italics** (a *slanted* style of print) are used for titles, foreign words, and words referred to as words.

Direct Quotations

▶ **Use quotation marks to indicate the beginning and the end of a direct quotation—a person's exact words.** The first word of a quotation introduced by words such as *she said* is capitalized. In a divided quotation, the first word of the second part is capitalized only if it begins a new sentence.

"Defense lawyers and prosecutors," remarked Mr. Blair, **"are on opposite teams."**

Do not use quotation marks to set off an indirect quotation.

Mr. Blair remarked that defense lawyers and prosecutors are on opposite teams.

Punctuation in Direct Quotations

Here are some guidelines on where to place punctuation when using quotation marks.

Placement of Punctuation with Quotation Marks	
Punctuation	**Guidelines**
. **,**	**Always put periods and commas inside quotation marks.** He said, "Everyone likes to win." "Everyone likes to win," he said.
; **:**	**Always put semicolons and colons outside quotation marks.** He said, "Trials are like games"; I'm not so sure I agree.
? **!**	**Put question marks and exclamation points inside the quotation marks if they are part of the quotation. If they are not, put them outside.** Ms. Yee asked, "Do you keep track of wins and losses?" Did the juror actually say, "I'm biased against gum chewers"?

Within a sentence, a direct quotation may end with a question mark or an exclamation point. However, a quotation that would normally end with a period must instead end with a comma if the surrounding sentence continues after it.

"When does the trial begin?" she asked. "It's set for noon," he said.

▶ **Use single quotation marks to set off a quotation within a quotation.** Place the single quotation marks inside the double quotation marks.

"'Never come to court unprepared' was the best advice I ever got from my mentor," remarked Mr. Rojas.

▶ **If a quotation consists of more than one paragraph, each paragraph should begin with a quotation mark.** However, a closing quotation mark should not be used until the end of the entire quotation.

You do not need to use quotation marks for a long quoted passage if you set off the entire excerpt in any of these ways: by indenting it, by setting it in smaller type, or by using single spacing instead of double spacing.

PUNCTUATION

Titles and Names

▶ **Use quotation marks to enclose titles of short works and for works that are contained within longer pieces (for example, chapters within books).**

Using Quotation Marks with Titles	
Kind of Title	Example
Short story	"A Worn Path" by Eudora Welty
Chapter	Chapter 4, "The Prosecution Rests"
Article	"Ants and Plants" in *National Geographic*
Essay	Thoreau's "Civil Disobedience"
Television episode	"Birds of the Sun Gods" on *Nova*
Short poem	"I, Too" by Langston Hughes
Song	Ricky Martin sings "Livin' La Vida Loca"

Use italics for titles of long works and for names of vehicles.

Using Italics			
Kind of Title or Name	**Example**	**Kind of Title or Name**	**Example**
Book	*The Scarlet Letter*	Movie	*Star Wars*
Newspaper	*Wall Street Journal*	Play	*The Crucible*
Magazine	*Newsweek*	Long poem	*Song of Myself*
Work of art	*Starry Night*	Long musical work	*Swan Lake*
Television series	*Law and Order*	Vehicle (ship, train, aircraft, spacecraft)	*Mariner IV*

Most software programs allow you to format your text in italics. However, if you're writing by hand or using a typewriter, use underlining to indicate italics.

While watching the classic film <u>Twelve Angry Men</u>, *viewers can almost feel the heat in the jury room.*

Other Uses

Use quotation marks to enclose slang words, unusual expressions, technical terms, and definitions of words.

The gangster hired a "mouthpiece" to represent him in court.
SLANG WORD

Dan White's lawyer used the "Twinkie defense" to explain his client's actions.   UNUSUAL EXPRESSION

Don't use quotation marks for emphasis.

The jury found the defendant "guilty."

> No quotes necessary

Italicize an unfamiliar foreign word or a word referred to as a word.

Her concern with **bella figura** made her look down on those who neglected their appearance.

> Italian term meaning "making a good impression"

The words **you** and **ewe** are homophones.

> Words referred to as words

❷ Practice and Apply

Find and correct errors in the use of quotation marks and italics. Use underscoring to indicate italics. If a sentence contains no errors, write Correct.

Example: "Put that crook in jail and throw away the key"! the mayor shouted at the district attorney.

Answer: key!"

The Winning Story

1. Even when a criminal is arrested in "flagrante delicto," which is Latin for 'caught in the act,' a prosecutor and a defense attorney still do battle.

2. "The closest most people will ever come to being in a courtroom, remarked Susan Knight, a court reporter, is by watching TV. Even then, they only see what the camera allows".

3. Unlike cases in the old Perry Mason television series, lawyers cannot call surprise witnesses, and no one ever breaks down, shouting, I confess!

4. These two books can help the layperson understand lawyers: "D.A.: Prosecutors in Their Own Words" and "The Trial Lawyers."

5. In describing a trial, attorney James F. Neal quoted his college football coach when he said, "The team that makes the fewest mistakes wins".

6. Attorney Arthur Liman was the subject of an article, The Gentle Lion of Litigation, that appeared in "The National Law Journal."

7. Liman, who listened intently to every witness, said, 'Without a follow-up pattern, your cross-examination is not going to be comprehensible.'

8. Just as Hemingway wrote stories such as The Killers that were complex yet told simply, prosecutors and defense lawyers try to tell simple but convincing stories to the jury.

9. "One prosecutor", recalled a law student, "said that the worst feeling in the world was to have a jury say, "You lose"".

10. The word "judicious," meaning *to show prudence and caution,* describes the best way for all court professionals to act, whether they are winning or losing.

➡ **For a SELF-CHECK and more practice, see the EXERCISE BANK, p. 622.**

Parentheses and Brackets

① Here's the Idea

Parentheses () enclose supplemental information in a sentence or text. **Brackets []** enclose explanatory information within quoted text or within text that is enclosed in parentheses.

Parentheses

▶ **Use parentheses to set off supplemental or explanatory material that is added to a sentence or text.**

Cases involving libel (pronounced LIE-bul) are rare in the age of tabloid journalism.

Here are some guidelines for punctuating parenthetical information.

Punctuating Parenthetical Material	
Rules	**Example**
If parenthetical material occurs within a sentence, do not capitalize the first word or put a period at the end. You may, however, put a question mark or exclamation point at the end.	Though the number of cases involving libel has fallen (see chart), the number of other kinds has risen. She sued me for libel (can you believe it?) and requested an immediate hearing.
Never put punctuation before the opening parenthesis. If punctuation is called for, put it after the closing parenthesis.	Sylvester Stallone (popularly called Sly), who grew up to be the muscular star of the Rocky movies, was a scrawny kid.
If a parenthetical sentence stands by itself, punctuate and capitalize the sentence as you normally would.	She sued me for libel and requested an immediate hearing. (Can you believe this?)

▶ **Use parentheses to enclose figures or letters that introduce items in a list within a sentence and to set off numerical information such as area codes.**

A person can harm the reputation of another person by three means: (1) libel, (2) slander, and (3) defamation of character.

Call the Legal Hotline, (999) 243-1000.

CHAPTER 10

Brackets

▶ **Use brackets to enclose an explanation or comment added to quoted material.**

She said, "This law [prohibiting the ridicule of vegetables] proves that libel cases are getting out of hand."

▶ **Use brackets as parentheses inside parentheses.**

Many free-speech advocates spoke out against veggie libel laws (laws against defaming food products [see insert]).

❷ Practice and Apply

CONCEPT CHECK: Parentheses and Brackets

Find and correct errors in the use of parentheses and brackets. If a sentence is correct, write Correct.

The "Cents" of Justice

1. James McNeill Whistler was the 19th-century equivalent of a media darling (his witty remarks were often quoted.
2. This famous painter was known for delivering a biting *bon mot* ["clever turn of phrase"] in the London salons.
3. In 1877, Whistler exhibited a painting (*Nocturne in Black and Gold: The Falling Rocket*) in a new art gallery.
4. The art critic John Ruskin wrote that he "never expected to hear a coxcomb (meaning Whistler) ask two hundred guineas for flinging a pot of paint in the public's face."
5. Whistler promptly sued for libel, demanding damages. [Was his real motive to get money]?
6. The attorneys focused on three points: 1 the critic's competence, 2 the artist's reputation, and 3 the painting's value.
7. During the trial, Ruskin's lawyer questioned Whistler harshly. (Ruskin himself didn't attend the trial, which lasted two days (November 25 and 26, 1878).)
8. Ruskin's lawyer asked if Whistler expected two hundred guineas (just over $1,000) for just two days' work.
9. Whistler gave his famous reply, "No, I ask it for a knowledge (that) I have gained in the work of a lifetime."
10. The jury found in favor of Whistler but awarded him one farthing, less than a penny, in damages.

➡ **For a SELF-CHECK and more practice, see the EXERCISE BANK, p. 623.**

PUNCTUATION

Grammar in Literature

Using Punctuation in Drama

Playwrights and fiction writers use the types of punctuation you've been studying in this chapter in order to help readers and performers understand the relationships among a text's ideas.

In the following model, notice how Arthur Miller uses punctuation to clarify his dialogue and stage directions. This excerpt is taken from Miller's play *The Crucible,* about the Salem, Massachusetts, witch trials of 1692.

The CRUCIBLE
ARTHUR MILLER

Mary Warren. I never knew it before. I never knew anything before. When she come into the court I say to myself, I must not accuse this woman, for she sleep in ditches, and so very old and poor. But then—then she sit there, denying and denying, and I feel a misty coldness climbin' up my back, and the skin on my skull begin to creep, and I feel a clamp around my neck and I cannot breathe air; and then—(*entranced*)—I hear a voice, a screamin' voice, and it were my voice—and all at once I remembered everything she done to me!

Proctor. Why? What did she do to you?

Mary Warren (*like one awakened to a marvelous secret insight*). So many time, Mr. Proctor, she come to this very door, beggin' bread and a cup of cider—and mark this: whenever I turned her away empty, she mumbled.

Elizabeth. Mumbled! She may mumble if she's hungry.

Mary Warren. But what does she mumble? You must remember, Goody Proctor. Last month—a Monday, I think—she walked away, and I thought my guts would burst for two days after. Do you remember it?

A semicolon indicates a pause in Mary's long sentence.

Parentheses enclose stage directions. Italics show that the words are to be read, not spoken, by the actors.

Dashes signal Mary's abrupt change of thought. Above, dashes set off stage directions.

Elizabeth. Why—I do, I
think, but—

Mary Warren. And so I told that to Judge Hathorne,
and he asks her so. "Sarah Good," says he, "what
curse do you mumble that this girl must fall sick
after turning you away?" (*And then she replies—
mimicking an old crone*)—"Why, your excellence,
no curse at all. I only say my commandments; I hope
I may say my commandments," says she!

> **Quotation marks**
> show that Mary
> must change her
> voice to convey
> that she's quoting
> the judge.

Using Other Punctuation in Drama

Apostrophe	Use an apostrophe to indicate missing letters when you want to create dialect.
Dashes	Use dashes to show a character's abrupt change of thought or to set off stage directions.
Ellipsis	Use an ellipsis to indicate that a character's voice is trailing off.
Parentheses	Use parentheses to enclose stage directions such as notes indicating how a line of dialogue should be spoken.
Quotation Marks	Quotation marks indicate that an actor must alter his or her voice to quote another.

PRACTICE AND APPLY: Writing

Write a script for a short dramatic scene that takes place in some
part of your school—for example, a classroom, the cafeteria, or
the parking lot. Include dialogue (either invented or overheard)
between at least two characters. Also include the following
features in your script, punctuating each example with at least
one of the marks listed in the chart above.

- stage directions that explain details (tone of voice, kind of
  gesture, etc.)
- a character's quoting someone else
- a character's sudden change of thoughts
- informal speech

When you're finished, exchange scripts with a classmate. Help
each other identify the uses of punctuation and correct mistakes.

A. Apostrophes, Hyphens, Dashes, and Ellipses Correct all errors in the use of apostrophes, hyphens, dashes, and ellipses.

The Trial of Jomo Kenyatta

1. Throughout Africas history, many political trials have only become well known after the fact.
2. In Kenya, for example, Africans and British colonists deaths resulted from guerrilla attacks.
3. Jomo Kenyatta was among many who were arrested . . . at the time he was the leader of an African political party.
4. The accusers charges of membership in the guerrilla group were un-founded.
5. The antiKenyatta faction feared this up and coming leader.
6. Initially Kenyattas and his colleagues rights to a lawyer were denied.
7. The government also shipped them to a remote village for trial, a ploy to avoid publicity.
8. The prosecution had no proof because the "Mau Mau . . . Society . . . appears to have no official list of members. . ."
9. Only one witness' testimony implicated Kenyatta.
10. Though the one witness's testimony was false, Kenyatta, he later became president of Kenya, served ten years hard labor.

B. Semicolons, Colons, Quotation Marks, Italics, Parentheses, and Brackets Correct all errors in the use of these punctuation marks. If a sentence is correct, write Correct.

The Trial of Nelson Mandela

(1) The book "Great World Trials" describes the ordeal of the African leader Nelson Mandela. **(2)** Mandela's trial 1963–1964 has many parallels with Kenyatta's trial a decade earlier. **(3)** Mandela had been an active political leader (He was on the executive board of the African National Congress (ANC).) **(4)** He and others had formed another group Umkhonto we Sizwe (MK), which means Spear of the Nation. **(5)** MK carried out acts of sabotage against government installations, consequently, its leaders were pursued relentlessly. **(6)** The government came down hard, it held political prisoners in solitary confinement for 90 days without trial. **(7)** Mandela's lawyer, Bram Fischer, was not given: a copy of the charges or the full time requested for preparation. **(8)** According to writer Eva Weber, "Mandela led off with, "My lord, the Government, not I, should be in the dock."" **(9)** The verdict which could have been predicted before the trial began was for life imprisonment. **(10)** However, he was freed in 1990, and four years later he was elected president of South Africa. **(11)** (Everyone should read Mandela's autobiography, Long Walk to Freedom.)

For each numbered item, choose the letter of the response that corrects the error.

Which is greater, <u>a thiefs' or a detective's cunning?</u> If the detective were
(1)
François Eugène Vidocq, the odds would be <u>twenty five to one</u> that even
(2)
the <u>most able bodied, catlike</u> crook wouldn't stand a chance. In the 1800s,
(3)
Vidocq gained fame as a daring rogue and master detective. His <u>training,</u>

<u>what irony, came</u> from life on the wrong side of the law. As a young man,
(4)
he was <u>a duelist, an escape artist, and a master of disguises,</u> however,
(5)
when faced with a long jail term, he decided to cooperate with officials. If <u>a</u>

<u>crook landed in jail at 3:00 P.M.,</u> by dinnertime <u>Vidocq would know: his life</u>
(6)   (7)
<u>story,</u> his accomplices, and his plans. Vidocq helped found the French police

agency known as the <u>*police de sûreté*, which means 'security police'.</u> His
(8)
philosophy was <u>"It takes a criminal to catch one".</u> His purported
(9)
autobiography <u>*Mémoires de Vidocq*</u> recounts many of his exploits.
(10)

1. A. thief
   B. thief's
   C. detectives'
   D. Correct as is

2. A. twenty-five-to-one
   B. twenty five-to-one
   C. twenty-five to one
   D. Correct as is

3. A. most-able-bodied
   B. most able-bodied
   C. cat-like
   D. Correct as is

4. A. training . . . what irony . . . came
   B. training-what irony-came
   C. training—what irony—came
   D. Correct as is

5. A. a duelist;
   B. escape artist;
   C. master of disguises;
   D. Correct as is

6. A. crook—landed in jail—at
   B. at 3:00 P.M.—
   C. at 3:00 P.M.;
   D. Correct as is

7. A. would know—his life story,
   B. would know his life story,
   C. would know; his life story,
   D. Correct as is

8. A. "police de sûreté,"
   B. "security police."
   C. security police
   D. Correct as is

9. A. "it takes a criminal to catch one".
   B. 'it takes a criminal to catch one'.
   C. "It takes a criminal to catch one."
   D. Correct as is

10. A. (*Mémoires de Vidocq*)
    B. [*Mémoires de Vidocq*]
    C. "Mémoires de Vidocq"
    D. Correct as is

Student Help Desk

Other Punctuation at a Glance

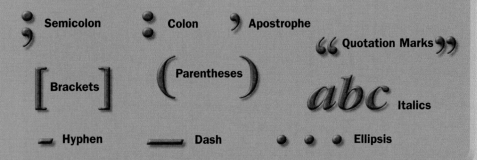

Semicolon

Colon   Apostrophe

Quotation Marks

[Brackets]   (Parentheses)   *abc* Italics

Hyphen   Dash   Ellipsis

Uses for Other Punctuation An Important Brief

Punctuation	Common Uses	Examples
Apostrophe '	to show possession to show contraction to identify missing letters	Dan's can't nothin'
Hyphen =	in numbers at the end of a line	twenty-two unbeliev- ably
Dash —	to show an abrupt thought change	Go—no, stay!
Ellipsis . . .	to identify missing text	"Oh say, can you see . . . what so proudly we hailed . . ."
Semicolon ;	to separate sentence elements	I cook; they do dishes.
Colon :	to signal a long quote to signal a series	He said this: Pack these items for camp:
"Quotation marks"	to enclose a direct quotation to enclose titles	I said, "Stay awhile." "Let It Be"
Italics	to designate titles to designate foreign words	*Newsweek* *un, deux, trois*
(Parentheses)	to enclose supplemental information	Inflation is down (see chart).
[Brackets]	to enclose supplemental info in parentheses or in quotations	The governor said, "I'll veto it [the welfare bill]."

Commas, Dashes, or Parentheses?
A Simple Verdict

- Use **commas** to show that the information is closely related to the rest of the sentence.

  The murder trial, **started in June,** lasted four months.

- Use **dashes** to indicate an abrupt change in thought.

  The murder trial—**such a controversial case!**—lasted four months.

- Use **parentheses** to show that the information is of incidental importance.

  The murder trial **(it made front-page headlines everywhere)** lasted four months.

The Bottom Line

Checklist for Other Punctuation

Have I . . .

_____ used apostrophes correctly in possessives, contractions, and special plurals?

_____ hyphenated compound words properly?

_____ divided words correctly at the end of lines?

_____ used dashes to set off explanations or changes in thought?

_____ indicated missing words in a quote by using an ellipsis?

_____ used semicolons as necessary in compound sentences or in series that contain commas?

_____ preceded a list correctly with a colon?

_____ used quotation marks and italics for titles?

_____ used parentheses and brackets properly?

Quick-Fix Editing Machine

You've worked hard on your assignment. Don't let misplaced commas, sentence fragments, and missing details lower your grade. Use this Quick-Fix Editing Machine to help you catch grammatical errors and make your writing more precise.

1 Sentence Fragments

What's the problem? Part of a sentence has been left out.

Why does it matter? A fragment doesn't convey a complete thought.

What should you do about it? Find out what is missing and add it.

What's the Problem?

Quick Fix

A. The subject is missing.

Is in question.

Add a subject.

My future is in question.

B. The verb is missing.

My plan no plan.

Add a verb.

My plan **is** no plan.

C. A helping verb is missing.

My parents saying I need a worthwhile goal.

Add a helping verb.

My parents **are** saying I need a worthwhile goal.

D. Both the subject and the verb are missing.

As an option.

Combine the fragment with an independent clause.

They don't accept clown school as an option.

E. The fragment is a dependent clause.

Because I love to perform.

Combine the fragment with an independent clause.

Because I love to perform, **I'll study acting.**

OR

Remove the conjunction.

~~Because~~ I love to perform.

For more help, see Chapter 3, pp. 76–103.

② Run-On Sentences

What's the problem? Two or more sentences have been run together.

Why does it matter? A run-on sentence doesn't show where one idea ends and another begins.

What should you do about it? Find the best way to separate the ideas or to show the proper relationship between them.

What's the Problem?

A. The end mark separating two complete thoughts is missing.

I play CDs Dad plays records.

B. Two sentences are separated only by a comma.

I say Dad's record player is an ancient artifact, he says it's a timeless piece of technology.

Quick Fix

Add an end mark between the ideas and create two sentences.

I play CDs. Dad plays records.

Add a conjunction.

I say Dad's record player is an ancient artifact, **but** he says it's a timeless piece of technology.

OR

Replace the comma with a semicolon.

I say Dad's record player is an ancient artifact; he says it's a timeless piece of technology.

OR

Replace the comma with an end mark and start a new sentence.

I say Dad's record player is an ancient artifact. **He** says it's a timeless piece of technology.

For more help, see Chapter 3, pp. 76–103.

QUICK FIX

3 Subject-Verb Agreement

What's the problem? The subject and the verb do not agree in number.

Why does it matter? The reader may regard your work as careless.

What should you do about it? Identify the subject's number and use a verb that matches it in number.

What's the Problem?

Quick Fix

A. The verb agrees with the object of a preposition, not the subject.

Mentally block out the prepositional phrase and make the verb agree with the true subject.

My appreciation of **teachers have** grown over the years.

My appreciation ~~of teachers~~ **has** grown over the years.

B. Part of a phrase has been mistaken for the subject.

Identify the true subject and make the verb agree with it in number.

I, like **others, are** becoming more sensitive through tutoring.

I, like others, **am** becoming more sensitive through tutoring.

C. The verb doesn't agree with an indefinite-pronoun subject.

Figure out whether the pronoun is singular or plural and make the verb agree with it.

Each of the kids I tutor **fill** me with pride.

Each of the kids I tutor **fills** me with pride.

D. A contraction does not agree in number with the subject.

Use a contraction that agrees in number with the subject.

The volunteer **program don't** accept tutors without any references.

The volunteer **program doesn't** accept tutors without any references.

For more help, see Chapter 5, pp. 130–151.

QUICK FIX

What's the Problem?

E. The verb doesn't agree with the true subject in a sentence beginning with *here* or *there*.

There was many **problems** in finding the right tutors.

F. A singular subject ending in *s* is mistaken for plural.

Measles are a common childhood disease.

Mathematics are the subject I teach.

G. A collective noun isn't treated as a single unit.

A high school **group tutor** at the neighborhood shelter.

H. A period of time isn't treated as a single unit.

A few hours a week **aren't** too much time to devote to helping others.

For more help, see Chapter 5, pp. 130–151.

Quick Fix

Mentally turn around the sentence so that the subject comes first, and make the verb agree with it.

There **were** many **problems** in finding the right tutors.

Watch out for these nouns and use singular verbs with them.

Measles is a common childhood disease.

Mathematics is the subject I teach.

If the collective noun refers to a single unit, use a singular verb.

A high school **group tutors** at the neighborhood shelter.

Use a singular verb whenever the subject refers to a period of time as a single unit.

A few hours a week **isn't** too much time to devote to helping others.

Pronoun Reference Problems

What's the problem? A pronoun does not agree in number, gender, or person with its antecedent, or an antecedent is unclear.

Why does it matter? Lack of agreement or an unclear antecedent can cause confusion.

What should you do about it? Identify the antecedent and make the pronoun agree with it, or rewrite a sentence to make the antecedent clear.

QUICK FIX

What's the Problem?

Quick Fix

A. A pronoun doesn't agree with an indefinite-pronoun antecedent.

Figure out whether the indefinite pronoun is singular or plural and make the pronoun agree with it.

Everyone has **their** favorite kind of music.

Everyone has **his or her** favorite kind of music.

B. A pronoun doesn't agree with the nearest part in a compound subject joined by *nor* or *or*.

Find the nearest part of the subject and make the pronoun agree with it.

Neither my friends nor my twin **sister** can make **themselves** listen to jazz.

Neither my friends nor my twin **sister** can make **herself** listen to jazz.

C. A pronoun doesn't have an antecedent.

Rewrite to eliminate the pronoun.

In our school newspaper **it** said that students prefer hip-hop music.

Our school newspaper said that students prefer hip-hop music.

D. A pronoun's antecedent is vague or indefinite.

Change the pronoun to a specific noun.

I think **they** would like jazz if **they** heard it.

I think my **friends** would like jazz if they heard it.

E. A pronoun could refer to more than one noun.

Substitute a noun for the pronoun to make the reference specific.

I asked my **principal** and my music **teacher** about forming a jazz club but **she** said no.

I asked my principal and my music teacher about forming a jazz club, but **the principal** said no.

For more help, see Chapter 6, pp. 152–179.

5 Incorrect Pronoun Case

What's the problem? A pronoun is in the wrong case.

Why does it matter? The reader may regard your writing, especially in formal situations, as sloppy and careless.

What should you do about it? Identify the pronoun and change it.

What's the Problem?

Quick Fix

What's the Problem?	Quick Fix
A. A pronoun in the wrong case follows a linking verb. The best trivia buff **is her.**	Always use the nominative case after linking verbs. The best trivia buff **is she.** <div align="center">**OR**</div>Reword the sentence. **She is** the best trivia buff.
B. A pronoun used as the object of a preposition is in the wrong case. Jen sometimes plays trivia games **with** Sharon and **I.**	Always use the objective case in a prepositional phrase. Jen sometimes plays trivia games with Sharon and **me.**
C. The wrong case is used in a comparison. I wish I could recall little details as quickly as **her.**	Complete the comparison and use the appropriate case. I wish I could recall little details as quickly as **she [can].**
D. Who or whom is used incorrectly. When we need a quirky question answered, **who** do we go to? Jen!	Figure out whether the pronoun is used as a subject (*who*) or as an object (*whom*). When we need a quirky question answered, **whom** do we go to? Jen!
E. A pronoun followed by an appositive is in the wrong case. **Us players** would lose more games without Jen.	Mentally eliminate the appositive to test for the correct case. **We** ~~players~~ would lose more games without Jen.

For more help, see Chapter 6, pp. 152–179.

6 *Who* and *Whom*

What's the problem? A form of the pronoun *who* or *whoever* is used incorrectly.

Why does it matter? If you just assume that *whom* and *whomever* are more formal versions of *who* and *whoever,* you may end up using these words incorrectly in formal writing situations.

What should you do about it? Figure out how the pronoun functions in the sentence to determine which form to use.

What's the Problem? / Quick Fix

What's the Problem?	Quick Fix
A. *Whom* **is used incorrectly as a subject.** **Whom** has borrowed my video game?	Use *who* as the subject of a sentence. Who has borrowed my video game?
B. *Who* **is used incorrectly as the object of a preposition.** **With who** are you going to the virtual reality center?	Use *whom* as the object of a preposition. With whom are you going to the virtual reality center?
C. *Who* **is used incorrectly as a direct object.** **Who** did you ask?	Use *whom* as a direct object. Whom did you ask?
D. *Whomever* **is used incorrectly as the subject of a clause.** **Whomever** can afford the price of admission can come.	*Whomever* is used only as an object. Use *whoever* as the subject of a clause. Whoever can afford the price of admission can come.
E. *Who's* **is used incorrectly as the possessive form of *who.*** **Who's** ticket is under the magnet on the refrigerator?	Always use *whose* to show possession. Whose ticket is under the magnet on the refrigerator?

For more help, see Chapter 6, pp. 152–179.

QUICK FIX

⑦ Confusing Comparisons

What's the problem? The wrong form of a modifier is used in making a comparison, or a double or illogical comparison is used.

Why does it matter? Incorrectly worded comparisons are confusing.

What should you do about it? Reword the comparison to make it clear.

What's the Problem?

What's the Problem?	Quick Fix
A. Both -er and *more* or -est and *most* are used in making a comparison. Jamal is the **most biggest** fan of roller coasters ever. He is a **more bigger** fan than I.	**Eliminate the double comparison.** Jamal is the ~~most~~ biggest fan of roller coasters ever. He is a ~~more~~ bigger fan than I.
B. The word *other* is missing in a comparison where logically it is needed. He has ridden on more roller coasters than any person I know.	**Add the missing *other*.** He has ridden on more roller coasters than any **other** person I know.
C. A superlative form is used where a comparative form is needed. Of the two big roller coasters in town, Jamal is **most** impressed with the one called Loop-de-Loop.	**When comparing two things, always use the comparative form.** Of the two big roller coasters in town, Jamal is **more** impressed with the one called Loop-de-Loop.
D. A comparative form is used where a superlative form is needed. Of all the roller coasters Jamal has ridden, the **more** thrilling one is called Rolling Thunder.	**When comparing more than two things, use the superlative form.** Of all the roller coasters Jamal has ridden, the **most** thrilling one is called Rolling Thunder.

For more help, see Chapter 7, pp. 180–199.

QUICK FIX

8 Verb Forms and Tenses

What's the problem? The wrong form or tense of a verb is used.

Why does it matter? The reader may regard your work as careless or confusing.

What should you do about it? Replace the incorrect verb with the correct form or tense.

What's the Problem?

Quick Fix

A. The wrong form of a verb is used with *have* or *had*.

The modern Olympic Games **had began** in 1896.

Always use the past participle with the helping verbs *have* and *had*.

The modern Olympic Games **had begun** in 1896.

B. A helping verb is missing.

Until 1984 only men **run** an Olympic marathon.

Add a helping verb.

Until 1984 only men **had run** an Olympic marathon.

C. An irregular verb form is used incorrectly.

Women **run** an Olympic marathon at the '84 event.

Look up the correct spelling and use it.

Women **ran** an Olympic marathon at the '84 event.

D. A past participle is used incorrectly.

Women athletes **shown** they can run distance races.

To refer to the past, use the past form of a verb.

Women athletes **showed** they can run distance races.

E. Different verb tenses are used in the same sentence without a valid reason.

Joan Benoit **became** famous when she **wins** the first women's Olympic marathon.

Match the tense of the other verb(s) to the tense of the first verb.

Joan Benoit **became** famous when she **won** the first women's Olympic marathon.

For more help, see Chapter 4, pp. 104–129.

Misplaced and Dangling Modifiers

What's the problem? The modifying word or phrase is in the wrong place, or it doesn't modify any other word in the sentence.

Why does it matter? The sentence can be confusing or unintentionally funny.

What should you do about it? Move the modifying word or phrase closer to the word it modifies, or add a word for it to modify.

What's the Problem?

Quick Fix

A. The adverb *even* or *only* is not placed close to the word it modifies.

Move the adverb to make your meaning clear.

Mall parking lots **only** confuse me.

Only mall parking lots confuse me.

OR

Mall parking lots confuse **only** me.

I usually don't remember where I **even** parked.

I usually don't **even** remember where I parked.

B. A prepositional phrase is too far from the word it modifies.

Move the prepositional phrase closer to the word it modifies.

In all the areas **of the lot** I wandered around.

I wandered around in all the areas **of the lot.**

C. A participial phrase is too far from the word it modifies.

Move the participial phrase closer to the word it modifies.

Sitting in a row of similar cars, mall security located my **car.**

Mall security located my **car, sitting in a row of similar cars.**

D. A participial phrase does not relate to anything in the sentence.

Reword the sentence, adding a word for the participial phrase to refer to.

Reaching into my backpack, the car keys were found easily.

Reaching into my backpack, I easily found the car keys.

For more help, see Chapter 7, pp. 180–199.

QUICK FIX

10 Missing or Misplaced Commas

What's the problem? Commas are missing or are used incorrectly.

Why does it matter? Incorrect use of commas can make sentences hard to follow.

What should you do about it? Determine where commas are needed and add or omit them as necessary.

What's the Problem?

Quick Fix

A. A comma is missing before the conjunction in a series.

Among the most popular attractions at Yellowstone Park are geysers, bears and bison.

Add a comma before the conjunction.

Among the most popular attractions at Yellowstone Park are geysers, bears, and bison.

B. A comma is placed incorrectly outside closing quotation marks.

"National parks are threatened by overcrowding", says the environmentalist.

Always put a comma inside the closing quotation mark.

"National parks are threatened by overcrowding," says the environmentalist.

C. A comma is missing after an introductory phrase or clause.

Because Yellowstone welcomes millions of tourists each year it has had to establish limits.

Find the end of the phrase or clause and add a comma.

Because Yellowstone welcomes millions of tourists each year, it has had to establish limits.

D. Commas are missing around a nonessential phrase or clause.

No wild animal no matter how long it has lived in the park can survive beyond the boundaries.

Add commas to set off the nonessential phrase or clause.

No wild animal, no matter how long it has lived in the park, can survive beyond the boundaries.

E. A comma is missing before the conjunction in a compound sentence.

National parks must consider ecological factors and parks must increase public awareness.

Add a comma before the conjunction.

National parks must consider ecological factors, and parks must increase public awareness.

For more help, see Chapter 9, pp. 222–239.

⑪ Using Active and Passive Voice

What's the problem? The use of a verb in the passive voice weakens a sentence.

Why does it matter? Sentences with strong active verbs are more interesting to the reader.

What should you do about it? Rewrite the sentence, using the active rather than the passive voice.

What's the Problem?

What's the Problem?	Quick Fix
A. The passive voice makes a sentence dull. Walkathons **have been participated** in by many who wish to support a charity.	**Revise the sentence to use the active voice.** Many who wish to support a charity **participate** in walkathons.
B. The passive voice takes the emphasis away from the people performing the action. Specified distances **are covered** by participants.	**Revise the sentence to use the active voice.** Participants **cover** specified distances.
C. The passive voice makes a sentence wordy. Walkathons **have been watched** by interested and supportive onlookers.	**Revise the sentence to use the active voice.** Interested and supportive onlookers **watch** walkathons.

For more help, see Chapter 15, pp. 347–363.

QUICK FIX

Note: The passive voice can be used effectively in the following situations:

To emphasize the receiver of an action or the action itself

The site for the next walkathon **was chosen** to avoid bike paths.

To indicate that the performer of an action is unknown

No injury **has been posted** in the event since 1992.

12 Improving Weak Sentences

What's the problem? A sentence contains repeated ideas or too many ideas.

Why does it matter? An empty or overloaded sentence bores the reader and weakens the message.

What should you do about it? Make sure that each of your sentences contains a substantial, clearly focused idea.

What's the Problem?

Quick Fix

A. An idea is repeated.

Srinivasa Ramanujan was **an astonishing math genius with an amazing grasp of numbers.**

Eliminate the repetition.

Srinivasa Ramanujan was ~~an astonishing~~ math genius ~~with an amazing grasp of numbers.~~

B. A stringy sentence contains too many weakly linked ideas.

Ramanujan grew up in a village in India, and, by the age of 13, he was doing advanced calculation, and all without the help of a proper teacher.

Divide the sentence into two or more sentences, using subordinate clauses to show relationships between ideas.

Ramanujan grew up in a village in India. By the age of 13, without the help of a proper teacher, he was doing advanced calculation.

C. Too much information about a topic is crammed into one sentence.

Ramanujan was asked to Cambridge University even though he did not have the proper qualifications, and he died at 32, and modern scholars have not been able to prove some of his theories.

Divide the sentence into two or more sentences, using subordinate clauses to show relationships between ideas.

Despite his lack of the proper qualifications, Ramanujan was asked to Cambridge University. Since his death at 32, modern scholars still have not been able to prove some of his theories.

For more help, see Chapter 3, pp. 76–103.

13 Avoiding Wordiness

What's the problem? A sentence contains unnecessary words. Sentences with too many words sometimes are called *padded sentences*.

Why does it matter? The reader may not be able to understand the meaning of such a wordy sentence.

What should you do about it? Use concise terms and eliminate extra words.

What's the Problem?

Quick Fix

A. A single idea is unnecessarily expressed in two ways.

In the 1800s, **many years ago,** quilts may have been used as signaling devices.

Delete the unnecessary words.

In the 1800s, ~~many years ago,~~ quilts may have been used as signaling devices.

B. A sentence contains words that do not add to its meaning.

Quilters may have **actually** stitched certain quilt patterns to warn **secretly** escaping slaves on the Underground Railroad.

Delete the unnecessary words.

Quilters may have ~~actually~~ stitched certain quilt patterns to warn ~~secretly~~ escaping slaves on the Underground Railroad.

C. A simple idea is expressed in too many words.

A participant might have **happened to have** displayed a coded quilt on a clothesline.

Simplify the expression.

A participant might have ~~happened to have~~ displayed a coded quilt on a clothesline.

D. A clause needlessly begins with *who is, that is,* or *which is.*

A quilt historian, **who is** someone devoted to finding facts, hopes to discover more evidence.

Reduce the clause to a phrase.

A quilt historian, ~~who is~~ someone devoted to finding facts, hopes to discover more evidence.

For more help, see Chapter 15, pp. 347–363.

QUICK FIX

14 Varying Sentence Beginnings

What's the problem? Too many sentences begin in the same way.

Why does it matter? Lack of variety in sentence beginnings makes writing choppy.

What should you do about it? Reword some sentences so that they begin with prepositional phrases, verbal phrases, or subordinate clauses.

What's the Problem?

Too many sentences in a paragraph start with the same word.

Stephen King is a popular writer. **His** books have broad appeal. **His** books sell many copies. **His** books become major motion pictures.

Quick Fix

Start a sentence with a prepositional phrase.

Stephen King is a popular writer. **With their broad appeal,** his books sell many copies and become major motion pictures.

OR

Start a sentence with a verbal phrase.

Having broad appeal, his books sell many copies and become major motion pictures.

OR

Start a sentence with a subordinate clause.

Because they have broad appeal, his books sell many copies and become major motion pictures.

For more help, see Chapter 15, pp. 347–363.

⑮ Varying Sentence Structure

What's the problem? A piece of writing contains too many simple sentences.

Why does it matter? Too much similarity of sentence structures makes writing dull and lifeless.

What should you do about it? Combine or reword sentences to create different structures.

What's the Problem?

The use of too many simple sentences leads to dull and choppy writing.

There is a famous dog sled race in Alaska. It is held every year. It's known as the Iditarod.

The race takes place in rough country. The distance is over a thousand miles. Competitors usually take two to three weeks to finish.

The Iditarod usually takes place in frigid weather. It is hard on dogs. It is even harder on drivers.

For more help, see Chapter 15, pp. 347–363.

Quick Fix

Combine the sentences to form a compound sentence.

There is a famous dog sled race held every year in Alaska, **and** it's known as the Iditarod.

OR

Combine the sentences in one complex sentence.

The race, **which takes place on a course covering over a thousand miles of rough country,** usually takes competitors two to three weeks to finish.

OR

Combine the sentences in a compound-complex sentence.

The Iditarod, **which usually takes place in frigid weather,** is hard on dogs; **but** it's even harder on drivers.

16 Adding Supporting Details

What's the problem? Unfamiliar terms aren't defined, and claims aren't supported.

Why does it matter? Undefined terms and unsupported claims weaken an explanation or a persuasive argument.

What should you do about it? Add information and details to support the sentence.

What's the Problem?

Quick Fix

A. A key term is not defined.

E-mailers are becoming more aware of **netiquette.**

Define the term.

E-mailers are becoming more aware of *netiquette,* **the etiquette or rules for writing and sending electronic mail.**

B. No reason is given for an opinion.

It's better to save rather than send an e-mail when you're upset.

Add a reason or reasons.

It's better to save rather than send an e-mail when you're upset **because you may express yourself more reasonably at a later time.**

C. No facts are given.

More and more people are e-mailing.

Add facts.

According to a Web expert, in 1998, more than 30 percent of adults in the United States and Canada used e-mail.

D. No examples are given.

It's a good idea to learn the rules of netiquette before e-mailing regularly.

Add examples.

It's a good idea to learn the rules of netiquette, **either through Internet manuals or magazine articles,** before e-mailing regularly.

For more help, see Chapter 14, pp. 333–345.

What's the problem? A piece of formal writing contains clichés or slang expressions.

Why does it matter? Clichés do not convey fresh images to the reader. Slang is inappropriate in formal writing.

What should you do about it? Reword sentences to replace clichés and slang with clear, fresh expressions.

What's the Problem?

Quick Fix

A. A sentence contains a cliché.

Because the athlete had been training strenuously for months, everyone knew he **would give 110 percent.**

Delete the cliché and use a different image that is more effective and accurate.

Because the athlete had been training strenuously for months, everyone knew he **would exceed his usual stellar performance.**

B. A sentence contains inappropriate slang.

The **dude** knew that he could **stomp the opposition** at the next day's race.

Remove the slang and use more appropriate language.

The **runner knew** that he could **outrace the competition** at the next day's event.

For more help, see Chapter 16, pp. 365–379.

QUICK FIX

18 Using Precise Words

What's the problem? Nouns, modifiers, or verbs are not precise.

Why does it matter? When a writer uses vague or general words, the reader's interest is not engaged.

What should you do about it? Replace the general words with precise and vivid ideas.

What's the Problem?

Quick Fix

A. Nouns and verbs are too general.

In the glow of the **light,** the aerialists **climbed** to the top of the pole.

Use specific nouns and verbs.

In the glow of the spotlight, the aerialists ascended to the top of the pole.

B. Modifiers are too general.

One of them performed a **nice** somersault on the **thin** high wire to the applause of the **watchful** crowd.

Use more precise or vivid adjectives and adverbs.

One of them performed a graceful somersault on the slender high wire to the applause of the captivated crowd.

C. A sentence tells about what happens instead of showing it.

The acrobats carried out each move calmly and carefully.

Use precise verbs and modifiers to show what happens.

With serene and supreme concentration, the acrobats executed each move with breathtaking precision.

For more help, see Chapter 15, pp. 347–363.

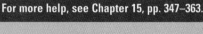

QUICK FIX

⑲ Using Figurative Language

What's the problem? A piece of writing is lifeless or unimaginative.

Why does it matter? Lifeless writing bores the reader. It doesn't help the reader to form mental pictures of what is described.

What should you do about it? Add figures of speech to make the writing lively and to help create pictures in the reader's mind. Do not, however, combine figures of speech that have no logical connection.

What's the Problem?

Quick Fix

A. The description is dull and lifeless.

The sand-sculpting contest was challenging. Working efficiently, our team sculpted a life-size replica of a race car.

OR

Add a simile to make the image more striking.

The sand-sculpting contest was challenging. Working **as efficiently as a pit crew at the Indy 500,** our team sculpted a life-size replica of a race car.

OR

Rewrite the sentence, adding a metaphor.

The sand-and-water mixture was molded and carved into a sleek design.

The sand-and-water mixture **was clay** in our hands that we molded and carved into a sleek design.

B. Figures of speech that have no logical connection have been used together.

A wave, **nature's eraser,** rolled in **like a rain cloud** and in effect flattened the car's two rear wheels.

Emphasize a single figure of speech.

A wave, **nature's eraser,** rolled in ~~like a rain cloud~~ and in effect flattened the car's two rear wheels.

For more help, see Chapter 16, pp. 365–379.

QUICK FIX

⑳ **Paragraphing**

What's the problem? A paragraph contains too many ideas.

Why does it matter? A long paragraph doesn't help signal new ideas and discourages the reader from continuing.

What should you do about it? Break the paragraph into smaller paragraphs, each focusing on one main idea. Start a new paragraph when the speaker, setting, or focus changes.

What's the Problem?

Too many ideas are contained in one paragraph.

The curtain was rising slowly. My heart rate was rising rapidly. Here I was, appearing as the Second Witch in our school's spring production of *Macbeth;* and my mind had suddenly gone blank. I looked out at the audience, a view that was blurred by the footlights. That was some comfort, at least. Alicia, the Third Witch, took my elbow firmly, as if she sensed my nervousness. "It's OK," she whispered. "Take a deep breath." "Thanks, Alicia," I said. "I'll be fine now. "

Quick Fix

The curtain was rising slowly. My heart rate was rising rapidly. Here I was, appearing as the Second Witch in our school's spring production of *Macbeth;* and my mind had suddenly gone blank.

Start a new paragraph to change the action, setting, or place.

I looked out at the audience, a view that was blurred by the footlights. That was some comfort, at least. Then Alicia, the Third Witch, took my elbow firmly, as if she sensed my nervousness.

Start a new paragraph whenever the speaker changes.

"It's OK," she whispered. "Take a deep breath."

"Thanks, Alicia," I said. "I'll be fine now. "

For more help, see Chapter 12, pp. 305–315.

What's the Problem?

The writing contains no paragraph breaks for logic or readability.

Have stories of young people who have launched successful businesses inspired or intimidated you? Either way, it's worthwhile to investigate what it might be like to be an entrepreneur, a person who takes on the risks of organizing and running a business. Polls have shown that although teenagers would like to start businesses of their own, most don't know how to begin. Help is out there, however, for the ambitious as well as for the merely curious. Attending a meeting of young entrepreneurs provides opportunities to share ideas and experiences with peers. In addition, making contact with entrepreneurs is a good way to gain an insider's view of business practices and opportunities. Whether you are seeking success or just a look at the workings of the business world, it can't hurt to get an early start.

For more help, see Chapter 12, pp. 305–315.

Quick Fix

Have stories of young people who have launched successful businesses inspired or intimidated you? Either way, it's worthwhile to investigate what it might be like to be an entrepreneur, a person who takes on the risks of organizing and running a business.

Start a new paragraph to introduce the first main idea.

Polls have shown that although teenagers would like to start businesses of their own, most don't know how to begin. Help is out there, however, for the ambitious as well as for the merely curious.

Start a new paragraph to introduce another main idea.

Attending a meeting of young entrepreneurs provides opportunities to share ideas and experiences with peers. In addition, making contact with entrepreneurs is a good way to gain an insider's view of business practices and opportunities.

Start a new paragraph for the conclusion.

Whether you are seeking success or just a look at the workings of the business world, it can't hurt to get an early start.

QUICK FIX

Essential Writing Skills

Getting the Point

Funny, isn't it? The more you use a pencil, the duller it becomes. Yet the more you explore writing, the sharper you become. The process of finding and fleshing out ideas takes work, but rewards do come. You'll discover that writing a piece that had once been a challenge now comes quite naturally. A good pencil may last only a week or two. Skill at writing can last for a lifetime.

Power Words
Vocabulary for Precise Writing

BLOCKED

at a loss

In Need of Inspiration

Even great literary figures have faced dry spells. Try words like these when you want to get your writing back on track.

The Lightbulb's Off . . .

Your teacher asks you to think of a name for an important class project, but you **draw a blank.** The request **baffles** you. Your imagination is **blocked,** and your thought processes **stall.** Every fresh attempt is **thwarted,** and you feel totally **at a loss.** Doubt **stymies** all possibilities. The challenge **perplexes** you and **frustrates** you at the same time. This request has you hopelessly **stumped.**

Storm of Creativity

You look for ways to be **creative.** A group discussion might produce an **inventive** name, something **conceptual,** based on the project's purpose. An **imaginative** idea might be to look in a **fertile** place like the Web for **associative** suggestions. The more places you try, the more **productive** your results and the better chance of finding an **innovative** and **ingenious** solution. Something's bound to help you achieve a **breakthrough.**

breakthrough

productive

frustrates

▷ Your Turn Words of Wisdom

What are some ways to deal with a sudden writing-related setback? Interview classmates about the challenges they have faced, and invite them to share advice or anecdotes, brief stories from their lives that focus on this topic.

creative

inventive

Writing Process in Action

The Far Side by Gary Larson

Edgar Allan Poe in a moment of writer's block.

Getting It Right

What suggestions would you offer Edgar Allan Poe to help him overcome his writer's block? What similar experience of your own could you share with the writer?

In the cartoon, Poe is groping for the right title, and he's very close to zeroing in on it. Writing is like that. One moment you experience the frustration of writer's block, the next you break through and find your focus. There is no right way to write. Along the way, you have to figure out what works best for you.

Write Away: Likes and Dislikes

What kind of writing do you like best? What kind do you dread? What is the biggest problem you face when you write? How do you overcome it? Place your response in your 📁 **Working Portfolio.**

Writing Process Overview

LESSON 1

The writing process generally involves five stages: **prewriting, drafting, revising, editing** and **proofreading,** and **publishing** and **reflecting.** The process is recursive. You can begin writing at one of the later stages or return to an earlier one throughout the process. As you write, you will develop an individual process that suits your style and the occasion for writing.

❶ Prewriting

When you prewrite, you experiment with writing ideas and let your imagination soar. The following may help you explore your ideas.

> **Here's How** **Choosing Writing Options**
>
> - **Find a Topic** Ideas for writing may be triggered by anything: a conversation, a book, a memory, a photo. Think about what interests you or what you would like to know more about.
> - **Establish Purpose** Purpose is why you write. You may write to express yourself, to analyze, to inform, to entertain, or to persuade—or you may combine these purposes.
> - **Identify Your Audience** Your audience is the group of people who will read your writing. Keep the following questions in mind as you think about audience: How much does my audience already know about my topic? What do they need to know? How can I engage their interest?
> - **Choose a Form** The form is the type of writing you choose to express your ideas. For example, you might choose to write a poem, a play, an article, or a speech.

Developing Ideas

Once you've chosen a topic, use one of the following techniques to develop your ideas and gather information on your topic.

- Freewrite, or write whatever comes to mind on your topic.
- Ask *who? what? where? when? why? how?* questions about your topic.
- Brainstorm, either alone or with a group, about your topic.

When you freewrite, don't worry about grammar or spelling. Just allow your thoughts to flow.

Organizing Information

After you've gathered information on your topic, you can start organizing it. How you organize your writing often depends on what you want to write about. For example, you might organize a report about an earthquake by considering its causes and effects. If you want to compare two athletes, you would probably begin by listing their similarities and differences. For a historical narrative on the women's rights movement, you might use a chronological ordering.

For more on organization methods, see pp. 326–327.

❷ Drafting

Drafting is the stage in the writing process when you start putting your thoughts on paper. You shape your raw material into sentences and paragraphs.

Depending on how focused your ideas are, you might write a discovery draft or a planned draft. A **discovery draft** is helpful when you're not sure of your ideas and just want to get your thoughts down—when you write a story or essay, for instance. A **planned draft** is appropriate when your ideas are well developed or your information needs to be presented in a logical order—as when you write a report or proposal.

Using Peer Response

After you've finished your draft, have another student read your work. A peer reader can sometimes spot problems you can't see and provide valuable feedback. Here are some response techniques to use when you share your writing.

Using Peer Response Techniques
Read your work aloud to a peer to hear how it sounds.
Ask your reader to restate what you've written.
Ask your reader to tell you what he or she liked best.
Have your reader summarize your main point.
Get feedback from your reader on specific problems.
Discuss your ideas with your reader.
Interrupt the reading and ask your peer what he or she is thinking.

❸ Revising

If possible, set aside your draft for at least an hour or two before you begin to revise it. Then, when you're ready, use the following six traits to help you evaluate your writing.

Six Traits of Effective Writing	
Ideas and Content	Make your ideas clear, focused, and well supported with relevant details.
Organization	Arrange your ideas in a logical order that moves the reader through the text.
Voice	Express your ideas in a way that shows your individual style and personality.
Word Choice	Use language that is precise, powerful, and engaging.
Sentence Fluency	Improve the rhythm and flow of your writing by using varied sentence length and structure.
Conventions	Eliminate grammar, capitalization, spelling, and punctuation errors.

For more on revising, see pp. 347–363.

❹ Editing and Proofreading

When you edit and proofread your work, you put the final touches on your writing. You check for errors in grammar, spelling, capitalization, and punctuation—errors that can distract your reader from understanding your ideas. In the following paragraph, proofreading symbols are used to mark errors for correction.

> **STUDENT MODEL**
>
> *DRAFT*
>
> When Jan began clerking at Style central, it
> wasn't just to earn some extra spending
> money. She needed the job because she
> couldn't depend on getting money for lunches
> and school supplies. Sometimes her dad
> would give her some money, but sometimes
> there just wasn't any money to be had.

Capitalize proper names.

Check spelling.

Check end punctuation.

Use a comma before the conjunction.

If you write using a computer, you may want to print out your work and do your editing and proofreading on the hard copy. It is often easier to spot errors on paper than on the screen.

For a list of commonly used proofreading marks, see p. 302.

❺ Publishing and Reflecting

Sharing your writing is usually the last stage of the writing process. However, even after you present your work, you can still choose to revise it again. You may want to place work that still needs polishing in your ▱ **Working Portfolio.** Your best writing—finished and ready for an audience—can go in your ▱ **Presentation Portfolio.**

Presenting Your Work

You can present your work in written form, in a performance, or in a media presentation.

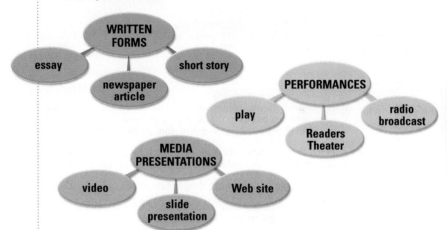

Reflecting

The best way to learn and grow as a writer is to reflect on your work after you've presented it. Ask yourself the following questions.

- What do I like about my work?
- What would I like to change?
- What part of the writing process caused me the least trouble? the most trouble?
- What did I learn about myself?
- What strategies can I use in my next writing project?

Adjusting Your Writing Process

You can adjust the writing process to fit any writing situation. By using different techniques for different kinds of writing and allotting your time to suit the situation, you can customize your writing process for many types of writing projects.

❶ Writing for Assessment

When you have to take a writing assessment, or answer an essay question, you respond to a specific prompt. You have a limited amount of time to organize and write down your ideas. There is no time to rewrite. In this situation, you should condense your writing process as you carefully plan your response. Here are some ways to adjust your writing process for a written exam.

1. Defend your position on the following question: Should the United States intervene militarily to help settle regional conflicts in other countries?

I believe that the U.S. government should not intervene militarily to settle conflicts in other countries b...

...tive

Adjusting for a Written Exam

Underline key words in the prompt to determine your purpose, the form of your writing, and your audience's needs.

Since time is limited, think ideas through before you begin writing. Restrict prewriting to a rough outline on scratch paper.

To focus your essay, write a thesis statement.

Draft an introduction that includes your thesis statement and previews the points you'll be making. Develop and support these points in the body. Summarize your thesis in a conclusion.

Allow time to reread your response and correct errors.

For more information on taking essay tests, see pp. 584–585.

❷ Informational Writing

Informational writing includes newspaper articles, essays, and reports of any kind, from research to business reports. Since this kind of writing must contain a great deal of accurate, factual information, you will probably spend a lot of time on the prewriting stage—planning, researching, and so on. Here are some ways to adjust your writing process for informational writing.

Adjusting for Informational Writing

Research and gather reliable information.	*I. Mars Polar Lander*
Use an outline like the one shown—or another kind of graphic organizer—to organize the information and write your draft.	*A. Mission time line* *1. Launch: January 3, 1999* *2. Land: December 3, 1999* *B. Mission purpose*
Use tables or other visuals to present information, if desired.	*1. Explore environment near South Pole*
During revision, be sure to define jargon or unfamiliar terms. Also check dates and spelling of names.	*2. Study planet's cyclic climate changes*
Include source lists and accurate citations in the finished product.	

HOT TIP

Ideas for other sections of your essay may occur to you while you're writing your response. Take notes as you write so you won't forget the ideas.

❸ Creative Writing

A short story, poem, and play are examples of creative writing. When you engage in creative writing, you may spend more time drafting and revising in order to get the details right. The chart below lists some ways to adjust your writing process for creative writing.

Adjusting for Creative Writing

During prewriting, you don't need to plan too much: creative writing is often a series of discoveries.	*Why is Yuri so angry? She could be mad at her parents, but that's obvious, dull. Okay.*
Use freewriting—as shown here—and other methods to experiment: let words and characters lead you in new directions.	*What makes me angry? Sometimes I'm not sure myself.*
As you draft and revise, spend time crafting: play with language, voice, structure.	*That's it. Yuri's mad at the world but doesn't know why.*
Use descriptions and figurative language to create a specific mood. Keep your audience, goals, and purpose in mind as you write.	*Maybe finding out could be the whole point of the story.*

For more on writing creatively, see pp. 434–443.

❹ Media Projects

Media projects combine written, visual, and audio elements. These elements should work together to create a unified whole. Here are some ways to adjust your writing process for such media projects as slide presentations, live performances, and videos.

Adjusting for a Media Project

Before you begin, consider what medium best suits your information.

During prewriting, use graphics or a storyboard like the one below to plan your project.

Coordinate written, visual, and audio elements.

Use peer response to evaluate your project and revise it accordingly.

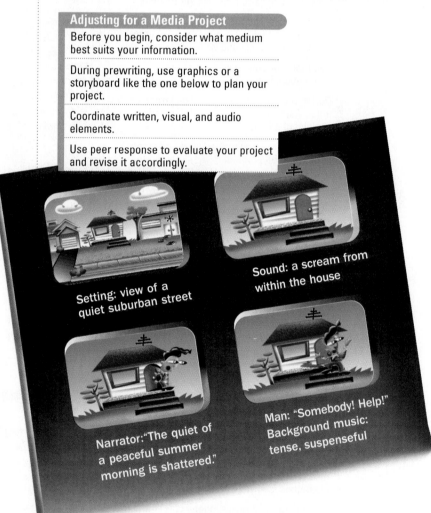

Setting: view of a quiet suburban street

Sound: a scream from within the house

Narrator:"The quiet of a peaceful summer morning is shattered."

Man: "Somebody! Help!"
Background music: tense, suspenseful

For more on media projects, see pp. 529–543.
See also the 📼 **Media Literacy Videotapes.**

Options for Publishing

You don't have to limit your audience to your teacher or other students. There are many forums available to you outside the classroom. Some lead directly into the world of professional writing.

❶ Public Forums

The web diagram below shows some of the public forums for your written work.

Before you submit your writing to a specific forum, use a writer's guide, such as the current issue of the *Market Guide for Young Writers,* to find out what kind of material the publication is looking for. You should also study the publication's guidelines. The chart below lists some general suggestions for submitting materials to a public forum.

> **Here's How** **Submitting Your Manuscript**
>
> **1.** Use a typewriter or computer to prepare your manuscript.
> **2.** Type your manuscript double-spaced on one side of the page.
> **3.** Print your name, address, and phone number in the upper-left corner of the first page. In the upper-right corner, indicate the word count.
> **4.** Number the pages of your manuscript.
> **5.** Include a cover letter explaining why your work is appropriate for that publication.
> **6.** Include an SASE (self-addressed, stamped envelope).
> **7.** Submit your manuscript to one publisher at a time.

Expect to wait a long time for a response—up to two or three months. View this time as a learning process and keep writing.

Here is an entry from the guide.

Asterisk indicates market of special interest to young people

* THE FUDGE CAKE, P.O. Box 197, Citrus Heights, CA 95611-0197. Bi-monthly newsletter designed to showcase the works of young writers 6–17.

Types of material accepted

Publishes: Short stories and poetry from writers ages 6–17. No artwork accepted.

Instructions for obtaining more detailed guidelines

Submission Info: Type or neatly print submissions on 8" x 11" white paper. Send SASE for information flyer and detailed guidelines. Sample copy $2.50.

Subscription Rates: Six issues $10 in U.S.; $12 Canada.

—Kathy Henderson
Market Guide for Young Writers

❷ Online Forums

These days, the Internet is probably one of the easiest ways to get published. You can create your own forum on the Internet by setting up a Web site. You can also publish your work on your school's online newspaper or tap into other electronic publications.

Web Site

You can use a Web site to provide information about yourself, your interests, or an issue that's important to you. Use graphics to clarify your written information and provide links to other Web sites. In the Web site below, the author shares his interest in movies.

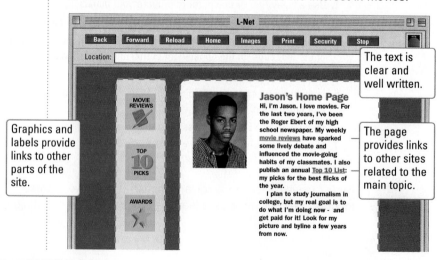

The text is clear and well written.

Graphics and labels provide links to other parts of the site.

The page provides links to other sites related to the main topic.

Jason's Home Page

Hi, I'm Jason. I love movies. For the last two years, I've been the Roger Ebert of my high school newspaper. My weekly movie reviews have sparked some lively debate and influenced the movie-going habits of my classmates. I also publish an annual Top 10 List: my picks for the best flicks of the year.

I plan to study journalism in college, but my real goal is to do what I'm doing now - and get paid for it! Look for my picture and byline a few years from now.

The Web offers excellent online tutorials and workshops about the technical skills required for creating a Web site.

For information on creating a Web site, see pp. 539–541.
See also the 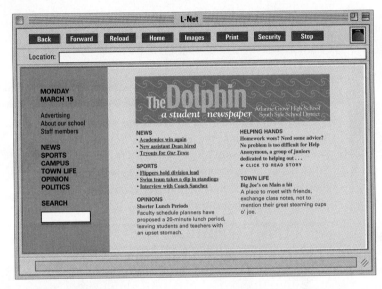 Media Literacy Videotapes.

Online School Newspaper

Your school may have an online newspaper that provides opportunities for you to publish your work. Here's an example of what an online school newspaper might look like.

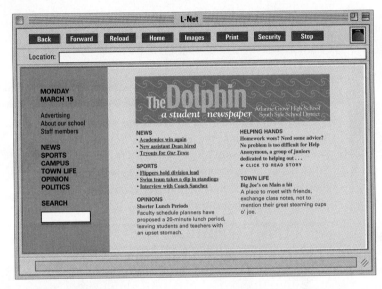

Other Electronic Forums

Here are some other possibilities for online publication.

- **Online student magazines.** Search for these by using keywords such as "student e-zines."

- **Letters to the editor.** Respond in an online letter to an article you read in a weekly news magazine.

- **Online contests.** Some sites hold year-round contests in writing and other creative pursuits. Search for these by using keywords such as "writing contests."

 Some Web sites disappear from the Net after a relatively short time. You might want to track a particular site for a while before submitting work to it.

Student Help Desk

Writing Process at a Glance

- Prewriting
- Drafting
- Writing, Editing, and Proofreading
- Publishing and Reflecting

Writing Breakthroughs: Hammering Writer's Block

Here are some techniques to overcome writer's block.

- Try rewriting the last few paragraphs from a previous writing session—don't just reread them.
- Write about the problems you're having with your topic.
- Play word-association games to get your ideas flowing.
- Have a peer reviewer read your work.

Proofreading Marks: Fix-It Symbols

Description	Symbol	Example
capitalize	(cap) ≡	I work for jim.
delete	ℐ	laptop commputers
insert	∧	She likes her job.
lowercase	(lc) /	He worked all Summer.
new paragraph	¶	¶"Thank you," I said.
change order	(tr) ∩	a item new
add period	⊙	It's time to go home⊙
close up	⌒	Here's the video cassette.
add space	#	Fill out this form.
don't delete	(stet)	He is a great athlete. (stet)

Computer Tips: Tools for Writing Electronically

- During freewriting, use a symbol such as # when you can't think of a particular word. Later, use the Search function to find the symbol and fill in the word.

- As you draft, type notes to yourself in capitals about changes you might make.

- Save each version of your draft in a separate file using the Save As command.

- Print out your drafts triple-spaced with wide margins so that you have plenty of room to write in changes and comments.

The Bottom Line

Checklist for Revising and Editing

Have you applied the six traits of effective writing? Ask yourself, have I . . .

____ presented my ideas clearly?

____ provided details and examples that support my ideas?

____ used a consistent organization method?

____ used a writing style that reflects my attitude toward the topic?

____ used precise, lively language?

____ used varied sentence length and structure?

____ checked for errors in grammar, capitalization, spelling, and punctuation?

Power Words
Vocabulary for Precise Writing

effective

the right stuff

Winning Ways

Is your future a big question mark? Whether you're focusing on present-day school activities or making future plans, the right words can be your keys to success.

A Success Story

You are running for class president. You need an **efficient** team to provide you with **effective** support. You must deliver a **forceful** address that will send a telling message. You will want to project the **dynamic** image of someone who has **the right stuff**—a person who can devise **efficacious** solutions to problems, a person who is the most **compelling** candidate to vote for.

Don't Defeat Yourself

Unless you plan well, you will have an **ineffective** campaign, and all your efforts will be **ineffectual** in gaining votes. Don't lose out through **inadequate** preparation and useless worrying. Don't let weak slogans and **pointless** issues and **feckless** helpers lead to a **fruitless** run for office.

▷ **Your Turn** All the Right Moves

In recent years, books have been published that detail the habits of successful people. Make a list of any habits you've developed that have led to positive results. What words would you use to describe your winning ways?

dynamic

ineffective

forceful

efforts

Writing Effective Paragraphs

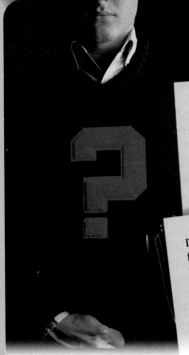

Which College Applicant Would You Choose?

I think I have a lot of good qualities for college. I'm from a large family of 5 kids. I'm the youngest. I have always loved to read, especially science fiction. In fifth grade, I learned to play the trumpet, and now I play the drums as well. Perseverance is one of my good traits. Even my teachers have praised me for not giving up. I think I will major in business or computer science.

Determination is my strong suit. Once I set a goal, I try to follow it through to the end. My experience on the swim team is a good example. At the end of my freshman year, I was dead last in the team standings due to my inexperience. The coach even mildly encouraged me to pursue another sport. However, I hung in there, and by the end of my junior year, I placed in the top 20% at the state meet.

PARAGRAPHS

Making the Grade

Consider this scenario: You're reviewing essays from college applications. The two paragraphs above land on your desk. Does the quality of the writing influence your decision?

One of the paragraphs is clear and orderly. A focused main idea and well-connected sentences make it easy to follow. In contrast, the other paragraph is cluttered with too many ideas. The reader has to strain to follow it. In its own way, each paragraph points up the importance of crafting an effective paragraph.

Write Away: A Paragraph for Your Thoughts

Try writing a paragraph about one of your personal strengths that could be included in a college application essay. Clearly state your strength; then support it with details or an example. Save your writing in your 🗂 **Working Portfolio.**

Effective Single Paragraphs

Paragraphs are often called the building blocks of longer writing. But sometimes you need to present your thoughts in a single independent paragraph—for example, when taking an essay test, completing an application, or writing a summary.

❶ What Makes a Good Paragraph?

Paragraphs are as different as snowflakes—the content and form of each is unique. But despite this, they share a few common characteristics. Every good paragraph focuses on one key idea, provides adequate support for that key idea, has a clear purpose, and smoothly flows from one sentence to the next.

LITERARY MODEL

This battle with Mr. Covey was the turning point in my career as a slave. It rekindled the few expiring embers of freedom, and revived within me a sense of my own manhood. It recalled the departed self-confidence, and inspired me again with a determination to be free. The gratification afforded by the triumph was a full compensation for whatever else might follow, even death itself.

—Frederick Douglass, *Narrative of the Life of Frederick Douglass, an American Slave*

Main Idea
The battle was a turning point.

Purpose
Narrator describes ways that battle was a turning point.

Unity
All sentences pertain to how life changed after battle.

❷ Developing the Main Idea

To be effective, every paragraph should have one—and only one—main idea. Before you write a paragraph, become clear yourself about the central point you want to make. Then stick to that thought.

Topic Sentences

Topic Sentence at the Beginning The main idea of a paragraph is often stated in one clear sentence called a **topic sentence.** Although a topic sentence can appear anywhere within a paragraph, it's often the first sentence. Placed there, it functions like a road sign, signaling to the reader what lies ahead. In the model you just read, all other sentences help to explain the beginning topic sentence.

Topic Sentence in the Middle Sometimes you may want to open your paragraph with catchy details. In that case, you might place your topic sentence in the middle of a paragraph.

> **PROFESSIONAL MODEL**
>
> The water is clear, calm and dark. As I drop off the rear of the boat with my fellow divers into the icy water, a chill runs up my spine—both from the cold and from my growing sense of anticipation. We are night diving in the Southern Ocean off the southwestern coast of Australia, in search of creatures that sound almost mythical. **We are hunting for dragons—more precisely, leafy sea dragons.** And for our breeding program at Underwater World Perth, we want to catch a male—a pregnant male.
>
> —Paul Groves, "Leafy Sea Dragons"
> *Scientific American*

Catchy details

Topic sentence

Topic Sentence at the End You can place a topic sentence at the end of a paragraph to summarize ideas, draw a conclusion, or emphasize a point.

Implied Main Idea

Some paragraphs do not require a topic sentence because the main idea is suggested by all the details. Such a paragraph is said to have an **implied main idea.**

PARAGRAPHS

At dozens of churches in Spring Valley and Columbia [South Carolina], and thousands more around the United States, teen-agers will stand at the exits, soup pots in hand, collecting money for people who have far less than they. They call it the Souper Bowl, playing off one of America's most conspicuous days of consumption, Super Bowl Sunday.

Implied Main Idea: Teens raise money for the poor on Super Bowl Sunday.

—"Banking on Super Bowl to Help Feed the Hungry,"
The New York Times

❸ Supporting the Main Idea

The main idea of a paragraph should be supported with illustrative details. While a main idea may be broad and general, supporting sentences are specific. They clarify your main idea for the reader by filling in the details, and they convince the reader that you know what you're talking about. Supporting sentences may include anecdotes, facts and statistics, examples, or sensory details. Notice how the main idea in the paragraph below is supported.

Actually, I've never met a pizza I didn't like. Make it from scratch or have it delivered; give me thick crust or give me thin; just give me a pizza lathered with tangy tomato sauce, generous amounts of pepperoni and olives, and smother that baby with as much mozzarella as the structural integrity of the crust can bear. From Perth to Pascagoula, I've found this basic pizza the stuff of an invariably satisfying meal. What's more, I've never had to look far to find it.

Jay Stuller, "As American as Pizza Pie"

Topic sentence

Supporting details show that the author has a passion for pizza.

For more on supporting details, see p. 326.

PRACTICE Crafting a Single Paragraph

Write a paragraph about your own favorite (or most detested) food. Include a topic sentence and at least three mouthwatering (or stomach-turning) supporting details.

Unity and Coherence in Paragraphs

LESSON 2

An effective paragraph is more than just several sentences about a main idea. The sentences in the paragraph must flow smoothly and logically from one to another. This smooth flow of ideas occurs when two important elements are present—unity and coherence.

❶ Unity in Paragraphs

A paragraph that has unity is fit and trim: every sentence contributes to the central point. As you write freely during the draft stage, you may find yourself cluttering a paragraph with too many ideas. If you think these ideas have merit, then develop them in new paragraphs of their own. Delete rambling ideas that relate only indirectly to your main idea. Notice how the following model has been edited to obtain unity.

STUDENT MODEL

1968 was clearly a year of crisis. The war in Vietnam escalated dramatically. ~~The Vietnam War had actually been raging for about twenty years by then, ever since Ho Chi Minh had launched the revolt for independence.~~ At home, the antiwar movement exploded and sometimes became violent. Over 50,000 protesters marched on the Pentagon in Washington, D.C. ~~That must have been an extraordinary sight.~~ On college campuses, antiwar activities often clashed with the police. Perhaps worst of all, 1968 brought the assassinations of two powerful leaders—Martin Luther King, Jr., and Robert Kennedy. ¶ By the end of the sixties, the turmoil was still raging.

> **Topic sentence**

> **Overloading:** Delete.

> **Off the point:** Delete.

> **New idea:** Begin new paragraph.

PARAGRAPHS

❷ Coherence in Paragraphs

In coherent paragraphs, each sentence leads into the next. The writing flows smoothly, and readers can clearly follow the writer's logic.

Patterns of Organization

To craft a coherent paragraph, organize your ideas in a consistent pattern. In addition, use **transitions**—words and phrases that link one idea to another. Below are examples of organizational patterns that you'll use again and again. Notice how the transition words in each example help to connect the ideas and make the pattern of organization obvious.

Sequential Order When you use the pattern of sequential order, you relate a sequence of events in the order that they occur. This pattern invites your readers to "watch" events unfold as they happen. Sequential order is useful when you tell a story, explain a process, or relate an event.

Our visit to the White House was remarkable.
First, we . . .
Next . . .
Then . . .
By the time we left . . .

1, 2, 3, 4...

Order of Degree You may want to order details based on their importance, usefulness, familiarity, or some other quality. This order can be from most to least or from least to most of the quality. Writers often use this pattern of organization when they are building a persuasive argument or giving information about several causes and effects.

A cramped student lunch period leads to several bad consequences.
For one thing . . .
Moreover . . .
Even worse . . .
Probably the worst effect of all is . . .

Comparison and Contrast Sometimes you want to show how two or more ideas are similar or different. In that case, organize your material by showing comparisons and contrasts, and by using transition words similar to the following.

Community colleges and state universities each have their own distinct advantages.
Both are . . .
Similarly . . .
But unlike state universities . . .
On the other hand . . .

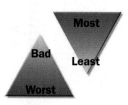

For more examples of transitions, see the Student Help Desk, p. 315.

Spatial Order Spatial order is order by space—near to far, top to bottom, and so forth. You can use this pattern effectively in descriptive paragraphs.

The child is waiting under the cool shade of the porch.

Near him is . . .
Farther away he sees . . .
Still farther, he notices . . .

❸ Connecting Ideas

Creating a **topic chain** within a paragraph is an effective method of achieving coherence. You create a topic chain when, instead of shifting topics, you refer to a single topic from one sentence to the next. Each link in a topic chain serves as a "stepping stone" for your reader, making it easy to follow your pattern of thinking.

STUDENT MODEL

DRAFT

 Friendliness is a strong trait of bottlenose whales. Many **sailors** have reported seeing bottlenose whales approaching their boats. **Loyalty** is another one of their traits. When a bottlenose whale is wounded, its **companions** won't leave it behind. **Whalers** found the bottlenose whales to be an easy target because of these traits. **They** killed tens of thousands of them before the commercial harvest ended in 1973.

> Several shifts in topics = **confusing**

REVISION

 Bottlenose whales are known for their friendliness. **They** are apt to approach boats as if they were curious reporters after a good story. These **midsize whales** are also loyal, refusing to abandon a companion that is wounded. The **endearing qualities of the bottlenose whale** actually made them an easy target to whalers. **Tens of thousands of bottlenose whales** were killed by whalers before the commercial harvest ended in 1973.

> Topic chain = **easy to follow**

PRACTICE   Smooth Moves

In your 📁 **Writing Portfolio,** find the paragraph you wrote for the **Write Away** on page 305. Revise your paragraph for unity and coherence by adding transitions and by organizing your ideas in a clear, consistent pattern.

PARAGRAPHS

Paragraphs in Longer Works

Most of the paragraphs you write do not exist independently; instead, they function as building blocks of longer works. The kind of paragraph you write will depend upon your purpose for writing.

❶ Types of Paragraphs

There are four basic types of paragraphs: narrative, descriptive, expository, and persuasive. You develop each type of paragraph differently, using different kinds of details and different content. Your purpose—the reason you are writing—determines the kind of paragraph you will choose. When writing longer pieces, you may use a number of different types of paragraphs in order to create particular effects or achieve certain purposes. The chart below can help you decide what type of paragraph to use.

Fitting Paragraphs to Purpose

What's your purpose?	Choose this paragraph type	Opportunities to use this paragraph
To describe a person, thing, or scene	Descriptive	For an engaging introduction; to describe people or settings; to enhance a definition
To tell a story or anecdote, either fictional or true	Narrative	For an engaging introduction; to support a point; to relate a scene or event
To give information	Expository	To give evidence for a claim; to support a point; to explain a process, event, or definition
To convince others or call them to action	Persuasive	To support a claim or an opinion; to call others to action; to solicit support

❷ Paragraphs at Work

Notice how each paragraph in the following model has its own purpose and function, yet contributes to the whole.

PROFESSIONAL MODEL

Jushua Illauq slid his hunting rifle onto the sled and yanked the starter cord of his battered black snowmobile. The aging machine sputtered in the frigid air, then roared to life. Soon all five of our snowmobiles were revving, and Jushua's sled dogs were howling from their nearby pens, pleading, it seemed to me, to join our journey across the ice toward the fjords of Baffin Island's east coast. . . .

> **Narrative paragraph** relates a scene to hook reader's interest.

We arrived at the base of Great Sail Peak, wind screaming, clouds boiling, cold biting. Bending my head back, I surveyed a peak as intimidating as anything I'd ever climbed. . . .

> **Descriptive paragraph** gives sensory details about a mountain peak.

We planned to climb Great Sail Peak in three stages. First, we'd haul our gear up a 1,400-foot cliff to set up ledge camp on a broad terrace, pulling our ropes up behind us. From there we'd climb the glassy plinth to a height of 3,750 feet above the frozen lake, and under a jutting lip of rock we called the Visor we'd set up wall camp, a shantytown of porta-ledges. Finally we'd climb the upper wall to the summit. On our scouting flight, we'd spotted a possible route up the blank northwest face.

> **Expository paragraph** classifies three stages of a mountain climb.

—Greg Child, "Hitting the Wall," *National Geographic*

PRACTICE ▸ Analyzing Types of Paragraphs

Examine in depth a long piece of writing in a current publication, such as a newspaper, magazine, Internet article, or textbook. Observe the different types of paragraphs and how they work together. You might highlight the paragraphs that seem particularly effective. Can you tell why these paragraphs drew your interest?

PARAGRAPHS

Student Help Desk

Paragraphs at a Glance

The Far Side by Gary Larson

An Effective Paragraph

- **States a main idea**
  ("the picture's pretty bleak")

- **Contains details that support the main idea**
  (reasons for the bleak picture)

- **Has unity and coherence**
  (sentences all explain main idea and are connected)

"The picture's pretty bleak, gentlemen. The world's climates are changing, the mammals are taking over, and we all have a brain about the size of a walnut."

Paragraphs Like Pencils: Sharpen the Point

Having trouble getting clear on your main idea for a paragraph? These strategies can help to get you focused.

- Compose your main idea as a headline or caption.

- Ask yourself: "What exactly is my point?" Then say your answer aloud so you can hear how your ideas fit.

- Sum up the target in three words or less (for example, benefits of exercise; the White House; puppy training).

Smooth Passage: Make the Transition

Make life easy for your readers. Using the following transitions will show readers how your ideas are related.

Sequential Order	Spatial Order	Comparison and Contrast	Order of Degree
after	behind	in the same way	first
before	to the right of	either . . . or	most important
the next day	below	likewise	less important
always	around	neither . . . nor	second
at that time	up	similarly	least important
preceding	on top of	also	mainly
while	at the bottom	like	best
meanwhile	in back	unlike	worst
second	in front	on the other hand	moreover
finally	over	in contrast	even more
during	beneath	on the contrary	mostly
every time	here	however	furthermore
soon	inside	instead	
simultaneously	above	nevertheless	

The Bottom Line

Checklist for Effective Paragraphs

Have I . . .

____ kept the paragraph focused on one idea?

____ clearly expressed the main idea in a topic sentence?

____ supported the main idea with convincing details?

____ used an organization that allows one sentence to flow logically to the next?

____ used transitions that help readers follow my logic?

Power Words
Vocabulary for Precise Writing

The Total Look

Picture this: you have many ideas and many words that help to put the ideas together.

Puzzling Pieces

You have a crime to solve. None of the witnesses **concur** on what they saw; they cannot **agree** on the facts. Stories don't **jibe;** times and dates don't **correspond** with the suspects' alibis. Nothing **tallies,** and you can't **correlate** one detail with another.

It All Comes Together

Suddenly, two bits of evidence **dovetail.** More pieces begin to **connect** and **interlock.** Everything starts to **fit together** and **harmonize.** Before, when nothing would **hang together** or **match,** you were discouraged. Then without warning, it all **melds**—what wouldn't **cohere** before, now makes perfect sense. You have **tessellated** the data into the mosaic of a solution. Reporters flock to you to learn your brilliant methods.

▷ **Your Turn** Working Parts

Sketch or find a cutaway drawing of a device with several working parts, such as a lock, a car engine, or a lightbulb. Explain to a partner how each part operates, either singly or in unison with other parts.

Effective Compositions

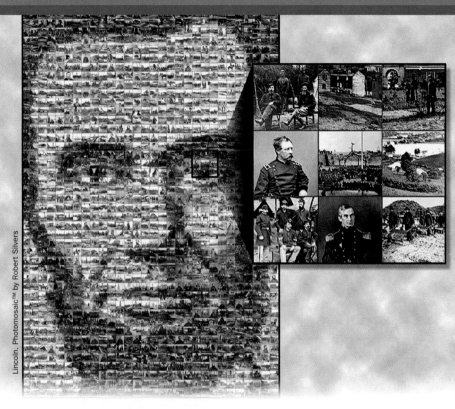

Lincoln. Photomosaic™ by Robert Silvers

Seeing the Big Picture

Step back and look at the image on this page. Now look at it more closely. How are the smaller pictures related to each other? How are they related to the bigger picture? The total effect is similar to that of a mosaic. In fact, the image is called a Photomosaic—a big picture made up of many smaller ones.

A composition is like a Photomosaic. All the paragraphs in a composition are related to each other and to the composition's thesis, or main point. The parts of a composition—its words, sentences, and paragraphs—form a unified, coherent whole.

Write Away: Picturing Your Composition
Find a composition you've already written and analyze it. What large picture would you use to illustrate its thesis? What smaller pictures would you use to illustrate the main idea in each paragraph? Place your ideas in your 📁 **Working Portfolio.**

The Complete Composition

Compositions take many different forms, such as essays in school, reviews, research reports, proposals, articles, and application essays. No matter what form they take, an effective composition is one in which you clearly convey your ideas or convincingly present your opinion. And contrary to what Calvin thinks, your audience will be impressed by its content, not by the binder you present it in.

Calvin and Hobbes by Bill Watterson

© 1989 Universal Press Syndicate

❶ Basic Structure

Generally, every composition has three basic parts: the introduction, the body, and the conclusion. As you read the following composition, notice how the parts work together.

STUDENT MODEL

Puffs of smoke rise from the ground as strange creatures—obviously actors in costumes—appear and disappear. A group of scientists land on the moon by crashing their rocket ship into the eye of a flat Man in the Moon. These images and scenes appear in *A Trip to the Moon*, a 14-minute feature created by French director Georges Méliès in 1902 and regarded as the first science fiction film ever made. Today's viewers would probably consider the pioneer film's technology simple and even laughable, but that first film paved the way for future sci-fi movies.

INTRODUCTION

This section grabs readers' attention with a vivid description.

THESIS STATEMENT

The main point of the work is stated in the introduction.

CHAPTER 13

However, for many years, the technology in science fiction films didn't improve much beyond the puffs of smoke and weird costumes in *A Trip to the Moon.* Even after sound opened up new possibilities for movies in the 1920s, science fiction films continued to use ridiculous costumes and unrealistic sets and tell predictable stories.

Finally, in 1968, sci-fi leaped into the future with the creation of *2001: A Space Odyssey.* Using slow-motion sequences, a talking computer named HAL, and spectacular light shows, director Stanley Kubrick raised the science fiction film to the level of a work of art. He also changed the conventional sci-fi plot by asking his audience thought-provoking questions about where humans came from and where they're going.

The development of the science fiction film continued in the decades that followed. In 1977, director George Lucas made the first of the *Star Wars* film series, using computer-imaging technology to create a host of strange intergalactic creatures. This technology was further refined in 1993 with Steven Spielberg's *Jurassic Park,* in which digitally generated dinosaurs—including a particularly frightening *Tyrannosaurus rex*—terrorize human actors.

In the 21st century, science fiction films will really come into their own. As audiences learn the full story of Darth Vader in George Lucas's *Star Wars* prequels, technology will take us to incredible new worlds. Interestingly enough, Lucas planned episodes one through three years ago but put off making them in part because early 1980s technology couldn't convincingly reproduce the aliens and settings he had in mind. At long last, technology has finally caught up with filmmakers' imaginations.

TOPIC SENTENCE
The paragraph's main idea is expressed in this topic sentence.

TOPIC SENTENCE
This topic sentence introduces a main idea that is related to the preceding one.

TOPIC SENTENCE
This main idea connects with and develops the other ideas in the body.

BODY
Each paragraph in the body supports the thesis.

CONCLUSION
This final paragraph summarizes the thesis and makes a prediction.

COMPOSITIONS

❷ Thesis Statement

In a composition, your **thesis statement** tells the main point of the work, just as the **topic sentence** tells the main idea of a paragraph. Each paragraph in the composition supports this thesis statement. Usually the thesis statement is directly stated in the composition's introduction. In some cases, however, it may not appear until the second paragraph, after an attention-grabbing opener.

A good thesis statement helps you control the direction of your composition. Compare the two thesis statements below. Notice that the revised sentence, the thesis statement from the composition you just read, provides more specific information than the earlier draft.

> **STUDENT MODEL**
>
> **DRAFT**
> The technology in early science fiction movies was simple.
>
> **REVISION**
> Today's viewers would probably consider the pioneer film's technology simple and even laughable, but that first film paved the way for future sci-fi movies.

A good thesis statement makes a point that you can support in the body of your composition. Here are some guidelines to help you write a good thesis statement.

Here's How Writing a Thesis Statement

1. Determine the central idea you want to explore. You might express this central idea in a general statement: Some movies are violent.

2. Write a thesis statement based on your central idea. The thesis should be more specific than the central idea: The increasing violence in movies is disturbing.

3. Revise to make your thesis statement more specific. A more detailed statement will help keep you from straying off your topic: The increasing violence in movies today reflects our increasingly violent society.

PRACTICE Identifying Composition Structure

Read over the composition that you "pictured" for the **Write Away** on page 317. Identify its introduction, thesis statement, body, and conclusion. Then use the notes you placed in your 🗀 **Working Portfolio** to pinpoint the main idea in each body paragraph.

LESSON 2 — Introductions and Conclusions

How you begin and end your composition will depend on the type of composition you're writing and what you want to say. No matter what you write, however, the introduction and conclusion should hold your reader's interest.

❶ Catch Your Reader's Attention

An effective introduction grabs your reader's attention and provides a reason to keep reading. In the following introduction, the writer uses a brief history of storytelling to hook the reader.

> **PROFESSIONAL MODEL**
>
> In the beginning there was nonfiction ("I was chased by a pterodactyl ...") and fiction ("...and killed it in one blow"). People told stories, wrote them in words or pictures or acted them out. From cavemen until 1895, that was about it. Then 33 people met in a café for the only new storytelling form of this millennium: They watched a movie.
>
> —*Life*, "The First Picture Show," October 1997

Here are some other ways to hook your audience.

Here's How ▸ **Writing Great Beginnings**

- **Tell an anecdote.** An anecdote, or very brief story, introduces your thesis, makes a point, and involves the reader.
- **Use a quotation.** A quotation not only introduces your topic but also lends credibility to your composition.
- **Present an unusual fact.** An unusual fact intrigues your readers and makes them want to keep reading.
- **Ask a question.** A question draws your readers in and involves them in your topic.

 WATCH OUT Avoid being too general in your introduction ("Everyone likes movies") on the one hand, or baldly stating your intention ("In this essay I will prove . . .") on the other.

COMPOSITIONS

PRACTICE Interesting Introductions

Rewrite the following introduction to make it more interesting.

Movie theaters in the late 20th century drew record crowds in spite of the widespread availability of VCRs, DVD players, and cable channels.

❷ Finish with a Flourish

A good conclusion ends on a strong note and leaves the reader with something to think about. This conclusion from the essay introduced on the preceding page uses humor to make a final point about film.

> **PROFESSIONAL MODEL**
>
> The nature of film, as opposed to, say, theater, means that the same images are banked in the consciousness of . . . people who would otherwise have little culture in common. After seeing *Jurassic Park*, kids from Beverly Hills to Bombay could suffer the same nightmare that they, too, were being chased by a pterodactyl.
>
> —*Life*, "The First Picture Show," October 1997

Here are some other good strategies for concluding a composition.

Here's How Writing Satisfying Endings

- **Summarize your ideas.** Summarizing your ideas allows you to emphasize your main points and provides a sense of closure.
- **Issue a call to action.** A call to action encourages readers to adopt your position and so is an effective way to end a piece of persuasive writing.
- **Ask a question.** Asking a question leaves the reader thinking about your topic or position.
- **Make a prediction.** Making a prediction also encourages the reader to think about your thesis.
- **Conclude with an anecdote.** Ending with a memorable or humorous anecdote may help you make your concluding point.

Be sure you don't introduce new ideas in your conclusion.

Unity and Coherence in the Body

Each paragraph in the body of a composition should support the thesis and flow logically from one to another. You can achieve this goal by making sure the paragraphs in your composition are unified and coherent.

❶ Unity Within Paragraphs

A unified paragraph supports a single main idea. To achieve unity, delete unrelated details. If your paragraph seems to cover too many ideas, break it into two or more paragraphs.

STUDENT MODEL

In science fiction movies, insects and other creatures often grow to the size of skyscrapers and threaten the existence of humans. Giant scorpions, ants, lizards, spiders, lobsters, and birds crawl, swim, fly, and eat their way across the screen. ~~Godzilla terrorized Tokyo in the original film and New York City in the sequel~~.

¶Usually the reason given in the story for the creature's amazing size is either a formula concocted by a mad scientist or a nuclear accident. However, the increases in size are actually physically impossible. When a creature doubles in size, its weight and volume quadruple. ~~In films featuring three-dimensional technology, the creatures seem even bigger~~. An ant the size of a dog would be crushed by its own weight.

> The topic sentence states the paragraph's main idea.

> This sentence strays from the main idea.

> A new related main idea is set off by a new paragraph.

> This sentence is an irrelevant detail.

COMPOSITIONS

Paragraphing

Paragraphing is the process of dividing ideas into paragraphs, as shown by ¶ in the model above. A topic change signals the need for a new paragraph. A composition that has been properly divided into paragraphs is easier for the reader to follow.

For more on writing single paragraphs, see pp. 306–308.

For guidelines on paragraphing, see p. 330.

❷ Unity Within a Composition

The topic sentence expressing the main idea in each paragraph in the body of your composition should relate to the thesis statement. An outline or diagram showing the thesis statement and the main ideas you want to cover can help you identify irrelevant ideas and keep your composition on track.

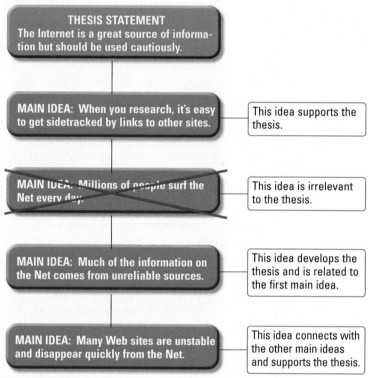

THESIS STATEMENT
The Internet is a great source of information but should be used cautiously.

MAIN IDEA: When you research, it's easy to get sidetracked by links to other sites.

This idea supports the thesis.

MAIN IDEA: Millions of people surf the Net every day.

This idea is irrelevant to the thesis.

MAIN IDEA: Much of the information on the Net comes from unreliable sources.

This idea develops the thesis and is related to the first main idea.

MAIN IDEA: Many Web sites are unstable and disappear quickly from the Net.

This idea connects with the other main ideas and supports the thesis.

Because you are too close to the material, you may need a peer reader to identify irrelevant ideas in your draft.

PRACTICE Listing Related Paragraphs

Create a diagram or outline listing the thesis statement and main ideas in the composition presented in Lesson 1. Add two or three ideas for new paragraphs that would support the thesis.

➌ Coherence Across Paragraphs

In a coherent composition, sentences flow smoothly, making ideas easy to understand. You can use transitions and word chains to create logical connections between your sentences and paragraphs.

Using Transitions

Transitions help link sentences and paragraphs in a composition by showing relationships between ideas. How your composition is organized can determine the transitions you use. For example, if your composition is structured using chronological order, you might use transitions like the ones in the following sentences.

> The **first** sound I hear is my cat purring loudly in my ear. **Then** there's the soft whir of my electric clock on the bedside stand. **Next** I tune into the sounds of my mother making breakfast.
> **After** I get up, I start making noises of my own.

TRANSITIONS

For more transition words and phrases, see p. 315.

For more transition words and phrases, see p. 315.

Using Word Chains

Another way to make your writing coherent is to use **word chains** that refer to something that came before. Common word chains include pronouns and repeated or reworded key words. Notice how the word chains in the following paragraphs help connect ideas.

COMPOSITIONS

STUDENT MODEL

The sun shone down on the field, revealing worlds of activity in its light. The sun illuminated the bees darting among the colorful wildflowers. Clouds of gnats danced in and out of the sun's rays. The sun even picked out the busily scurrying ants as it beamed down on the grass.

The girl wandered lazily onto the sunny scene. She sat on the grass and lifted her face, like a flower, to the warmth.

REPEATED KEY WORD

PRONOUN USED TO REFER BACK TO *SUN*

WORD USED TO REWORD *SUN*

Patterns of Organization

A well-organized composition logically leads the reader from one idea to the next. The organization method you choose should fit your content and be clear to your readers. However, don't feel that you have to restrict your writing to only one organizational method. You can combine different methods in a single composition.

1 Arranging the Details

What you're writing about will determine how your composition should be organized. The chart below lists a few organizational methods and when they are most commonly used.

Organization Methods	
Methods	**Common Uses**
Chronological or sequential order the order in which events happened	To narrate stories and historical accounts or to explain a process.
Spatial order the order in which objects are located in a physical space	To describe a scene.
Comparison-and-contrast order an arrangement in which one subject is measured against another	To compare two or more people, objects, or concepts.
Cause-and-effect order an arrangement showing that one event took place as a result of another event	To explain scientific findings or an historical or current event.
Problem-and-solution order an arrangement in which a problem is presented and details provide the solution	To explain how a problem or obstacle can be overcome; to present a proposal.
Deductive organization an arrangement in which a general statement is supported by specific details	To build a convincing argument or explain a generalization.
Inductive organization an arrangement beginning with specific details and ending with a general conclusion drawn from the information	To lead a reader to draw a general conclusion.

Once you have decided what organizational method you want to use, you can use a graphic organizer to help you order your information. For example, a Venn diagram can help you organize information you want to compare and contrast. A time line can help you organize information in chronological order.

❷ Paragraph by Paragraph

Your composition should have a single overall structure, but you can use different organizational methods in the body paragraphs. Notice the different patterns of organization that could be used to write a composition on digital television.

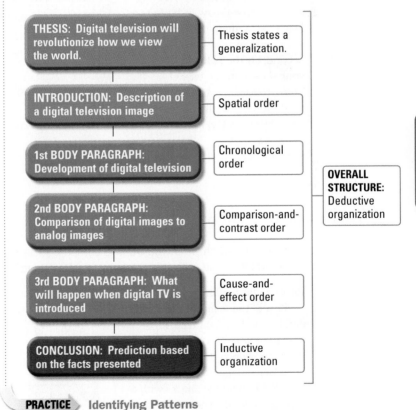

THESIS: Digital television will revolutionize how we view the world.	Thesis states a generalization.
INTRODUCTION: Description of a digital television image	Spatial order
1st BODY PARAGRAPH: Development of digital television	Chronological order
2nd BODY PARAGRAPH: Comparison of digital images to analog images	Comparison-and-contrast order
3rd BODY PARAGRAPH: What will happen when digital TV is introduced	Cause-and-effect order
CONCLUSION: Prediction based on the facts presented	Inductive organization

OVERALL STRUCTURE: Deductive organization

COMPOSITIONS

PRACTICE Identifying Patterns

Select a composition from your 🗂 **Working Portfolio** and determine the pattern or patterns of organization used to structure it.

Incorporating Visuals

In today's busy world, everyone wants information presented as briefly and clearly as possible. Visuals, including bulleted lists, tables, and diagrams, can make information in a composition clearer and easier to understand.

❶ Bulleted Lists

Processes, rules, and instructions are much clearer in a bulleted list format. Compare the paragraph below with the same information given in a bulleted list. Which steps are easier to follow?

Written Information

Here's the secret to shooting a perfect free throw in basketball. First, bounce the ball until your arms and shoulders relax. Second, lift the ball and line up your shot with the basket. Third, release the ball using a fluid motion. Finally, complete the motion with a smooth follow-through.

In Visual Form

To shoot a free throw:

- Bounce the ball until you feel relaxed.
- Line up your shot with the basket.
- Release the ball using a fluid motion.
- Be sure to follow through.

❷ Tables and Diagrams

Use a table or graph when you want to compare facts or present figures. Which of the following is easier to understand?

Written Information

Most of the teams in our varsity division are in a tight race. Right now, the Pumas lead the league with 10 games won and 4 games lost. Their percentage of games won is .714. Next come the Sharks with 8 wins and 6 losses. Their percentage is .571. Trailing the pack are the Tigers, with 3 wins and 11 losses. Their percentage of wins is .214.

In Visual Form

Team Rankings			
Teams	W	L	Pct
Pumas	10	4	.714
Sharks	8	6	.571
Tigers	3	11	.214

You can draw or use a scanned diagram to show the parts of a whole or to demonstrate how something works. Why is the hand-drawn diagram below a better choice than the written description of the information?

Written Information

   A desktop computer is made up of several basic parts. The monitor perches on top of the CPU, which contains the disk drive and the CD-ROM and DVD drive. The keyboard sits in front of the CPU/monitor setup, and the mouse rests beside the keyboard.

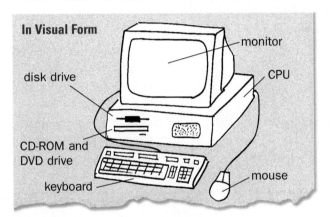

In Visual Form

monitor
disk drive
CPU
CD-ROM and DVD drive
keyboard
mouse

For more on visuals, see pp. 342–343.

Keep your tables and diagrams simple. Limit your information to one purpose. Too much information will make them hard to decipher.

PRACTICE Visualizing Information

Read the paragraph below. Then present the information in a table or graph.

   Experts predict that immigration patterns in the United States will have a significant impact on the ethnic and racial makeup of the population. In 1998, the makeup was as follows: 73% non-Latino white; 12% African American; 11% Latino; and 4% Asian. By 2050, the Census Bureau predicts that the population will consist of the following: 53% non-Latino white; 25% Latino; 14% African American; and 8% Asian.

Student Help Desk

Compositions at a Glance

INTRODUCTION	BODY	CONCLUSION
• Grabs the reader's interest • Presents the thesis • Sets the tone	• Supports the thesis • States the main supporting ideas • Follows a logical pattern of organization	• Reinforces the thesis • Ties ideas together • Leaves the reader with a strong impression

Transitions Seeing the Connection

Techniques	Examples
Show chronological relationships	after, next, before, first, second, last, then, again, finally, soon
Show spatial relationships	above, below, next to, near, behind, around, here, there
Show degree of importance	first, second, primarily, mainly, more important, least important
Show comparison and contrast	similarly, like, also, in contrast to, on the other hand, unlike, however, nevertheless
Show cause and effect	because, consequently, therefore, as a result, so, for that reason

Guidelines for Paragraphing
Looking for a Break

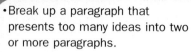

- Break up a paragraph that presents too many ideas into two or more paragraphs.
- Begin a new paragraph when you introduce a new idea or your topic shifts.
- Begin a new paragraph when you introduce a change in place.
- Begin a new paragraph when you introduce a time shift.
- Begin a new paragraph when the action changes.
- Begin a new paragraph when the speaker changes.

Visual Presentation   A Feast for the Eyes

Here are some pointers on how and when to use visuals.

- Decide which type of visual best fits your data.
- Use the Internet or print sources to find ready-made graphics on your topic.
- Introduce the visual before it appears in your composition.
- Explain in your text how the data in the visual supports your ideas.
- Label all parts of the visual clearly.
- Credit your sources, including those downloaded from Web sites or scanned electronically.

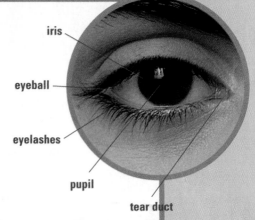

iris

eyeball

eyelashes

pupil

tear duct

The Bottom Line

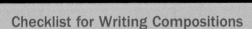

Checklist for Writing Compositions

Have I . . .

_____ stated my thesis in the introduction?

_____ stated main ideas related to my thesis in the body paragraphs?

_____ supported the main ideas in the body paragraphs with details?

_____ organized my ideas clearly?

_____ used transitions and word chains to link sentences and paragraphs?

_____ incorporated visuals if appropriate?

_____ tied all my ideas together in the conclusion?

Power Words
Vocabulary for Precise Writing

festoon

Just the Right Touch

If you've ever dressed for a formal occasion, you know the importance of eye-catching details. Experiment with words like these to boost the appeal of your writing.

Beauty Is What Beauty Does

This year the city is going to be really **decked out** for New Year's Eve. The plan is to **enhance** every nook and cranny. Ice sculptures will **adorn** the park; the streets will be **decorated** with lights; banners will **festoon** storefronts. Citizens will **trim** their houses with bright lights. Horses with carriages **caparisoned** in colorful costumes will parade the streets, and fireworks will **emblazon** the night sky.

Room with a View

You've decided it's time to **spruce up** your room at home, maybe **ornament** the walls with some cool posters. The computer could be **bedecked** with decals, and the entertainment unit **embellished** with a **handsome** CD holder and **elegant** picture frames. Why stop with the inside? **Beautify** the door to your room with a picture of yourself; perhaps **trick it out** with a warning sign or two. Make "Redo Now!" your motto.

▷ **Your Turn** Lovely to Look At

Consider the sayings "the more the better" and "less is more." The first saying implies that the way to improve is to add lots of details. The second saying suggests that decoration should be minimal. Which saying matches your view? Think of an example that supports your opinion and describe it to a friend.

spruce up

Adorn

decorated

EMBLAZON

elegant

Elaboration

Details, Details

Compare this truck with one you're familiar with. What has been added to the truck? What's your favorite touch? What could you do without? Do you think it's overdone or just right?

Just as the details on this truck make it stand out from others, details in your writing can make the difference between an effective piece and one that falls short. **Elaboration**—the details and information you use to support your ideas—makes your writing more interesting and meaningful. You might even say that elaboration helps you get more mileage out of your writing.

Write Away: Elaborate Description
Use vivid details to describe the "elaborated" truck shown above. Place your description in your 📁 **Working Portfolio.**

The Importance of Elaboration

Calvin and Hobbes by Bill Watterson

Calvin has filled his report with descriptive details and attention-grabbing facts. Unfortunately, most of them are wrong. Elaboration helps you convey what you have to say, so it's important to know how to use different types of details to elaborate your writing. Of course, it also helps to know what you're talking about.

❶ Common Types of Elaboration

Common types of elaboration include facts, statistics, examples, sensory details, anecdotes, reasons, and expert testimony. The types of elaboration you use will depend on what you want your writing to achieve. Here's a chart of some types of elaboration and ways they can be used.

Uses of Elaboration	
Type	**Uses**
Facts and statistics	To support an opinion or develop a point
Examples	To strengthen your writing by making it more concrete
Sensory details	To bring a description to life by creating a vivid word picture
Anecdotes	To engage your reader and bring your subject to life
Reasons	To strengthen an argument
Expert testimony	To use the words of experts to validate a point

Now read the paragraph at the top of the next page. How does each type of elaboration strengthen the writing?

Since the industrial age, people have worried that machines would take over their jobs. In some modern factories, a silent, cold-steel blur of activity suggests that this fear has become a reality. Robots "man" an assembly line in car plants, repeatedly picking up parts and welding them together. But these robots haven't taken over. Humans still do the jobs that robots can't. In fact, in some U.S. factories there is only about one robot for every 300 workers. And most humans welcome their robotic coworkers because the robots work quickly, perform dangerous jobs, and never complain that they're bored.

Topic sentence

SENSORY DETAILS

EXAMPLE

FACT

STATISTIC

REASONS

❷ Elaboration Techniques

As you read over your writing, try using the following techniques to elaborate your work.

Here's How Elaborating Your Writing

Ask questions	Present a complete picture of your subject. Ask and answer the questions *who, what, when, where, why,* and *how.*
Show, don't tell	Use specific details to enrich your descriptions. Don't say "Jana felt sad"; say "Jana bit her lip as tears welled in her eyes."
Zoom in on details	Like a zoom lens, focus on small details. How will your readers know about a scar on a character's wrist unless you tell them?
Fill in the gaps	Look for holes in an argument by assuming the opposing viewpoint. What points need strengthening? What points haven't you addressed?

Be careful when you're fleshing out your writing with details. Don't include any that don't support your main idea.

Developing Ideas

When you elaborate your ideas, you should constantly ask yourself, Why do I think that? What do I mean? You can often show readers what you mean by supporting your ideas with facts, statistics, and examples.

❶ Using Facts and Statistics

A **fact** is a true statement that can be proved with reference materials or through observation. **Statistics** are facts expressed as numbers. Here are some purposes for which you might use facts and statistics.

- To support an opinion
- To prove a point
- To provide evidence for a general statement
- To grab readers' attention (if the information is startling or unusual)
- To provide a tone of authority and believability

In the following paragraph, facts and statistics are used to convey the horror of high-tech war.

PROFESSIONAL MODEL

It took a blitzkrieg to start World War II, but only two bombs to end it. The first, on August 6, 1945, leveled most of Hiroshima, annihilating some 80,000 people in a blinding flash. The second hit Nagasaki three days later, killing 40,000. After three years of top-secret work, the Manhattan Project had translated Einstein's theory of relativity into devastating reality: a weapon that harnessed the energy released by the splitting of the atom.

—*Life,* "The Day That Time Stood Still," Fall 1997

> This fact grabs the reader's attention by posing a contrast.

> These statistics reveal the devastation of the bombs.

WATCH OUT Make sure your source is reliable before you use any fact or statistic. **For information on where to find reliable sources, see pp. 466–470.**

❷ Using Examples

Examples are specific instances that illustrate general ideas. Here are some purposes for which you might use examples.

- To flesh out a description
- To give weight to informative or persuasive writing
- To help define a new term
- To support a generalization
- To add interest to a piece of writing
- To hook readers' attention

What examples has the writer of the following paragraph used to illustrate his idea?

PROFESSIONAL MODEL

Bigger wasn't only better during the 1950s and '60s, bigger was best. The Cadillac Coupe de Ville was as long as a city block, with tail fins extending to the suburbs. Elvis had big hair, the Beatles came along with even bigger hair, and the Jackson Five arrived with stupendously massive hair.

—Karl Taro Greenfeld, "Voracious, Inc."

PRACTICE ▸ Elaborating About Working Women

Use these facts, statistics, and examples to write a paragraph about women in the workplace.

In 1900, women made up about 18 percent of the work force.

In 1900, women were mostly employed in factories, on farms, and as servants.

In 1999, women made up about 47 percent of the work force.

Many women are underpaid and work in low-level jobs.

Women who have thrived in male-dominated businesses include Ann Fudge, a division president at Kraft Foods, and Muriel Siebert, the first woman to buy a seat on the New York Stock Exchange.

Details That Enrich Writing

When you write a story or description, use details that show rather than tell what you want to express. Sensory details, figurative language, and anecdotes will help you bring your writing to life.

❶ Sensory Details

Sensory details are details that appeal to the five senses. Here are some writing purposes for which you might use sensory details.

- To describe a person, object, or scene
- To reveal characters' personalities
- To create a mood

In this passage, notice how the writer has included details that appeal to sight, hearing, and touch.

LITERARY MODEL

The hardest weather in the world is there. Winter brings blizzards, hot tornadic winds arise in the spring, and in summer the prairie is an anvil's edge. The grass turns brittle and brown, and it cracks beneath your feet.... At a distance in July or August the steaming foliage seems almost to writhe in fire. Great green and yellow grasshoppers are everywhere in the tall grass, popping up like corn to sting the flesh, and tortoises crawl about on the red earth, going nowhere in the plenty of time.

—N. Scott Momaday, *The Way to Rainy Mountain*

Details that appeal to touch help you feel the winds and grass.

Details that appeal to hearing help you hear the cracking grass.

Details that appeal to sight help you see the fiery foliage and giant grasshoppers.

❷ Figurative Language

You can also use figurative language, such as similes and metaphors, to create images and enrich descriptions. Compare the examples of simile and metaphor at the top of the next page. Then see if you can identify a simile and a metaphor in the passage above.

**Relief washed over her like a warm
spring rain.**

> A **simile** is a comparison
> expressed with *like* or *as*.

**His face, a stone mask, revealed
nothing.**

> A **metaphor** is an implied
> comparison that does not
> contain *like* or *as*.

❸ Anecdotes

An anecdote is a very short story that is often true. Here are
some writing purposes for which you might use anecdotes.

- To provide insight into a biographical or autobiographical subject
- To illustrate a point
- To reveal a character's personality, motivation, or emotions
- To set a mood

As you read the following anecdote, think about what makes
it effective.

PROFESSIONAL MODEL

One evening a few years ago I walked back
into my office after dinner and found roughly a
hundred black widow spiders frolicking on my
desk. I am not speaking metaphorically and I
am not making this up: a hundred black
widows. It was a vision of ghastly, breathtaking
beauty, and it brought on me a wave of nausea.
It also brought on a small moral crisis—one
that I dealt with briskly, maybe rashly, in the
dizziness of the moment, and that I've been
turning back over in my mind ever since.

—David Quammen, "The Face of a Spider: Eyeball to
Eyeball with the Good, the Bad, and the Ugly"

> The first sentence
> sets a mood of
> horrified wonder.

> The anecdote
> makes you want
> to keep reading.

PRACTICE Giving a Detailed Description

In your 📁 **Working Portfolio,** find the paragraph you wrote for
the **Write Away** on page 333. Use sensory details, figurative
language, or an anecdote to enrich your writing.

ELABORATION

Supporting Opinions

When you write to persuade, you try to convince your readers to agree with your opinion. Supporting your ideas with details will help you present a convincing argument.

❶ Presenting a Detailed Argument

You can use various kinds of details to present an argument, including facts and statistics, examples, and anecdotes. Notice how the writer of the following passage uses different kinds of details to make the point that homework can be beneficial.

STUDENT MODEL

Researchers at the University of California, San Diego, surveyed 6,000 students over five years. The achievement levels of students who began doing an extra 30 minutes of nightly math homework in 7th grade were, by 11th grade, two grades higher then those of other students. It is also a fact that students in Japan and China spend much more time on homework than the average American student—and score higher on standardized tests.

The answer, though, is not just to double or triple homework assignments. Endless worksheets are boring, time-consuming, and turn kids off to learning. The quality of the work assigned should be an important consideration. In Hinsdale, Illinois, parents complained that their children received too much homework from some teachers and not enough from others. As a result, a committee of teachers, parents, and administrators came up with a policy requiring "meaningful and purposeful" homework at all grade levels but limiting the amount given by age.

> These statistics support the value of homework.

> This fact adds weight.

> This example stresses that homework shouldn't be just busywork.

> This anecdote makes a point about the quality of homework.

For more on supporting an argument, see pp. 424–433.
For more on revising for logic, see p. 349.

❷ Using Reasons and Expert Testimony

Although the sign in the cartoon might persuade the chicken to cross the road without a reason, your readers will demand stronger elaboration before your argument convinces them. In the following model, the writer uses reasons and expert testimony—the words of an authority or someone with firsthand experience—to support his opinion that e-mail has changed the workplace.

The Far Side by Gary Larson

> **PROFESSIONAL MODEL**
>
> Most experts agree that E-mail has changed the workplace for the better. It allows some employees to work from home, conduct business after hours and while traveling, and transmit information more efficiently, without the unnecessary chitchat of a phone conversation....
>
> But perhaps the biggest change E-mail has wrought is in its snowballing use as legal evidence—whether in cases brought against workers or companies....
>
> "Everyone has got to be aware that whatever they put in their E-mail could be retrieved and used against them, now or in 10 years," says Craig Cornish, a privacy-law attorney.
>
> —Dana Hawkins, "E-mail Nation"

Reasons support the assertion that e-mail has changed the workplace for the better.

An **expert** explains the downside of using e-mail in the workplace.

ELABORATION

 Beware of quoting nonexperts, such as a celebrity who is endorsing a product or supporting a particular cause.

PRACTICE Defending Your Opinion of Homework

Use any combination of facts, statistics, examples, anecdotes, reasons, and expert testimony to write a paragraph supporting your opinion of the value of homework.

Elaborating with Visuals

Visuals—including graphs, charts, and maps—literally let you show what you have to say. Using visuals to elaborate helps you engage your readers and present information more clearly and sometimes more effectively than you could by using words alone. As you look at the visuals in this lesson, think about what it would take to present each idea in words.

❶ When to Use Visuals

Use a visual when it makes information easier to understand. Compare the written instructions and picture below. Which is easier to grasp?

Written Information

1. Hold a pair of chopsticks parallel to each other. 2. Grip the top chopstick, which moves up and down, between your thumb and index and middle fingers. The bottom stick should rest at the base of the thumb and be supported by the fourth finger. 3. Use the ends of the chopsticks to pick up and hold food.

Visual Information

❷ How to Use Visuals

Use visuals that are appropriate to your purpose and to the form of your writing.

Graphs

Graphs—including bar graphs, line graphs, and pie graphs—are usually used to present and compare statistics. The bar graph shown here might appear in an essay on the Civil War. What does the graph tell you about the suffering caused by the war?

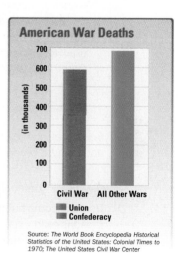

American War Deaths

Source: The World Book Encyclopedia Historical Statistics of the United States: Colonial Times to 1970; The United States Civil War Center

Charts

Charts are used to organize, simplify, and summarize facts and statistics for easy reference and comparison. This chart might appear in an article on physical fitness. What are the advantages of presenting the information in this form?

Exercise Pros and Cons		
Exercise	Benefits	Dangers
Running	Exercises cardio-respiratory system, strengthens bones	Shin splints, knee problems, stress fractures
Swimming	Exercises arms and legs, strengthens heart	Some possibility of injury, particularly to back
Walking	Exercises lower body, raises heart rate	None

Maps

Maps are used to present information about geographical features and historical events. This map of the Oregon Trail could appear in a historical narrative about U.S. westward expansion. What conclusions can you draw about the pioneers' journey by studying the map?

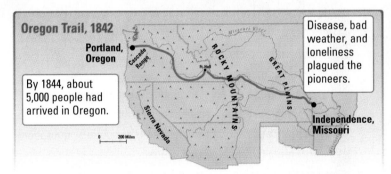

Oregon Trail, 1842
Portland, Oregon
Cascade Range
Missouri River
ROCKY MOUNTAINS
GREAT PLAINS
Ft. Hall
Sierra Nevada
Disease, bad weather, and loneliness plagued the pioneers.
By 1844, about 5,000 people had arrived in Oregon.
Independence, Missouri
0   200 Miles

HOT TIP

You can use the Internet to download maps and other visuals, but be sure to credit your sources.

PRACTICE Using Visuals

In a small group, discuss and take a survey of your tastes in music. Choose the best way to present the information in a visual.

ELABORATION

Student Help Desk

Elaboration at a Glance

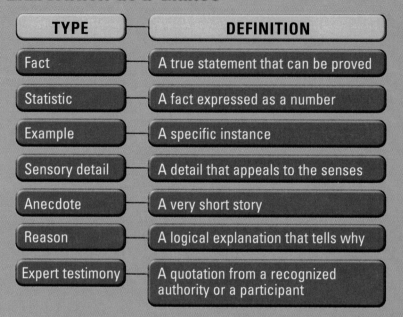

TYPE	DEFINITION
Fact	A true statement that can be proved
Statistic	A fact expressed as a number
Example	A specific instance
Sensory detail	A detail that appeals to the senses
Anecdote	A very short story
Reason	A logical explanation that tells why
Expert testimony	A quotation from a recognized authority or a participant

Elaboration Sources

References That Work

Almanacs: facts, statistics

Atlases: maps

Encyclopedias: facts, statistics, examples, visuals

Biographies: facts, statistics, quotations, anecdotes

Periodicals: facts, statistics, sensory details, quotations

Internet: facts, statistics, visuals

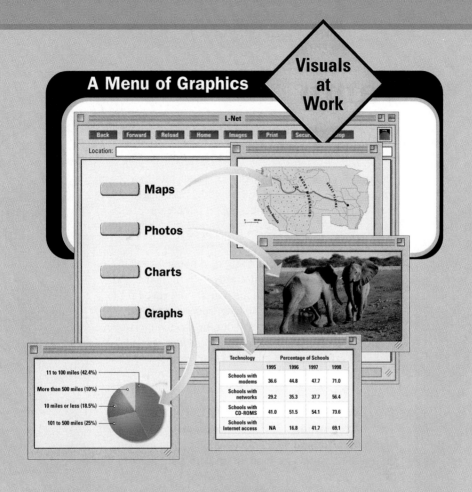

A Menu of Graphics

L-Net

Back | Forward | Reload | Home | Images | Print | Secur... | ...top

Location:

- Maps
- Photos
- Charts
- Graphs

11 to 100 miles (42.4%)
More than 500 miles (10%)
10 miles or less (18.5%)
101 to 500 miles (25%)

Technology	Percentage of Schools			
	1995	1996	1997	1998
Schools with modems	36.6	44.8	47.7	71.0
Schools with networks	29.2	35.3	37.7	56.4
Schools with CD-ROMS	41.0	51.5	54.1	73.6
Schools with Internet access	NA	16.8	41.7	69.1

ELABORATION

The Bottom Line

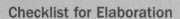

Checklist for Elaboration

Have I . . .

____ provided facts, statistics, and examples that develop my ideas?

____ enriched my writing with sensory details, figurative language, and anecdotes?

____ used details to present a logical argument?

____ included reasons and expert testimony to support my opinion?

____ used visuals to make information easier to understand?

____ eliminated details that don't support my main idea?

Re**vamp**

UPDATE

Here We Go Again

Whump! Another wadded piece of paper hits the wastebasket, and you're still at work. Try using words like these to describe making changes.

If at First You Don't Succeed . . .

You have just written something that doesn't sound quite right. Now you should **clarify** your thoughts and **emend** your phrasing. Perhaps you should **revamp** the entire thing: **modify** your thinking, **reconceptualize** the theme, and **update** your facts, not to mention **rectifying** any errors. After a while you may find it easier to **edit** writing.

. . . Try, Try Again.

The **reworking** of a piece of writing ought to improve it on each **rewriting.** The job of **reconstruction** and **amendment** will lead to understanding. The second time around, try some **innovation** with a fresh idea or two. The more careful your **revision,** the closer it is to being a **recension.**

▷ **Your Turn** Improvise a Change

In small groups, brainstorm a few everyday situations, and perform them as improvisational skits. At least twice during each performance, an audience member can call out "freeze" to stop the action and to suggest a change to the situation. Observe how well each group handles any added twists.

reworking

AMENDMENT

EDIT

revision

Revision Strategies

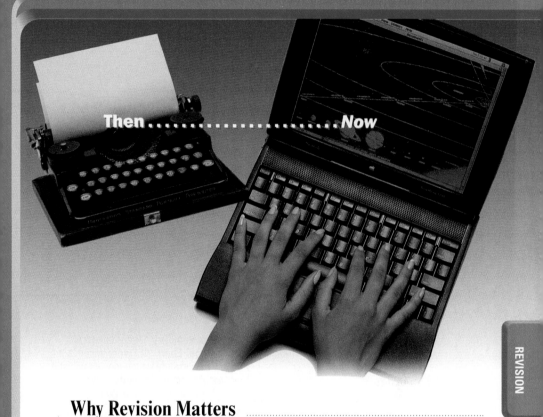

Then............................Now

Why Revision Matters

Where would we be if no one had tried to improve the typewriter? Just about any invention or creation can benefit from a second look and some rethinking. Even writing can almost always be improved from the original version.

When you write a draft, you first get all your ideas down on paper—often quickly, concentrating on just getting things said. When you revise, however, you focus on how to say them best.

Write Away: **A Quick Revise**

Compare the old-fashioned typewriter with the modern laptop computer shown above. For three minutes, write quickly about how that technological change affects you. Afterward, try to sharpen and focus what you wrote by revising several sentences and replacing at least three words in each sentence. Save your writing in your ▭ **Working Portfolio.**

Ideas and Content

The strategies in this lesson will help you revise the "big picture" of your draft—your ideas and content.

❶ Elaborating Unsupported Ideas

Your writing will lack credibility if your opinions and ideas are not well-supported. Perform the quick diagnostic activity below to see if the ideas in your draft are sufficiently supported.

Examine Your Draft for Unsupported Ideas

✔ Look for places where you give your opinion, make a claim, or express generalities. Are these statements followed with convincing details—or do they hang there without support?

If you find any unsupported ideas, then dig out your research materials again. Look for facts, statistics, quotations, anecdotes, and other compelling details that you can add to your draft.

Adding Details to Your Draft

Unsupported Ideas	Ways to Support Ideas
The *Star Wars* films stand among the world's all-time greatest movies.	**Quote an authority.** According to film critic Roger Ebert, "If I were asked to say with certainty which movies will still be widely known a century or two from now, I would list . . . *Star Wars."*
Many Americans faced desperate circumstances during the Great Depression of the 1930s.	**Provide an anecdote.** For example, one Philadelphia woman had to borrow 50 cents to buy stale bread for 3½ cents per loaf. She and her family ate nothing but bread for several days.
Deer have become a nuisance in our New York suburb.	**Add facts.** The deer have destroyed the bottom level of our woods. Nothing green grows anymore below five feet off the ground. Robbed of a habitat, our small mammals have disappeared.
At 16, he was gangly, yet his appetite was already enormous.	**Embellish with details.** He ate three lunches a day, three dinners at night, and cleaned off the plates of anyone at his table.

For more ways to elaborate with details, see pp. 308 and 326.

② Correcting Errors in Logic

A **logical fallacy** is a statement or an argument that may appear to be logical but actually isn't. When you revise any of your expository or persuasive pieces, check for the two common fallacies in logic discussed below.

> **Examine Your Draft for Errors in Logic**
>
> ✔ **Overgeneralization** Do you use sweeping terms such as *all, no one, never, everyone?* Can you really support the statements that contain these terms?
>
> ✔ **Circular Reasoning** Do you try to "prove" a statement by simply repeating it?

If you find these errors in logic in your draft, you can correct them with the following strategies.

Revise Overgeneralizations

Overgeneralizations include everyone or everything without qualification or backup. They can sometimes be corrected by using qualifiers, such as *most, some, usually, sometimes.* You can also correct them by referring to a specific case.

OVERGENERALIZATION **Pit bulls are vicious dogs.**

REVISED **My neighbor's pit bull is a vicious dog.** `SPECIFIC CASE`

[or] Some pit bulls can be vicious. `QUALIFIER ADDED`

Learn to recognize overgeneralizations even when signal words do not appear. In this sentence, the word *all* is implied: [All] *Kids these days are wild.*

Fix Circular Reasoning

Statements that do nothing more than restate the same idea in different words are examples of circular reasoning. Revise the second part of these statements by giving valid reasons or support.

CIRCULAR REASONING **I like Zeno's because it's my favorite restaurant.**

REVISED **I like Zeno's because the spaghetti is plentiful and cheap.**

REVISION

Organization

Well-organized writing flows so smoothly that the reader hardly thinks about the structure. Strategies suggested in this lesson help you to achieve a sound organization with sequencing that is logical and effective.

❶ Revising Your Thesis

The organization of your entire composition follows from your thesis. A poorly written thesis makes it hard for your readers to understand the structure of your writing. Use this checklist to diagnose the effectiveness of your thesis.

> ### Examine Your Thesis Statement
>
> ✔ Does your thesis only mention the topic without making a statement about it?
>
> ✔ Does it focus on only one part of your composition and exclude other parts?
>
> ✔ Does it circle around your main point, but not state it directly?

If your diagnosis uncovers problems with your thesis, you can revise it by following these guidelines.

Here's How **Improving Your Thesis Statement**

Correct the scope. The scope of your thesis statement should be large enough to cover all your major ideas but narrow enough to provide a clear focus. A weak thesis statement often focuses on only the first two or three paragraphs of a composition.

Give it an angle. Your thesis should say something specific about your topic.

NONSPECIFIC **This paper is about couch potatoes.**

REVISED **Lack of physical activity is taking its toll on the health and well-being of many Americans.**

Adjust it. In the process of writing a draft, you may shift the key idea of your composition. You'll need to revisit your thesis statement to make sure it still fits the content of your composition.

For more on writing a thesis, see p. 320.

❷ Reordering Paragraphs

Each paragraph should clearly follow the one preceding it, and all the paragraphs about one key idea should be grouped together. To spot organization problems, read through your draft with these questions in mind.

> **Examine the Order of Paragraphs in Your Draft**
>
> ✔ Are paragraphs about similar subjects or ideas grouped together?
>
> ✔ Do paragraphs flow from one to the next so readers can follow the train of thought?

Sometimes you may be too close to your work to detect disorganization. A helpful strategy is to list your topic sentences on a separate sheet. You can see more clearly at a glance what paragraphs need to be shifted and how to group your big ideas.

STUDENT MODEL

LIST OF TOPIC SENTENCES
"A Nation of Couch Potatoes"

- There are several reasons why Americans don't get enough exercise.
- Machines perform many of our tasks—another reason for lack of exercise.
- The benefits of exercise on personal health are enormous.
- Increased physical activity even improves your sleep.
- Motorized vehicles move us from place to place.
- Fitness experts suggest several ways to get fit.
- If you don't like exercise, you can increase the activity in your daily routine.
- Exercise improves your mental outlook.

> Group this with reasons for lack of exercise.

> This mentions a benefit of exercise. Move up.

HOT TIP

Check your outline of topic sentences against the thesis statement. You know your thesis statement is well-focused if all the topic sentences follow from it.

Fluency

When you revise for fluency, you bring rhythm and flow to your writing. Fluent sentences hum along—they are easy to follow and enjoyable to read.

❶ Combining Sentences

To make your writing flow, you may need to combine some of your short sentences. Perform this diagnostic activity to see if sentence combining could improve your draft.

> **Examine Your Draft for Choppy Sentences**
>
> ✔ Have you written several short, choppy sentences in a row?
>
> ✔ Are the relationships between ideas in a paragraph not clear?

You can use these strategies to combine short, related sentences and make your writing smoother, livelier, and clearer.

Move a Word or Group of Words

See if you can move a word, or even a group of words, from one sentence into another that contains a related idea. You may have to change the form of the words you're moving.

Future ovens will be able to regulate the heat. They will do this automatically.

Future ovens will automatically **regulate the heat.**

The future will usher in huge changes. The changes will occur in the realm of technology.

The future will usher in huge technological **changes.**

Combine with *Who, Which, That*

You can eliminate repetition by using the introductory words *who, which,* or *that* to combine sentences.

New hybrid cars can go 60 to 70 miles on one gallon of gas. They combine electric and gasoline motors.

New hybrid cars that combine electric and gasoline motors

can go 60 to 70 miles on one gallon of gas.

Electric-powered vehicles can go about 100 miles before their batteries must be recharged. They have low-pollution benefits.

↓

Electric-powered vehicles, which have low-pollution benefits, **can go about 100 miles before their batteries must be recharged.**

Combine with Conjunctions

You can combine sentences that express related ideas of equal importance by using a **coordinating conjunction:** and, but, or, for, yet. To connect ideas that are not equal in importance, use **subordinating conjunctions,** such as whenever, though, unless, until.

The wild ponies of Chincoteague gallop fast. They tire fairly quickly.

↓

The wild ponies of Chincoteague gallop fast, but they tire fairly quickly.

Gorillas look ferocious. **They are actually gentle creatures.**

↓

Although gorillas look ferocious, **they are actually gentle creatures.**

Combine with Appositive Phrases

An **appositive** explains a noun in a sentence. You can combine two sentences about the same subject by placing one as an appositive phrase.

Steveland Morris had his first hit single at the age of 12. Steveland Morris is better known as Stevie Wonder.

↓

Steveland Morris, better known as Stevie Wonder, **had his first hit single at the age of 12.**

For more on coordinating and subordinating conjunctions, see pp. 21–22.

Sentence Combining

Combine each pair or set of sentences into one fluent sentence.

1. Some experts predict human settlements on the moon during the next century. Experts also predict that people will settle on a few nearby asteroids during the next hundred years.

2. Plants and animals will be grown on various asteroids and planets. These plants and animals will be genetically engineered.

3. Mars presents greater challenges for human habitation. It may be colonized, too.

4. Mars is our nearest planetary neighbor. Mars is more than 34 million miles from Earth at its closest approach.

5. Liquid water lies deep under Mars's frozen ground. At least, that's what many scientists believe.

❷ Reducing Wordiness

Wordiness is not usually hazardous—the case in the cartoon is obviously an exception—but it can destroy the fluency of your writing. Empty words and rambling phrases can bury your best ideas and make your writing difficult to read. Use the following checklist to inspect your draft for wordiness.

© 2000 by Sidney Harris

Examine Your Draft for Wordiness

✔ Do you use words that could be deleted and never missed?

✔ Does your phrasing seem loose and rambling instead of trim and compact?

✔ Do you needlessly use words with similar meanings?

Eliminate Wordy Phrases

Many wordy phrases can be stated more directly, often with only a single word. Notice how you can revise the following wordy phrases by replacing them with one concise word.

Wordy	Revision
at this point in time	now
by means of	by
due to the fact that	because
in spite of the fact that	although
in the vicinity of	near
in the not too distant future	soon
the fact is that	actually

A common mistake in writing is to announce what you're going to say. Don't announce; just say it. Delete references to your intentions, such as these: *I intend to persuade you . . . My point is . . .*

Delete Redundant Phrasing

Redundancy is the needless use of words that have similar meanings. When you revise, trim redundant phrases by eliminating unnecessary words, as shown in the following examples.

picked ~~out~~	dates ~~back~~ from	might ~~possibly~~
returned ~~back~~	~~entirely~~ complete	never ~~at any time~~
~~most~~ unique	~~every~~ now and then	~~on the occasion~~ when
~~but~~ nevertheless	last ~~of all~~	over ~~and done with~~

The judges picked ~~out~~ five winners.

The other entries were returned ~~back~~ to their owners.

For examples of common redundancies, see the Student Help Desk, p. 362.

PRACTICE B Reducing Wordiness

Rewrite the following paragraph to reduce wordiness.

Car manufacturers are cranking out hybrid cars that run along on both gasoline engines and electric motors. The engine keeps the batteries charged and all. But nevertheless the fact is that the motor runs the car. Electric vehicles are a great environmental advance because of the fact that they produce low pollution. Before in the past, electric vehicles had to come to a stop and recharge their batteries about every 100 miles. At this point in time, electric cars with a booster engine can run over 800 miles on one and only one tank of gas.

REVISION

Style

LESSON 4

If you have ever listened to someone speak in a monotone, you know how boring it can be compared to a voice that's engaging. Strategies suggested in this lesson can bring style and grace to your writing voice.

❶ Creating Sentence Variety

Too many sentences with the same structure make your writing seem lifeless, dull, and gray. Varying your sentences adds color and energy to your writing.

Vary Sentence Beginnings

One way to spice up your writing is to vary the beginnings of your sentences. Perform this quick diagnosis to see if your sentences need new starts.

Examine Your Draft for Sentence Variety

✔ Do you start too many of your sentences in the same way, especially by repeating the words *the, he, she, I, it,* or *there?*

If you find that your sentences sound dull because the beginnings are all the same, then choose from the menu of sentence starters in the following chart.

Sentence Starters	Original	Fresh Start
Begin with a subordinate clause.	Movies went through a period of adjustment when sound was introduced.	**When sound was introduced,** movies went through a period of adjustment.
Begin with a prepositional phrase.	Scents may be added to movies in the future.	**In the future,** scents may be added to movies.
Begin with an adjective.	Animation is now cheaper and better and is being used more than ever in movies.	**Now cheaper and better,** animation is being used more than ever in movies.
Begin with an infinitive.	Filmmakers spend a lot of money to attract top stars.	**To attract top stars,** filmmakers spend a lot of money.

❷ Creating Parallelism

Copyright © The New Yorker Collection 1940
Charles Addams

Any skier can tell you that you need to keep your skis parallel for a smooth ride. The same principle of parallelism applies to smooth writing.

If some of your sentences sound awkward, it may be because the parts within it don't have parallel structure. A noun should be paired with a noun, a prepositional phrase should be paired with a prepositional phrase, and so on.

Revising for Parallelism

	Faulty	Revised
Make parts of speech parallel.	Laws should be passed to protect passengers from **harm** or even **being killed.**	Laws should be passed to protect passengers from **harm** or even **death.**
Make phrases parallel.	John Wilkes Booth became infamous for **assassinating President Lincoln during a play** and **having escaped the theater on horseback.**	John Wilkes Booth became infamous for **assassinating President Lincoln during a play** and **escaping the theater on horseback.**
Make clauses parallel.	During the drought, the crops **shriveled** and **died,** the **livestock on the range were suffering from heat exhaustion,** and the stream beds **dried** up.	During the drought, the crops **shriveled** and **died,** the livestock on the range **suffered from heat exhaustion,** and the stream beds **dried** up.

REVISION

Make Parts of a Series Parallel

When you have a series of items in one sentence, make sure that each item in the series has the same grammatical form as the others.

FAULTY SERIES **Edgar Allan Poe is said to be a man who often brooded, was rarely caught smiling, and no one ever heard him laugh aloud.**

PARALLEL SERIES **Edgar Allan Poe is said to be a man who often brooded, rarely smiled, and never laughed aloud.**

Use Parallelism with Paired Conjunctions

Check your draft for these pairs of **correlative conjunctions:**

either . . . or	**as . . . as**
neither . . . nor	**both . . . and**
not only . . . but also	**whether . . . or**

Make sure that the structure after the second part of the pair is exactly parallel in form to the structure after the first part.

NOT PARALLEL **Heather loves both seeing old black-and-white movies and to go to big-screen blockbusters.**

REVISION **Heather loves both seeing old black-and-white movies and going to big-screen blockbusters.**

PRACTICE Revising for Parallelism

Revise these sentences to make their structure parallel.

1. The history of the computer is long and attracts your interest.
2. Crude forerunners of "computers" include both the abacus of ancient China and the calculating machine was invented in nineteenth-century England.
3. Famous mathematicians in the history of the computer were Alan Turing for using a binary code of 1's and 0's and John von Neumann to create the concept of a stored program.
4. The first modern computer was not only slow, its size could fill an entire room.
5. Today's computers are smaller, lighter, and even the price is less than early models.

Word Choice

Strategies suggested in this lesson will help you energize your writing by replacing dull words with lively ones and by making general language specific.

❶ Activating Verbs

Your writing will almost always be more direct and energetic if you write in the active voice instead of the passive. Check your draft for how often you use the passive voice.

> **Examine Your Draft for Passive Voice**
>
> ✔ In the active voice, the subject performs the action. In the passive voice, the subject receives the action. Are many of your sentences written in the less energetic passive voice?

If you find that you use the passive voice too often, revise your draft by making the voice active.

> **Here's How** **Changing Passive Voice to Active**
>
> 1. In a passive sentence, find the receiver of the action.
> 2. Make that receiver the *subject* of the sentence.
>
> **Passive** The Milky Way *is circled* by the sun every 225 million years.
>
> **Active** The sun *circles* the Milky Way every 225 million years.

Notice how this story springs to life when the verbs are "activated."

STUDENT MODEL

DRAFT IN PASSIVE VOICE

It seemed that the winner would be the Rockets when the first two touchdowns **were scored** by them. Nothing **was going** well on the Lions' side. The ball **was fumbled** five times by them in the first half. Then the Lions were able to recover. Three touchdowns **were scored** by that team and the game **was won**.

REVISED FOR ACTIVE VOICE

It seemed that the Rockets would win Saturday's game when they **scored** the first two touchdowns. The Lions **could do** nothing right. They **fumbled** five times in the first half. But the Lions were able to recover and **scored** three touchdowns to win 20–14.

➋ Replacing Overused Words

Your writing may be uninteresting if you often repeat the same words or if you choose language that is generally overused, such as clichés.

Examine Your Draft for Worn-Out Words
✔ Do you keep repeating certain words—especially those associated with your topic?
✔ Do you use clichés and other worn-out language?

Substitute Synonyms for Repetitive Words

When you write about a particular subject, there's a natural tendency to repeat key words or phrases. Use a thesaurus to find interesting replacements for these overused words. In the following model, notice how synonyms are used to replace the key word *exercise*.

STUDENT MODEL

    Aerobic workouts
Exercise has many benefits. ~~Exercise~~ strengthens your heart
      physical activity
and lungs. Weight loss is another benefit of ~~exercise~~. Exercise
         fitness
improves physical appearance. Accomplishing ~~exercise~~ goals

enhances self-esteem and improves self-confidence. People who
work out   *rigorous activity*
~~exercise~~ regularly also report more energy. And ~~exercise~~

improves concentration and ability to focus. Finally, regular

exercise helps people sleep better.

Replace Tired Language

"How are you?" The automatic answer is "Fine," but does that answer have real meaning anymore? Like *fine,* some words and expressions have lost their impact from overuse. An overworked expression is called a **cliché.** When you find tired language in your draft, replace it with words and images that are fresh and original.

TIRED WORDS   **awesome, beautiful, great, incredible, nice**

CLICHÉS   **bite the bullet, have a loose screw, sink or swim**

❸ Choosing Specific Language

General language, vague and indirect, creates only fuzzy pictures in your reader's mind. Concrete language, by contrast, creates images that help your readers imagine that they can see, hear, and feel.

Examine Your Draft for Specific Language

✔ Do too many general words make your writing vague in places?

✔ Do you give concrete and specific images that your reader can easily visualize?

The following strategies will help you replace general language with language that is concrete and specific.

Revising for Specificity

	General	Specific
Use *nouns* that are concrete and specific.	They served **food** and **beverages.**	They served **gooey cinnamon buns** and **hot apple cider.**
Use *verbs* that relate vivid actions.	Refugees **moved** from war-torn countries.	Refugees **fled** from war-torn countries.
Use *adjectives* that describe specific or precise details.	She wore a **pair of** earrings and **some** sandals.	She wore **fluorescent** earrings and **ankle-strap** sandals.
Use *adverbs* that clarify the action.	She decided not to attend the party.	She decided **reluctantly** not to attend the party.

PRACTICE Revising Word Choice

In your 🗇 **Working Portfolio,** find your **Write Away** paragraph from page 347. Diagnose your draft for the passive voice, overused words, and nonspecific language. Then revise your word choice using the strategies in this lesson.

REVISION

Student Help Desk

Revision at a Glance

Keep the six traits of good writing in mind as you revise.
It may help to approach the revision process in stages—
starting with the big picture and moving to the small.

The Big Picture
Scan the entire piece.

Paragraph Level
Check individual paragraphs.

Sentence Level
Check individual sentences.

Word Level
Examine individual words and phrases.

Revise for:

Ideas and Content

Organization

Fluency

Style and Voice

Conventions

Word Choice

Deleting Redundancies   Yak Yak Yak

In a redundant phrase, too many words are used to
express the same idea. When you revise, you need
to be especially aware of choosing redundant phrases,
many of which are now in common usage.

~~advance~~ warning	~~close~~ proximity
~~major~~ breakthrough	~~end~~ product
~~serious~~ danger	~~grateful~~ thanks
~~true~~ facts	~~habitual~~ custom
~~young~~ infant	~~important~~ essentials
hurry ~~up~~	~~more~~ superior
return ~~back~~	~~necessary~~ requisite
never ~~at any time~~	~~root~~ cause
~~a pair of~~ twins	might possibly (choose one)
filled ~~to capacity~~	separate and distinct (choose one)
strangled ~~to death~~	any and all (choose one)

Clichés As Old As The Hills

Replace clichés like those in the following list with more original phrases.

light as a feather	fresh as a daisy
deep as the ocean	few and far between
sweet as sugar	by leaps and bounds
bite the bullet	boggle the mind
right as rain	in the nick of time
cool as a cucumber	make a killing
pretty as a picture	play by ear
straight as an arrow	cute as a button

ISN'T HE CUTE AS A BUTTON?

© John C. Long 1999

Self-Editing Tips Help Yourself

- **Allow mellowing time.** Put your draft aside for a couple of days before you revise. When you return to it, you'll see it with fresh eyes.
- **Read your draft aloud.** You'll hear problems that you might not see.
- **Read from your reader's point of view.** You know what you're talking about, but will your readers know?
- **Make an outline of your work.**

The Bottom Line

Checklist for Revision Strategies

Have I . . .

____ fully supported my ideas?

____ detected and corrected errors in logic?

____ clearly organized my ideas so that the reader can easily follow my train of thought?

____ focused my thesis statement?

____ combined sentences for greater fluency?

____ corrected wordiness and deleted redundancies?

____ varied sentence beginnings?

____ revised for parallelism?

____ used specific details?

Power Words
Vocabulary for Precise Writing

meticulous   *ill-kept*

It Takes All Kinds

The lockers on the next page illustrate that a wide range of personalities often exist side by side. Here are words you can use to make distinctions between opposites.

Seeking Perfection

A scientist is typically a **careful** sort of person, who is very **precise** in thinking and **conscientious** in following procedures. Her record keeping is **meticulous,** and she conducts experiments with **painstaking** care. She is both **finicky** and **fastidious** about every detail. You can be sure that her **impeccable** laboratory is **pristine** in its cleanliness. She is **exacting** of her students and **demanding** of her fellow scientists.

Seeking Help

A **careless** housekeeper will probably have an **ill-kept** and **disorganized** home. You can tell that chores are done in a **slapdash** and **haphazard** manner. The kitchen looks **messy,** newspapers are thrown into **disorderly** piles, and toys are **scattered** in **jumbled** heaps. Clothes are strewn in a **negligent** way. This is a totally **disarrayed** and **chaotic** environment.

▷ **Your Turn** When Worlds Collide

With a partner, plan and perform a skit in which two opposite personalities are forced to interact with each other. The encounter might take place in a crowded situation, such as a subway train at rush hour, a line for playoff tickets, or any other situation that has dramatic potential. As you plan, make notes about how to portray the characters' different natures and how to resolve any possible conflicts.

careful *jumbled*

Stylistic Choices

Why It Matters

What can you learn from peeking into a student's locker? What might it tell you about the person's interests, activities, and characteristics? Every person reveals something about his or her personality in every activity, from furnishing a locker to giving a speech. The choices that an individual makes show his or her personal style. In this chapter, you will learn about the specific choices that determine a writer's style.

Write Away: Secrets Unlocked
Choose one of the lockers shown above and write a paragraph describing the type of person who uses it. Keep your paragraph in your 📁 **Working Portfolio.**

Using Language Precisely

Making good stylistic choices in your writing can help you express your ideas clearly and memorably. Using the right words is the key. Choose the best language level for each piece, and find words that express exactly what you want to get across.

❶ Choosing a Language Level

Standard English is the language of business and success—for both written and oral communication. Depending on your audience and purpose, you can use either a formal or an informal level of standard English.

Levels of Standard English			
	Situations	**Characteristics**	**Example**
Formal	School, business, serious occasions, news reporting, speeches, reports	• precise, often long words • conventional' spelling, no slang, usually no contractions • complete, often complex sentences	Beyond the development of CD-ROM technology, improvements in communications began to open new opportunities for better education. —*The Americans*
Informal	Personal letters, fiction or humorous writing, everyday conversation	• simple, often short words • some unconventional spelling, slang, and contractions • many simple sentences and fragments	Have you ever listened to a computer hacker? It's not speech.... It's code. —Jim "the Mad Monk" Crotty, *How to Talk American*

Although people often use nonstandard English—*ain't, don't have none, I'm gonna, How ya doin'?,* for example—in informal speaking situations, it is not appropriate for speaking or writing in school or in the business world.

❷ Putting Connotations to Work

After you choose formal or informal language to match your situation and audience, choosing your words carefully helps you get your precise meaning across. Each word has two types of meaning. Its **denotation** is its literal, dictionary meaning. Its **connotation** is the associations or emotions it evokes.

I was struck by the woman's pale complexion.

> Neutral connotation merely describes a lack of color.

I was struck by the woman's ghostly complexion.

> Negative connotation suggests illness.

I was struck by the woman's creamy complexion.

> Positive connotation suggests beauty.

LITERARY MODEL

She looked **bloated,** like a body long submerged in motionless water, and of that **pallid** hue. Her eyes, lost in the **fatty** ridges of her face, looked like two small pieces of coal pressed into a **lump** of dough. . . .

—William Faulkner, "A Rose for Emily"

> Negative connotations paint a picture of a disagreeable woman.

STYLE

PRACTICE ▶ Using Connotations

The connotations of the words in the description below do not fit with the picture on the movie poster. Rewrite the description, using words with appropriate connotations.

Enjoy the wonders of nature as you meet the fascinating, adorable varieties of insect life up close and personal.

Using Language Creatively

Getting your message across is obviously important. Add creative language to the message, and people will not forget what you say.

❶ Figurative Language

Figurative language is language that communicates ideas beyond the literal meanings of words. It can help open readers' minds.

Imagery and Symbolism

An **image** conveys a sensory impression—something seen, heard, tasted, touched, or smelled—that enriches your message. A **symbol** is an image that represents something beyond itself. For example, in "The Devil and Tom Walker," the main character sells his soul to the Devil. How is the swamp a symbol of this situation?

> **LITERARY MODEL**
>
> The swamp ... often betrayed the traveler into a gulf of **black, smothering mud**; there were also **dark and stagnant pools** ... where the trunks of pines and hemlocks lay **half-drowned, half-rotting, looking like alligators sleeping in the mire.**
>
> —Washington Irving, "The Devil and Tom Walker"

> Vivid sight images

Personification

Personification is figurative language in which human qualities are attributed to animals and inanimate objects.

> **PROFESSIONAL MODEL**
>
> There were fat, **sassy** triggerfish and homely groupers with big lips. There were tons of long, silvery barracuda whose toothy, jutting jaws and **"bite-me!" attitudes**. . . .
>
> —Ellen Alperstein, "Fauna Follies"

> Writer attributes human mental attitudes and behavioral traits to fish.

Simile and Metaphor

A **simile** is a direct comparison between two unlike persons or things. It always contains the word *like* or *as*. A **metaphor** is an implied comparison that does not use the word *like* or *as*.

> **LITERARY MODEL**
>
> The clean profiles of the musicians, . . . the restless, wind-tossed forest of fiddle necks and bows—I recalled how, in the first orchestra I had ever heard, those long bow strokes seemed to draw the heart out of me, as a conjurer's stick reels out yards of paper ribbon from a hat.
>
> —Willa Cather, "A Wagner Matinee"

Metaphor comparing violins being bowed to waving tree branches

Simile (using *as*) comparing bows to a magician's wand

Avoid mixed metaphors. They dilute the impact of creative language, as in this promotional blurb about a novel.

Divine Justice—The crime-thriller novel that shows the frightening results when the wheels of justice come apart at the seams.

Hyperbole

Another way of being creative with language is through careful use of exaggeration, or **hyperbole,** which can add humor or a light tone.

> **PROFESSIONAL MODEL**
>
> [My mother] laughs at me these days when I call her to announce, excitedly, that I have **absolutely, totally, fully, wholly, 100 percent nothing to do.**
>
> —Deborah Mathis, "What's So Bad About a Little Boredom?"

Too bad she's so busy!

PRACTICE A Using Figurative Language

Revise these sentences, replacing stale expressions with original figurative language.

1. The soprano sang like an angel.

2. The storm howled.

3. His presentation went over like a lead balloon.

STYLE

❷ Sound Devices

People experience life with all their senses, and the more senses writers can appeal to, the more powerful their messages will be. Devices for appealing to the sense of hearing include alliteration, consonance, assonance, rhyme, and onomatopoeia.

Sound Devices

	Description	Example
Alliteration	Repeated consonant sounds at the beginning of words	hammering, hopeful heartbeat
Consonance	Repeated consonant sounds in the middle or at the end of words	most deceitful kiss
Assonance	Repeated vowel sounds in words	ice-like fright
Rhyme	Repeated sounds at the end of words, often at the end of lines	They stand and **gawk** Afraid to **talk**
Onomatopoeia	Words that sound like their meanings	the **titter** of laughter and **sigh** of relief

PRACTICE B Using Figurative Language and Sound Devices

Look at this cartoon, then write a paragraph describing what happens next. Use all of the sound devices you have learned about, as well as figurative language.

The Far Side by Gary Larson

Using Tone and Mood for Effect

LESSON 3

❶ Identifying Tone and Mood

As you read the following passages, notice how their overall effects differ.

PROFESSIONAL MODEL

> The one time I did sit through [an opera], it lasted approximately as long as fourth grade and featured large men singing for 45 minutes in a foreign language merely to observe that the sun had risen.
>
> —Dave Barry, "Should Government Force Taxpayers to Admire Art As Well As Pay for It?"

Audience: Readers of newspaper column
Purpose: To entertain

PROFESSIONAL MODEL

> An opera's characters and plot are revealed through song, rather than the speech used in ordinary drama. Once we accept this convention, opera offers great pleasure; its music both delights the ear and heightens the emotional effect of the words and story. Music makes even a complicated plot believable by depicting mood, character, and dramatic action.
>
> —Roger Kamien, *Music: An Appreciation*

Audience: Readers of music textbook
Purpose: To instruct

STYLE

Each of these models shows a very different **tone,** or attitude toward a subject, and each tone contributes to a distinctive **mood,** or general feeling. The ironic tone of the first excerpt helps to create its humorous mood; the straightforward tone of the second establishes a serious mood that serves the work's instructional purpose. Some possible tones and moods are listed below.

Tones and Moods	
Tones	formal, informal, critical, admiring, straightforward, ironic
Moods	suspenseful, calm, gloomy, hopeful, serious, humorous, pessimistic, optimistic

② Creating Tone and Mood

You can use many of the stylistic elements you have learned about—and others—to establish the tone and mood of a piece of your writing.

> **Here's How** **Creating Tone and Mood**
>
> - **Choose appropriate word choice or diction** to match the situation and audience. Use words with connotations that evoke the appropriate feelings.
> - **Use figurative language** to paint precise word pictures.
> - **Vary sentence length and complexity** to mirror meaning (for example, short, simple sentences for fast-paced action).
> - **Use punctuation** to create a sense of motion or absence of motion (for example, long sentences punctuated with commas, semicolons, and colons that pull readers breathlessly along).

Humor

You can use humor to make advertisements, speeches, parodies, comic strips, and other forms of writing memorable as well as entertaining. **Diction** is a writer's choice of words. It can be both formal and informal and often plays a part in the creation of a humorous mood.

PROFESSIONAL MODEL

When I plead, as I often do, for greater precision in our use of words, perhaps it is because I am so prone to confusion. . . .

I may have been more stupid than most, but when I heard in fourth grade that a special class was being formed for "backward readers," I silently wondered how many of my classmates possessed that marvelous gift of being able to read backward.

—Sydney J. Harris,
"In Case of Fire, Break Glass"

Straightforward diction with few adjectives establishes little boy's innocence.

Misinterpretation of *backward* creates humorous contrast.

In humorous writing, your subject, word choice, and sentence structure have to be suited to your readers, or they won't find your writing funny.

Irony

If you give your humor a cutting edge, it becomes irony. Use words and sentence structures that give readers hints that what you are saying shouldn't be taken at face value.

My wife almost always resorts to the Interrogative Putdown to let me know that I have done something stupid, such as driving past our turnoff on the freeway again. What she usually says is: "Where are you going?"

This suggests genuine curiosity. She had been expecting me to take the usual turnoff but I have gone past it, and now, excited by the prospect of adventure, she simply can't wait to find out where I'm taking her.

—Jack Smith, "The Interrogative Putdown"

> Literal interpretation of wife's question establishes irony, because what she really meant was, "You dope, you did it again."

Suspense

You can use suspense to create anticipation about what hasn't yet happened and keep readers' attention. Diction, sentence structure, and imagery can contribute to suspense.

The figure was tall and **gaunt, and shrouded** from head to foot in the habiliments of the grave. The mask which concealed the visage was made so nearly to resemble the countenance of a **stiffened corpse** that the closest scrutiny must have difficulty in detecting the cheat. . . . His vesture was dabbed in *blood.* . . .

—Edgar Allan Poe, "The Masque of the Red Death"

> Precise, frightening words create an ominous mood.

> Readers can't help but wonder who this horrible figure is and what he will do.

STYLE

PRACTICE ▸ Altering Tone and Mood

Rewrite the following passage, changing the sentence structure, diction, and imagery to create a different tone and mood.

The alarm clock went off like a nuclear attack warning. I was catapulted out of bed and started running before I even hit the floor. Halfway out the door, I realized it was Saturday.

Choosing a Point of View

Whether telling a story, reporting the news, or trying to sell a product, a writer needs to decide what **point of view,** or perspective, to use. The choice of a point of view depends on how much and what kind of information the writer wants to give and on how personally he or she wants readers to relate to the writing.

There are three points of view—**first person, third person,** and **second person.**

Be sure to stick with a point of view throughout a piece of writing. If you switch points of view, do so for a specific purpose that is clear to your readers.

❶ First Person

First-Person Point of View

Use: To express personal ideas or experiences

Signal: Writer/narrator who takes part in events and uses first-person pronouns (*I, me, my, mine, myself, we, us, our, ours, ourselves*) to refer to himself or herself

Types of writing: Editorials, autobiographies, advertising testimonials, personal essays, first-person fictional narratives

Advantage: Personal and forceful, drawing readers in

Disadvantage: Insights limited to those of one person

LITERARY MODEL

At certain times I have no race. I am *me*. When I set my hat at a certain angle and saunter down Seventh Avenue, Harlem City, feeling as snooty as the lions in front of the Forty-Second Street Library, for instance.... The cosmic Zora emerges. I belong to no race nor time. I am the eternal feminine with its string of beads.

—Zora Neale Hurston, "How It Feels to Be Colored Me"

> First-person point of view makes readers feel that they know Hurston.

❷ Third Person

Third-Person Omniscient

In the **third-person omniscient** point of view, the writer or narrator is "all-knowing" and can present events from the perspectives of many people. It gives readers a broad understanding of characters but may lack the depth of a first-person point of view.

> **LITERARY MODEL**
>
> "I'm here to help you," said the psychiatrist, frowning. Something was wrong with the room. . . . He glanced around. The prisoner laughed.
>
> "If you're wondering why it's so quiet in here, I just kicked the radio to death."
>
> Violent, thought the doctor.
>
> The prisoner read this thought, smiled, put out a gentle hand. "No, only to machines that yak-yak-yak."
>
> —Ray Bradbury, "The Murderer"

Writer gives readers access to both characters' actions and thoughts.

STYLE

Third-Person Limited

In the **third-person limited** point of view, the writer or narrator presents events from the perspective of a single person. Readers get an in-depth view of that person's observations, feelings, and thoughts but perceive other characters only through his or her eyes. Ambrose Bierce's powerful short story "An Occurrence at Owl Creek Bridge" is told from a third-person limited point of view.

❸ Second Person

PROFESSIONAL MODEL

Just follow these steps:

1. Turn to Part Two of this User Manual and choose the topic area that most closely describes the image you are seeking. . . .
2. Pinpoint the image that best meets your needs. . . .
3. Take mental note of the image's location. . . .
4. Insert the CD-ROM that contains the desired category. . . .
5. . . .Add the desired clip art image to your document. . . .

—*Art Explosion User Manual*

> Information is addressed to readers. (*You* is implied, not stated.)

 Although parts of this textbook are written in the second person, many educational and professional standards discourage the use of the second-person point of view except for directions and instructions.

PRACTICE Changing Point of View

Rewrite this first-person excerpt, using a different point of view. How does the impact of the rewritten passage compare with that of the original?

> I lived with Mr. Covey one year. During the first six months, of that year, scarce a week passed without his whipping me. I was seldom free from a sore back. My awkwardness was almost always his excuse for whipping me.
>
> —Frederick Douglass, *Narrative of the Life of Frederick Douglass*

Developing a Voice

The stylistic choices you make as a writer contribute to your **voice**—the distinctive sound of your work. The techniques you learned about in the previous lessons—word choice, creative use of language, tone and mood, point of view—all play a part.

> **Here's How** **Developing Your Writing Voice**
>
> - Don't try to imitate other writers.
> - Read your writing aloud to see if it sounds natural.
> - Write, write, write.
> - Don't become discouraged. This process isn't quick or easy.

Although a writer may use different styles when writing for different audiences and purposes, a writer's voice runs through all his or her work and makes it immediately recognizable.

LITERARY MODELS

How easy it is to make people believe a lie and how hard it is to undo that work again! Thirty-five years after those evil exploits of mine I visited my old mother, whom I had not seen for ten years; and being moved by what seemed to me a rather noble and perhaps heroic impulse, I thought I would humble myself and confess my ancient fault.

—Mark Twain,
The Autobiography of Mark Twain

I found Simon Wheeler dozing comfortably by the barroom stove of the dilapidated tavern in the decayed mining camp of Angel's, and I noticed that he was fat and baldheaded and had an expression of winning gentleness and simplicity upon his tranquil countenance.

—Mark Twain,
"The Notorious Jumping Frog of Calaveras County"

Both passages show Twain's fondness for descriptive details, long sentences, and first-person point of view.

STYLE

PRACTICE **Developing Your Voice**

In your 📁 **Working Portfolio,** find the paragraph you wrote for the **Write Away** on page 365. Rewrite it, using the techniques you learned in this chapter.

Student Help Desk

Stylistic Choices at a Glance

Figurative Language
imagery, symbolism, personification, simile, metaphor, hyperbole

Language Level
formal, informal

Word Choice
appropriate denotation and connotation

Sound Devices
alliteration, consonance, assonance, rhyme, onomatopoeia

Point of View
(first person, third person omniscient or limited, second person)

Tone and Mood
tone—attitude toward subject

mood—general feeling

Choosing Appropriate Connotations  Pinpoint Accuracy

POSITIVE	NEUTRAL	NEGATIVE
thrifty	economical	stingy
relaxed	inactive	lazy
solid	heavy	obese
slender	thin	anorexic
clear away	dismantle	demolish
preserve	save	hoard
traditional	old-fashioned	reactionary
discriminating	selective	picky
brilliant	intelligent	know-it-all

Avoiding Clichés   Put a New Spin on It

Avoid clichés like these in your writing.

kill two birds with one stone

the cream of the crop

hit the nail on the head

hide your light under a bushel

easier said than done

last but not least

let your hair down

the whole ball of wax

bite the bullet

can't see the forest for the trees

boggle the mind

play it by ear

over the hill

by leaps and bounds

in the nick of time

few and far between

busy as a bee

free as a bird

clear as mud

quiet as a mouse

sound as a dollar

stubborn as a mule

fit as a fiddle

wise as an owl

light as a feather

deep as the ocean

sweet as sugar

cute as a button

right as rain

cool as a cucumber

pretty as a picture

straight as an arrow

STYLE

The Bottom Line

Checklist for Style

Can I improve my style by . . .

____ clarifying the purpose of my writing?

____ adjusting the level of language to better suit my audience?

____ choosing words with more appropriate connotations?

____ creating fresh, concrete images?

____ using a variety of sentence structures?

____ choosing words and images that create a more appropriate tone and mood?

____ changing the point of view?

____ experimenting with my writing voice?

Writing Workshops

Reach for the Sky

Weave a story. Research and write about a topic. Help a fellow worker by explaining how to perform a task. Shed light on a problem and urge others to take action. Bring a memorable experience to vivid life. The amazing thing about writing is that there's no limit to what you can produce.

Reflective Essay

Learn What It Is

You have probably learned important lessons from certain experiences in your life. When you write about a personal experience and what it has meant to you, you are writing a **reflective essay.** You can find reflective writing in letters, memoirs, autobiographies, and other similar literature. Here's how to write a reflective essay.

Basics in a Box

REFLECTIVE ESSAY AT A GLANCE

personal experience

thoughts observations connections

lesson learned

RUBRIC

Standards for Writing

A successful reflective essay should

- be written in the first person
- describe an important experience in your life or the life of someone you admire
- use figurative language, dialogue, sensory details, or other techniques to re-create the experience for the reader
- explain the significance of the event
- make an observation about life, based on the experience
- encourage readers to think about the significance of the experience in light of their own lives

See How It's Done: *Reflective Essay*

Student Model
Jennifer Stiers
R.O.W.V.A. High School

RUBRIC
IN ACTION

Untitled

My body sank in the thick brown mud, causing the ice-cold water to rise above my scratched and already muddy knees. But the freezing water and disgusting mud didn't bother me. I was on a mission. My brother, the neighbor boys, and I were attempting to catch one of the ugliest and meanest beasts that lived in the small stream that ran behind my house. The beast was a gigantic, four-inch, brown crawdad with long antennae, a scaly tail, and enormous claws that could take off a finger; so we thought.

That small creek was visited almost daily by the kids in my neighborhood. For us it was full of adventure and mysterious objects and creatures buried underneath rock and mud. But that was nearly five years ago. Since then, we've all been too busy or too mature to put on grubby clothes and see what the creek had for us to discover. Never did I think I would begin another journey in the long-forgotten creek. But this past summer, after reminiscing about the wonderful past experiences that I had had as a child in the creek, my neighbor, Jason Dixon, and I found ourselves on another mission: catching minnows and crawdads as bait for a future fishing trip.

. . . As we started toward the creek, I almost felt nervous. What if I couldn't remember how to carefully position the poles in the mud, trudge through the swampy water, and with all my might, lift the net out of the water?. . . When we approached the steep bank before the creek, Jacob jumped right in. I stood back and watched him stand in the cloudy water and untangle the broom handles from the stiff, dirty net. I hesitantly lowered myself over the edge, gripping the side of the rocky bank. I noticed how I was so much

① Written in first person

② This writer opens with a flashback to introduce the theme and setting of an important experience in her life.

Other Options:
• Start by describing the experience itself.
• Open with an unexpected statement.

③ Makes transition from flashback to the main experience

④ Uses specific details to re-create the experience for readers

REFLECTIVE

more careful than I had been years before. Instead of thinking how cool the water and mud would feel, I was worried about bug bites, poison ivy, and getting my clothes dirty. . . .

I realized this trip would be more difficult. The weeds that grew along the bank formed a mangled tunnel of vegetation. The water stood above my waist, and insects swarmed all around me. I began to ease myself down the bank again, but I remembered how I shouldn't worry about the dangers of the creek and should just have fun. I let go of the bank and slid into the muddy water with a splash. Jacob followed close behind me, and we set up the net quickly. I was filled with excitement, and when we began to walk, I marched in front of him.

As we silently trudged through the creek, the water felt much warmer, the colorful insects and weeds were more beautiful, and even the mud felt slick and cool against my skin. When we had walked far enough, we raised the net with all of our strength. Again the water gushed from the net. After all the water and debris had cleared, we discovered, to our delight, numerous red-bellied flopping minnows and a considerable number of angry crawdads that didn't seem as large as they had when I was younger.

The older I get, the more I think I know all the answers. But when I stopped and reflected on the lessons of my childhood, I realized that as a child, I was already wiser than most adults. In order to become successful, I had to follow Annie Dillard's advice: point myself, forget myself, aim, and dive. As a child, I knew wholehearted effort and total concentration were the keys to achieving my goals. The creek is responsible for teaching me those valuable lessons. I plan to visit it often.

❺ This writer tells readers how she felt during the experience.

❻ Implies that readers should think about the significance of this experience in light of their own lives

Another Option: State directly how readers should apply the experience to their lives.

❼ Makes an observation about life, based on the experience

Do It Yourself

Writing Prompt Write a reflective essay about an experience from which you learned an important lesson.

Purpose To show what the experience means to you

Audience School literary magazine, classmates, family

❶ Prewriting

Choosing a Topic To find a topic, try listing some vivid memories. Then make notes of why you remember each. Or reverse the process by listing important lessons you have learned in your life. Then note the experience that led to each lesson. After you have picked your topic, complete the following activities.

- **Think about your experience.** Why do you remember it? What details do you remember most clearly? What emotions did you go through at the time?

- **Explore the significance.** Does the experience hold one obvious meaning for you? What else did your experience teach you? Try to uncover as many levels of meaning in it as you can.

- **Consider your audience.** What parts of the experience do you need to re-create for your readers? How can you encourage them to apply the lessons from your experience to their own lives?

For more help, see the Idea Bank, p. 388.

❷ Drafting

Starting to Write You might begin by picturing the experience in your mind and jotting down sights, sounds, and dialogue. Or you could try writing a moral to your story. The important thing is to keep your ideas flowing. Later you can rearrange your material to fit the organization you choose.

Organizing Your Ideas Should you begin with the lesson you learned and then share your experience? Or should you begin with your experience, and then explain what it taught you? It doesn't matter. If you feel that your organization is not working, you can stop at any point and try a different approach.

For information about getting feedback from your peers, see p. 388.

REFLECTIVE

❸ Revising

TARGET SKILL ▶ **Avoiding Clichés and Slang** To keep your writing fresh and interesting, avoid clichés (phrases that have been used so often they are now stale). If you want your work to seem polished and well-considered, avoid slang. For more help with revising, see the rubric, page 382.

> But when I stopped and reflected on ∧ ~~being a kid,~~ *the lessons of my childhood,* I realized
> that as a ~~kid,~~ *child,* I was already ~~sharp as a tack~~ *wiser than most adults.*

❹ Editing and Proofreading

TARGET SKILL ▶ **Misplaced Modifiers** Putting a prepositional phrase too far away from the word it modifies in a sentence can confuse readers. This type of error is called a **misplaced modifier**. By placing a phrase next to the word it modifies, you can avoid confusing your readers. Notice how moving the modifiers in the following passage makes the meaning of each sentence clearer.

> For us it was full of adventure ~~buried underneath rock~~
> *buried underneath rock and mud*
> ~~and mud~~ and mysterious objects and creatures ∧ But that
> *nearly*   ⊙
> was ∧ five years ago ∧ ~~nearly.~~

For more help with misplaced modifiers, see p. 191.

❺ Sharing and Reflecting

Share your finished essay with a friend, family member, or your peer reviewer by reading it aloud. Ask for feedback from your audience to improve your communication skills.

For Your Working Portfolio Did your feelings about your experience change as you wrote about it? Did you encounter any problems? What went especially well? Which responses from your audience surprised you? Attach your answers to your finished work, and save the essay in your 🗀 **Working Portfolio.**

Real World Reflective Essay

Often when people write letters, they write about important things that have happened to them in their lives. In autobiographies, people write about their entire lives in a book. You might keep a journal of important things that happen to you day to day. These are all examples of reflective writing:

- Letters
- Autobiographies
- Interviews
- Magazine articles
- Speeches
- Journals

College Application Essay

from *Essays That Worked*

There is a little demon that lurks in my conscious and unconscious mind that has done me more ill than any conventional ailment could. It is a stealthy creature that preys upon my life and in the lives of many. The demon's name is procrastination, and he mocks me even as I type up the final draft of this essay. For the demon has triumphed again, and stolen my sleep, and he may triumph again after this. But I think not for a while, for this time he has stung me sorely, and my guard shall be up.

For the complete text of the essay, see MODEL BANK, pp. 624–625.

JOURNAL

BOOK

Letters *from the* Lake

by Julian Yin

MAGAZINE ARTICLE

Peace of Mind
by Tom Taylor

It wasn't easy, I can tell you that. I fought the idea kicking and screaming. Why would I ever be crazy enough to give up some of the best foods the world has to offer? Give up hamburgers and hot dogs? Give up steak and seafood? Say good-bye to chicken and turkey? These were the definitions of healthy dinners, holiday feasts, and All-American meals.

I had a couple of close friends who were vegetarians. I thought they were crazy and vowed over and over that I would never change my diet. Finally, they dared me. They were so sure that I would be happier without all that meat in my system, that I figured, "What have I got to lose?"

I wasn't about to alter my whole diet overnight, but I decided to go for one month without any red meat, just to see if I noticed any difference in how I felt.

Student Help Desk

Reflective Essay at a Glance

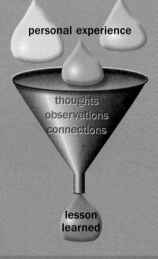

personal experience

thoughts
observations
connections

lesson
learned

Idea Bank

- **Brainstorm familiar proverbs.** Which morals or adages apply to your life? How did they become important to you?
- **Reflect on your favorite stories.** Do any of them remind you of an experience in your life that was important to you?
- **Borrow inspiration.** Read an essay such as Joan Didion's "Letter from Paradise, 21° 19' N., 157° 52' W." (*Language of Literature,* Grade 11).

Friendly Feedback   Questions for Your Peer Reader

- Why do you think this experience was important to me?
- What do you see as the main point of my piece?
- In what ways did my story relate to anything you have experienced?
- Which parts did you like? Why?
- Which parts could have been made more clear or interesting?

Publishing Options

Print	Submit your reflective essay to your school newspaper or to a student magazine.
Oral Communications	Present a class reading to share your essay with your classmates. Leave time afterward to discuss what you learned from each other.
Online	Check out **mcdougallittell.com** for more publishing options.

Elaboration Techniques

What did you say? What did others say?

Use **dialogue** wherever appropriate.

How did it smell? taste? sound? look? feel?

Use **sensory words** to re-create the physical world.

How exactly did it move?

Use **specific verbs** and **concrete nouns** to describe actions and objects.

The Bottom Line

REFLECTIVE

Checklist for Reflective Essay

Have I . . .

____ used first person?

____ described an important experience?

____ used sensory details, figurative language, or other methods to give the reader a picture of the experience?

____ explained the significance of the event?

____ presented a moral or an observation about life, based on the experience?

____ encouraged readers to think about the significance of the experience in their own lives?

Eyewitness Report

Learn What It Is

You are there. The only thing more exciting than experiencing an event is reading a well-written eyewitness account of it. Writers for newspapers, magazines, radio, and television attract and keep their audience by presenting vivid sensory details that transport them to the scenes of events. Here is how to create an effective **eyewitness report.**

Basics in a Box

EYEWITNESS REPORT AT A GLANCE

What? the event	**Who?** the people involved	**Where?** the place
When? the date, year, time	**Why?** the cause	**How?** the details of what happened

= **Re-Creation of Event**

RUBRIC

Standards for Writing

A successful eyewitness report should

- focus on an event that has personal or historical significance
- answer the five W's: *who, what, when, where, why,* and *how*
- create a sense of immediacy with precise language and sensory images
- present occurrences in a clear, logical order
- capture the mood of the event

See How It's Done: *Eyewitness Report*

Student Model
Yursa Ahmad
Glenbard East
High School

RUBRIC
IN ACTION

Flood

"Water, water, everywhere, nor any drop to drink."
Coleridge's lines flashed through my mind as the
muddy Ganges water gently lapped the prow of our
wooden *nowka*, or riverboat. All around were the
flooded streets of Dhaka, Bangladesh. As we
approached our apartment building, the *nowka-wala*
[person handling the boat] had trouble maneuvering
through our narrow alleyway. As the *nowka* stopped,
my father and I scrambled up a rope ladder to the
second floor of our building. The first floor had
vanished overnight under the flood waters. I
immediately ran out to our balcony and gasped at
what I saw. The wide dirt road that separated our
building from the great Ganges had disappeared. Now
there was only water.

The swollen river was streaked with long ripples
that splashed up the building wall. I realized with a
shudder that some of these silver streaks were actually
snakes! People clambered onto wooden boats from a
makeshift platform of floating straw. I saw a mullah, or
religious leader, vigorously whipping his staff in the air
and shouting, causing the platform to rock
dangerously. My eyes widened as I saw what upset
him. A huge iguana had coiled its tail around his staff,
clinging for dear life. The struggle seemed funny at the
time. Now I see it as a tragic symbol of the struggle
for survival that went on in Bangladesh in the summer
of 1988.

I was there at the flood of '88, the worst flood in
50 years. Water swept away entire villages. Pain and
suffering were everywhere and left their mark on
everyone's life. Sorrow became my constant
companion. I had been spared but was helpless to
ease the misery, hunger, disease, and death around me.
Water, the life giver, had now become the destroyer.

1 Tells where

2 Tells who

3 Includes precise
language

4 Tells what, and
explains the event's
historical
significance

EYEWITNESS

Although I was born in Dhaka, living abroad had lulled me into believing that all children could be happy. It was only when I passed through the slums that summer that my innocence was shattered in the face of abject human distress. The sight was like something I had seen on the news, but the news always happened somewhere else, unreal and beyond my reach. Now I was in the midst of a tragic disaster, and I was affected.

I can still smell the stench from the bloated bodies that lay piled high for lack of a dry burial ground. My ears ring with the sound of children crying from hunger and women wailing for their drowned families. I see frightened villagers fleeing death and feel the raw courage of relief workers battling to provide food, shelter, and comfort. I cried many times, knowing that there were other kids just like me who lived around the corner but had lost their homes in one horrible night.

The flood marked a turning point in my life. Now I know that I am not special or protected from disaster. My life is as fragile—and as precious—as everyone else's. I've learned that what happens in the world is not "somewhere out there" but right in my own back yard and very close to my heart.

❺ This writer presents events in a clear, logical order: first the flood itself, then the aftermath.

Another option: Present the aftermath, then flash back to the flood itself.

❻ Presents sensory details: smell, sound, sight

❼ Captures the mood of the event

Do It Yourself

Writing Prompt Choose an event of personal or historical significance and write an eyewitness report describing it.

Purpose to inform

Audience general readers, family, friends

❶ Prewriting

Choose an event to write about. Remember that the topic has to be something you have experienced or you expect to experience in the near future. If you choose to write about a future event, take notes as the event unfolds. If the event has already occurred, make sure you remember the details clearly enough to describe them. Once you decide on your topic, try the following activities.

- **Answer the five W's.** Be sure to list the *who, what, where, when, why,* and *how* of the event.
- **Use your senses.** Record details experienced through the senses.
- **Fill in the gaps.** Check print or online sources or talk to others who witnessed the event to fill in missing details.
- **Check newspapers and magazines.** Look for other examples of eyewitness reports. Analyze the strategies the writers used to compose them.

For more help, see the Idea Bank on p. 396.

❷ Drafting

Organize your essay. One good way to start writing your draft is to list events in **chronological order,** the order in which they occurred. Try filling in a flow chart like the one below.

First event ▸ Second event ▸ Third event ▸ Last event

Once you have organized your material chronologically, you might experiment with different ways of presenting it. For example, you could begin with the last event, then flash back to the beginning and give the rest of the events in order. You also might consider beginning by setting the scene, presenting a striking image, or including a memorable quotation.

For information about getting feedback from your peers, see p. 396.

EYEWITNESS

❸ Revising

TARGET SKILL ▶Effective Introductions To get your eyewitness report off to a good start, capture your readers' attention immediately. You might try using a question, a quotation, or a bold statement. For more help with revising, review the rubric on page 390.

> *"Water, water, everywhere, nor any drop to drink."*
> ^A flood is bad when it happens, but what it leaves behind is
>
> worse. That is what I experienced recently.
>
> *Coleridge's lines flashed through my mind as the muddy Ganges water gently lapped the prow of our wooden nowka, or riverboat.*

❹ Editing and Proofreading

TARGET SKILL ▶Pronoun-Antecedent Agreement A good eyewitness report must clearly explain who did or felt what. To make sure that yours does, check that pronouns agree with their antecedents in number, gender, and person.

> *their*
> Pain and suffering were everywhere and left its mark on
> everyone's life. Sorrow became my constant companion.

For more on pronoun-antecedent agreement, see pp. 162–164.

❺ Sharing and Reflecting

Share your eyewitness report with an audience. Consider including photographs, videotapes, or audiotapes to make your presentation more lively.

For Your Working Portfolio What did you learn about the event? about observation? about your own writing process? Attach your answers to your finished work and save it in your
📁 **Working Portfolio.**

Real World Eyewitness Report

When police conduct an investigation, they get statements from people who saw what happened. Scientists write detailed accounts of experiments they perform, and books are written by people who were present when historical events took place. You may encounter many eyewitness reports every day:

- News stories
- Historical accounts
- Sports reports
- Police reports
- Documentaries
- Courtroom transcripts

Newspaper Article

Section

Heavy Tread of Elephants Makes Hearts Lighter

By Michael T. Kaufman   *The New York Times*

The night was cool and the wind was churning as the 18 elephants prepared to cross by foot into Manhattan from Queens. It was a little before midnight, and up ahead, the Empire State Building shone brightly as the mahouts and keepers slid open the animal cars on the circus train.

Without a single snort of protest, without an elephant sneer, they emerged wallowing in grace like fat chorus girls happy to be back in town. Without anyone saying a word to them, they lined up and bowed their heads to make it easier for their handlers to put on the red bridles with the Ringling Brothers and Barnum & Bailey insignia.... **For the complete text of the article, see MODEL BANK, pp. 626–627.**

MAGAZINE

An announcer uses binoculars for a closer look as he observes the team's pre-season training.

COURT TRANSCRIPT

MR. DANIELS: I just want to be absolutely sure I answer as precisely as I can, Your Honor. It's not that I didn't understand the question.

THE COURT: Simply state exactly what you saw after the defendant left the building. That was the point you were after, wasn't it?

MR. MORTON: Yes, Your Honor, essentially.

THE COURT: Perhaps you should repeat the question.
... Daniels, after you saw the defendant leave the

Student Help Desk

Eyewitness Report at a Glance

What? the event	**Who?** the people involved	**Where?** the place
When? the date, year, time	**Why?** the cause	**How?** the details of what happened

= **Re-Creation of Event**

Idea Bank

- **Check your calendar.** Look for sports events, performances, town meetings, and family gatherings. Plan to attend one of the events and take notes.

- **Expect the unexpected.** Carry a notebook with you for the next several days. Be on the lookout for planned events you hadn't thought of or for unexpected events. Take notes!

- **Play it back.** If you were at an event where you or someone else made a video, use the video to trigger and verify your own memories of the event.

Friendly Feedback Questions for Your Peer Reader

- Why do you think I chose to report on this event?
- Which details were most vivid? Which details seemed unnecessary?
- What would you like to know more about?
- What did you like best about my report?

Publishing Options

Print	Post your report in a "You Are There" space on your classroom bulletin board.
Oral Communication	Present your eyewitness report as a multimedia, on-the-scene news broadcast with sound and video clips.
Online	Check out **mcdougallittell.com** for more publishing options.

Elaboration: Flesh It Out

Use a chart like the one below to record details about your event.

The Five Senses: How did it . . .

sound?	look?	smell?	taste?	feel?

The Bottom Line

Checklist for Eyewitness Report

Have I . . .

____ made the significance of the event clear?

____ shown who, what, where, when, why, and how?

____ created a sense of immediacy?

____ used precise words and sensory images?

____ presented occurrences in a logical order?

____ captured the mood of the event?

Literary Interpretation

Learn What It Is

You know you liked the book or the movie, but can you explain why? What did the work mean to you? A **literary interpretation** allows you to explore your own ideas about the meaning of a literary work and analyze the elements in the work that support that meaning. Here are the basic elements of a literary interpretation.

Basics in a Box

LITERARY INTERPRETATION AT A GLANCE

Introduction
Introduces the literary work and includes a clear thesis statement that introduces the interpretation

Body
Supports the interpretation with evidence from the literary work

- Explanation
- Evidence
- Evidence
- Evidence

Conclusion
Summarizes the interpretation

RUBRIC

Standards for Writing

A successful literary interpretation should

- clearly identify the title and author of the literary work
- give a clearly stated thesis statement at or near the beginning of the essay
- present evidence and quotations from the text to support the interpretation
- take into account other interpretations and contradictory evidence

CHAPTER 19

See How It's Done: *Literary Interpretation*

Student Model
Sarah Hospelhorn
New Trier High School

RUBRIC
IN ACTION

Tragic Hero in *The Crucible*

Arthur Miller's play *The Crucible* takes place during the Salem witchhunts of 1692. The final scene in the play is one of great tragedy, yet John Proctor's final act reveals his heroic character. He sacrifices himself for a greater cause and exhibits such courage and honor that he must be regarded as a tragic hero.

Despite Proctor's goodness, however, he has a tragic flaw. He has had a relationship with Abigail, one of the teenagers in Salem who practices witchcraft. Proctor's relationship with Abigail, followed by his rejection of her, makes the girl spiteful. She makes accusations against Proctor's wife that lead to Elizabeth's arrest as a witch.

Proctor is respected in the town but regards himself as a sinner and a fraud. He was unable to resist Abigail. Worse yet, his involvement with her results in the witchcraft hysteria that overtakes the town. His weakness leads to his downfall and that of the community.

Proctor has been asked to sign a document in which he confesses his involvement with witchcraft and implicates others. He confesses to his relationship with Abigail but is imprisoned when he refuses to confess to practicing witchcraft.

After Proctor confesses to his relationship with Abigail, many people continue to believe that he is a good man. The Reverend Hale, a "witchcraft expert" brought in from a neighboring town, believes that Proctor deserves to live—and so should confess to being in league with the Devil. He says to Elizabeth, "Life, woman, life is God's most precious gift; no principle, however glorious, may justify the taking of it. I beg you, woman, prevail upon your husband to confess. Let him give his lie."

① Clearly identifies the title and author of the work

② Presents a thesis statement that introduces the interpretation

③ Cites contradictory evidence

④ Explains the interpretation in more detail

⑤ Draws a conclusion from quoted evidence to support the interpretation

LITERARY INTERP.

Even Elizabeth, who is the real victim of Proctor's sins, continues to have faith in him. But she believes he will do the right thing. Before he decides whether to confess or die, she comforts him: "Only be sure of this, for I know it now: Whatever you will do, it is a good man does it."

Proctor rejects the "salvation" that is offered him in return for speaking against his friends. He signs but then refuses to hand over the document saying, "I have three children—how may I teach them to walk like men in the world, and I sold my friends?" He has confessed to his real sins, and his repentance is so powerful that he will not sin again, even to save his own life. He tears up the document.

Proctor sacrifices himself for the good of his friends and family. By doing so, he redeems himself. His wife understands this. When Hale begs Elizabeth to stop Proctor, she replies, "He have his goodness now. God forbid I take it from him!" Proctor's self-sacrifice liberates him from his sins and makes him a true tragic hero.

❻ Uses a strong quotation as further support

❼ Summarizes the interpretation in the conclusion

Other Options
• End with a quotation from the work
• End by restating the interpretation

Do It Yourself

Explore the meaning of a literary work through a literary interpretation.

Purpose To explain your interpretation

Audience People who are familiar with the work

❶ Prewriting

Decide what to write about. You might choose to explore a piece you had some difficulty understanding. On the other hand, you might choose to analyze a work you feel confident you understand. Once you have chosen your topic, follow the steps below.

Read and reread.

Take notes about the literary elements in the work. Freewrite about the characters, the central conflict, and the theme. Then choose what elements you will focus on.

Write a working thesis statement.

Try to capture the main point of your interpretation in a sentence.

Gather evidence.

List significant passages and quotations from the text and write a few sentences explaining how they support your interpretation.

Challenge your interpretation.

Does the evidence support your interpretation? Did you find evidence that contradicts it? If so, how can you revise your interpretation to account for more of the evidence?

---

❷ Drafting

A good way to start your essay is to list or outline the points you want to make. Jot down evidence from the text that supports each point. You can refer to these notes as you work. As you write your draft, organize it into the following basic parts:

- **Introduction**—identifies the author and title of the work and states the main point of the interpretation
- **Body**—presents specific evidence from the work to support the interpretation
- **Conclusion**—restates or summarizes the interpretation

For information about getting feedback from your peers, see p. 405.

❸ Revising

TARGET SKILL ▶**Elaborating with Evidence** To make your interpretation convincing, you will need to support your main ideas with evidence—specific references and quotations—from the literary work. Integrate these references smoothly into your writing. Don't just insert them between sentences. For more help with revising, review the rubric on page 398.

> *Hale begs Elizabeth to stop*
> When ^ ~~someone talks to Elizabeth about~~ Proctor, she replies ^
> *"He have his goodness now. God forbid I take it from him!"*
> ^ ~~that he is doing the right thing and she doesn't want to~~
> ~~interfere.~~

For more on elaboration, see pp. 333–345.

❹ Editing and Proofreading

TARGET SKILL ▶**Correcting Sentence Fragments** As you polish your work, watch for incomplete sentences, or fragments. Be sure to change capitalization and punctuation marks as needed when you change the fragments to complete sentences.

> After Proctor confesses to his relationship with Abigail ^ Many
> people continue to believe that he is a good man.

For more information on correcting sentence fragments, see p. 27.

❺ Sharing and Reflecting

Share your interpretation in a discussion group with people who have read the work. Reread your work aloud before you begin your discussion.

For Your Working Portfolio What helped you the most in developing your literary interpretation? How did your interpretation change as you wrote? Attach your answers to your finished work. Save your literary interpretation in your ▱ **Working Portfolio.**

Real World Literary Interpretation

Literary interpretations come in a wide variety of forms. People get together in book clubs to discuss works they've read. Actors translate written words into performances based on their interpretations. Book reviews analyze specific works. You can find literary interpretation in any of these places:

- Book clubs
- Live performances
- Book reviews
- Interviews with writers
- Literary Web pages
- Film adaptations

Star Wars: Episode I— The Phantom Menace

By Roger Ebert   *Chicago Sun-Times*

"Star Wars: Episode I—The Phantom Menace," to cite its full title, is an astonishing achievement in imaginative filmmaking. If some of the characters are less than compelling, perhaps that's inevitable: This is the first story in the chronology and has to set up characters who (we already know) will become more interesting with the passage of time.... At the risk of offending devotees of the Force, I will say that the stories of the "Star Wars" movies have always been space operas and that the importance of the movies comes from their energy, their sense of fun, their colorful inventions, and their state-of-the-art special effects. I do not attend with the hope of gaining insights into human behavior. **For the complete text of the review, see MODEL BANK, pp. 628–629.**

POETRY CONTEST WINNERS

STUDENT WEB PAGE

Laura's Favorite Books Page:

#5: A Separate Peace By John Knowles
This book made my list because it's one of the few books I've had to read for school that actually made me cry. It's about a man named Gene remembering his days at the Devon School, a boy's school he attended in 1942. Gene has a competitive friendship with his roommate Finny, who is an excellent athlete with a winning personality. One day, as Finny is about to jump from a tree into the river, Gene jounces the branch and Finny falls and breaks his leg.

Ten Books That Changed My Life

One Man's journey from prisoner to poet

by John Brooks

BOOK

Student Help Desk

Literary Interpretation at a Glance

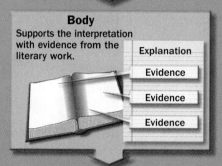

Introduction
Introduces the literary work and includes a clear thesis statement that introduces the interpretation

Body
Supports the interpretation with evidence from the literary work.

Explanation

Evidence

Evidence

Evidence

Conclusion
Summarizes the interpretation

Idea Bank

- **Read a favorite author.** In the library, look for new or unfamiliar works by your favorite authors.

- **Take on a challenge.** Choose a selection that challenges you.

- **Read a movie.** Read the book or story that was the basis for a movie you've enjoyed.

- **Find something you hate.** Pick something you know you'll hate so that you can explain why.

- **Choose a song.** Choose one or two songs by your favorite recording artist or group.

- **Talk to your friends.** Ask your friends for recommendations.

- **Check out the library.** Browse the library or bookstore shelves until something catches your eye.

Friendly Feedback
Questions for Your Peer Reader

- What is the main point of my interpretation?
- What evidence did I provide to support my interpretation?
- Are you convinced that my interpretation is reasonable? Why or why not?
- What other points could I have included to support my ideas?

Publishing Options

Print	• Submit your interpretation to your school's literary magazine.
	• E-mail your interpretation to friends who are familiar with the literary work.
	• Publish your interpretation on a literary Web site—yours or someone else's.
Oral	• Hold a literary roundtable in which you and several others discuss your interpretations of a particular work.
	• Debate your interpretation with someone who holds a contradictory position.
	• Organize a reading of your interpretation and ask the audience to come dressed as characters in the work.
Online	• Visit **mcdougallittell.com** for more publishing options.

The Bottom Line

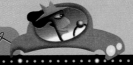

Checklist for Literary Interpretation

Have I . . .

_____ clearly identified the title and author of the literary work in my introduction?

_____ clearly presented my thesis statement at or near the beginning of the essay?

_____ supported my interpretation with evidence from the work?

_____ taken into account other interpretations and contradictory evidence?

_____ summarized my interpretation in the conclusion?

Comparison-and-Contrast Essay

Learn What It Is

Think about two people you know. What do they have in common? How are they different? When you consider these questions, you compare and contrast the pair. You can compare and contrast any time you want to analyze the similarities and differences between objects, people, or events. Here's how to put it all together in a **comparison-and-contrast essay.**

Basics in a Box

COMPARISON-AND-CONTRAST ESSAY AT A GLANCE

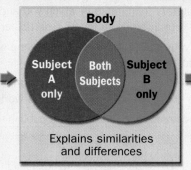

Introduction
- Identifies the **subjects** being compared
- Tells the **purpose** for the comparison

Body

Subject A only   Both Subjects   Subject B only

Explains similarities and differences

Conclusion
- Restates the **main idea** or draws a **conclusion**

RUBRIC

Standards for Writing

A successful comparison-and-contrast essay should

- identify the subjects being compared
- establish a clear reason for the comparison
- include both similarities and differences, and support them with specific examples and details
- follow a clear organizational pattern
- use transitional words and phrases to make the relationships between ideas clear
- summarize the comparison in the conclusion

See How It's Done: *Comparison-and-Contrast Essay*

Student Model
Stephanie Butler
Glenbard East High School

RUBRIC
IN ACTION

We Need Plays Too

Fast-paced. Action-filled. Dramatic. Fanciful. These words describe modern-day movies, our most prevalent form of entertainment. In a sense, movies are an "upgrade" of plays, which have been a source of entertainment since antiquity. Some people feel that movies have so many advantages over live theater that theater will ultimately disappear as an important form of entertainment. However, since specific benefits can be attributed to movies and plays, both forms will endure.

1 Identifies the subjects being compared: movies and plays

2 Establishes a clear reason for the comparison

Movies undoubtedly have some advantages over theater. For one thing, movie tickets are cheaper than theater tickets. Movie showings are also more convenient for audiences. One movie can be shown in more places—and more often—than an individual play.

3 Discusses the advantages of movies over plays

Furthermore, movie settings have many advantages over theater settings. For instance, one scene can take place in New York and the very next second, the scene can shift to Paris. Settings can seem more authentic because they are filmed on location or on a realistic set. Moviemakers can also use special effects to create imaginary worlds. They can show dinosaurs chasing humans across the screen or whole cities being toppled by an earthquake.

4 Supports advantages with specific examples

Unlike film, a play production is limited to the stage on which it is being performed. However, actors and audiences in a theater share a special intimacy that cannot be achieved in a movie theater. At times, actors talk directly to the audience. This is possible in theater because the performance is live. The intimacy shared by the audience and actors makes this entertainment vehicle ideal for expressing emotion. While limited in its ability to create exciting action, the theater excels in conveying human drama.

5 This writer follows a clear subject-by-subject organizational pattern: first movies, then plays.

Other option:
• Use a feature-by-feature organizational pattern.

COMPARISON

Another advantage of a play is that it is a dynamic production, capable of growing and changing. Once a movie is released, it is finished and cannot be changed. But a play can be modified and adapted over time. For example, in the Gilbert and Sullivan play *The Mikado,* a song originally written to criticize contemporary politicians is updated in new performances to include attacks on modern officials.

Though movies and plays are vastly different, in some ways they are very much alike. Both are meant to entertain. Both tell a story. Both deal with basic human nature and moral issues. Both provide a wide range of genres. Comedies, war stories, love stories, and mysteries are all presented on stage and on the big screen.

Movies and plays have different appeals. Movies are cheaper, more convenient, and have a greater range of visual effects than plays. Live theater provides a more intimate setting and the possibility for human interaction. Live theater also can change and adapt in response to audience reaction. However, both strive to entertain, to tell a good story, and to deal with basic human issues. For that reason, each medium will continue to find an audience.

6 Uses transitional phrases

7 Discusses how subjects are similar

8 Summarizes the comparison in the conclusion

Do It Yourself

Writing Prompt Explore the similarities and differences between two subjects that interest you by writing a comparison-and-contrast essay.

Purpose To explain, clarify, or make a point

Audience People interested in the subjects being compared

❶ Prewriting

Choose your subjects. Start making a list of things you might be interested in comparing. It will help if you think about why you are interested in comparing them. Do you have a choice to make? Do you want to show that one thing is better than another? Once you've chosen your subjects, follow the steps below.

- **Focus on features.** Think about the main idea of your essay. Focus on features—similarities and differences—that are important to this main idea.

- **Pick a pattern.** There are two basic patterns for organizing a compare-and-contrast essay: subject-by-subject and feature-by-feature. When you organize by subject, you discuss one subject thoroughly before you discuss the other. When you organize by feature, you compare and contrast each subject one characteristic at a time.

For more on these organizational patterns, see pp. 326–327.

❷ Drafting

Write an introduction. You can work on creating a lively introduction now or write it during the revision stage. Be sure to identify the subjects you are comparing in your introduction.

Stick to an organizational pattern. If the pattern you chose isn't working, change it—but use a pattern consistently.

Use transitions. You can help your reader keep track of your ideas by using transitional words and phrases. Words such as *both, similarly,* and *also* indicate similarities. Words such as *instead, in contrast,* and *however* indicate differences.

Write a conclusion. Write a paragraph that summarizes your comparison.

For information about getting feedback from your peers, see p. 412.

COMPARISON

➌ Revising

TARGET SKILL ▶ **Paragraphing and Transitions** Each paragraph in your essay should develop one main idea. A change in idea, place, speaker, action, or time signals the need for a new paragraph. Use transitions to connect the paragraphs and show relationships between the ideas. You should also use transitions to achieve coherence within paragraphs. For more help with revising, review the rubric on page 406.

> Settings can seem more authentic because they are filmed on
> location or on a realistic set. Moviemakers can *also* use special effects
> to create imaginary worlds. . . . ¶ *Unlike film,* A play production is limited to
> the stage on which it is being performed.

➍ Editing and Proofreading

TARGET SKILL ▶ **Subject-Verb Agreement** When you are polishing your work, look for verbs that do not agree with their subjects in number. When the subject and verb in a sentence are separated by one or more words, mentally screen those words out and make the subject and verb agree.

> The intimacy ~~shared by the audience and actors~~
> make*s* this entertainment vehicle ideal for expressing emotion.

For more on subject-verb agreement in person and number, see pp. 132–133.

➎ Sharing and Reflecting

Share your essay by e-mailing it to a group of friends and encouraging feedback.

For Your Working Portfolio What did you learn about the two subjects you compared and contrasted? What would you do differently the next time you analyze two subjects? Attach your answers to your finished work. Save your comparison-and-contrast essay in your 📁 **Working Portfolio.**

Real World Comparison-and-Contrast

When you look in the sports section of the paper, you may see two teams' records weighed against each other. In advertisements, one car's price is often compared to another. Newspaper articles may show the contrast between two political candidates. Comparisons and contrasts are everywhere:

- Sports articles
- Print advertisements
- Consumer magazines
- TV commercials
- Scientific articles
- Movie reviews

Consumer Magazine

Consumer Reports
March 1999

Mmmm Chocolate

To the connoisseur, chocolate can be as subtle, as varied, and as rewarding as fine wine or exotic coffee.

Milk chocolate, the favorite type in the U.S., is sweeter, with a mellower, less chocolaty flavor than dar[k] dark chocolate dominates. Whether swe[et] or extra-bittersweet, dark chocolate is c[   ] bitter; it's a sophisticated treat favored b[   ] intense chocolate hit. (The difference be[tween] bittersweet is determined by the amount [of] the substance produced when cacao bea[ns] and that makes chocolate taste like choc[olate.]

For the complete text of the article, see MODEL BANK, pp. 630-631.

SCIENCE LESSON

Classifying Organisms

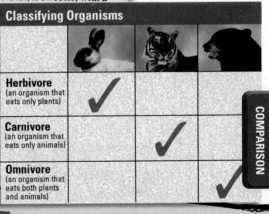

Herbivore (an organism that eats only plants)	✓		
Carnivore (an organism that eats only animals)		✓	
Omnivore (an organism that eats both plants and animals)			✓

COMPARISON

TEXTBOOK GRAPHIC

Greek City-States

ATHENS ONLY
economy: moved from farming to trading
government: democracy
values: beauty, individuality, creativity

BOTH
language: Greek
religion: same
slavery: in both
economy: began as farming communities

SPARTA ONLY
economy: remained farming community
government: military dictatorship
values: duty, strength, discipline

411

Student Help Desk

Comparison-and-Contrast Essay at a Glance

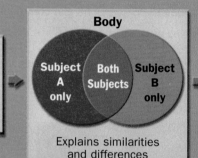

Introduction
- Identifies the **subjects** being compared
- Tells the **purpose** for the comparison

Body

Subject A only | Both Subjects | Subject B only

Explains similarities and differences

Conclusion
- Restates the **main idea** or draws a **conclusion**

Idea Bank

- **Compare your interests.** Compare and contrast subjects you're interested in, such as clothing styles, movies, food, music, or books.

- **Find subjects for debate.** Think of topics such as sports teams or school activities that you and your friends disagree about. Choose two specific subjects and prove your point by comparing them.

- **Browse periodicals.** Skim magazines and newspapers for ideas. Look for a current event to compare with a past one or a new form of technology to compare with an older one.

- **Contrast characters.** Compare characters from two different works of fiction. Or compare historical figures from two different periods.

Friendly Feedback Questions for Peer Readers

- What is my reason for comparing and contrasting these subjects?
- Did my opening make you want to read on?
- Which examples did you find most striking?
- Which examples did you think were dull?
- Did I use enough examples to prove my point?

Publishing Options

Print If you compared two products, submit your essay to a consumer's guide. If you compared two movies, submit them for publication in your school newspaper.

Oral Communications Read your essay aloud to your class. Then ask your audience whether they agree with your analysis. Engage the class in a debate on the topic.

Online Visit **mcdougallittell.com** for more publishing options.

Organizational Patterns   Putting It All Together

Subject-by-Subject	Feature-by-Feature
Introduction	**Introduction**
Subject A	Feature 1
Feature 1	Subject A
Feature 2	Subject B
Subject B	Feature 2
Feature 1	Subject A
Feature 2	Subject B
Conclusion	**Conclusion**

The Bottom Line

Checklist for Comparison-and-Contrast Essay

Have I . . .

____ identified the subjects being compared?

____ established a clear reason for the comparison?

____ included both similarities and differences?

____ supported my comparisons with specific examples and details?

____ followed a clear organizational pattern?

____ used transitional words and phrases effectively?

____ summarized my comparison in the conclusion?

Business Writing

Business writing refers to the kinds of writing you encounter in the workplace. In this chapter, you'll learn three common forms of business writing—a **procedural narrative,** a **summary,** and a **résumé.**

Learn What It Is: *Procedural Narrative*

On your first day at a new job, you may be given an employee manual that explains how certain tasks or procedures are performed at that workplace. That manual is an example of a **procedural narrative.** It explains, step by step, how to perform tasks or procedures. Like all business writing, a procedural narrative should be clear, informative, and to the point. Here are guidelines for writing one.

Basics in a Box

PROCEDURAL NARRATIVE AT A GLANCE

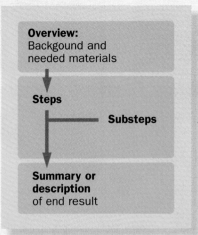

Overview:
Backgound and
needed materials

Steps

Substeps

Summary or description of end result

GUIDELINES

Standards for Writing

A successful procedural narrative should

- begin with a clear statement of the topic and your purpose
- provide a step-by-step explanation of how to carry out the procedure
- describe each step of the procedure clearly and in sequence
- state the time frame for each step, if appropriate
- if necessary, clearly identify who will perform each step

See How It's Done: *Procedural Narrative*

Office Transits

This section of your employees' manual outlines the procedures for opening the office as well as for entering and leaving the office during the workday.

❶ Begins with a clear statement of the topic and purpose

I. Opening the Office

If you are one of the persons likely to enter the office first in the morning, you will be assigned three keys: a bright blue key for the dead-bolt lock, a cardkey for the ID slot, and a small gold key for the control panel.

❷ Gives background information, such as necessary supplies

1. Slip your cardkey in the ID slot to gain authorization to open the building.

2. Use the bright blue key to unlock the dead-bolt lock. Turn the key to the right.

❸ Provides a detailed, step-by-step explanation

3. The alarm buzzer will sound as soon as you unlock the door. Upon entering, immediately turn off the alarm, following these steps:

   a. Go to the security panel on the wall to the left of the receptionist's desk.

   b. Unlock it with the small gold key.

   c. Flip the red switch to OFF.

❹ Presents another set of steps (substeps) in the correct sequence

IMPORTANT ALERT: The alarm must be switched off within 30 seconds. If not, it alerts our security company at a substantial cost to us.

❺ States the time frame for the step

II. Checking In and Out of the Office

All employees need to check in and out of the office on the Who's Here Board, which is located on the north wall of the reception area.

❻ Identifies who will perform the step

- **Entering the office** Each time you enter the office, place a **green** magnetic marker in the box beside your name on the Who's Here Board.

- **Leaving the office** Each time you leave the office, place a **red** magnetic marker in the box beside your name on the Who's Here Board.

BUSINESS

Choose a task or process that you know how to perform well and write a procedural narrative that explains how to do it.

Purpose To explain or teach a process

Audience Fellow workers, a person learning the task, friends

❶ Prewriting

Choose a procedure to explain. Pick something you know how to do well. For instance, you might describe a process that you have followed on a job. The work does not have to be for a company. For example, if you baby-sit or do odd jobs in the neighborhood, you can write out procedures for specific parts of your job.

- **Consider what your audience knows.** How much do your readers already know about the procedure you're explaining? Do you need to define basic terms and concepts?

- **Do a trial run of the procedure.** Pretend you are talking a person through the procedure. Go through the procedure once without writing anything down. Then go through it again, taking notes on each step.

❷ Drafting

Use the outline on page 414 to help you organize your content. Write an introduction that gives an overview of the process and that describes necessary materials. Then explain the process step-by-step, keeping these points in mind:

- **Use the active voice.** It often helps to use imperative sentences as well, in which each sentence starts with the verb. *Measure the frame . . . Plug the adapter into . . . Double click on the . . .*

- **Address problems.** Think of any difficulties your reader may have while doing the procedure. If necessary, include what should *not* be done as well as what should be done.

- **Keep it simple.** Stick to instructions only, not theory or philosophy.

- **Number your steps** Do this only if they must be performed in a particular order. If not, consider using a word processing program for bulleting each step or setting the steps apart with boldfaced heads.

When you finish your draft, ask someone to follow your directions, and to note where information is missing, confusing, or out of order.

Summary
Safety Recommendations: Report
by Safety First, Inc.
DATE: January 6, 2000
TO: Storeroom and Loading Dock Personnel

Last month, health and safety consultants from Safety
First conducted an intensive, 80-hour study of safety
conditions at our storeroom and loading dock. They
recently submitted an initial report of their findings and
recommendations. The key points of that report are
summarized here.

Accidents from Falling
Slips and falls account for 35% of the accidents involving
our moving and loading personnel. The majority of falls
occurred on rainy or snowy days when loading docks
were slippery and when employees tracked water into the
storeroom. Another large percentage of falls was caused
by obstructions in the aisles. These accidents occurred
most frequently to employees who were moving or lifting
boxes or whose vision was obstructed.

New Safety Measures
The study recommended that the following safety
measures be initiated immediately in order to prevent or
minimize accidents in the future.
- On days when there is precipitation (rain, snow,
  sleet), all employees must wear rubber boots on the
  loading dock. If employees lose, misplace, or forget
  their boots, they should ask Supplies for a temporary
  issue.
- On days when there is precipitation, managers
  should lay down extra floor mats at all doorways and
  in all the loading aisles. Employees should wear wet
  boots only when walking on these mats. Otherwise,
  they should remove wet footgear.
- All spills should be cleaned up at the time of
  occurrence. Employees can page I-Help for assistance.
- Pathways should be kept clear of obstructions at all
  times.

❶ Identifies the
title, writers, and
date of the original
10-page report

❷ Gives the
purpose and scope
of the original
document

❸ Briefly states
the main ideas of
the report

❹ Includes
recommendations
made in the full
report

❺ Bulleted points
are easy to scan

❻ Sticks to
essential
information

BUSINESS

Learn What It Is: *Résumé*

You might think of your résumé as a self-portrait. Usually, it will be the only "picture" that an employer has of you, so it should be as excellent as you can make it. In a résumé, you describe your skills, experience, and knowledge. A well-done résumé may open the door to a good job.

Basics in a Box

RÉSUMÉ AT A GLANCE

Personal Data

Job Objective _____

Skills _____

Education _____

Achievements _____

Activities _____
(optional) _____

References _____

GUIDELINES

Standards for Writing

A successful résumé should

- give a clear statement of your employment objective
- present details of relevant experience gained at school, at work, and in extra-curricular activities
- present your abilities in a positive light
- be well-organized, attractive, and free of errors

⑦ Tips for Writing a Résumé

Keep these points in mind as you prepare your résumé:

- **Gather important information.** It may include personal data (address, phone number), job objective, work experience, education, other experiences such as volunteer work, achievements and abilities, names and addresses of references.
- **Make your information specific.** Include numbers, dates, and names, such as "junior camp counselor for two summers" or "Chess Club, 7 years."
- **Decide what information to highlight or eliminate.** Emphasize the parts of your experience or education that are most important to the job you're applying for.

Benita Payo
768 Crescent Drive
Austin, Texas 78708
(512) 555-1212

❶ Gives name, address, and telephone number

Job Objective: Assistant camp counselor

❷ Clearly states job objective

Related Experience

Summer 1999   **Junior camp counselor**
- Mountain Sunshine Summer Camp
  Elmo, Texas
- Supervised nine- and ten-year-olds.
- Organized and coached outdoor sports:
  swimming, basketball, soccer, volleyball.
- Taught swim lessons.

Summers 94–98   **Experienced camper**
- Mountain Sunshine Summer Camp
  Elmo, Texas
- Attended camp for four weeks each
  summer. Voted Cabin Leader, 1997.
  Received Morale Booster Trophy, 1998.

❸ Gives details of work experience

1994–99   **Baby sitter**
- Cared for young boys two hours each
  night after school. Managed emergencies,
  played games and sports, gave baths,
  cooked, read books.

Education

1996–99
- Austin High School
- Grade average: B
- Course work includes Home Economics,
  Health, Physical Education (swimming,
  basketball, volleyball, soccer)

❹ Lists educational background

Achievements

1999   Earned life-saving certificate, American
Red Cross

1998–99   Co-captain of Junior Varsity Swim Team

❺ Mentions special skills and extra-curricular activities

References   Available on request

BUSINESS

Student Help Desk

Business Writing at a Glance

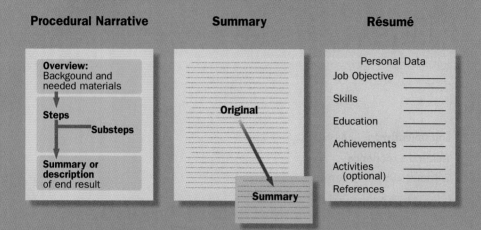

Procedural Narrative

Overview:
Backgound and
needed materials

Steps
Substeps

**Summary or
description**
of end result

Summary

Original

Summary

Résumé

Personal Data

Job Objective _____

Skills _____

Education _____

Achievements _____

Activities _____
(optional)

References _____

Writing Procedural Narratives One Step at a Time

- **Clearly identify each step of the process.** It helps
  to do a trial run of the procedure before you write a
  draft. Take notes of what's involved in each step.

- **Test your directions.** Before revising, ask a friend
  to try to follow your directions.

- **Troubleshoot**. Try to predict problems that a person may
  have in doing the procedure for the first time.

- **Use printing features for clarity**. Number or bullet the
  steps. Use headings. Boldface essential information.

CHAPTER 21

Writing Summaries Special Tips

- **Use the active voice.** That will automatically make your language more concise and direct.
- **Stick to the main points.** Think of your reader as the busy executive or coworker who wants to get the facts and move on.
- **Make sure that you include all essential information.** After reading your summary, readers should know all the important information without having to read the original.

Writing Résumés Putting Your Best Foot Forward

- **Make it attractive.** Use the printing features of boldface, indenting, and underlining to make your résumé look its best.
- **Put it in chronological order.** List your work and educational experience in order, starting with the present.
- **Make it concise.** Use language that is short and direct. Your entire résumé should fit on one page.
- **Highlight your best skills.** List all your accomplishments, experiences, and responsibilities that you think might interest your potential employer.

The Bottom Line

Checklist for Business Writing

Have I . . .

____ conveyed information clearly and concisely?

____ clearly identified my purpose or goal?

____ used printing features (boldface, underlining, numbering, bulleting) to make the information attractive and easy to scan?

____ used a writing voice that is direct and informative?

____ included all the essential or important details and eliminated unnecessary information?

____ checked to make sure my facts and details are accurate?

Persuasive Argument

Learn What It Is

"The best solution is . . ." "No one should . . ." Do lines like these sound familiar? Almost everywhere you look in the media—from newspapers to the Internet—you can find **persuasive arguments,** which ask you to think or act in a particular way. Writers and speakers use persuasion to present a wide range of topics. Here's how to write an effective persuasive argument for a topic you feel strongly about.

Basics in a Box

PERSUASIVE ARGUMENT AT A GLANCE

WHAT I BELIEVE

Opinion or belief — Introduction

WHY YOU SHOULD BELIEVE IT

| Supporting evidence | Supporting evidence | Supporting evidence | Body |

Summary of opinion
WHAT READERS SHOULD DO — Conclusion

RUBRIC

Standards for Writing

A successful persuasive argument should

- clearly state the issue and your position on it in the introduction
- be geared to the audience you're trying to convince
- support your position with evidence, such as facts, statistics, and examples
- answer possible objections to your position
- show clear reasoning
- conclude with a summary of your position or a call to action

CHAPTER 22

See How It's Done: *Persuasive Argument*

Student Model
Paige Blake
New Trier High School

RUBRIC
IN ACTION

Teenage Drivers Need More Education

I recently read an article in our weekly community newspaper about the large number of "fender-benders" in our area. As a sixteen-year-old driver in the busy suburbs, I too am concerned about this problem. I am extremely observant of the drivers around me, and in my experience, today's drivers, especially new ones, are careless. However, I believe two simple changes could reduce this problem.

First, the adults in our community could vote to keep the age requirement for a learner's permit at 15 but raise the legal age for receiving a driver's license to 18. Then the state could change the number of required driver's education courses from one to two. With these changes, the number of car-related accidents would be lowered considerably, making the roads a safer place.

When teenagers are first learning to drive, practice is a crucial factor. The more one practices driving, the better driver one becomes. According to the National Highway Traffic Safety Administration, in 1997, teenagers aged 16 to 19 had the highest percentage of crashes involving specific violations such as speeding, failing to stop, not focusing on driving, and following too closely. New drivers make these violations because they do not understand the consequences of such errors. Under the present system, students take one driver's education course and are then sent off to correct driving mistakes by themselves. Additionally, driver's education can be as minimal as a three-week course. Three weeks is not enough time for students to experience a range of mistakes and learn how to handle them.

Of course, some people may consider requiring two driver's education courses instead of one to be too expensive. However, consider the long-term savings

❶ Writer uses specific language—such as the word "our"—to show that her audience is her own community.

❷ This writer states the issue in the opening paragraph, then presents her position on it in the next paragraph.

Other Options:
• Open with an anecdote.
• Quote an expert.

❸ Supports her position with facts

❹ Addresses possible objections to her position

PERSUASION

that could result. Not only would a reduced accident rate lower our insurance costs, but, most important, better drivers may also save lives lost in automobile accidents.

My proposal includes a three-year permit for teens, with one instructional course in the first year and another in the second. This plan offers several benefits. With more supervised practice, students can make mistakes under adult guidance and then learn how to correct those mistakes. The second course would allow student drivers and an adult supervisor to monitor the student's progress. This would help break any bad habits that teens may have formed after the first course. The second course will also allow time for students to ask additional questions and receive more information than allowed in a single course. Plus, having more practice will allow students to anticipate specific problems that may arise while driving, a necessary skill for "driving defensively."

As a product of the current teaching system, I feel that after learning all the rules, I was left to make mistakes and fix them on my own. The easiest, most efficient way to achieve safer streets is to produce more careful drivers. If safer roads are what everyone wants, then we need three-year learning permits and two separate driver's education courses.

❺ Provides a detailed explanation of her proposed solution

❻ Shows clear reasoning

❼ This writer concludes with a summary of her position.
Another Option:
• Urge readers to take action.

Do It Yourself

Writing Prompt Write a persuasive argument for your stand on an issue.

Purpose To persuade others to agree with you and possibly to act

Audience Community members, people affected by the issue

❶ Prewriting

Find a worthwhile topic. Look for an issue that you care about and that others will care about too, whether or not they agree with you. Here are some possibilities to help you decide.

- **Read the news.** Try looking for issues in the news, particularly in your community or school newspaper.

- **Be an inquiring reporter.** You might interview people to find out what issues concern them.

- **Fill in the blank.** Brainstorm ways to complete this statement: Everybody complains about _____ .

After you have chosen your topic, the following suggestions will help you decide what you want to say and how you want to say it.

Develop a position. Think about how you feel about your topic and why. Try to clarify your thoughts enough that you can write a tentative thesis statement.

Zero in on your readers. Who is your audience? What do they already know? What do they need to know? How do they feel about the issue? What reasoning is most likely to get them to see things your way?

Rank your reasons. Order your reasons, labeling each from strongest to weakest. This will help you when you begin to build your case.

Bring in the evidence. What reference materials or experts will be good sources of facts and statistics that support your position? Where can you find some good quotations or anecdotes? What are some specific incidents that help prove your point?

For more help, see the Idea Bank, p. 432.

❷ Drafting

Building Your Case

Although you'll need to use careful logic to draft a convincing argument, the main purpose of your first draft is just to get your ideas on paper. As you develop your persuasive argument, you might want to experiment to find the most natural and effective way to present the body of your argument.

INTRODUCTION
Clearly state what the issue is and where you stand on it.

⬇

BODY
Support your position with facts, statistics, examples, and other evidence. Below are two possible methods for organizing your ideas.

Introduce your reasons and supporting evidence, from weakest to strongest, and then address all possible objections.	Immediately after introducing a reason and its supporting evidence, answer any objections to it that your readers may have.
1st Paragraph Reason and supporting evidence	**1st Paragraph** Reason and supporting evidence
2nd Paragraph Reason and supporting evidence	**2nd Paragraph** Answer to possible objections
3rd Paragraph Reason and supporting evidence	**3rd Paragraph** Reason and supporting evidence
4th Paragraph Answer to all possible objections	**4th Paragraph** Answer to possible objections
	5th Paragraph Reason and supporting evidence
	6th Paragraph Answer to possible objections

⬇

CONCLUSION
Present a strong closing argument in which you either summarize your position, call for a particular action on the part of your readers, or both.

Staying Logical

Remember that your essay will only be effective if you use sound reasoning as you write. Here are some common faulty or deceptive arguments that you should avoid.

Illogical Arguments	
Circular reasoning	Saying the same thing two different ways *CDs are popular because people often buy them.*
Over-generalization	Making a statement that is too broad to prove *Nobody likes school lunches.*
Either-or fallacy	Saying there are only two alternatives *Either we ban the Internet or children will be exposed to harmful ideas.*
Cause-and-effect fallacy	Assuming that because one event follows another, the first event caused the second *Because television newscasts report more crime, there is more crime.*
Bandwagon appeal	Trying to get people to follow the crowd *Don't be the only one without the Ziz.*
Name calling	Attacking the person instead of the idea *She doesn't deserve the office because she's an airhead.*

For more on logical fallacies and sound reasoning, see pp. 485–495.

Presenting Facts and Opinions to Elaborate

Your thesis in a persuasive argument presents your opinion on the issue. To convince your readers that your thinking is sound, you can elaborate on the ideas in the body of your draft with facts, statistics, and other evidence that supports your argument. Use the following chart to guide you as you choose details to use.

Stating Facts and Opinions		
Fact	A statement that can be proved	In 1997, teenagers aged 16 to 19 had the highest percentage of crashes involving specific violations.
Unsupported opinion	A statement that cannot be proved, although you might agree with it	Teens need more supervised driving practice.
Informed opinion	An opinion that includes facts to support it	The percentage of accidents involving teen drivers indicates that they need more supervised driving practice.

For information about getting feedback from your peers, see p. 433.

PERSUASION

➌ Revising

TARGET SKILL ▶Using Appropriate Language Your language should fit your audience. If you're appealing to teenagers, you might use informal language to relate to your audience. If you are appealing to adults, you may want to use a serious tone so that your audience will listen to your ideas. For more help with revising, review the rubric on page 424.

> *If the voters want to reduce the hazards of our streets, they*
> ~~If you guys want to get this thing fixed, just make~~
> *can call for*
> ~~these~~ two simple changes: raise the legal driving age to

➍ Editing and Proofreading

TARGET SKILL ▶Shifts in Verb Tense Check your work for consistent use of past, present, and future verb tenses. Mistakes in tense can confuse readers.

> According to the national highway traffic safety administration,
> in 1997, teenagers aged 16 to 19 ~~have~~ *had* the highest
> percentage of crashes involving specific violations.

For more on verb tenses, see pp. 110–116.

➎ Sharing and Reflecting

After you've completed your persuasive argument, **share** it with an audience. Create a "soapbox" podium and give a speech!

For Your Working Portfolio As you wrote your argument, did you find yourself changing your mind on any points, or did you become even more sure that your position is right? Later, after you shared your work, did any reactions from your audience surprise you or make you rethink your position? Attach your answers to your finished work, and save the essay in your 🗀 **Working Portfolio.**

Real World Persuasive Essay

Persuasive essays are a common form of expression in the real world. Newsgroups on the Internet allow people to post their ideas and opinions on important issues. Almost any advertisement is trying to persuade you to use a certain product or service. You've probably seen persuasive essays in all of these places:

- Letters to the editor
- Magazine articles and advertisements
- Junk mail advertisements
- Internet newsgroups
- Newspaper editorials
- Public service posters

MAGAZINE ADVERTISEMENT

Live the life you want . . .
Drive the car you love . . .

POLITICAL CAMPAIGN

Terri for School Board!

Newspaper Opinion Essay

How do we decide who gets another chance at life?

Don't tie gift of life to recipient's location

By G. Bruce Weir   *USA Today*

Eleven years ago, I was told I needed a heart transplant or I would be dead in six months.

I was lucky: I made it. I got my transplant in four weeks; today, it would be closer to three months.

In 1998, there were 17,000 people waiting; today, there are more than 65,000. Every day, 90 more names get added to the national organ transplant list. Every day, 10 people on that list die because their organs did not come in time. **For the complete text of the essay, see MODEL BANK, pp. 632–633.**

WEB BANNERS

If you haven't told your family you're a donor, you're not.

Ad SHARE YOUR LIFE. SHARE YOUR DECISION. Organ & Tissue DONATION

Expect The Best From A Girl. That's What You'll Get. WOMEN'S COLLEGE COALITION

Ad **BUY RECYCLED.**

PERSUASION

Student Help Desk

Persuasive Argument at a Glance

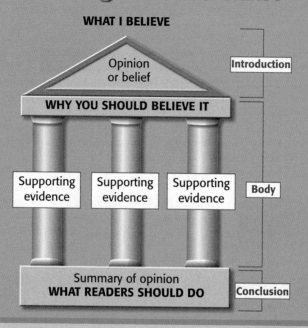

WHAT I BELIEVE

Opinion or belief — Introduction

WHY YOU SHOULD BELIEVE IT

Supporting evidence | Supporting evidence | Supporting evidence — Body

Summary of opinion
WHAT READERS SHOULD DO — Conclusion

Idea Bank

See if one of these seems worth writing about:

- one of the school's "you can't" policies
- a problem featured in the news
- students holding jobs

Complete one of these statements:

Why can't we fix _____?

I'd really like to change _____.

Parents should _____.

Reading someone else's persuasive argument may help you generate your own ideas. Read and analyze a persuasive argument such as "Letter from Birmingham Jail" by Martin Luther King, Jr. (*Language of Literature*, Grade 11).

Friendly Feedback · Questions for Your Peer Reader

- Where do you think I stand on this issue?
- Which of my points do you find most convincing? least convincing?
- What more do you need to know to understand the issue?

Publishing Options · Go Public

Print Submit your writing to your local newspaper as a "letter to the editor."

Oral Communications Use your persuasive argument to prepare a debate with classmates or to give a speech at a public forum.

Online Visit **mcdougallittell.com** for more publishing options.

Consider the Source · Who Says?

If you got it from:
- the Internet, make sure the source is reliable.
- an almanac or encyclopedia, make sure the source is up-to-date.
- a person who says "all my friends are. . . ," try to find out if the friends make up a representative sample.

The Bottom Line

Checklist for Persuasive Argument

Have I . . .

____ made my position clear?

____ geared my argument to my audience?

____ supported my position with evidence?

____ answered possible objections to my position?

____ shown clear reasoning?

____ concluded with a summary of my stand or a call for action?

Short Story

Learn What It Is

Through the wonderful flexibility of creative writing, you can follow your imagination wherever it leads. In this chapter, you'll focus on the short story. However, you will also explore how you can express your ideas in a poem or dramatic scene.

A **short story** is a work of fiction that is usually short enough to be read in one sitting. The short story combines the key elements of plot, character, and setting to produce one total effect.

Basics in a Box

SHORT STORY AT A GLANCE

Introduction	Body	Conclusion
Sets the stage by • introducing characters • describing setting	**Develops the plot by** • introducing the conflict • telling a sequence of events • developing main characters • building toward a climax	**Finishes the story by** • resolving the conflict or • telling the last event

RUBRIC

Standards for Writing

A successful short story should

- use the elements of character, setting, and plot to create a convincing world.
- use techniques such as vivid sensory language, concrete details, and dialogue to create believable characters and setting.
- develop and resolve a central conflict.
- present a clear sequence of events.
- maintain a consistent point of view.

CHAPTER 23

See How It's Done: *Short Story*

RUBRIC
IN ACTION

Chess

The man struggled up the marbleized steps to the row of hard benches. He set his leather briefcase down on one of the worn chess tables. Sitting down, he removed his dark brown hat to reveal a full head of gray hair. Looking out at the lake in front of him, he removed a large thermos of black coffee and poured himself a cup.

❶ Opens story with clear description

A homeless man sat up and pointed to one of the many boards. "Game of chess?" he asked. His blue eyes glowed like the early-morning lake.

The first man looked over, his gray eyes responding with a crinkled sadness.

❷ Uses dialogue to establish the story's conflict (the characters' initial unfamiliarity)

"Oh, uh, sure, I guess. Want some coffee?"

The homeless man shook his head, holding up a paper cup.

"Hot chocolate," he said.

"Oh, okay," said the first man. "I'm William. . . . I uh, don't have any pieces."

❸ Advances the plot with specific description of setting up for the game

"That's okay," said the other, taking out a plastic bag from within his remarkably unfaded jungle-green shirt. "I'm Billy, nice to meet you."

"Same to you," said William, standing up to remove his black suit jacket. The early-morning lake air was chilly, but he was somehow warmed by the homeless man's presence.

Billy emptied the pieces onto the nearest chess board. To William's surprise, they were beautifully hand-carved, polished wood. One side was a deep, rich baker's fudge color and the other was a creamy seashell tan.

❹ Includes vivid sensory imagery

"Your choice," said Billy.

William instantly reached for the brown pieces, almost knocking them from the table.

"Same color as my hat," he said, trying to hide his clumsiness.

SHORT STORY

Billy smiled slightly and then calmly reached to move his pawn. His plump red fingers seemed to know the pieces. Even before Billy had finished retreating from the table, William had already made his move.

They continued in this way for a while. Billy waited long, stretched-out moments before making his slow, deliberate moves, which ended in the soft click of his pieces on the table. William quickly countered with a fidgety move that rattled his piece against the others. Their game was like a heartbeat. Click, rattle. . . . Click, rattle. . . . Click, rattle.

> ❺ Uses description to contrast the characters' personalities

William coughed and readjusted himself. He was angered by the waiting. His eyebrows came together in a squint that he threw across the table. His lips pressed together in a tight frown while he cracked the knuckles on his long, bony fingers.

Billy played silently. When one of his pieces was taken, he showed no disappointment; when he captured a piece, he showed no joy.

And then suddenly they both noticed something.

"Oh . . ." said William.

"Mmm . . ." said Billy.

The game was a stalemate. William shook his head while Billy slowly nodded.

After an endless, still moment, William stood up to put on his jacket. Billy began to place the pieces back inside the plastic bag.

> ❻ Resolves the conflict with a surprise ending
>
> **Another Option:** Earlier in the story, provide additional clues about William's complex behavior.

As he walked away, William almost turned to say good-bye, but there was no need to. They did this every day.

Do It Yourself

Writing Prompt   Write a short story about an incident or a person.

Purpose To entertain

Audience Friends, classmates, a writing club or contest

❶ Prewriting

Find an idea. Do you enjoy stories that are charged with gripping action? Perhaps you prefer subtle character studies or tales that transport you to another place or time. Freewriting about your reading choices can spark ideas for your own short story.

Identify your audience. Deciding on your audience and purpose can help you choose the characters and the mood of the story. For example, if your intended readers are your age, you might appeal to them by presenting a young main character who has interests and struggles similar to theirs.

Plan your plot. Most short stories center around some sort of conflict or struggle. Be sure to think through a beginning, events that occur as the conflict unfolds, and a resolution of the conflict.

To develop more story possibilities, see the Idea Bank, p. 442.

❷ Drafting

These strategies can help you to elaborate on your story ideas.

Show, don't tell.

Don't tell your readers everything directly. Description, dialogue, and action are tried-and-true storytelling tools. Use them like brush strokes to reveal characters' thoughts and personalities and to move the plot along.

Stick to a point of view.

Whether you choose a first-person narrator or a third-person narrator, keep your readers on track by maintaining a consistent point of view.

Be convincing.

Your story must be believable. Ask yourself questions like these:
• Is this really the way the character would respond to this event?
• In the situation I have set up, what is most likely to happen as a result?
• Would this ending cause the members of my audience to shake or nod their heads?

SHORT STORY

➌ Revising

TARGET SKILL ▶Using Dialogue Allow your characters to speak for themselves. Use dialogue to show their thoughts and plans. Dialogue also is used to break up long paragraphs and make the story easier to read. For more help with revising, review the rubric on page 434.

> The first man looked over, his gray eyes responding with a
> ¶*"Oh, uh, sure, I guess. Want some coffee?"*
> crinkled sadness. ~~He agreed to the game and asked whether~~
> ~~the other man would like some coffee~~¶The homeless man
> ¶*"Hot chocolate," he said.*
> shook his head, holding up a paper cup, ~~and explained that~~
> ~~he already had hot chocolate.~~

➍ Editing and Proofreading

TARGET SKILL ▶Punctuating Dialogue It is important to punctuate dialogue correctly so that the reader will be able to tell who is talking. Double quotation marks frame the exact words of the speaker. A comma or a period is usually used between the speaker's words and the end quotation mark.

> "Same color as my hat," he said, "trying to hide his clumsiness."

For more on punctuating dialogue, see pp. 252–253.

➎ Sharing and Reflecting

Think of ways to **share** your short story with others. You might read it aloud to a small group of friends or get others to act it out as a skit. Develop your own standards or criteria for analyzing or evaluating the performance.

For Your Working Portfolio Think about what you've discovered. Did you gain any unexpected insights into a character? What did you learn from the responses of your audience? Jot down some thoughts, attach the answers to your finished short story, and place this material in your ◻ **Working Portfolio.**

Learn What They Are: *Poem and Dramatic Scene*

Whatever form of creative writing you choose, you're sure to come to know and use the power of well-chosen words. If you create a poem, you will be able to experiment with the sounds of language, to capture a moment in nature, or to convey a feeling or a certain message. If you enjoy the intensity of a live performance, you might create a dramatic scene. Then you will see how elements like dialogue and stage directions can put an audience in direct contact with the characters and action.

Basics in a Box

CREATIVE WRITING AT A GLANCE

Poem

A successful poem should

- focus on a single experience, idea, or feeling.
- use precise, sensory words in a fresh, interesting way.
- incorporate figurative language such as similes and metaphors.
- include sound devices as appropriate.

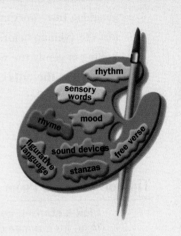

Dramatic Scene

A successful dramatic scene should

- introduce the setting and characters in the opening stage directions.
- use the setting and characters to create a convincing world.
- develop a clear and interesting situation or conflict.
- use actions as well as dialogue to advance the story and present the characters.
- include stage directions as necessary.

SHORT STORY

See How They're Done

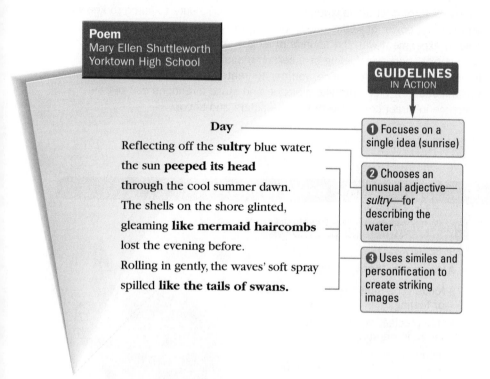

Poem
Mary Ellen Shuttleworth
Yorktown High School

GUIDELINES
IN ACTION

Day

Reflecting off the **sultry** blue water,

the sun **peeped its head**

through the cool summer dawn.

The shells on the shore glinted,

gleaming **like mermaid haircombs**

lost the evening before.

Rolling in gently, the waves' soft spray

spilled **like the tails of swans.**

❶ Focuses on a single idea (sunrise)

❷ Chooses an unusual adjective—*sultry*—for describing the water

❸ Uses similes and personification to create striking images

Tips for Writing a Poem

Pick a starting point. Begin with an image that lingers in your mind from a memorable experience. Try to associate sensory words with that experience.

Decide on the speaker and the voice. Your choice might depend on the mood or tone you wish to convey. Keep in mind that a first-person speaker might be appropriate for a personal, lyric poem, while a third-person speaker might fit a narrative poem.

Decide on the mood. Are you going to write a humorous poem, or are you planning a serious one? How does the topic make you feel? What do you want your audience to feel?

Experiment with sound devices. Imagine, for example, that you're creating a poem about a walk on an ocean shore. You might use sound devices such as onomatopoeia and rhythm to suggest the sound of waves.

Read as you go. Reading your poem aloud can help you to experience it as a listener would. Rereading can help you as you experiment with the poem's sound or as you refine elements such as phrasing.

GUIDELINES
IN ACTION

After the Storm

Characters: **Mariana,** *high school teacher;* **Joy,**
Regina, Kris, *high school students*

Setting: *outdoors in a poor village in a Central*
American country, following a severe hurricane; the
high school students and teacher have come to the
village to help rebuild; there is debris all around, but
a small house is being reconstructed

Mariana. Gang! We need to make a trip to get more
  two-by-fours for this room. Joy, you did bring your
  driver's license, didn't you?

Joy *(somewhat petulantly).* Of course. Do you need
  to see it? I have my passport, too. Here, want to see?

Regina *(laughing nervously, as though she knows*
  Joy can be difficult). No need to get snippy, Joy.
  We can't afford that attitude at this point!

Kris. Come on. Let's get to it. I'll drive. We really
  need to get the roof started today before sundown.

❶ Introduces
setting and
characters

❷ Reveals conflict
between
characters through
dialogue

❸ Stage directions
show actors the
attitudes they
should take.

Tips for Writing a Dramatic Scene

Take advantage of the properties of drama. For a short dramatic
scene, pick a subject that will lend itself to action. Consider how
the scene's physical production—the lighting, costumes, and
props—can enhance your audience's interest.

Experiment with types of speeches. A **monologue** is a long
speech spoken by a single character. A **soliloquy** is a speech that
reveals a character's private thoughts. An **aside** is a short
comment a character delivers directly to the audience. These
devices spice up basic dialogue and can reveal characters' traits
or motivations.

Make the best use of staging. As you develop your scene, draw
stage diagrams to help you visualize the characters' interactions.

SHORT STORY

Student Help Desk

Short Story at a Glance

Introduction

Sets the stage by
- introducing characters
- describing setting

Body

Develops the plot by
- introducing the conflict
- telling a sequence of events
- developing main characters
- building toward a climax

Conclusion

Finishes the story by
- resolving the conflict

  or
- telling the last event

Idea Bank   Tips for Tale Telling

- **Draw from your life.** Your story ideas may come most readily from memorable events in your life. An idea can also come from a current event or an issue that has captured your attention or stirred your emotions.

- **Focus on a theme.** What theme or lesson about life do you want to communicate? Think about how your characters' actions and the story's events can be manipulated to convey an idea that is important to you.

- **Ask yourself "What if?" questions.** Find your plot by teasing out the possibilities you can find in familiar situations.

- **Read literature.** Novelist Ernest Hemingway was also a celebrated writer of short stories. Pay attention to his authentic-sounding dialogue in "The End of Something" (*Language of Literature*, Grade 11). Note how he uses dialogue economically to reveal the characters' attitudes.

Friendly Feedback   Questions for Your Peer Reader

- What do you think my main objective was in writing this piece?
- How could I make the conflict and resolution more convincing?
- What is your favorite part of the story?
- Where could I have made a description more vivid?

Publishing Options

Print As a class, publish a yearly or twice-yearly collection of short stories. Use a software program to enhance formatting and graphics.

Oral Communication Since many short stories read like ready-made scripts, it may be easy to adapt your story into one for a Readers Theater presentation.

Online Check out **mcdougallittell.com** for more publishing options.

The Five-Minute Sprint

Exercise your writing muscles by writing five minutes every day. It doesn't matter what you write—just write. Nonsense rhymes, a ridiculous grocery list, or a description of the person you just passed in the hall will keep your writing muscles flexed.

The Bottom Line

Checklist for Short Story
Have I . . .

____ used character, setting, and plot to create a convincing world?

____ included sensory language and concrete details?

____ presented dialogue where it is most helpful?

____ developed and resolved a conflict?

____ presented a clear sequence of events?

____ kept to one point of view?

Research Report

Learn What It Is

In this exciting information age, new data becomes available every minute. One way to keep up to date with subjects that interest you is to do a **research report.** While researching and writing about your topic, you have an opportunity to learn new ideas, to present them in your own way, and to share them with others.

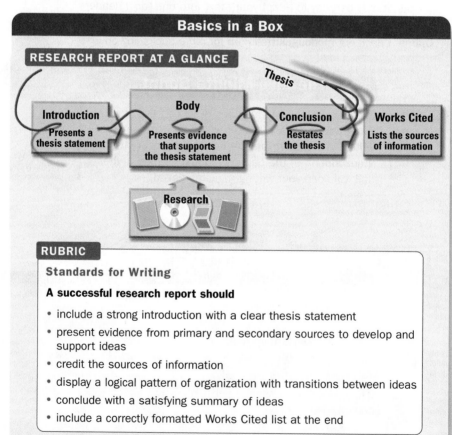

Basics in a Box

RESEARCH REPORT AT A GLANCE

Thesis

Introduction	Body	Conclusion	Works Cited
Presents a thesis statement	Presents evidence that supports the thesis statement	Restates the thesis	Lists the sources of information

Research

RUBRIC

Standards for Writing

A successful research report should

- include a strong introduction with a clear thesis statement
- present evidence from primary and secondary sources to develop and support ideas
- credit the sources of information
- display a logical pattern of organization with transitions between ideas
- conclude with a satisfying summary of ideas
- include a correctly formatted Works Cited list at the end

See How It's Done: *Research Report*

Dave Donaldson

Ms. Carter-Jones

English III

14 May 2000

The Real American Cowboy

What American doesn't remember playing cowboys and Indians or even wanting to become a cowboy when he or she was a child? During an interview, even my elderly neighbor mentioned spending Saturday afternoons watching Westerns at the movies and "shooting 'em up" with toy cap pistols (Edwards).

Our cowboy heroes were good-looking, exciting, larger-than-life men who rode a horse, carried a gun, and always got the girl. There are enormous contrasts between this legendary cowboy and the real cowboy, however.

Despite all the common stereotypes, the first cowboy wasn't even an American. According to the Encyclopaedia Britannica, the original cowboy was the *vaquero*, which is the Spanish word for "cowboy." The real cowboy was a tender of cattle. He had his "roots in antiquity" since herders of animals have existed since biblical times (Frantz 248), and even today "such people exist all over the world, from those who tend yaks in Central Asia to the *gardians* of the Camargue or the *gauchos* of Argentina" (Morgan 268).

The heyday of the American cowboy did not begin until after the Civil War and lasted for only about 25 years. By the late 19th century, a combination of factors—including the westward expansion of the railroads, the invention of barbed wire, and disastrously low cattle prices—led to the end of the free-roaming cowboy (Frantz 249).

Far from a being the romantic hero that legend has turned him into, the real cowboy was just that—a boy who

---

RUBRIC
IN ACTION

❶ This writer opens with an engaging question.
Other options:
• Use a quotation.
• Cite a startling fact or statistic.

❷ Includes a clear and detailed thesis statement

❸ Effectively uses and correctly cites quotations from secondary sources

❹ Presents information in chronological order

REPORT

worked with cows. He was young—about 24 years old on the average. He worked long, hard hours on the prairies for little pay. Modern cowboys have just as hard a time. In fact, cowboys today work so hard and are paid so little that few people want to do it any longer. The Jobs Almanac ranked the occupation 246th in terms of desirability out of 250 jobs.

❺ Cites a primary source

Not only were cowboys hard-working and underpaid, but they weren't even the romantic gunslingers of legend. Cowboy gunfighters did exist, but "they were the exception" (Rosa 11). In fact, cowboys earned so little money that they could hardly afford cartridges.

❻ Uses appropriate transitions between ideas

Works Cited

"Cowboy." <u>Encyclopaedia Britannica Online</u>.Vers. 00.1
　　Encyclopaedia Britannica. 31 Mar. 2000
　　<http://www.eb.com:180/bol/topic?eu=27108>.

Edwards, Martin. Personal interview. 14 July 1999.

Frantz, Joe B. "Cowboys." <u>Dictionary of American</u>
　　<u>History</u>. Vol 2. New York: Scribner's, 1976.

<u>Jobs Almanac</u>. Holbrook: Adams, 1999.

Morgan, Ted. <u>A Shovel of Stars: The Making of the</u>
　　<u>American West, 1800 to the Present</u>. New York:
　　Simon, 1995.

Morris, Michele. <u>The Cowboy Life</u>. New York: Fireside,
　　1993.

Rosa, Joseph G. <u>The Taming of the West: Age of the</u>
　　<u>Gunfighter</u>. New York: Smithmark, 1993.

Works Cited List
- Identifies all sources of information credited in the report
- Presents entries in alphabetical order
- Gives complete publication information
- Contains correct punctuation in entries
- Is double-spaced throughout
- Follows an accepted style, such as the Modern Language Association (MLA style)

CHAPTER 24

Do It Yourself

Writing Prompt   Write a research report on a topic that interests you.

Purpose To learn and share information about your topic

Audience Your classmates, teacher, or other people interested in the topic

❶ Developing a Research Plan

The basis of a good research report, of course, is research. Be sure to plan ahead and allow yourself enough time to investigate a variety of sources.

Defining Information Needs

The best research reports develop out of a writer's personal interest in a topic. Even if you are assigned a topic, look for a perspective on it that makes it truly your own. Dave Donaldson's assigned topic, for example, was the American West. He had always loved Westerns and even convinced his parents to send him to a dude ranch one summer. Doing a research report was a good way for him to explore this personal interest in depth.

Dave first did some preliminary reading to get a broad background on cowboys. He found a great deal of information about real cowboys and about legendary cowboys portrayed in the movies and on television.

For more ideas on finding a research topic, see p. 458.

Developing Researchable Questions

As he read, Dave soon discovered that the life of the real cowboy was very different from the one he had imagined. He then made a list of questions to help him look for specific information.

- Who were the first cowboys, and where did they come from?
- How did their lives differ from those of cowboys in movie Westerns?
- Are there still cowboys today?
- What personal characteristics do good cowboys need?
- Do cowboys exist only in the United States?
- What forces led to the cowboy's heyday and then to his decline in the United States?

REPORT

The more specific your questions are, the better your research and your report will be. Evaluate your questions by asking

- Is the question interesting? relevant to my topic?
- Will answering the question give me insight into my topic?
- Can I find a source that will answer the question?

❷ Using and Documenting Sources

Finding and Prioritizing Sources

There are two basic kinds of information sources you can use. **Primary sources** give firsthand information. **Secondary sources** provide interpretations, explanations, and comments on material from primary and other secondary sources.

Research Resources	Characteristic	Examples
Primary source	Provides direct, firsthand knowledge	Letters, journals, diaries, original manuscripts, questionnaires, interviews
Secondary source	Provides information gathered from primary and other secondary sources	Encyclopedias, textbooks, newspapers, magazines, biographies and other nonfiction books

Evaluating Sources

Not all sources are equally helpful for your needs. Ask yourself these questions to evaluate each source you find.

- **Is the source up to date?** Particularly in rapidly developing fields like computer technology, recent information is best.
- **Is the source reliable?** The author should be from a reputable university, business, or other institution. He or she should be a recognized authority in the field.
- **What are the author's viewpoints and biases?** Try to discover if the author has a political, an ethnic, a gender, or other type of bias. Ask how this bias might affect his or her objectivity.

Using a wide variety of sources will help to make your report more interesting. Although it's important to capture your readers' interest, make sure that the facts you present are correct.

For more help, see Using Information Resources, pp. 464–473.

Making Source Cards

Once you have located a variety of sources, decide which ones you might use in your report, and record all the relevant information about each on an index card. (Remember to include the call number of a library book.) You will need this information when you make your Works Cited list. Number each source card so that you can refer to it when you take notes and add documentation to your report.

Here's How Making Source Cards

Follow these guidelines when you make source cards.

- **Book** Write the author's or the editor's complete name, the title, the location and name of the publisher, and the copyright date.
- **Magazine and Newspaper** Write the author's complete name (unless the article is unsigned), the title of the article, the name and the date of the publication, and the page number(s) of the article. For a newspaper article, also include the city and edition number (if available).
- **Encyclopedia** Write the author's complete name (unless the article is unsigned), the title of the article, and the name and copyright date of the encyclopedia.
- **Online Source** Write the author's or the editor's complete name (if available), the title of the document, publication information for any print version of it, the date of the document's electronic publication (if available) or of the latest update, the name of the institution or organization responsible for the site, the date when you accessed the site, and the document's electronic address (in angle brackets).

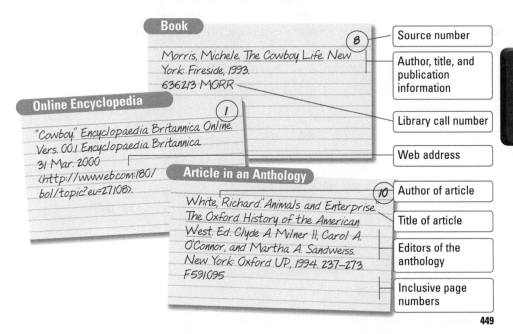

Book

Morris, Michele. *The Cowboy Life.* New York: Fireside, 1993.
636213 MORR

8 — Source number

Author, title, and publication information

Library call number

Online Encyclopedia

"Cowboy." *Encyclopaedia Britannica Online.* Vers. 00.1 Encyclopaedia Britannica. 31 Mar. 2000
<http://wwwebcom:180/bol/topic?eu=27108>.

1

Web address

Article in an Anthology

White, Richard. "Animals and Enterprise." *The Oxford History of the American West.* Ed. Clyde A. Milner II, Carol A. O'Connor, and Martha A. Sandweiss. New York: Oxford UP, 1994. 237–273.
F591.095

10 — Author of article

Title of article

Editors of the anthology

Inclusive page numbers

REPORT

❸ Taking Notes

As you read your sources, note information that answers your research questions, as well as other interesting facts. Follow these guidelines as you take notes.

> **Here's How** Taking Notes
>
> - **Use a separate index card** for each idea or bit of information.
> - **Write a heading** on each card indicating the subject of the note.
> - **Write the number of the corresponding source card** on each note card.
> - **Put direct quotations in quotation marks.**
> - **Record the number of the page** in the source where you found the material.

Paraphrasing

Paraphrasing is restating someone else's ideas in your own words. Most of the note taking you do will involve paraphrasing. Be sure to enclose in quotation marks any of the author's exact words that you include in your paraphrase.

> **PROFESSIONAL MODEL**
>
> The editor's graphic portrait of the typical gunfighter refutes the loud-mouthed, troublemaking "shoot at anything that moves" Texas cowboy of the 1860s and early 1870s. Nevertheless, there were cowboy-gunfighters but they were the exception. For most of the men who lived and died by the gun were indeed a breed apart.
>
> —Joseph G. Rosa, *The Taming of the West: Age of the Gunfighter*

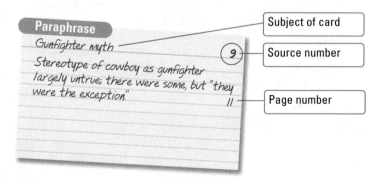

Paraphrase

Gunfighter myth ———————————— ⑨

Stereotype of cowboy as gunfighter largely untrue; there were some, but "they were the exception." //

Subject of card

Source number

Page number

Quoting

Sometimes an author explains an idea so well that you'll want to quote the original in your report. Be sure to copy the words exactly as the author wrote them and to enclose them in quotation marks. Include quotations only for

- extremely important ideas that might be misstated in a paraphrase
- explanations that are particularly concise and easy to understand
- statements presented in unusually lively or original language

Avoiding Plagiarism

Plagiarism is presenting someone else's work as your own. It is dishonest and must be avoided. Borrowing, buying, or stealing someone else's work obviously constitutes plagiarism. You are also guilty of plagiarism when you use either an author's ideas or his or her exact words without enclosing them in quotation marks and giving credit to the author.

> **PROFESSIONAL MODEL**
>
> But this "ordinary bow-legged human," whose actual span of activity on the trail drives was a fleeting twenty years, has been buried under a heavy tonnage of pulp and celluloid.
>
> —Ted Morgan, *A Shovel of Stars*

STUDENT MODEL

PLAGIARIZED

The ordinary bow-legged cowboy, who was active only a fleeting 20 years, has been buried under heavy tons of pulp fiction and movies.

> Some words were changed, but no quotation marks were inserted and no credit was given to the author.

PROPERLY CITED

As Ted Morgan notes in *A Shovel of Stars*, the real American cowboy was just "an ordinary bow-legged human" who rode the trails for only two decades (268). You would never know that from the heroes created by popular fiction and the movies, though.

> The author was credited.

> The author's lively words were included in quotation marks.

> A page citation was included.

REPORT

❹ Crafting a Good Thesis Statement

After you have collected information from a variety of sources, you will have to begin to organize it. A good way to start is to create a **thesis statement,** or a statement of the main idea you want to present in your report. You should be able to support your thesis statement with various kinds of evidence from your research sources. Here are some examples of thesis statements for research reports.

- The writer Zora Neale Hurston was a complex woman with many interests and skills.
- Computer technology has had negative effects on young people.

This checklist will help you create a good thesis statement for your research report.

Thesis Statement Checklist

☑ Is my thesis sufficiently limited and sharply focused?

☑ Have I stated it concisely in a sentence that my readers will understand?

☑ Do I have the time and resources to fully develop my thesis?

☑ Will writing about my thesis fulfill the assignment?

For more on thesis statements, see pp. 320, 350.

❺ Organizing and Outlining

Once you have done your research and written a good thesis statement, you must decide how you want to organize your report and then write a preliminary outline.

Choosing an Organizational Pattern

A good first step in organizing your information is to arrange your index cards according to their key ideas. Try several arrangements, such as chronological order and comparison-contrast order, to determine which works best. Also remember that you can use different organizational patterns in different parts of your paper. Then create an outline using your key ideas as the main entries.

Dave Donaldson decided to begin his report on cowboys with a question to capture his readers' attention and some information he gathered from a personal interview. He then presented information about the origins of the cowboy in chronological order and compared and contrasted the mythical cowboy with the real historical person. Here is the beginning of the outline he used.

The Real American Cowboy

Thesis Statement: There are enormous contrasts between the legendary cowboy and the real cowboy.

    I. Introduction

    II. Origins

    III. Reality versus Myth

        A. Unromantic daily life

        B. Extremely low pay

        C. Not a gunslinger

Once you have an outline, you can group your index cards according to the entries in it. Remember that an outline is intended to be a helpful guide. If you find it is not working well, you can always make changes as you continue to draft your report.

Although making an outline can be time-consuming, doing this early on will save you time during the later stages of your writing.

❻ Drafting

Armed with your notecards, your thesis statement, and your outline, you can begin writing. It doesn't matter which part of the report you write first—just so you get started. You'll probably want to begin with a section you feel comfortable with, whether it's in the beginning, the middle, or the end of the report. Once you have something down on paper, you'll find it easier to write the more challenging or complicated sections.

As you write, remember that your goal is to develop your thesis statement. Look back at that statement frequently to make sure you haven't gotten off track. Also be sure that the information from your sources truly supports the ideas you are presenting.

Integrating Your Notes into Your Report

In preparing to write his report, Dave Donaldson had taken many notes about the cowboy's daily life. As he drafted that section of his paper, he had to decide which information to use and how to organize it effectively. He knew that he definitely wanted to include vivid descriptions and facts such as these.

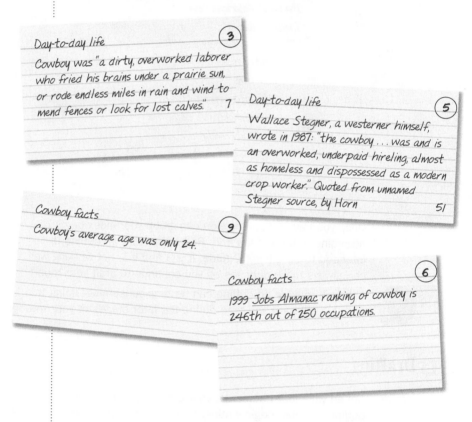

Day-to-day life   3
Cowboy was "a dirty, overworked laborer
who fried his brains under a prairie sun,
or rode endless miles in rain and wind to
mend fences or look for lost calves."   7

Day-to-day life   5
Wallace Stegner, a westerner himself,
wrote in 1987: "the cowboy . . . was and is
an overworked, underpaid hireling, almost
as homeless and dispossessed as a modern
crop worker." Quoted from unnamed
Stegner source, by Horn   51

Cowboy facts   9
Cowboy's average age was only 24.

Cowboy facts   6
1999 Jobs Almanac ranking of cowboy is
246th out of 250 occupations.

Note how Dave integrated this information from four separate sources into a single paragraph in his report.

Far from a being the romantic hero that legend has turned him into, the real cowboy was just that—a boy who worked with cows. He was young—about 24 years old on the average. He worked long, hard hours on the prairies for little pay. Modern cowboys have just as hard a time. In fact, cowboys today work so hard and are paid so little that the 1999 Jobs Almanac ranked the occupation 246th in desirability out of 250 jobs.

Sharing Your Own Ideas and Interpretations

Writing a research report involves more than just collecting and restating what other people have said. It is a great opportunity for you to think about the information, make inferences, analyze and interpret the evidence, and draw your own conclusions. Make sure, however, that your conclusions make sense and are well supported by your research.

In writing his research report, for example, Dave came up with his own interpretation of two conflicting ideas about cowboys. One idea was the myth of the cowboy that he had grown up with—the one he had seen in the movies, heard in popular songs, and read in books. The other evolved as he learned more details about a real cowboy's life that he collected in his research. He accounted for this contradictory information in his thesis statement. His report provided the details to support that statement.

❼ Documenting Information

The most common method of crediting sources in a research report is parenthetical documentation. In this method of documentation, a detailed record of sources appears at the end of the report, in a Works Cited list. Brief references in parentheses within the body of the report allow readers to locate the complete information about the sources in that list. You must be sure to credit each quotation, paraphrase, or summary that you include in your report.

You do not have to credit information that is common knowledge or your own original ideas.

Here's How **Using Parenthetical Documentation**

- **Work by One Author** Give the author's last name and the page number in parentheses: **Not until after the Civil War did the cowboy become prominent (Morgan 268).** If you mention the author's name in the sentence, give only the page number in parentheses: **As Morgan notes, the cowboy didn't become prominent until after the Civil War (268).**

- **Work by More than One Author** Give the authors' last names and the page number in parentheses: **(Frantz and Choate 55).** If a source has more than three authors, give the first author's last name followed by *et al.* and the page number: **(Durham et al. 212).** You may also list all the authors' last names, if you wish.

- **Work with No Author Given** Give the title (or a shortened version of it) and the page number: **("Maybe Your Job" 1).**

- **One of Two or More Works by the Same Author** Give the author's last name, the title or a shortened version of it, and the page number: **(Westermeier, Trailing the Cowboy 78).**

- **Two or More Works Cited at the Same Place** Use a semicolon to separate the entries: **(Horn 261; White 4).**

- **Electronic Source** Give the author's last name, or if no author is named, give the title: **("Cowboy").**

Preparing a Works Cited List

First, gather all your source cards. Then read your report and put a check mark on the card for every work you have cited. Put the other cards aside. (You should include only the works you actually referred to in your report in your Works Cited list.) Alphabetize the checked cards according to the authors' last names. Alphabetize anonymous works by the first word (except *A, An,* or *The*) in their titles. Follow the instructions below when typing the list.

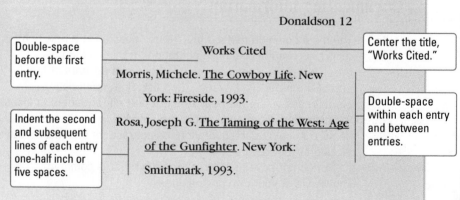

Donaldson 12

Works Cited

Double-space before the first entry.

Center the title, "Works Cited."

Morris, Michele. The Cowboy Life. New
    York: Fireside, 1993.

Indent the second and subsequent lines of each entry one-half inch or five spaces.

Rosa, Joseph G. The Taming of the West: Age
    of the Gunfighter. New York:
    Smithmark, 1993.

Double-space within each entry and between entries.

For more help, see the MLA citation guidelines, pp. 650–657.

TARGET SKILL ▶**Varying Sentences** Strings of sentences of the same type and length can bore your readers and lessen the impact of your message. As you revise, look for opportunities to vary your sentences.

> Even in his heyday, the cowboy earned only $25 to $40 a
> month, ~~He also got~~ *plus* room and board (White 261). ~~The cowboy's~~
> ~~salary~~ in the mid-1990s, ~~ranged~~ *American cowboys earned* between $700 and $1,200 a
> month, ~~He still gets~~ *including* room and board. ~~That is not much when you~~ *Sounds pretty good, doesn't it?*
> *But* consider that a custom saddle, ~~then~~ costs about $2,000 (Morris 7). *two- to three-months' salary*
> *necessity for the modern cowboy, his*

9 Editing and Proofreading

TARGET SKILL ▶**Parallel Construction** To help readers understand your ideas, make sure that you use parallel construction, or express sentence parts that serve the same function in the same grammatical form.

> Some cowboys were ~~from~~ Mexico, *an* others Native
> American, and many others ~~of~~ African-American ~~descent~~.

10 Sharing and Reflecting

Once you have revised and proofread your report, **share** it with people who might be interested in your subject. Consider photocopying it to pass around or posting it on the Internet.

For Your Working Portfolio After sharing your report, **reflect** on what you learned by writing it. What did you find out about your topic? What questions do you still have? What was the most difficult part of writing the report? How might you do research more efficiently next time? Attach your answers to your finished report and save it in your ☐ **Working Portfolio.**

REPORT

Student Help Desk

Research Report at a Glance

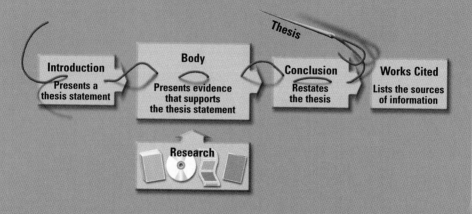

Thesis

Introduction
Presents a
thesis statement

Body
Presents evidence
that supports
the thesis statement

Conclusion
Restates
the thesis

Works Cited
Lists the sources
of information

Research

Idea Bank

Tiptoe through your interests. List topics that you know something about but want to explore further. Circle the topic that you would most like to share with others in your writing.

Scratch a mental itch. Brainstorm to identify topics that excite your intellectual curiosity. Do some preliminary reading and follow up on related ideas that might make good topics for a research report. Make sure, though, that these ideas are mainstream enough that other people have written about them too.

Be a creative problem solver. Don't be discouraged by an assigned topic that seems uninteresting to you. Try looking at it from an unusual angle, comparing and contrasting it with something else, or asking "what-if" questions about it. You're sure to find an aspect of it that you can get excited about.

Read literature. In his essay "Why Soldiers Won't Talk" (*Language of Literature*, Grade 11), John Steinbeck gives a unique perspective on the personal experience of war. Reading selections such as that one can suggest topics you might want to explore as well as angles or approaches you might take.

Friendly Feedback

Questions for Your Peer Reader

- What did you like best about my report?
- What information did you think was unnecessary?
- What parts of the report didn't seem to flow smoothly or were confusing?
- What new information did you learn?
- What questions do you still have about my topic?

Publishing Options

Print	Compile the reports of your classmates who wrote about related topics into a "Perspectives on . . ." notebook. Share this with members of your class and others.
Oral Communication	Have a panel discussion with classmates about your research reports. You might also want to use hypertext software to create a multimedia presentation of your report.
Online	Visit **mcdougallittell.com** for more publication options.

The Bottom Line

Checklist for Research Report

Have I . . .

_____ provided an interesting introduction with a clear thesis statement?

_____ used evidence from primary and secondary sources to develop and support my ideas?

_____ properly credited my sources of information?

_____ used an effective organizational pattern?

_____ used appropriate transitions between ideas?

_____ summarized my ideas in a satisfying conclusion?

_____ provided a properly formatted Works Cited list at the end of the report?

REPORT

Communicating in the Information Age

The Mouse That Soared

Perhaps you rely on a the click of a computer mouse to bring you information. Or you may prefer the more direct methods of telephoning or face-to-face interviews. Whether your resources are technical or human, you need to make many critical decisions about what you find. Is the material sound? Who is the best audience? What is the most effective way to present it? As a communicator in the Information Age, you must be wise as well as resourceful.

Power Words
Vocabulary for Precise Writing

Which Way Do You Turn?

Sometimes using words to describe the nature of a confusing place or problem can lead you down the pathway to understanding it.

Getting Lost

Imagine yourself an archaeologist among the **mazy** ruins of an ancient city. Can you find your way along the **complex** pattern of its **meandering** streets? No mistake, this town had an **elaborate** and **complicated** design, full of **involuted, tangly** streets reaching **dead ends.** Somewhere among these **snaky** byways must be a town square. Taking a **circuitous, roundabout** approach to find it may become too **involved,** too **oblique** to get you where you want to go. So you try several **twisty** paths and **serpentine, tortuous** alleys.

Attach a String and Unwind

After hours of going **astray,** you are first **bewildered,** then **distracted** with worry, and then absolutely **discombobulated.** Still, you have managed to create a new map so others won't become **confounded** in the future.

▷ **Your Turn** Take Alternative Routes

What's the most confusing place you've ever visited? Describe it to a partner, using any of the words presented above. Explain what steps you took to find your way to your destination.

Using Information Resources

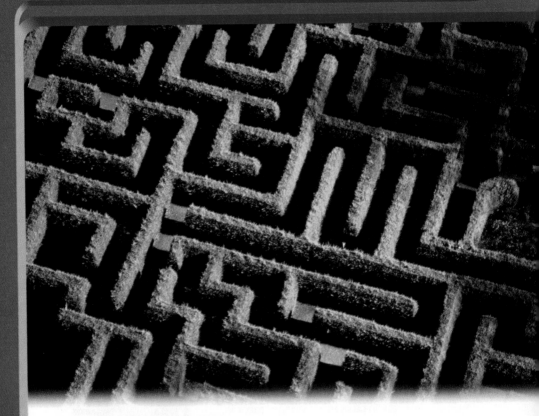

Directory Assistance

In today's information age, a wealth of knowledge is available on just about every imaginable topic. So doing your schoolwork, learning about the world, and finding your place in it should be easy, right? Not necessarily. Knowing the information is out there is one thing; tracking it down is another.

This chapter will help you successfully navigate the information maze to find what you need to know.

Write Away: Finding Yourself

Write a paragraph about what might await you after school. Focus on a career you might be interested in pursuing, listing questions you have about the career and ideas about where to find the answers. Keep your paragraph in your 📁 **Working Portfolio.**

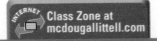
Class Zone at
mcdougallittell.com

INFO. RESOURCES

Accessing Information

Before you begin looking for information, you need to decide what you need to know and figure out how to locate it.

❶ Identifying Information Needs

To find information, you must have a clear idea about what you're looking for. Focus your research by asking yourself the following questions:

- What do I already know?
- What do I still need to find out?
- What are the most appropriate resources to consult?

For more help on planning a research strategy, see p. 447.

❷ Locating Library and Media Center Resources

Even in this electronic age, public libraries still may be the most important source of information. Most libraries offer a wide range of materials:

- **print resources**—manuscripts, books, journals, newspapers, and magazines
- **multimedia materials**—films, CDs, audio-cassettes, videos, records, and CD-ROMs
- **electronic access**—Internet and other online databases

Libraries also provide helpful guides for navigating these materials: online catalogs and databases and librarians.

Online Catalogs and Databases

Online catalogs and databases help users conduct specialized searches for information. Electronic catalogs have mostly replaced the card catalogs of book listings filed in labeled drawers. These online catalogs may include specific databases, such as indexes to periodicals or special subjects, and listings of holdings at nearby libraries. By following the on-screen commands, you can search for material by author, title, or subject.

Online Catalog

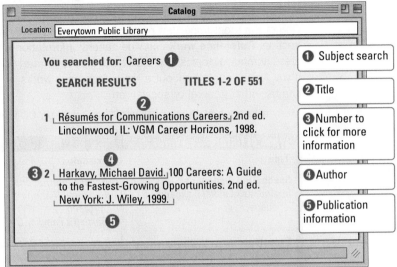

To find the most up-to-date information on a topic, consult articles in periodicals such as newspapers, magazines, and journals. Indexes to these articles, such as the *Readers' Guide to Periodical Literature* and *The New York Times Index*, can be printed, computerized, or stored as small photographs of printed pages. You can read these photographs, or **microforms,** on a special magnifying machine.

Databases vary greatly. To conduct efficient research, pay attention to the procedures and commands for the database you are using.

Reference Librarians

To get the most out of a visit to the library, first find out what it has to offer. **Librarians** are research professionals trained to locate information. Some specialize in areas such as reference or children's books. If you are unsure how to begin your research, the librarian can explain the special resources of the library, such as the computer lab. He or she also can show you how to use the resources and help you get started.

Reference librarians often can look up information for you or direct you to the appropriate resources over the phone.

Using Print Resources

❶ Reference Works

One of the most important parts of the library is the reference section. **Reference works** provide general information about a great number of topics and are useful places to start your research if you know very little about a topic. Reference works can be either general or specialized.

Many reference works are available online or on CD-ROM.

Types of Reference Works

Type	Examples
Specialized dictionaries—detailed treatments of special aspects of language	*Roget's International Thesaurus* *Historical Dictionary of American Slang* *Bartlett's Familiar Quotations*
Encyclopedias—multivolume collections of articles on a number of subjects, alphabetized by topic, usually with an index of topics covered	*Encyclopaedia Britannica* *Encyclopedia Americana* *World Book Encyclopedia* *Collier's Encyclopedia*
Atlases—geographical or historical, including maps, charts, and other graphics	*Hammond Medallion World Atlas* *National Geographic Atlas of the World* *Rand McNally Atlas of the World*
Biographical works—biographical information about notable people, arranged alphabetically or by subject matter	*Webster's New Biographical Dictionary* *The International Who's Who* *Dictionary of American Biography* *Cyclopedia of World Authors*
Vertical files—up-to-date information, including pamphlets, news clippings, and photographs	*Government files* *Business pamphlets* *Educational brochures*
Periodical indexes—alphabetized listings of magazine and newspaper articles	*Readers' Guide to Periodical Literature* *The New York Times Index*
Career guides—information about various occupations and careers	*Peterson's Annual Guide to Careers* *Dictionary of Occupational Titles* *The Encyclopedia of Careers and Vocational Guidance*

Armed with a list of questions about your topic, you can use reference works to begin gathering information as illustrated on the next page.

CHAPTER 25

Career possibilities: veterinarian or landscaper

Questions	Where to Look for Answers
• What is the field all about?	*The Dictionary of Occupational Titles*
• What kinds of jobs are available?	*VGM Opportunities Series*
• What are the educational requirements?	*The Encyclopedia of Careers and Vocational Guidance*
• What does the future look like for people in this field?	*Occupational Outlook Handbook*
• Does the government offer careers in this field?	*Guide to Federal Jobs*

For more information about formulating research questions, see pp. 447–448.

❷ Primary and Secondary Sources

Initial research should give you both a general overview of your subject and ideas about the specific information for which you need to look. You can find more specific information by using primary and secondary sources.

Primary Sources

Primary sources are firsthand documents written at the time that events took place. They can be written by either participants in or observers of events.

Types of Primary Sources		
	Advantages	**Disadvantages**
Historical document	Reliable factual information	Often incomplete or in need of interpretation
Diary, autobiography, letter	True emotional account, interesting details	Personal bias, limited perspective
Eyewitness report	Personal insights, interesting details	Limited perspective
Interview	Good source of quotations	Generally not in-depth

INFO. RESOURCES

Secondary Sources

Secondary sources are written after an event by people who did not witness it firsthand. The writers often gather information from a number of primary sources and even other secondary sources. Secondary sources offer interpretations and judgments as well as facts about events.

Types of Secondary Sources

	Advantages	Disadvantages
General and specialized encyclopedias	Easy-to-access facts and statistics	No personalized, subjective information
Textbook	Organized, general overview	Not as in-depth as a specialized source
Biography	Focused view of an individual	May be colored by biographer's biases
News article	Factual information in narrative format	May be colored by reporter's and newspaper's biases

Here's How) **Evaluating Secondary Sources**

To quickly evaluate whether a secondary source will be useful, check the following items:

- **Publication date**—Does the work include up-to-date information?
- **Author's credentials**—Is the author a recognized expert?
- **Table of contents**—Does the work cover topics you're interested in?
- **Introduction or preface**—Is the focus or point of view appropriate?
- **Index**—Is the material easy to find?
- **Specific entry**—Is the material understandable?
- **Critical reviews**—Do other experts endorse the work?

Consult a variety of sources in your research. A combination of primary (fairly subjective) and secondary (generally more objective) sources will give you a balanced picture of your topic.

CHAPTER 25

Doing Online Research

The **Internet** is a powerful global network of computers. It provides access to information presented on individual **Web pages** and on multidocument **Web sites** on the **World Wide Web.** The Internet and Web are wonderful informational tools, but you need to consider their strengths and weaknesses.

Go to ClassZone at mcdougallittell.com for a complete tutorial on using the Web for research.

Advantages and Disadvantages of the Internet

Advantages	Disadvantages
24-hour access to a tremendous variety of information	Increasing numbers of services are not free.
Easy and quick access to a variety of sites	Amount of information can be confusing and unmanageable.
Up-to-the-minute information	Information may be unreliable.
Summaries and condensed overviews on many sites	Complete material is often not available.

❶ Using Search Engines

Search engines, or browsers, such as Excite or Infoseek, can help you navigate the complicated Internet pathways. These computerized databases sort through the information available on the Web. Each search engine uses a different database, so you may need to try several to find what you need.

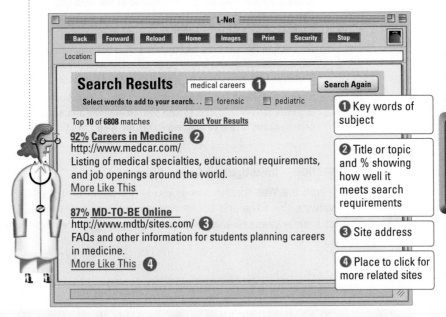

L-Net

Back | Forward | Reload | Home | Images | Print | Security | Stop

Location:

Search Results   medical careers ❶   Search Again

Select words to add to your search... ☐ forensic   ☐ pediatric

Top **10** of **6808** matches   **About Your Results**

92% Careers in Medicine ❷
http://www.medcar.com/
Listing of medical specialties, educational requirements, and job openings around the world.
More Like This

87% MD-TO-BE Online
http://www.mdtb/sites.com/ ❸
FAQs and other information for students planning careers in medicine.
More Like This ❹

❶ Key words of subject

❷ Title or topic and % showing how well it meets search requirements

❸ Site address

❹ Place to click for more related sites

When you find a useful site, either bookmark it (add to your favorite sites) or print it out so you can return to it easily whenever you need to.

Be sure to include complete citation information when printing research materials from the Internet. This information usually appears at the end of the material in a form like the following:

To cite this page:
"medicine" *Encyclopaedia Britannica Online*

❷ Evaluating Online Sites

The fact that the Internet is so available and easy to use has two important implications:

• Anyone can get online, create a Web site, post information, and register the site with a search engine.

• No one is required to verify sources of information.

Therefore, you cannot assume that the information you find is accurate, reliable, or up to date. It is extremely important to keep this in mind and evaluate a Web site carefully before deciding to use any information it includes. The following guidelines can help you.

Here's How **Evaluating Internet Web Sites**

• **Check the URL.** Those ending in .edu (educational institution sites) and .gov (government agency sites) or posted by well-known newspapers and magazines generally are reliable.

• **Review the credentials and affiliations of the Web site author.** Personal Web sites (e.g., "Elena's Top 10 Careers") may not be good sources of reliable information.

• **Note when the site was last updated.** This will help you determine if the information on the site is up to date. Be aware that even though a site recently was updated, not all information may be current.

• **Read any online reviews and ratings of Web sites.** Many established organizations offer these. (Some search engines and educational organizations also give online awards for Web sites.)

PRACTICE **Investigating Online Sites**

Search the Web for the career you wrote about on page 463. Evaluate the sites and bookmark or print out useful ones. Also, list their addresses and keep them in your **Working Portfolio.**

Collecting Your Own Data

Sometimes you'll find all the information you're looking for in library and Internet resources. But you may want or need to do original research to

- investigate a totally new issue
- compare your findings with other researchers' results

❶ Networking

An easy, effective way of getting information from organizations, agencies, and individual experts is **networking**, or communicating with a series of people. This process can give you

- specialized information
- suggestions on where you can find more information
- referrals to other people who might be able to help

NETWORKING

❶ **Use the phone book or Directory Assistance** to find the name and phone number of a person or organization that might have useful information.

❷ **Write a list of questions** to ask.

❺ **Follow up on referrals** (beginning with step 3) **or start a new search** (beginning with step 1).

❸ **Make the call,** stating your name, the information you need, and if you were referred by someone.

❹ **Take notes and ask questions,** including requests for referrals to other people or organizations that might help.

❷ Interviewing

A good way to get in-depth firsthand information is by **interviewing** a person knowledgeable about your subject.

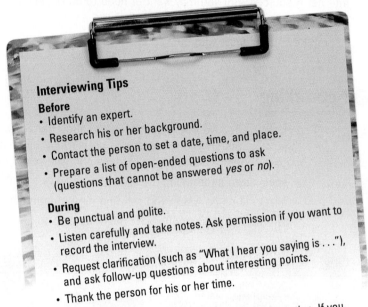

Interviewing Tips

Before
- Identify an expert.
- Research his or her background.
- Contact the person to set a date, time, and place.
- Prepare a list of open-ended questions to ask (questions that cannot be answered *yes* or *no*).

During
- Be punctual and polite.
- Listen carefully and take notes. Ask permission if you want to record the interview.
- Request clarification (such as "What I hear you saying is . . ."), and ask follow-up questions about interesting points.
- Thank the person for his or her time.

After
- Review your notes, and summarize the conversation. If you recorded the conversation, you might want to transcribe it while it is fresh in your mind.
- Identify strong statements you might want to quote directly.
- Send a note of appreciation—and possibly a copy of the material you use from the interview—to the interviewee.

❸ Conducting a Survey

While an interview can tap an individual's knowledge, a **survey** can provide information from a broad range of people.

Creating the Questionnaire

Conducting a survey involves creating, administering, and evaluating the results of a **questionnaire**. The results of a survey are only as good as the questionnaire, so construct it carefully.

What Do You Think?
Please answer the following questions
completely and honestly.

1. What type of work do you like best?
   Check one in each column.

   | with people | intellectual |
   | alone | physical |

2. Which career category are you most
   interested in? Check one.

   business (management, consulting)
   professional (law, medicine)
   academic (teaching, research)
   trade (electrical, plumbing, carpentry)
   service (sales, child care)

Encourage truthful
responses.

Ask clear, direct
questions and
present them in a
logical order.

Offer answer
options if possible.

Keep it short and
simple!

Administering the Survey

To get the most useful information from a survey, you must
administer it to a large and varied group of people and make sure
you don't influence the way they respond.

Targeted Audience Choose people who know something about the
subject of your survey but who might have different opinions about
it. For example, if you're surveying teenagers, get responses from
people with varied interests and outlooks—not just your friends.

Reliable Responses Make sure that the survey-taker is open and
friendly and presents the questions neutrally. The person should
never suggest his or her own opinions.

Interpreting Survey Results

Here's How Interpreting Survey Results

1. Compile and tally the responses to each survey question.
2. Look for patterns, such as boys responding one way and girls another.
3. Think of possible explanations for the response patterns.
4. Choose the interpretation that explains the results in the most simple,
   complete way.

Try to keep an open mind when interpreting survey results. Pay
special attention to information that contradicts your expectations
and be prepared to alter your view.

For more help interpreting and evaluating data, see pp. 485–487.

INFO. RESOURCES

Incorporating Information

Although sometimes you will gather information just to satisfy your curiosity, often you will want to incorporate that information into a written, oral, or other type of presentation. There are several ways to do this: quoting, paraphrasing, and summarizing.

❶ Quoting

A **direct quotation** is a statement copied word for word from a source. Use quotations only when the author's or speaker's words help you make your point more strongly and succinctly. Weave them into your writing smoothly and credit the source of a quotation where it appears in your paper or presentation. You must also provide complete publication information in a Works Cited list.

> **PROFESSIONAL MODEL**
>
> Fighting fires is dangerous and stressful. As firefighter Teresa Taylor says, though, it is also incredibly rewarding: "I love my job because I know I'm saving lives and making a difference" (Working World 8).

For more help using and documenting direct quotations, see pp. 451 and 477.

❶ Paraphrasing and Summarizing

Other ways to incorporate information are to paraphrase or summarize it.

Paraphrasing

Paraphrasing, or restating information in your own words, is a good way to present all the details of someone else's ideas. A paraphrase often is as long as the original material.

> **Here's How** Paraphrasing
>
> 1. Identify the main idea and supporting details of the passage and restate them in your own words.
> 2. Simplify difficult vocabulary without changing the meaning.
> 3. Review your paraphrase for plagiarism and misleading statements.
> 4. Credit the source of the ideas where they appear in your writing and in the Works Cited list.

Summarizing

Probably the most common way of incorporating information is **summarizing,** or presenting a condensed version of someone else's ideas in your own words. The steps in writing a summary are similar to those used in creating a paraphrase, except that you present only the main points and leave out minor details. A summary should be about one-third the length of the original, as these cows wish their owner remembered.

The Far Side by Gary Larson

STUDENT MODEL

Original: "For me, being a doctor is a rich and rewarding experience. It gives me a front-row seat on all the hopes and fears, joys and sorrows of people's lives. To be part of this mysterious cycle of birth and death and to effect change within it—this is something that is indescribable and unforgettable. I can think of no better way to live a life."
—Alice Mann, M.D.

Paraphrase: According to Dr. Alice Mann, being a doctor is very fulfilling. She feels honored to take part in the varied experiences of other people's lives—both happy and sad—and to make a positive contribution to them. To her, the doctor's life is a life well-lived.

Summary: Dr. Alice Mann says that being a doctor is a rewarding experience. She's glad she chose medicine as a career.

HOT TIP

You don't need to document information that is common knowledge.

INFO. RESOURCES

Student Help Desk

Using Information Resources at a Glance

Information Resources

Accessing Information

Print resources
- Reference works
- Primary sources
- Secondary sources

Electronic resources
- Web sites
- CD-ROMs

Original data collection
- Interviewing
- Networking
- Conducting surveys

Incorporating Information
- Quoting
- Paraphrasing
- Summarizing

Online Search Strategies

WWWhere in the World Wide Web?

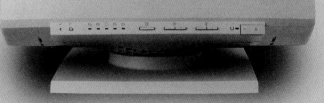

Think ahead. Make a list of questions and circle the key words. Use these to start your search.

Stick to the first sites listed. These usually match your key words most closely.

Look at the URL: .edu—educational site, **.gov**—government site, **.com**—commercial site, **.org**—organizational site

Use the Help or Search Tips features of the search engine to refine your search.

Incorporating Information

When Citing Sources

Use these symbols and abbreviations

Quotation marks (" ") enclose a statement quoted directly from a source

Ellipses (. . .) indicate material you have omitted from a quotation

ed. editor or edition

et al. and the rest (used to cite multiple authors)

P Press (used to cite publishers' names)

trans. translator

vol. volume

Include this information

In the text:
- last name(s) of the author(s)
- page number(s) where the information is located
  (Ginsberg 77)

In the Works Cited list:
- complete name(s) of the author(s)
- complete title of the work
- publisher's name
- place and date of publication
  (Ginsberg, Leon H. *Careers in Social Work.* Needham Heights: Allyn, 1997.)

For more help using and documenting direct quotations, see p. 456.

The Bottom Line

Checklist for Using Information Resources

Have I . . .

____ clearly identified my information needs?

____ used various resources to help search for source material?

____ done preliminary research using general reference works?

____ consulted both primary and secondary sources?

____ accessed information through the Internet?

____ evaluated the reliability of both print and online sources?

____ collected my own data, if necessary?

____ incorporated information by quoting, paraphrasing, or summarizing?

____ properly documented my sources of information?

INFO. RESOURCES

Power Words
Vocabulary for Precise Writing

impractical

Bright Ideas

It's beyond belief that there are so many words that describe thinkers and thoughts. Here are words you can use to evaluate ideas.

Wise in Disguise

The ideas of the great scientist Albert Einstein were often called **impractical** at first. Other scientists sometimes said they were even **untenable** and **illogical,** perhaps going so far as to call them **inconceivable** and **irrational.** But what seemed **farfetched** to others, **incoherent, flimsy,** and **ill-thought-out,** simply showed how much deeper Einstein could see into things than his colleagues could. His thinking was unusual, but not **inconsistent** and never **inconsequential.**

Mind at Work

The world eventually came to realize that many of his ideas were **brilliant.** Fellow scientists came to see Einstein's thoughts as **intelligent** and **cogent.** His reasoning was **logical** and **consistent,** each detail **well-thought-out.** All his calculations were **relevant** and **germane** to his main thesis.

Nowadays we realize how **perspicacious** Einstein was. He had the **profound** mind of a scientific genius, and he is celebrated for his **compelling** and **farsighted** discoveries.

▷ **Your Turn** Share Your Ideas

What qualities or behaviors do you think sound thinkers display? What individual do you admire for his or her ability to solve a problem or present a fresh idea? Discuss your thoughts with a partner.

CHAPTER 26

flimsy

PROFOUND

brilliant

compelling

ill-thought-out

Evaluating Information

Believe It or Not!

Information is coming your way all the time in all kinds of forms. You might read headlines similar to those above while standing in line at a drugstore. You see billboards while driving. You read editorials and you listen to speeches. Commercials and ads confront you in magazines and the media. So, how do you decide what information is valuable—or even believable? Sharpening your evaluation skills is what this chapter is all about.

Write Away: Convince Me

Write a few paragraphs for the kind of article you would expect to accompany one of the headlines in the *Weekly Whisper*. How many facts do you think would be included? Who would your sources be? Add your writing to your 🗂 **Working Portfolio.**

VIDEO
Media Focus

EVALUATING INFO.

Preparing to Evaluate Information

LESSON 1

Before you can evaluate information, you must do two things:
- establish a set of standards, or **criteria**, for making evaluations;
- determine the quality of the information source.

❶ Developing Criteria

Is being a lifeguard the right summer job for you? Before you could answer that question, you'd need to establish criteria, or determine the qualities you'd look for in the "right job." Establishing criteria is an important way to compare options and make life decisions. It is also a necessary step in judging the value of what you read and hear. The criteria shown below were developed by two students. One was looking through reviews for a movie to recommend to some friends; the other was looking through ads to buy a computer.

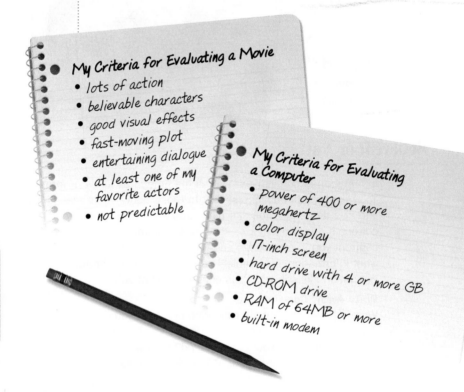

My Criteria for Evaluating a Movie
- lots of action
- believable characters
- good visual effects
- fast-moving plot
- entertaining dialogue
- at least one of my favorite actors
- not predictable

My Criteria for Evaluating a Computer
- power of 400 or more megahertz
- color display
- 17-inch screen
- hard drive with 4 or more GB
- CD-ROM drive
- RAM of 64MB or more
- built-in modem

Using Criteria

Copy the criteria below. Then write the part of the ad that corresponds to each criterion and tell whether or not the criterion is met, or whether you can't tell.

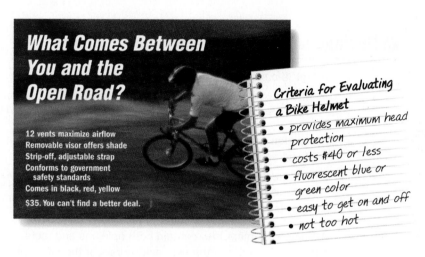

❷ Evaluating a Source of Information

Sometimes you can tell a lot about the credibility of printed material before you even read it. Use the following criteria to help assess the reliability of an information source.

- **Author** Analyze the author's credentials. Is the book or article written on a topic in the author's area of expertise? Evaluate, as well, the author's objectivity. Is the author biased? Does he or she have a reason to favor one view?

- **Timeliness** Note the publication date. Is this a topic for which information may change quickly? A ten-year-old source may be reliable for information about World War II, but not for the use of computers in classrooms.

- **Supporting Information** Does the information seem to be soundly researched and well supported? Look for a bibliography or a list of credits and sources at the back of the book.

- **Publisher** Magazines known for trendy articles or gossip will not be as factual and reliable as news or science magazines. Books published by university presses are likely to have information that is sound and well researched.

Facts and Opinions

LESSON 2

"The best player of this generation . . ." "The most innovative musician . . ." "Biggest crime of the century . . ." Do these phrases lead into facts or opinions? Knowing the difference between the two is a key skill in evaluating information.

❶ Distinguishing Between Facts and Opinions

A **fact** is a statement that can be proved.

> **Ms. Lee, an incumbent for 20 years, lost the November election by a few hundred votes.**

> Can be proved by counting votes

An **opinion** is a statement that cannot be proved. Usually, it contains someone's view or feeling about a subject.

> **The Foreign Relations Committee will suffer without the benefit of Miss Lee's expert knowledge of international affairs.**

> Someone's view— can't be proved

A single statement may contain both opinions and facts. To differentiate between the two, ask yourself if the information is subjective (an opinion) or objective (a fact).

> **The greatest invention in history was Johann**   **OPINION**
> **Gutenberg's movable-type system, which he used**   **FACT**
> **to print the Bible in 1455.**

It's a common tendency to consider a statement factual simply because it fits in with your own opinion. Remember that just because you agree with an opinion, that doesn't make it a fact.

❷ Critically Assessing Facts

Facts and statistics strengthen an argument or claim because they appear to be objective. However, facts alone do not mean that a piece of writing is valid or credible. Almost anyone can find a fact—however small, outdated, or irrelevant—to "support" an idea.

> **Four out of five doctors recommend this pain killer.**

That statement itself may be true, but you may need to know, for example, how many doctors were surveyed and if they were paid by the manufacturer.

To judge the value of facts, ask yourself questions like these.

> **Can I Trust These Facts?**
> ✓ Are the facts relevant to the issue?
> ✓ Do they tell the whole story?
> ✓ Are the facts still current and applicable?
> ✓ How reliable are the sources?

❸ Critically Assessing Opinions

Writing that contains opinions should not be considered untrustworthy or lacking in credibility. On the contrary, many nonfiction pieces are filled with opinions that may be thoughtful and well-informed. Persuasive pieces are strongly based on opinions. Narrative nonfiction— including biographies, histories, and eyewitness accounts— contains many personal observations. Even objective scientific material may contain opinions. Use the checklist to determine if opinions are well founded.

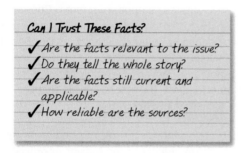

> **Are These Well-Informed Opinions?**
> ✓ Are these opinions supported by facts?
> ✓ Are they based on accurate eyewitness observations?
> ✓ Do they result from logical thinking?
> ✓ Are they supported by expert opinions?

PROFESSIONAL MODEL

The Galápagos [Islands] are without peer as a marine ecosystem too. Located at the juncture of several major Pacific currents, the undersea mountains help generate a massive cold-water upwelling that feeds the entire chain of sea life, from the tiniest planktonic creatures to the greatest of the whales.

—Peter Benchley, "Galápagos: Paradise in Peril," *National Geographic*

> Author states opinion

> Objective data support opinion

❹ Opinions That Appear as Facts

Sharp thinking skills are required to evaluate information about controversial issues. Opinions may sometimes be skillfully manipulated to appear as facts. Careful readers and listeners uncloak "false facts" by asking themselves whether sound evidence is being presented. In the following model, President Jackson tries to convince the U.S. Congress that the Cherokee should be moved from their native lands. He sounds authoritative and factual—but where are his facts?

PROFESSIONAL MODEL

... **All preceding experiments for the improvement of the Indians have failed. It seems now to be an established fact that they can not live in contact with a civilized community and prosper. Ages of fruitless endeavors have at length brought us to a knowledge of this ... no one can doubt the moral duty of the Government of the United States to protect and if possible to preserve and perpetuate the scattered remnants of this race which are left within our borders.**

—President Andrew Jackson,
"Message to Congress," 1835

> Which experiments?

> Based on what?

> Of course, someone can doubt this!

PRACTICE Identifying Facts and Opinions

Identify the opinion contained within each statement below. If a statement contains no opinions, write *none*.

Example: Daw Aung San Suu Kyi is the daughter of General Aung San, the wildly popular founder of modern Burma, or Myanmar.
Answer: wildly popular

1. Suu Kyi, seen internationally as a symbol of heroic resistance, was awarded the Nobel Prize for Peace in 1991.
2. After receiving a university education in Britain, Suu Kyi returned to Burma in 1988 where she became a courageous foe of the military regime.
3. By the time she was awarded the Nobel Prize in 1991, she had already been under house arrest for two years.
4. Suu Kyi has led her party, the National League for Democracy, with humor and resolve.
5. Although her party won 82% of the vote in national elections, the brutal military junta refused to relinquish power.

Logical Fallacies

A **logical fallacy** is a faulty argument built on unsound reasoning. Some logical fallacies can sound convincing, but they often present incomplete information or don't address the issue directly.

❶ Incomplete Information

The reasoning in the following logical fallacies is faulty because essential information is missing.

Either-Or Thinking
This type of fallacy reduces a solution or situation to only two extremes. It leaves no room for alternatives.

> **Either we stop the construction of a new airport, or the surrounding suburbs will become ghost towns.**

There are less extreme alternatives, such as the surrounding suburbs' maintaining their populations by passing protective zoning laws or by airport employees' moving in.

Oversimplification
A complex situation is explained by omitting key information. Clues to oversimplified thinking include phrases like these: "It's a simple question of . . ." "It all boils down to. . ." "It's clear to anyone that. . . ."

> **Getting a good job all boils down to whom you know.**

Securing a good job isn't really that simple. Other factors are also important, such as educational background, work record, employers' recommendations, interviewing skills, experience, and so on.

Half-Truths
These statements are misleading because they contain part of the truth but not all of it.

> **The fire chief is obviously incompetent because it now takes firefighters five minutes longer to report to a fire than it took five years ago.**

The argument does not state the fact that the fire department's budget was cut in half during the last five years.

Overgeneralization

A sweeping statement includes everything and everyone without exceptions. You can often recognize overgeneralizations by key words such as *all, everyone, every time, any, anything, no one,* or *none.*

None of the sanitation workers in our city really care about keeping the environment clean.

In all probability, there are many exceptions. The writer can't possibly know the feelings of every sanitation worker in the city.

❷ Dodging the Issue

Circular Reasoning

A person tries to prove or support a statement simply by repeating it in different terms. A circular argument seems to lead to a conclusion, but actually it just circles back to the starting point.

Larry Rosner deserves your vote for Deputy Commissioner. Rosner is the best guy for the job. This city needs the kinds of improvements that Rosner can make.

Every statement repeats the idea that Rosner deserves the vote. None of the statements offer any evidence.

"This CD player costs less than players selling for twice as much."

Evading the Issue

An opinion is "supported" with arguments that fail to address its central point. A child may use this defense when faced with a mistake: "Why don't you scold my brother? He does that all the time."

QUESTION

"Why did you break your campaign promise not to raise taxes if elected?"

ANSWER

"Increased revenues greatly benefited the citizens of this state. Crime was lowered because of more police patrol, highways were paved, and overcrowding was lessened in the schools."

The speaker evades the issue of breaking a campaign promise and focuses instead on the benefits from the raised taxes.

Attacking the Person

Instead of addressing the issue, a person tries to discredit an argument by attacking the person making it. This fallacy is sometimes referred to as *ad hominem,* meaning literally, "to the person." In some political campaigns, candidates use this form of name-calling to attack each other.

My liberal opponent is so soft on crime that violence in our city will surely escalate.

No solutions are offered for the crime problem. Instead the speaker focuses on insulting an opponent.

PRACTICE Identifying Logical Fallacies

Identify and evaluate the logical fallacy in each of the following statements. Then change the statements to correct the logical fallacies.

1. I've never favored our high school's adopting a uniform dress policy because I've always disliked the idea.
2. Either we choose the kind of clothes we want to wear to school, or our rights as citizens will be demolished.
3. No one wants to wear the same outfit each and every day.
4. The only reason people want a dress code is to try to control our tastes.
5. Those who support the idea are unimaginative and controlling.

Persuasive Techniques

LESSON 4

You encounter persuasion every day. It can be the simple appeal of a friend convincing you to go somewhere, the emotional appeal of a TV commercial to support a charity, or the ideological claims in a political campaign. Persuasion can be an effective way to stir people's feelings. It helps, however, to recognize persuasive techniques so that you can objectively decide whether you want to be persuaded or not.

❶ Slanted Language

Language is a powerful tool that can be shaped to the user's purposes. Slanted language is language that is purposely "bent" in order to persuade others.

Connotation and Denotation

Denotation is the literal meaning of a word. **Connotation** is the attitude or feelings associated with a word, as opposed to its dictionary definition. Skilled persuaders will carefully select connotations that support their purposes.

John Knots is a shrewd negotiator.
Suggests competence and insight

John Knots is a crafty negotiator.
Suggests slightly devious methods

Loaded Words

Someone who has a **bias** leans toward one side in an argument or issue. To be unbiased is to be neutral. Writers who have a strong bias tend to use loaded words that carry especially strong connotations—either positive or negative. For example, writers with different aims could describe the same person as *thorough* or *nit-picking, courageous* or *foolhardy, sensitive* or *wimpy.* Used well, these words can add flair and passion to a persuasive speech or appeal. Misused, they can appeal to the emotions at the expense of reason.

Notice how the positive and negative connotations of the bold-faced synonyms give two totally different meanings to the movie reviews on the next page.

In this **touching** film, the **delightful** Tina Tomley plays a **spirited** safari guide. The film opens with a **tender** scene in which Tomley **discovers** an **undernourished** tiger cub. Henry Young makes a **brief** appearance, but delivers some **stirring oratory** about environmental issues. The plot is **full of surprises** and the ending is very **moving**.

Positive Connotations

In this **sappy little** film, the **irritating** Tina Tomley plays a **reckless** safari guide. The film opens **melodramatically** when Tomley **stumbles upon** a **scrawny** tiger cub. Henry Young makes a **rushed** appearance, apparently to do some **heavy-handed ranting**. The plot is **erratic** and the ending is **maudlin**.

Negative Connotations

❷ Advertising Appeals

Advertisers may not legally present false claims. However, they can and do use a variety of the following persuasive techniques to slant the truth in their favor.

Testimonial

Testimonials are claims made by celebrities or paid "experts" who attest to the merits of a person, product, or service. The person paid to make the appeal is carefully chosen to inspire confidence. Thus, who the person *is* inspires more confidence than the *facts* behind the claim.

> **Olympic track star: "To keep on the fast track, I take my Vitabest every day."**

Appeals by Association

In using **appeals by association,** advertisers are appealing to people's desires to be popular and special.

Plain folks
Ordinary, average people are shown to support a product or candidate. The underlying message here is "People like you are on 'our side.'"

> **I wouldn't think of starting my day without Hearty Oats. If it was good enough for Gramps, it's good enough for me.**

EVALUATING INFO.

Bandwagon

Bandwagon appeals urge you to step in line with the crowd. The underlying message is "You don't want to be left out, do you?"

Every day, hundreds of new users discover the joy of Pocket Phones.

Snob Appeal

The opposite of the plain-folks approach, this appeal engages your need to be distinctive and set apart. Snob appeal addresses the human desire to be "somebody."

Treat yourself to Tropical Paradise because, after all, you deserve the best under the sun.

Transfer

In this approach, a company or campaign tries to transfer the positive feelings associated with certain images to its product or candidate. For example, a sparkling mountain stream may be used to symbolize the pure clean feeling you get from an advertised soap.

Appeals to Fear

This is an emotional appeal that plays on common fears. It veils a subtle threat: If you don't buy our product, bad things may result.

You depend on Durable Tires because precious lives depend on you.

PRACTICE Identifying Advertising Appeals

Identify the advertising technique used in the ad below. Then create an ad campaign of your own in which you design a billboard and use at least one or more of the appeals you learned.

Sound Reasoning

Building strong reasoning skills helps you reach accurate conclusions. In addition, it helps you assess whether or not the reasoning behind another's argument is sound.

❶ Inductive Reasoning

When you use inductive reasoning, you start with specific facts. By studying these facts, you reach a general conclusion. Inductive reasoning always goes from the *specific* to the *general*.

Specific Facts

Fact 1 Johann Sebastian Bach started playing violin at the age of 4.

Fact 2 At the age of 3, Ludwig van Beethoven was taking piano lessons.

Fact 3 Johannes Brahms was composing music at age 5.

Fact 4 Frederic Chopin taught himself to play melodies on the piano at 5.

Fact 5 Stephen Foster was playing both guitar and organ by the time he was 2.

Generalization

Many musical geniuses showed talent during their preschool years.

Testing the Soundness of Inductive Arguments

Use these questions to test the validity of an inductive argument.

- **Is the evidence accurate?** Inaccurate information almost inevitably leads to an inaccurate conclusion.

- **Does the conclusion follow logically from the evidence?** This generalization does not follow reasonably from the facts listed above: "Many musical geniuses must have parents who push them into music at a young age."

- **Is the evidence drawn from a large enough sample?** If the only engineers you ever met were men, you may conclude that all engineers are male. Your conclusion would be wrong because your sampling of engineers was too small.

In the next model, Umberto Eco puts together facts to arrive at an inductive conclusion. His sampling of evidence is large enough to fit his argument because his conclusion is purely personal.

In 1918, at the age of 40, my maternal grandfather was stricken by a form of viral influenza, popularly known as the Spanish flu, which was decimating much of Europe. Within a week, despite the best efforts of three physicians, he died.   **FACT 1**

In 1972, at the age of 40, I was stricken by a serious illness that seemed very similar to la spagnola. Thanks to penicillin, after a week I was up and about.   **FACT 2**

So it is easy to understand why, forgetting about atomic energy, space travel and the computer, I persist in thinking that the most important invention of our century is penicillin. . . .   **GENERALIZATION**

—Umberto Eco, *The New York Times Magazine*

❷ Deductive Reasoning

Whereas inductive reasoning ends with a generalization, **deductive reasoning** begins with a general statement. It then uses that generalization to arrive at a conclusion about a specific situation.

Air pollution is aggravated by car exhaust.   GENERALIZATION

We want to have cleaner air.   SPECIFIC

We need to drive less or fix auto emissions.   SPECIFIC

Testing the Soundness of Deductive Arguments

In order to be valid, a deductive argument must be correctly structured. The conclusion must follow logically from the premise.

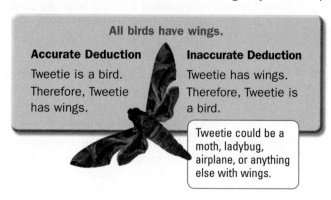

All birds have wings.

Accurate Deduction
Tweetie is a bird. Therefore, Tweetie has wings.

Inaccurate Deduction
Tweetie has wings. Therefore, Tweetie is a bird.

Tweetie could be a moth, ladybug, airplane, or anything else with wings.

In addition to a logical construction, a deduction must have a sound premise in order to be valid. In the model below, Gandhi explains his premise to make sure that his followers understand its logic.

> . . . no State is possible without two entities, the rulers and the ruled. You [the British government] are our sovereign, our Government, only so long as we consider ourselves your subjects. When we are not subjects, you are not the sovereign either. . . . If you make laws to keep us suppressed in a wrongful manner and without taking us into confidence, these laws will merely adorn the statute-books. We will never obey them.
>
> —Mohandas K. Gandhi, "On Civil Disobedience"

Generalization

❸ Reasoning by Analogy

An **analogy** is a comparison between a subject and something else. It suggests that since the two things being compared are alike in some ways, they will probably be alike in other ways as well.

> **Gossip works like a contagious virus. Its toxic effects spread unseen from one bearer to the next.**

A **false analogy** is an inaccurate comparison between two people, things, or ideas. It implies that the two things are more similar than they really are. The following example is a false analogy because it ignores many essential differences between the people being compared.

> **The president of a country is like the father of a family.**

This analogy fails to take into consideration several important facts, for example, that the people of many countries elect the president but that children don't choose their parents, and that a country usually has a series of presidents but that children have only one biological father.

EVALUATING INFO.

Inferences and Conclusions

The critical evaluation of ideas is an active process that calls upon you to think for yourself. You must draw your own conclusions and infer meanings that are not overtly or directly stated.

❶ Making Inferences

Writers do not always state their information directly. Instead, readers need to **make inferences,** or "read between the lines," to understand their deeper meanings. When you make an inference, you analyze facts and details, and interpret them by using your common sense and prior knowledge. Make inferences of your own as you read the following passage.

> **LITERARY MODEL**
>
> We should never forget that everything Adolf Hitler did in Germany was "legal" and everything the Hungarian freedom fighters did in Hungary was "illegal." It was "illegal" to aid and comfort a Jew in Hitler's Germany. Even so, I am sure that, had I lived in Germany at the time, I would have aided and comforted my Jewish brothers.
>
> —Martin Luther King, Jr., "Letter from Birmingham Jail,"
> April 16, 1963

You know from your prior knowledge that Adolf Hitler led the Nazis in exterminating millions of Jews during World War II. In addition, you know that many ordinary citizens of Germany and other Nazi-occupied countries risked their lives by hiding Jews or helping them to escape Nazi terror. Prior knowledge also informs you that Martin Luther King, Jr., was a leading civil rights activist in the United States. By piecing together this prior knowledge with the facts in the excerpt, you can arrive at the following inferences:

- Hitler had unlimited power in Germany.
- The freedom fighters helped the Jews.
- King would refuse to obey immoral laws.

❷ Drawing Conclusions

You draw a conclusion after studying information that may include facts, observations, arguments, and opinions. Drawing valid conclusions requires you to synthesize these various data and make your own judgment. Conclusions are not mere opinions or guesses; they are decisions reached after carefully weighing the evidence.

> **Fact**
>
> The median income for high school graduates is $32,000 compared to $19,000 for those without a high school diploma.

> **Reasoning**
>
> A diploma helps me get a good job. A good job enhances the quality of life.

> **Observation**
>
> My relatives who earned high school degrees have better jobs than my relatives who didn't.

> **Conclusion**
>
> Earning a high school diploma will help me get a better job and a better life.

Often when you draw a conclusion or make an inference, you form a generalization. A **generalization** is a broad, or general, statement that expresses a principle or reaches a conclusion based on examples or instances.

PRACTICE Drawing Conclusions

Read the following sets of statements. For each set, write a valid conclusion that you might draw.

1. In the nineteenth century, few female writers succeeded in becoming published authors. However, Charlotte Brontë had her novel *Jane Eyre* published in 1847. Her sister, Emily Brontë, wrote *Wuthering Heights* in 1848. Both novels were highly popular.

2. During the 1930s, farmers in the Great Plains were unable to sell their crops because of a large economic depression that swept the country. During the same period, the Great Plains were ravaged by dust storms that ruined their crops.

Student Help Desk

Evaluating Information at a Glance

information *information* *information* *information* *information*

Identify persuasive techniques

Distinguish facts from opinions

Watch for logical fallacies

Draw conclusions and make inferences

Use sound reasoning

Establish criteria

information

Logical Fallacies   Come Again?

Watch for these errors in logic.

Logical Fallacies	Example
Either/Or Thinking Only two extremes	America: Love it or leave it.
Oversimplification Key information omitted	Deciding what college to go to all boils down to how much money you have.
Overgeneralization A sweeping statement	Hollywood actors are always seeking more publicity.
Circular Reasoning "Conclusion" repeats the beginning	I like jazz because it's my favorite kind of music.
Evading the Issue Central point avoided	"I don't deserve this parking ticket. The police should be using their time to get real criminals."
Attacking the Person Argument discredited by attack on the person making it	How could you vote for a spineless teacher's pet like Joe for student council?

Facts and Opinions

Facts can be proven.

The world's largest plant, a giant sequoia in Sequoia National Park, California, is about 272 feet tall and about 3,500 years old.

Opinions cannot be proven.

The giant sequoia is a priceless treasure that must be protected by strict preservation laws.

Persuasive Techniques — Smart and Savvy

Testimonial	Movie star: "Eating Okey Dokey Oats gives me a fresh start to every day."
Appeals to fear	Get your tickets now. This concert is sure to sell out quickly.
Bandwagon	Join the thousands of fans discovering the joy of windsurfing.
Plain folks appeal	Hey, I'm easy. Some laughs with my friends. A cool glass of Sparkling Lemon. What more does a guy need?
Snob appeal	Mountain Bike Magic. Pity the riders eating your dust. It's not your problem.

The Bottom Line

Checklist for Evaluating Information

Have I . . .

____established criteria for forming judgments?

____distinguished facts from opinions?

____identified errors in logic?

____used sound reasoning in forming opinions?

____recognized flawed or sound reasoning in arguments?

____evaluated persuasive claims?

____drawn legitimate conclusions?

____made sound inferences?

sonorous

orotund

Loud and Clear

We can't state loudly enough that the human voice can produce a range of sounds. You can elaborate about the vocal qualities with words like these.

Listen Up

Great singers or actors can use their voices like musical instruments. Such a voice can be **deep, sonorous,** and **imposing,** or **soft, murmurous,** and **whispery.** (A really **loud** one sounds **stentorian;** a really **low** one, **breathy.**) A **resonant, booming** voice will be heard throughout an auditorium, but you have to strain to hear a **cooing** voice.

Set the Right Tone

You've all heard a rock or pop singer with a **reverberating, thrilling** voice—one that gives you goosebumps. Singers from the early days of radio sounded **honey-voiced** and **mellifluous.** An operatic soprano, who has a **high-pitched** voice, can sound **lilting** and **melodious,** while an operatic bass has a **throbbing** and **plummy** sound.

If you had to give a speech or sing a song in public, how do you think it would sound—**rich** and **orotund, ringing** and **vibrant?** Or would it sound **shrill** and **screechy,** like nails scraping across the chalkboard? If you answered *yes* to the second question, keep a big supply of earplugs on hand.

reverberating

melodious

▷ **Your Turn** Stay Tuned

Write a brief review of one of your favorite singers. Using words from this page as well as your own, describe the quality of the singer's voice.

loud   resonant

Oral Communication

Do I Make Myself Clear?

What strategies do you use to make yourself heard? Screaming might work in some situations, but you probably wouldn't want to try it in the classroom. Sometimes the most effective way to make your point is to remain quiet and let others do the talking. There's no magic formula for successful oral communication. The approach you choose will depend on the situation, your audience, and what you're trying to say.

In this chapter, you'll learn a variety of techniques that will help you speak your mind without losing your head.

Write Away: You Said *What*?

Write a paragraph about a time when you either succeeded or failed to get your point across orally. Include a sentence or two about why you think you got the results you did. Keep your paragraph in your **Working Portfolio.**

Listening Critically

"I hear you!" Many people use this phrase to express understanding and sympathy with the speaker. Its widespread use indicates how important the spoken word is in communicating information. For this reason, it is extremely important to know how to listen effectively and evaluate what you hear.

❶ Establishing a Listening Purpose and Strategies

The first step in being a good listener is understanding why you are listening. Once you understand the purpose of what is being said, you'll be able to choose the appropriate listening strategy.

Listening Purposes and Strategies	
Purpose	**Strategies**
Informational—to learn who, what, where, when, and why (classes, lectures)	Taking notes, asking questions, making connections, making inferences
Critical—to evaluate information and distinguish fact from opinion (speeches, news)	Asking for explanations, analyzing ideas and logic
Creative—to solve problems and play with ideas (group discussions, brainstorming)	Developing new perspectives, building on others' ideas
Empathetic—to understand others' feelings (conversations)	Offering supportive verbal and nonverbal feedback

❷ Applying Listening Skills and Strategies

Even if you use the appropriate listening strategy, you may still have trouble following speakers who do not state their main ideas clearly. Paying attention to verbal and nonverbal clues can help you get the point.

- **Verbal clues**—the information that follows such statements as "There are three main reasons," "My next point is," "It's important to note," and "To summarize"; repetition of ideas; change in tone or emphasis
- **Nonverbal clues**—facial expressions, gestures, posture, and tone and pitch of voice that indicate emphasis and stress; charts, slides, and illustrations that communicate or clarify ideas visually

Making Inferences and Predictions

Much of what you learn from listening is not directly stated by the speaker. You learn by combining what you hear with what you already know and by making inferences and predictions. **Inferences** are logical conclusions based on both old and new information. **Predictions** are guesses of what might happen, based on your inferences.

Listening Event

You answer the telephone at 6:00 P.M. The person calling asks to speak to "Mr. or Mrs. ___."

Prior Knowledge

A caller who knows your family would ask for one person by name and probably wouldn't call at dinnertime.

Inference

The caller is a telephone solicitor.

Prediction

The person will try to sell you something.

Taking Notes

You make inferences and predictions in your head, but taking notes can help you process and remember both what you hear and what you think about it.

Here's How Taking Notes While Listening

- Use phrases, key words, or your own symbols and abbreviations.
- Write main points, including important details. If you're given any handouts, use them to take notes on, filling in details and examples.
- Think about ideas as you write them, and jot down questions, related ideas, or comments.
- Try making simple concept webs, diagrams, or charts to show the relationships among ideas.

ORAL COMM.

❸ Evaluating the Message

As a thinking being, you constantly evaluate what you hear. That process involves judging both the "what" of the message—its content—and the "how"—its delivery.

Assessing Content

To be a good listener, you must judge the content of an oral message as objectively as possible. Think about points like the following:

- **Reliability of sources** Where does the speaker get his or her information? Are the sources respected authorities?

- **Supporting information** What facts, opinions, and specific details does the speaker use to support ideas and arguments? How effective is this information? Are the arguments presented logically?

- **Persuasiveness** How convincing is the message? Which points do you disagree with? What questions do you still have?

For more information about persuasive techniques, see pp. 488–490.

Weighing Verbal and Visual Input

In evaluating an oral message, weigh both the speaker's words and his or her method of presentation.

Notice how both verbal and nonverbal techniques help Maya Angelou get her powerful message across.

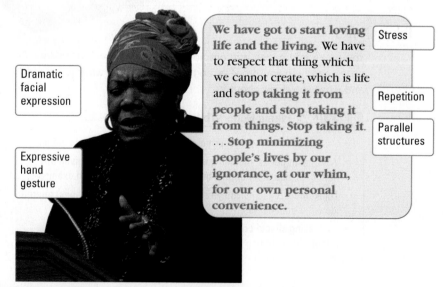

Dramatic facial expression

Expressive hand gesture

We have got to start loving life and the living. We have to respect that thing which we cannot create, which is life and stop taking it from people and stop taking it from things. Stop taking it. ...Stop minimizing people's lives by our ignorance, at our whim, for our own personal convenience.

Stress

Repetition

Parallel structures

CHAPTER 27

Planning an Oral Presentation

There are many types of oral presentations—from informal discussions to formal speeches, teleconferences, and debates. Any effective presentation, however, must include both oral and visual elements that are appropriate to your subject, audience, and purpose.

❶ Considering Audience and Purpose

This story, which former president Ronald Reagan used to tell, illustrates the importance of audience and purpose in an oral presentation:

> The speaker at an agricultural show arrived to find that only one farmer showed up. He wondered aloud if he should go ahead with his talk. "When I bring a hay wagon out to the field and only one cow shows up, I feed it," the farmer replied. After finishing the two-hour presentation, the speaker asked for the farmer's thoughts. "Well, I said I'd feed the cow; but I wouldn't give it the entire wagon load."

The chart below shows how knowing your audience and purpose can help you determine the best way to deliver your presentation.

Oral Presentation—Topic: Blaketon College		
Audience	**Purpose**	**Delivery Method**
High school students	To inform prospective students about the college	Informal multimedia presentation, including pictures of students involved in campus activities and live or taped interviews with current students and graduates
Businesspeople and community members	To persuade people and businesses to donate money	Formal multimedia presentation, including charts of statistics about faculty qualifications, student population and graduates, and allocation of funds

❷ Preparing the Content

Preparing the material for an oral presentation is very much like preparing for a written report.

Researching and Organizing the Text

Begin by gathering and organizing information on your topic.

- **Make a research plan.** Make a list of questions about your topic and write down ideas about where to begin looking for the answers.

- **Gather information.** Use as many sources as you can—books, newspapers, reference works, Internet sites, interviews, and personal observation.

- **Organize your material.** Group together information about similar topics and create an outline of the order in which to present it.

For more information about gathering material, see pp. 464–473.

Incorporating Audiovisual Aids

To make the most of audiovisual materials in an oral presentation, identify the information that can be best presented through the media and the best medium to present it.

- audiotapes
- actual objects
- charts and graphs
- maps
- illustrations and photographs

- slides and overhead transparencies
- videotapes
- software presentations
- graphics programs
- simulations

Although audiovisual aids can add interest to an oral presentation, remember that they may require some explanation. Integrate these materials into your oral delivery by using such phrases as "As you can see in this chart" or "The graph clearly shows this trend."

Make sure the visuals you use are large enough to be seen clearly in the back of the room. Also check sound equipment before you begin to make sure it is working.

LESSON 3 — Rehearsal and Delivery

❶ Methods of Presentation

You can choose several methods of presentation, depending on your audience, purpose, topic, and personal style.

Delivering a Presentation	
Method	**Effective Uses**
Manuscript—Read word for word from a prepared script	Official addresses, award acceptance speeches
Memorized—Delivered word for word from memory with occasional glances at a script	Short political speeches, introductions of speakers
Extemporaneous—Prepared beforehand, but presented in a conversational manner with reference to notes or an outline	Classroom instruction and business presentations
Impromptu—Delivered knowledgeably, but without preparation	Training sessions, question-and-answer forums

❷ Practicing the Delivery

You don't have to be an actor to make dramatic techniques work for you. Try out these verbal and nonverbal methods to hold your audience's interest and make your presentation memorable.

Verbal Elements

Think about the following aspects of your oral delivery when rehearsing.

- **Articulation** Pronounce words clearly and distinctly, especially those your audience might not know.
- **Volume** Speak loudly enough to be heard, but don't shout.
- **Tone and pitch** Use a tone and pitch that convey the appropriate attitude and emotions about your topic.
- **Pace** Speak slowly enough for your audience to understand you, but not so slowly that you put them to sleep.
- **Emphasis** Change the volume, tone, pitch, and pace of your speech to emphasize important words or concepts. Well-placed pauses can also lend emphasis and variety.

Nonverbal Elements

Remember that your body language is an essential part of your presentation.

Eye contact and posture help the speaker establish a close connection with the audience.

Hand gestures reach out to the audience and draw them in.

❸ Dealing with Stage Fright

If you're afraid to speak in front of a group, you're not alone. Many successful speakers, actors, performers, and teachers get stage fright. The famous actor Sir Richard Burton had a secret method of dealing with stage fright—curling his toes. His secret was revealed, however, when he had to wear sandals for his role in Shakespeare's *Julius Caesar.*

Dealing with Stage Fright		
Common Fears	**Symptoms**	**What to Do**
I'll . . . • forget everything. • make a fool of myself. • get sick. **The audience will . . .** • think I'm stupid. • laugh at me. • get up and leave.	sweating trembling increased pulse rate elevated blood pressure shallow breathing queasy stomach	Remember that stage fright is normal. Stretch arms, legs, neck, and face muscles. Take slow, deep breaths. Focus on a friendly face in the audience.

Arrive for your presentation early so you can familiarize yourself with the room, test equipment, and practice a line or two—preparation is a good way to relieve tension and ease nervousness.

Group Communication Skills

LESSON 4

Humans are social beings—most of our work, play, and learning is done in groups or teams. To be successful, such activities require similar group communications skills.

❶ Setting a Purpose

Every group activity has a purpose, even if that purpose is only to enjoy the company of others. Certain groups have tasks to accomplish, however, and group members need to determine that purpose either before they meet or as the first task. Such purposes might include:

- **Planning projects** (class meeting to plan and create homecoming float)
- **Sharing information** (reporting on a group science project)
- **Solving problems** (discussing how to deal with a friend's problems)
- **Taking part in competition** (attending a state debate meet)

❷ Playing an Active Role

Because you may participate in many different groups and won't always know your role, it's important to develop your skills as both a speaker and a listener. Essential skills include **giving feedback, asking questions,** and **checking interpretations.** These skills help groups function as a unit and achieve their goals.

Giving Feedback

When you're working in a group—as either speaker or listener—look for opportunities to provide or ask for the following types of feedback:

- agreement or disagreement
- information and ideas
- opinions

- encouragement
- solutions
- summaries

Try to give clear, direct, specific verbal feedback. Nonverbal feedback—eye contact, smiling, nodding—shows your support but doesn't give the speaker concrete help.

Asking Questions

Asking questions can help group members clarify points, gain information, or make sure the group is moving in the right direction:

Questions to Ask	
Listener	**Speaker**
Can you say more about that?	What more could we add?
Do I hear you saying . . . ?	What points are still unclear?
Does that mean . . . ?	Who has a different point of view?

Checking Interpretations

Each member of a group has different life experiences and listening skills, and so interprets information differently. Group members should compare their interpretations often to make sure that everyone is "on the same page."

Notice the different ways three group members interpret a statement and then the techniques they use to resolve those differences.

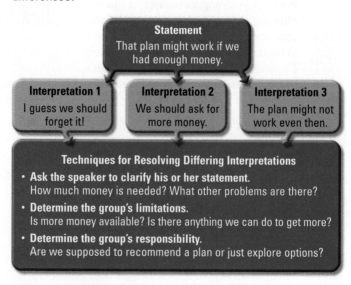

Statement
That plan might work if we had enough money.

Interpretation 1
I guess we should forget it!

Interpretation 2
We should ask for more money.

Interpretation 3
The plan might not work even then.

Techniques for Resolving Differing Interpretations
- **Ask the speaker to clarify his or her statement.**
  How much money is needed? What other problems are there?
- **Determine the group's limitations.**
  Is more money available? Is there anything we can do to get more?
- **Determine the group's responsibility.**
  Are we supposed to recommend a plan or just explore options?

❸ Dealing with Conflict

Because group members can interpret statements differently, conflict sometimes arises. Conflict can be a positive sign because it indicates that the group members are involved and expressing their individual viewpoints.

Sometimes, however, conflict can lead discussions off track. One group member should act as a monitor to keep the group focused on the meeting's purpose.

Here's How Dealing with Conflict

- **Listen to each other.** Keep the lines of communication open. All group members must feel comfortable voicing their opinions.
- **Treat each other with respect.** Disagreement doesn't have to mean being disagreeable. Respect helps groups resolve conflict.
- **Use reason rather than emotion as a basis for discussion.** The group should make decisions based on the issues, not on individual personalities or agendas.
- **Work toward consensus.** To achieve a solution that all group members can support, some—or even all—may have to compromise.

Conflict
Two group members want a salsa music theme, and two want a Star Wars theme for the junior prom.

Discussion
A. A salsa music theme will let us be really creative with lights and sounds.
B. A Star Wars theme can be even more creative, since the universe is the limit!
C. Yeah, we could even show scenes from the movies on the walls and ceiling.
D. But think of the foods we could serve in a salsa-inspired setting.

Resolution
A. I guess if we want to be creative, either theme will work.
B. True, but I still think Star Wars would make us seem more out there.
C. How about combining the themes into "Salsa-in-Space"?
D. I can live with that. What about the rest of you?

Debating

Formal debating is a special type of oral communication that involves both oral presentation and group discussion skills. Even if you never take part in a formal debate, the analytic, organizational, persuasive, and speaking skills debate requires will serve you well in many academic, business, and social situations.

❶ Preparing for the Debate

A debate is basically an argument—but a very structured one that requires a good deal of preparation. The basis of a debate is the **proposition,** a formal statement of the issue to be debated. One team of debaters—the affirmative—argues for the proposition; the negative team argues against it. Debaters research both their side and their opponents' side of the proposition, creating a **brief,** or a complete outline of the debate. They also prepare a **rebuttal,** or a follow-up speech intended to support their own arguments and rebut, or undercut, their opponents'.

Preparing a Brief

Winning a debate depends largely on thorough preparation of a brief.

> **Here's How** **Preparing a Brief**
>
> 1. **Gather information.** Consult a variety of primary and secondary sources to gather the most reliable, up-to-date information about the proposition. Record the information on note cards.
> 2. **Identify key ideas.** Sort out the important points and arrange them in order of importance.
> 3. **List arguments for and against each key idea.** Look for strong arguments that support your side of the proposition and for ones that support your opponents' side.
> 4. **Support your arguments.** Find facts, quotations, expert opinions, and examples that support your arguments and counter your opponents'.
> 5. **Write the brief.** Begin your brief with a statement of the proposition. Then list the arguments and evidence that support both sides of the proposition.

For more information about organizing material, see pp. 326–327.

Write just one idea, fact, or argument on each note card and number each card in pencil. That way, you can easily rearrange the order to answer your opponents' arguments in your rebuttal.

Planning a Rebuttal

If you've prepared a thorough brief, you will already have predicted many of your opponents' arguments. The rebuttal is your chance to refute those arguments, as well as others they present, and to solidify your own position.

> **Here's How** **Planning a Rebuttal**
>
> - **Listen carefully and identify the issues** your opponents have attacked.
> - **Target weaknesses** in their arguments, points they overlooked, and lack of solid evidence.
> - **Present counterarguments** and additional evidence that support your side.
> - **Summarize your original argument** and its strengths.

 Don't be fooled by political or other public debates you may have seen in which the participants attack their opponents personally rather than dealing with the issues. These tactics are not good debating etiquette and are not effective in the long run.

❷ Participating in a Debate

There are several debate formats. Generally, however, each side makes its case in one or more **constructive speeches,** and replies to its opposition in one or more **rebuttals.** A chairperson is usually chosen to make sure the procedures are followed. The diagram shows a common order of presentation of speeches in a debate.

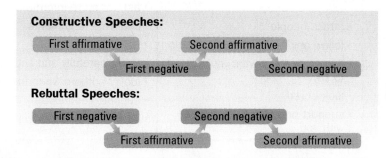

Constructive Speeches:

First affirmative — Second affirmative

First negative — Second negative

Rebuttal Speeches:

First negative — Second negative

First affirmative — Second affirmative

Student Help Desk

Oral Communication at a Glance

Listening Critically
asking questions/ providing feedback

Planning
research/organization

Rehearsing
verbal/nonverbal elements

Delivering a Speech
dealing with stage fright

Participating in a Group
speaking/listening, reaching consensus

Note-Taking Tips From Hear to Here

Keep listening while you write so you don't miss important points.

Highlight main points with underlining, a star, or your own creative doodle.

Review your notes as soon as you can in order to
1) fill in details while they're fresh in your mind.
2) record your own critical responses.
3) rewrite unclear or illegible statements.

Commit important points to memory so you don't have to rely exclusively on your written notes.

Group Participation Guidelines Talk This Way

Don't . . .	Do . . .
• ask for attention	• ask for more information
• attack people	• challenge arguments
• follow any thought that comes up	• follow the agenda
• think only about what you're going to say	• listen carefully and actively
• look bored	• look at others when they speak
• support only those who agree with you	• support good ideas
	• be willing to compromise

CHAPTER 27

Interviewing Techniques

Ask open-ended questions. "I see; can you say more about that?" "Tell me more about the implications of that theory."

Restate information. "So that means . . .?" "In other words, you're saying that . . .?"

Offer interpretations. "From what you've said, it seems that . . . ."

Probe specific issues. "Tell me more about the first step of the procedure." "Did you ever try reversing the order of the steps?"

Pause. Silence encourages others to keep talking and shows that you are listening.

The 5th Wave by Rich Tennant

© The Fifth Wave by Rich Tennant

The Bottom Line

Checklist for Oral Communication

Have I . . .

_____ listened carefully and critically to oral presentations?

_____ identified the audience and purpose of my presentation?

_____ researched my topic thoroughly?

_____ organized my main points and supporting evidence?

_____ selected the best method of delivery?

_____ incorporated appropriate audio or visual aids into my presentation?

_____ worked with others to achieve group consensus?

lavish

posh

simulated

Let the Buyer Beware

Words like these will help you think more critically about the ways advertisers go after your money.

The Best Money Can Buy

How would you spend a ton of money? Would you buy **extravagant** gifts for your family and **luxurious** presents for yourself? Would you travel **first-class** to a **deluxe** resort, where the guests wore **elegant** clothes and drove **posh** cars and carried **costly** luggage? Perhaps you'd order a **top-of-the-line** entertainment center with a **top-shelf** DVD and a **cutting-edge** high-definition TV. **Precious** gems might be a temptation, or **expensive** series tickets to concerts or ball games. On the other hand, you might make a **lavish** donation to charity.

Check the Label

Look for things of **authentic** value, making sure that you have bought the **genuine article,** the **real McCoy,** the **bona fide** item. Stay away from the **artificial.** Watch out for **simulated** jewels, **sham** leather, **ersatz** designer clothes, **counterfeit** celebrity autographs, and other **bogus** offerings.

▷ **Your Turn** Is the Appeal Real?

In a small group, discuss any advertising campaign for clothing or entertainment that is currently gaining popularity. What words are used to make that product appealing? Offer your opinions of whether the product lives up to its claims.

bogus

sham

luxurious

precious

Persuasion and the Media

Thinking for Yourself

What influences the decisions you make about the clothes you wear? Many people find the media play a major role in shaping their perceptions on topics ranging from fashion to health to politics. Every day, the media send thousands of messages that are specially designed to influence teens. If you're aware of the ways that the media use persuasion, you are more likely to make informed and balanced decisions regarding any topic.

Write Away: Fashion Fads

Write a paragraph about a time the media convinced you to change your opinion of a new fashion or another matter. Save your paragraph in your  **Working Portfolio.**

VIDEO **Media Focus**

Becoming Media Aware

Remember that the term *media* includes more than television and newspapers. Becoming **media aware** means thinking critically about messages in a wide range of media sources, from billboards to CDs to Internet sites.

❶ Recognizing Media Elements

The term **media** refers to various types of communication, including the following:

newspapers	flyers	videocassette tapes
magazines	letters	audio tapes
books	junk mail	compact discs (CDs)
billboards	radio	e-mail
posters	television	Internet
brochures	films	

As technology evolves, the media's potential to reach more people and to create messages with greater impact also develops. Think about the various media in which the following types of persuasive messages appear. Which types of messages and media do you encounter most often? Which do you find the most compelling?

Finding Persuasion in the Media	
Type of Persuasive Message	**Where You Might Find It**
Consumer advertisement	TV and radio commercials, print ads in magazines and newspapers, Web sites, billboards, flyers, junk mail
Political campaign	Speeches, TV and radio ads, bumper stickers, campaign buttons, posters
Public service announcement	Newspaper articles, letters to the editor, TV and radio commentaries
Editorial or commentary	Newspaper and magazine articles, letters to the editor, TV and radio commentaries

All persuasive media messages—from consumer advertisements to editorials—rely on audio elements, visual elements, or both to communicate effectively. **Multimedia** such as television, film, and the Internet combine text, graphics, sound, and video to increase the power of a persuasive message.

Audio Elements

When you listen to television, radio, or film, the spoken words and other sounds often blend together to capture your attention and convey a specific message. However, isolating audio elements such as the following can help you understand why a message affects you the way it does.

- **Speaker's tone and volume** May create a certain impression of speaker; for example, a firm yet quiet voice may convey leadership

- **Sound bites** These excerpts from longer passages can be powerful and engaging, but watch for remarks taken out of context

- **Music** Can create a mood or imply an association with certain ideas or values

- **Sound effects** Can create humor, emphasize a point, or contribute to the mood

- **Repetition** May reinforce a particular idea presented in the music or narration

Zits by Jerry Scott and Jim Borgman

Reprinted with special permission of King Features Syndicate

Advertisers may use a catchy tune or popular music by your favorite artists to grab your attention and build the mood they want you to associate with their products or services.

Visual Elements

Print and multimedia may also use any or all of the following visual elements to create a more persuasive message.

- **Printed text** May use headlines and other graphic elements to grab your attention and create persuasive appeals
- **Film techniques** Can use camera angles, lighting, special effects, and other techniques to create a mood and influence your perception of reality
- **Design** May use intriguing settings, props, colors, symbols, logos, and images to focus your attention on an idea
- **Special effects** Can manipulate reality through the sequence of events, design, and other film techniques
- **Body language** Can relay nonverbal signals and set a tone

Examine this print advertisement for examples of persuasion.

Magazine Ad

Camera angle and lighting reinforces focus on children, creates serious tone

Setting creates a surprising contrast—children in an adult situation

Printed text grabs attention with size and a startling statement

For more on visual elements, see pp. 526–527.

PRACTICE Finding Visual Elements

Identify at least two other visual elements in this ad. How do these elements contribute to the meaning/message of the ad?

❷ Recognizing Source, Audience, and Purpose

Just as you think about a specific audience and purpose when you write, the media devise messages with specific audiences and purposes in mind. Recognizing the source, audience, and purpose of a persuasive message will help you determine its reliability.

Source and Sponsor

The **source** of a media message is its creator or point of origin. Creating a media message requires resources such as money, so each message also needs a sponsor. A **sponsor** is the group or individual who pays for a message to appear in the media. When you hear or view a message, keep in mind *who* is behind it and *what* his or her possible motivations might be. For instance, how differently might a record company promoter and a newspaper music critic present messages about the same CD?

Target Audience

The members of a **target audience,** or the people a sponsor hopes to persuade, often share characteristics such as age, gender, values, and lifestyle. You can usually determine a sponsor's target audience by looking at the kinds of audio and visual elements used to create a message. For example, do you think a sponsor who stresses the health benefits of a cereal hopes to appeal to children or to adults?

Purpose or Intent

The **purpose or intent** of a media message is why it was made. A media message can include multiple purposes. For instance, a Super Bowl commercial may try to entertain you, while a political speech may try to inform you. However, the primary purpose of each message is to persuade you to take a specific action—such as to buy a certain product, to change a behavior or point of view, or to vote for a particular candidate or issue.

Try watching an especially entertaining television commercial with the volume muted. Its persuasive intent may become surprisingly obvious.

MEDIA

LESSON 2 Identifying Persuasion in the Media

Most persuasive appeals aren't as obvious as the ones used in this cartoon. In fact, one trend has been to make television and print advertisements so subtle that you may wonder what the sponsor is advertising. Using critical listening and thinking skills will help you recognize both the obvious and more subtle persuasive appeals in media messages.

Shoe by Jeff MacNelly

❶ Identifying Persuasive Appeals

While consumer advertisements, editorials, political campaigns, and other persuasive media messages may appeal to your sense of logic, they often rely heavily on emotional appeals, as well. Use your awareness of the following techniques to help you evaluate persuasive media messages and identify misleading information.

Bandwagon Tries to make you think you should do what everybody else is doing. **Example:** An ad for a new film might read, "See the movie that everyone's talking about . . . ."

Loaded language Uses words such as *rotten* or *beautiful* that carry strong positive or negative connotations. **Example:** The persuasive message in a commercial might begin, "It's the smartest way to . . . ."

Snob appeal Implies that only the elite or wealthy can appreciate or afford a certain product. **Example:** A luxury car ad might assert, "Some people know they're worth the best . . . ."

Testimonial Presents endorsements from hired experts or celebrities. **Example:** A popular local athlete might appear in a print ad that reads, "I always eat at . . . ."

Unfinished claims Offers statements or comparisons that don't provide all the supporting evidence. **Example:** A campaign for an airline service might state, "Giving you more freedom to fly," leaving you to wonder, "Giving me more freedom than what?"

Polling results Presents survey results, usually in the form of percentages or other numerical formats, about a topic. **Example:** An editorial might state, "Sixty-eight percent of the teenagers surveyed said that they prefer to wear school uniforms . . . ."

Transfer appeal Tries to transfer feelings associated with a certain product or person to another product or person. **Example:** The voice-over introducing a song might say, "If you like the Space Monkeys, then you'll love the new CD by Generation Y . . . ."

A persuasive media message can have a positive intent. For instance, some public service announcements use persuasive appeals to shed light on important social issues. Look for well-supported claims and facts to determine a message's reliability.

For more on emotional and logical appeals, see p. 488.

❷ Distinguishing Facts from Opinions

When looking at persuasion in the media, keep in mind the difference between facts and opinions. **Facts** are statements that can be proven. **Opinions** are statements of belief that cannot be proven. The following statements reflect the types of claims that a persuasive media message might use.

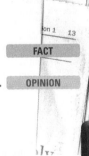

> . . . your voice heard, the Students' League is hosting a demonstration against U.S. Representative Sharon Bullhorn on Saturday.
>
> **Just last week, Representative Bullhorn voted against raising the minimum wage. Obviously, Representative Bullhorn doesn't care about teens.** If she did, she would have helped pass the much-needed minimum wage increase, so that teens could earn the money they deserve.

FACT

OPINION

A media message may present facts to create a logical argument, but then use those facts to reach a faulty conclusion. For instance, Senator Bullhorn may have voted against a minimum wage increase because she fears it would result in fewer jobs for teens, not because she doesn't care about them.

For more on fact and opinion, see p. 482.

MEDIA

LESSON 3 **Analyzing Media Persuasion**

❶ Persuasion in Print

Deconstructing a media message, or breaking the whole into parts, makes it easier to analyze. When deconstructing persuasion in print media, consider the ways that the content and other visual elements affect you.

Here's How   Deconstructing Persuasion in Print

1. Look for any logos or attributions to find the source and sponsor.
2. Identify as many visual elements as possible, such as logos, colors, etc.
3. Analyze each visual element and the content by asking:
   • What emotions and ideas do the visual elements convey?
   • Does the content present facts or opinions?
4. Finally, consider all of the elements together to decide:
   • What does the message ask readers to do or believe?
   • Who is the target audience?
   • What viewpoints are left out of this message?
   • Do you agree or disagree with this message?

Notice the features of the following public service ad. Use the deconstructing tips to get the main point of the message.

Magazine Ad

Purpose To persuade parents that their children need to get more exercise

Target Audience Adults, especially parents

Printed Text Words support the images to emphasize message

Image Child in front of television superimposed on a traffic sign

Logo Identifies American Heart Association as the sponsor

CAUTION:
CHILDREN NOT AT PLAY.

Once, children spent their time running and playing. Today, they're more likely to be found in front of the TV And that could mean trouble. Because lack of exercise can lead to weight problems and high blood cholesterol. Encourage your children to be more active. Fighting heart disease may be

as simple as child's play. To learn more, contact your nearest American Heart Association. *You can help prevent heart disease and stroke. We can tell you how.*

American Heart Association ♥

CHAPTER 28

❷ Persuasion in Television

Television combines visual and audio elements so well that you may find it tricky to analyze a message. You may need to watch a TV message a few times to deconstruct both types of elements.

> **Here's How** **Deconstructing Persuasion in Television**
>
> 1. Use the images and narration to determine the source and sponsor.
> 2. Identify the message's other visual and audio elements.
> 3. Analyze each element by asking:
>   - What emotions and ideas do the visual elements convey?
>   - What moods do the music and other sounds evoke?
>   - Does the narration present facts or opinions?
> 4. Finally, consider all of the elements together to decide:
>   - What does the message ask viewers to do or believe?
>   - Who is the target audience?
>   - What viewpoints are left out of this message?
>   - Do you agree or disagree with this message?

The following image and script segments are taken from a television commercial. A closing shot of a tearful Native American is used as a comment on the worsening state of America's natural environment.

Television Commercial

Keep America Beautiful, Inc.

Sound: Drumming shifts to dramatic mainstream music; music continues.

Male voice: *(sternly)* Some people have a deep, abiding respect for the natural beauty that was once this country.

Camera: Shot of people in moving car, throwing garbage at man's feet.

Male voice: *(sternly)* And some people don't.

Camera: Profile shot of man; zooms in closer as he turns toward camera

Male voice: *(firmly)* People start pollution. People can stop it.

> **Facial Expression/Body Language** Man's tear shows his sadness about the littering.

> **Film Techniques** Close-up focuses on sadness and creates intimacy

❸ Persuasion on the Internet

The Internet can target messages to you in ways that other media can't. By tracking your selections on search engines and Web sites, sponsors learn about your interests and use this information to send messages to you. The following example shows the type of persuasive message that might appear on a search engine if you entered the keywords "budget travel books."

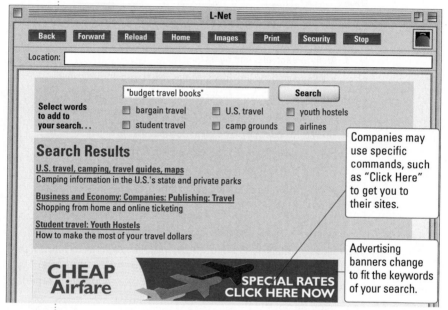

Companies may use specific commands, such as "Click Here" to get you to their sites.

Advertising banners change to fit the keywords of your search.

Never reveal personal information on the Internet.

For more on the Internet, see p. 469, and for more on evaluating information, see p. 479.

PRACTICE ⟩ Deconstructing Media Messages

Recording Impressions Find a current example of a persuasive message in print, on TV, or on the Internet. Briefly record your initial emotional response to the message.

Analyzing and Reflecting List the specific audio and visual elements used in the message, and then use those to identify its audience, sponsor, purpose, and overall message. With a group of classmates, discuss how the process of analyzing a message helped you understand it or changed your initial response to it.

Responding to Persuasive Messages

After you've analyzed a persuasive media message, you know exactly what values, ideas, and actions the message wants you to follow. If you agree with the message, should you simply do what it tells you to do? What if you disagree? Here are some ways to take the next step.

❶ Weighing Personal Factors

Even if you agree with a media message you've analyzed, important personal factors such as your own needs, resources, or experiences may lead you to respond differently than the message advises.

Taking Personal Factors into Account	
Persuasive media message	Green hair gets you noticed. Buy our new green hair coloring!
Do you agree?	Yes. People with green hair do stand out!
What response do your experiences suggest?	The last time I dyed my hair green, my parents were furious, my scalp itched, and I looked funny. I'm not changing my hair color.

❷ Consulting Multiple Sources

Consulting multiple sources may help you learn more about a subject, even if the additional sources have their own biases. For example, imagine that you're researching used cars. One auto manufacturer's Web site raves about the model you want to buy. Another site, sponsored by a consumer awareness organization, criticizes the car. Checking out several sources can help you gauge how credible each one might be.

For more on evaluating sources, see p. 479.

PRACTICE Comparing and Contrasting Media Coverage

In a small group, choose a political or social issue that interests you, then locate at least three examples of media coverage on it. Make sure the examples represent different viewpoints. Using what you've learned about media analysis, compare and contrast the examples. Write a brief critique of the three persuasive messages and the techniques used. Report your team's findings to the class.

MEDIA

Student Help Desk

Evaluating Media Persuasion at a Glance

Get in the Flow

To deal with the persuasive media messages bombarding you every day, use the following tips:

Identify audio and visual elements

Identify persuasive techniques

Media Message

Choose a Response

Identify source, purpose, and target audience

Decide whether you agree or disagree

Sights and Sounds — Media Monitoring

Elements	Tips
Visual	**Look for . . .**
Printed text	persuasive appeals in headlines and graphic elements
Design	the use of symbols, logos, settings, props, colors, and other images
Film techniques	the manipulation of reality through special effects, camera angles, make-up and actors, and other techniques
Audio	**Listen for . . .**
Music	the mood or image that a sponsor is trying to convey via a song's lyrics, rhythm, or popular appeal
Language/spoken words	repetition, remarks taken out of context, emotional appeals, and the speaker's tone and volume
Sound effects	the way sound effects emphasize a point or create a mood

Visual Symbols

The Power of Pictures

Some persuasive media messages use images to symbolize certain ideas or values. Think of political campaigns and consumer advertising in which you've seen these symbols.

Innocence, purity

Strength, power

Rebirth, romance

Patriotism

Subtle Persuaders — Ads in Disguise

Magazines and newspapers	Advertorials	Print advertisements designed to look like news or feature articles or editorials; the small print on these pages often says "paid advertisement"
Television	Infomercials	Lengthy commercials for a product, service, or idea disguised as an information-based program
Film	Product placement	Intentional display of a brand name product in a movie

The Bottom Line

Checklist for Analyzing Media Messages

Have I . . .

____ analyzed the audio and visual elements of the message?

____ identified the message's purpose, source, and target audience?

____ weighed the message's emotional and logical appeals?

____ checked the message's credibility by consulting more than one source?

____ made an informed decision that is based on a thorough analysis of the message and my own needs?

Power Words
Vocabulary for Precise Writing

forceful

dynamite

arresting

vital

captivatin

Showstoppers

If you want to spark the kind of excitement that's depicted on the opposite page, create a presentation that fits words like these.

Is It Something You Said?

This is your chance to create a **compelling, vital** ad campaign for your favorite cause. First, you need an **appealing, memorable** slogan—one that will be **entrancing** to your audience. Your **vigorous** advertising copy must lure people by being **thought-provoking.** It must be so **riveting** and **mesmerizing** that viewers and readers find it **irresistible. Dazzling** video and **arresting** photography help deliver a **potent** message. A Web site can be an **energizing** means of attracting attention. An **exhilarating** design can draw an enthusiastic response.

Make a Splash

Use your friends as guinea pigs to see if your ideas are **forceful** enough, if you have created an attractive and **alluring** story that's **persuasive.** The more **imaginative** your presentation, the more **tempting** it will be—a **captivating** display can win many **awe-struck** customers. Add to that some **beguiling** graphics, and you'll have a **dynamite** campaign. Its strong images can make a lasting impression; and your **incisive** words, a **convincing** case.

▷ **Your Turn** Show and Tell

Make an acrostic, a series of written lines in which the first letter in each line forms a word. Choose a word from above (or its base word) and write each letter vertically. For each letter, write a tip or suggestion for a successful presentation.

Creating Media Products

Media Mania

What do you suppose this audience is watching? Whatever it is, it has their undivided attention. Imagine an audience hanging on your every word. What kind of presentation might hold their interest? An oral report on the latest finds from the pyramids of Giza? It might, but it might not. However, if you added graphics, sound, and video, you'd probably stand a better chance.

This chapter presents an overview of the kinds of media products you can create with such basic equipment as a video camera and a computer. Reading the chapter and exploring your options will help you decide which media products are right for your needs.

Write Away: Multimedia Dreaming

Make a list of topics you would like to explore using multimedia. For instance, you might want to explore a sport, current event, or historical figure. Then place your list in your 📁 **Working Portfolio.**

MEDIA PRODUCTS

VIDEO 📼 **Media Focus**

Going Beyond Print

You were born in the information age, so it is only fitting that you use information-age tools to express yourself. Of course, videos and computers haven't replaced print as the primary medium for mass communication—not yet, anyway. As students, you still need paper to take notes and tests and to write essays, reports, letters, and party invitations. But you've probably also found yourself in situations such as these.

- watching a how-to video instead of reading a manual
- using e-mail to communicate
- researching a topic on the Internet
- using a CD-ROM atlas
- visiting a Web site

❶ Why Use Media Other Than Print?

Visual and electronic media offer possibilities of expression that print media can't. For example, a written report on the Harlem Renaissance could include a lot of insightful information. But a **multimedia presentation**—including text, graphics, sound, and video—could really make the subject come alive.

HARLEM RENAISSANCE — Artists

Presenter explains the subject.

Recording of jazz plays in the background.

From this screen the presenter can link to a biography of Johnson or a video clip of Harlem in the 1920s.

Street Life-Harlem by William H. Johnson

Don't use visual or electronic media as a crutch or a flashy substitute for thoroughness. Remember that you still need to communicate worthwhile information about your subject.

❷ Selecting a Format

Your selection of a particular form of presentation may depend on your personal preference or the kind of equipment available to you. Your subject matter could also dictate your choice. For example, information on the Civil War, an event for which there is a wealth of documentation, would work very well in a multimedia presentation. Knowing the advantages of each kind of product can help you decide.

Advantages of Media Products	
Product	**Advantages**
Video	• Easy to work with • Captures live action as well as still photos • Includes sound (audio) • Allows artistic expression
Multimedia Presentation	• Allows interactive presentation of information, permitting the presenter to return to or skip screens • Shows a variety of information: text, graphics, images, sound, video • Easy to customize material for different audiences and situations
Web Site	• Can include links to related information in the site and in other Web sites • Has space for in-depth text • Easy to update information • Allows the audience to interact with and control the presentation • Can reach a larger audience than the other two products

PRACTICE Choosing a Format

Look at the topics you listed in the **Write Away** and placed in your **Working Portfolio.** Select one of the topics and choose the format that you believe would be best suited to the subject. Write a paragraph in which you identify the format and some of the graphics, sound, and video elements you might use to enliven it.

Creating Media Products **531**

Videos

All you need to make a video is a video camera, or camcorder, and some blank tapes. Then get your creative juices flowing by thinking of the kinds of projects you could create. Which of the following would you be interested in making?

- a visual narrative
- a news story
- a music video
- a montage (series of related images)
- an advertisement for a product or candidate
- a documentary
- an adaptation of a literary work

❶ Focusing Your Topic and Storyboarding

Refine the topic you or your group has chosen so that it can be presented with your equipment and within your time frame. Then create a **storyboard**—a series of descriptions or sketches of the scenes that will appear in your video. This storyboard scene details the beginning of a documentary on homelessness.

Page #: 1   **Date:** Oct. 19
Title: Homelessness on Our Streets   **Characters:** Joe and passersby
Setting: downtown, present day   **Scene:** 1, corner of Elm and Oak

VIDEO

Camera: Long shot of Joe
Lighting: Joe shaded by building

AUDIO
Music: Sound of Joe's playing; then fade as voice-over begins
Voice-Over: You probably don't see him. You may not even hear him. But he's there in the shadows of your town.

❷ Elements of a Video

The basic elements of a video are the script, the camera, and the sound. If you produce your video with a group, you can divide the responsibilities. If you work alone, you'll need to tackle each element on your own.

Script

A script includes all the words to be spoken in your video, plus basic directions and notes about camera angles and sound. You may want to write your script before you begin storyboarding. Here's part of the script for another scene in the documentary.

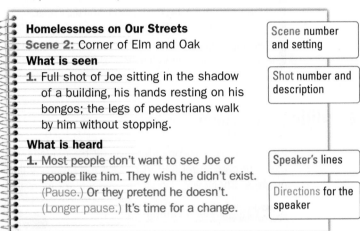

Homelessness on Our Streets
Scene 2: Corner of Elm and Oak

What is seen

1. Full shot of Joe sitting in the shadow of a building, his hands resting on his bongos; the legs of pedestrians walk by him without stopping.

What is heard

1. Most people don't want to see Joe or people like him. They wish he didn't exist. (Pause.) Or they pretend he doesn't. (Longer pause.) It's time for a change.

Scene number and setting

Shot number and description

Speaker's lines

Directions for the speaker

Camera Operation

When you frame a shot, you decide how far the camera will be from the subject and how the camera will move. You also decide what the shot will include and what it will leave out. Here are some common framing techniques.

Framing Techniques

A **long shot** is good for showing the action and background of a scene.

A **full shot,** showing the full length of a subject, is used most often.

A **close-up** shows facial expressions, which provide insight into character.

Professionals follow the "five-second rule": Start filming five seconds before you want the action to start, and stop filming five seconds after you want the scene to end.

Sound

An audio track consists of three basic parts: voices, sound effects, and music. You can use the microphone on your camcorder to record sounds. Here are some tips on getting good sound quality.

Audio-Track Tips

Go to a prospective location, close your eyes, and listen. These are the sounds your camcorder will pick up.

Choose a location where you can control the sound. Try to find a place where the background noise is minimal.

Rehearse on location, using all the sounds you want to record. Then play your tape on your VCR to hear what the audio track sounds like.

❸ Editing Your Video

Professionals use computers to edit their videos, but you can use your camcorder and VCR. Here's a broad outline of the process. Check your camcorder manual for more information.

Here's How Video Editing

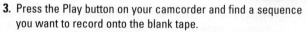

1. Hook up your camcorder to your VCR.
2. Place the tape with your rough footage in the camcorder. Put a blank tape in the VCR.
3. Press the Play button on your camcorder and find a sequence you want to record onto the blank tape.
4. Rewind to the beginning of the sequence. Then push the Play button on your camcorder and the Record button on your VCR. Press Pause on the VCR to stop recording.
5. Search for another sequence on your camcorder while your VCR is paused.

❹ Evaluating Your Video

Before you finalize your video, show it to a group of peer reviewers. Ask the group to discuss these points.

• Is the story or message clear?

• Does the narration flow coherently? Which scenes need work?

• How is the sound quality? Too loud? Too soft? Inconsistent?

• Are the camera techniques effective, distracting, or dull?

Multimedia Presentations

LESSON 3

Multimedia refers to the use of multiple media—text, graphics, sound, and video—in presenting information. A multimedia presentation is created with a hypertext program, such as PowerPoint, Action, or Harvard Graphics. This software also allows you to present the multimedia product interactively to a group of people, using a computer and a projection screen. Here are just a few of the projects you could create for a multimedia presentation.

- a biography
- a literary analysis
- a report
- a proposal
- an instructional program

❶ Designing Your Presentation

Before beginning a multimedia project, you need to design your presentation. First, create a rough outline of the content. Then make a flow chart that shows how your screens will connect to each other. Depending on the complexity of your project, you may also need to create a storyboard for each screen in your presentation.

This storyboard details the organization of a challenging math project. It takes you step by step through the presentation, which shows a real-world application of quadratic equations.

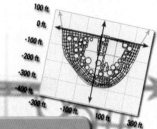

Diagram: Graph of a quadratic equation (parabola)

Audio: Brief explanation of graph

Diagram: Drawing of Pueblo Bonito superimposed over graph

Audio: Overview of parabolic design of this Great House built by Anasazi Indians

Video Clip: Footage of Great Houses, with commentary on construction

Photo: Bird's-eye shot of Pueblo Bonito

Audio: Brief description of dimensions

MEDIA PRODUCTS

535

❷ Elements in Your Presentation

You can choose any number of ways to present information using text, sound, graphics, images, and video.

Text

No matter how much fancy technology you use, the text is the most important element of your presentation. It's often the glue that holds everything else together. For a typical multimedia presentation, you'll need to write brief informational paragraphs and lists. This text should always be placed in the central part of the screen so that your audience can follow along while you read it aloud.

Don't overload the screen with too much text.

Sound

Sound elements, including music, sound effects, and voice recordings, can help your audience understand information in your text. You can record your own sound, download audio clips from the Internet, or buy a CD-ROM of audio clips. Here are some examples of sound clips you could use.

- a brief speech or interview featuring someone you discuss in your presentation
- a musical selection that ties in with your topic
- a voice-over narration explaining a graphic or image
- sound effects that draw attention to a graphic or image

Here are some tips on using audio clips.

> **Here's How** **Using Audio Clips**
>
> - Use a hyperlink on a keyword or an image to launch an audio clip. That way your audience will have something to look at while they're listening.
> - Keep audio segments to about 10 or 15 seconds.
> - Use sound effects, but go easy on them. Remember, it's a presentation, not an action movie. A few sound effects go a long way.
> - Edit out awkward pauses and *um*'s from voices you record yourself. But don't change a historical speech!
> - Be sure to get permission to use copyrighted audio clips.

Graphics and Images

Graphics and images, such as charts, diagrams, maps, time lines, photos, and drawings, present information in a form that can be quickly and easily understood. Here are some examples of visuals you can create, download, or scan.

Clicking on the photo launches a video clip on the Anasazi Great Houses.

- a flow chart that details a process you are discussing
- a graph that supports a point you're making
- a photo or drawing of a person or setting that is important to the topic

In your presentation, you can use a still image to introduce a video clip. Imagine the photo above springing to life.

Video Clips

Video clips can energize your presentation. You can find CD-ROMs with collections of video clips, or you can film your own. Here are some examples of video clips you can use.

- a video that develops or expands on an image you have shown
- a video of a person or event you are discussing
- a video of a musical performance to accompany an audio clip

Here are some tips on using video clips.

Here's How Using Video Clips

- Use only a few video clips in a presentation. Too many will bore your audience after a while.
- Keep video segments to 30 seconds or shorter.
- Think about separating a video from its soundtrack. You might want to talk or play background music while the video is playing.
- Learn from TV news programs. Watch how the shows are edited, how one video image fades into another, and how the spoken text and video are integrated.
- If the material is copyrighted, get permission before you use it.

MEDIA PRODUCTS

❸ Evaluating and Revising

Have a group of peer reviewers act as audience for your presentation before you finalize it. To help them focus on what you need to know, give them a questionnaire.

Sample Questionnaire

1. Is the purpose of the presentation clear?
❑ yes ❑ no

2. Do all the elements—text, graphics, images, audio, and video—support the purpose? If not, which elements need work?
❑ yes ❑ no _____
_____

3. Does the presentation flow smoothly and coherently? If not, where are the rough spots?
❑ yes ❑ no _____
_____

4. Is the presenter knowledgeable about the subject and at ease with the equipment? What does he or she need to work on?
❑ yes ❑ no _____
_____

---

❹ Running Your Presentation

To run your presentation, you'll need a computer that is hooked up to a TV monitor or to a projector that projects your visuals onto a large screen. It's not enough to have all the right hardware, though. You also have to know what you're doing once you get in front of your audience. Here are some tips on delivering your presentation.

> **Here's How** **Giving Your Presentation**
>
> - Make sure that your equipment works and that you know how to use it.
> - Rehearse several times, preferably in the room you'll be using.
> - Turn off the lights around the screen, but leave some lights in the room on, perhaps at the back. A dark room tends to make people drowsy.
> - Know where every link is. You shouldn't be fumbling around looking for something during the presentation.
> - If something goes wrong, relax, keep talking, and move on. Remember, it's what you say that's really important.

Web Sites

LESSON 4

❶ Why Create a Web Site?

A site on the World Wide Web is similar to a multimedia presentation in that you can use a combination of text, graphics, images, sound, and video. One difference lies in the software and the language you use to input commands. The biggest difference, though, is in the audience for a Web site—potentially the whole world! Here are some reasons why you might consider creating a Web site.

- to provide information that's easy to update
- to allow the audience some control over the information
- to get feedback and interact with people around the world
- to link to other sites that support and expand on your topic
- to learn skills that you will use later in college or on the job

To protect your privacy, **do not** give out any personal information— your last name, street address, or phone number. Talk to people anonymously through an e-mail address on your Web site.

❷ Web Site Basics

Web sites can be created with programs such as SimpleText and PageMill. You can also find online tutorials that give you step-by-step instructions in creating Web pages. (Search for the tutorials by using the keywords "creating Web pages.") Here are the basic elements to keep in mind when planning your Web site.

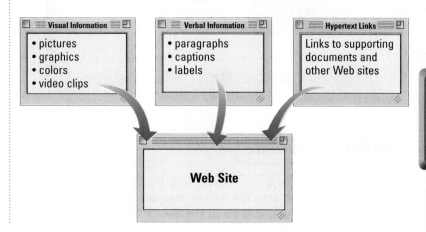

MEDIA PRODUCTS

❸ The Home Page

Your home page, the first page of your Web site, tells visitors what your site is about, who created it, and what other pages are available. Which page would you want to visit in this Web site?

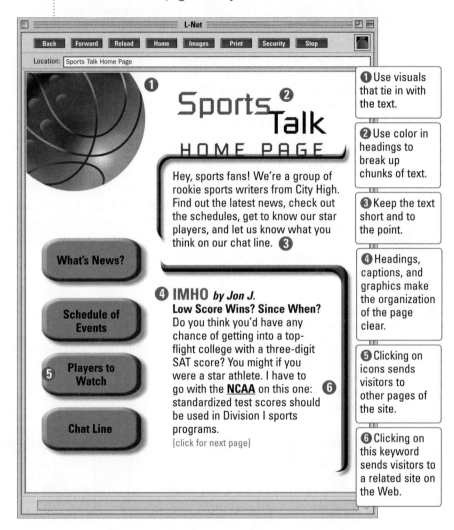

❶ Use visuals that tie in with the text.

❷ Use color in headings to break up chunks of text.

❸ Keep the text short and to the point.

❹ Headings, captions, and graphics make the organization of the page clear.

❺ Clicking on icons sends visitors to other pages of the site.

❻ Clicking on this keyword sends visitors to a related site on the Web.

❹ Building the Site

Develop a site map showing the connections between the parts of your site. The map on the next page shows the connections between the parts of the Sports Talk site.

After you design your site map, create a blueprint for each screen. Here's the blueprint for the What's News? screen.

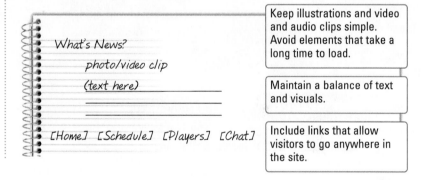

What's News?

photo/video clip

(text here)

[Home] [Schedule] [Players] [Chat]

Keep illustrations and video and audio clips simple. Avoid elements that take a long time to load.

Maintain a balance of text and visuals.

Include links that allow visitors to go anywhere in the site.

❺ Evaluating and Revising

Ask a group of your peers to review your site before you put it on the Internet. Prepare a feedback form to focus their review, using questions such as those below.

- Are all the pages consistent with the purpose or main idea of the Web site? Note any problem areas.
- Is the home page clearly organized, attractive, and inviting? What could make it better?
- Do all the links work? Are there any problems in navigating through the site?
- Are there any confusing parts? What needs more work?
- What are the most interesting parts? Why?

Student Help Desk

Media Products at a Glance

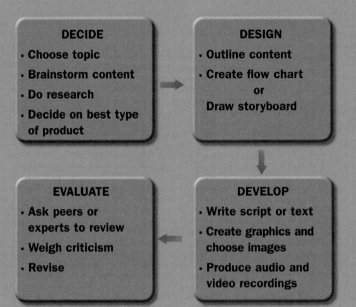

DECIDE
- Choose topic
- Brainstorm content
- Do research
- Decide on best type of product

DESIGN
- Outline content
- Create flow chart
  or
  Draw storyboard

EVALUATE
- Ask peers or experts to review
- Weigh criticism
- Revise

DEVELOP
- Write script or text
- Create graphics and choose images
- Produce audio and video recordings

Web Screen · Freeze Frame

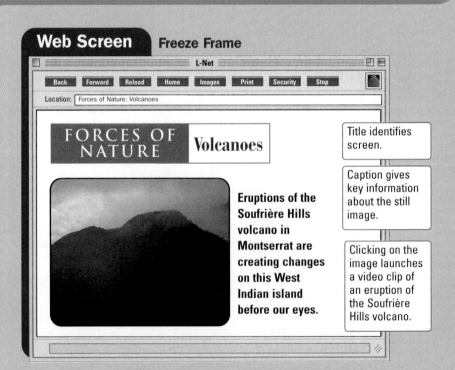

L-Net

Back Forward Reload Home Images Print Security Stop

Location: Forces of Nature: Volcanoes

FORCES OF NATURE · **Volcanoes**

Eruptions of the Soufrière Hills volcano in Montserrat are creating changes on this West Indian island before our eyes.

Title identifies screen.

Caption gives key information about the still image.

Clicking on the image launches a video clip of an eruption of the Soufrière Hills volcano.

The Rule of Thirds

Take Your Best Shot

- Think of frame as divided into vertical and horizontal thirds.
- Frame heads in top third of screen, with faces in full view.
- Place dramatic elements in right or left third.
- If subject is walking toward right, place him or her in left third of frame.
- If subject is reacting to something in left third, place him or her in right third.

Glossary of Video Terms

Backdrop: Background of a shot, showing setting

Close-up: Shot showing only head and shoulders of subject

Dead zone: Center of frame

Framing: Controlling distance of camera from subject, movement of camera, and arrangement of objects in view

Freeze-frame: Effect showing action electronically stopped

Full shot: Shot showing full length of subject

Headroom: Space in frame for subject's full head and face

Leadroom: Space in frame for subject to walk into

Long shot: Shot showing setting as well as subject

Voice-over: Narration off screen

The Bottom Line

Checklist for Media Products

Have I . . .

____ designed my project thoroughly, using outlines, flow charts, and storyboards, before beginning to record, develop, or write?

____ clearly expressed the main idea of my project?

____ made sure that all the parts of my project work together to present a coherent whole?

____ used the technology effectively?

____ kept my project simple, without unnecessary, distracting, or confusing effects?

tranquil

plunging

All at Sea

Although settings in nature can seem beautiful beyond words, there is a wealth of words available to describe them.

The Open Sea

Many a sailor has become entranced with the **vast** and **mysterious** ocean and its **changeable** moods. The sea can be an **endless, tranquil** expanse, its **sparkling** surface dancing in the sunlight. At times its waters are **translucent,** even **transparent**. A storm can make it terrifyingly dangerous, with **raging** winds, **towering** waves, **plunging** troughs, and **swirling** eddies. The **frothy** water can seem alive, almost **threatening**. With the passage of the storm, the sea's gently **undulating** roll can soothe the sailor's fears.

Below the Surface

Beneath the waves, the water is **quiet** except for sometimes **swift** currents. Near the surface, the water is a **luminous** realm, but it becomes **murky** and **opaque** the deeper you go, until finally it is completely lightless. In the **fathomless** depths of the **bottommost** trenches, strange and **bizarre** forms of life thrive in the **inky** darkness. It is a **tantalizing** but mostly unknown and **inscrutable** world that humankind can explore but may never know well.

swirling

vast

▷ **Your Turn** Scenic Views

Find a postcard or any photograph of a scene in nature. Create a cluster diagram based on the image. Refer to the image as you and a partner add as many descriptive words as you can to the diagram.

inky

Vocabulary Development

"It's, like, wow!"

When 'Wow' Won't Do

Imagine that you are the person sitting on the cliff overlooking the Grand Canyon. What words would you use to describe the scene to your friends or family? Expressions like *wow* or *awesome* don't quite measure up to the job, do they? Fortunately, the English language comes with an immense storehouse of words for expressing our thoughts and ideas. Building a large vocabulary of your own will increase the power of anything you say and write.

Write Away: A Grand Vocabulary
Write a paragraph describing this view of the Grand Canyon. Try to use words as majestic as the scene itself, something that conveys the experience to someone who is not there to see it. Place your work in your ▭ **Working Portfolio.**

VOCABULARY

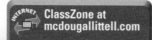
ClassZone at
mcdougallittell.com

LESSON 1

Context Clues

You probably read and hear new words every day—in books, on the Internet, in class, on TV, during conversations. What do you do when you encounter these new words? Using the strategies in this lesson can help you understand unfamiliar words so they can become part of your vocabulary.

❶ Types of Context Clues

The sentence or passage in which a word appears is called its **context.** There are several different types of **context clues,** or hints that suggest the meaning of unfamiliar terms. The most common context clues are shown in this chart.

Types of Context Clues

	Explanation	Example
Definition and restatement	The meaning of the unfamiliar word is provided immediately after the word. **Signals:** Punctuation marks such as commas and dashes, or words such as *or, that is, in other words*	The **dermis**—that is, the second layer of skin—is where the sense receptors are located.
Example	An unfamiliar word is followed by an example of it. **Signal Words:** *including, such as, for example*	Mrs. Bryce was well known for her acts of **philanthropy, such as her million-dollar donation to the state university.**
Contrast	The meaning of an unfamiliar word is suggested by contrasting it to something different or opposite. **Signal Words:** *however, but, although, unlike*	Ana is usually pretty **adept** at board games; **however, today all her moves were wrong.**
Cause and effect	When an unfamiliar term is used to describe a cause or effect, the rest of the relationship can help you figure out the meaning. **Signal Words:** *because, since*	Because one juror was so **intransigent, the jury could not come to a unanimous agreement.**
Synonym	An unfamiliar term is followed by a familiar synonym.	You're not the only one with an **insolvency** problem—I'm **broke** too!

CHAPTER 30

546 Communicating in the Information Age

❷ General Context

Be alert not only for context clues involving key words but also for clues suggested by the main idea of a passage. The supporting details, individually or collectively, may also suggest the meaning.

> **PROFESSIONAL MODEL**
>
> . . . the [wild] dogs themselves appear at first to have **no great enthusiasm** [for the hunt.] They **drag** themselves up from the heap and mill around greeting one another. They lean forward and **languidly** bridge their back legs out behind. One of them **moseys** off. . . . The others **tag along** in loose file, with a desultory wagging of tails.
>
> —Richard Conniff, "Africa's Wild Dogs," *National Geographic*

Details suggest that *languid* means "lazily slow."

HOT TIP

Create a personal word bank for collecting new words. Personalize each entry by writing the context in which you encountered the word.

PRACTICE **Using Context to Identify Words**

Use context to help determine the meaning of each italicized word in the paragraph below. Write the meaning of each word and be prepared to describe the clues that you used. Check your answers in a dictionary.

> **PROFESSIONAL MODEL**
>
> Roller coasters have been around for more than 100 years, but for most of that time, they've been in a state of **(1) arrested** development. In fact, it's only recently that ride technology has advanced much beyond the principles of the first roller coaster, . . . which opened in 1884. Then, passengers had to climb up a 45-foot tower to enter cars that were set in motion with a simple push. Seems awfully **(2) primitive**, but **(3) variations** on that basic model—a wood-frame structure on which cars are **(4) propelled** by gravity along a track—are still being built today, with steeper drops and friction-reducing materials (like **(5) metallastic**, a blend of rubber and metal) for faster, smoother rides.
>
> —Ted Oehmke, "High Rollers," *New York Times Magazine*

Word Structure: Roots and Bases

Context is not the only clue you can have for determining a word's meaning. You can also look at the word itself and analyze its component parts.

❶ Recognizing Word Parts

If you know one part of a word, sometimes you can figure out the meaning of the whole word. Every English word includes one or more of the following parts.

Word Parts	Meaning	Example
Prefix	a word part that is added to the beginning of a word or a word part	dis**similarity** **prefix** = dis
Suffix	a word part that is added to the end of a word or a word part	dissimilar**ity** **suffix** = ity
Base Word	a complete word to which a prefix and/or a suffix can be added	dis**similar**ity **base word** = similar
Root	a word part to which a prefix and/or a suffix can be added; roots cannot stand alone.	**simil**ar **root** = *simil*, from the Latin word *similis*, meaning "like"

❷ Word Families

A group of words that has a common root or base word is called a **word family.** When you learn the meaning of a common root or base, you help unlock the meaning of every word within that word family.

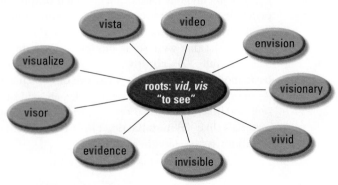

CHAPTER 30

❸ Greek Roots

The core meaning of a word is contained in its root. English borrows words from many languages, but many English words have Greek or Latin roots. This is why learning common Greek and Latin roots is an important step in improving your vocabulary.

ROOT MEANS "SAME" ↘   ↙ ROOT MEANS "SOUND"

Homophones

> **Homophones** are words that sound the same, like *chord* and *cord*.

Common Greek Roots

	Meaning	English Words
biblio, bibl	book	bibliography, Bible
bio	life	biology, biography
chron	time	chronological, chronic
cosm	order, universe	cosmic, microcosm
crac, crat	govern	democratic, aristocrat, bureaucracy
gen	birth, race	genetic, genesis
geo	earth, ground, soil	geography, geology
graph	write	graphic, telegraph
hydr	water	hydrant, hydraulics
log, logo	word, speech	logical, dialogue
logy	study of	biology, theology
phob	fear	phobia, claustrophobia
phono	sound, voice	phonics, microphone
pol	city	metropolis, police
therm	heat	thermometer, thermostat

On standardized tests, knowing the meanings of word parts can often help you choose correctly from among the answer options.

❹ Latin Roots

Although the ancient language of Latin is no longer spoken, it lives on by forming the roots of many common English words.

Common Latin Roots

	Meaning	Examples
ag, act	do, make	agent, action
aud, audit	hear	audible, auditorium
bene	good, well	benefit, beneficiary
capt, cap, cip, cept	take, seize	capture, accept
ced, cess	go; withdraw	recede, recess
cred	believe	incredible, creed
ject	throw	inject, reject
jur, just	law, right	jury, justice
luc	shine	lucid, translucent
mand	order	command, mandate
mitt, miss	send	mission, transmit
port	carry	portable, transport
scrib, script	write	describe, manuscript
spec, spect	look at, examine	spectacle, inspect
vaca, vacu	empty	vacate, vacuum
vid, vis	see	video, visible

PRACTICE Identifying Greek and Latin Roots

Listed below are several pairs of words that share a common root. For each pair, give the meaning of the root. Then add two other words to each pair to create a word family.

1. geometry
   geophysics
2. discredit
   credence
3. phonograph
   biography
4. speculate
   retrospect
5. chronology
   synchronize

6. phonetic
   symphony
7. auditorium
   audible
8. vision
   video
9. zoology
   psychology
10. evacuate
    vacuum

LESSON 3 Word Structure: Prefixes and Suffixes

A working knowledge of certain prefixes and suffixes can help you decipher the meanings of many unfamiliar words. When you encounter a word made up of multiple word parts, look at each part and then combine the individual meanings to determine the meaning of the entire word.

MEANS "BAD" ↘   ↗ MEANS "STATE OF"

mal|nourish|ment
        BASE WORD

> **Malnourishment** is the state of being badly nourished.

❶ Prefixes

Prefixes typically change the meaning of a base word. For example, the prefix *in–* means "not." When it is added to a base word such as *formal,* it creates the new word *informal,* which means "not formal."

Common Prefixes

	Meaning	Examples
anti-	against, opposed to	antiseptic, antisocial, antitrust
auto-	self	autonomous, autograph, autobiography
de-	down; away from	degrade, descend; deflect
dis-	opposite of; free from	disappear, disagree; dislodge
equi-	equal	equator, equation, equilibrium
hyper-	over, excessive	hyperactive, hypersonic, hyperspace
in-, il-, im-, ir-	not	indirect, illegal, improper, irresponsible
inter-	between, among	intercom, Internet, interstate
micro-	small, minute	microscope, microcosm, microphone
mono-	one, alone	monologue, monotone, monopoly
para-	near, beside	paraphrase, paramedic; parallel
poly-	many	polygraph, polygon, polygamy
post-	behind, after	postmortem, postscript, posterity
quasi-	to some degree, in some manner	quasi-judicial, quasi-stellar, quasi-public
semi-	half, partial	semicircle, semidarkness, semiformal
sub-	below, under	submarine, subterranean; subplot
super-	over, above	superior, superego, superlative

Using Prefixes

For each word below, give the meaning, first, of the prefix and then of the entire word. Check your answers in a dictionary.

1. equidistant
2. postpone
3. monorail
4. hypertension
5. paralegal
6. antibody
7. automate
8. disadvantage
9. semifinal
10. microburst

"They have very strict anti-pollution laws in this state."

❷ Suffixes

A **suffix** is a word part added to the end of a word. Notice how the suffixes shown below determine the part of speech of the word *joy*.

joy   joyous   joyless   joyfulness

Most suffixes that are useful for figuring out word meanings are used to form adjectives and nouns. Once you know the meanings of certain suffixes, it's easier to determine the meanings of the words they form. For each of the charts that follow, challenge yourself to think of additional examples.

Adjective Suffixes		
	Meaning	**Examples**
-able, -ible	inclined to be	tolerable, durable, possible
-ate	characterized by	desolate, passionate, fortunate
-ful	full of	eventful, wasteful, cheerful
-ous	full of	joyous, nervous, religious
-some	characterized by a quality, state, or action	awesome, tiresome, lonesome

CHAPTER 30

Noun Suffixes

	Meaning	Examples
-ance, -ence	action, condition	acceptance, repentance, turbulence
-ant	one that performs or causes an action	defendant, accountant, informant
-cide	killer, killing	homicide, pesticide, germicide
-cy	state, condition	hesitancy, accuracy, potency
-dom	quality, office	boredom, freedom, kingdom
-ian	of, relating to	musician, technician, physician
-ice	state, quality	malice, justice, cowardice
-ion	state, condition, action, process	vacation, expansion, nutrition
-ism	action, practice	criticism, heroism, patriotism
-ment	result, process	development, amazement, contentment
-ness	state, condition	happiness, loneliness, friendliness
-tude	state, condition	fortitude, gratitude, solitude

Verb Suffixes

	Meaning	Examples
-ate	act upon, cause to be	liberate, activate, confiscate
-en	cause to be, become	straighten, sharpen, lengthen
-fy	make, form	intensify, satisfy, terrify
-ize	cause to be, make, become	standardize, idolize, realize

PRACTICE B Using Suffixes

For each word below, give the meaning, first, of the suffix and then of the whole word. Check your answers in a dictionary.

1. genocide
2. amendment
3. perishable
4. spacious
5. popularize
6. defiance
7. magician
8. wisdom
9. jaundice
10. servant
11. meddlesome
12. wondrous
13. desperate
14. starkness
15. falsify

Shades of Meaning

Those who use the English language precisely choose words that capture the specific meanings that they intend. The enormous array of word choices in the English language makes it possible to find a word to fit any situation.

❶ Denotation and Connotation

There are two types of meaning—denotation and connotation. The **denotation** of a word is simply its dictionary meaning. However, the **connotations**—emotions attached to the words— vary considerably. The words at the beginning of the series have positive connotations, while those at the end have negative ones.

─────────────── **determined** ───────────────

POSITIVE CONNOTATIONS
persevering iron-willed tenacious

inflexible relentless obstinate
NEGATIVE CONNOTATIONS

Selecting words with the precise connotations you want will add force to your writing and speaking.

Choosing the Right Synonym

As you develop your vocabulary, search for words that capture the exact shade of meaning you need. (Note the variations in meaning for each synonym for the word *look*.)

Synonyms for *Look*	Definition	In Context
spy	catch sight of	He *spied* a snake.
gawk	stare stupidly	He *gawked* at a snake.
observe	watch attentively	He *observed* a snake.
gaze	look with wonder	He *gazed* at a snake.

❷ Vocabulary Resources

What is a *shunt*? How do you pronounce *segue*? What's another word for *grand*? To find the answers to questions like these, look in a general dictionary, a thesaurus, or both.

General Dictionary A general dictionary provides a wide range of vocabulary information, as shown in the entry below.

con•fine (kən fīn'), *v.* **–fined, –fin•ing, –fines.** —*tr.*
1. To keep within bounds; restrict. **2.** To shut or keep in, especially to imprison: *The governor wishes to confine the prisoners in a better state facility.* **3.** To restrict in movement. —*intr. Archaic.* To border. —**confine** (kŏn' fīn') *n.* **1. confines.**
a. The limits of a space or an area; the borders.
b. Restraining elements: *the confines of politics.*
[Lat. *cōnfīne,* from the neuter of *cōnfīnis,* adjoining : *com–,* com– + *fīnis,* border.] —**con•fin'a•ble, con•fine'a•ble** *adj.* —**con•fin'er** *n.*

— MAIN ENTRY
— PRONUNCIATION
— PART OF SPEECH
— OTHER FORMS
— DEFINITION
— EXAMPLE
— ETYMOLOGY-WORD HISTORY
— RELATED WORD FORMS

—Adapted from *The American Heritage College Dictionary,* Third Edition.

Thesaurus A thesaurus is a book of synonyms. Use it to find a replacement for an overused word or to find a word with the precise shade of meaning that you need.

When you use a thesaurus, remember that synonyms are not always interchangeable. For example, which synonyms for "grand" could be substituted in the following sentence? Which words would not be appropriate?

The view at the top of the mountain was grand.

grand *adjective*
1. Large and impressive in size, scope, or extent : august, baronial, grandiose, imposing, lordly, magnific, magnificent, majestic, noble, princely, regal, royal, splendid, stately, sublime, superb. see BIG, GOOD.

—from *Roget's II The New Thesaurus*

PRACTICE Using a Thesaurus

In your 🗂 **Working Portfolio,** find the paragraph you wrote for the **Write Away** on page 545. Use a thesaurus to help you improve your description of the Grand Canyon by replacing overused words with fresh ones.

Specialized Vocabularies

If you've taken algebra, you may have used words like *function, equation, variables, coefficients, exponents, factors, polynomial, binomial,* and *quadratic.* In other words, you used a specialized vocabulary—special terms suited to a field of study or work.

❶ Acquiring Specialized Vocabularies

Building a strong vocabulary is an ongoing process. As you encounter new experiences, you also encounter new sets of specialized vocabularies. For example, almost every job has its own language—words specifically suited to that particular occupation. So does every academic field or professional niche, for example. If you work with computers, you may be familiar with some of the specialized words and terms that appear in this ad.

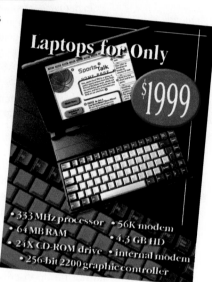

❷ Specialized Dictionaries

Does the above ad seem like it was written in a foreign language? If it does, you could find help in a dictionary that specializes in computer terms—in other words, in a **specialized dictionary.** Every specialized dictionary provides information on a specific subject, such as music, medicine, law, language, or biography. You might refer to one to find out the meaning of unfamiliar lingo (such as in the computer ad). You might also consult a specialized dictionary when writing a report to help you understand the terminology used by professionals in a specific field and to make your writing more credible and convincing.

You can use the same skills that you use for a general dictionary to find information in a specialized dictionary. The following excerpt is from a dictionary of computer terms.

mega– Abbreviated **M 1.** A prefix indicating 1 million (10^6), as in *megahertz*. **2.** A prefix indicating 1,048,576 (2^{20}), as in *megabyte*. This is the sense in which mega– is generally used in computing, which is based on powers of two.

megabyte Abbreviated **MB, meg**   A unit of measurement of computer memory or data storage capacity, equal to 1,048,576 (2^{20}) *bytes*. One megabyte equals 1,024 *kilobytes*.

memory 1. See **RAM. 2.** The capacity of a computer, chips, and *storage devices* to preserve data and programs for retrieval. Memory is measured in bytes. **3.** A system for preserving data and programs for retrieval. *Volatile memory*, or RAM, stores information only until the power is turned off. *Nonvolatile memory* stores memory even when the power is off. Nonvolatile memory includes *ROM, PROM, EPROM,* and *EEPROM*, as well as such external devices as *disk drives* and *tape drives*. See also *expanded memory, extended memory, flash memory, main memory,* and *virtual memory*.

—*Dictionary of Computer Words,*
American Heritage Dictionaries

PRACTICE ▸ Defining Specialized Terms

Make a list of specialized terms for any topic. Include words and abbreviations that are unfamiliar to someone who knows little about your subject. Then create a list of your terms. Model your list on the one shown below.

STUDENT MODEL

Jake's Skateboarding Terms

3-60 A kickflip that involves rotating the board 360 degrees.

Fakie Riding backward.

Goofy-foot A skate stance in which the right foot is positioned forward.

Grind Scraping the trucks, or metal framework, along an edge.

Lipslide A slide in which the tail of the skateboard is over the deck.

Mongo-foot A style of pushing in which the foot positioned in the rear is kept on the board and the other foot is used to push.

VOCABULARY

Student Help Desk

Vocabulary Building at a Glance

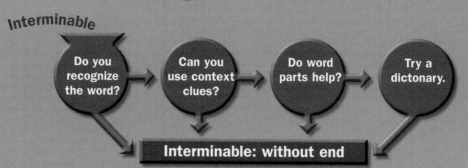

Interminable

| Do you recognize the word? | → | Can you use context clues? | → | Do word parts help? | → | Try a dictonary. |

Interminable: without end

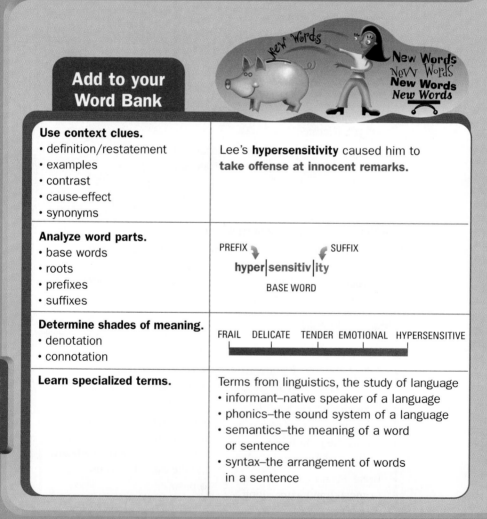

Add to your Word Bank

Use context clues. • definition/restatement • examples • contrast • cause-effect • synonyms	Lee's **hypersensitivity** caused him to **take offense at innocent remarks.**
Analyze word parts. • base words • roots • prefixes • suffixes	PREFIX ↘ ↙ SUFFIX **hyper│sensitiv│ity** BASE WORD
Determine shades of meaning. • denotation • connotation	FRAIL DELICATE TENDER EMOTIONAL HYPERSENSITIVE
Learn specialized terms.	Terms from linguistics, the study of language • informant–native speaker of a language • phonics–the sound system of a language • semantics–the meaning of a word or sentence • syntax–the arrangement of words in a sentence

Learning New Words   Owning the Language

Memory tips for expanding your vocabulary

Read	Three words sum up the best way to build a strong vocabulary: read, read, read.
Visualize	Picture new words, if you can, or associate them with visual images.
Speak and write	When learning a new word, say it out loud and/or write it down. The more senses you bring into play, the greater the chance that a new word will register permanently in your memory.
Associate	Compare unfamiliar words with other words that look or sound like them. You could remember *polarize* (to separate) by thinking of the north and south poles, which are as separate as two things can be.
Build gradually	A manageable goal is to add three new words per day to your vocabulary. Look for new words when reading or listening. Then find opportunities for using them in your speech or writing three times a day.

The Bottom Line

Checklist for Vocabulary Development

Have I . . .

____ analyzed any prefixes, and suffixes, or both to help me understand the word?

____ examined the root on which a word is based to see if I recognize its meaning?

____ understood the various connotations of a word?

____ used vocabulary resources (general dictionary, thesaurus, specialized dictionary) to get information about words?

____ used context clues to understand the meaning of a new word?

____ consistently added new words to my vocabulary?

pungent

fresh

ambrosial

sweet-smelling

What's on the Menu?

What isn't edible but can make a meal seem mouthwatering? Words that stir appetites by appealing to readers' senses.

A Taste Sensation

Time to rustle up some dinner for the gang. They'll want something **luscious** and **delectable,** a **flavorsome, toothsome** meal to remember. Maybe start with a **peppery** appetizer, or a **zesty** salsa, and a salad of **succulent** greens and tomatoes. The **scrumptious** main course should have a **delicate** but **tasty** flavor, perhaps fish with a **tart, lemony** seasonings that aren't too **salty.** The vegetables should be fresh and crisp, and topped with **buttery** sauces. Dessert will be something **tangy** and **savory,** like a **creamy-smooth,** key lime pie. Guests won't forget this **ambrosial** meal.

Mmmm—What's Cooking?

One of the most satisfying things about cooking is the **aromas** from the kitchen. Not the **acrid, piercing** smell of something burning, but the **hickory-smoked** aroma of food being charbroiled. Imagine breathing in the strong, **pungent** scents of onions and garlic, and the fresh smell of herbs, or aroma of **fragrant, sweet-smelling** apples and peaches, and the **spicy** smell of cinnamon. A kitchen **perfumed** with such odors is as welcoming as a hug.

▷ **Your Turn** You've Said a Mouthful

Survey the food preferences of a small group. List not only a favorite food but sensory words that each person associates with that food's taste, smell, or texture. Later, compare your choices.

succulent

lemony

AROMAS

History of English

Food for Thought

There's nothing unusual about each of these foods, right? Wrong! None of the words that describe them are native to the English language. Take the everyday orange. Its name comes from Arabic. Coleslaw and cookie—both Dutch. Minestrone, of course, is Italian. But how about the all-American hamburger, you say? Sorry, it's German. Other common foods aren't any less exotic: for example, chow mein (Chinese), jambalaya (French), squash (Naragansett), anchovy (Portugese), and yam (Wolof). Just read on in the chapter to get more food for thought about our amazing language.

Write Away: Eat Your Words

Imagine that you're sitting down to your favorite meal. Describe it from start to finish, including an appetizer, main course, vegetable, beverage, and dessert. Now look up the name of each food in the dictionary, and list its origin. Keep your writing in your **Working Portfolio**.

ENGLISH LANG.

History of the English Language

Like a person, a language is a living thing that continuously grows and changes. The English language—with its long and colorful history—is no exception. New words are added and old words die out. Words and phrases take on different meanings, and even pronunciation, spelling, and grammar change. Today, English is spoken in more places in the world than any other language.

❶ Indo-European Language Family

Linguists categorize languages into families with ancestors and descendants. English is a member of the most extensively studied and well-defined language family—Indo-European. All Indo-European languages are descended from Proto-Indo-European, a language that was spoken in Asia Minor about 5,000 years ago. Although no records of this language remain, linguists have reconstructed it based on its descendants.

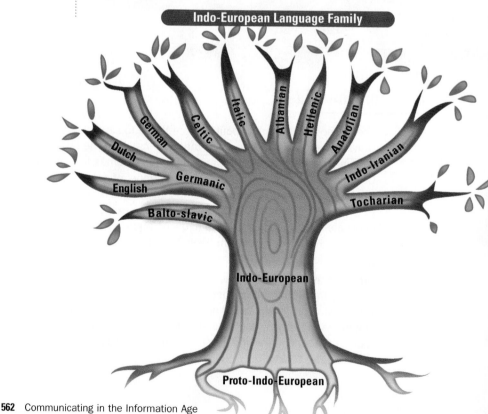

Indo-European Language Family

Italic · Albanian · Hellenic · Anatolian · German · Celtic · Dutch · Indo-Iranian · English · Germanic · Tocharian · Balto-slavic · Indo-European · Proto-Indo-European

❷ Old English

The linguistic roots of Old English were planted in the fifth century, when the Romans recruited the Germanic peoples known as the Angles and the Saxons into their army. The Anglo-Saxons eventually claimed the southern part of Britain as the "land of the Angles," which became known as Engla land, and eventually as England. They spoke Englisc, or what we now call Old English.

Old English Words and Their Modern Equivalents			
Old English	**Modern English**	**Old English**	**Modern English**
freond	friend	writan	write
nama	name	boc	book
modor	mother	hus	house
leornere	learner	cnif	knife

❸ Middle English

Between the 9th and 11th centuries, the Norse people of Scandinavia invaded and settled in Britain, contributing some Scandinavian words to the English language. Then in 1066, the French Normans invaded England, making French and Latin the official languages of the country. It wasn't until the 14th century that English came back into common use. By that time, many words like these had been borrowed from those other languages.

- **French**—army, dinner, letter, palace, serve, table
- **Latin**—alphabet, index, library, student

Publication of *The Canterbury Tales* by Geoffrey Chaucer in his native English dialect in the late 14th century was a major milestone in English literature. As the following passage shows, he worried about its lack of uniformity, though.

> **LITERARY MODEL**
>
> And for ther is so gret diversite
> In Englissh and in writyng of oure tonge . . .
> That thow be understonde, God I biseche!
>
> —Geoffrey Chaucer, *Troilus and Criseyde*

❹ Modern English

Although the passage from Chaucer on the previous page is not difficult to understand, it definitely doesn't look like modern English—and sounds even less like it. Several events kept the language changing.

Invention

Before the mid-15th century, manuscripts were written by hand. The invention of the printing press around 1450 made it possible to produce books cheaply and in large quantities. This helped increase literacy and bring about the standardization of English that Chaucer hoped for.

Migration

Language spreads and changes as the people who speak it move around. Starting in the early 1600s, the British were bitten by the travel bug, journeying to and settling in countries around the world.

British Settlements—17th-18th Centuries

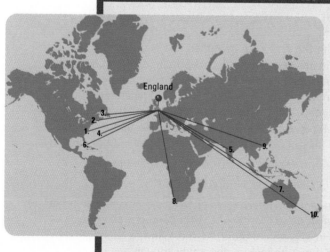

England

1. Virginia 1607
2. Massachusetts 1620
3. Newfoundland 1610
4. Bermuda 1612
5. India 1612
6. Bahamas 1647
7. Australia 1788
8. Cape of Good Hope, South Africa 1820
9. Hong Kong 1821
10. New Zealand 1840

Industrialization

In the late 18th century, the Industrial Revolution thrust England into the center of global trading. Traders not only exchanged goods but also influenced each others' languages.

Development of American English

One of the places the early British colonists chose to settle was the New World. In this new environment, their language began to change and take on a character of its own. The development of American English can be divided into three distinct periods: Colonial (1607–1776), National (1776–1898), and International (1898 to present).

❶ Colonial Period

Arriving in the New World in the early 1600s, the British colonists must have been grateful to have survived their journey.

LITERARY MODEL

Being thus arrived in a good harbor, and brought safe to land, they fell upon their knees and blessed the God of Heaven who had brought them over the vast and furious ocean, and delivered them from all the perils and miseries thereof, again to set their feet on the firm and stable earth, their proper element.

—William Bradford, *Of Plymouth Plantation*

The colonists discovered, however, that many aspects of their lives—including their language—would have to change as they adapted to their new circumstances. They needed to communicate with the Native Americans and to find words to describe unfamiliar wildlife, vegetation, and landscape. Their survival depended on the growth of their language.

Vocabulary Changes in Colonial English	
Words Borrowed from Native American Languages	**Words Developed in the New World**
skunk, squash, moose, coyote, hammock	muskrat, groundhog, hot cake, bank (as in river bank)

Colonial writers such as William Bradford, Roger Williams, and Mary Rowlandson also helped change the language. They introduced innovations such as new spellings (*spoil* rather than *spile*) and new past forms for verbs (*drunk* for *drink*).

ENGLISH LANG.

➋ National Period

By 1776, when the original 13 colonies declared their independence from Britain, the English language of the Americas had already changed considerably from that spoken in England. These changes were so great that American English was considered a distinct variety of—if not a totally separate language from—British English.

Noah Webster helped standardize American English with his dictionary and spelling book, the "Blue-Backed Speller." His spellings also distanced American English even further from British English, which still uses the original spellings.

centre ➡ center	flavour ➡ flavor
theatre ➡ theater	practise ➡ practice
colour ➡ color	standardise ➡ standardize

As settlers moved westward, the frontier culture also left its mark on the language, contributing words such as *prairie, voyage,* and *kin.* Another important influence was the Spanish spoken by earlier settlers of the West, which supplied words such as

estampida ➡ stampede	cañon ➡ canyon
la reata ➡ lariat	vaquero ➡ buckaroo

➌ International Period

By the end of the 19th century, the United States was heavily engaged in foreign trade, wars, and other world affairs. This global involvement helped establish English as the language of international commerce. It also gave—and continues to give—English vocabulary an international flavor.

Mutual Language Influences	
Other Language Influences on English	**English Influences on Other Languages**
Santa Claus (Dutch)	le weekend (French)
lacrosse (French)	pullover (German)
pizza (Italian)	hottu doggu (Japanese)
hibachi (Japanese)	archivo (Spanish)
rodeo (Spanish)	
smorgasbord (Swedish)	
banjo (West African)	

Varieties of American English

Just as American English diverged from British English, regional varieties of American English developed in different geographic areas of the country. Migration, cultural interaction, and geographic isolation all played a part in the development of regional dialects.

Regional Dialects

A **dialect** is a form of speech used in a particular region. Although a dialect is considered a branch or sub-group of a more widely spoken language, its vocabulary, pronunciation, and grammatical variations distinguish it from other dialects. One classification of the regional dialects of American English includes four regions— **New England, North, Midland,** and **South.**

Regional Dialect Variations

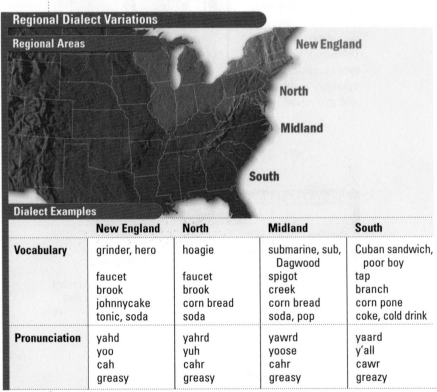

Regional Areas

New England

North

Midland

South

Dialect Examples

	New England	North	Midland	South
Vocabulary	grinder, hero	hoagie	submarine, sub, Dagwood	Cuban sandwich, poor boy
	faucet	faucet	spigot	tap
	brook	brook	creek	branch
	johnnycake	corn bread	corn bread	corn pone
	tonic, soda	soda	soda, pop	coke, cold drink
Pronunciation	yahd	yahrd	yawrd	yaard
	yoo	yuh	yoose	y'all
	cah	cahr	cahr	cawr
	greasy	greasy	greasy	greazy

HOT TIP

Don't expect people from the same geographic area to speak the same variety of dialect. In fact, each individual speaks his or her own special version, or idiolect, of the language.

ENGLISH LANG.

English Around the World Today

Today, English is spoken all over the world. It is the official language of business and diplomacy in many countries—from Belize, Botswana, and Kenya to India, Malaysia, and New Zealand. English is also the second, third, or fourth language of many people around the globe. Although these varieties of English are mutually comprehensible, they also differ in many ways.

❶ American and British English

The gap between American and British English that opened in Colonial times has continued to widen until the two are now essentially separate languages. Differences include pronunciation, spelling, vocabulary, and grammar.

© The New Yorker Collection, 1995, Lee Lorenz

"He's like, 'To be or not to be,' and I'm, like, 'Get a life.'"

Differences Between American and British English		
	American English	**British English**
Spelling	jail humor aluminum	gaol humour aluminium
Pronunciation	ad´ vur tyz muhnt huh ras´ muhnt kahn´ troh vur see	ad vur´ tihs muhnt hair´ uhs muhnt kahn troh´ vur see
Vocabulary	trash can sweater pants apartment	dust bin jumper trousers flat
Grammar	I have a car. She was in the hospital.	I have got a car. She was in hospital.

❷ Global Language

The leading role of the United States in politics, business, science and technology, and entertainment has led to the international use of English and has also enabled the language to grow and change. And as English gives widely dispersed people a common means of communication, it helps build a tightly knit global community.

International Interaction

Two major ways that English has gained international influence are through global transportation and mass media such as television and the World Wide Web. As technology continues to bridge cultural differences and bring people closer together, English and other world languages will continue to influence each other and continue to change.

Future Talk

But what directions will that change take? What new influences will affect English? Will the number of English speakers increase or decrease? As international power shifts, could another language become more universally spoken than English is?

Some people have suggested that the rise of a global community will lead to the development of a global language that everyone speaks and understands. Will that language be like English? Will it be a computer-generated language based on all the world's languages? Will it include gestures and signs? Or will it be some means of communication that we can't even imagine? Only time will tell.

Student Help Desk

The History of English at a Glance

3,000 B.C.

Proto-Indo-European
(before 3,000 B.C.)

Indo-European
(3,000 B.C.)

2,000 B.C.

1,000 B.C.

A.D. 1

Germanic
3rd-6th
centuries

A.D. 1000

Old English
6th-11th
centuries

Middle English
11th-15th
centuries

Modern English
15th century to present

A.D. 2000

American English
17th century to present

American
regional dialects
(ongoing)

English Through Time — Word Watch

Old English	Middle English	Modern English
abidan	abidyng	awaiting
scyp	shippe	ship
freond	freend	friend
geocynde	natyf	natural
deorc	derke	dark
faegernis	beautee	beauty

Meaning Shifts — My, How You've Changed!

Type of Change	Word	Original Meaning	Modern Meaning
Extension	salary arrive	soldier's payment with salt to reach a shore	wages of any kind to reach any destination
Narrowing	starve deer wife	to die wild animal woman	to die of hunger hoofed ruminant mammal married woman

English Around the World

Country Where English Is Spoken	Primary Language	Other Languages Spoken
Argentina	Spanish	Italian, German, French, native languages
Brunei	Malay	Chinese
Cameroon	French, English	Fang, Bulu, Fulani, YaundÈ, Duala, Mbum,
Canada	English, French	Cree, Ojibwa, Micmac, Mohawk, Inuit, Tsimshian, Nootka, Kawkiutl, Haida
Egypt	Arabic	French
Fiji	Fijian	Hindi
Guyana	English	English Creole, Hindi, Urdu, Arawak, Carib
Kenya	Swahili	Kikuyu, Luhya, Kamba, Kisii, Meru, Luo, Masai, Kalenjin, Suk, Somali, Oromo
Libya	Arabic	Tuareg, Italian
Monaco	French	Monegasque, Italian
Singapore	Chinese	Malay, Tamil
Suriname	Dutch	Sranang Tongo, Hindi, Javanese, Carib, Saramacca
Thailand	Thai	Chinese, Malay, Mon, Khmer, Karen, Miao
Trinidad and Tobago	Arabic	Hindi, French, Spanish

The Native American Influence

As American as Potatoes

More food for thought: all these common English words were borrowed from various Native American languages.

Chicago	totem	hickory	petunia
Manhattan	shark	jaguar	opossum
Appalachian	moccasin	cocoa	kayak
Dakota	potato	chipmunk	chocolate
Minnesota	raccoon	cashew	teepee

ENGLISH LANG.

Power Words
Vocabulary for Precise Writing

Over the Top

Warning! This is a burnout alert! Too much of anything could lead you to use words like these.

Enough Is Enough!

You finally recognize the **unparalleled** level of disorder in your room. The surface of your desk is a mess, covered with **needless** and **unnecessary** layers of paper. Books are **crammed** into your bookcase, which would topple over if not for the **overwhelming** number of books stacked around it. A pile of dirty clothes in one corner is so **prodigious** in size, it's casting a hulking shadow. Your TV remote control has been missing for two days. Family members are threatening to take **extreme** measures. You don't have **heaps** of choices. You have an **exorbitant** amount of cleaning to do.

Achieving a Balance

One possible reason for all the **overload** is your calendar, which is **chock full** of appointments. You can't afford to be so **extravagant** with your time. Instead, **lavish** more attention on using your time well. Delete the **superfluous** activities. You'll be **brimming over** with relief.

▷ Your Turn Measure the Pressure

Taking tests, juggling school and work, and preparing for the future are situations that are trying to many people your age. With a partner, devise a stress scale to rate such situations. Position each situation on the scale according to its level of stressfulness, ranging from *Mildly Stressful* to *Over the Top*.

brimming over *overload* lavish extreme

Taking Standardized Tests

Test-Taking Burnout

Does this student look like anyone you know? Do you recognize the glazed eyes? the hand stiff from gripping number two pencils too tightly? Before you take your next standardized test, look in the mirror. This student might bear an uncomfortable resemblance to you.

You've taken standardized tests throughout your student life. During your junior year, however, you will be bombarded with them—state tests, national tests, college entrance exams. Don't panic. Take a deep breath. Knowing how to prepare and what to expect will help you get through it.

Write Away: A Nonstandard Celebration
Imagine that you've taken your last high school standardized test. How do you feel? What are you going to do to celebrate? Write a short paragraph about your celebration and place it in your
📁 **Working Portfolio.**

 **ClassZone at
mcdougallittell.com**

Taking Standardized Tests **573**

TAKING TESTS

State and National Tests

When you take a standardized test, you take the same test in the same amount of time as the other students in your grade level. This allows test reviewers to measure your progress and compare it with that of other students. It also ensures that no one taking the test has any unfair advantages or disadvantages.

❶ Categories of Tests

Here are some of the standardized tests that you are probably most familiar with.

- **Achievement Tests** Achievement tests measure how much you've learned about a single subject or many subjects.

- **College Entrance Exams** One or both of these tests are usually required when you apply to a college. The SAT tests math and verbal skills. The ACT tests achievement in English, math, reading, and science reasoning.

- **Aptitude Tests** These are designed to measure your interest and potential ability in a certain type of activity. This kind of test can help you select a course of study or a career path.

- **Personality Tests** These are designed to help you identify personal preferences that could help you choose career or school goals that suit your own style.

 HOT TIP

You can earn college credit by taking standardized achievement tests and advanced placement exams in various subjects. Talk to your guidance counselor about these tests.

❷ Test-Taking Tactics

Test-preparation courses and study groups can help you get ready for a standardized test. There are also some tactics you can use before, during, and after the test.

EXAM TUESDAY! 4 PM!

Taking a Standardized Test
Before the Test Begins

- Arrive on time.
- Wear a watch so that you can keep track of the time and make sure you don't take too long on any one part of the test.
- When you receive your test, listen carefully to guidelines and directions, especially those concerning how to mark your answer sheet. Ask questions, if necessary.
- Find out whether there is a penalty for guessing. Some tests take off points for incorrect answers; some don't.
- If allowed, scan the entire test so that you can plan your time.

During the Test

- Do the items you are certain about first. Then go back and do the harder ones.
- Don't panic and don't rush. Take a deep breath and work steadily.
- Check your answer sheet from time to time to make sure you're marking the correct answer space.
- Use the final minutes of the test to answer the items you left blank and to recheck answers.

After the Test

- Avoid rehashing the test with your friends. Second-guessing yourself at this point won't accomplish anything.
- Relax.

❸ Test Scores

The answer sheets for most standardized tests are sent to a scoring center, where they are corrected by scoring machines. Test scores are often issued at the end of school marking periods, along with report cards. Once you have a chance to review your scores, you can decide whether you want to schedule an appointment with a teacher or counselor to discuss your results.

LESSON 2 SAT and ACT Overview

If you're planning to go to college, you'll probably take the Scholastic Aptitude Test (SAT) and the American College Test (ACT) in your junior year. Scores from these standardized tests are sent to the colleges to which you apply. Check with your guidance counselor to find out when and where you should take the SAT and ACT, and what the fee will be.

❶ How They Compare

The SAT and ACT are often mentioned in the same breath, but they are significantly different tests. Since some colleges require scores from only one of the tests and allow you to choose which one to send, knowing how the tests differ can help you decide which is more suited to your test-taking abilities.

ACT Versus SAT

ACT	SAT
Content-based	Tests critical-thinking and problem-solving skills
Tests achievement in English, math, reading, and science reasoning	Tests math and verbal skills
Tests grammar	Doesn't test grammar
Places little emphasis on vocabulary	Places much more emphasis on vocabulary
All multiple choice	Not all multiple choice
Does not penalize for wrong answers	Does penalize for wrong answers
Each section worth 36 points	Each part worth 800 points
Four scores are averaged to reach a composite score	Two scores are added together

 Some colleges or programs require minimum ACT or SAT scores for admission. Check with individual colleges to find out about their policies.

❷ How to Prepare

The year the S.A.T. creators decided to mess with students' minds.

CLOSE TO HOME copyright 1993 John McPherson. Reprinted with permission of UNIVERSAL PRESS SYNDICATE.

Contrary to what the cartoon suggests, test creators aren't trying to trick you. The questions on the SAT and ACT require thoughtful reading and attention to details and clues. The best way to prepare for the tests is to practice taking them. In your sophomore year, you probably took the PSAT, which was practice for the SAT. However, you can also practice taking the tests in your junior year.

> **Here's How** **Practicing for the Tests**
>
> - Enroll in classes designed to hone your test-taking skills. These classes may be offered by private organizations or by your school.
> - Form SAT/ACT study groups with other students.
> - Find software programs that allow you to take practice SATs and ACTs and review the answers.
> - Locate on-line sites that specialize in SAT and ACT preparation. Use the keywords "SAT" or "ACT" to locate these sites.

If you're not satisfied with your scores, you can retake either or both tests. Only your best SAT and ACT scores will be sent to the colleges you apply to.

TAKING TESTS

Test Item: Reading Comprehension

A reading comprehension item tests your ability to read and understand material seen for the first time. Don't panic—you aren't expected to know anything about the subject beforehand. Once you understand the item's format and learn some strategies for answering the questions, you will feel more confident about this test item.

A reading comprehension item usually has two parts: a reading selection and several questions about the selection. Here's a sample reading comprehension item from an essay on fashion.

Directions: Answer the questions below, based on the information in the accompanying passage.

(1)   The concept of fashion as we know it originated around 1350. Before that time, people wore loose garments draped according to the national style. Clothing styles changed after the Crusaders returned
(5) from the East with the button, which they had seen used by the Turks and Mongols. Court tailors began attaching buttons to clothes that fastened tightly around the human form. These garments resulted in fashion's first scandal when the Catholic Church
(10) objected to the revealing clothes.

     The objections posed by the Church did not halt the progress of fashion, however. As merchants and other members of the emerging middle class acquired new wealth, they wanted to dress like the
(15) nobility. The aristocrats, in turn, struggled to keep a step ahead of the middle class, and as a result, styles quickly became obsolete. By 1380 tailors were kept busy with the rapidly changing fashions.

     As fashions changed, some odd styles emerged.
(20) One of the strangest was that worn by women in Venice, Italy, in the 1600s. Venetian noblewomen began wearing platform shoes that lifted them nearly a foot off the ground. The wearer required an attendant on either side to support her as she
(25) walked on the stiltlike shoes. The shoes might have been designed to keep the women's feet dry when water from the surrounding lagoons rose and flooded some of the city's streets, but they were far from practical. The women who wore them might be
(30) considered among the earliest slaves to fashion.

❶ Before you read the selection, scan the questions and answer choices so that you can focus on relevant information.

❷ Read the passage carefully, and then reread or scan it to establish understanding.

❸ Pay special attention to topic sentences, which contain the key ideas.

1. The Crusaders saw the Turks and Mongols wearing
  A. loose garments
  B. clothes fastened with buttons
  C. clothes fastened with zippers
  D. high platform shoes

> This question asks you to recall information from the passage.
> *Answer:* **B**

2. What is meant by the phrase "styles quickly became obsolete" in lines 16–17?
  A. Styles came into fashion.
  B. Strange styles developed.
  C. No one cared about styles anymore.
  D. Styles became dated.

> You can often use context clues in the passage to determine the meanings of unfamiliar words.
> *Answer:* **D**

3. Which of the following DOESN'T explain why Venetian women wore high platform shoes?
  A. They wanted to keep their feet dry.
  B. They wanted to maintain the height of fashion.
  C. They wanted to scandalize the Catholic Church.
  D. They wanted to attract attention.

> When a wrong answer is called for, look for an answer choice that provides insufficient or incorrect information.
> *Answer:* **C**

4. According to the selection, who were among the earliest slaves to fashion?
  A. Venetian noblewomen in the 1600s
  B. the attendants who supported the Venetian women
  C. the tailors who tried to keep up with the changing fashions
  D. the Turks and Mongols

> The phrase "according to the selection" means that you should base your answer on information in the selection only.
> *Answer:* **A**

For more practice answering reading comprehension items, see ClassZone at mcdougallittell.com.

 You won't always be able to find the answer to a reading comprehension item in the selection. You may have to infer, or "read between the lines," to arrive at an answer.

TAKING TESTS

LESSON 4 Test Item: Analogy

Do you think you can't mix apples and oranges? You can when you answer an analogy item. This item tests your ability to recognize the relationship between a pair of words and to apply that relationship to a second word pair.

❶ Format

Most analogy items provide a related pair of words and ask you to choose a second word pair that expresses the same relationship as the first. A single colon separates each pair of words; a double colon shows that the pairs express the same relationship.

Directions: Choose the word pair that expresses the relationship most like that expressed in the given pair.

DISK : COMPUTER : :

A. remote control : television   **C.** typing : keyboard

B. audiotape : cassette player   **D.** printer : paper

Answer: **B**

---

❷ Strategies for Answering

Here are some strategies to help you answer analogy items.

> ### Strategies for Answering Analogy Items
>
> • Read the item as a question: "A disk is to a computer as what is to what?"
>
> • Make up a sentence that precisely expresses the relationship between the words in the given pair: "A disk records information from a computer."
>
> • Try the answer choices in the made-up sentence. Answer choice **A** would be "A remote control records information from a television." Does this word pair express the same relationship as the given pair?
>
> • Make sure that the order of the words in the second pair is the same as that in the given pair. In answer choice **D** above, printer : paper presents a similar relationship, but the word order is reversed.
>
> • Look for answer choices with the same parts of speech as the given pair. In the item above, the words in the given pair are both nouns. Therefore, you can eliminate answer choice **C** because *typing* is a verb or gerund.

For practice answering analogy items, see ClassZone at mcdougallittell.com.

❸ Common Relationships

Here are some of the relationships you might find in analogy items.

Common Relationships in Analogies

Relationship	Example
Synonyms	REASON : LOGIC : : generosity : munificence
Antonyms	ALERT : DULL : : present : absent
Part to whole	TEACHER : FACULTY : : toe : foot
Cause to effect	INSOMNIA : EXHAUSTION : : fast : hunger
Tool to user	WRENCH : PLUMBER : : brush : painter
Product to source	NOVEL : NOVELIST : : film : director
Action to object	DRIVE : VEHICLE : : toss : ball
Connotative differences	CHEAP : INEXPENSIVE : : weird : exotic

PRACTICE ▶ **Analogy Test Items**

Choose the word pair that completes each of the following analogy test items.

1. ACCOUNTANT : CALCULATOR : :
   A. mathematics : graph
   B. gardener : shovel
   C. pen : writer
   D. clock : wind

2. ERROR : INACCURACY : :
   A. unusual : typical
   B. wrong : incorrectly
   C. form : contour
   D. vacation : travel

3. RAIN : FLOODS : :
   A. fire : matches
   B. earthquake : volcanoes
   C. crop loss : drought
   D. plane crash : casualties

4. VOLUME : ENCYCLOPEDIA : :
   A. musician : orchestra
   B. book : page
   C. poet : poetry
   D. menu : restaurant

5. INAUDIBLE : WHISPER : :
   A. speech : lengthy
   B. resounding : yell
   C. dejected : delighted
   D. jest : joke

6. SUPERVISOR : FACTORY : :
   A. conductor : orchestra
   B. drummer : drum
   C. boss : command
   D. spectator : applause

7. HILARIOUS : COMEDY : :
   A. stunt : dangerous
   B. edit : scene
   C. performance : triumphant
   D. gloomy : tragedy

8. ELEGANT : OSTENTATIOUS : :
   A. observant : nosy
   B. rich : poor
   C. pretentious : haughty
   D. gaudy : flamboyant

Test Items: Vocabulary and Usage

Vocabulary and usage items test your knowledge of words, language, and mechanics.

❶ Vocabulary Items

Vocabulary items measure your ability to recognize and define words. The best way to prepare for these items is to expand your vocabulary through reading. You can also take practice tests to become familiar with the items and their format.

Format

A typical vocabulary item asks you to identify a word's synonym or antonym. Read the directions carefully so that you know which form to look for.

> **Directions:** Choose the best synonym for the underlined word.
>
> <u>Persevere</u>
>
> **A.** give up   **C.** anger
>
> **B.** perspire   **D.** persist
>
> *Answer:* **D**

Strategies for Answering

Here are some strategies to help you answer vocabulary items.

Strategies for Answering Vocabulary Items

- Examine word parts, including prefixes, suffixes, roots, and base words, to determine the meaning of an unfamiliar word.

  > Example: **monotone**
  > **prefix:** *mono-* means "one" or "single"
  > *Monotone* means "a single tone."

- Use context clues in a sentence item to help you figure out unfamiliar words.

  > Example: **The opulent apartment reflected its owner's wealth.**
  > The context clue "reflected its owner's wealth" suggests that *opulent* means "lavish."

- Use your knowledge of word families to figure out a word's meaning. For example, knowing that the Latin root *vid* or *vis* means "see" can help you figure out the meaning of words like *vista* or *visor*.

For more on parts of words, see pp. 548–553.

❷ Usage Items

Usage items test your knowledge of capitalization, punctuation, grammar, and language. Reviewing lessons on these subjects in your language textbooks will help you prepare for the items.

Format

Usage items take many forms, depending on the skill being tested. The item below tests your knowledge of verbs.

> **Directions:** Choose the best way to write the underlined phrase.
>
> While the final seconds in the game were ticking away,
>
> our star forward <u>will soar</u> through the air and scored
>
> what would be the winning basket.
>
> **A.** No Change **C.** soars
>
> **B.** soared **D.** soar
>
> *Answer:* **B.**

The action in the sentence takes place in the past. The verb "will soar" refers to a future action rather than a past one.

Strategies for Answering

Here are some strategies to help you answer usage items.

Strategies for Answering Usage Items

- Read the directions for these items carefully, since they can vary from item to item.

- Look for logical relationships between parts of a sentence, including compare-and-contrast and cause-and-effect.

- Within a sentence, make sure that subjects agree with verbs.

- Within a passage, make sure that verb tenses and pronouns are used correctly and consistently.

- If you're unsure of an item, repeat the sentence mentally, using each answer choice.

For practice answering vocabulary and usage items, see ClassZone at mcdougallittell.com.

Test Item: Essay

Peanuts by Charles Schulz

Does the thought of taking an essay test keep you awake at night? Actually, an essay test gives you more freedom than an objective test item, because you can often develop your own ideas and draw your own conclusions.

❶ Strategies for Answering

The most important thing to know about an essay test item is what is expected in the answer. You can glean this information from keywords in the writing prompt.

Understanding Writing Prompts

An essay question, or writing prompt, contains specific keywords that tell you how the question should be answered. For example, the keyword *summarize* asks you to provide a brief overview of a subject's key ideas. Can you identify the keywords in this prompt?

> **Directions:** Write an essay on the following.
>
> **1.** Define *perestroika* and explain its impact on the Russian economy.

Define asks for a precise meaning; *explain* asks you to tell about and show how.

For a list of keywords and the type of information they require, see p. 586. For suggestions on adapting the writing process to an essay question, see p. 296.

HOT TIP

Underline the keywords in the prompt and refer to them as you write. By doing so, you will keep your response focused.

Drafting a Response

Once you understand the prompt and what is required, you can start to compose your answer.

> **Here's How** **Writing Your Answer**
>
> - Write your thesis on scratch paper.
> - Jot down a quick outline to organize your ideas, and refer to this as you begin to write.
> - If ideas come to you while you're writing about something else, take notes so you won't forget the new ideas.
> - Use facts, statistics, examples, and other details to support your ideas.
> - Be aware of time restraints and pace yourself.
> - Try to reserve a little time at the end to read over your answer and correct any misspellings and punctuation errors.

If you're running out of time, outline the rest of your answer. This shows the evaluator that you know the material but didn't have time to write it all down. You may not receive full credit, but you will probably get some credit.

❷ Standards for Evaluation

Test examiners for a particular test use the same criteria to score essay items. These criteria are often contained in a rubric, a set of standards for evaluating writing. Here is a typical rubric.

Rubric	
Score	Evaluation
5	Answer is complete. Ideas are well organized and supported. Student understands the subject very well.
4	Answer is good but not complete; all major points are not addressed. Student understands the subject reasonably well.
3	Answer provides only a minimum amount of information. Student has only a basic understanding of the subject.
2	Answer is mostly padded with irrelevant material. Student reveals little knowledge of the subject.
1	Answer is completely off the mark. Student has no understanding of the subject.

Student Help Desk

Standardized Tests at a Glance

Achievement Tests	Tests that measure how much you've learned
College Entrance Exams	• The SAT tests math and verbal skills. • The ACT tests achievement in English, math, reading, and science reasoning.
Aptitude Tests	Tests that measure your interest and potential abilities
Personality Tests	Tests that help you identify your personal preferences.

Keywords in Essay Prompts

Looking for Clues

Keyword	Your Task
Analyze	Break something into its parts, and discuss how the parts are related.
Compare/contrast	Point out similarities and differences.
Define	Provide a precise meaning or list a subject's distinguishing characteristics.
Discuss	Examine a subject in detail.
Evaluate	Assess and judge a subject by carefully examining it.
Explain	Make a problem or relationship understandable by providing reasons.
Identify	Point out specific distinguishing details.
Interpret	Give your opinion on what something means.
Persuade	State your opinion on an issue, and use logical arguments to convince the reader it is correct.
Prove	Take a stand, and support it by citing evidence.
Summarize	Present the main points of a subject.
Synthesize	Logically derive a theory or a general idea from the facts.

Test-Taking Strategies   Your Plan of Attack

Test Item	Strategy
Reading comprehension	Scan the questions and answer choices before you read the selection.
	Read the passage carefully once, and then reread it to establish understanding.
	Notice how ideas are related within the selection.
Analogy	Make up a sentence that expresses the relationship in the given word pair.
	Make sure that the order of the relationship is maintained.
	Eliminate answer choices that don't present the same parts of speech as the given pair.
Vocabulary and usage	Use context clues to figure out unfamiliar words.
	Make sure that subjects and verbs agree.
	Make sure that verb tenses and pronouns are used correctly and consistently.
Essay	Use keywords in the prompt to figure out what information is expected.
	Jot down your thesis and a quick outline to organize your ideas.
	Use details to support your ideas.
	Be aware of time restraints, and pace yourself.

The Bottom Line

Checklist for Taking Standardized Tests

Have I . . .

____ taken practice tests when possible?

____ reviewed verbal and grammar skills in appropriate textbooks?

____ read written directions and listened to oral directions?

____ found out what materials— calculators or other supplies—I can bring to the test?

____ prepared myself both mentally and physically for the test?

Student Resources

Exercise Bank

Parts of Speech

1. Nouns (links to review on p. 8)

Write all of the nouns in the following sentences. Use the following categories to identify each noun: concrete noun, proper noun, abstract noun, possessive noun, and compound noun. You will use two categories to identify some nouns.

1. A pond is a small, still body of water that is generally shallow enough for light to penetrate to the bottom.
2. This sunlight makes it possible for a carpet of rooted aquatic plants to grow over the pond's floor.
3. Many animals live in and around ponds, and new creatures are continually being introduced to the habitat via wind and streams.
4. Birds, fish, insects, turtles, frogs, various plants, and microscopic organisms can be part of a pond's ecosystem.
5. The sort of life found around a pond is decided largely by the type of soil in the area, the makeup of the water, and the pond's location.
6. One kind of pond, a bog pond, often develops in low-lying, cool areas of the Northern Hemisphere and has acidic water.
7. Another variety, the riverine pond, forms in places where old stream beds are stopped up.
8. A pond evolves naturally over time with changes in the climate around it.
9. Floods and ice movement, along with the continual change of the seasons over time, help ponds grow.
10. When human beings and their creations interfere in this natural cycle of renewal, the quality of a pond can seriously deteriorate.

2. Pronouns (links to review on p. 12)

Write the pronouns and identify them as personal, intensive, possessive, relative, demonstrative, indefinite, or interrogative.

1. Did you know that many of the wedding customs that are practiced today originated during ancient times?
2. For example, the convention of wearing a veil most likely dates back to Roman brides, who may have covered their faces for weddings more than 2,000 years ago.
3. One of the practices that definitely started with the ancient Romans is that of giving a wedding ring.

4. Wearing a wedding ring on the left-hand ring finger is another familiar custom, itself begun because people believed that a vein or a nerve ran straight from that finger to the heart.
5. According to a long-lived superstition, a bride and a groom should not catch sight of each other prior to the ceremony on the wedding day.
6. The act of throwing rice at a couple after their wedding probably began because rice was once thought to bring fertility, joy, and prolonged life.
7. If a bride follows the French custom of tossing her bouquet to the single females at the wedding, everyone expects the woman who catches it to be married next.
8. Many of the couples getting married these days uphold the customs and superstitions that have been preserved from the past.
9. But who can blame some of the young couples if they want to deviate somewhat from tradition to create a more personalized ceremony?
10. A couple may go so far as to write a wedding service that is uniquely theirs.

3. Verbs (links to review on p. 15)

For each of the following sentences, write the verbs or verb phrases and identify them as linking or action verbs. Circle the auxiliary verbs.

1. Members of the crow family, ravens are large and entirely black.
2. These birds can be found throughout the Northern Hemisphere.
3. Ravens are extremely hardy, and they may inhabit the northern tundra and even the desert.
4. The raven is an omnivore that will eat insects, worms, frogs, rodents, birds' eggs, grains, and fruits.
5. Ravens call to each other with deep, rumbling croaks, which vary in tone and length.
6. If a raven is taken into captivity when it is very young, it may learn a few human words too.
7. Odin, a god of Norse mythology, kept two sacred ravens as his servants.
8. These ravens would fly around the world every day and report what they had seen to Odin in the evening.

9. This myth was created long before the bird was immortalized in American literature by Edgar Allan Poe's poem "The Raven."
10. Poe used a raven as an omen of death in his poem.

4. Adjectives and Adverbs (links to review on p. 18)

Write every word used as an adjective or an adverb in the following sentences. Identify each modifier as an adjective or adverb and tell the word or words it modifies.

1. A plant that is growing where humans do not want it to grow is often called a weed.
2. Whether a certain type of plant is seen as a weed depends on where it is growing.
3. When a morning glory grows in an alfalfa field, for example, it causes the crop to be less healthy, so it is considered a weed in this situation.
4. In gardens, however, people often cultivate morning glories for their beautiful flowers and hearty nature.
5. Most weeds detract from the health of surrounding crops by depriving neighboring plants of necessary sunlight, water, and nourishing nutrients in the soil.
6. Weeds can also shelter harmful insects and diseases that can damage crops planted by humans.
7. In some cases, however, weeds are quite helpful in preserving natural areas, because their roots actually reduce soil erosion.
8. Birds and other wildlife can also benefit from the food and shelter that weeds provide.
9. It can be hard to eliminate weeds from an area, because they often spread and germinate quickly.
10. The seeds of some weeds, like those of the dandelion, have special devices that allow the wind to carry them far from their parent plant.

5. Prepositions (links to review on p. 20)

Write the prepositional phrases in the following sentences. Circle the prepositions.

1. Mary Flannery O'Connor was an Amerian author who was born in Savannah, Georgia, in 1925.
2. She went to school at the Georgia State College for Women and the State University of Iowa.
3. For much of her life, O'Connor raised peacocks and wrote novels and stories in Milledgeville, Georgia.

4. Influences on Flannery O'Connor's work included the culture of the South and her Roman Catholicism.
5. The characters of her writing are often physically disfigured or emotionally or spiritually troubled.
6. Despite these disturbing people, O'Connor's books are frequently humorous as well.
7. Because she was afflicted by bad health during the last ten years of her life, she was not able to finish many works.
8. O'Connor published two novels and one collection of short stories during her lifetime.
9. Another book of stories was printed posthumously, and all of Flannery O'Connor's stories were compiled into one book in 1971.
10. *Flannery O'Connor: The Complete Stories* won the National Book Award for fiction in 1972.

6. Conjunctions (links to review on p. 23)

Write the conjunctions and the conjunctive adverbs in the following sentences.

1. Because the trees of the genus *Populus* grow so quickly, they are quite useful to humans.
2. These trees can provide protection against the elements by blocking both sun and wind to make an area more hospitable.
3. Poplar, aspen, and cottonwood trees are all members of the genus *Populus.*
4. Although the wood of the cottonwood tree is soft and weak, it can be used to make plywood, pulpwood, furniture, boxes, and matches.
5. Kansas, Wyoming, and Nebraska have named the cottonwood as their state tree; nevertheless, it grows in other areas of the United States, too.
6. The leaves of the cottonwood are green and shiny; moreover, they are triangular in shape.
7. Furthermore, cottonwood leaves can be identified by their edges, which are wavy and toothed.
8. Cottonwood trees grow long clusters of little greenish flowers before summer begins.
9. After they wilt, these flowers produce large quantities of cottony seeds.
10. Trees of the genus *Populus* are prolific; indeed, a single tree can generate millions of seeds each season.

Parts of the Sentence

1. Subjects and Predicates (links to exercise A, p. 28)

➜ **2.** Flying <u>lizards</u> | <u>are</u> an entirely different matter.
   5. <u>It</u> | <u>soars</u> from tree to tree on these outstretched "wings."

Copy each sentence. Draw a vertical line between the complete subject and the complete predicate. Then underline the simple subject once and the simple predicate twice.

1. Everyone knows about swimming fish.
2. Some fish actually "walk" on land, though.
3. Certain catfish crawl from one body of water to another on their tails and side fins.
4. These fish often spend days out of the water.
5. The roaming fish breathe through special air-breathing organs on land.

2. Compound Sentence Parts (links to exercise A, p. 30)

➜ **1.** <u>ranked, took</u>   **5.** <u>tornadoes, hurricanes</u>

Write the sentences below, and underline the compound subjects once and the compound verbs twice.

1. Depending on the circumstances, almost any kind of weather can seem normal or can feel odd.
2. For example, low precipitation levels seldom occur in rain forests but are normal in deserts.
3. Deserts and other hot, dry areas sometimes experience dust devils.
4. These whirlwinds resemble small tornadoes and carry dust, sand, and debris up into the air.
5. Dust devils neither last long nor do much damage.
6. Tornadoes and smaller whirlwinds over lakes and oceans are called waterspouts.
7. The swirling wind and spray can be quite dangerous to boaters.
8. Winter and early spring in the Rocky Mountains sometimes include chinooks, or warm, dry winds.
9. These warm, dry winds sweep down the eastern mountain slopes and quickly melt the snow in their path.
10. Skiers and newcomers to the region can be taken by surprise.

3. Subjects in Sentences (links to exercise A, p. 34)

➡ **2.** Ex; S, tree; V, stands   **4.** D; S, nothing; V, is

Identify each sentence below as declarative, imperative, interrogative, or exclamatory, and write its simple subject and simple predicate.

1. Do some bristlecone pines live even longer than redwoods and giant sequoias?
2. Yes, Methuselah, a bristlecone pine in eastern California, is more than 4,000 years old!
3. Imagine living that long.
4. How can bristlecones possibly survive for such a long time?
5. There are few harmful insects and diseases in the cool, dry environment of the bristlecones.

4. Complements (links to exercise A, p. 37)

➡ **1.** residents, tourists, IO; abundance, DO
   5. cathedrals, PN; castles, PN

Identify each italicized complement as a direct object (DO), an indirect object (IO), an objective complement (OC), a predicate nominative (PN), or a predicate adjective (PA).

1. Some caves are so *spectacular* that they deserve a place on anyone's list of natural oddities.
2. Crystal Ice Cave in Idaho gives *visitors* the *shivers.*
3. One reason is the *beauty* of the cave's frozen waterfall, frozen river, and other ice formations.
4. Many people consider Kentucky's *Mammoth Cave one* of the world's great natural wonders.
5. There, trickling water has carved rock *formations* that resemble trees, flowers, icicles, draperies, and other living and nonliving things.

② Using Phrases

1. Prepositional Phrases (links to exercise A, p. 52)

➡ **2.** of the Chicago Bulls, Michael Jordan, adjective phrase; from basketball, retiring, adverb phrase

For each sentence, write each prepositional phrase. Then write the word or words it modifies and tell whether it is an adjective phrase or an adverb phrase.

1. In 1849, over 80,000 fortune seekers arrived in California.
2. It was the beginning of the California Gold Rush.
3. Among the new arrivals was a man named Joshua Abraham Norton.
4. Norton was born in England but had spent most of his life in South Africa.
5. Once settled in San Francisco, Norton made a fortune as a merchant and a speculator.
6. A disastrous investment in the rice market forced him into bankruptcy after a few years, however.
7. Norton reacted badly to the disaster.
8. He became psychologically unstable and, in 1858, proclaimed himself "Emperor of the United States and Protector of Mexico."
9. During his 21-year "reign," the "emperor" wore a gold-braided uniform and issued royal documents, inspected construction projects, and performed other activities in a highly dignified manner.
10. He captured the imagination and the affection of the people of San Francisco, and 30,000 attended his funeral.

2. Appositives and Appositive Phrases (links to exercise on p. 54)

➡ 1. Bertrand Piccard, essential; Brian Jones, essential

For each sentence, write each appositive or appositive phrase. Also indicate whether it is essential or nonessential.

1. The Edsel, a Ford car introduced in 1957, was at the center of one of the oddest chapters in the company's history.
2. The car was named after Edsel Ford, the son of the company's founder.
3. Just how did this automobile, a sporty model that failed to sell, get its unusual name?
4. The story begins with company executive R. E. Krafve.
5. During the development of the car, Krafve suggested the name "Edsel" to Edsel Ford's three sons, Henry II, Benson, and William Clay.
6. Henry II, the president who had to choose the name, and his brothers objected to the commercial use of their father's name.

7. As a result, marketing manager David Wallace conducted research into names such as "Mars," "Jupiter," "Ariel," and "Phoenix" for the car.
8. Because of inconclusive results, the New York advertising agency Foote, Cone, and Belding was hired to suggest a name for the car.
9. When the deadline arrived, Ernest R. Breech, the chairman of the company, did not like any of the names under consideration.
10. Breech convinced Henry Ford II to agree to "Edsel," the original name proposed for the car.

3. Verbals: Participial Phrases (links to exercise A, p. 58)

➜ 1. Envisioning better automobile production

For each sentence, write the participial phrases.
1. All the penguins, seals, whales, and other animals living in Antarctica make their homes in coastal areas.
2. Found in the water and on rocky shores, these creatures obtain their food from the sea.
3. Until recently, Antarctica was a land uninhabited by humans.
4. Even today, the only people living there are scientists and military personnel.
5. Not belonging to any country and having no government of its own, Antarctica is governed by an international treaty.

4. Verbals: Gerund Phrases (links to exercise on p. 60)

➜ 2. Clicking your mouse
4. e-mailing someone, researching a topic on a computer

For each sentence, write the gerund phrases.
1. Millions of American men and women participated in World War II by fighting in Europe and in the Pacific.
2. Meanwhile men, women, and children at home were urged to help by working on the home front.
3. Helping the war effort from home took several different forms.
4. Working in defense plants was one way civilians, such as millions of women who had never worked outside the home before, contributed.
5. Huge amounts of metal were needed for building planes, tanks, and weapons.
6. For many youngsters, collecting scrap metal was a daily activity.

7. Wartime shortages also led to food and gasoline rationing.
8. People started growing their own vegetables on plots of land that became known as "victory gardens."
9. Efficiently using space for food production at home was the goal of every victory gardener.
10. Thanks to victory gardens, more farm products could be sent to soldiers instead of being needed for home use.

5. Verbals: Infinitive Phrases (links to exercise on p. 62)

➡ **1.** to tap her as a potential astronaut, noun

Write each infinitive or infinitive phrase. Indicate whether it functions as a noun, an adjective, or an adverb.

1. To study the world's oceans, scientists have developed specialized ships and equipment.
2. The H.M.S. *Challenger* was one of the first ships to embark on a solely scientific voyage.
3. This ship, which sailed from England in 1872, was outfitted to explore the ocean.
4. The crew's goal was to study the depth of the ocean, the chemical composition of its waters, and the life within it.
5. Scientists used data from the *Challenger*'s voyage to write the 50-volume *Report on the Scientific Results of the Voyage of H.M.S. Challenger.*

6. Avoiding Problems with Phrases (links to exercise on p. 65)

➡ **1.** dangling modifier; Now hailed as a substance that changed the world, the first all-synthetic plastic was invented by Leo Baekeland.
4. misplaced modifier; Instead of abandoning science, the chemist continued to perform experiments involving new substances.

For each sentence, indicate whether there is a problem caused by a faulty modifier. Write *misplaced modifier, dangling modifier,* or *no error.*

1. In the late 1500s, modern historians say that a Dutch botanist named Clusius received tulip seeds from Turkey and planted them in the botanic garden in Leiden.
2. Becoming wildly popular, people throughout Holland fell in love with the flower.

3. Before long, a speculative market developed in tulip bulbs.
4. Some people made huge fortunes while others lost everything overnight from 1634 to 1637.
5. Speculating on tulip bulbs, the situation became so unstable that the government finally decided to impose regulations.

3 Using Clauses

1. Kinds of Clauses (links to exercise A, p. 80)

→ **2.** independent

Identify the underlined clause in each sentence below as independent or subordinate.

1. According to Hippocrates, a cheerful, easygoing person had excess blood in his or her body, <u>and Hippocrates called this personality type "sanguine."</u>
2. <u>When a person had too much "black bile,"</u> he or she was dubbed the melancholic type—that is, moody and depressed.
3. <u>Hippocrates labeled aggressive, excitable people choleric</u> because they supposedly had excess choler, or yellow bile, in their bodies.
4. People still use words such as *sanguine* and *melancholic* to describe temperament and behavior, <u>although most may not understand Hippocrates' use of the words.</u>
5. <u>While scientists no longer agree with Hippocrates' ideas about body fluids and personality,</u> the idea of four basic personality categories still exists.
6. <u>For example, the 16 personality types of the Myers-Briggs system grow out of four "preference scales,"</u> and David Keirsey describes four main personality types.
7. Keirsey acknowledges his debt to the Myers-Briggs system, <u>even though he uses names and descriptions different from those of Myers and Briggs.</u>
8. <u>According to Keirsey and other personality classifiers, every person is unique,</u> yet every person also fits into one of the 16 types.
9. <u>If 50 people of the same personality type gathered in one room,</u> they would all be different, not only in appearance but also in attitude, interests, values, and behavior.
10. They also would have a great deal in common, <u>or so personality classifiers say.</u>

2. Adjective and Adverb Clauses (links to exercise A, p. 84)

➡ **1.** if you look in magazines and on the Internet; adverb clause
3. which anyone can use; adjective clause

For each sentence below, write the adjective or adverb clause and identify the type of clause.

1. Many personality tests are based on the Myers-Briggs system of personality types or on a related system, although some grow out of very different theories.
2. For example, some books offer self-reporting personality questionnaires that are based on the Enneagram system.
3. *Enneagram* comes from the Greek word *ennea,* which means "nine," and the Enneagram system includes nine personality types.
4. Still, the Myers-Briggs Type Indicator® (MBTI), while not the only personality test available, is probably the most widely used.
5. Since it was published in 1962, the MBTI has been translated into more than two dozen languages and has been taken by millions of people around the world.

3. Noun Clauses (links to exercise on p. 87)

➡ **1.** Why even the youngest children differ in irritability, calmness, shyness, and other traits
2. what that role is

Write the noun clauses in the following sentences.

1. Some experts claim that genes are crucial in determining many aspects of personality.
2. The nagging problem for these researchers is how they can isolate various genes and verify their effects on personality.
3. In truth, present-day scientists cannot answer, with certainty, the question of whether genes or life experiences have the greater impact on personality.
4. One might ask whoever believes in the importance of genes why siblings' personalities are often quite different.
5. One probable reason is that siblings have only about 50 percent of their genes in common, unless they are identical twins.
6. In addition, how parents treat their children affects their children's personality.
7. That parents treat different children differently is an important part of the argument for the influence of birth order on personality.

8. Different treatment for different children also must be taken into account when considering how a person's gender helps to determine personality.
9. For example, are girls genetically "programmed" to be less aggressive than boys, or do girls simply respond to their parents' expectations about how girls should behave?
10. Of course, some experts believe we overestimate the influence of genes and parents on personality.

4. Sentence Structure (links to exercise A, p. 90)

➡ **1.** simple **2.** compound-complex

Identify the structure of each sentence as either simple, compound, complex, or compound-complex.

1. People acknowledge the importance of personalities in relationships when they say that someone else either is or is not their "type."
2. Personalities can clash when two people differ about whether they pay more attention to thoughts (Person A) or feelings (Person B).
3. Person A may call Person B "oversensitive," and Person B may call Person A "heartless."
4. Person A may wonder why Person B never thinks logically; Person B may wonder how Person A can be so cold.
5. If Person A and Person B make an effort to understand one another, they may come to appreciate what each person can bring to a relationship; moreover, they may find they actually get along quite well.
6. Unfortunately, something quite different often happens.
7. Attracted by the differences in their personalities, Person A and Person B get married, become best friends, or start a business together.
8. After a while, their differences lead to disagreements, and they begin to view one another's differences as flaws.
9. They might use methods such as criticism, sarcasm, and tears to accomplish the goal of changing the other's personality.
10. Such an effort is doomed to fail; the only results are likely to be frustration, hurt feelings, and a possible breakdown of the relationship.

5. Fragments and Run-Ons (links to exercise A, p. 93)

Identify each of the following as a phrase fragment (PF), clause fragment (CF), run-on sentence (RO), or complete sentence (C).

    1. People trying to choose a career aren't the only ones who can make use of personality tests, companies sometimes use personality tests for their own purposes.
    2. Publishers of personality tests do not recommend that employers use their tests to screen job applicants.
    3. To make decisions about promotions.
    4. Nevertheless, employers do use personality tests for many reasons.
    5. If a job applicant or a candidate for promotion is likely to succeed.
    6. For counseling employees, improving employee communication, and building effective employee teams.
    7. Even when personality tests are used in ways their supporters consider appropriate.
    8. The results can seem a bit strange.
    9. One writer reported visiting a factory where the managers wore color-coded badges these indicated the wearer's personality type according to the personality test the person had taken.
    10. The idea was that communication would be more effective if everyone could tell what kind of personality each manager had.

④ Using Verbs

1. Principal Parts of Verbs (links to exercise A, p. 108)

➜ **2.** emphasizing   **3.** won

Complete each sentence by writing the principal part of the verb indicated in parentheses.

    1. Socrates (be—past) a Greek philosopher who lived from 470 to 399 B.C.
    2. Although Socrates never (write—past) anything himself, his philosophy has been preserved in the works of Plato.
    3. Socrates taught the people of Athens to think rationally by (question—present participle) their ideas.
    4. He carefully (create—past) a questioning strategy.
    5. This strategy became (know—past participle) as the Socratic method.
    6. The strategy (ask—past) people to define concepts such as justice and goodness.

7. His pupils were (force—past participle) to admit their ignorance, and this, according to Socrates, was the beginning of knowledge.
8. Socrates always had (say—past participle) that he was the wisest man because he realized that he knew nothing.
9. For (offend—present participle) many influential people, Socrates was tried and convicted of corrupting the youth of Athens.
10. After being offered either banishment or death, he (choose—past) death by drinking hemlock.

2. Verb Tenses (links to exercise A, p. 113)

➡ **2.** had begun, past perfect   **4.** adopted, past

Write the verb in each of the following sentences and identify its tense.

1. The first notable use of the telescope was in 1609 by Galileo.
2. Within months, he had proved Copernicus right.
3. According to Copernicus's theory, the earth circled the sun, and not the reverse.
4. It is not surprising that the telescope has evolved considerably since the 1600s.
5. With the help of the telescope and other new instruments, scientists probably will have answered many questions about the universe by the end of the century.

3. Progressive and Emphatic Forms (links to exercise A, p. 116)

➡ **2.** had been working, past perfect progressive
  3. did fight, past emphatic

Write each progressive and emphatic verb in the following sentences and identify its form.

1. Before the era of consumer advocacy, people had been spending their money on dangerous and even life-threatening products.
2. Some manufacturers literally were getting away with murder.
3. Ralph Nader, one of the first consumer activists, will have been fighting for consumer rights for over 45 years by the year 2005.
4. Earlier, Nader was practicing law in Connecticut.
5. In 1965 he published his best-selling book *Unsafe at Any Speed,* which did succeed in improving auto safety regulations.
6. In 1969 he founded the Center for Study of Responsive Law, which does document the government's failure to enforce regulation.
7. Up until 1980, he had been serving as the head of the Public Citizen Foundation, a consumer activist group.

8. Nader did attack the nuclear power industry and the manufacturers of harmful pesticides.

9. Nader is still encouraging the establishment of powerful citizens' lobbies.

10. One goal that Nader and his followers did accomplish was informing consumers about their rights.

4. Active and Passive Voice (links to exercise A, p. 118)

➡ **1.** were underpaid, passive   **4.** had, active

Write the verbs in the following sentences and identify each as either active or passive voice.

1. Abraham Lincoln was born in a log cabin in Kentucky in 1809.

2. His grandfather had been killed at a young age.

3. As a result, Lincoln's father received little education.

4. The loss of their farm forced the Lincolns to move to Indiana in 1816.

5. Then at age nine, Abe lost his mother, Nancy Hanks.

6. His sister died ten years later.

7. In Lincoln's adult years, four children were born to him and his wife, Mary Todd.

8. However, only one of them, Robert, lived to adulthood.

9. Lincoln was also deeply saddened by the splitting of the country and the loss of lives during the Civil War.

10. Nevertheless, he met these tragedies with courage and perseverance.

5. Mood of Verbs (links to exercise A, p. 120)

➡ **4.** imperative

Identify the mood of the underlined verbs.

The French philosopher Jean-Paul Sartre <u>believed</u> that philosophy should help people live in the world. His philosophy, known as existentialism, demands that we <u>define</u> ourselves by making conscious choices. According to Sartre, most people would prefer that they <u>were</u> not free. <u>Imagine</u> yourself, like Sartre, living in Nazi-occupied Paris during World War II, where you could be killed or sent to a concentration camp at any time. If you <u>were living</u> that way, how would you express your freedom of choice and action? Sartre spent the rest of the war fighting against the Nazis. After the war, Sartre <u>continued</u> to live his existentialist philosophy. Among his causes <u>were</u> an end to the war in Vietnam and to the nuclear arms race. <u>Think</u> of all the causes that Sartre <u>would be involved in</u> if he <u>were</u> alive today.

6. Problems with Verbs (links to exercise A, p. 123)

➡ **1.** had not been   **4.** sit

Correct the verb errors in the following sentences.

1. In ancient times, the first astronomers had gazed in wonder at the stars.
2. The Greek astronomer Ptolemy has devised an explanation of the universe that had stood for over a thousand years.
3. In Ptolemy's system, the fixed earth laid at the center of the solar system with the sun and the other planets revolving around it.
4. In the early 17th century, the Italian astronomer Galileo had proved Ptolemy wrong.
5. Through Galileo's careful methods, astronomy was risen to the status of a true science.
6. After he showed Ptolemy's error, Galileo opened the door for the acceptance of the Copernican theory, which puts the sun at the center of the solar system.
7. By the time the 20th century arrived, astronomers demonstrate that our sun is part of an enormous galaxy containing billions of other stars.
8. Perhaps the most astonishing development of the 20th century will have been the discovery of the vast size of the universe.
9. In the early 1920s, Edwin Hubble discovered that the faint, glowing clouds of dust beyond our own galaxy have been other galaxies similar to our own.
10. Learning so much from the study of astronomy during the last century, we now know that we inhabit only a tiny corner of a huge galaxy among billions of galaxies in an expanding universe.

5 Subject-Verb Agreement

1. Agreement in Person and Number (links to exercise A, p. 134)

➡ **1.** are   **4.** was

For each of the following sentences, choose the correct verb form.

1. The writings of Amy Tan (has, have) made her one of the best-known American authors.
2. While Tan is American-born, her parents (was, were) born and raised in China.

3. Conflicts between Chinese tradition and the American lifestyle (figure, figures) prominently in her books.
4. The harshness of the upbringing of Tan's mother in China (was, were) responsible for her strong will.
5. Tan's relationship with her mother (was, were) marked by arguments and rifts.
6. Tension between such a mother and her stubborn daughter (appear, appears) as a major theme in Tan's novel *The Joy Luck Club.*
7. The main character of her novel *The Kitchen God's Wife* also closely (resemble, resembles) Tan's mother.
8. Refusal to suffer abuse by her husband (contributes, contribute) to the heroism of this character.
9. Clearly, Tan's feelings toward her mother (have, has) been mixed.
10. Tan's work, in addition to her novels for adults, (includes, include) books for children.

2. Indefinite Pronouns as Subjects (links to exercise A, p. 136)

➜ **3.** think   **5.** has

Correct the errors in the verbs that are in boldface type.

Many **thinks** that it is impossible to turn an animated film into a stage play effectively. Yet no one who **have** seen *The Lion King* on Broadway would doubt that it can be done. Most of the credit for this stunning achievement **belong** to Julie Taymor. There's little question that few **possesses** the talent and vision that Taymor brought to this show. All of the animal characters from the film **comes** to life, thanks to talented actors and to Taymor's costume designs. Everybody connected with the production **have** praised her innovative direction as well. Both achievements **deserves** the Tony Awards she received. Although none of Taymor's prior work **have** earned her the acclaim given *The Lion King,* most of those in the theater world **has** been aware of her brilliance for many years. In all likelihood, all her future work **are** going to receive much attention.

3. Compound Subjects (links to exercise A, p. 139)

➜ **2.** Neither difficult sacrifices nor lack of recognition was enough to discourage her.

For each of the following sentences, choose the correct verb form.

1. Popular music and acting (is, are) fields in which few manage to succeed.

2. Almost every ambitious young man and woman eventually (has, have) to admit defeat.

3. Neither the odds against success nor the hard struggle (was, were) enough to keep Ruben Blades from success in both fields, though.

4. Millions of fans and Latin music enthusiasts (regard, regards) Blades as a leading artist in salsa music.

5. Songwriting and performing (remain, remains) important aspects of Blades's life.

4. Other Confusing Subjects (links to exercise on p. 142)

➡ **1.** is   **3.** stem

For each of the following sentences, choose the correct verb form.

1. With the emergence of Jakob Dylan in the music world, the Dylan family (claim, claims) two stars in two generations.

2. What is amazing (is, are) that his father, Bob Dylan, has been a major figure in popular music for four decades.

3. Nineteen years (was, were) the age at which Bob Dylan moved to New York to start his musical career.

4. A host of would-be stars (invades, invade) New York every year, but few have had such an immediate impact as Bob Dylan.

5. Writing one's own songs (seems, seem) commonplace now, but Dylan started that trend.

5. Special Agreement Problems (links to exercise A, p. 145)

➡ **1.** There are few athletic training and competition programs as respected as Special Olympics.

4. Aren't Special Olympics events held only every four years?

For each of the following sentences, choose the correct verb form.

1. There (have, has) been few performers of popular music more precocious than Stevie Wonder.

2. Blindness (seem, seems) to have helped his enormous talents blossom early.

3. (Was, were) any other musician able to compose, sing, and perform on several instruments at age 12?

4. "Here (is, are) a genius," his first producer must have thought on first hearing the 11-year-old prodigy.

5. Into the pop music scene (was, were) the youngster introduced—billed as "Little" Stevie Wonder.

6. His songs (remain, remains) a popular commodity today.

7. There (is, are) a number of other issues that occupy Wonder today, however.

8. How many performers of popular music (have, has) been singled out by Nelson Mandela for their work against apartheid?
9. Issues of equality in the United States (is, are) another field that Wonder focuses on, both in his music and his life.
10. (Is, are) there any doubt that "Little" Stevie Wonder has grown to be a human being of huge stature?

6 Using Pronouns

1. Nominative and Objective Cases (links to exercise on p. 156)

➡ **2.** her   **5.** she

Write the correct form of the pronoun in parentheses. Identify the pronoun as nominative (N) or objective (O).

1. In 1527 Álvar Núñez Cabeza de Vaca joined an expedition to Florida, and (he, him) was immediately appointed second in command by the leader, Pánfilo de Narváez.
2. The raft conveying Cabeza de Vaca and his men was shipwrecked off the coast of what is now Texas and cast (they, them) ashore.
3. It was up to (he, him) to lead his men to safety.
4. Ultimately three men and (he, him) were the only survivors of the entire Narváez expedition.
5. Cabeza de Vaca returned to Spain in 1537, where he wrote *La Relación,* a report to the king of Spain about the adventures (he, him) and his men encountered.

2. Possessive Case (links to exercise on p. 158)

➡ **1.** his   **4.** my

For each sentence, choose the correct word in parentheses.

1. The Han dynasty (second century B.C.–A.D. second century) owes much of (its, it's) longevity and accomplishments to Chang Ch'ien, China's "Marco Polo."
2. In the early years of the Han dynasty, the Chinese struggled against the barbarians to the north. (Their, Them) constant fighting with the Huns was particularly damaging.
3. In response, Emperor Wu Ti transformed Chinese military tactics, which resulted in (his, him) being called the "Martial Emperor."

4. The Han fought many battles against the Huns; however, even when victory was (theirs, there's), the Chinese suffered many casualties.
5. Wu Ti decided to seek allies among other barbarian tribes. (His, Him) request for volunteers to lead a mission resulted in Chang Chi'en's stepping forward.
6. In 138 B.C., Wu Ti sent (his, him) journeying through the Huns' army lines.
7. (His, Him) traveling through enemy territory resulted in Chang's capture.
8. Chang was a captive for ten years. However, (his, him) marrying a Hun may have helped convince his captors to allow him to move to the western part of their territory.
9. Therefore, they didn't see (his, him) escaping and setting off on a journey through several Central Asian states.
10. (His, Him) traveling outside the Chinese empire helped open up trade and resulted in the collection of valuable information about empires lying to the south and west of Han China.

3. *Who* and *Whom* (links to exercise on p. 161)

→ **2.** whoever   **3.** who

Choose the correct pronoun in parentheses.

1. Mary Henrietta Kingsley, (who, whom) was born in London in 1862, fearlessly explored regions of West and Central Africa.
2. Kingsley had no relatives in England to (who, whom) she was close, so she visited her native country only briefly in 1894 before returning to Africa.
3. Kingsley, for (who, whom) everything was an adventure, climbed 14,435-foot Mount Cameroon before returning again to England.
4. She went to South Africa when war broke out there between the British and the Boers, (who, whom) were settlers of Dutch descent.
5. While nursing Boer prisoners of war in Cape Town, Kingsley, (who, whom) was only 38 years old, died of typhoid fever.

4. Pronoun-Antecedent Agreement (links to exercise A, p. 164)

➜ **2.** its

For each sentence, choose the correct pronoun in parentheses.

1. Amelia Earhart learned to fly and bought (his, her) first airplane at age 24.
2. However, (she, they) sold the airplane three years later because of family problems.
3. When Earhart returned to flying four years later, (she, they) became the first woman to make a solo transcontinental flight.
4. Earhart achieved international fame in 1932 after (he, she) became the first woman to fly solo across the Atlantic Ocean.
5. In 1937, Earhart and navigator Frederick Noonan took off on (his, their) 29,000-mile flight around the world.
6. When the pair flew over the Pacific Ocean, radio contact with (it, them) was lost.
7. Earhart and Noonan were never found after (his, their) plane disappeared.
8. A team formed by the U.S. Navy and Coast Guard searched for Earhart and Noonan, but (it, they) never found any trace of the flyers.
9. Earhart's and Noonan's fate has been the subject of much speculation over the years, but (he, they) most likely died at sea.
10. Neither Earhart nor any other early women aviators knew that (she, they) would inspire future female astronauts.

5. Indefinite Pronouns as Antecedents (links to exercise A, p. 167)

➜ **1.** their   **2.** his or her

For each sentence, choose the correct pronoun in parentheses.

1. Most would not want to spend (his or her, their) time on Macquarie Island near Antarctica.
2. However, everyone on Australia's sub-Antarctic base— researchers and wildlife rangers—seems to enjoy (his or her, their) work there—at least, for a while.
3. Eventually, though, each claims that (he or she, they) will "go feral," or become stir-crazy.
4. That most people go a little stir-crazy is not surprising, considering that (he or she, they) are surrounded by animals.
5. After nine months on the island, few of the researchers are sorry to see (his or her, their) work come to an end.

6. Other Pronoun Problems (links to exercise on p. 170)

➡ **1.** us   **3.** he

For each sentence, choose the correct pronoun in parentheses.

1. For years, my parents have told us, my sister and (I, me), about the town's famous lost treasure.
2. One day, (we, us) sisters decided to hunt for the missing treasure in the old Jackson house.
3. The house seemed to welcome us, my sister and (I, me), from the moment we opened the door.
4. Still, no one was more surprised than (we, us) when a beam of light suddenly revealed a large box.
5. Imagine our horror, though, when we opened the box and found (us, ourselves) face to face with a large skunk!

7. Pronoun-Reference Problems (links to exercise A, p. 173)

➡ **3.** His findings were ignored until 1900.
    4. Mendel's theory—that traits handed down from parent plants to offspring could be predicted—transformed agriculture.

Rewrite the following sentences to correct instances of general, indefinite, and ambiguous pronoun references.

1. British navigator James Cook commanded three voyages to the Pacific Ocean and sailed around the world twice, which suggests how ambitious he was.
2. Cook and his crew were the first known Europeans to reach the Hawaiian Islands. That, Cook believed, gave him the right to name the islands.
3. Cook named them the Sandwich Islands after the Earl of Sandwich because he was Britain's lord of the admiralty.
4. While exploring America's northwest coast, Cook and his crew encountered treacherous storms and huge walls of ice in the Arctic Ocean. It forced them to turn back and return to Hawaii.
5. Cook's men and the Hawaiian people enjoyed a feast that they had provided.

7 Using Modifiers

1. Using Adjectives and Adverbs (links to exercise A, p. 183)

➜ **1.** adjectives: leading, chronic; adverb: now
3. adjectives: prominent, medical, 79; adverb: nearly

Write the words used as adjectives or adverbs in the following sentences. Do not include articles.

1. For a long time, people have commonly believed that sugar is addictive.
2. Many people still believe that high sugar consumption can lead to all sorts of behavioral changes.
3. Some of these behavioral changes include hyperactivity in children and aggressiveness in adults.
4. But there is no real proof that sugar is addictive.
5. People who completely eliminate sugar from their diets do not experience physical withdrawal symptoms as they would with truly addictive substances.
6. Most well-designed studies have found that sugar consumption does not cause or worsen hyperactivity in children.
7. Some scientists reportedly believe that the hyperactivity may be due to a child's excitement over a sugary treat instead of the actual sugar.
8. Studies on the exact relationship between sugar and behavior are ongoing.
9. Earlier experiments reported that excess sugar intake can possibly lead to aggressive or criminal behavior in adults.
10. Low blood sugar, which is actually caused by high sugar intake, diminishes brain function and can result in difficulties in emotional control.

2. Making Comparisons (links to exercise A, p. 186)

➜ **2.** fitter   **3.** better

Choose the correct form of comparison for each sentence.

1. If you would like to feel stronger and (more energetic, most energetic) than you do now, look closely at the types of foods you eat.

2. Obtaining healthy nutrition for your body is (simpler, simplest) than you probably think.
3. Of all the nutrition aids out there, one of the (better, best) ones is the Food Guide Pyramid.
4. The pyramid does (much, more) than simply divide foods into types.
5. It allows you to be (more flexible, most flexible) in your food choices than you may have thought possible.
6. The pyramid promotes balance and moderation in diet (more well, better) than the four food groups of the 1950s did.
7. It is also a (visual, more visual) approach to food selection than the four food groups were.
8. In the Food Guide Pyramid, none of the five listed food groups is (less essential, least essential) than the rest.
9. No foods are identified as (badder, worse) than others.
10. Use the Food Guide Pyramid to help you make the (more nutritious, most nutritious) food selections possible for your age and lifestyle.

3. Problems with Comparisons (links to exercise A, p. 189)

➡ 1. Can a robot be a more skillful surgeon than a real doctor?
  3. The accuracy rate of a robotic arm is higher than that of a human doctor.

Rewrite the following sentences to make the comparisons clear and correct. If there are no problems in a sentence, write Correct.

1. Although bread and potatoes are both high in complex carbohydrates, potatoes are a more better source of vitamin C than bread is.
2. The fat content of croissants is higher than English muffins.
3. Deep-yellow and dark-green leafy vegetables are better sources of beta carotene, which forms vitamin A, than any other vegetables are.
4. Broccoli, bell peppers, and tomatoes have more vitamin C than any vegetables.
5. Peas are less usefuller sources of vitamins A and C than other vegetables are.
6. The fiber obtained from fruits is better or at least as good as vegetable fiber.

7. A half cup of three-bean salad contains three times as much fiber as a whole cup of lettuce does.
8. Legumes are a more versatiler food than most because they can be substituted for foods in the vegetable and meat groups.
9. The vitamin C in citrus fruits and berries is more plentiful than peaches and apricots.
10. Of all foods, meat, poultry, and fish are some of the body's most best sources of iron.

4. Other Modifier Problems (links to exercise A, p. 193)

➜ 3. The pain didn't bother him when he was playing soccer, though.
4. However, he didn't do well in several of his classes.

Correct the sentences with modifier errors. If a sentence has no errors, write *Correct.*

1. Trying to build strong bodies for the future, a healthful diet is a must for teenagers.
2. Many teenagers don't never get enough of certain nutrients, particularly calcium and iron.
3. These here nutrients are vital for good physical development.
4. Calcium, which you need if your bones are to grow good, comes from foods like milk and cheese.
5. Since almost half of your adult bone mass is formed during your teenage years, your body will react badly to a shortage of calcium.
6. A teenager can't hardly get along with fewer than 1,200 to 1,500 milligrams of calcium daily.
7. A diet of fast foods will never get them needed milligrams into your body.
8. If you want to feel good and have lots of energy, iron is another nutrient that your body requires.
9. Chicken, eggs, and green leafy vegetables: these kind of foods are good sources of iron.
10. If you know a teenager who doesn't barely have enough energy to get through the day, maybe he or she is low on iron.

8 Capitalization

1. Names (links to exercise on p. 204)

➜ **1.** President Lyndon B. Johnson, America's
4. Dad, James O. Hill, Ph.D.

For each sentence, write the words that should be capitalized.

1. On July 10, 1999, mia hamm, michelle akers, and the other members of the American women's soccer team played a World Cup final match against China.
2. My aunt jane managed to get tickets for the match and took mom and me.
3. The game-winning penalty kick belonged to brandi chastain.
4. However, the biggest winners were all the cheering mothers and daughters watching the game—and that number included aunt jane, my mother, and me.
5. You don't need a ph.d. to figure out that the World Cup match was good for young girls who need positive female role models.

2. Other Names and Places (links to exercise A, p. 207)

➜ **2.** British, Christian, Sundays, Jew, anti-Semitism

For each sentence, write the words that should be capitalized.

1. In 1528, Hernán Cortés was eager to impress the king of spain, who also ruled most of europe.
2. During the post-conquest era, damaging rumors about Cortés had horrified powerful catholic bishops.
3. Cortés desperately wanted to please the spanish king.
4. He brought aztec athletes east across the atlantic ocean to the iberian peninsula.
5. Cortés and his men had been the first non-americans to see a game of tlachtli.
6. This nahuatl word was strange to their ears, but the game itself intrigued them.
7. After Cortés's arrival in toledo, both the spanish nobles and the native americans must have been astounded.
8. The christian europeans had never seen a "pagan" ball game like tlachtli.
9. Likewise, the aztecs had never seen moorish castles, french lace, or spanish ladies before.
10. The gifts must have worked, for in 1530, Cortés returned to new spain.

3. Organizations and Other Subjects (links to exercise A, p. 211)

➡ **3.** junior, Lincoln-Sudbury High School
   5. World Games for the Disabled

For each sentence, write the words that should be capitalized. If the sentence contains no errors, write *Correct*.

1. Athletes in olympic competitions often want gold medals and contracts with athletes' choice shoes or crispy cracklin' cereal.
2. In contrast, the athletes in the special olympics just want to run, jump, skate, or ski.
3. For them, the commercial aspects of athletics are as foreign as life on mars or a trip to the moon.
4. Organizers at the special olympics international headquarters promote the joy of participation.
5. In 1999, the special olympics world summer games were held in North Carolina.
6. One athlete, Leslie, practiced sprinting at the track at the university of oregon.
7. As anyone who has taken psychology 101 knows, positive reinforcement is important.
8. So in Leslie's event, everyone got a medal—as precious to them as a vintage sportster zs to a collector.
9. Leslie gave an oscar-winning performance on the victory stand.
10. Her smile was so wide that it probably could have been seen from the orbiting *discovery* space shuttle.

4. First Words and Titles (links to exercise on p. 213)

➡ **2.** The, "That

For each sentence, write the words that should be capitalized. If the sentence contains no errors, write *Correct*.

1. In 1940, listeners heard the first *superman* radio show.
2. The music swelled and the announcer said, "faster than a speeding bullet!"
3. today that announcer might use Richard Noble's Thrust SSC (supersonic car) as the epitome of speed.
4. In his article "Magnificent supersonic car," Stan Goldstein described the speed record on land.
5. "At 768 mph," he wrote, "the surface of Nevada's Black Rock Desert was literally pulverized."
6. the pilot, Andy Green, set the record with an average of 763.035 miles per hour.

7. An office worker seven miles from the course said, "Never have i seen pictures on a wall move on their own!"
8. "The culprit wasn't a poltergeist," explained one expert. "the shock waves from the jet car tilted the pictures."
9. In 1965, Ralph Nader wrote the book *unsafe at any speed,* which attacked the U.S. car industry.
10. "What we need today," remarked one critic, "is someone like Nader to expose the problems with speed demons."

5. Abbreviations (links to exercise A, on p. 215)

➡ **1.** A.D. **4.** ESPN, ABC, NBC

For each sentence, write the abbreviations that should be capitalized.

1. At 6:30 a.m., my parents have fuzzy brains.
2. So when I told them about needing money for the rca, they asked why I wanted an old record player.
3. I explained that I had to pay my dues to the Rodeo Cowboys Association by 2 p.m.
4. Later, I asked Joe for a pin number, but he didn't know that I was talking about the Police Information Network.
5. When Polybius commented about umpires in 247 b.c., he didn't have to make nl and al distinctions.
6. Likewise, Dio Chrysostom wrote about Greek sports in the second century a.d. without one single abbreviation.
7. Recently, I saw "ak" after a player's name but couldn't remember whether it stood for Alaska or Arkansas.
8. I also wondered who decided that "mn" would be Minnesota, "me" would be Maine, and "mt" would be Montana.
9. After all this confusion, I've decided to call eric—not my friend, but the Educational Resources Information Center.
10. The alphabet soup is getting thicker, and I need help asap.

9 End Marks and Commas

1. Periods and Other End Marks (links to exercise on p. 225)

➡ **1.** If someone said that you could earn money with your driving skills, what would your response be?

2. As a part-time driver, you could probably earn more than minimum wage, without working from 9 A.M. to 5 P.M. every Saturday and Sunday.

Add periods, exclamation marks, and question marks where they are needed.

1. After seeing today's sleek, sophisticated racing cars, you might ask yourself what their predecessors were like

2. Think about the 19th century's level of technology, and you'll get an idea of how the first race car looked

3. When a racing car driver like A J Foyt or Al Unser, Jr, sees an original racing car, he must wonder what it would be like to drive such a car

4. Those racing cars were simply motorized variations of horse-drawn carriages and carts

5. After seeing an early car, you might exclaim, "Wow Engineers certainly have improved the performance capabilities and design of racing cars"

6. Today, engineers are able to produce complex high-performance racing machines

7. Did you know that modern racing cars are categorized into two different types

8. The first category consists of one-person, open-wheeled cars with open cockpits

9. The second category includes closed-wheeled cars with enclosed cockpits

10. What do these machines cost A lot

2. Commas in Sentence Parts (links to exercise A, p. 229)

➡ **1.** model, but   **3.** money, here

Add or delete commas to clarify the following sentences.

1. Once Carl a friend of mine was a passenger in a car involved in a collision.

2. By the way, Carl drives no one would ever guess how nervous he was in driver's education class.

3. To pass the written exam Carl studied every night.
4. The instructor Mr. Hughes asked Carl, to be the first driver to take the road test.
5. "You're prepared Carl" Mr. Hughes said. "Don't worry. Just drive defensively."
6. After buckling his seat belt, and adjusting the rearview mirror Carl started the car's ignition.
7. His palms were sweaty and he felt sick to his stomach.
8. However once Carl drove out of the parking lot he began to relax, and enjoy the challenge.
9. At Mr. Hughes's request, Carl calmly negotiated every turn parallel parked and smoothly merged back into traffic.
10. Now a confident capable driver, Carl who has been driving for six years drives with caution rather than fear.

3. Using Commas for Clarity (links to exercise A, p. 231)

➡ 1. rallies, unlike the Grand Prix or Indy 500,
2. road, rallies

Insert commas to clarify sentences as needed, and revise sentences that contain comma splices.

1. Some people enjoy the speed of air travel; others the independence of car travel.
2. A long automobile trip not just air or rail travel requires a lot of advanced planning.
3. With a good plan and a well-maintained car road trips can offer a great way to see the nation.
4. Motorists should be prepared for anything that can go wrong probably will.
5. Any road traveler will tell you that preparation is key; patience vital.
6. Before hitting the road travelers should check that their tires are in good condition and their turn signals in working order.
7. Always keep a good map, a gasoline can, and a blanket in your car when you travel, having a first-aid kit, a snack, and water in the car is a good idea, too.
8. Problems from inopportune breakdowns to congested traffic can make drivers wish they had never left home.
9. The Motor Club provides this safety tip for road travel in bad weather: "If you must drive drive cautiously!"
10. Some people say that driving on the open road is relaxing, others prefer to let someone else do the driving.

4. Other Comma Rules (links to exercise A, p. 233)

➡ **1**. Last month, the; Lee, Would

Insert commas as needed to clarify the following sentences.

1. "Women have been in the driver's seat since cars gained popularity in the late 1800s" the noted lecturer began.
2. She continued "An adventurer named Alice Huyler Ramsey founded the first United States Women's Motoring Club."
3. I soon discovered that Alice Ramsey club president organized an auto race exclusively for women.
4. With New York as the starting point, the race began on January 12 1909.
5. "The racers traveled in pairs" reported the local papers "and drove fine automobiles."
6. The exhausted winners reached the finish line in Pennsylvania two days later on January 14 1909.
7. On June 6 1909 Ramsey began a history-making trip from New York to San Francisco.
8. Ramsey a tireless driver faced hardships, such as being stuck in the mud for long periods of time.
9. At the end of the trip, she might have sent a telegram to fans in New York to exclaim "Dear Friends I've made it!"
10. Auto manufacturers quickly realized that women all over the country from Portland Maine to Portland Oregon constituted a viable target market.

⑩ Other Punctuation

1. Apostrophes (links to exercise A, p. 244)

➡ **2**. FBI's, people's   **4**. sister's, brother-in-law's

Identify and correct errors in the use of apostrophes.

1. In the 1890's, France feared Germanys power.
2. In 1894, evidence that a French spy was leaking information to Germany surfaced in a wastebaskets contents.
3. From torn pieces of a memorandum, authorities conclusions led to a Jewish captain, Alfred Dreyfus.
4. Dreyfus was convicted of someone's else's crime, stripped of his' rank, and sent to prison.

5. After two years time, proof of Dreyfus' innocence was found; however, the French Armys honor was at stake and nothing was done.
6. Through his brother's and wifes efforts and the publics outcries, Dreyfus won another trial after five years.'
7. The defenses case should have been easy because the guilty party, Major Esterhazy, had confessed and fled the country.
8. To no ones surprise, however, the judges declared Dreyfus guilty.
9. Dreyfus brother appealed to the French president, whose' decision was to grant a pardon.
10. Justice wasnt done until 1906, when Dreyfus' rank was restored and he was awarded the Legion of Honor.

2. Hyphens, Dashes, and Ellipses (links to exercise A, p. 248)

➡ 3. de-emphasizing, con-vinced
   4. people—reporters, businessmen—by

Insert hyphens, dashes, and ellipses where they are needed. If necessary, consult a dictionary.

1. Impostors can sometimes be well intentioned do gooders.
2. Three fourths of their motivation may come from a desire to be respected and all important.
3. One famous, chameleon-like impostor, Ferdinand Demara, said, "We impostors. . . . are unaccountable people."
4. With great selfconfidence but scant medical knowledge, Demara enlisted in the Royal Canadian Navy as a doctor.
5. Remarkably, his patients soldiers wounded during the Korean War survived his six month medical career.
6. Possibly the most famous impostor of all, that is, if the story is true, was the ninth century Pope, John VIII, who was also called Pope Joan.
7. Trained by an English monk, Joan became well versed in countless disciplines, including theology.
8. The ordained clergy priests, monks, and bishops did not accept women in their ranks; nonetheless, Joan rose to a post in the Vatican as "Father John."
9. The impostor was elected Pope John VIII, an unbelievable feat of fakery though her term was cut short when she died giving birth during a procession.
10. Colin Wilson wrote: "According to the Church, the story of Pope Joan is just an amusing . . . legend. But it persisted throughout the Middle Ages . . . "

3. Semicolons and Colons (links to exercise on p. 251)

➜ **1.** stated the following: **2.** term;

Correct all errors in the use of semicolons and colons.

1. In real-life battles, issues of right and wrong aren't always clear, both sides may be right.
2. In the early 1980s, Detroit's mayor, Coleman Young, faced these civic problems, high crime rates, high unemployment, and very few economic opportunities.
3. In order for Detroit to be the site: of a new General Motors factory and benefit from the job opportunities, the city had to act quickly.
4. The city selected an area for the factory site and made deals with more than 3,400 residents, nonetheless, about 300 residents did not want to sell.
5. In the end, Poletown lost its case to the majority interests, the remaining residents finally agreed to leave.

4. Quotation Marks and Italics (links to exercise on p. 255)

➜ **1.** *flagrante delicto,* "caught in the act,"
3. *Perry Mason,* "I confess!"

Correct errors in the use of quotation marks and italics. Use underlining to indicate italics.

1. Sophocles once wrote, How dreadful it is when the right judge judges wrong!
2. Centuries later, that same fear is still being voiced in books such as "Out of Order."
3. In the chapter The Injudicious Judiciary, author Max Boot describes the powers and problems of judges.
4. He explains that judges are influential because more than 90 percent of criminal and civil cases "are settled, not tried before a jury. . .".
5. Of course, TV shows such as "The Practice" and "Ally McBeal" focus on jury trials because they have more dramatic appeal.
6. Those shows do occasionally depict a judge who suffers from what Boot has called gavelitis.
7. "Your fellow man", wrote Boot, "invariably addresses you as "Your Honor" or "Judge.""
8. For some judges, this treatment is "heady stuff;" consequently, they grow out of touch with everyday life.

9. Afflicted judges often do whatever they want "carte blanche," which is French for without restrictions.

10. Who wouldn't feel powerful when, as Boot suggests, the whole world "bows and scrapes and genuflects before you?"

5. Parentheses and Brackets (links to exercise on p. 257)

➡ **4.** [meaning Whistler]   **5.** (Was . . . money?)

Correct errors related to the use of parentheses and brackets. If a sentence is correct, write *Correct.*

1. The movie *Rasputin and the Empress* (1932) was remarkable for two reasons: 1 it starred John, Ethel, and Lionel Barrymore; and 2 it was the subject of two lawsuits.

2. The movie was produced by Metro-Goldwyn-Mayer [MGM].

3. Grigory Rasputin was a Russian monk who gained great power over Nicholas II and Alexandra through their only son who (suffered from hemophilia).

4. In 1916, a group of Russian noblemen conspired to have Rasputin (the "Mad Monk") murdered.

5. One of the main conspirators was Prince Feliks Yusupov [He was still living when MGM made the movie].

6. The movie was the only film the Barrymores made together. (It was Ethel's first "talkie" (talking picture).)

7. According to one source, "The studio sought to avoid [legal] trouble with Prince Yusupov."

8. Someone, no one knows who, came up with the name Prince Chegodieff for Yusupov's character.

9. First, Yusupov sued MGM for depriving him of credit for the conspiracy. (he won!)

10. Then Prince Chegodieff (the real one!) sued MGM for libel to his good name, and he won a handsome sum.

Model Bank

Reflective Essay

College Application Essay
from *Essays That Worked*

PROMPT: Write a personal essay that gives readers a sense of who you are.

RUBRIC
IN ACTION

There is a little demon that lurks in my conscious and unconscious mind that has done me more ill than any conventional ailment could. It is a stealthy creature that preys upon weakness and appetite and has ruined many a fair weekend in my life, and in the lives of many. The demon's name is procrastination, and he mocks me even as I type up the final draft of this essay. For the demon has triumphed again, and stolen my sleep, and he may triumph again after this. But I think not for a while, for this time he has stung me sorely, and my guard shall be up.

❶ Begins by engaging the reader's interest in a humorous way

This autumn and winter have been a hectic time in my life, and the hectic time is when the demon thrives. In late October I began rehearsal for a play. The rehearsal schedule was not rigorous at first, and did not rule my life, but it was there. It was there and the demon seized upon it and assured me I had nothing to worry about; January and deadline time were still a long way off. And I was persuaded, and the further into rehearsal I went, the less I resisted the imp's devious advice. It was not long into rehearsal when the other, smaller deadlines began to creep up and rear their ugly heads, and paper after paper after test struck me unmercifully. And then the play was over. It was almost Christmas and now the responsibilities of shopping allied themselves with my academic obligations and thrashed me mercilessly while the demon chuckled, knowing that the real deadline was obscured and would be staggeringly painful to meet. Finally, Christmas was past, and the real deadline loomed ahead, frighteningly unobscured. Now the diabolical creature convulsed in unrestrained laughter, while I shuddered with a tinge of fear of imminent discomfort.

❷ Describes the situation in precise and humorous detail

Another option: Use dialogue to further personify the "demon"

I then began the ordeal that would geometrically increase my misery daily until the Epiphany, when the deadline must be met. I cursed the demon, loudly at first, then more softly and then not at all. I stopped and I could only laugh an ironic laugh. For I realized that the demon does not exist; that he is merely an apparition that I have created. And discovering the power of creation, I realized that I also have the power to dispel the creature. I know now that all I need do is seize the deadline in the distance and never shall the demon haunt me.

❸ Maintains the humorous tone while also showing the lesson learned

Eyewitness Report

Heavy Tread of Elephants Makes Hearts Lighter
by Michael T. Kaufman
The New York Times
March 24, 1995

The night was cool and the wind was churning as the 18 elephants prepared to cross by foot into Manhattan from Queens. It was a little before midnight, and up ahead, the Empire State Building shone brightly as the mahouts and keepers slid open the animal cars on the circus train.

Without a single snort of protest, without an elephant sneer, they emerged wallowing in grace like fat chorus girls happy to be back in town. Without anyone saying a word to them, they lined up and bowed their heads to make it easier for their handlers to put on the red bridles with the Ringling Brothers and Barnum & Bailey insignia. . . .

Midnight came and Mark Oliver Gebel, the 24-year-old lion tamer and chief animal trainer, said, "Go, Jenny, Go." And Jenny, the pleasant lead elephant, led the way across Jackson Boulevard and down 50th Avenue to the Queen's Midtown Tunnel entrance. There were not many pedestrians around, but the drivers of cabs who had to stop as the animals crossed were all smiling. . . .

Jenny walked past the toll booth. No one paid. Mr. Gebel said, "Hatri," a command that the elephants understand to mean "grab the tail of the elephant in front of you with your trunk." The trainer said, "Jaldi, jaldi," which Hindi speakers and elephants understand to mean "step on it."

Jenny set the pace for the chain of elephants and for the 23 horses, 4 zebras, 5 camels, and 2 llamas that trailed behind them. For 25 minutes, the animals trudged in silence. Under the river, their surrealistic menagerie formed a peaceable kingdom. . . .

As the bipeds strained to keep up, the elephants glided, their lined faces and introspective eyes looking wise. One of the trainers said he thought they could probably get to where they were going without the guides. . . .

RUBRIC
IN ACTION

❶ Sets the scene by telling what is happening and when

❷ Uses vivid sensory images and a simile to set the tone

❸ Presents events in a clear logical order

RESOURCES

When the procession came around the final bend in the tunnel to the Manhattan night, Mayor Rudolph W. Giuliani was waiting with his son, Andrew. The mayor posed with the elephants. . . . He urged Andrew to meet Jenny up close and personal, but Andrew maintained a more formal distance.

Then the procession moved on, heading crosstown. Now there were people on every street. There were loud cheers for the animals. People started marching along on the sidewalks, shouting and yelling. At Stern College, hundreds of female students jumped up and down and danced to welcome the huge beasts. . . .

❹ Captures the mood of the event

Among those who joined the elephant march were two brothers, Richard and Jonny Rosch, musicians who welcome the elephants every year. . . .

[Richard] was asked if he thought this city would be a better place if it had elephants on the street all the time.

"Definitely," he replied.

Literary Interpretation

**Looks Like a Winner: 'Phantom' Fulfills Destiny by
Astounding the Eyes**
by Roger Ebert
Chicago Sun-Times
May 17, 1999

RUBRIC
IN ACTION

"Star Wars: Episode I—The Phantom Menace," to
cite its full title, is an astonishing achievement in
imaginative filmmaking. If some of the characters are
less than compelling, perhaps that's inevitable: This is
the first story in the chronology and has to set up
characters who (we already know) will become more
interesting with the passage of time. . . .

❶ Clearly
identifies the
work being
reviewed

At the risk of offending devotees of the Force, I will
say that the stories of the "Star Wars" movies have
always been space operas and that the importance of
the movies comes from their energy, their sense of fun,
their colorful inventions, and their state-of-the-art
special effects. I do not attend with the hope of gaining
insights into human behavior. Unlike many movies,
these are made to be looked at more than listened to,
and George Lucas and his collaborators have filled "The
Phantom Menace" with wonderful visuals.

❷ Gives a
clearly stated
interpretation
near the
beginning of
the piece

There are new places here—new *kinds* of places.
Consider the underwater cities, floating in their
transparent membranes. The Senate chamber, a vast
sphere with senators arrayed along the inside walls, and
speakers floating on pods in the center. And other
places: the cityscape with the waterfall that has a
dizzying descent through space. And the other cities:
one city Venetian, with canals, another looking like a
hothouse version of imperial Rome, and a third that
seems to have grown out of desert sands.

❸ Uses details
from the film to
support the point
about new kinds
of places

Set against awesome backdrops, the characters in
"The Phantom Menace" inhabit a plot that is little more
complex than the stories I grew up on in science-
fiction magazines. . . .

The plot details (of embargoes and blockades) tend
to diminish the size of the movie's universe—to shrink
it to the scale of a 19th century trade dispute. The stars
themselves are little more than pinpoints on a black
curtain, and "Star Wars" has not drawn inspiration from

the color photographs being captured by the Hubble Telescope. The series is essentially human mythology, set in space, but not occupying it.... Lucas gives us the universe domesticated by man. His aliens are really just humans in odd skins. For "The Phantom Menace," he introduces Jar Jar Binks, a fully realized computer-animated alien character whose physical movements seem based on afterthoughts. And Jabba the Hutt (who presides over the Podrace) has always seemed positively Dickensian to me.

4 Continues with another aspect of the interpretation—the characters

Yet within the rules he has established, Lucas tells a good story. The key development in "Phantom" is the first meeting between the Jedi Knight Qui-Gon Jinn (Liam Neeson) and the young Anakin Skywalker (Jake Lloyd)—who is, the Jedi immediately senses, fated for great things. . . .

The discovery and testing of Anakin supplies the film's most important action, but in a sense all the action is equally important, because it provides platforms for special-effects sequences. . . .

As surely as Anakin Skywalker points the way into the future of "Star Wars," so does "The Phantom Menace" raise the curtain on this new freedom for filmmakers. And it's a lot of fun. The film has correctly been given the PG rating; it's suitable for younger viewers and doesn't depend on violence for its effects. As for the bad rap about the characters—hey, I've seen space operas that put their emphasis on human personalities and relationships. They're called "Star Trek" movies. Give me transparent underwater cities and vast hollow senatorial spheres any day.

5 Answers opposing opinions and ends strongly

Comparison and Contrast

Mmmm Chocolate (excerpt)
Consumer Reports
March 1999

RUBRIC
IN ACTION

To the connoisseur, chocolate can be as subtle, as varied, and as rewarding as fine wine or exotic coffee.

❶ Begins by clearly identifying the subjects being compared

Milk chocolate, the favorite type in the U.S., is sweeter, with a mellower, less chocolaty flavor than dark chocolate. In Europe, dark chocolate dominates. Whether sweet, semisweet, bittersweet, or extra-bittersweet, dark chocolate is complex and somewhat bitter; it's a sophisticated treat favored by those who crave a more intense chocolate hit. (The difference between, say, sweet and bittersweet is determined by the amount of chocolate liquor—the substance produced when cacao beans are roasted and ground and that makes chocolate taste like chocolate.) Some dark chocolates have a pronounced nutty or woody character; others have a distinct fruity note, too. And dark chocolate should feel smooth and silky as it melts in the mouth.

❷ Describes the first subject, dark chocolate

Milk chocolate bars vary the most in flavor. Some have more chocolate than milk flavor; others, more milk than chocolate. They tend to have a thicker, creamier melted texture in the mouth than dark chocolate.

❸ Describes the second subject, milk chocolate

For many, it's enough that chocolate just tastes good. That's what treats are for, after all. But the medical verdict on chocolate is also more favorable than you might expect:

- You don't have to feel guilty about an occasional indulgence. A 1½-ounce serving of a typical chocolate bar contains around 200 calories and 12 to 15 grams of fat. That's a fair percentage of a single day's intake of fat and calories. But unless people eat chocolate every day, chocolate bars don't contribute much to the overall calorie and fat intake.

❹ Gives background on the overall subject

- A majority of the fat in cocoa butter (which contributes to the fat in a chocolate bar) is saturated fat. But about half that fat is stearic acid, a saturated fat believed to have a neutral effect on cholesterol.

- You can tell doubting teenagers that chocolate doesn't beget acne.

- There's even some preliminary research indicating that chocolate may help people live longer. In a recent study of 7,841 male college graduates, the ones who ate a moderate amount of chocolate lived almost a year longer than those who abstained. The reason may lie with phenols, antioxidants that can help prevent fatlike substances from forming in the blood and clogging arteries. This study is very tentative, however.

For this report we tested 37 chocolate bars: plain dark chocolate, plain milk chocolate, and milk chocolate with extras like nuts, toffee crisps, or nougat bits. They ranged from classic ... milk chocolate bars that cost less than a dollar to the superpremium ... dark chocolate bar that costs nearly $8. We also included three "dietetic" bars, sweetened with maltitol or fructose and promoted to diabetics. ...

⑤ Describes the way in which the comparison was made

Persuasive Essay

How Do We Decide Who Gets Another Chance at Life?
Don't Tie Gift of Life to Recipient's Location
by G. Bruce Weir
USA Today
February 24, 1999

> **RUBRIC**
> IN ACTION

Eleven years ago, I was told I needed a heart transplant or I would be dead in six months.

❶ Begins with an attention-getting fact

I was lucky: I made it. I got my transplant in four weeks; today, it would be closer to three months.

In 1988, there were 17,000 people waiting; today, there are more than 65,000. Every day, 90 more names get added to the national organ transplant list. Every day, 10 people on that list die because their organs did not come in time.

❷ Provides important background information

Yet we decide who gets another chance at life—and who does not—in an organ distribution system that simply is not fair. Where you live can be more important than how sick you are.

❸ States his opinion clearly

As it now works, the nation is divided into 63 local and 11 regional organ fiefdoms. When an organ becomes available, priority is given to patients in the same local area.

If no local patients are suitable, then the United Network for Organ Sharing (UNOS), the federal subcontractor that matches patients with organs, searches for a suitable recipient in the region where the organ was donated. If no one who is suitable for the transplant can be located in that specific region, then UNOS looks at patients on waiting lists in the rest of the country.

❹ Gives more background information on this complex issue

A recent report by UNOS underscores the unfairness of this system. It shows, for example, that median waiting times for liver transplant patients were 439 days in the Baltimore area but only 147 days in nearby Washington, D.C. In New York City, the median wait was 511 days; across the river in New Jersey, it was 56 days.

❺ Provides support for his opinion that the system is unfair

U.S. Health and Human Services Secretary Donna Shalala knows this isn't right.

"You shouldn't be discriminated against on the basis of where you live," she told a national television audience this month. "Your life shouldn't depend on geography. Organs are a national treasure. Organ distribution in this country must depend on medical criteria."

Last year, Shalala tried to even up the wide disparities by allocating organs over broader geographic areas and giving patients with "medical urgency" priority, within certain limits. But UNOS successfully lobbied Congress to block her plan until at least this fall.

This is a complex issue that opponents oversimplify into a battle between national and local control. They've so alarmed legislators in some states— Oklahoma, Wisconsin, South Carolina, and Louisiana— that these legislators have passed laws saying organs donated within their borders must be offered first to patients living in the state.

That idea is not only unfair, but often won't work; a nonresident listed in one of the state's transplant centers may get the organ.

But, more importantly, if an organ is donated as a gift—a gift of life—does that giver really care where the organ goes? I don't think so. The giver wants to come to the aid of those who need help most—be they in the next hospital room or across the country.

Until we have sufficient organs donated to guarantee there's one for every transplant candidate, we should base our decisions on who gets the limited supply on something more rational than where an ill person happens to live.

❻ Quotes an expert who supports his position

❼ Answers objections to his position

❽ Ends strongly by restating his opinion

Writing for History

PROMPT: What were some of the major changes in American life after the Civil War?

The Civil War caused great changes in the lives of Americans. The most significant changes occurred in the areas of politics, economics, and, especially, the population.

> ❶ Begins by listing three areas of change

Before the war, states' rights became a huge political issue, one that Southern states used frequently to fight national policies they opposed. After the war, the threat of secession could no longer be used, and states' rights were, in effect, squashed as an issue. The power that the Southern states wielded because of that threat was lost.

> ❷ Discusses the first area: politics

The war widened the economic gap between the North and the South. The North was relatively undamaged by the war; the war actually fed the industrialization of its cities. During the war, Northern cities actually produced more goods than the entire country had created a few years earlier.

> ❸ Continues the logical organization by discussing the second area: economics

On the other hand, the South was economically devastated. Since the majority of battles were fought on Southern soil, farmland and the entire railway system were destroyed. Cities like Atlanta were burned or crippled. Technological development came to a standstill. The labor force, consisting not only of slaves but also of many owners of small farms, was lost.

> ❹ Uses a transition to connect ideas

Most important to the country was the death toll of the war. Almost as many Americans were killed in the Civil War as in all later American wars combined. There was one dead or wounded soldier for every four slaves set free. Men who were physically crippled and mentally devastated returned to homes and farms that would take years to rebuild. Families were indelibly scarred by the war.

> ❺ Discusses the third area: the impact of war-related deaths on the population

Life in post–Civil War America was entirely different from life before 1860. The changes were far-reaching, and in many cases, insurmountable. Politically, economically, socially, and demographically, the Civil War changed America forever.

> ❻ Summarizes the changes discussed earlier in the essay

Writing for Science

PROMPT: What observations led scientists to believe that the Earth's continents were once joined together?

Scientists studied different evidence from all over the world to come to the conclusion that all the continents were once joined together in a supercontinent called Pangaea.

❶ Gives a brief overview of the answer in the introduction

The most obvious evidence that scientists noticed was that the eastern coastline of South America seemed to fit perfectly into the western coastline of Africa like pieces of a puzzle. Not only were the shapes of the coastlines very similar, but there were mountain ranges in South America that seemed to continue in Africa.

❷ Gives evidence to support the answer

In Antarctica, scientists found fossils of tropical plants and animals that never could have grown in such a cold climate. This led them to believe that at one point Antarctica must have been much closer to the equator than it is now.

Fossils of a specific plant were found in both India and Australia. Since the plants could not have crossed the ocean by any known means, this finding meant that India and Australia had to have been joined at some time in the past.

There were other theories to explain these similarities, however. Proponents of one theory said that the land between South America and Africa had been eroded and had become the Atlantic Ocean. Another said that the continents were once joined by bridges of land that had sunk into the oceans over time. No evidence was ever found to support these theories, though.

❸ Alternate ideas are offered.

Later, the theory of continental drift explained how the continents could move. This made the idea of Pangaea much more believable, and now it is generally accepted as the truth.

❹ Concludes with the reason that the Pangaea idea is so widely accepted

Business Letter

21 McPike Place
Memphis, TN 40075
August 21, 2001

Michael Claudius
Kitty Konniption, Inc.
100 East Monroe
Chicago, IL 60606

Dear Mr. Claudius:

I bought the Kitty Konniption tree house at my local Pets and Me store in June of this year. As an owner of two cats, I thought the product looked terrific.

My cats played in the tree house, and I didn't think to worry about their safety. Much to my shock, however, one of my cats was cut quite badly by a sharp-edged bolt on the forward right-hand corner of the tree house. I had to take the cat to the veterinarian, who gave her five stitches in her back left thigh.

This cat toy looks neat but could be lethal to cats. I would like my money back—enclosed is my receipt. In addition, I hope you will redesign the tree house to eliminate the danger for other cats.

Sincerely,

Hillary Johnson

Hillary Johnson

❶ Heading includes the sender's address and the date.

❷ The inside address directs the letter to a specific person.

❸ Greeting

❹ The body gives clear background information relative to the complaint.

❺ The writer clearly states the action she requests.

❻ Closing

Job Application

421 Katis Drive
San Francisco, CA 90090
May 26, 2001

❶ Sender's address and date

Dave Schneider
Zamboni Chase Productions
6371 N. Waverly Avenue
San Francisco, CA 90089

❷ The inside address directs the letter to a specific person.

Dear Mr. Schneider:

❸ Greeting

I am responding to your ad in the paper announcing a video technician position at your studio this summer. I am very eager to get into the video production field, and I hope I will have an opportunity to do so at Zamboni Chase Productions.

❹ Opens with a reference to the position and expresses enthusiasm for the job

I am currently in my junior year at Pepper Pike High School. Since my freshman year I have been an avid member of the school's audio-visual department. In my time there I have become well-acquainted with various video-editing systems, cameras, and sound systems. With my friends, I have produced a dozen short videos ranging in style from documentary to comedy to horror. One of our productions, *Keep Your Head in the Game,* is currently entered in three local film festivals.

❺ Gives a brief history that demonstrates his qualifications

Enclosed us my résumé, which gives further details about my other projects. I look forward to hearing from you soon. I hope there is an opportunity at your company requiring my experience and talent.

❻ Directs attention to the enclosed résumé and ends on a positive note

Sincerely,

James Kochalka

James Kochalka

❼ Closing

Personal Letters

Letter of Thanks

November 28, 2000

Dear Mrs. Spaly,

    I want to tell you what a great time I had at the lake last weekend. Thanks so much for letting Joe bring me along. I know space was tight in the cabin and it couldn't have been easy having an extra person there, but I want you to know how much I appreciated it.

    I've been talking nonstop about the trip since I got back. I hope I can come along again some time.

Yours,

Mike

❶ Date

❷ Greeting

❸ Thanks the reader and mentions a specific reason for being grateful

❹ Closing

Letter of Condolence

July 25, 2000

Dear Uncle Paul and Aunt Dalia,

    I don't know how to tell you how sorry I am about Amy. She was one of the finest people I knew. I will miss her.

    She told me once how happy it made her when you and she took trips together. I will always remember her warm smile.

    Please know that I am thinking about you now.

Love,

Sarah

❶ Date

❷ Greeting

❸ Identifies the reason for writing and shares the personal pain of the loss with the readers

❹ Closing

Guidelines for Spelling

Forming Plural Nouns

To form the plural of most nouns, just add -s.

prizes   **dreams**   **circles**   **stations**

For most singular nouns ending in o, add -s.

solos   **halos**   **studios**   **photos**   **pianos**

For a few nouns ending in o, add -es.

heroes   **tomatoes**   **potatoes**   **echoes**

When the singular noun ends in s, sh, ch, x, or z, add -es.

waitresses   **brushes**   **ditches**   **axes**   **buzzes**

When a singular noun ends in y with a consonant before it, change the y to i and add -es.

army—armies   **candy—candies**   **baby—babies**
diary—diaries   **ferry—ferries**   **conspiracy—conspiracies**

When a vowel (a, e, i, o, u) comes before the y, just add -s.

boys—boys   **way—ways**   **array—arrays**
alloy—alloys   **weekday—weekdays**   **jockey—jockeys**

For most nouns ending in f or fe, change the f to v and add -es or -s. Since there is no rule, you must memorize such words.

life—lives   **calf—calves**   **knife—knives**
thief—thieves   **shelf—shelves**   **loaf—loaves**

For some nouns ending in f, add -s to make the plural.

roofs   **chiefs**   **reefs**   **beliefs**

Some nouns have the same form for both singular and plural.

deer   **sheep**   **moose**   **salmon**   **trout**

For some nouns, the plural is formed in a special way.

man—men   **goose—geese**   **ox—oxen**
woman—women   **mouse—mice**   **child—children**

For a compound noun written as one word, form the plural by changing the last word in the compound to its plural form.

stepchild—stepchildren   **firefly—fireflies**

If a compound noun is written as a hyphenated word or as two separate words, change the most important word to the plural form.

brother-in-law—brothers-in-law   **life jacket—life jackets**

Forming Possessives

If a noun is singular, add 's.

mother—my mother's car   **Ross—Ross's desk**

Exception: the s after the apostrophe is dropped after *Jesus'*, *Moses'*, and certain names in classical mythology (*Zeus'*). These possessive forms, therefore, can be pronounced easily.

If a noun is plural and ends with s, just add an apostrophe.

parents—my parents' car   **the Santinis—the Santinis' house**

If a noun is plural but does not end in s, add 's.

people—the people's choice   **women—the women's coats**

Spelling Rules

Words Ending in a Silent *e*

Before adding a suffix beginning with a vowel or *y* to a word ending in a silent *e*, drop the *e* (with some exceptions).

amaze + -ing = amazing   **love + -able = lovable**
create + -ed = created   **nerve + -ous = nervous**

Exceptions: *change + -able = changeable; courage + -ous = courageous*

When adding a suffix beginning with a consonant to a word ending in a silent *e*, keep the *e* (with some exceptions).

late + -ly = lately   **spite + -ful = spiteful**
noise + -less = noiseless   **state + -ment = statement**

Exceptions include *truly, argument, ninth, wholly,* and *awful.*

When a suffix beginning with *a* or *o* is added to a word with a final silent *e*, the final *e* is usually retained if it is preceded by a soft *c* or a soft *g*.

bridge + -able = bridgeable   **peace + -able = peaceable**
outrage + -ous = outrageous   **advantage + -ous = advantageous**

When a suffix beginning with a vowel is added to words ending in *ee* or *oe*, the final silent *e* is retained.

agree + -ing = agreeing   **free + -ing = freeing**
hoe + -ing = hoeing   **see + -ing = seeing**

Words Ending in *y*

Before adding a suffix to a word that ends in **y** preceded by a consonant, change the **y** to *i.*

easy + -est = easiest   crazy + -est = craziest

silly + -ness = silliness   marry + -age = marriage

Exceptions include *dryness, shyness,* and *slyness.*

However, when you add *-ing,* the **y** does not change.

empty + -ed = emptied   but   empty + -ing = emptying

When adding a suffix to a word that ends in **y** and is preceded by a vowel, the **y** usually does not change.

play + -er = player   employ + -ed = employed

coy + -ness = coyness   pay + -able = payable

Exceptions include *daily* and *gaily.*

Words Ending in a Consonant

In one-syllable words that end in one consonant preceded by one vowel, double the final consonant before adding a suffix beginning with a vowel, such as *-ed* or *-ing.* These are sometimes called 1+1+1 words.

dip + -ed = dipped   set + -ing = setting

slim + -est = slimmest   fit + -er = fitter

The rule does not apply to words of one syllable that end in a consonant preceded by two vowels.

feel + -ing = feeling   peel + -ed = peeled

reap + -ed = reaped   loot + -ed = looted

In words of more than one syllable, double the final consonant (**1**) when the word ends with one consonant preceded by one vowel and (**2**) when the word is accented on the last syllable.

be·gin´   per·mit´   re·fer´

In the following examples, note that in the new words formed with suffixes, the accent remains on the same syllable.

be·gin´ + -ing   = be·gin´ning = beginning

per·mit´ + -ed   = per·mit´ted = permitted

In the following examples, the accent does not remain on the same syllable; thus, the final consonant is not doubled.

re·fer´ + -ence   = ref´er·ence = reference

con·fer´ + -ence   = con´fer·ence = conference

SPELLING

Prefixes and Suffixes

When adding a prefix to a word, do not change the spelling of the base word. When a prefix creates a double letter, keep both letters.

dis- + approve = disapprove re- + build = rebuild
ir- + regular = irregular mis- + spell = misspell
anti- + trust = antitrust il- + logical = illogical

When adding *-ly* to a word ending in *l,* keep both *l*'s. When adding *-ness* to a word ending in *n,* keep both *n*'s.

careful + -ly = carefully sudden + -ness = suddenness
final + -ly = finally thin + -ness = thinness

Special Spelling Problems

Only one English word ends in *-sede:* supersede. Three words end in *-ceed:* exceed, proceed, and succeed. All other verbs ending in the sound *-seed* are spelled with *-cede.*

concede precede recede secede

In words with *ie* and *ei,* when the sound is long *e,* the word is spelled *ie* except after *c* (with some exceptions).

i before *e*	thief	relieve	piece	field	grieve	pier
except after *c*	conceit	perceive	ceiling	receive	receipt
Exceptions:	either	neither	weird	leisure	seize

Commonly Misspelled Words

abbreviate
accidentally
achievement
amateur
analyze
anonymous
answer
apologize
appearance
appreciate
appropriate
argument
associate
awkward
beginning
believe
bicycle
brief
bulletin
bureau
business
calendar
campaign
candidate
certain
changeable
characteristic
column
committee
courageous
courteous
criticize
curiosity
decision
definitely
dependent
description
desirable
despair
desperate

development
dictionary
different
disappear
disappoint
discipline
dissatisfied
efficient
eighth
eligible
eliminate
embarrass
enthusiastic
especially
exaggerate
exceed
existence
experience
familiar
fascinating
February
financial
foreign
fourth
fragile
generally
government
grammar
guarantee
guard
height
humorous
immediately
independent
indispensable
irritable
judgment
knowledge
laboratory
license

lightning
literature
loneliness
marriage
mathematics
minimum
mischievous
mortgage
necessary
nickel
ninety
noticeable
nuclear
nuisance
obstacle
occasionally
occurrence
opinion
opportunity
outrageous
parallel
particularly
permanent
permissible
persuade
pleasant
pneumonia
possess
possibility
prejudice
privilege
probably
psychology
pursue
realize
receipt
receive
recognize
recommend
reference

rehearse
repetition
restaurant
rhythm
ridiculous
sandwich
schedule
scissors
seize
separate
sergeant
similar
sincerely
sophomore
souvenir
specifically
strategy
success
surprise
syllable
sympathy
symptom
temperature
thorough
throughout
tomorrow
traffic
tragedy
transferred
truly
Tuesday
twelfth
undoubtedly
unnecessary
usable
vacuum
vicinity
village
weird
yield

Commonly Confused Words

Good writers master words that are easy to misuse and misspell.
Study the following words, noting how their meanings differ.

accept, except *Accept* means "to agree to something" or "to receive
something willingly." *Except* usually means "not
including."
Did the teacher accept your report?
Everyone smiled for the photographer except Jody.

adapt, adopt *Adapt* means "to make apt or suitable; to adjust." *Adopt*
means "to opt or choose as one's own; to accept."
The writer adapted the play for the screen.
After years of living in Japan, she had adopted its culture.

advice, advise *Advice* is a noun that means "counsel given to
someone." *Advise* is a verb that means "to give counsel."
Jim should take some of his own advice.
The mechanic advised me to get new brakes for my car.

affect, effect *Affect* means "to move or influence" or "to wear or to
pretend to have." *Effect* as a verb means "to bring about."
As a noun, *effect* means "the result of an action."
The news from South Africa affected him deeply.
The band's singer affects a British accent.
The students tried to effect a change in school policy.
What effect did the acidic soil produce in the plants?

all ready, *All ready* means "all are ready" or "completely prepared."
already *Already* means "previously."
The students were all ready for the field trip.
We had already pitched our tent before it started raining.

all right *All right* is the correct spelling. *Alright* is nonstandard and
should not be used.

a lot *A lot* may be used in informal writing. *Alot* is incorrect.

all together, *All together* means "in a group."
altogether *Altogether* means "completely."
The news story is altogether false.
Let's sing a song all together.

among, between *Among* and *between* are prepositions. *Between* refers to two people or things. The object of *between* is never singular. *Among* refers to a group of three or more.

Texas lies *between* Louisiana and New Mexico.
What are the differences *among* the four candidates?

anywhere, nowhere, somewhere, anyway *Anywhere, nowhere, somewhere,* and *anyway* are all correct. *Anywheres, nowheres, somewheres,* and *anyways* are incorrect.

I don't see geometry mentioned *anywhere*.
***Somewhere* in this book is a map of ancient Sumer.**
***Anyway,* this street map is out of date.**

borrow, lend *Borrow* means "to receive something on loan." *Lend* means "to give out temporarily."

He *borrowed* five dollars from his sister.
Please *lend* me your book.

bring, take *Bring* refers to movement toward or with. *Take* refers to movement away from.

I'll *bring* you a glass of water.
Would you please *take* these apples to Pam and John?

can, may *Can* means "to be able; to have the power to do something." *May* means "to have permission to do something." *May* can also mean "possibly will."

We *may* not use pesticides on our community garden.
Pesticides *may* not be necessary, anyway.
Vegetables *can* grow nicely without pesticides.

capital, capitol, Capitol *Capital* means "excellent," "most serious," or "most important." It also means "seat of government." *Capitol* is a "building in which a state legislature meets." The *Capitol* is "the building in Washington, D.C., in which the U.S. Congress meets."

Proper nouns begin with *capital* letters.
Is Madison the *capital* of Wisconsin?
Protesters rallied at the state *capitol*.
A subway connects the Senate and the House in *the Capitol*.

choose, chose *Choose* is a verb that means "to decide or prefer." *Chose* is the past tense form of *choose*.

He had to *choose* between art and band.
She *chose* to write for the school newspaper.

desert, **dessert**	*Desert* (des´ ert) means "a dry, sandy, barren region." *Desert* (de sert´) means "to abandon." *Dessert* (des sert´) is a sweet, such as cake. **The Sahara in North Africa is the world's largest** *desert.* **The night guard did not** *desert* **his post.** **Alison's favorite** *dessert* **is chocolate cake.**
differ from, **differ with**	*Differ from* means "to be dissimilar." *Differ with* means "to disagree with." **The racing bike** *differs* **greatly** *from* **the mountain bike.** **I** *differ with* **her as to the meaning of Hamlet's speech.**
different from	is used to compare dissimilar items. *Different than* is nonstandard. **The hot sauce is much** *different from* **the yogurt sauce.**
farther, further	*Farther* refers to distance. *Further* refers to something additional. **We traveled two hundred miles** *farther* **that afternoon.** **This idea needs** *further* **discussion.**
fewer, less	*Fewer* refers to numbers of things that can be counted. *Less* refers to amount, degree, or value. *Fewer* **than ten students camped out.** **We made** *less* **money this year on the walkathon than** **last year.**
good, well	*Good* is always an adjective. *Well* is usually an adverb that modifies an action verb. *Well* can also be an adjective meaning "in good health." **Dana felt** *good* **when she finished painting her room.** **Angela ran** *well* **in yesterday's race.** **I felt** *well* **when I left my house.**
imply, infer	*Imply* means "to suggest something in an indirect way." *Infer* means "to come to a conclusion based on something that has been read or heard." **Josh** *implied* **that he would be taking the bus.** **From what you said, I** *inferred* **that the book would be** **difficult.**
its, it's	*Its* is a possessive pronoun. *It's* is a contraction for *it is* or *it has*. **Sanibel Island is known for** *its* **beautiful beaches.** *It's* **great weather for a picnic.**

kind of, sort of	Neither of these two expressions should be followed by the word *a*.
	What *kind of* **horse is Scout?**
	What *sorts of* **animals live in swamps?**
	The use of these two expressions as adverbs, as in "It's kind of hot today," is informal.
lay, lie	*Lay* is a verb that means "to place." It takes a direct object. *Lie* is a verb that means "to be in a certain place." *Lie,* or its past form *lay,* never takes a direct object.
	The carpenter will *lay* **the planks on the bench.**
	My cat likes to *lie* **under the bed.**
lead, led	*Lead* can be a noun that means "a heavy metal" or a verb that means "to show the way." *Led* is the past tense form of the verb.
	Lead is used in nuclear reactors.
	Raul always *leads* **his team onto the field.**
	She *led* **the class as president of the student council.**
learn, teach	*Learn* means "to gain knowledge." *Teach* means "to instruct."
	Enrique is *learning* **about black holes in space.**
	Marva *teaches* **astronomy at a college in the city.**
leave, let	*Leave* means "to go away from." *Leave* can be transitive or intransitive. *Let* is usually used with another verb. It means "to allow to."
	Don't *leave* **the refrigerator open.**
	She *leaves* **for Scotland tomorrow.**
	Cyclops wouldn't *let* **Odysseus' men** *leave* **the cave.**
like	as a conjunction before a clause is incorrect. Use *as* or *as if*.
	Ramon talked *as if* **he had a cold.**
loan, lone	*Loan* refers to "something given for temporary use." *Lone* refers to "the condition of being by oneself, alone."
	I gave that shirt to Max as a gift, not a *loan.*
	The *lone* **plant in our yard turned out to be a weed.**
lose, loose	*Lose* means "to mislay or suffer the loss of something." *Loose* means "free" or "not fastened."
	That tire will *lose* **air unless you patch it.**
	My little brother has three *loose* **teeth.**

majority means more than half of a group of things or people that can be counted. It is incorrect to use *majority* in referring to time or distance, as in "The majority of our time there was wasted."

Most of our time there was wasted.

The *majority* of the students study a foreign language.

most, almost *Most* can be a pronoun, an adjective, or an adverb, but it should never be used in place of *almost,* an adverb that means "nearly."

Most of the students enjoy writing in their journals. (pronoun)

Most mammals give birth to live young. (adjective)

You missed the *most* exciting part of the trip. (adverb)

Almost every mammal gives live birth. (adverb)

of is incorrectly used in a phrase such as *could of.* Examples of correct wordings are *could have, should have,* and *must have.*

I *must have* missed the phone call.

If you had played, we *would have* won.

principal, principle *Principal* means "of chief or central importance" and refers to the head of a school. *Principle* is a "basic truth, standard, or rule of behavior."

Lack of customers is the *principal* reason for closing the store.

The *principal* of our school awarded the trophy.

One of my *principles* is to be honest with others.

quiet, quite *Quiet* refers to "freedom from noise or disturbance." *Quite* means "truly" or "almost completely."

Observers must be *quiet* during the recording session.

We were *quite* worried about the results of the test.

raise, rise *Raise* means "to lift" or "to make something go up." It takes a direct object. *Rise* means "to go upward." It does not take a direct object.

The maintenance workers *raise* the flag each morning.

The city's population is expected to *rise* steadily.

real, really *Real* is an adjective meaning "actual; true." Really is an adverb meaning "in reality; in fact."

Real skill comes from concentration and practice.

She doesn't *really* know all the facts.

seldom	should not be followed by *ever,* as in "We seldom ever run more than a mile." *Seldom, rarely, very seldom,* and *hardly* ever all are correct. **I** *seldom* **hear traditional jazz.**
set, sit	*Set* means "to place" and takes a direct object. *Sit* means "to occupy a seat or a place" and does not take a direct object. **He** *set* **the box down outside the shed.** **We** *sit* **in the last row of the upper balcony.**
stationary, stationery	*Stationary* means "fixed or unmoving." *Stationery* means "fine paper for writing letters." **The wheel pivots, but the seat is** *stationary.* **Rex wrote on special** *stationery* **imprinted with his name.**
than, then	*Than* is used to introduce the second part of a comparison. *Then* means "next in order." **Ramon is stronger** *than* **Mark.** **Cut the grass and** *then* **trim the hedges.**
their, there, they're	*Their* means "belonging to them." *There* means "in that place." *They're* is the contraction for *they are.* **All the campers returned to** *their* **cabins.** **I keep my card collection** *there* **in those folders.** **Lisa and Beth run daily;** *they're* **on the track team.**
way	refers to distance; *ways* is nonstandard and should not be used in writing. **The subway was a long** *way* **from the stadium.**
whose, who's	*Whose* is the possessive form of *who. Who's* is a contraction for *who is* or *who has.* *Whose* **parents will drive us to the movies?** *Who's* **going to the recycling center?**
your, you're	*Your* is the possessive form of *you. You're* is a contraction for *you are.* **What was** *your* **record in the fifty-yard dash?** *You're* **one of the winners of the essay contest.**

MLA Citation Guidelines

Forms for Source Cards and Works Cited Entries

The following are some basic forms for bibliographic entries. Use these forms on the source cards that make up your working bibliography and in the list of works cited that appears at the end of your paper.

Whole Books

The following models can also be used for citing reports and pamphlets.

A. One author

Liptak, Karen. <u>Coming-of-Age: Traditions and Rituals Around the World</u>. Brookfield: Millbrook, 1994.

B. Two authors

Dolan, Edward F., and Margaret M. Scariano. <u>Illiteracy in America</u>. New York: Watts, 1995.

C. Three authors

Rand, Donna, Toni Parker, and Sheila Foster. <u>Black Books Galore!: Guide to Great African American Children's Books</u>. New York: Wiley, 1998.

D. Four or more authors

The abbreviation *et al.* means "and others." Use *et al.* instead of listing all the authors.

Quirk, Randolph, et al. <u>A Comprehensive Grammar of the English Language</u>. London: Longman, 1985.

E. No author given

<u>Science Explained: The World of Science in Everyday Life</u>. New York: Holt, 1993.

F. An editor but no single author

Radelet, Michael L., ed. <u>Facing the Death Penalty: Essays on a Cruel and Unusual Punishment</u>. Philadelphia: Temple UP, 1989.

G. Two or three editors

Langley, Winston E., and Vivian C. Fox, eds. <u>Women's Rights in the United States: A Documentary History</u>. Westport: Greenwood, 1994.

H. Four or more editors
The abbreviation *et al.* means "and others." Use *et al.* instead of listing all the editors.

Brain, Joseph D., et al., eds. <u>Variations in Susceptibility to Inhaled Pollutants: Identification, Mechanisms, and Policy Implications</u>. Baltimore: Johns Hopkins University Press, 1988.

I. An author and a translator
Rabinovici, Schoschana. <u>Thanks to My Mother</u>. Trans. James Skofield. New York: Dial, 1998.

J. An author, a translator, and an editor
La Fontaine, Jean de. <u>Selected Fables</u>. Trans. Christopher Wood. Ed. Maya Slater. New York: Oxford UP, 1995.

K. An edition other than the first
Metcalf, Robert L., and Robert A. Metcalf. <u>Destructive and Useful Insects: Their Habits and Control</u>. 5th ed. New York: McGraw, 1993.

L. A book or a monograph that is part of a series
Simon, Rita James. <u>The Jury System in America: A Critical Overview</u>. Sage Criminal Justice System Annuals 4. Beverly Hills: Sage, 1975.

M. A multivolume work
If you have used only one volume of a multivolume work, cite only that volume.

Tierney, Helen, ed. <u>Women's Studies Encyclopedia</u>. Rev. ed. Vol. 2. Westport: Greenwood, 1999. 3 vols.

If you have used more than one volume of a multivolume work, cite the entire work.

Tierney, Helen, ed. <u>Women's Studies Encyclopedia</u>. Rev. ed. 3 vols. Westport: Greenwood, 1999.

N. A volume with its own title that is part of a multivolume work with a different title
Cremin, Lawrence A. <u>The National Experience, 1783–1876</u>. New York: Harper, 1980. Vol. 2 of <u>American Education</u>. 3 vols. 1970–88.

O. A republished book or a literary work available in several editions

Give the date of the original publication after the title. Then give complete publication information, including the date, for the edition that you have used.

Hemingway, Ernest. <u>The Sun Also Rises</u>. 1926. New York: Scribner, 1954.

P. A government publication

Give the name of the government (country or state). Then give the department if applicable, followed by the agency if applicable. Next give the title, followed by the author if known. Then give the publication information. The publisher of U.S. government documents is usually the Government Printing Office, or GPO.

United States. Dept. of Labor. Bureau of Labor Statistics. <u>Perspectives on Working Women: A Databook</u>. By Howard Hayghe and Beverly L. Johnson. Washington: GPO, 1980.

- - -. Dept. of Health and Human Services. U.S. Public Health Service. Centers for Disease Control and Prevention. <u>The ABCs of Safe and Healthy Child Care: A Handbook for Child Care Providers</u>. Washington: GPO, 1996.

Parts of Books

A. A poem, a short story, an essay, or a chapter in a collection of works by one author

Hawthorne, Nathaniel. "Young Goodman Brown." <u>The Portable Hawthorne</u>. Ed. Malcolm Cowley. Rev. ed. New York: Viking, 1969. 53–68.

B. A poem, a short story, an essay, or a chapter in a collection of works by several authors

Faulkner, William. "Race and Fear." <u>Voices in Black and White</u>. Ed. Katharine Whittemore and Gerald Marzorati. New York: Franklin Square, 1993. 83–94.

C. A novel or a play in an anthology

Cather, Willa. <u>My Mortal Enemy</u>. <u>The Norton Anthology of American Literature</u>. Ed. Nina Baym. 4th ed. Vol. 2. New York: Norton, 1994. 975–1025.

D. An introduction, a preface, a foreword, or an afterword written by the author(s) of a work

Bloom, Harold. Introduction. <u>Modern Crime and Suspense Writers</u>. Ed. Bloom. New York: Chelsea, 1995. xi–xii.

E. An introduction, a preface, a foreword, or an afterword written by someone other than the author(s) of a work

Primack, Marshall P. Foreword. <u>Phobia: The Crippling Fears</u>. By Arthur Henley. Secaucus: Stuart, 1987. 1–4.

F. Cross-references

If you have used more than one work from a collection, you may give a complete entry for the collection. Then, in the separate entries for the works, you can refer to the entry for the whole collection by using the editor's last name or, if you have listed more than one work by that editor, the editor's last name and a shortened version of the title.

French, Warren G., ed. <u>A Companion to</u> The Grapes of Wrath. New York: Viking, 1963.

- - -. "What Did John Steinbeck Know About the 'Okies'?" French, <u>Companion</u> 51–53.

Steinbeck, John. <u>Their Blood Is Strong</u>. 1938. French, <u>Companion</u> 53–92.

G. A reprinted article or essay (one previously published elsewhere)

If a work that appears in a collection first appeared in another place, give complete information for the original publication, followed by *Rpt. in* and complete information for the collection.

Searle, John. "What Is a Speech Act?" <u>Philosophy in America</u>. Ed. Max Black. London: Allen, 1965. 221–39. Rpt. in <u>Readings in the Philosophy of Language</u>. Ed. Jay F. Rosenberg and Charles Travis. Englewood Cliffs: Prentice, 1971. 614–28.

Magazines, Journals, Newspapers, and Encyclopedias

A. An article in a magazine, a journal, or a newspaper

Allen, Jodie. "Working Out Welfare." <u>Time</u> 29 July 1996: 53–54.

"Dumping by the Coast Guard." Editorial. <u>New York Times</u> 6 Sept. 1998, late ed., sec. 4: 10.

Eisenberg, David M., et al. "Unconventional Medicine in the United States: Prevalence, Costs, and Patterns of Use." <u>New England Journal of Medicine</u> 328.4 (1993): 246–52.

B. An article in an encyclopedia or other alphabetically organized reference work

Give the title of the article, the name of the reference work, and the year of the edition.

"Storytelling." The World Book Encyclopedia. 1999 ed.

C. A review

Schwarz, Benjamin. "Was the Great War Necessary?" Rev. of The Pity of War, by Niall Ferguson. Atlantic Monthly May 1999: 118–28.

Miscellaneous Print and Nonprint Sources

A. An interview you have conducted or a letter you have received

Jackson, Jesse. Personal interview [or Letter to the author]. 15 July 1992.

B. A film

Star Wars. Screenplay by George Lucas. Dir. Lucas. Perf. Mark Hamill, Harrison Ford, Carrie Fisher, and Alec Guinness. 20th Century Fox, 1977.

C. A work of art (painting, photograph, sculpture)

Ward, John Quincy Adams. The Freedman. Art Institute of Chicago.

D. A television or a radio program

Give the episode name (if applicable) and the series or the program name. Include any information that you have about the program's writer and director. Then give the network, the local station, the city, and the date of the airing of the program.

"A Desert Blooming." Writ. Marshall Riggan. Living Wild. Dir. Harry L. Gorden. PBS. WTTW, Chicago. 29 Apr. 1984.

E. A musical composition

Chopin, Frédéric. Waltz in A-flat major, op. 42.

F. A recording (compact disc, LP, or audiocassette)

If the recording is not a compact disc, include *LP* or *Audiocassette* before the manufacturer's name.

Marsalis, Wynton. "Fuchsia." Think of One. Columbia, 1983.

G. A lecture, a speech, or an address

Give the name of the speaker, followed by the name of the speech or the kind of speech (*Lecture, Introduction, Address*). Then give the event, the place, and the date.

King, Martin Luther, Jr. Speech. Lincoln Memorial, Washington. 28 Aug. 1963.

Electronic Publications

The number of electronic information sources is great and increasing rapidly, so please refer to the most current edition of the MLA Handbook for Writers of Research Papers *if you need more guidance. You can also refer to the page on "MLA Style" on the Modern Language Association Web site <http://www.mla.org/>.*

Portable databases (CD-ROMs, DVDs, laserdiscs, diskettes, and videocassettes)

These products contain fixed information (information that cannot be changed unless a new version is produced and released). Citing them in a research paper is similar to citing printed sources. You should include the following information:

- Name of the author (if applicable)
- Title of the part of the work used (underlined or in quotation marks)
- Title of the product or the database (underlined)
- Publication medium (CD-ROM, DVD, videodisc, diskette, or videocassette)
- Edition, release, or version if applicable
- City of publication
- Name of publisher
- Year of publication

If you cannot find some of this information, cite what is available.

"Steinbeck's Dust Bowl Saga." Our Times Multimedia Encyclopedia of the 20th Century. CD-ROM. 1996 ed. Redwood City: Vicarious, 1995.

Eyes on the Prize: America's Civil Rights Years, 1954–1965. Prod. Blackside. 6 videocassettes. PBS Video, 1986.

Beowulf. Great Literature. CD-ROM. 1992 ed. Parsippany: Bureau Development, 1992.

"Jump at the Sun: Zora Neale Hurston and the Harlem
Renaissance." <u>American Stories</u>. Laserdisc. McDougal, 1998.

Online Sources

Sources on the World Wide Web are numerous and include
scholarly projects, reference databases, articles in periodicals, and
professional and personal sites. Not all sites are equally reliable,
and therefore material cited from the World Wide Web should be
evaluated carefully. Entries for online sources in the Works Cited list
should contain as much of the information listed below as available.

- Name of the author, editor, compiler or translator, followed by
  an abbreviation such as *ed., comp.,* or *trans.* if appropriate
- Title of the material accessed. Use quotation marks for
  poems, short stories, articles, and similar short works.
  Underline the title of a book.
- Publication information for any print version of the source
- Title (underlined) of the scholarly project, database
  periodical, or professional or personal site. For a professional
  or personal site with no title, add a description such as
  Home page (neither underlined nor in quotation marks).
- Name of the editor of the scholarly project or database
- For a journal, the volume number, issue number, or other
  identifying number
- Date of electronic publication or of the latest update, or date
  of posting
- For a work from a subscription service, list the name of the
  service and—if a library is the subscriber—the name of the
  library and the town or state where it is located.
- Range or total number of pages, paragraphs, or other
  sections if they are numbered
- Name of any institution or organization that sponsors or is
  associated with the Web site
- Date the source was accessed
- Electronic address, or URL, of the source. For a subscription
  service, use the URL of the service's main page (if known) or
  the keyword assigned by the service.

Scholarly project
Documenting the American South. Aug. 1999. Academic Affairs
   Lib., U of North Carolina at Chapel Hill. 11 Aug. 1999
   <http://metalab.unc.edu/docsouth/>.

Professional site
American Council of Learned Societies Home Page. 1998. Amer.
   Council of Learned Societies. 13 Aug. 1999 <http://
   www.acls.org/jshome.htm>.

Personal site
Fitzgerald, Evan. A Students' Guide to Butterflies. 5 July 1999.
   Butterfly Farm. 11 Aug. 1999 <http://www.butterflyfarm.co.cr/
   farmer/bfly1.htm>.

Book
Poe, Edgar Allan. Tales. New York: Wiley, 1845. Documenting the
   American South. 16 Sept. 1998. Academic Affairs Lib., U of
   North Carolina at Chapel Hill. 13 Aug. 1999 <http://
   metalab.unc.edu/docsouth/poe/poe.html>.

Article in reference database
"Dickinson, Emily." Encyclopaedia Britannica Online. Vers. 99.1.
   Encyclopaedia Britannica. 11 Aug. 1999 <http://
   www.eb.com:180/bol/topic?eu=30830&sctn=1>.

Article in journal
Wagner, Diana, and Marcy Tanter. "New Dickinson Letter Clarifies
   Hale Correspondence." Emily Dickinson Journal 7.1 (1998):
   110–117. 29 July 1999 <http://muse.jhu.edu/demo/
   emily_dickinson_journal/7.1wagner.html>.

Article in magazine
Swerdlow, Joel L. "The Power of Writing." National Geographic
   Aug. 1999. 28 July 1999 <http://
   www.nationalgeographic.com/ngm/9908/fngm/index.html>.

Work from a subscription service
"Cinco de Mayo." Compton's Encyclopedia Online. Vers. 3.0.
   1998. America Online. 29 July 1999. Keyword: Compton's.

Weiss, Peter. "Competing Students' Science Skills Sparkle."
   Science News 30 Jan. 1999: 71. General Reference Center.
   InfoTrac SearchBank. Evanston Public Lib., IL. 16 Aug. 1999
   <http://www.searchbank.com/searchbank/evanston_main>.

Glossary for Writers

Allegory — a story in which the major events and characters have hidden or symbolic meanings. A quarrel between friends, for example, might represent a conflict between their native cultures.

Alliteration — the repetition of beginning sounds of words in poetry or prose; for example, the "c" sound in "creeping cat"

Allusion — a reference to a historical or literary person, place, event, or aspect of culture

Analogy — a comparison used to explain an idea or support an argument. For example, an analogy for how a government works might be a family.

Analysis — a way of thinking that involves taking apart, examining, and explaining a subject or an idea

Anecdote — a brief story told as an example to illustrate a point

Argument — speaking or writing that expresses a position or states an opinion with supporting evidence. An argument often takes into account other points of view.

Audience — one's readers or listeners

Autobiography — a biography (life story) told by the person whose life it is

Bias — a preference to lean toward one side in an argument; to be unbiased is to be neutral

Bibliography — a list of sources (articles, books, encyclopedias) in a paper or report used to document research or to recommend further study

Body — the main part of a composition, in which its ideas are developed

Brainstorming — a way of generating ideas that involves quickly listing ideas as they occur without stopping to judge them

Cause and Effect — a strategy of analysis that examines the reasons for actions or events, and the consequences or results of those actions

Characterization the way people (characters) are portrayed by an author

Chronological organized according to time sequence

Clarity the quality of being clear and easy to understand

Classification a way of organizing information by grouping or categorizing items according to some system or principle

Cliché an overused expression, such as "quiet as a mouse"

Clustering a brainstorming technique that involves creating an idea or topic map made up of circled groupings of related details

Coherence connectedness; a sense that parts hold together. A paragraph has coherence when its sentences flow logically from one to the next. A composition has coherence when its paragraphs are connected logically and linked by transitional words and phrases.

Collaboration the act of working with other people on projects or to problem solve

Colloquial characteristic of conversational style in speech or writing; linguistically informal, the way people ordinarily speak in conversation

Comparison and Contrast a pattern of organization in which two or more things are related on the basis of similarities and differences

Conclusion a judgment or a decision that is reached based on evidence, experience, and logical reasoning; also, the final section of a composition that summarizes an argument or main idea with added insight, and points the reader toward action or further reflection

Connotation the meaning of a word that carries ideas and feelings, as opposed to the word's strictly literal definition (denotation)

Context the setting or situation in which something happens; the parts of a statement that occur just before and just after a specific word and help determine its meaning

Controversy	a disagreement, often one that has attracted public interest
Counter-argument	a refutation; an argument made to oppose (counter) another argument
Critical Thinking	what a writer *does* with information; thinking that goes substantially beyond the facts to organize, analyze, evaluate, or draw conclusions about them
Criticism	discourse (usually an essay) that analyzes something (usually a literary or artistic work) in order to evaluate how it does or does not succeed in communicating its meaning
Cubing	a method for discovering ideas about a topic by using six strategies of investigation (in any order): describing, comparing, associating, analyzing, applying, and arguing for or against
Deconstruction	the process of taking apart for the purpose of analysis
Deductive Reasoning	the process of deriving a specific conclusion by reasoning from a general premise
Denotation	the meaning of a word that is strictly literal, as found in the dictionary, as opposed to the ideas and feelings the word carries (connotation)
Descriptive Writing	an account, usually giving a dominant impression and emphasizing sensory detail, of what it is like to experience some object, scene, or person
Dialect	a form of a language (usually regional) that has a distinctive pronunciation, vocabulary, and word order
Dialogue	spoken conversation of fictional characters or actual persons; the conversation in novels, stories, plays, poems, or essays
Documentation	the identification of documents or other sources used to support the information reported in an essay or other discourse; usually cited in footnotes or in parentheses
Editorial	an article in a publication or a commentary on radio or television expressing an opinion about a public issue

Elaboration the support or development of a main idea with facts, statistics, sensory details, incidents, examples, quotations, or visual representations

Evaluation writing that purposefully judges the worth, quality, or success of something

Expository Writing writing that explains an idea or teaches a process; also called informative writing

Expressive characterized by expression; refers to descriptive discourse full of meaning or feeling, often used by writers in personal writing to explore ideas

Fiction made-up or imaginary happenings as opposed to statements of fact or nonfiction. Short stories and novels are fiction, even though they may be based on real events; essays, scientific articles, biographies, news stories are nonfiction.

Figurative Language language that displays the imaginative and poetic use of words; writing that contains figures of speech such as simile, metaphor, and personification

Formal Language language in which rules of grammar and vocabulary standards are carefully observed; used in textbooks, reports, and other formal communications

Freewriting a way of exploring ideas, thoughts, or feelings that involves writing freely—without stopping or otherwise limiting the flow of ideas—for a specific length of time

Gender Neutral refers to language that includes both men and women when making reference to a role or a group that comprises people of both sexes. "A medic uses his or her skills to save lives" and "Medics use their skills to save lives" are two gender-neutral ways of expressing the same idea.

Generalization a statement expressing a principle or drawing a conclusion based on examples or instances

Gleaning a method of picking up ideas to write about by observing events, by scanning newspapers, magazines, and books, and by talking to others

Graphic Device a visual way of organizing information. Graphic devices include charts, graphs, outlines, clusters, and diagrams.

Idea Tree	a graphic device in which main ideas are written on "branches" and related details are noted on "twigs"
Imagery	figurative language and descriptions used to produce mental images
Inductive Reasoning	a method of thinking or organizing a discourse so that a series of instances or pieces of evidence lead to a conclusion or generalization
Inference	a logical assumption that is made based on observed facts and one's own knowledge and experience
Informative Writing	writing that explains an idea or teaches a process; also called expository writing
Interpretation	an explanation of the meaning of any text, set of facts, object, gesture, or event. To interpret something is to try to make sense of it.
Introduction	the opening section of a composition, which presents the main idea, grabs the reader's attention, and sets the tone
Invisible Writing	writing done with a dimmed computer screen or with an empty ballpoint pen on two sheets of paper with carbon paper between them
Irony	a figure of speech in which the intended meaning is the opposite of the stated meaning—saying one thing and meaning another
Jargon	the special language and terminology used by people in the same profession or with specialized interests
Journal	a record of thoughts and impressions, mainly for personal use
Learning Log	a kind of journal used for recording and reflecting on what one has learned and for noting problems and questions
Literary Analysis	critical thinking and writing about literature that presents a personal perspective
Looping	a repetitive process for discovering ideas on a topic through freewriting, stopping to find promising ideas, then producing another freewrite on that subject, and repeating the loop several times

Media various forms of mass communication, such as newspapers, magazines, radio, television, and the Internet; the editorial voice and influence of all of these

Memoir an account of true events told by a narrator who witnessed or participated in the events; usually focuses on the personalities and actions of persons other than the writer

Metaphor a figure of speech that makes a comparison without using the word *like* or *as.* "All the world's a stage" is a metaphor.

Monologue a speech by one person without interruption by other voices. A dramatic monologue reveals the personality and experience of a person through a long speech.

Mood the feeling about a scene or a subject created for a reader by a writer's selection of words and details. The mood of a piece of writing may be suspenseful, mysterious, peaceful, fearful, and so on.

Narrative Writing discourse that tells a story—either made up or true. Some common types of narrative writing are biographies, short stories, and novels.

Onomatopoeia the use of words (usually in poetry) to suggest sounds; examples are "the clinking of knives and forks," and "the trilling of a flute."

Order of Degree a pattern of organization in which ideas, people, places, or things are presented in rank order on the basis of quantity or extent. An example is listing items in order from most important to least important.

Paraphrase a restatement of an original passage in one's own words that stays true to the original ideas, tone, and general length

Parenthetical Documentation the placement of citations or other documentation in parentheses within the text

Peer Response suggestions and comments on a piece of writing provided by peers or classmates

Personal Writing writing that focuses on expressing the writer's own thoughts, experiences, and feelings

Personification a figure of speech in which objects, events, abstract ideas, or animals are given human characteristics

Persuasive Writing writing that is intended to convince the reader of a particular point of view or course of action

Plagiarism the act of dishonestly presenting someone else's words or ideas as one's own

Point of View the angle from which a story is told, such as first-, second-, or third-person point of view

Portfolio a container (usually a folder) for notes on work in progress, drafts and revisions, finished pieces, and peer responses

Précis a short summary or abstract of an essay, story, or speech, capturing only the essential elements

Proofreading the act of checking work to discover typographical and other errors; usually the last stage of the revising or editing process

Propaganda discourse aimed at persuading an audience, often containing distortions of truth; usually refers to manipulative political discourse

Prose the usual language of speech and writing, lacking the special properties of meter and form that define poetry; any language that is not poetry

Satire a literary form that ridicules or mocks the social practices or values of a society, a group, or an important individual

Sensory Details words that express attributes of the five senses—the way something looks, sounds, smells, tastes, or feels

Sequential Order a pattern of organization in which information is presented in the order in which it occurs, as in telling a story chronologically or describing the sequence of steps in a process

Simile a figure of speech that uses the word *like* or *as* to make a comparison. "Trees like pencil strokes" is a simile.

Spatial Order a pattern of organization in which details are arranged in the order that they appear in space, such as from left to right

Style	the distinctive features of a literary or artistic work that collectively characterize a particular individual, group, period, or school
Summary	a brief restatement of the main idea of a passage
Symbol	something (word, object, or action) that stands for or suggests something else. For example, a flag can stand for or symbolize a nation; a withered plant may suggest or symbolize a failing relationship.
Synthesis	the combining of separate elements to form a coherent whole
Theme	the underlying idea or central concern of a work of art or literature
Thesis Statement	a statement in one or two sentences of the main idea or purpose of a piece of writing
Tone	the writer's attitude or manner of expression—detached, ironic, serious, angry, and so on
Topic Sentence	a sentence that expresses the main idea of a paragraph
Transition	a connecting word or phrase that clarifies relationships between details, sentences, or paragraphs
Tree Diagram	a graphic way of showing the relationships among ideas; particularly useful in generating ideas; also known as an idea tree or spider map
Trite Phrase	a phrase overused so much that it loses meaning and suggests a lack of imagination on the part of the user
Unity	a consistent focus on a single writing purpose. A paragraph has unity if all its sentences support the same main idea or purpose; a composition has unity if all its paragraphs support the thesis statement.
Venn Diagram	a way of visually representing the relationship between two items that are distinct but that have common or overlapping elements
Voice	the "sound" of a writer's work determined by stylistic choices such as sentence structure, diction, and tone

Index

RESOURCES

Advertorial, 527
Advice and *advise,* 644
Affect and *effect,* 644
Agencies, abbreviations of names of, 214
Agreement
  of pronoun with antecedent, 9, 162–167, 270, 394
  of verb with subject, 130–151, 268–269, 410
Airplanes, names of
  capitalization of, 210
  italicization of, 210, 254
Allegory, 658
Alliteration, 370, 658
All ready and *already,* 644
All right, 644
All together and *altogether,* 644
Allusion, 658
Almanac, 344
Almost and *most,* 648
A lot, 644
A.M., 214
Ambiguous reference of pronoun, 172, 175, 179, 270
Among and *between,* 645
Analogy, reasoning by, 493, 658
Analogy test item, 580–581, 587
Analysis, 658
Anecdote, 658
  in conclusion of composition, 322
  elaborating with, 334, 339, 340, 344, 348
  in introduction of composition, 321
  as supporting detail, 308, 348
Antecedent, 7, 11
  agreement of pronoun with, 9, 162–167, 270, 394
  determining number of relative pronoun, 141–142
  pronoun reference and, 171, 172, 175, 270
Antithetical phrase, 230, 239
Antonyms
  in analogy test items, 581
  in vocabulary test items, 582
Anyway, 645
Anywhere, 645
Apostrophe, 242–244
  in contraction, 243, 262

for omitted digits in year number, 243
for omitted sound, 243, 259, 262
other punctuation with, 243
in plural, 243
in possessive, 7, 242–243, 262, 640
Appeals in advertisement, 489–490, 517, 518, 520, 522–523, 527
Appositive, 53–55, 70, 353
  commas with, 53, 75, 228
  diagramming, 66–67
  essential and nonessential, 53, 75, 228
  noun clause as, 85
  pronouns in and with, 168, 178, 271
Appositive phrase, 53–55, 74
  diagramming, 66–67
  essential or nonessential, 53, 228
  sentence combining with, 353
  in writing, 53–54, 71
Aptitude test, 574, 586
Argument, 424–433, 658
  in debate, 510–511
  deceptive techniques of, 429, 485–487
  deductive organization for, 326, 428
  elaborating, 334, 335, 340
  evaluating, 491–493
  inductive organization for, 428
Articles (part of speech), 16
  in titles, 213
Articles (written works). *See also* Encyclopedias; Magazines; Newspapers.
  documenting, in research report, 449, 653–654, 657
  quotation marks with titles of, 253
Artwork
  italicization of title of, 254
  MLA citation form for, 654
Aside, 441
As in comparison, 169, 188
Assessment. *See* Tests.
Association, appeal by, 489–490
Assonance, 370
Astronomical terms, capitalization of, 209–210

C

RESOURCES

Drama
    punctuation in, 258–259
    writing, 439, 441
Drawing conclusions. *See* Conclusion
    (of reasoning).

E

Editing and proofreading, 294–295
    comparison-and-contrast essay,
        410
    eyewitness report, 394
    literary interpretation, 402
    persuasive argument, 430
    procedural narrative, 417
    reflective essay, 386
    research report, 457
    short story, 438
    symbols used in, 302
    video, 534
Effect and *affect,* 644
Either-or fallacy, 429, 485, 496
Elaboration, 333–345, 661
    for developing ideas, 336–337,
        429, 437
    for enriching writing, 338–339,
        397
    sources for, 344
    for supporting opinions, 336,
        340–341, 348, 402
    techniques for, 335, 389
    types of, 334–335, 344
    with visuals, 342–343, 386,
        394
Electronic sources, 464–465, 536,
    537
    MLA citation forms for, 655–656
Ellipsis, 245, 247, 259, 262, 477
Elliptical adverb clause, 83, 169,
    178
E-mail
    capitalization in, 221
    as publishing option, 405, 410
Emotional appeals. *See* Persuasion,
    techniques of.
Emphatic verb forms, 114, 115,
    116
Encyclopedia, 466, 468
    MLA citation form for article in,
        654

as source for elaboration, 344
End marks, 224–225. *See also*
    Exclamation point; Period;
    Question mark.
    for fixing run-on sentences,
        267
English
    American, 565–568
    British, 566, 568
    globalization of, 569, 571
    history of, 561–571
    standard, 366
Essay
    MLA citation forms for, 652, 653
    quotation marks with title of, 253
Essay test item, 296, 584–585, 586,
    587
Essential (restrictive) adjective
    clause, 81, 82, 83, 102, 228,
    238
Essential (restrictive) appositive, 53,
    75
Ethnic groups, capitalization of
    names of, 205
Evading the issue, 487, 496
Evaluating
    arguments, 491–493
    facts and opinions, 482–484
    information, 479–497
    media messages, 515–527
    multimedia presentation, 538
    oral messages, 502
    sources, 433, 448, 468, 470,
        481, 502
    video, 534
    Web site, 470, 541
Events, capitalization of names of,
    206, 211, 217
Ever with *seldom,* 649
Evidence
    for generalizations, 336, 491
    for supporting ideas, 401, 402,
        427, 429, 455
Examples
    as context clues, 546
    elaborating with, 334, 337, 340,
        344
    as supporting details, 282, 308
Except and *accept,* 644
Exclamation point
    in exclamatory sentence, 224, 238

Graphics, 661
    charts, 343, 393, 537
    diagrams, 328–329, 537
    elaborating with, 342–343, 537
    graphs, 342, 537
    images, 386, 518, 522, 527,
        537, 539
    maps, 343, 537
    in multimedia presentation, 537
    for oral presentation, 504
    for organizing information, 327,
        393
    tables, 328–329
    in Web site, 539, 540
Graphs, 342, 537
Greek roots, 549
Group communication, 507–509,
    512

H

Half-truth, 485
Hardly
    in double negative, 192
    with *ever,* 649
Have as auxiliary verb, 111, 274,
    648
Helping verbs. *See* Auxiliary
    verbs.
He or she with antecedent of
    indeterminate gender, 163
Here
    sentences beginning with, 33, 46,
        47, 143, 151, 269
    with *this* or *these,* 190
Highways, capitalization of names of,
    206
His or her with antecedent of
    indeterminate gender, 163, 165
Historical events and periods,
    capitalization of names of, 206
Historical present tense, 111
History of English, 561–571
Holidays, capitalization of names of,
    206
Home page, 540
Hospitals, capitalization of names of,
    209
Humorous writing, 372
    informal language for, 366
Hyperbole, 369

Hyphen
    to avoid confusion, 246
    in compound word, 7, 245, 262
    double, to represent dash, 247
    for line break, 245, 262
    with prefix, 246

I

I, capitalization of, 213
Ideas
    connecting, 311
    developing, in prewriting, 292
    main, in paragraphs, 287,
        306–308, 314, 323, 324
    nouns as names of, 6
    revising for, 294, 348–349
    unsupported, 348
Idea tree, 662
Illogical comparison, 187–188, 273
Imagery, 368, 662
Images
    in media message, 518, 522, 527
    in multimedia presentation, 537
    in reflective essay, 386
    in Web site, 539
Imperative mood, 119, 124, 125
Imperative sentence, 32, 33
    period with, 224, 238
    in procedural narrative, 416, 417
    subject-verb agreement in, 143,
        151
Implied main idea, 307–308
Imply and *infer,* 646
Incomplete comparison, 187–188,
    273
Indefinite pronouns, 11
    agreement of personal pronouns
        with, 165–167, 270
    agreement of verbs with,
        135–137, 147, 150, 268
    possessive forms of, 242
    singular or plural, 11, 135–136,
        165–166
    used as adjectives, 182
Indefinite reference of pronoun, 171,
    175, 179, 270
Independent clauses, 22, 78, 102
    colons between, 250
    comma and conjunction to
        separate, 92, 228, 238

in complex sentences, 89
in compound-complex sentences, 89, 97
in compound sentences, 88, 94, 238
conjunctive adverbs with, 21, 249
semicolons between, 249–250, 262
in simple sentences, 88
in writing, 99
Indexes of periodicals, 464, 465, 466
Indicative mood, 119
Indirect object, 35
   diagramming, 39
   gerund as, 59
   noun clause as, 85
   pronoun as, 155, 159, 178
Indirect question, 224
Indirect quotation, 252
Indo-European language family, 562
Inductive organization, 326, 428
Inductive reasoning, 491–492, 662
Infer and *imply,* 646
Inference, 455, 494, 501, 662
Infinitive phrase, 61–63, 74
   agreement of verb with, 140
   comma with, 226
   diagramming, 68–69
   in sentence revising, 356
   in writing, 62, 70, 71
Infinitives, 56, 61–62, 68
   split, 61, 75
Infomercial, 527
Informal language, 366
Information. *See also* Sources of information.
   evaluating, 479–497
   finding, 463–477, 504
   organizing, 293
Informative/expository writing, 312, 313, 390–405, 414–423, 444–459, 662
   adjusting writing process for, 296–297
   elaboration in, 337
Informed opinion, 429
Initial
   capitalization of, 202

period with, 224
Institutions, capitalization of names of, 209
Intensive pronouns, 10, 169
Interjections, 23
   commas with, 226
   exclamation points with, 23, 224
Internet. *See* World Wide Web.
Interrogative pronouns, 10
Interrogative sentence, 32, 33. *See also* Questions.
   question mark with, 224
   word order in, 32, 46, 143
Interrupters
   commas with, 226–227, 238, 246, 263
   dashes with, 246, 262, 263
   parentheses with, 246, 256, 262, 263
Interview, 472
   MLA citation form for, 654
   in multimedia presentation, 536
   as primary source, 467
   techniques for, 513
Intransitive verbs, 13
Introduction (of composition), 318, 321, 330, 662
   in comparison-and-contrast essay, 406, 409
   in eyewitness report, 394
   in literary interpretation, 398, 401
   in persuasive argument, 424, 428
   in procedural narrative, 414, 416
   in research report, 444
   in short story, 434
Introductory element, comma with, 226, 238, 249, 276
Inverted sentence, 32, 46
   subject-verb agreement in, 143, 151
Invisible writing, 662
Irony, 373, 662
Irregular comparison, 185
Irregular verbs, 106, 107, 108, 129, 274

Italics
  for foreign words, 254, 262
  for titles of works, 254, 262
  underlining to represent, 254
  for vehicle names, 210, 254
  for words referred to as words, 254
Its and *it's,* 157, 243, 646

J, K

Jargon, 662
Journals, MLA citation forms for articles in, 653, 657
Kind of, 647

L

Landforms, capitalization of names of, 206
Landmarks, capitalization of names of, 210
Language. *See also* English; Word choice.
  appropriateness of, 366, 430
  colloquial, 659
  figurative, 285, 338–339, 368–369, 372
  gender-neutral, 661
  levels of, 366
  slanted, 488–489
  usage test items on, 583
Languages, capitalization of names of, 205
Latin roots, 550
Lay and *lie,* 122, 647
Lead and *led,* 647
Learn and *teach,* 647
Learning log, 662
Leave and *let,* 122, 647
Lend and *borrow,* 645
Less and *fewer,* 185, 646
Letter (epistle)
  business, 234–235, 250
  commas in, 232, 234–235
  MLA citation form for, 654
  as primary source, 467
Letter (of alphabet)
  in list, 256
  in outline, 212, 224
  plural of, 243

Levels of language, 366
Library, 464–465
Lie and *lay,* 122, 647
Like, misuse of, 647
Limited point of view, 375
Line breaks, hyphens for, 245, 262
Linking verbs, 13–14, 15, 17, 106
  complements with, 36, 154, 271
List
  colon introducing, 250, 262
  commas in, 228, 238
  in composition, 328
  in multimedia presentation, 536
  parentheses for numbers or letters in, 256
  periods in, 224
Listening skills, 500–502
Literary interpretation, 398–405
Literary present tense, 111
Loaded words, 488–489, 520
Loan and *lone,* 647
Logical fallacies, 349, 485–487, 496
  attacking the person, 487, 496
  cause-and-effect fallacy, 429
  circular reasoning, 349, 429, 486, 496
  either-or fallacy, 429, 485, 496
  evading the issue, 487, 496
  false analogy, 493
  half-truth, 485
  overgeneralization, 349, 429, 486, 496
  oversimplification, 485, 496
Lone and *loan,* 647
Looping, 662
Loose and *lose,* 647

M

Magazines
  advertorials in, 527
  italicization of titles of, 254
  MLA citation forms for articles in, 653, 657
  online, 301
  submitting writing to, 299–300
Main clause. *See* Independent clauses.

O

Place names, 6
  abbreviations of, 214
  capitalization of, 206, 217
  commas in, 232, 238, 239
Plagiarism, 451, 664
"Plain folks" appeal, 489, 497
Planets, capitalization of names of,
    209–210
Planned draft, 293
Play. *See also* Drama.
  italicization of title of, 254
  MLA citation form for, 652
  punctuation in, 258–259
Plot, 434, 437
Plural
  apostrophe in, 243
  indefinite pronouns, 11, 165
  nouns, 6, 133, 639
  verbs, 132
P.M., 214
Poetry
  apostrophes in, 243
  capitalization in, 212–213
  italicization of titles of, 254
  MLA citation forms for, 652
  quotation marks with titles of, 253
  writing, 439, 440
Point of view, 374–376, 437, 664
Political parties, capitalization of
    names of, 209
Positive degree, 184
Possessive
  apostrophe in, 7, 242–243, 262
  nouns, 7, 10, 242, 640
  pronouns, 9, 10, 16, 154,
    157–158, 178, 182, 242, 243,
    646, 649
Predicate, 26–28
  complete, 27, 46, 57
  compound, 29, 88, 228, 238
  simple, 26, 38, 46
Predicate adjective, 13, 17, 36
  diagramming, 40
Predicate nominative, 13, 36
  diagramming, 40
  gerund as, 59
  noun clause as, 85
  pronoun as, 9, 13, 154, 159,
    178
  subject-verb agreement and, 144,
    151

who as, 103
Predicate pronoun, 154, 159
Prediction
  in conclusion of composition, 322
  in oral communication, 501
Prefixes, 548, 551
  hyphens with, 246
  with proper nouns and adjectives,
    202, 203
  spelling and, 642
  in vocabulary test items, 582
Prepositional phrase, 19, 50–52, 74
  adjective, 50, 74
  adverb, 50, 74
  comma with, 226
  diagramming, 66
  indirect object and, 35
  positioning of, 51, 275
  for sentence variety, 356
  in writing, 51, 70, 71, 280
Prepositions, 4, 19–20, 50
  compound, 20
  objects of, 9, 19, 20, 50, 59, 85,
    103, 155, 159, 178, 271,
    272
  in titles, 213
Present participle, 56
  gerund distinguished from, 59
  as principal part of verb,
    106–107, 114
Present perfect tense, 110, 111,
    112, 128
  progressive form of, 114, 128
Present tense, 110–111, 128
  emphatic form of, 115
  as principal part of verb,
    106–107, 110, 115
  progressive form of, 114, 124,
    128
Prewriting, 292–293
  for comparison-and-contrast essay,
    409
  for eyewitness report, 393
  for literary interpretation, 401
  for persuasive argument, 427
  for procedural narrative, 416
  for reflective essay, 385
  for research report, 447–453
  for short story, 437
Primary source, 448, 467
Principal and *principle,* 648

Principal parts of verb, 106–109, 110, 111
Print media. *See also* Books; Magazines; Newspapers; Periodicals.
  deconstructing messages in, 522
Problem-solution order, 326
Procedural narrative, 414–417, 422
Progressive verb forms, 114, 115, 128
Pronouns, 4, 9–12, 152–179
  adjectives as modifiers of, 16, 182
  agreement of, with antecedents, 9, 162–167, 270, 394
  appositives and, 168, 178, 271
  cases of, 9, 154–156, 159, 178, 271
  for coherence, 325
  in comparisons, 169, 271
  in contractions, 14, 157, 243, 272, 646, 649
  demonstrative, 11, 16, 182
  indefinite, 11, 135–137, 147, 150, 165–167, 182, 242, 268, 270
  intensive, 10, 169
  interrogative, 10
  introducing noun clauses, 86
  personal, 9, 154–158, 162–169, 178, 243, 270, 271
  persons of, 9, 10, 162, 163
  plural, 11, 135, 165
  possessive, 9, 10, 16, 157–158, 178, 182, 242, 243, 646, 649
  as predicate nominatives, 9, 13, 154, 159, 178
  reference problems with, 171–173, 175, 179, 270
  reflexive, 10, 169
  relative, 11, 81, 141–142
  singular, 11, 135, 165
Proofreading, 664. *See also* Editing and proofreading.
Propaganda, 664. *See also* Persuasion, techniques of.
Proper adjectives, 17, 202
Proper nouns, 6, 202
  proper adjectives formed from, 17

Proposition, 510
PSAT, 577
Publishing, 295. *See also* Sharing.
  options for, 299–301, 389, 397, 405, 413, 433, 443, 459
Punctuation, 222–263. *See also names of particular punctuation marks.*
  as style element, 372
  usage test items on, 583
Purpose
  of comparison-and-contrast essay, 409
  establishing, as prewriting strategy, 292
  of eyewitness report, 393
  of group communication, 507
  for listening, 500
  of literary interpretation, 401
  of media message, 519, 522
  of oral presentation, 503
  in paragraph, 306, 312–313
  of persuasive argument, 427
  of procedural narrative, 416
  of reflective essay, 385
  of research report, 447
  of short story, 437

Q

Question mark
  with declarative sentence asking question, 224
  with interrogative sentence, 224
  in parentheses, 256
  with quotation marks, 252, 253
Questions. *See also* Interrogative sentences.
  in conclusions of compositions, 322
  for elaborating, 335
  for evaluating facts and opinions, 483
  for exploring topic, 292, 393, 401, 437, 447–448
  indicative mood in, 119
  indirect, 224
  interrogative pronouns in, 10
  in introductions of compositions, 321, 394

in oral communication, 500, 508
subject-verb agreement in, 143,
151
for survey, 472–473
who and *whom* in, 159, 272
Quiet and *quite,* 648
Quotation
brackets with explanation in, 257,
262
capitalization in, 212, 217, 252
colon introducing, 250, 262
comma with, 232, 239
divided, 217, 252
ellipsis in, 247
in eyewitness report, 393
indirect, 252
of information from research, 450,
451, 474
in introduction of composition,
321, 394
in literary interpretation, 402
of more than one paragraph, 253
quotation marks with, 252–253,
259, 262, 438, 450, 451,
477
within quotation, 253
in research report, 455
Quotation marks
with definitions, 254
with direct quotations, 252–253,
259, 262, 438, 450, 451, 477
other punctuation marks with,
252–253, 276, 438
single, 253
with slang, unusual, and technical
terms, 254
with titles of works, 253

R

Restatement clue, 546
Restrictive adjective clause. *See* Essential adjective clause.
Restrictive appositive. *See* Essential appositive.
Résumé, 420–421, 423
Review, MLA citation form for, 654
Revising, 294, 347–363
  comparison-and-contrast essay, 410
  to correct errors in logic, 349
  eyewitness report, 394
  literary interpretation, 402
  multimedia presentation, 538
  for organization, 294, 350–351
  persuasive argument, 430
  procedural narrative, 417
  reflective essay, 386
  research report, 457
  sentences, 278–281, 352–355
  short story, 438
  for style and word choice, 356–361
  to support ideas and opinions, 348
  thesis statement, 350
  video, 538
  Web site, 541
Rhyme, 370
Rise and *raise,* 122, 648
Roots, 548, 549–550
  in vocabulary test items, 582
Run-on sentence, 91, 92, 267

S

Sacred days and writings, capitalization of names of, 205
Salutation of letter, 232, 234, 235, 250
SAT (Scholastic Assessment Test), 574, 576–577
Scarcely in double negative, 192
Schools, capitalization of names of, 209
School subjects and years, names of, 210, 217
Script for video, 533
Search engines, 469, 476

Seasons, names of, 206
Secondary source, 448, 468
Second-person point of view, 376
Seldom, 649
Semicolon
  in compound sentence, 88, 249
  for fixing run-on sentence, 92, 230, 267
  between independent clauses, 249–250, 262
  with quotation marks, 252
  in series, 250
Sensory details, 664
  elaborating with, 334, 338, 344, 389
  as supporting details, 308, 393
Sentence combining, 281, 352–354
  with adjective clauses, 352–353
  with appositive phrases, 353
  with compound subjects, 138–139
  with conjunctions, 353
  by moving words, 352
Sentence fragment, 27, 91, 92, 93, 266, 402
  in informal language, 366
Sentences, 26
  capitalization of first words in, 212
  combining, 138–139, 281, 352–354
  complex, 88, 89, 95–96, 281, 366
  compound, 88, 94, 228, 235, 238, 239, 249, 276, 281
  compound-complex, 88, 89, 97, 281
  compound parts in, 29–31, 38, 43, 47, 88, 138–139, 147, 150, 154, 162, 228, 238, 270
  declarative, 32, 33, 224
  diagramming, 38–41, 66–69, 94–97
  exclamatory, 32, 33, 224, 238
  imperative, 32, 33, 143, 151, 224, 238, 416, 417
  interrogative, 32, 33, 46, 143, 224
  inverted, 32, 46, 143, 151
  overloaded, 278
  padded, 279

INDEX

with phrase as subject, 140, 150

in question, 143, 151

with relative-pronoun subject, 141–142

in sentence beginning with *here* or *there,* 143, 151, 269

in sentence containing predicate nominative, 144, 151

with singular subject that ends in *s,* 141, 150, 269

with title as subject, 141, 150

when words separate subject and verb, 133, 136, 150, 268, 410

Subjunctive mood, 119, 120, 125

Subordinate clauses, 11, 78–79, 102

adjective, 81–82, 83, 95, 98, 102, 141–142, 227–228, 239, 352–353

adverb, 81, 82–83, 95, 98, 102, 169, 178, 226

in complex sentences, 89, 95–96

in compound-complex sentences, 89, 97

noun, 85–87, 89, 96, 102, 140

as sentence fragments, 91, 266

in sentence revising, 278, 280, 356

subordinating conjunctions introducing, 22, 78–79, 82, 86

who and *whom* in, 81, 103, 141, 160

in writing, 79, 83, 86, 98–99

Subordinating conjunctions, 22, 78–79

introducing adverb clauses, 82

introducing noun clauses, 86

sentence combining with, 353

Suffixes, 548, 552–553

hyphens with, 246

spelling and, 640–642

in vocabulary test items, 582

Summary, 665

in business writing, 418–419, 423

in conclusion of composition, 322, 414

of information from research, 475

in research report, 455

Superlative degree, 184–185, 273

Supporting details, 348

adding, to sentences, 282

as context clues, 547

in oral communication, 502

in paragraphs, 308, 314

in response to essay test item, 585

Survey

conducting, 472–473

use of, in media message, 521

Suspense, 373

Symbolism, 368, 665

Synonyms

in analogy test items, 581

for avoiding repetition, 360

as context clues, 546

shades of meaning in, 554, 555

in vocabulary test items, 582

T

Tables, 328–329

Take and *bring,* 645

Teach and *learn,* 647

Teams, capitalization of names of, 209, 217

Technical terms. *See also* Specialized vocabulary.

quotation marks with, 254

Television

deconstructing messages on, 523

infomercials on, 527

italicization of titles of shows on, 254

MLA citation form for program on, 654

quotation marks with titles of episodes on, 253

Tenses of verbs, 14, 110–116, 124–125, 128. *See also names of particular tenses.*

avoiding shifts in, 121, 274, 430

misuse of, 121

perfect, 110, 111–112

simple, 110–111

Testimonial, 489, 497, 520

U

Underlining. *See* Italics.
Unity, 665. *See also* Coherence.
  in composition, 324
  in paragraph, 286, 306, 309, 314, 323
Unsupported ideas, revising to avoid, 348
Unsupported opinion, 429
Usage test item, 583, 587
Us with appositive, 168, 178, 271

V

Variety in sentences, 43, 47, 89, 98–99, 280–281, 294, 356, 372, 457
Vehicles, names of
  capitalization of, 210
  italicization of, 210, 254
Venn diagram, 327, 665
Verbal elements in oral communication, 500, 502, 505
Verbal phrase, 56
Verbals, 56–63, 85, 280. *See also* Gerunds; Infinitives; Participles.
Verb phrase, 14
Verbs, 5, 13–15, 104–129, 274. *See also* Subject-verb agreement; Verbals.
  action, 13, 14, 15, 35, 106, 117
  adverbs as modifiers of, 16, 182
  auxiliary, 14, 56, 111, 112, 114, 115, 117, 266, 274
  commonly confused, 122, 644, 645, 646, 647, 648, 649
  compound, 29, 30, 38
  conjugation of, 110, 111, 132, 133
  emphatic forms of, 114, 115, 116
  intransitive, 13
  irregular, 106, 107, 108, 129, 274
  linking, 13–14, 15, 17, 36, 106, 154, 271
  moods of, 14, 119–120, 125

objective complements occuring with, 35
  principal parts of, 106–109, 110, 111
  progressive forms of, 114, 115, 116
  regular, 106, 107
  as simple predicates, 26
  suffixes in, 553
  tenses of, 14, 110–116, 121, 124–125, 128, 274, 430
  transitive, 13, 117
  using specific, 284, 361, 389
  voices of, 14, 117–118, 125, 277, 359, 416, 423
Vertical file, 466
Video, 531
  editing, 534
  elements of, 532–534
  evaluating, 534
  with eyewitness report, 394
  in multimedia presentation, 537
  storyboarding, 532
  terms, 543
  topic for, 532
  in Web site, 539, 541
Viewing skills, 502, 515–527
Visual aids. *See* Audiovisual materials; Graphics.
Visual elements in media message, 518
Vocabulary, 545–559. *See also* Language; Words.
  memory tips for expanding, 559
  "power words" for, 290, 304, 316, 332, 346, 364
  specialized, 556–557
  test items, 582, 587
Voice (in writing), 665
  evaluating, in revising, 294
  in poem, 440
  revising for, 294, 356–358
  as style element, 377
Voice (of verb), 14, 117–118, 125, 277, 359, 416, 423

W

Ways, misuse of, 649
Web. *See* World Wide Web.

INDEX

Y

Acknowledgments

Cover Art

top right Dennis O'Clair/Tony Stone Images; *bottom left* Copyright © SuperStock; *bottom center* Tabletop by Sharon Hoogstraten; Illustrations by Jenny Adams.

Table of Contents Art

viii *top* Illustration by Jenny Adams; *bottom* Copyright © 1999 PhotoDisc, Inc.; **ix** Copyright © Ron Lowery/The Stock Market; **x** Copyright © Elizabeth Crews/Stock Boston/PNI; **xi** Illustration by Jenny Adams; **xii** AP/Wide World Photos; **xiii** Illustration by Jenny Adams; **xv** Photo by Jim Marvy/The Stock Market; **xvi, xvii, xviii** Illustrations by Jenny Adams; **xix** Copyright © Andrew Willsheer; **xxi** Copyright © Bonnie Kamin/PhotoEdit; **xxii** *left* Copyright © 1999 PhotoDisc, Inc.; *right* Photo by Sharon Hoogstraten; **xxvi** Copyright © Jason Hawkes/Tony Stone Images; **xxvii** Copyright © Paul S. Howell/Tony Stone Images; **xxviii** Copyright © 1994 Ron Chapple/FPG International; **xxix, xxxi** Copyright © 1999 PhotoDisc, Inc.

Illustrations by Jenny Adams

9, 10, 15, 16, 17, 23, 27, 33 *top right,* **34, 38, 43, 46, 47, 54, 57, 61, 88, 91, 108, 128, 129, 132, 140, 151, 159, 166, 168, 172, 178, 179, 182, 185, 191, 204, 206** *top right,* **210** *top,* **213, 221, 229, 238, 239, 248, 255, 263, 264, 266, 269, 298, 302, 308, 314** *bottom,* **321, 323, 330, 337, 339, 342, 349, 350, 360, 362, 367, 372, 378, 388, 396, 423, 467, 469, 507, 512** *bottom, center,* **532, 534** *top,* **538, 540** *top left,* **550, 554, 558, 562, 586.**

Art Credits

REVIEW 2–3 Copyright © Al Francekevich/The Stock Market; **4–5** Copyright © Ken Fisher/Tony Stone Images; **7** Copyright © 2000 by Sidney Harris; **9, 13** Copyright © 1999 PhotoDisc, Inc.; **19** Copyright © 1985 FarWorks, Inc. All rights reserved. Reprinted by permission; **21** Photo by Sharon Hoogstraten.

CHAPTER 1 24 Copyright © E. R. Degginger/Natural Selection; **28** Copyright © 1999 PhotoDisc, Inc.; **29** Copyright © The New Yorker Collection 1999 David Sipress from cartoonbank.com. All rights reserved; **31** AP/Wide World Photos; **33** *bottom left* Copyright © Michael Doolittle/Rainbow/PNI; **42** NASA.

CHAPTER 2 48 NASA; **51** Copyright © Jerry Wachter Photography, Ltd.; **52** Photograph from The Historical Collection of Herb and Dorothy McLaughlin/FPG International; **55** Corbis-Bettmann; **59** *Calvin and Hobbes* copyright © 1988 Watterson. Distributed by Universal Press Syndicate. Reprinted with permission. All rights reserved; **62** Copyright © Christopher Morris/Blackstar/Time Life; **70** Copyright © SuperStock; **71** Richard T. Nowitz/Corbis.

CHAPTER 3 79 Copyright © Bob Daemmrich/Stock Boston/PNI; **82** Copyright © Michael Newman/PhotoEdit; **85** Copyright © Jean-Luc Dubin/Tony Stone Images; **90** Copyright © Paul Conklin/PhotoEdit; **102** Copyright © Jean-Luc Dubin/Tony Stone Images; **103** Copyright © 1999 PhotoDisc, Inc.

CHAPTER 4 104 *background* AP/Wide World Photos; **106** *Calvin and Hobbes* copyright © 1993 Watterson. Dist. by Universal Press Syndicate. Reprinted with permission. All rights reserved; **109** Alfred Eisenstaedt/*Life* Magazine. Copyright © Time Inc.; **116** AP/Wide World Photos; **121** Copyright © Diana Walker/Time Inc.; **124** Courtesy of the Heye Foundation, National Museum of the American Indian, Smithsonian Institution (33738).

CHAPTER 5 130 Copyright © 1998 Ron Kimball/Ron Kimball Photography, Inc.; **135** AP/Wide World Photos; **137** Photo courtesy of Dr. Nicholas C. Metropolis; **144** AP/Wide World Photos; **146** Copyright © Mary Kate Denny/PhotoEdit.

CHAPTER 6 152 *background* Copyright © Firefly Productions/The Stock Market; *foreground* Copyright © Chris Salvo/FPG International/PNI; **156** The Granger Collection, New York; **160** Copyright © 2000 by Sidney Harris; **174** The Granger Collection, New York.

CHAPTER 7 180 Copyright © 1999 PhotoDisc, Inc.; **187** Copyright © 1992 Thaves/Reprinted with permission; **188, 193** Copyright © 1999 PhotoDisc, Inc.; **198** Reprinted with special permission of King Features Syndicate.

CHAPTER 8 200 *left, right* Copyright © 1999 PhotoDisc, Inc.; **203** Major League Baseball and Minor League Baseball trademarks and copyrights are used with permission of Major League Baseball Properties, Inc.; **206** *left* Map by Bruce Burdick; **209** NASA; **210** *bottom* Copyright © 1999 PhotoDisc, Inc.; **214** Copyright © 1995 The Washington Post Writers Group, Reprinted with permission; **217, 218** Copyright © 1999 PhotoDisc, Inc.

CHAPTER 9 222 Copyright © Garry Gay/The Image Bank; **227** Copyright © Tribune Media Services, Inc. All rights reserved. Reprinted with permission; **230** Copyright © 1999 PhotoDisc, Inc.; **231** Copyright © Archive Photos/PNI; **234** Copyright © Stephen Frisch/Stock Boston/PNI.

CHAPTER 10 240 Copyright © Jeff Cadge/The Image Bank; **244** *top, bottom* Archive Photos; **247** *Dilbert* reprinted by permission of United Feature Syndicate, Inc.; **258, 259** Martha Swope. Copyright © Time Inc.; **260** Copyright © Peter Magubane/*Time* Magazine.

CHAPTER 11 288–289 Copyright © The Stock Market; **290** Copyright © 1999 PhotoDisc, Inc.; **291** Copyright © 1987 FarWorks, Inc. All rights reserved. Reprinted by permission; **293** Copyright © 1999 PhotoDisc, Inc.; **303** Copyright © Stockbyte.

CHAPTER 12 304 *background* Copyright © David Young-Wolff/PhotoEdit; *foreground* Copyright © 1999 PhotoDisc, Inc.; **305** Copyright © 1993 Jim Marvy/The Stock Market; **307** Copyright © Kelvin Aitken/Natural Selection; **313** Copyright © Art Wolfe/Tony Stone Images; **314** *top* Copyright © 1985 FarWorks, Inc. All rights reserved. Reprinted by permission.

CHAPTER 13 316 Copyright © Elizabeth Crews/Stock Boston/PNI; **317** Photomosaic™ by Robert Silvers/www.photomosaic.com; **318** *Calvin and Hobbes* copyright © 1989 Watterson. Distributed by Universal Press Syndicate. Reprinted with permission. All rights reserved; **331** *top* Copyright © 1999 PhotoDisc, Inc.

CHAPTER 14 332 Copyright © Andy Sacks/Tony Stone Images; **333** Photo copyright © Andrew Willsheer; **334** *Calvin and Hobbes* copyright © 1989 Watterson. Distributed by Universal Press Syndicate. Reprinted with permission. All rights reserved; **341** Copyright © 1991 FarWorks, Inc. All rights reserved. Reprinted by permission; **345** *center right* Copyright © 1999 PhotoDisc, Inc.

CHAPTER 15 346, 347 *left* Copyright © 1999 PhotoDisc, Inc.; **347** *right* Photo by Sharon Hoogstraten; **354** Copyright © 2000 by Sidney Harris; **357** Copyright © The New Yorker Collection 1940 Charles Addams from cartoonbank.com. All rights reserved; **358** Copyright © 1999 PhotoDisc, Inc.; **363** Copyright © 1999 John C. Long.

CHAPTER 16 364 Copyright © 1999 PhotoDisc, Inc.; **365** Copyright © Bonnie Kamin/PhotoEdit; **370** Copyright © 1983 FarWorks, Inc. All rights reserved. Reprinted by permission.

CHAPTER 17 380–381 Copyright © Ron Lowery/The Stock Market; **387** *bottom left* Darrell Gulin/Corbis; *bottom middle* By permission of Tom Taylor.

CHAPTER 18 395 *top* Copyright © John Iacono/Sports Illustrated/Time Inc.; *bottom* Copyright © Jose L. Pelaez/The Stock Market.

CHAPTER 19 403 *top* AP/Wide World Photos; *center* Photo by Sharon Hoogstraten; *bottom* Copyright © Steffen Jagenburg/Nonstock/PNI.

CHAPTER 20 411 *top* Copyright © Sue Klemens/Stock Boston/PNI; *center* United States Environmental Protection Agency; *bottom* Photo by Sharon Hoogstraten.

CHAPTER 22 431 *top left* Copyright © Donald Johnson/Tony Stone Images; *bottom left* Photo by Sharon Hoogstraten; *bottom right* Courtesy of The Advertising Council.

CHAPTER 24 455 Montana Historical Society, Helena.

CHAPTER 25 460–461 Copyright © Mendola/Doug Chezem/The Stock Market; **462** Copyright © Magellan Geographic/PNI; **463** Copyright © Jason Hawkes/Tony Stone Images; **464** Copyright © 1999 PhotoDisc, Inc.; **471** D. Boone/Corbis; **472** Photo by Sharon Hoogstraten; **475** Copyright © 1986 FarWorks, Inc. All rights reserved. Reprinted by permission; **476** Copyright © Stockbyte.

CHAPTER 26 478 Copyright © Archive Photos/PNI; **479** *top* Copyright © 1994 Ron Chapple/FPG International; *center* Copyright © Vedros/Vedros & Asso/Tony Stone Images; **480** Photo by Sharon Hoogstraten; **481** Copyright © Curtis O'Shock/Adventure Photo & Film; **484** AP/Wide World Photos; **485** Copyright © 1999 PhotoDisc, Inc.; **486** Copyright © The New Yorker Collection 1989 Robert Weber from cartoonbank.com. All rights reserved; **489, 490** Photos by Sharon Hoogstraten; **492** Copyright © 1999 PhotoDisc, Inc.; **497** Copyright © Greg Probst/Tony Stone Images.

CHAPTER 27 498 Copyright © Bob Daemmrich/Stock Boston/PNI; **499** National Gallery, Oslo, Norway/Bridgeman Art Library, London/New York/SuperStock; **501** Copyright © Paul S. Howell/Tony Stone Images; **502** AP/Wide World Photos/Bill Mueller/The Dallas *Times Herald;* **503** Paul A. Souders/Corbis; **504** Copyright © 1999 PhotoDisc, Inc.; **506** AP/Wide World Photos; **509** Copyright Lawrence Migdale/Stock Boston/PNI; **512** *top* Copyright © 1999 PhotoDisc, Inc.; **513** *center* Copyright © The 5th Wave by Rich Tennant, Rockport, Massachusetts. E-mail: the5wave@tiac.net.

CHAPTER 28 514 Copyright © 1999 PhotoDisc, Inc.; **515** *left* Copyright © 1997 Zephyr Pictures; *right* Photo by Sharon Hoogstraten; **517** Reprinted with special permission of King Features Syndicate; **518** The Advertising Council; **520** Copyright © Tribune Media Services, Inc. All rights reserved. Reprinted with permission; **522** Reproduced with permission. *Caution: Children Not At Play,* Winter/Spring Ad Kit 1992. Copyright © American Heart Association; **523** Copyright © 1999 PhotoDisc, Inc.; *inset* Courtesy of Keep America Beautiful, Inc.; **527** Copyright © 1999 PhotoDisc, Inc.

For Literature and Text

Denise Smith: Excerpt from "The Interrogative Putdown," from *How to Win a Pullet Surprise* by Jack Smith. Copyright © 1982 by Jack Smith. Reprinted by permission of Mrs. Denise Smith.

Jenny Stiers: "Untitled" by Jenny Stiers, from Best Illinois Student Poetry and Prose, 1997, Fall 1998 issue of Illinois English Bulletin. Reprinted by permission of Jenny Stiers.

Jay S. Stuller: Excerpt from "As American as Pizza Pie" by Jay Stuller, originally published in *Smithsonian,* June 1997. Copyright by Jay S. Stuller. Used with the permission of the author.

Time: Excerpt from "Voracious Inc." by Karl Taro Greenfeld, *Builders & Titans of the 20th Century,* special issue of *Time,* December 7, 1998. Copyright © 1998 Time Inc. Reprinted by permission.

Excerpt from "The Day That Time Stood Still," *The Millennium: 100 Events That Changed the World,* special issue of *Life,* October 1997. Copyright © 1997 Time Inc. Reprinted by permission.

Excerpts from "The First Picture Show," *The Millennium: 100 Events That Changed the World,* special issue of *Life,* October 1997. Copyright © 1997 Time Inc. Reprinted by permission.

Excerpt from "Tim Berners-Lee" by Joshua Quittner, *The Century's Greatest Minds,* special issue of *Time,* March 29, 1999. Copyright © 1999 Time Inc. Reprinted by permission.

Universal Press Syndicate: Excerpts from "Looks Like a Winner" by Roger Ebert, *Chicago Sun-Times,* May 17, 1999. Copyright © 1999. Distributed by Universal Press Syndicate. Reprinted with permission. All rights reserved.

U.S. News & World Report: Excerpt from "E-mail Nation," *U.S. News & World Report,* March 22, 1999. Copyright © 1999 U.S. News & World Report. Reprinted with permission.

Viking Penguin: Excerpt from *The Crucible* by Arthur Miller. Copyright © 1952, 1953, 1954, renewed 1980, 1981, 1982 by Arthur Miller. Used by permission of Viking Penguin, a division of Penguin Putnam Inc.

G. Bruce Weir: "Don't Tie Gift of Life to Recipient's Location" by G. Bruce Weir, from "How Do We Decide Who Gets Another Chance at Life?" USA Today, February 24, 1999. Reprinted by permission of G. Bruce Weir.

Writers House: Excerpts from "Letter from Birmingham Jail" by Martin Luther King, Jr. Copyright © 1963 by Martin Luther King, Jr., renewed 1991 by Coretta Scott King. Reprinted by arrangement with the Heirs to the Estate of Martin Luther King, Jr., c/o Writers House Inc. as agent for the proprietor.

Wylie Agency: Excerpt from "The Man to Send Rain Clouds" by Leslie Marmon Silko. Copyright © 1981 by Leslie Marmon Silko. Reprinted with the permission of The Wylie Agency, Inc.

McDougal Littell Inc. has made every effort to locate the copyright holders of all copyrighted material in this book and to make full acknowledgment for its use.